Dynamic Macroeconomics

Instability, Fluctuation, and Growth in Monetary Economies

Peter Flaschel
Reiner Franke
Willi Semmler

The MIT Press
Cambridge, Massachusetts
London, England

This book was set in Palatino by Windfall Software using ZzTEX.

Printed and bound in the United States of America.

Library of Congress Cataloging-in-Publication Data

Flaschel, Peter, 1943–
Dynamic macroeconomics : instability, fluctuation, and growth in monetary economies / Peter Flaschel, Reiner Franke, and Willi Semmler.
p. cm. — (Studies in dynamical economic science)
Includes bibliographical references and index.
ISBN 0-262-06191-0 (alk. paper)
1. Equilibrium (Economics) 2. Econometrics. I. Franke, Reiner. II. Semmler, Willi. III. Title. IV. Series.
HB145.F556 1997
330′.01′5195—dc21 96-39443
CIP

Contents

Series Foreword ix
Preface xi

1 General Introduction 1
1.1 Introduction 1
1.2 Market-Clearing Approach to Dynamic Macroeconomics 2
1.3 Nonmarket-Clearing Approach to Dynamic Macroeconomics 4
1.4 On Stylized Empirical Facts 6
1.5 Perspective of the Book 7
1.6 A Brief Outlook 10
1.7 Dynamic Tools and Econometric Issues 13
1.8 Notation and Abbreviations 14

I Market Mechanisms and Macrodynamics: Basic Models 19

2 Micro- and Macroeconomic Adjustment Mechanisms: A Brief Overview 23
2.1 Introduction 23
2.2 Microeconomic Adjustment Mechanisms 23
2.3 Macroeconomic Adjustment Mechanisms 27

3 Market Mechanisms and Boundedness of Market Fluctuations 33
3.1 Introduction 33
3.2 Walrasian Price-Quantity Adjustments 34
3.3 Keynesian and Composite Adjustment Processes 44
3.4 Proportional and Derivative Control 48

3.5 Concluding Remarks 57
3.6 Appendix: Market Adjustments and the Newton Method 58

4 Non-Neoclassical Variants of Dynamic Macroeconomics 61
4.1 Introduction 61
4.2 Instability in Real and Monetary Models 63
4.3 Boundedness in Real and Monetary Models 73
4.4 Classical Growth Dynamics and Viability 81
4.5 Supply-Driven Keynesian Growth Dynamics 90
4.6 Effective Demand in Classical Growth Dynamics 96
4.7 Some Conclusions 101

5 Neoclassical Variants of Dynamic Macroeconomics 103
5.1 Introduction 103
5.2 The Solow Version and the Labor Market 105
5.3 The Intertemporal Version of the Solow Model 109
5.4 Stochastic Growth and Equilibrium Business Cycles 112
5.5 Endogenous Technical Change and Growth 115
5.6 Growth, Money, and Finance 121
5.7 Concluding Remarks 126

II Price Flexibility, Nominal Rigidity, and Macrodynamics 127

6 Wage Flexibility and Stability in the Short Run 131
6.1 Introduction 131
6.2 The Walrasian Adjustment Process 133
6.3 The Keynesian Adjustment Process 137
6.4 Conclusion 143
6.5 Mathematical Appendix 144

7 Price Flexibility and Instability in the Medium Run 147
7.1 Introduction 147
7.2 In Defense of Adaptive Expectations 149
7.3 Adaptive Expectations and Extrapolative Regression Forecasts 156
7.4 Basic Features of the Tobin and the Sargent Model 162
7.5 The Case of Adaptive Expectations 166
7.6 The Case of Myopic Perfect Foresight 172
7.7 Conclusion 176
7.8 Appendix: Mathematical Proofs 177

III AD-AS and IS-LM Models of Monetary Growth 183

8 Keynesian Growth Dynamics, Perfect Foresight, and Viability 187
- 8.1 Introduction 187
- 8.2 RE Propositions in Fully Specified AD-AS Growth Models: A Reconsideration 189
- 8.3 Hyperperfect Foresight: An Exceptional Case in an Exceptional Environment 196
- 8.4 Myopic Perfect Foresight and Cyclical IS-LM Growth 210
- 8.5 IS-LM Growth Dynamics and Viability 217
- 8.6 Concluding Remarks 224

9 Adaptive Expectations or Myopic Perfect Foresight: The Wrong Alternative 227
- 9.1 Introduction 227
- 9.2 The AD-AS Growth Model in Discrete Time 233
- 9.3 A Numerical Analysis of the AE Case 238
- 9.4 AE and MPF I: Cases of No Difference 241
- 9.5 AE and MPF II: Why Can There Be a Difference? 247
- 9.6 AE and MPF III: The Basic Fallacy 254
- 9.7 Appendix: Forecasted Price Changes and Adaptive Learning 262

IV Supply and Demand Side Models of Keynesian Growth Dynamics 267

10 Supply Side Keynesianism and the Classical Growth Cycle 271
- 10.1 Introduction 271
- 10.2 A General Keynes-Wicksell Model of Monetary Growth 274
- 10.3 Local Stability Analysis 278
- 10.4 The Neoclassical Case: Savings and Monetary Growth 279
- 10.5 The Classical Case: Cross-Dual Monetary Growth Dynamics 281
- 10.6 Conclusions 288
- 10.7 Appendix 1: Stein (1982) 289
- 10.8 Appendix 2: Proofs of Theorems 10.1–10.3 292

11 Inflation, Distribution, and Cycles in a Keynesian Monetary Growth Model 299
- 11.1 Perspective of the Model 299

11.2 Formulation of the Model 305
11.3 Local Analysis 311
11.4 Simulation Results for the Original Model 316
11.5 A Modification of Adaptive Expectations 321
11.6 Simulation Results with Flexible Adaptive Expectations 326
11.7 Conclusion 332

V Finance, Long-Term Expectations, and Macro Fluctuations 335

12 Finance, Expectations Dynamics, and Macro Fluctuations 339
12.1 Introduction 339
12.2 Investment and Long-Term Expectations 341
12.3 The IS-LM Configuration 348
12.4 Analysis of Temporary Equilibria 351
12.5 Long-Run Dynamics 357
12.6 Computer Simulations 363
12.7 Conclusion 368
12.8 Mathematical Appendix 369

13 Trends and Cycles in the Capital Structure 373
13.1 Introduction 373
13.2 A Simple Dynamic Approach 376
13.3 The Dynamics of the Capital Structure: Constant Trend 378
13.4 The Dynamics of the Capital Structure: Trend Variations 386
13.5 Conclusion 389
13.6 Appendix 392

14 Conclusions 397

Notes 401
References 427
Index 447

Series Foreword

Studies in Dynamical Economic Science is devoted to theoretical, mathematical, and empirical research concerning economic change and the forces causing it. It encompasses business cycles, economic growth, economic development, and the underlying microeconomic processes that govern individual, household, firm, market, and government behavior. It is eclectic as to theory and method, encompassing equilibrium, disequilibrium, optimizing, and adaptive evolutionary points of view. Theory and models that emphasize realistic assumptions and that are buttressed by an appeal to facts are especially encouraged. The ultimate goal of the series is to contribute to more effective policies for enhancing the benefits and ameliorating the costs of rapid change.

Preface

The expectations revolution and the equilibrium market clearing approach have challenged macroeonomics and Keynesian variants in particular. Macroeconomics has to a great extent shifted away from aggregate analysis and the traditional IS-LM framework that was introduced to model the Keynesian nonmarket-clearing approach and now emphasizes microfoundations and rationality. This book deals with the challenges arising from this new development by attempting to revive the traditions of nonmarket-clearing approaches to macroeconomics. Our work is concerned less with developing microfounded macro theory than with building dynamic macroeconomics on sound adjustment principles originating in longstanding discussions on market mechanisms and their stability properties.

Yet rationality we believe should not be a claim of only one school. Economic agents in Keynesian macroeconomics, for example, do not behave irrationally. They may also act rationally when faced with situations characterized by disequilibria. Agents may act rationally while "groping in the dark," describing situations where the future equilibrium path of decision variables is unknown.[1]

In our book we avoid the rational expectations perfect foresight methodology according to which variables, when out of the steady-state equilibrium, are allowed to jump to their stable paths in order to ensure convergence back to the steady state. We rather work with out-of-equilibrium disequilibrium adjustment processes where prices can change only gradually and where expectations can be perfect or also gradually adjusting.

In putting forth our view we do not follow a strategy to present an all-encompassing model that is, or appears to be, appropriate for dealing with all macroeconomic problems. After surveying related models, we rather discuss and employ different variants of the dynamic macroeconomic tradition that help us to highlight particular issues in macroeconomics and obtain definite results.

Although this book employs recent tools from dynamic analysis, this is not a book about tools. There are now a number of books on sophisticated tools in macrodynamics, for example, Chiarella 1990, Lorenz 1993, Tu 1994. Our book attempts instead to use these tools to draw out significant economic results within a unified framework rather than to focus on the exposition of the tools. Although the book requires some mathematics, the chapters are not too demanding. In our study of dynamic macroeconomics we combine analytical and numerical methods. References to analytical tools are made in the introductory chapters of the book. Computer simulations are generally not included in the book but can be obtained from the authors upon request.

There are many important writers in the macroeconomic tradition. We apologize for being able to include discussions only on those scholars who have undertaken more formal work in this tradition.

We owe thanks to many generations of students who took our classes in macroeconomics and economic dynamics at the University of Bielefeld and the New School for Social Research. Many chapters of the book were presented at other universities or at conferences and seminars on macroeconomic themes. We thank the participants of conferences and seminars at the University of Bielefeld; the University of Southern California and the University of California, Los Angeles; the State University of New York, Stony Brook; the University of Montreal; the University of Technology, Sydney; the University of Technology, Vienna; the Asia University; the Chuo and Waseda Universities, Tokyo; the UNAM and Metropolitana Universities, Mexico; the Viennese Workshop on Economic Dynamics; the Society of Nonlinear Dynamics and Econometrics; the Society of Computational Economics; and the Society of Economic Dynamics and Control.

We thank the colleagues at our own universities whose discussions have helped us improve the book. We also would like to acknowledge helpful discussions with Toichiro Asada, Jess Benhabib, Phil Cagan, Gustav Feichtinger, Geoffrey Heal, Stefan Mittnik, James Ramsey, Rajiv Sethi, Malte Sieveking, John Sterman, and James Tobin. We are particularly grateful to Richard Day, who has provided support with suggestions on the exposition of the book, with clarifying the main themes, and with detailed comments on major chapters. We also want to thank our research assistants Xiaoyun Wang, Friedrich Hübler, Gang Gong, and Raul Zambrano. We want to thank many anonymous referees who have read an earlier version of the manuscript and have very much helped the book to become a better product. We are also grateful to Ann Sweeny for editorial assistance. Finally we want to thank Terry Vaughn from the MIT Press for his unflagging support and his assistance in keeping the book focused and readable for a broader audience.

1 General Introduction

1.1 Introduction

Since the 1970s there have been a variety of schools designing frameworks for macroeconomic analysis ranging from Keynesians, monetarists, and the rational expectations school to the new Keynesians. What has been increasingly understood across schools is that macroeconomic theory has to choose an intrinsically dynamic approach. In fact the need for dynamic macroeconomics was already recognized in the 1930s and 1940s when the first models of macro fluctuations and business cycles were put forward by theorists such as Michael Kalecki, Ragnar Frisch, Nicholas Kaldor, John Hicks, Paul Samuelson, and Richard Goodwin. In those contributions it was shown that the dynamic interaction of the multiplier and the accelerator in Keynesian macroeconomic models can generate fluctuations in output and employment. Those theories focused mainly on the dynamics of the product markets. The IS-LM framework allowed the inclusion of the money market and—in more elaborate extensions—the labor market dynamics by including a Phillips curve. Further extensions of this approach incorporating price and price expectations dynamics in disequilibrium models have been undertaken since the 1970s from the supply side by Stanley Fischer, Jerome Stein, Hugh Rose, and Thomas Sargent and from the demand-side perspective by James Tobin.

Macroeconomic theory of that tradition, however, has been criticized since the 1970s, when a search for a new microeconomic framework of macroeconomics began. Areas in this quest have included the rational expectations revolution that adopted a market-clearing, intertemporal equilibrium approach based on stochastic growth models. While some pursued this new research perspective, others continued the investigation of various variants of nonmarket-clearing and out-of-equilibrium adjustment models in the spirit of Keynes and Wicksell, taking up the challenge of reformulating expectations formation. In the latter type of work the fluctuations of macroeconomic data are frequently explained by referring to strong endogenous propagation mechanisms. By contrast, the market-clearing approach has relied on the Slutsky-Frisch impulse-propagation mechanism emerging in the 1930s to explain the variability of macroeconomic times series. An example of this is found in the Real Business Cycle (RBC) model in which stochastic shocks to real activity—initiated by technology shocks—are assumed to impinge on output and employment. It is worthwhile to contrast the essential elements of both the nonmarket-clearing and market-clearing approaches.

1.2 Market-Clearing Approach to Dynamic Macroeconomics

The market-clearing approach to macrodynamics has focused on equilibrium models. Work of this type can be found in Benhabib 1992, Cooley 1995, and is evaluated in, for example, Blanchard and Fischer 1989 and Turnovsky 1995. The starting point of those macrodynamic models are the Ramsey type of optimal growth or overlapping generations models (Grandmont 1988; Benhabib 1992; Azariadis 1993; Stokey and Lucas 1989). The following list highlights a few essentials of the equilibrium business cycle models regarding their view of microeconomic behavior, dominant adjustment mechanisms, determination of spending behavior, and dynamic properties.

- Macrotheory is built on microeconomic principles, using the competitive equilibrium model with given endowments of agents, preferences and technology as a reference model. The equilibrium approach posits that representative agents (e.g., consumers, firms) are rational, have full information, and optimize intertemporally. The paths of prices, wages, and rental rates of capital are usually assumed to be known in advance. The decision-making process is modeled as if decisions are undertaken by an idealized policy maker and as if this were a good approximation of the complex decision making in an industrial society.
- The dominant adjustment mechanisms are price adjustments, which are supposed to equilibrate markets infinitely fast. A perfect foresight

path of prices is often assumed so that markets can instantaneously clear. In intertemporal models with typical saddle point properties, prices are assumed to jump in order to bring about convergence to the long-run equilibrium. Product markets are cleared, and imbalances in the labor market are seen to be a result of the choice between leisure-work effort. On empirical grounds, those adjustment processes are problematic, however, since empirical prices move rather slowly and market institutions frequently do not exist to allow for infinitely fast equilibrations of market imbalances.

• Assumptions on the determination of spending behavior of economic agents—particularly consumption and investment spending—are crucial for macro fluctuations. Within the competitive equilibrium framework capital markets are assumed to be perfect and spending is determined by an equilibrium path. Because of the possibility to borrow against future income, consumption, in general, is conceived as smooth. Liquidity and borrowing constraints resulting from imperfect capital markets, which means that one cannot borrow against future income without collaterals, are mainly disregarded. Investment is also determined by an equilibrium path, through the pricing on asset markets. Fluctuations in output, employment, investment, and consumption are the result of technology shocks.

• Most of the equilibrium macromodels exhibit monotone convergence toward the steady state, the fluctuations being brought about by exogenous shocks and the impulse dynamics. There are deterministic variants of this model type where nonlinear mechanisms can generate oscillatory and chaotic motions in intertemporal optimizing variants.[1] Nonlinear data-generating mechanisms that produce a variety of dynamics, such as chaotic orbits (Boldrin and Montrucchio 1986), are admissible, as are bounded fluctuations with an unstable steady state (Dockner and Feichtinger 1991). If we assume complete markets and decreasing returns to scale, however, optimal growth models can display interesting fluctuations only when extreme parameter constellations, for example, extremely high discount rates, are assumed.[2]

With respect to economic policy, real business cycle theorists frequently stress that "The policy implication of this research is that costly efforts at stabilization are likely to be counterproductive. Economic fluctuations are optimal responses to uncertainty in the rate of technological change. . . . Attention should be focused not on fluctuations in output but rather on determinants of the average rate of technological advance" (Prescott 1986, 21). Thus, equilibrium macroeconomists suggest a noninterventionist policy.

1.3 Nonmarket-Clearing Approach to Dynamic Macroeconomics

The nonmarket-clearing theories have focused on diverse sources of instability and macroeconomic fluctuations. Instabilities are seen to originate in: (1) stock-flow relationships (for example, accelerator-multiplier or output-inventory interactions); (2) price dynamics and price expectations dynamics (nominal-real interaction); (3) large demand shocks; (4) the conflict over distributive shares; and (5) the financial sector and the financial-real interaction. These kinds of instabilities were addressed extensively in Keynesian-oriented work.[3] Models of this type have proved useful in econometric modeling, forecasting, and economic policy analysis.[4] The essentials of the nonmarket-clearing approach may be briefly summarized as follows.

• Agents behave adaptively regarding microeconomic behavior. Given an uncertain and complex environment agents cannot have full information on future states of the world and the consequences of their action. They cannot fully optimize since the "cost of optimization"—properly computed—might be very large and, even worse, not known in advance. This often results in the presupposition of bounded rationality or procedural rationality in which agents imitate the behavior of others, follow rules of thumb, and adjust gradually to a changing environment. In addition to this notion of rationality one finds the supposition that expectations are changing gradually. The dominant expectations-generating mechanism is most conveniently specified as adaptive expectations.

• Contrary to widespread prejudice, "Keynesian macroeconomics neither asserts nor requires nominal wage and/or price rigidity. It does assert and require that markets not be instantaneously and continuously cleared by prices" (Tobin 1994, 166). Although some markets may adjust faster than others and for analytical purposes could be considered in temporary equilibrium (e.g., the money market), others, e.g., the labor market, might generally be out of equilibrium. In particular, price adjustments in the product and labor markets are rather slow and are dominated by quantity adjustments. Given gradual price adjustments, accelerator-multiplier models are still often perceived as valid macrodynamic adjustment mechanisms. Prices are perceived to change, but the changes occur slowly and are seen to be driven by labor cost and markups. An important view is that there is a nominal-real interaction with a role for price expectations dynamics and nominal rigidities for quantity adjustments in the business cycle. It also is frequently demonstrated that price flexibility and the speed of price expectations formation may add to instability, not remove it.

• Economic agents may be constrained by liquidity and credit. Because of the view that capital markets are imperfect and agents—not having sufficient collateral—cannot borrow against future income, a large fraction of agents in the economy (e.g., households and firms) are seen to spend what they receive. These agents' current spending is determined by their current income, which may exacerbate economic fluctuations. Thus, financial markets matter for spending and real activity. Although there are agents whose spending is determined by asset positions and permanent income, the majority of the population does not own shares; thus, their spending is curtailed by current income, and with income changing in the business cycle, spending may accelerate business cycle downturns.

• This general perspective shows an attentiveness to positive feedback mechanisms according to which market mechanisms are locally unstable but bounded fluctuations may arise. Such possibilities are already anticipated in the work of Kaldor, Hicks, and Goodwin. Convergence to equilibrium can also exist, but it may be so slow that it becomes nearly irrelevant in real time. Apart from that, there might be multiple equilibria and the economy may end up in a socially undesirable equilibrium.

With the instability of the steady state, adjustment processes that are too slow, or multiple equilibria, even if convergence occurs, interventionist policies may have welfare-improving effects. Labor markets are unlikely to be self-stabilizing—or the stabilizing forces are too weak to be of consequence. Moreover, financial market dynamics and financial instability may add substantially to economic fluctuations. Keynesian macrodynamic theory, therefore, suggests discretionary stabilization policies and, in addition, shows how changes in monetary aggregates affect real activity through the credit channel.

1.4 On Stylized Empirical Facts

Both market clearing and nonmarket-clearing approaches pay great attention to stylized empirical facts in order to match the models' characteristics with properties of macroeconomic times series data. In fact, to contrast macroeconomics with stylized facts presently appears to be a promising route for demonstrating the relevance of macrodynamic theory, although one is obliged to admit that what the stylized facts in macroeconomics are still remains ambiguous and debatable. This may depend on the macroeconomic view one takes and the chosen filtering procedure.[5] It is only consequent, therefore, that each school of thought points out particular stylized facts.

In the equilibrium school of macrodynamics, fluctuations are seen to result from the impulse-propagation mechanism originating in a sequence of randomly occurring shocks to endowment, preferences, or technology. Technology shocks are regarded as the major driving force in the dominant version of the equilibrium macrodynamic theory, that is, RBC models. The theory usually claims that its theoretical properties are empirically matched by the following three types of stylized facts:[6]

- Persistence, that is, a serial correlation, in the time series of technology shocks, GNP, employment, consumption, and investment;
- A hierarchy in volatility, whereby the investment exhibits the highest volatility, followed by the GNP, the Solow-residual, and consumption (as the smoothest time series);
- Positive correlation between GNP, investment, employment, consumption, and hours worked.

Since equilibrium business cycle theory has to demonstrate the existence of unemployment as a result of labor-leisure trade-off—with real wages varying only weakly over the business cycle—it has to postulate an unrealistically high elasticity of labor supply to changes in the real wage. This supposition, however, appears to be strongly at odds with actual macroeconomic time series data. In fact the "available empirical evidence suggests only a minimal response of labor to transitory wage changes" (Summers 1986, 176). In general, equilibrium business cycle models exhibit empirically implausible properties in regard to the time series properties of labor market variables.[7]

The Keynesian tradition[8] attempts to account for the following stylized facts:

• There is a strong cyclical covariation of the (detrended) levels of output, capacity utilization, employment, and labor productivity. In fact, procyclical direct productivity and total factor productivity are the best documented empirical facts about the business cycle; however, in the Keynesian view these reflect less technology shocks than demand changes.

• Compared to output, prices and money wages are relatively sluggish when macroeconomic fluctuations occur (although, as generally recognized, there are some exceptional areas where prices move faster). Real wages fluctuate only minimally, as does the real interest rate. There is only a very weak positive covariation of the real wage (and interest rate) with output and employment.

• Distributional factors, though often neglected in standard models, are important for macrodynamics. Empirical evidence seems to show that the income distribution is strongly impacted not solely by the money (or real) wage but also by the variation of productivity, although there is no clear empirical pattern of the wage share over the business cycle.

• It is commonly accepted that nominal shocks have real effects. In addition, even anticipated monetary shocks may have real effects for economies with lagged price and wage changes.

• Credit and financial factors are considered important in the business cycle (credit-output relation). Financial propagation mechanisms are seen to have amplifying effects on real output and employment. Thus, financial structure and transmission mechanisms, that is, the financial-real interaction should be important building blocks in macrodynamic models.

1.5 Perspective of the Book

The specific perspective taken in the book is as follows. We refer to sources of macroeconomic instabilities and study the out-of-equilibrium dynamics.[9] This first requires a careful specification and examination of adjustment mechanisms that originally arose in traditional studies of market mechanisms. We take the view that prices as well as quantities adjust, although they may react at different speeds. For analytical purposes, some markets could be considered in temporary equilibrium, for example, money or financial markets, while others, for example, the labor market, adjust slowly.

We seek to integrate both growth and fluctuations, in contrast to the traditional IS-LM framework as well as to the earlier multiplier-accelerator approach, which abstracted from growth in order to study fluctuations. In integrating growth and fluctuations, however, we do not employ models of endogenous growth or stochastic optimal growth but rather build on traditional monetary growth models that attempt to integrate the short-, the medium-, and the long-run in a macrodynamic framework.[10] In doing so we will contrast our framework with recent intertemporal approaches on growth and fluctuations.

By studying the interaction of the major markets in a framework of complete and integrated models of IS-LM growth, we avoid the necessity that the building blocks of the IS-LM subsector be of conventional type. It is also worth noting that the full dynamic interaction of complete models are rarely investigated in the literature. Their dynamic properties are basically unknown, even in the case of a conventional IS-LM subsector. Therefore, abandoning these types of models is—even today—premature. They still represent plausible models of monetary growth with both labor and capital under- or overemployed, especially when compared with competing models in this area. This fact is very obvious from, for example, the survey of Orphanides and Solow (1990) on "Money, Inflation and Growth."

An alternative to our aggregate analysis is the conventional aggregate demand/aggregate supply (AD-AS) approach and its extension to a growing economy. However, Barro (1994) has recently pointed out that there is a contradiction in the AD-AS framework because it assumes market-clearing.[11] Barro's (1994, 5) conclusion, therefore, is that the AD-AS model is logically flawed. In chapters 8–9 we perform a thorough investigation of the problematic implications of the AD-AS model under myopic perfect foresight and in the context of economic growth and arrive at this same conclusion, independently of Barro. Like Barro (1994, 1), we conclude from the logical inconsistencies of the AD-AS framework that the AD-AS model should be abandoned. The consequences of this conclusion are far-reaching since they imply that the model of the neoclassical synthesis[12] from which the Keynesian and classical versions of macroeconomic temporary equilibrium are generally obtained as special cases, as, for example, in Sargent 1987, chapter 1–5 and McCallum 1989, chapter 5, is wrong and should be abandoned as a theoretical framework.

If the AD-AS model is no longer employed, does anything Keynesian remain? Our response is again in line with Barro's observations:

> We have available, at this time, two types of internally consistent models that allow for cyclical interactions between monetary and real variables. The conventional IS/LM model achieves this interaction by assuming that the price level and nominal wage rate are typically too high and adjust only gradually toward their market-clearing values. The market-clearing models with incomplete information get this interaction by assuming that people have imperfect knowledge about the general price level. (Barro 1994, 4)

Given these two coherent perspectives, our book primarily extends the first type of internally consistent macrotheory to model fluctuating growth with or without myopic perfect foresight in chapters 8 through 12. These chapters in particular show that the IS-LM method is in fact very general, meaning that goods- and asset-markets equilibria of various types are investigated for gradually adjusting wages and prices (in a growing economy). The outcome is that under- or overemployment of labor or capital generally occurs in a way that does not clear markets.

Conversely, the market-clearing approach is investigated in this book in chapter 5, where we demonstrate how various markets are supposed to clear through wage and price jumps when not on the stable branch of the saddle paths. In contrast to the latter view, most parts of this book take the perspective of gradually adjusting wages and prices by not employing the rational expectations/perfect foresight jump variable technique. We also show that Sargent (1987, chapter 5) uses the jump variable technique in his AD-AS model with perfectly flexible prices and wages, thus resulting in the classical version of the full market-clearing type.[13] Moreover, we demonstrate that the internally consistent IS-LM approach can be extended to the study of fluctuating growth that is highly neglected in the rational expectations/jump variable approach in monetary growth dynamics literature.

The result of fluctuating growth, and thus a sufficient variability of macroeconomic time series, is naturally obtained in an extended IS-LM framework by emphasizing nonlinearities in the shock propagation mechanisms. Recently, a formidable body of economic literature has been published that elaborated on such feedback loops—often in discrete time—in dynamic macroeconomics.[14] In earlier times these nonlinearities have first been studied in the multiplier-accelerator models.

Nonlinearities have also been viewed to be important for the wage-employment dynamics (Goodwin 1967), IS-LM models (Dana and Malgrange 1984; Schinasi 1982), and even Solow-type of growth models (exhibiting chaotic dynamics in discrete time [see Day 1982]), Keynesian versions of monetary-real interaction (Day and Shafer 1987; Day and Lin 1991), or in Keynesian variants of the financial-real interaction (see the diverse papers in Semmler 1989, 1994).

Although we recognize that there is a rich tradition in macroeconomics employing the discrete-time approach—especially since this method may more easily give rise to complex (chaotic) dynamics, as for example, represented by the work of Day[15]—we prefer to work in continuous time. The main reason is that this framework facilitates a mathematical analysis (chaos-generating mechanisms will play no role in this book). Our models must be made discrete ones when we undertake computer simulations, but this is done in such a way that the chosen adjustment period can be arbitrary in order to stay close to the continuous time model. Studying global dynamics, we employ what one might call "essential nonlinearities." These nonlinearities can be roughly conceived of as regime changes and might directly result from thresholds of the state variables beyond which, for example, some reaction coefficients begin to vary. Other essential nonlinearities are created by viability constraints, by which we mean economically reasonable conditions that define dynamic path boundaries, so that they cannot become totally unstable. A last type of important nonlinearity that results from the extension of a proportional control mechanism by a further autocontrol where the time rate of change of variables (derivative control) additionally impacts the adjustment processes.

1.6 A Brief Outlook

This book is organized into five parts. In part I we deal with background models of nonmarket-clearing and market-clearing type, where the emphasis is on nonmarket-clearing models. chapter 2 classifies market adjustment mechanisms at the micro- and macrolevel that are relevant in the nonmarket-clearing tradition literature and which will prove important for subsequent parts of the book. Notably, we present variants, both with and without cross effects between prices and quantities (classical and Keynesian traditions, respectively). Chapter 3 explores the dynamic properties of a variety of microeconomic adjustment mechanisms that have arisen independently from each other in the Walrasian excess demand function tradition and in the classical and Keynesian traditions of economic dynamics. Chapters 4 and 5 then contrast nonmarket- and market-clearing-type macromodels, which have become prototypes for dynamic macroeconomics: The non-neoclassical macro models as developed by Harrod-Domar, Kaldor, Goodwin, and others for goods- and labor-market dynamics, and the neoclassical tradition in macroeconomics originally based on Solow's work but now extended to intertemporal models of growth, stochastic growth, and RBC models in addition to endogenous growth models. In the latter variants income distribution is typically fixed. In both strands, money and money mechanisms are not well integrated, if they are present at all. These issues are addressed in the remainder of the book.

Part II introduces short-run monetary models of macro fluctuations that attempt to build on the dynamic interaction of product, labor, and financial markets. In both this section and part III we pursue the question of price and price expectations dynamics as sources of real macroeconomic instability. The nominal-real interaction, a topic that Tobin (1994) has recently revived, is studied here with respect to a still stationary economy. For simplicity, we also abstract from capital accumulation. Models with adjustment mechanisms akin to the ones discussed in part I are introduced where adjustment speeds appear to be essential for the monetary models' stability properties. We also introduce Keynesian versions of monetary models where wage and price flexibility will indeed give rise to instability. The obtained result on price flexibility resembles the Harrod knife edge problem, which now arises, however, from the wage-price dynamics, not from the quantity dynamics.

In part III we continue to investigate monetary instability in variants with capital accumulation and growth. With respect to inflationary expectations we often contrast adaptive expectations (AE) and the limiting case of myopic perfect foresight. Occasionally multiperiod ahead forecasts are also considered (the use of the concept of AE's is defended in chapter 7). In this context we focus particularly on conventional aggregate demand–aggregate supply (or AD-AS) approaches to monetary growth where an instantaneous adjustment of the price level to the equilibrium value is generally assumed. In chapter 8 the AD-AS approach as presented in Sargent's book *Macroeconomic Theory* (1987, especially chap. 5) is translated into so-called Keynes-Wicksell models, which are presented in great detail, for example, in Stein 1982. We also provide a criticism of myopic perfect foresight versions of such macromodels, and of the jump-variable technique by showing that they can become logically inconsistent and extremely unrealistic. We conclude these models should be replaced by IS-LM growth models, thereby allowing gradual wage and price adjustment throughout, as well as perfect or gradual expectations formations. Subsequently, in chapter 9, we develop a more classically oriented version of macro fluctuations that stresses the role of income distribution, money, and expectations formation in an IS-LM growth context. This integrated model appears to be more consistently formulated and better attuned to the stylized facts of the business cycle than the AD-AS growth variant assuming market-clearing price jumps. This holds true not only in the case of an adaptive formation of expectations as well as for multiperiod ahead forecasts of decision variables, but also for the "limit case" of myopic perfect foresight.

In part IV supply- and demand-side Keynesian business cycles and monetary-type growth models are explored. Macroeconomic adjustment mechanisms exhibiting both cross-effects between prices and quantities (classical tradition) and no cross-effects (Keynesian tradition) are employed to study fluctuations in the context of such monetary macromodels. In chapter 10 we study the tradition of supply-side-oriented Keynesian business cycle theory, the Keynes-Wicksell approach of monetary growth as put forward by Stein and Rose, and further investigated by Fischer and by Sargent and others. Here, prices are gradually adjusted with price adjustments being a sign-preserving function of excess demand. By contrast, the model in chapter 11 is definitely demand constrained. It drops marginal productivity theory, builds on markup pricing, and the markup itself adjusts dynamically. The resulting variations in income distribution may add to macroeconomic instability and fluctuations. As a central stabilizing force we introduce a flexibilization in the rigid mechanism of adaptive inflationary expectations. The model addresses stylized facts of price, real wage, and productivity changes over the business cycle. It is calibrated in such a way that the fluctuations can account for a number of empirical regularities over the business cycle.

Part V is concerned with the role of the financial sector as a source of instability and fluctuations. In chapter 12 we present a model with finance and financial structure that builds on credit-dependent firms and emphasizes the credit view of economic activities. Furthermore, inflation is dropped as the central expectational variable. It is replaced with long-term expectations of the general business climate, where we draw heavily on chapter 12 of Keynes's *General Theory*. By determining the adjustments in investors' sentiments by subjective as well as objective factors, we work out the stabilizing and destabilizing potential for the economy. This interplay can again lead to oscillatory behavior (inclusive of corridor stability of the steady state). Here, too, we attempt to account for some empirical regularities. Aspects of the financial structure of firms are stylized in a dynamic model and empirically analyzed in chapter 13. A decomposition of the capital structure into trend and cyclical components—as well as into different components determining the long-run trend—is undertaken to study low-frequency movements and the role of inflation in the financial structure of firms in the aggregate. This last chapter serves as background for chapter 12, where these issues are disregarded.

1.7 Dynamic Tools and Econometric Issues

We may say that recently the nonmarket-clearing as well as the market-clearing approaches apply similar technical tools in studying macroeconomic dynamics. Both borrow from recent advances in the mathematical literature on nonlinear system dynamics.

We want to mention what particular technical tools are involved in our study. We use the established toolbox of local stability analysis based on linear approximations and the global stability analysis of planar systems. We also make use of special limit-cycle configurations—so-called relaxation oscillations—and employ Liapunov functions and their stability implications from a local as well as a global perspective. We employ the Poincaré-Bendixson and related theroems. Also, local Hopf bifurcation theory is frequently used in this book. Presentations of this material that are not too technical are provided in Hirsch and Smale 1974; Guckenheimer and Holmes 1983; Arrowsmith and Place 1990; and Wiggins 1990, and with many economic applications in Gandolfo 1985; Gabisch and Lorenz 1989; Lorenz 1993; and Azariadis 1993. In addition we employ some elementary tools of dynamic optimization (see Stokey and Lucas 1989) for the intertemporal models in chapter 5.

Our mathematical tools, therefore, consist of the more traditional theorems on nonlinear dynamical systems. This is mainly due to the continuous-time approach (without delays) here adopted, which minimizes the use of lags in the formulation of models of real and monetary growth and their stationary forerunners. In our view, significant economic lags may be introduced and motivated in a second step, after the macrodynamic interactions that abstract from them have been thoroughly understood. There may also be some scope for less regular dynamics.[16] This book consequently investigates two-, three-, and four-dimensional dynamical systems which, as far as we have explored them, do not yet give rise to really "complicated dynamics." We expect, however, that the further investigation and extension of these IS-LM growth cycle approaches will also reveal more complicated dynamics in this continuous time framework.

Lastly, it is worthwhile to note the relation of this book to recent developments in dynamic econometrics. A large number of empirical studies have focused on nonlinear dynamic interactions in macroeconomic time series data and on chaos. New methods have been proposed to detect nonlinear propagation mechanisms (e.g., business cycle data, financial data), such as the Brock, Deckert, and Scheinkman (BDS) chaos test (see Brock, Hsie, and LeBaron 1991), univariate and multivariate threshold models, as well as time irreversibility, and wavelet models. In particular threshold models appear to be well suited to capture regime changes in the cross-effects between variables. These types of studies have been growing increasing common recently. They address the problem of detecting strong and asymmetric propagation and impulse-response mechanisms.[17] This new work in dynamic econometrics aims at capturing limit cycles, jump phenomena, thresholds, and asymmetric behaviors. These phenomena test positively in many recent studies on macroeconomic time series such as output, unemployment, real wage, prices, monetary aggregates, interest rates spreads, stock returns, and exchange rate data. As these econometric methods indicate, compelling nonlinearities may be involved in a large number of economic and financial time series (see Ramsey 1988). It is therefore useful to initiate a cross-fertilization between dynamic macroeconomics and dynamic econometrics. We hope that our book might help to further this pursuit.

1.8 Notation and Abbreviations

As a general rule, constant behavioral parameters are denoted by a Greek letter, mostly β. A subscript is often added that is derived from context. The (indexed) letter f stands for a behavioral or technical functional relationship that may be nonlinear.[18] In all other cases, subscripts are usually employed to denote partial derivatives, for example, F_K in the production function. The functions f are assumed to be at least twice continuously differentiable. Steady state or (in the case of productivity) trend values are indicated by an asterisk. A dot over a dynamic variable $x = x(t)$ denotes the time derivative, $\dot{x} = dx/dt$; a caret its growth rate, $\hat{x} = \dot{x}/x$. Occasionally, a superscript d or s is used to refer to demand or supply terms.

The main variables and parameters of the various models are designated as follows:

B outstanding government (fixed-price) bonds
C real private consumption
E number of equities
F neoclassical production function; $F = F(K, L)$
G real government demand
H high-powered money
I real net investment of fixed capital
K stock of fixed capital
L volume of employment (working hours)
L^s labor supply (with respect to normal working hours)
M stock of money supply (if the banking sector is suppressed)
S total saving; $S = S_h + S_g$
S_g government saving
S_h private saving
T real tax collections
W real wealth of the private sector
Y real output (net of intermediate inputs) or total income, respectively
Y^d disposable income
Y^p potential (maximal) output
Z inventories of finished goods
c consumption per unit of capital; $c = C/K$
c_h households' propensity to consume; $c_h = 1 - s_h$
e employment rate; $e = L/L^s$
g_k growth rate of fixed capital; $g_k = I/K$
g_m (constant) growth rate of money supply
h the length of the adjustment period (in years) in a discrete-time setting for the computer simulations
i nominal rate of interest on government bonds, or on loans (in chapters 12 and 13)
k capital intensity; $k = K/L$
l labor intensity; $l = L/K$
m real balances relative to capital stock; $m = M/pK$
n growth rate of labor supply; $n = \hat{L}^s$
p price level
p_b price of bonds; $p_b = 1$
p_e price of equities

p_k demand price of capital
q Tobin's (average) q; $q = p_e E/pK$
r rate of return on capital (specification depends on context)
i_f investment function parameter
s_f retention ratio of firms
s_h propensity to save of households
u unemployment rate; $u = 1 - e = (L^s - L)/L^s$
v wage share (in gross product); $v = wL/pY$
w nominal wage rate
x output-capital ratio (utilization of capital); $x = Y/K$
x^c utilization of productive capacity; $x^c = Y/Y^p$
x^p potential (maximal) output-capital ratio; $x^p = Y^p/K$
y labor productivity; $y = Y/L$
y^p potential (maximal) labor productivity; $y^p = Y^p/L$
$y^\star$ trend (normal) value of labor productivity
z inventories per unit of capital; $z = Z/K$
β_π speed of adjustment of the rate of inflation in adaptive expectations
γ government expenditures per unit of capital; $\gamma = G/K$
δ constant rate of capital depreciation
$\eta_{e,\sigma}$ elasticity of equity holding with respect to $\sigma = r + \rho - (i - \pi)$
$\eta_{m,i}$ interest elasticity of money demand (expressed as a positive number)
θ real taxes (net of interest) per unit of capital; $\theta = (T - iB/p)/K$
Λ stock of loans of firms from commercial banks
λ debt-asset ratio; $\lambda = \Lambda/pK$
μ markup rate over unit labor cost
π current rate of inflation; $\pi = \hat{p}$
π^e expected rate of inflation
ρ state of confidence (investor sentiment; difference between expected and present rate of profit), in chapter 12; or discount rate, in chapter 5
σ difference between profit rate and expected real interest rate; $\sigma = r - (i - \pi^e)$ ($\sigma = r + \rho - (i - \pi^e)$ in chapter 12)
ϕ high-powered money relative to capital stock; $\phi = H/pK$
χ proportion of net investment financed by equity issuance
ω real wage rate; $\omega = (w/p)$ (in chapter 11 deflated by trend productivity $y^\star$, i.e. $\omega = (w/p)/y^\star$)
τ tax rate on gross profits of firms

To avoid the repetition of lengthy standard expressions we shall make use of the following abbreviations:

IS-LM	IS-LM Model (gradual adjustment of p or μ)
AD-AS	Aggregate Demand–Aggregate Supply Model (instantaneous adjustment of p)
RE	Rational Expectations
ARE	Asymptotically Rational Expectations
MPF	Myopic Perfect Foresight
AE	Adaptive Expectations
CTM	Continuous Time Model
DTM	Discrete Time Model

I

Market Mechanisms and Macrodynamics: Basic Models

The first part of the book begins with a reconsideration of dynamic market mechanisms. Here Walrasian adjustment rules have usually been defined as price adjustments under fixed quantities, whereas Keynesian adjustments—attributed to the influence of Marshall on Keynes—have been viewed as quantity adjustments in the presence of fixed prices. In addition, we take up the classical tradition where prices impact on quantities and quantities on prices. Chapter 2 accordingly classifies the combinations of these adjustment rules.

Chapter 3 provides an analytical treatment of the stylized market mechanisms. Some of the variants, especially the versions with cross-effects between prices and quantities and a derivative auto-control, may give rise to a locally unstable equilibrium but globally bounded fluctuations, which furthermore can be of a rather complex type. The stability analysis itself is undertaken by constructing a measure of a distance from the equilibrium, a so-called Liapunov function, and by means of numerical simulations. A comparison to the advanced literature on market mechanisms is given in the appendix of the chapter.

Chapters 4 and 5 turn to macrodynamic systems. Both nonmarket- and market-clearing approaches are discussed. Chapter 4 studies non-neoclassical disequilibrium models. Originating in the growth theory influenced by classical or Keynesian economics, they often exhibit local instability of the growth equilibrium. Their prototype character allows the application of elegant analytical tools from dynamical systems analysis. The economic concepts put forward in these models will prove to be relevant in parts III and IV of the book.

In the dynamic macroeconomic market-clearing tradition, the Solow model and its extension to Ramsey-type intertemporal resource allocation models have become central. They are based on representative agents—consumers and firms—and intertemporally optimizing behavior. In chapter 5 it is demonstrated that with the standard assumptions on production and utility functions, these models primarily display monotone paths toward the steady-state position. They are brought about by the requirement of the rational expectations hypothesis that initial adjustments to unanticipated shocks let the economy jump onto the stable branch of the saddle-point equilibrium. Stochastic optimal growth models, popularized as real business cycle models, employ the Slutsky-Frisch methodology of impulse-propagation mechanisms to explain the variability of macroeconomic time series data by exogenous shocks. More specifically, the fluctuations in output and employment that we observe in reality are here generated mainly by sequences of technology shocks. We also include a brief discussion of other variants of equilibrium dynamics: endogenous growth models and intertemporal models with money and finance.

2 Micro- and Macroeconomic Adjustment Mechanisms: A Brief Overview

2.1 Introduction

Price and quantity adjustments have become central in macroeconomic controversies.[1] There are two polar versions. One represents the sticky-price model where quantities adjust primarily when markets are out of equilibrium, and the other is a version where prices move infinitely fast to clear markets. The first position is advanced by the new Keynesians. In new Keynesian versions the imperfect market/imperfect information framework is employed to justify sluggish price and fast quantity adjustments.[2] The other position can be attributed to the equilibrium approach in macroeconomics. An evaluation of this position in the context of the AD-AS model is given in chapters 8 and 9.[3]

Though in both the new Keynesian and the rational expectations school micro theories are invoked to explain why prices are sticky, or, in the other extreme, prices move quickly to clear markets, neither school is much concerned with the interaction of the price and quantity dynamics. There is, however, a long microeconomic tradition on the matter of price-quantity adjustments that is worth investigating. A variety of market adjustments have been stylized in the history of economic analysis that are equally important for the nonmarket-clearing tradition. In this introductory chapter we will briefly classify them but will not yet elaborate on the behavioral assumptions, the implied market structure, and the dynamic properties of the different types of mechanisms.

2.2 Microeconomic Adjustment Mechanisms

The study of market adjustment mechanisms began with the works of the great classical economists.[4] Market adjustments were perceived to be stable and even converging because of cross-effects between prices and quantities: Imbalances between price and cost lead to changes in quantities; imbalances in demand and supply drive prices toward long-run "natural prices." Although verbal statements of this kind can be found in the writings of all classical economists, the statements are not supported by a detailed analytical stability demonstration of such mechanisms. Since the 1950s there have been important contributions to the analysis of this type of dynamics employing more formal tools.[5]

With the contributions of John Hicks (1939) and Paul Samuelson (1947), the classical study of market dynamics was turned into the dynamic study of excess demand functions where only one law of motion was perceived: the law of excess demand. Here, in general, stability is obtained when goods are gross-substitutes or when the weak axiom of revealed preferences can be shown to hold. A stability results survey of the studies originating in Hicks and Samuelson is given in Hahn 1982.

Resuming the discussion along classical lines, Goodwin (1953, 1983) made an early contribution to a classification of microeconomic adjustment mechanisms and a thorough study of the dynamics of them by using Liapunov functions and gradient processes. The contributions by Goodwin appear to be of particular importance since they also point out the relation between micro- and macroeconomic adjustment mechanisms. In Goodwin and Punzo 1987, for example, one finds the following four basic types of market adjustments classified:

(I) as $p_i \lesseqgtr cost_i$, p_i falls (rises)

(II) as $p_i \lesseqgtr cost_i$, q_i rises (falls)

(III) as $d_i \lesseqgtr q_i$, q_i rises (falls)

(IV) as $d_i \lesseqgtr q_i$, p_i rises (falls)

where $p_i =$ prices, $q_i =$ quantities supplied, $d_i =$ quantities demanded. In addition, they note that "of course, there are various combinations of the cases. This, with at least three types of control routine, makes rather a lot of cases"(ibid, 78). The three types of control routine mentioned are proportional, derivative, and integral control (see chapter 3 for further discussions on this matter).[6]

The classical market adjustment process with cross-effects between prices and quantities has been called cross-dual dynamics by Morishima (1976, 1977). It can be portrayed by the twin concepts II and IV above. More specifically it reads

$$\text{price} > \text{cost} \quad \longrightarrow \text{increase in supply}$$

$$\text{demand} > \text{supply} \longrightarrow \text{increase in prices}$$

and, of course, "decrease" in place of "increase" in the "<" case. As noted above, the origin of this approach to general market dynamics is not necessarily Walrasian, though a description of it, for the case of an economy with production, can be found in Walras 1977, chapters 12 and 18. The adjustment rules II and IV are a description of a proportional autocontrol mechanism operating through cross-effects between prices and quantities. The one-sided process based on the law of demand as introduced by Hicks (1939), however, is commonly stylized through adjustment rules of type IV, with quantities determined by the planned demand and supply of households and firms.

Price-quantity adjustments II and IV were first formally modeled by Goodwin ([1953] 1983) in terms of a Walrasian competitive economy, then later in the context of a von Neumann growth economy (Goodwin 1983), and further explored by Duménil and Lévy (1987), Franke (1987), and Flaschel and Semmler (1987), and many other contributions. A Leontief input-output framework is also a convenient way to formalize the two dynamic processes. Details of such a formulation are given in Flaschel and Semmler 1988. The cross-dual dynamics is investigated for Walrasian general equilibrium models in chapter 3.

In the Keynesian tradition, however, adjustment processes such as II and IV have been considered unsatisfactory. In Keynesian literature, building on imperfect competition and oligopolistic market structure, adjustments such as I and III have been favored where no cross-effects between prices and quantities occur. These adjustment processes have been called "dual dynamics."[7] Here, price and quantity movements may even be completely independent of each other. These two dynamic processes can be stylized as follows:

$$\text{price} > \text{cost} \quad \longrightarrow \text{decrease in price}$$

$$\text{demand} > \text{supply} \longrightarrow \text{increase in supply}$$

Again, of course, in the "<" case "increase" in place of "decrease" and vice versa. Economies in which only the process III prevails have been called fix-price economies since prices are considered to be fixed when quantities change.[8] It has been maintained that the above dual dynamics can already be found in Keynes.[9] In fact, the quantity adjustment process III has become an essential element in non-Walrasian models on quantity rationing and disequilibrium analysis. The price adjustment I has been elaborated by many Keynesians. For the most part, some kind of markup pricing is involved to justify these dynamics.[10] It might, however, be fair to state that recent microeconomic theories of quantity and price adjustment do in rare cases put forward dynamic formulations of such adjustment processes.

Early dynamic versions of the adjustment processes I and III can be found in Jorgenson 1960 where the so-called dual (in)stability theorem is derived on the basis of the assumption of full utilization of capacity and perfect foresight path of prices. Mathematical formulations of such dual dynamics can also be found in the work of Morishima (1976, 1977), Goodwin (1988), and Aoki (1977); also see Mas-Colell 1986 for a slightly different version. Here, for the most part, the assumptions of full utilization of capacity and perfect foresight are dropped when a stability analysis of the dynamics is provided. Again one can stylize such market mechanisms I and III in the context of a von Neumann growth model or by employing a Leontief input–output framework (see Goodwin and Punzo 1987; Flaschel and Semmler 1987, 1988), or by utilizing a Walrasian general equilibrium approach as in Mas-Colell 1986.

It is worth noting that the above two traditions in quantity and price dynamics—the classical dynamics, based on cross-effects between prices and quantities, and the Keynesian variant, relying on two independent adjustment mechanisms—can be integrated into one unifying framework, a composite system where both the quantity and the price adjustments simultaneously follow two laws instead of only one.

A study of those composite adjustment processes where cross-dual and dual dynamics emerge as special cases is undertaken in Flaschel and Semmler 1988. In this study output changes are considered to be initiated by two laws: in the long run, differentials in rates of return affect output, but in the short run, output is changed in addition by the level of excess demand. Similarly, price changes are brought about by two adjustment mechanisms. Firms, from the long-run perspective, are presumed to price their products by computing their marked up normal costs, which are assumed to be corrected by the actual level of excess demand.

The stability properties of those composite models are not easily explored. Under certain restrictive conditions concerning the reaction speeds, stability results can be obtained. We further pursue this modeling approach to microdynamics in chapter 3 in the context of Walrasian general equilibrium theory. We also will introduce, additionally to the proportional control, the concept of derivative control as a promising extension of the market mechanisms II and IV.

This concept of derivative control, though from a purely formal point of view, was first discussed by Kose (1956) in the framework of input-output models. It means that in the context of our above market dynamics with cross-effects supply might not react solely to differentials in rates of return among activities but also to the rate of change of those differentials. Similarly, price adjustments are not only a sign-preserving function of excess demand, but prices also respond to the rate of change in excess demand. Formally, these adjustment processes can be stylized as follows:

$$\text{(price} - \text{cost)} + \Delta\text{(price} - \text{cost)} \longrightarrow \text{change in supply}$$

$$\text{(demand} - \text{supply)} + \Delta\text{(demand} - \text{supply)} \longrightarrow \text{change in prices}$$

where Δ means the time rate of change of excess demand or excess of price over cost. As will be seen for micro adjustment processes—and also for macroeconomic adjustment processes—introducing such derivative forces may enhance the stability properties of the dynamics significantly. In addition, the concept of a derivative autocontrol may not be applicable in the vicinity of steady states, but may become increasingly important far away from them, where it then helps to understand why price-quantity fluctuations are globally bounded, though not necessarily convergent. Finally, the question of "universal stability" of market mechanisms—built on the concept of derivative control—will be discussed in chapter 3.

2.3 Macroeconomic Adjustment Mechanisms

From the formal point of view there is a clear relation of the dynamics with cross-effects II and IV and classical growth dynamics to be introduced in chapter 4. The Goodwin (1967) version of the classical growth dynamics, for example, is characterized by the interaction of employment and wages with cross-effects from one to the other. In fact the classical growth cycle model gives rise to the same type of neutral cyclical behavior that characterizes the classical microeconomic price-quantity adjustments, namely, center-type dynamics. Due to these cross-effects—between prices and quantities on the micro, and employment and wages on the macro level—pure oscillatory movements arise. For both micro as well as macro dynamics, however, it holds that small perturbations may easily alter the conservative oscillations, thereby producing totally stable or unstable trajectories. The latter case gives rise to the question of what bounds these trajectories far off the steady state.

It is in the Keynes-Wicksell tradition of real or monetary macrodynamics[11] where one again finds macroeconomic adjustment mechanisms that mirror the micro mechanism with cross-effects between prices and quantities as in II and IV. According to the adjustment rule IV, price adjustments occur when there are imbalances between demand and supply. Correspondingly, for aggregate economic activity it has been posited that the following adjustment mechanisms for the goods and labor market prevail

$$\hat{w} = \beta_w(L/L^s - 1) + \pi_p^e$$

$$\hat{p} = \beta_p(I - S)/K + \pi_w^e$$

where a caret as in $\hat{x}$ denotes the growth rate of a variable, w is the money wage, p the price level, L, L^s labor demand and supply, and I, S investment and saving (β_p and β_w are given adjustment speeds). These two cross-dual adjustment rules are—as is customary now in macroeconomics—augmented by terms π_p^e, π_w^e, which represent the expected rate of price and wage inflation. In the above context one can make use of a variety of formulations of the dynamics that drives expectations π_p^e, π_w^e. Different variants of expectations formations are studied in chapters 7–10 in particular. The above two dynamic equations provide a straightforward application of cross-dual price adjustment rules, or of the law of demand, to two basic markets of the macroeconomy.

The microeconomic quantity adjustment rule of type II is also present in the above type of disequilibrium monetary macro theory. This is quite obvious if we consider the case where the growth path of the capital stock is determined by net investment that is not necessarily equal to savings in the present context. The growth rate of capital stock is then made dependent in these Keynes-Wicksell models on the expected differential between the rate of return on physical capital and on financial assets, for example in the following simple way:

$$\hat{K} = I/K = i_f(r - \delta - (i - \pi_p^e)) + n$$

where i_f is an adjustment parameter, r, the marginal product of capital, δ the depreciation rate, i the nominal rate of interest, and n the rate of population growth. This formulation of an investment function relates the real and the financial sector in a classical way, and it stresses the point that price discrepancies are the primary sources of quantity adjustments.

Lastly, we want to add that the adjustment rules based on cross-effects of prices and quantities as in II and IV are not confined to descriptive (nonoptimizing) macro models. Intertemporal versions with optimizing behavior of firms or households frequently also exhibit cross-effects between state variables (or state and control variables), often with intriguing dynamics resulting from them.[12]

The microeconomic dynamics with no cross effects between prices and quantities as proposed in I and III also find their counterparts in macroeconomic theory. The simplest example of a pure quantity feedback mechanism is given by the dynamic multiplier process of Keynesian theory as it finds, for example, application in all models adopting Kaldor's approach to the trade cycle (see section 4.3). Furthermore, the Keynesian growth theory originating in the work of Harrod (1948) is also based on pure quantity adjustments as stylized in III. In the famous knife-edge problem of Harrod an at least locally unstable macrodynamic mechanism is generated through the interaction of the static multiplier with an accelerator mechanism based on expected sales. Appropriate assumptions on expectations formation then guarantee that deviations from the "warranted growth path" (where expectations are confirmed and stationary) are always amplified, even when they are of the myopic perfect foresight type. This latter situation can, for example, be derived as follows: Assume the Keynesian multiplier (in its equilibrium formulation) in the following simple form $Y = \frac{1}{s}I$, where s is a constant savings propensity and Y, I output and net investment. Assume furthermore that the growth rate of investment per unit of capital I/K depends in the following simple and straightforward way on the deviation of actual capacity utilization $x = Y/K$ (correctly anticipated) from the given desired level $x^\star$:

$$\widehat{I/K} = \beta_x(x - x^\star), \qquad \beta_x > 0$$

Since output must grow at the same rate as investment, in this model the rate $\widehat{I/K}$ can be replaced by the rate of change in capacity utilization $\hat{x}$, whereby a direct and positive feedback of the rate of capacity utilization onto itself is established. Deviations of the rate of capacity utilization from its desired level are therefore not corrected but amplified. A Harrodian instability of this kind is further investigated in section 4.2.

One often finds corresponding to this macroeconomic pure quantity adjustment in models of Keynesian variety the presumption that price adjustments take the form of type I. This is frequently justified with reference to the theory of full-cost or markup pricing. Hicks (1965, chap. 7) already notes that the full-cost or markup theory is the counterpart of the Keynesian theory of quantity adjustment. A similar view is expressed in Kaldor (1985, chap. 4). The markup, in the context of such an adjustment rule does not, however, need to be arbitrary. Starting with Kalecki (1943), a number of economists have offered theories that have attempted to provide a microeconomic foundation of proper markups set by firms.

A particularly simple example for a pure price adjustment mechanism can be provided as follows. Assume that prices p are modified in the direction of a target level $p^\star$ and that this target level is given by marked-up unit wage costs $p^\star = (1+\mu)wL/Y$, μ the markup and w again the level of money wages. If the level of wages is given and if it is assumed that labor productivity Y/L is constant, we get the following price adjustment rule

$$\dot{p} = \beta_p((1+\mu)wL/Y - p), \qquad \beta_p > 0$$

which again describes a direct effect of the price level onto its rate of change; in contrast to the quantity side, however, a negative and thus stable one. Such a mechanism will find application in various parts of the book.

We also want to mention that price dynamics of cross-dual type in its interaction with expected price changes—the latter formulated, for example, as adaptive expectations—may, however, again give rise to totally unstable dynamics similar to the quantity dynamics of Harrodian type. In price models of this type the instability of the price side typically arises from the assumption that there is a positive feedback of inflationary expectations onto the level of economic activity and thus on the actual rate of inflation (see Tobin 1975). There the dynamic multiplier process of Keynesian economics interacts with a money wage Phillips curve as presented above and a static markup theory of the price level ($\beta_p = \infty$), and thus with a Phillips curve as used in the debate between Keynesians and monetarists.[13] This combination of two dual price and quantity adjustment mechanisms[14] combined with one cross-dual price adjustment mechanism has led to corridor stability and instability scenarios in Tobin (1975) and in subsequent work on his approach. A thorough study of this problem of price and wage flexibility and instability is undertaken in chapter 7 there on the basis of a finite adjustment speed of the price level to its target level, too.

We have sketched major types of micro- and macroeconomic adjustment mechanisms that will reappear in the remainder of the book. We have, however, neither introduced specific behavioral theories that provide justifications for the assumed different types of adjustments, nor did we study more thoroughly the stability properties of those mechanisms. These will be studied next, on the microlevel in chapter 3 and for partial models of macrodynamics in chapter 4.

3 Market Mechanisms and Boundedness of Market Fluctuations

3.1 Introduction

In the nonmarket-clearing approaches, market adjustments can be stylized as dynamics with cross-effects (classical view) or no cross-effects (Keynesian view) between prices and quantities. This chapter[1] demonstrates focusing on the former but admitting for utility-maximizing households and profit-maximizing firms that classical market dynamics can also be presented in the framework of general equilibrium analysis of Walrasian type and related to Walras's view on the working of competition in a production economy. This perspective is presented in section 3.2, where the cyclical nature of the dynamics with cross-effects is investigated for the one-input/one-output case. A proposition describing how to obtain local asymptotic stability in the general multicommodity case is also provided. In section 3.3 Keynesian adjustment processes and their integration with the classical view are introduced and investigated. It is shown that the Keynesian adjustment process is locally asymptotically stable under well-known conditions on the production structure of the economy. It is furthermore argued that its integration with the classical process does not improve the stability properties of the latter.

In section 3.4, we pursue the question of how classical or other market adjustment processes, based on the traditional proportional control of prices by the levels of excess demands, will be impacted by the inclusion of a derivative control term. We show how trajectories of prices and quantities—if not locally—may be globally bounded. This property carries over to the general multicommodity case. Although the local and global stability results obtained here are valid only for restricted choices concerning the strength of the derivative control terms, the approach is rather encouraging when compared with the results for the various purely proportional controls of prices considered in the literature.

In the appendix, our method of making arbitrary equilibria of a Walrasian production economy asymptotically stable, or at least viable (bounded in its dynamics) by an appropriate choice of a derivative control, is contrasted with recent studies on excess demand functions, Walrasian *tâtonnement* processes and other dynamics such as the Newton Method (Smale 1976) and elaborations on it (Varian 1977; Saari and Simon 1978; and Jordan 1983). It is shown that our extended dynamics, which add derivative control mechanisms to the conventional Walrasian tâtonnement procedure, represent in fact a Generalized Newton Method for which, however, only information provided by the market mechanism itself is required to make it converge under quite general conditions. We should also note that we do not claim that the following processes are necessarily realistic. Many complicated feedbacks of a consistently formulated economic environment are set aside. But to lay bare the essentials of an economic adjustment mechanism in an (extremely) stylized environment may represent one useful approach on the way to construct proper types of market adjustment processes.

Technically, we study the local dynamics in this chapter by employing linearization and its indirect stability assertions as well as local bifurcation theory. This latter theory is presented in its details, including economic applications, in for example, Lorenz 1993 and Tu 1994. From a more global point of view, we refer to the Poincaré-Bendixson theorem and to theorems on Liapunov functions. These mathematical techniques are thoroughly explained in, for example, Hirsch and Smale 1974. Since these mathematical tools for the analysis of dynamical systems are well documented in the economic literature, we do not present them here, but instead confine ourselves to visual and intuitive characterizations when using these tools.

3.2 Walrasian Price-Quantity Adjustments

We begin with the one-input / one-output case of Walrasian economics to introduce market dynamics with cross-effects between price and quantity adjustment. This replaces the one-sided price adjustment process that is generally considered in a Walrasian approach. In the next section the adjustments with cross-effects are compared with, and augmented by, dual or direct price-quantity adjustments, thereby giving rise to richer dynamic features though the stability properties are in general not enhanced. Subsequently, our modified dynamics including derivative forces will be introduced and investigated. Which of the obtained results can be extended to a fully developed general equilibrium model of Walrasian type are indicated throughout this chapter.

We first describe the Walrasian general equilibrium model and the Walrasian price-quantity adjustment process.[2] The general formulation and investigation are extensively treated in Mas-Colell 1986, whereas Mas-Colell 1985 provides a general introduction to the there-employed differentiable approach to the theory of general equilibrium. In this setup, profits of firms and utilities of households are maximized subject to the usual budget constraints. They give rise to supply and demand correspondences which in Mas-Colell 1985 and 1986 are reduced to smooth supply and demand functions by means of appropriate assumptions. The corresponding excess functions are the starting point of our investigation of Walrasian (and classical) adjustment processes in stationary production economies. This provides a convenient framework to study those dynamics and their simple stylized laws of motion. Occasionally, we will, however, also refer to nonstationary economies as described by the von Neumann model of economic growth and dynamic input-output approaches.

We posit an economy where a commodity Y is produced solely by means of labor L with a smooth production function $Y = f(L)$, which in general may exhibit decreasing, constant, or increasing returns to scale. We assume that demand for the produced commodity can be represented by a smooth function $D = D(p, w)$, p denoting the price and w the nominal wage rate. Profits Π are defined by $\Pi = pf(L) - wL$. w is taken as the numéraire, $w = 1$.[3] Households' initial endowments consist of labor only, and labor supply L^s can be derived from the above demand function by means of Walras's Law $pd(p, \Pi) = L^s(p, \Pi) + \Pi$. Owing to this law we can focus on the goods market and neglect the labor market.

The demand function d can obviously be rewritten as a function of the two variables p and L, which is denoted by $d(p, L)$ in our model for simplicity. According to Mas-Colell (1986, 65) this function is nondecreasing, that is, $d_p \leq 0$ if and only if the weak axiom of revealed preference holds, an assumption from which we will frequently depart. We denote by $L = L(Y)$ the inverse of the production function (i.e., planned employment as a function of planned output). The function $L = L(Y)$ also represents the (minimum) cost function of producers.

Consider an interior equilibrium of the above model, that is, a situation where demand equals supply and where prices equal marginal wage costs,

$$d(p^\star, L(Y^\star)) = Y^\star > 0 \tag{3.1}$$

$$L'(Y^\star) = p^\star > 0 \tag{3.2}$$

Assume that $L''(Y) \geq 0$ for the second derivative of the cost function $L(Y)$ at least in a neighborhood of $Y^\star$ (i.e., locally decreasing or constant returns to scale prevail). Because of the assumption of (short-run dynamic) profit maximization we shall not consider those points of rest where increasing returns to scale prevail, though of course segments with such returns to scale may exist for the assumed production function.[4]

Out of equilibrium the following type of *tâtonnement* adjustment process has been suggested by Mas-Colell (1986, 53 f.) as a formalization of Walras's views on the market dynamics in a production economy,

$$\dot{p} = \beta_p[d(p, L(Y)) - Y] \tag{3.3}$$

$$\dot{Y} = \beta_y[p - L'(Y)] \tag{3.4}$$

$\beta_p > 0$, $\beta_y > 0$. Equations (3.3), (3.4) posit that prices are adjusted in the direction of the excess demand on the market for goods, and that goods supply is adjusted following the discrepancy between the current price for the goods and the marginal wage costs of producing the current supplies. Such a process of a proportional control of prices as well as quantities has long been related to the writings of Walras by a few authors, most notably by Morishima (1959, 1977) and Goodwin (1953, 1989); compare also the reconsideration of Walras's disequilibrium-production model in Walker 1987. Most of the literature on *tâtonnement* processes, however, has confined itself to pure exchange economies and has neglected an extension to production economies, despite its long tradition in neoclassical—as well as classical—nonmathematical analysis.[5]

For the Jacobian J of the process (3.3), (3.4) we get *at the equilibrium point* $p^\star, Y^\star$,

$$J = \begin{pmatrix} \beta_p & 0 \\ 0 & \beta_y \end{pmatrix} \begin{pmatrix} d_p & -1 \\ 1 & -L'' \end{pmatrix} \tag{3.5}$$

since in obvious shorthand notation $d_Y = d_\Pi \Pi'(L)L'(Y) = 0$ at $L(Y^\star)$ owing to the assumption of profit maximization. We will generally consider only equilibria with det $J \neq 0$.[6] In the case of the weak axiom of revealed preference ($d_p \leq 0$) we in particular have trace $J^\star \leq 0$ (since $L''(Y^\star) \geq 0$) and det $J > 0$. Thus *local asymptotic stability*[7] is ensured if either $d_p < 0$ or $L''(Y) > 0$ holds true in addition, that is, in case of a negatively sloped $d(\cdot, L)$-curve or for strictly increasing marginal costs.[8] The stability results actually turn out to be the same as in the partial model by Beckmann and Ryder (1969). The model (3), (4) can, however, be considered as being genuinely Walrasian (see again Walker 1987) and need not be characterized as a combination of "Walrasian" and "Marshallian" features, as these two authors have suggested.

It is illuminating to compare the process (3.3), (3.4) with the conventional one-sided process of a pure price adjustment, as it has been employed since Hicks 1939 in general equilibrium theory. This process reads in our notation

$$\dot{p} = \beta_p[d(p, L(Y)) - Y], \qquad Y = L'^{-1}(p) \tag{3.6}$$

In this treatment output is given at each moment of time and determined as the profit-maximizing output $[p = L'(Y)]$ with regard to arbitrarily given prices p. Output is an upward-sloping function of prices p in the case of decreasing returns: $Y'(p) = 1/L''(Y(p))$. For $L'' > 0$, the local asymptotic stability condition for the above pure price adjustment is consequently given by

$$d_p - Y' = d_p - \frac{1}{L''} = \frac{(d_p L'' - 1)}{L''} < 0$$

The second partial derivative of the function d with respect to Y continues to be zero. This stability condition represents one of the two necessary and sufficient conditions for the asymptotic stability of the price–quantity dynamics with cross-effects, namely, det $J > 0$.

For any given demand function d, for example, also for $d_p > 0$, stability is always ensured when decreasing returns to scale (at the equilibrium) exist that are sufficiently close to the case of constant returns (i.e., the above one-sided adjustment process is *always* stable for appropriate returns to scale on the production side). This is due to the fact that stabilizing output reactions with respect to price changes approach infinity when the technology approaches the constant returns case.

Though this stability property of process (3.6) may appear superior over process (3.3), (3.4), it in fact only mirrors the extreme and implausible supply side reactions of the goods supply function when the economy is close to the situation of constant returns and subject to price shocks. From an economic point of view, process (3.3), (3.4) is indeed the more general one, since it is also well defined in the important subcase of a constant returns technology. It exhibits in this case as Jacobian the matrix

$$J = \begin{pmatrix} \beta_p d_p & -\beta_p \\ \beta_y & 0 \end{pmatrix} \tag{3.7}$$

that is, it is locally asymptotically stable if $d_p < 0$ holds true and unstable for $d_p > 0$. It thus does not lead to an undefined situation for this basic case of economic model building ($L'' \equiv 0$).

Our first important result, therefore, is that the price-quantity adjustment process, which includes a cross-effect of finite speed, is the more appropriate one when viewed from the perspective of modeling of market dynamics—though its stability properties may be less reliable than the conventional price dynamics in certain cases.

The adjustment processes (3.3), (3.4) can be generalized to a Walrasian economy with m sectors producing n goods by means of these goods (no joint production) and labor (one type for simplicity); see Mas-Colell 1986, 2–3 for details. The Jacobian J of the dynamics in the multisectoral economy then consists of square and rectangular matrices in place of the scalars in (3.5):

$$J = \begin{pmatrix} <\beta_p> & 0 \\ 0 & <\beta_y> \end{pmatrix} \begin{pmatrix} A & -B \\ B^t & C \end{pmatrix}.$$

Here, $<\beta_p>$, $<\beta_y>$ denote diagonal matrices of adjustment coefficients and the superscript t stands for the transposed matrix. The matrix A is augmented by an additional term, $Z_p(p, Y)$, the matrix of partial derivatives of the net output mapping Z with respect to prices p, which is zero in the one–input/one–output case.[9] With respect to this general situation the following proposition is proved in Mas-Colell 1986, 56.[10]

Proposition 3.1 If near the equilibrium $(p^\star, Y^\star)$ the weak axiom of revealed preference (WA) holds and if the matrix B has full rank, then $(p^\star, Y^\star)$ is locally asymptotically stable for any speeds of adjustment $<\beta_p>, <\beta_y>$.

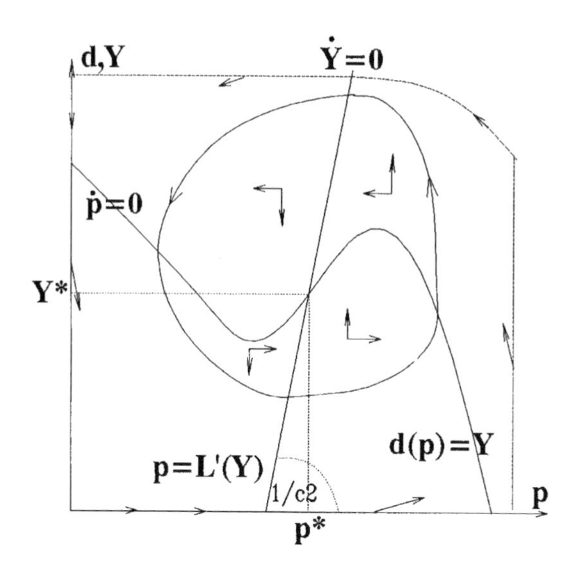

Figure 3.1
Cross-dual dynamics: Local instability and global boundedness

The result of this generalization is that the conditions of the one–input one–output case have their natural equivalent in the general case. The case of constant returns is represented by, now $C = 0$.

Let us now dispense with the weak axiom of revealed preference for the demand function in (3.3) and admit for $d_p > 0$ at the steady state, such that instability prevails if either β_y or L'' are sufficiently small.[11] The simplest situation in which this occurs is illustrated by figure 3.1. This, however, represents only a very special case of what can actually hold in a general Walrasian production economy.

We, following Mas-Colell 1986, 64, have assumed that demand is independent of profit income, so that the demand function is simply given by $d = d(p)$, as in Beckmann and Ryder 1969.

Figure 3.1 provides the basic phase–diagram information on the process (3.3), (3.4) in the case of a locally positively sloped demand curve. We employ a linear marginal cost function in the examples throughout this chapter for simplicity, $L'(Y) = c_1 + c_2Y$, implying that $Y = (p - c_1)/c_2$ represents the $\dot{Y} = 0-$ isocline. A production function with piecewise decreasing and increasing returns to scale would add further complexity to the situation shown in figure 3.1.

In the above shown case the unique equilibrium is unstable if the adjustment speed of outputs is chosen sufficiently low, since[12]

$$\text{trace } J = \beta_p d(p^\star) - \beta_y L''(Y^\star)$$

Furthermore, if $c_2 \uparrow$ and the $\dot{Y} = 0-$ isocline is rotated around the equilibrium point and becomes flatter, $d'(p^\star)$, this equilibrium point turns into a saddlepoint, since det $J < 0$ iff $c_2 < d'(p^\star)$. There will then exist two further equilibria to the right and to the left of the original one, which must be locally asymptotically stable if c_2 is chosen sufficiently high ($\dot{Y} = 0$ sufficiently flat), since $d'(p)$ is negative at the outer equilibrium points.

Independently of the local stability characteristics of the equilibria, the above phase diagram has already been supplemented by information that implies the global stability or viability of the price–quantity dynamics. In this respect, the assumed boundedness of goods demand for $p = 0$ and the existence of a positive price where this demand becomes zero are of decisive importance. An invariant domain from which trajectories cannot escape can always be found. Note here that situations exist where the dynamics may hit the boundary of the positive orthant—where it is then to be modified in a natural way (see figure 3.1) so that it will stay in the nonnegative orthant of $\mathbb{R}^2$. Figure 3.1 suggests that the Poincaré–Bendixson theorem[13] can be applied if the shown steady state is unstable. It follows that there exists at least one closed orbit (see also Mas-Colell 1986, 64 ff.).

To illustrate the above assertions, let us assume a demand function d of the polynomial form

$$d(p) = a_0 p^3 + a_1 p^2 + a_2 p + a_1 = -0.02p^3 + 0.8p^2 - 9p + 50$$

With respect to $L'(Y)$, we consider variations in the coefficients that imply the above shape over the price range $p \in [0, 26.6]$. The marginal wage cost function $c_1 + c_2 Y = L'(Y)$ is rotated around the point[14] $(p^\star, d(p^\star)) = (13, 24.26)$ on the graph of the demand function, that is, we assume as side condition $c_1 = 13 - 24.26c_2$ whenever the parameter values c_1, c_2 are modified.

Figure 3.2a[15] shows the case of three equilibria—always with a positively sloped demand function in their vicinity; the isoclines are shown as dotted curves in all of the subsequent graphs. This picture shows that the two outer equilibria are nevertheless asymptotically stable, one with a fairly limited basin of attraction. This results from the choice of the output adjustment speed parameter β_y. There are no closed orbits in this situation. Figure 3.2b, by contrast, exhibits the situation of

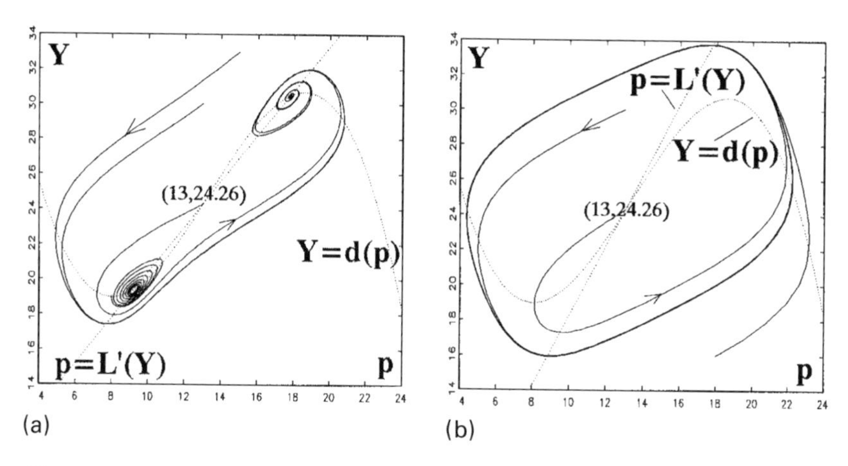

Figure 3.2
(*a*) Bounded or (*b*) viable types of cross-dual dynamics

a uniquely determined unstable steady state resulting globally in a stable limit cycle. This orbit lies in the interior of the interval $[0, 26.6] \times [0, 50] \in \mathbb{R}^2$ in the phase space of the given price–quantity dynamics due to the boundary conditions on the demand function $d(p)$.[16]

The present example also allows the application of the Hopf bifurcation theorem,[17] including a determination of the nature of the bifurcation that takes place when the parameter β_y in the right-hand figure is increased from 1 to, say 4. As figure 3.2b suggests, the resulting bifurcation is supercritical.[18] The global information provided by the Poincaré–Bendixson theorem here coincides with the local information provided by the Hopf theorem. The figure 3.3 shows how this local–global stable limit cycle shrinks to the steady state when the parameter β_y is increased to its bifurcation value $\beta_y^H = 3.22$. From then on, the steady state of the dynamics is locally and even globally asymptotically stable.

It is conjectured in Mas-Colell 1986, 64ff. that this is not the only limit cycle. The curves represented in figure 3.1 may also imply the existence of a globally stable limit cycle (via outer bounds and the Poincaré–Bendixson theorem) and a smaller unstable one (via a so-called subcritical Hopf bifurcation with respect to the parameter β_y).[19] In the subcritical case there exists a corridor for asymptotic stability around the steady state, surrounded by the limit cycle, which shrinks to

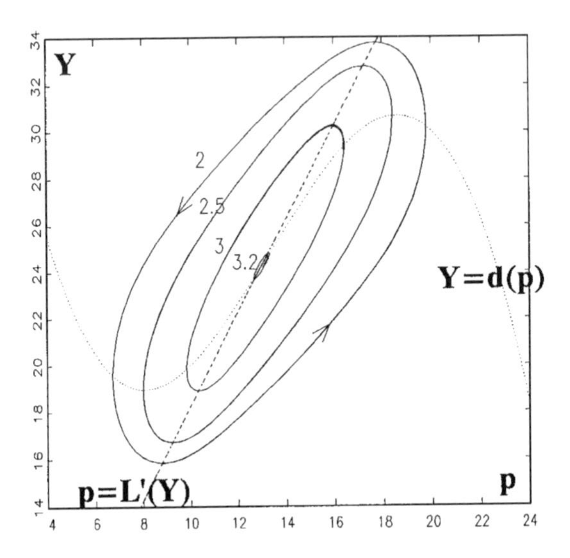

Figure 3.3
Stable limit cycles for $\beta_y = 2, 2.5, 3, 3.2$ $[c_2 = 0.5, \beta_p = 1]$

zero, that is, to the steady state as the bifurcation parameter approaches its bifurcation value. The following simulation provides an example for this situation and supports the Mas-Colell conjecture.

Figure 3.4 shows the unstable limit cycle—surrounding the corridor of asymptotic stability—as dashed curve and the stable one as solid bold. The convergent trajectories are generated via shocks of p and Y of the depicted sizes.

It is not difficult to show[20] that a polynomial of type $d(p) = -a_0p^3 + a_1p^2 \pm a_2p \pm a_3$ with positive a_i must give rise to a supercritical Hopf bifurcation if a_1 is chosen sufficiently small, while $d(p) = a_1p^2 \pm a_2p \pm a_3,\ a_i > 0$ implies the subcritical case with respect to the parameter β_y (presupposing that $1/c_2 > d(p^\star)$ holds). In view of these assertions, the polynomial underlying the isocline $d(p) = Y$ of the figure 3.4 has been chosen as $d(p) = 0.1p^2 - 2.6p + 32$ for $p \leq 30$. Note that the added kinked straight line part of this curve (for $p > 30$) simply serves the purpose of making the Poincaré–Bendixson theorem applicable to the global situation, generating a stable limit cycle from this global perspective, which is definitely unrelated to the forces that generate the local one. Note also that the global validity of the assumed polynomial form of the $\dot{p} = 0$– isocline (also for $p > 0$) would generate a further (upper) steady state of saddlepoint type (det < 0) in the above figure.

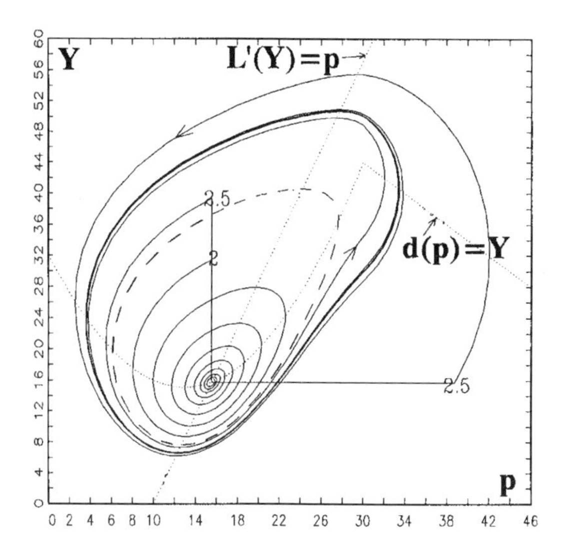

Figure 3.4
Global viability and a subcritical Hopf bifurcation [$\beta_y = 2, 2.5, c_2 = 0.35, \beta_p = 1$]

The dynamics would in this case be globally unstable outside the stability corridor, the basin of attraction, of the lower steady state.

We conclude this section with several observations:

- Owing to the Debreu–Sonnenschein theorem[21] on the fairly arbitrary nature of admissible (excess) demand functions in general equilibrium theory, it is obvious that market adjustment processes of the above type can be made arbitrarily complex by considering economies of higher dimension than the one here considered, and by manipulating the shape of the employed demand schedules appropriately.
- The conditions that have so far served to generate the global boundedness of market fluctuations are somewhat special. They may not work very well in higher dimensions and depend too much on conditions on the demand function at extreme boundary values for prices and quantities.

The question therefore arises whether other economic mechanisms can be found that may keep market fluctuations within more narrow bounds. We explore in the next section other mechanisms that may also not be entirely convincing, whereas those of the then following section may serve the purpose of generating economically meaningful viability.

3.3 Keynesian and Composite Adjustment Processes

The preceding section appears to have suggested that not too much can be gained from a dynamics with cross-effects between prices and output, compared to the standard one–sided pure price dynamics of neoclassical economics—even though the former type of dynamics appeared as more convincing. Important similarities in the formulation of Walrasian dynamics with those cross-effects[22] suggest, on the one hand, that this type of dynamics has a much wider economic background and plausibility than its neoclassical one–sided counterpart. On the other hand, the long tradition that the excess demand approach now has in the economic theorizing of various schools of thought demands that further modifications might be considered as well.

A modern alternative to the Walrasian or classical adjustment process (3.3), (3.4) that arose in the tradition of Keynesian economics is given by the following feedback structure,[23]

$$\dot{Y} = \beta_y[d(p, L(Y)) - Y] \tag{3.8}$$

$$\dot{p} = \beta_p[L'(Y) - p] \tag{3.9}$$

Here, quantities react to quantity discrepancies and prices to cost–price differentials. Except for the reassignment, and the sign change contained in the second equation, the differential equations on the right-hand side of (3.8) and (3.9) are the same as in the preceding section. The above "Keynesian" adjustment procedure, here formulated in a Walrasian framework, has been discussed in chapter 2. It is also called "dual adjustment process" because of its similarity to the dual adjustment rules (and the dual instability theorem) of input–output analysis (see Jorgenson 1960).

The Jacobian of this process at an interior equilibrium is given by

$$J = \begin{pmatrix} -\beta_y & \beta_y d_p \\ \beta_p L'' & -\beta_p \end{pmatrix}$$

The trace of this Jacobian is always negative ($-\beta_y - \beta_p$), which shows that this type of price–quantity adjustment is of a very "direct" type. Its determinant is given by

$$\det J = \beta_y \beta_p (1 - d_p L'')$$

This demonstrates that one of the two conditions of the preceding sec-

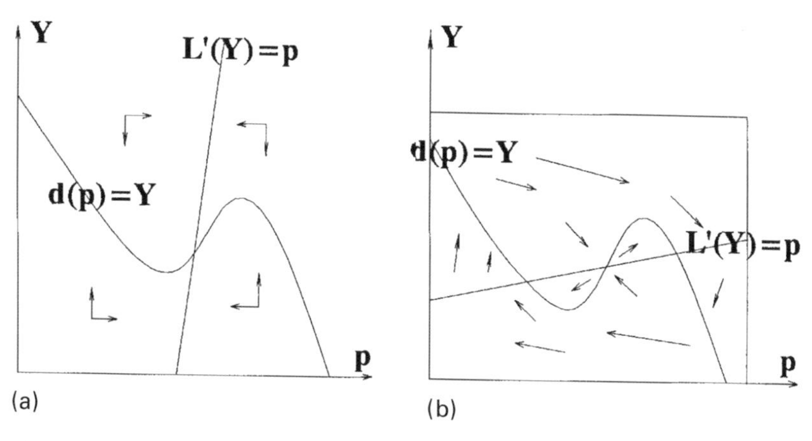

Figure 3.5
Keynesian dual dynamics with (*a*) a unique and (*b*) multiple equilibria

tion, det $J^\star > 0$, is now already sufficient for the local asymptotic stability of the given equilibrium. In the opposite case: det $J^\star < 0$, the given equilibrium is a saddlepoint. This implies that there is no possibility for a Hopf bifurcation in the present situation.

The phase diagram in the case of det $J^\star > 0$ and with the $d(\cdot)$-curve of figure 3.1 is given by the phase plot on the left-hand side in figure 3.5a ($d = d(p)$ again for simplicity), while one with det $J^\star < 0$ is shown in the plot on the right-hand side.

Figure 3.5b again exhibits three equilibria for the case det $J < 0$ (where the determinant is calculated at the middle equilibrium). Two equilibria are locally asymptotically stable, and one is a saddle. The figure again shows that viability of the global dynamics can be achieved in a way similar to that in the preceding section, in general also with cyclical motions. The local stability of the various equilibria is now completely independent of adjustment speeds.[24]

Process (3.8), (3.9) can be generalized too, only now to an economy with n goods and n sectors (and no joint production) (see Mas-Colell 1986, 60 ff.). Its Jacobian at an equilibrium is then given by (compare the preceding section):

$$J = \begin{pmatrix} <\beta_y> & 0 \\ 0 & <\beta_p> \end{pmatrix} \begin{pmatrix} -B & -A \\ -C & -B^t \end{pmatrix}$$

With respect to this situation the following proposition is proved in Mas-Colell 1986:

Proposition 3.2 Suppose that the matrix B has a positive diagonal, negative off–diagonal entries and is a productive matrix, and that there are constant returns to scale ($C = 0$). Then the Jacobian matrix J at the steady state of system (3.8), (3.9) is a stable matrix. This is true independently of the particular matrix A and the diagonal matrices of the speeds of adjustment coefficients $< \beta_y >$, $< \beta_p >$.

The difference in the stability conditions of Proposition 3.1 and 3.2 is remarkable. In the case $C \neq 0$, the conditions on the submatrix A that support stability in Proposition 3.1 for the cross–dual case need no longer be sufficient to guarantee the stability of the dual mechanism (3.8), (3.9) in the multicommodity case; see Mas-Colell 1986 for further observations in this matter.

Since stability conditions are so different, the question arises whether an integrated version of the two processes (3.3), (3.4) and (3.8), (3.9) will exhibit stronger attractive forces than the isolated cross–dual and dual adjustment rules. Such an integration is of importance from an economic point of view because it synthesizes classical and Keynesian adjustment features. Price changes then depend not only on supply and demand imbalances, but also on price–cost differentials, while supplied quantities are adjusted not only in the light of such price–cost differentials, but also with respect to supply and demand discrepancies. In formal terms this is described by

$$\dot{p} = \beta_p^1(d(p, L(Y)) - Y) + \beta_p^2(L'(Y) - p) \tag{3.10}$$

$$\dot{Y} = \beta_y^1(p - L'(Y)) + \beta_y^2(d(p, L(Y)) - Y) \tag{3.11}$$

Certainly, this system with composite dynamics has the same steady states as the isolated variants, that is, they are determined by $d(p^\star, L(Y^\star)) = Y^\star$ and $p^\star = L'(Y^\star)$. They are all Walrasian equilibria owing to the assumption $L'' > 0$. This assertion follows from

$$\det \begin{pmatrix} \beta_p^1 & \beta_p^2 \\ \beta_y^2 & -\beta_y^1 \end{pmatrix} = -\beta_p^1\beta_y^1 - \beta_p^2\beta_y^2 < 0$$

Note that—though steady states are identical—the isoclines are different to the isolated cases. The Jacobian of the dynamics (3.10), (3.11) at (one of) the steady states and its sign pattern are given by

$$J = \begin{pmatrix} \beta_p^1 d_p - \beta_p^2 & -\beta_p^1 + \beta_p^2 L'' \\ \beta_y^1 + \beta_y^2 d_p & -\beta_y^1 L'' - \beta_y^2 \end{pmatrix} = \begin{pmatrix} \pm & \pm \\ + & - \end{pmatrix}$$

This gives for det J the expression

$$(\beta_p^1\beta_y^1 + \beta_p^2\beta_y^2)(1 - d_pL'')$$

that is, the condition $d_pL'' < 1$ is—as in the two preceding situations—necessary and sufficient for det $J > 0$. It thus appears that the critical case $d_p > 0$ of the cross–dual adjustment process is now less severe due to the extra minus signs in the diagonal of J resulting from the dual adjustments. In this simple situation, the composite process seems to be superior to the Walrasian classical one with cross–effects, since

$$\beta_p^1 d_p - \beta_y^1 L'' - (\beta_p^2 + \beta_y^2) < 0$$

is now already sufficient for obtaining trace $J < 0$.

In the multi-goods case the Jacobian J at the steady state of these dynamics is of the following form:

$$J = \begin{pmatrix} <\beta_p^1> & 0 \\ 0 & <\beta_y^1> \end{pmatrix} \begin{pmatrix} A & -B \\ B^t & C \end{pmatrix} + \begin{pmatrix} <\beta_p^2 & 0 \\ 0 & <\beta_y^2> \end{pmatrix} \begin{pmatrix} -B^t & -C \\ A & -B \end{pmatrix}$$

which is quite a complicated summation of various types of matrices. Assuming constant returns ($C = 0$) and a fixed vector of final demand ($A = 0$) as in conventional input–output analysis and positing that all adjustment speeds are equal to one gives the particularly simple composite matrix

$$J = \begin{pmatrix} -B^t & -B \\ B^t & -B \end{pmatrix}$$

We state

Proposition 3.3 There exist simple input–output matrices B (of the type as in Proposition 2) for which the matrix J is not a stable matrix.

See Flaschel and Semmler 1990 for a proof of this proposition (there in the context of dynamic input-output models of Leontief type).

Even for simple input–output characterizations of the above composite price and quantity adjustment process one therefore cannot obtain local asymptotic stability by adding to the purely cyclical Walrasian, or classical, substructure[25]

$$\begin{pmatrix} 0 & -B \\ B^t & 0 \end{pmatrix}$$

the asymptotically stable Keynesian substructure

$$\begin{pmatrix} -B^t & 0 \\ 0 & B \end{pmatrix}.$$

Composite adjustment processes—though interesting from the point of view of economic theory—do not perform better with respect to local stability than their classical and Keynesian component structures.[26] Boundedness of market fluctuations cannot, in general, be obtained by adding Keynesian dual adjustment components to the cross–dual structure of Walrasian-classical nature.

3.4 Proportional and Derivative Control

It has already been stressed in section 3.1 that there are important similarities in the formulation of Walrasian dynamics, with its cross-effects between prices and quantities, and the classical market dynamics. Above we have extended the cross-dual process by introducing dual elements into it, but have found that the composite process does not necessarily stabilize the market dynamics, though it looks richer now in its economic structure.

It is appealing to introduce derivative control, as mentioned in chapter 2, into classical market dynamics where the reactions then take place not only to levels but also to the state of change of levels. Thus, we posit that prices and quantities do not react only with respect to the level of excess demands and the excess of prices over costs (proportional control), but also with regard to their time rates of change (derivative control). In economic terms this says that *rising disequilibria exercise an influence on the dynamics of prices and quantities different from that of falling ones* even if the levels of those disequilibria are the same. These ideas will now be applied to the Walrasian dynamics of section 3.2.

Let $\gamma_p, \gamma_y = \text{const} > 0$ denote further adjustment parameters and consider the cross-dual dynamics of section 2:

$$\dot{p} = \beta_p \cdot (d(p, L(Y)) - Y) + \gamma_p \cdot \overbrace{(d(p, L(Y)) - Y)}^{\cdot} \tag{3.12}$$

$$\dot{Y} = \beta_y \cdot (p - L'(Y)) + \gamma_y \cdot \overbrace{(p - L'(Y))}^{\cdot} \tag{3.13}$$

Of course, this system has the same points of rest as (3.3), (3.4) above. In the above formulation the first terms on the right-hand side of the differential equations denote the proportional control of prices and quantities, and the second terms, a derivative control, which pays attention to the time rate of change of the discrepancies.

Partial derivative control—either the influence of the rate of change of excess profitability on supply conditions, or the impact of the rate of change of excess supply on prices—has already been used in Flaschel and Semmler 1987 in the context of a linear Sraffa–von Neumann model. There global stability results were obtained (where in the course of convergence process either production processes or products go extinct). The present study differs from this earlier approach insofar as it also allows for decreasing returns to scale, neglects "normal profits," and considers the joint effect of the above two partial derivative forces.[27] As it turns out, this ensures stability even if the original cross-dual dynamics themselves are unstable, and it stresses the importance of the adjustment speeds γ_i for obtaining stability for one or all equilibria of a given economy. As in Flaschel and Semmler 1987, derivative control terms for price as well as quantity adjustments turn out to be a strong stabilizing force and may be considered as plausible components of real economic adjustment mechanisms.

Let us make use of the following notation in order to represent the above dynamics in a more compact and general form. We denote the system of differential equations (3.3),(3.4) that represents the Walrasian cross-dual process by $\dot{z} = DF(z)$, $z = (p, Y)^t$, where the matrix D is the diagonal matrix formed by the adjustment speeds β_p, β_y of this process. This matrix D is suppressed in the following via its integration into the function F. The remaining adjustment coefficients γ_i are collected in the diagonal matrix $< \gamma >$:

$$< \gamma >= \begin{bmatrix} \gamma_p & 0 \\ 0 & \gamma_y \end{bmatrix}$$

We use these condensed formulations of the components of process (3.12), (3.13) in order to show by the following propositions and their proofs that they can be easily extended in this way to multiproduct economies as they were considered in the preceding sections of this chapter.

In compact form the system (3.12), (3.13) can then be represented as follows:

$$\dot{z} = F(z) + < \gamma > \overset{\cdot}{\overbrace{F(z)}} \tag{3.14}$$

Since $\dot{F}(z) = F'\dot{z}$ we have

$$\dot{z} = Z(z) = (I - <\gamma> F'(z))^{-1} F(z) \tag{3.15}$$

as long as the matrix $I - <\gamma> F'(z)$ is regular (I the identity matrix). It goes without saying that the dynamics (3.12), (3.13) have the same points of rest as our original Walrasian dynamics (3.3), (3.4).

The Jacobian of the original cross-dual dynamics at the steady state is given by:

$$F'(z^\star) = \begin{bmatrix} \beta_p d_p(p^\star, L(Y^\star)) & -\beta_p \\ \beta_y & -\beta_y L''(Y^\star) \end{bmatrix}, \qquad z = \begin{bmatrix} p \\ Y \end{bmatrix}$$

Owing to $F(z^\star) = 0$ at the steady state, the Jacobian of process (3.15) is therefore given by

$$J = (I - <\gamma> F'(z^\star))^{-1} F'(z^\star) \tag{3.16}$$

It is well defined whenever $det(I - <\gamma> F'(z^\star) \neq 0$ holds true. The original nonlinear dynamics (3.15) are then well defined in a neighborhood of the steady state.

It is not difficult to prove, by means of eigenvalue comparison, the following proposition.[28]

Proposition 3.4 Consider an interior equilibrium $z^\star$ of system (3.12), (3.13) and assume that $\gamma_p = \gamma_y$ holds. Then there exists $\gamma_0 > 0$ such that $z^\star$ is *locally asymptotically stable* for all $\gamma_p = \gamma_y > \gamma_0$ with regard to the adjustment process (3.12), (3.13). A corresponding statement holds true for the multi-commodity generalization.

Note, that the γ_0 of Proposition 3.4 may also be chosen large enough to become independent of the considered particular equilibrium of the given economy, if the number of these equilibria is finite. However, γ_0 cannot be chosen independently of the functions d and L', that is, independently of the particular economy considered. The above proposition thus shows how market dynamics—in combination with price-cost considerations—can be reformulated in such a way that the stability of all economic equilibria of a given economy is ensured. Yet, the proposition also shows the information "markets" need in order to admit adjustment processes that are generally locally asymptotically stable. This, however, exceeds the information that markets commonly provide to ensure the existence of equilibria.

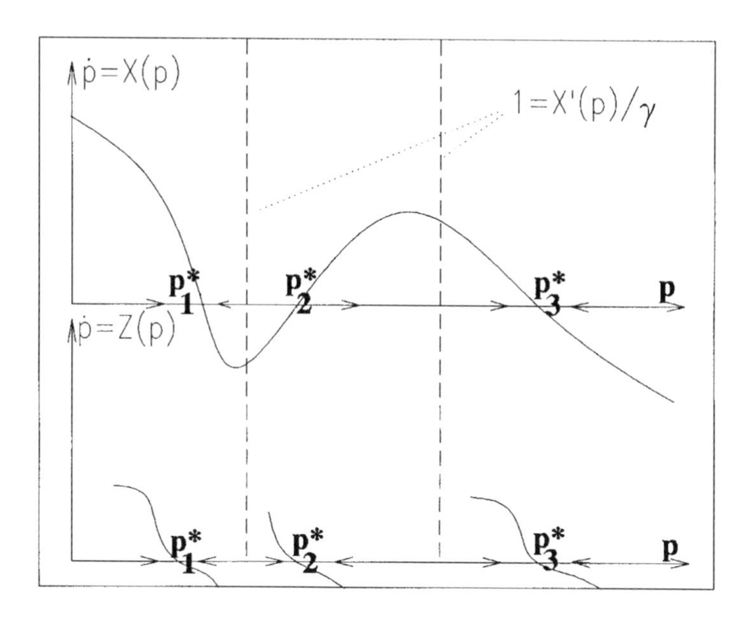

Figure 3.6
Universal stability for pure price adjustment processes

Figure 3.6 provides an illustration of the change in the Walrasian dynamics with proportional control that is brought about by our addition of a derivative auto-control mechanism. For simplicity, we consider the case of a one-sided price adjustment mechanism $\dot{p} = X(p)$ based on an excess demand function solely, in which case the comparison between the original type of adjustment and its enrichment by means of derivative feedbacks, $\dot{p} = Z(p)$, is particularly easy to depict. Figure 3.6 shows that universal asymptotic stability is obtained through the partitioning of the domain of definition of the original dynamics into isolated basins of attraction for each Walrasian point of rest.[29]

One weakness in the arguments put forth in sections 2, 3 to support the global stability of the dynamics with or without cross-effects is that they rely on situations where a well-defined economic behavior is not really to be expected, that is, on boundary conditions for $y = 0$ or $p = 0$. These are simply too extreme to suggest that the true forces that keep an economic system within economically sensible bounds have thereby been represented. Derivative forces like those in (3.12) and (3.13), which depend on the direction and the amount of change of disequilibrium situations, may provide a more reliable mechanism for the generation of global stability. Furthermore, a great disadvantage of the above Proposition 4 concerning composite proportional and derivative adjustment mechanisms is the assumption that the γ-adjustment terms are all equal. This was convenient in the eigenvalue calculations employed in the proof of the theorem. We now proceed to a proof strategy that admits differentiated adjustment speeds $\gamma_i > 0$ as well as for global statements.[30]

Let us therefore return to the dynamics (3.15) from this extended point of view:

$$\dot{z} = Z(z) = (I - <\gamma> F'(z))^{-1} F(z) \tag{3.17}$$

The parameters in the diagonal of the matrix $<\gamma>$ are all positive but not necessarily identical to each other. This explicit system of differential equations is well defined as long as the matrix $I - <\gamma> F'(z)$ is regular.

Since the choice of a sufficiently large common adjustment parameter γ makes all points of rest of such a system locally asymptotically stable, we know (by index considerations, cf. Dierker 1974, for example) that system (3.17) cannot be well defined in the whole positive orthant if there are multiple equilibria as shown in figure 3.6. A general investigation of the global properties of (3.17) may therefore be quite complicated and demanding.

To simplify our considerations let us assume that there exists an equilibrium $z^\star$ and an open and connected domain D containing $z^\star$ as a unique equilibrium such that the function

$$G(z) = z - z^\star - <\gamma> F(z)$$

is sufficiently smooth and has a regular Jacobian at all points in D, such that the above dynamics are well defined. To study the system (3.17) on an appropriately chosen subset of D the following auxiliary function H is of great help

$$H(z) = \|G(z)\|^2 = \|z - z^\star - <\gamma> F(z)\|^2 \tag{3.18}$$

where $\|\cdot\|$ denotes the Euclidean distance, derived from the Euclidean scalar product $\ll x, y \gg = \sum x_i y_i$).

Proposition 3.5 The function H is a *strict Liapunov function* at $z^\star$ if the adjustment parameters in $<\gamma>$ are chosen sufficiently large. Hence, the equilibrium $z^\star$ is locally asymptotically stable with respect to (3.17).[31]

Briefly, a Liapunov function has the following properties: $H(z) > 0$ for $z \neq z^\star$, $H(z^\star) = 0$, $\dot{H}(z) < 0$ for $z \neq z^\star$. See Hirsch and Smale 1974, 193 for the definition and the application of this concept.

Proof of Proposition 3.5 By the definition of H we have $H(z^\star) = 0$. Because of the regularity of the function $G(z) = z - z^\star - <\gamma> F(z)$ at $z^\star$ we also know that $H(z) > 0$ must hold true in $U - z^\star$ for a suitably chosen neighborhood U of the equilibrium $z^\star$. According to Liapunov's stability theorem[32] it remains to be shown that the condition $\dot{H} < 0$ holds $U - z^\star$.

q.e.d.

Differentiating H along the trajectories of (3.17) gives (see Dieudonné 1960, 144)

$$\dot{H} = 2 \ll (I - <\gamma> F'(z))\dot{z},\ z - z^\star - <\gamma> F(z) \gg$$

$$= 2 \ll F(z), z - z^\star - <\gamma> F(z) \gg$$

$$= 2[\ll F(z), z - z^\star \gg - \ll F(z), <\gamma> F(z) \gg]$$

Now, since $z^\star$ is a regular equilibrium of F, we can apply the mean value theorem (cf. Dieudonné 1960, 155) with regard to the function F^{-1} in order to get

$$\|F^{-1}(q) - F^{-1}(0)\| \leq c \cdot \|q - 0\| \quad \text{or} \quad \|z - z^\star\| \leq c \cdot \|F(z)\|$$

must hold true for all z of a suitably chosen neighborhood U′ of $z^\star$ and a positive constant $c > \gamma_{min}$. This gives

$$\dot{H} \leq 2[\|F(z)\| \cdot \|z - z^\star\| - \gamma_{min} \cdot \|F(z)\|^2]$$

$$\leq 2[\|F(z)\|^2 \cdot c - \gamma_{min} \cdot \|F(z)\|^2]$$

$$= 2(c - \gamma_{min})\|F(z)\|^2$$

where $\gamma_{min} > 0$ is the minimal parameter in the set of all adjustment parameters γ_i in $<\gamma>$. The choice $\gamma_{min} > c$ then immediately implies that $\dot{H} < 0$ must hold true in $U' - z^\star$, that is, H is a strict Liapunov function for $z^\star$, which is strictly decreasing along the trajectories of (3.17) in $U - z^\star$ toward 0.

Consider now a positive real number a such that the compact set $K = H^{-1}([0, a])$ is contained in the domain D. Let us furthermore denote the maximum of $\|z - z^\star\|$ for $z \in K$ by k_1 and the minimum of $\|F(z)\|$ on the set $K - U^\epsilon$ by k_2 where U^ϵ is an open set around the equilibrium point $z^\star$ and where $K - U^\epsilon$ denotes the set of points in K that are not in U^ϵ. Since the set $K - U^\epsilon$ is also compact and since $z^\star$ is the only equilibrium in K it follows that k_2 exists and is positive. On the basis of these assumptions we can show:

Proposition 3.6 The function H is *a nonlocal Liapunov function* for the equilibrium $z^\star$, which means that $\dot{H} < 0$ holds true in the set $K - U^\epsilon$ if all adjustment parameters γ_i are larger than k_1/k_2.

Proof Calculations, as in the proof of Proposition 3.5, give rise to

$$\begin{aligned}\dot{H} &\le 2[\|F(z)\| \cdot \|z - z^\star\| - \gamma_{min} \cdot \|F(z)\|^2]\\ &\le 2[\|F(z)\|^2 \cdot k_1/k_2 - \gamma_{min} \cdot \|F(z)\|^2]\\ &= 2(k_1/k_2 - \gamma_{min})\|F(z)\|^2 < 0\end{aligned}$$

since we have $\|F(z)\| \neq 0$ on $K - U^\epsilon$ and $\|z - z^\star\|/\|F(z)\| \le k_1/k_2$ by the choice of the constants k_1, k_2.

q.e.d.

Of course, the above estimation is very crude, so that $\dot{H} < 0$ may generally be expected to hold true for much smaller γ_i than have been used to prove the proposition. Verbally stated, Proposition 3.6 says[33] that all trajectories of process (3.17) that start in K will reach the set U^ϵ after some finite time. From there on, their further behavior is no longer obvious, since $z^\star$ need not be an asymptotically stable equilibrium of (3.17). The "limit set" of the invariant set K must therefore be contained in U^ϵ, but may have quite a complicated structure (in higher dimensions). Note finally that a larger set U^ϵ will in general admit a choice of a smaller bound k_1/k_2.

We conclude that the dynamics (3.17) permit a variety of possibilities to tailor them to the particular equilibrium under consideration. In particular, one may endogenize the parameters γ_i by making them dependent on the discrepancies in supply and demand as well as in prices and marginal costs—or alternatively on the distance that actual prices and quantities $z = (p, Y)^t$ will have from their equilibrium values $z^\star$. For example, we may impose the conditions

- $\gamma_i \equiv 0$ in a neighborhood of $z^\star$, that is, derivative forces are only operative if price-cost or supply-demand differences become sufficiently pronounced;

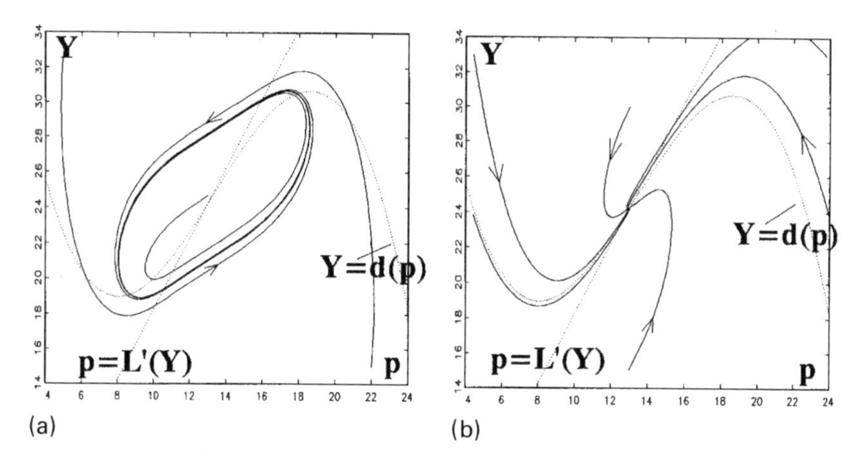

Figure 3.7
(*a*) Decreased amplitude and (*b*) global asymptotic stability for the unique and stable limit cycle of section 3.2, fig 3.2b, by means of a constant derivative auto-control

- γ_i = const large enough to ensure $\dot{H} < 0$ (at least) far off the steady state;
- γ_i a continuous function of z.

Such conditions should generally imply that the dynamics (3.17) are bounded or viable but they do not imply anything definite on their behavior in neighborhoods of the steady if the dimension of the considered commodity space is sufficiently high.

In order to provide some numerical presentations of such effects of a derivative control we return to the example of section 3.2, figure 3.1, employing now, however, the following numerical specifications. The subsequent figures show the effect of a derivative auto-control on the limit cycle that was depicted in figure 3.2b in section 3.2, first (figure 3.7a) for speeds of adjustment $\gamma_p, \gamma_y = .9$ and second for $\gamma_p, \gamma_y = 10$ (figure 3.7b). It can be seen that the limit cycle of figure 3.2b is somewhat compressed in the first situation, while this stable cycle is completely eliminated in the second case of a very strongly acting derivative control. Derivative control thus may not only lead to persistent cyclical movements with a reduced amplitude but is also capable of removing the cyclical nature of cross-dual dynamics in a very radical fashion.

As shown, derivative control may ensure boundedness of the cross-dual dynamics through its strong impact far off the steady state, but may not give rise to an asymptotically stable dynamics. In order to

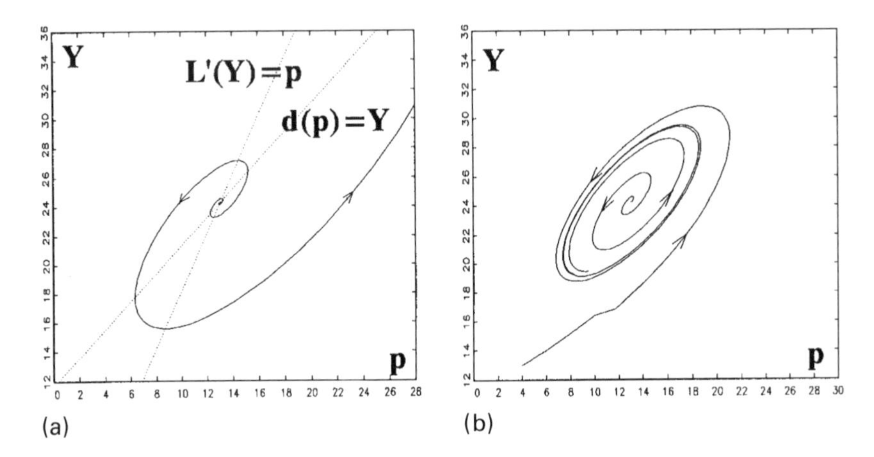

Figure 3.8
An explosive cross-dual dynamics (*a*) without and (*b*) with derivative control far off the steady state

illustrate this, let us again consider the case of no derivative control first ($\gamma_p, \gamma_y = 0$). Figure 3.8 shows on the left-hand side the result of this cross-dual mechanism in the linear context[34] where local instability is equivalent to global instability. The boundary conditions of section 3.2 are therefore here not operative. The figure to the right then adds a derivative auto-control to this dynamics that varies in strength with the (Euclidean) distance from the equilibrium point according to the following formula,

$$\gamma_p = \gamma_y = 0.9\sqrt{(p - p^\star)^2 + (Y - Y^\star)^2}/10$$

At distance 10 from the equilibrium we thus get a strength of the derivative control term that equals the weaker one in the left panel of figure 3.7, but now applied to a totally unstable system.

This little exercise demonstrates that the inclusion of derivative control mechanisms—which are plausible whenever existing imbalances exceed certain thresholds—does not necessarily give rise to the "world of point attractors", but may create—in higher dimensions—arbitrarily complex dynamics in certain neighborhoods of the steady state.

It may also be noted that we have made use of the possible combinations of cross-effects between prices and quantities and derivative control mechanisms only in a very preliminary way. Many further results may be expected for other types of combinations, different parameter sizes, and in particular for different types of economic environments.

Also, the possibility of only a partial derivative control (where some of the adjustment parameters are set equal to zero, for example, by excluding the law of demand but not the law of profitability from the derivative control mechanism) should be investigated in much more detail. This, however, will require different strategies of proof if global stability results are to be obtained. Such questions must be left for future investigations, however.

3.5 Concluding Remarks

We have demonstrated and exemplified in this chapter that cross-effects in price and quantity adjustments should be considered as important building blocks in the construction of market adjustment mechanisms, though their main dynamic implication may be one of generating oscillatory movements and not necessarily asymptotic stability. Keynesian adjustments without such cross-effects appear as much more direct in their feedback mechanism in this regard. Their stabilizing potential may also be fairly limited. Boundedness of market fluctuations is thus not clearly supported by these two basic types of economic adjustment mechanisms, even when tested in the artificial environment of Walrasian tâtonnement procedures.

The addition of derivative control in each component of these proportionally controlled tâtonnement processes is, however, sufficient to establish the needed boundedness of market fluctuations by generating convergence if their presence is assumed to be universal and sufficiently strong. If we assume the existence of sufficiently strong derivative forces only at certain distances from the steady state of the economy, this will already establish persistent fluctuations of any—meaningful—magnitude.

In the next chapter we shall deal with non-neoclassical theories of the business cycle at the macroeconomic level. Here, too, cross-effects between some of the variables involved may be present—often also side by side with Keynesian dual adjustment procedures. This, as will be discussed, might represent a central cause for the cyclical features observed in particular types of these macromodels.

Yet, such macromodels are often based on further (intrinsic) laws of motion as well as on dynamical features as they derive from the inclusion of backward- and forward-looking processes of expectation formations. The structure of macromodels is therefore generally not of the uniform type of the price-quantity adjustment processes we have considered in this chapter. The results obtained on composite proportional and derivative control cannot easily be extended to questions of macrodynamics. Nevertheless, the dynamic processes considered in this chapter can be applied to some of the macromodels treated in later chapters and are thus also of interest at the macro level (see in particular chapters 6 and 10.)[35]

3.6 Appendix: Market Adjustments and the Newton Method

It is worthwhile to contrast the market adjustment mechanisms as introduced in (3.12), (3.13) to recent advanced work on excess demand functions and market dynamics. In particular, we refer to the so-called Global Newton Method (Smale 1976) and to subsequent work by Varian (1977), Saari and Simon (1978) and Jordan (1983). In this literature the question has been pursued of whether there exist adjustment processes with universal stability properties and informational requirements that render applicable a Walrasian tâtonnement procedure.

Formally, the starting point of this type of investigation was methods that had been invented to compute the fixed points of a map from any point near the boundary of its domain. One such method is discussed in Smale's (1976) paper on convergent price adjustment through "Global Newton Methods" applied to the excess demand functions of general equilibrium systems. Smale's approach offers not only a new method of computing price equilibria, but it also bridges the gap between the early optimistic views of Arrow, Hurwicz and others on the stability of general equilibrium systems and the subsequently developing pessimistic characterizations of this problem based on the counterexamples by Scarf and Gale and the theorems of "Debreu-Sonnenschein" type. The view by Saari and Simon (1978) has been that informational requirements are too strong to render the Newton process operative in Walrasian general equilibrium models that cannot be relaxed. As will be seen, our above proposed adjustment processes exhibit a Newton-like form, are able to generate "universal stability," and need less information than the standard Newton method.

Let $p \in \mathbb{R}^n$ be a regular equilibrium of the excess demand function X, $X(p) \in \mathbb{R}^n$, which in the conventional setup depends only on prices p. Assuming regularity, Smale's Global Newton Method is given by the following system of differential equations,

$$\dot{p} = -\lambda(p) X'(p)^{-1} X(p)$$

where $\lambda(p)$ is assumed to be determined by det $X'(p)$. This Global Newton Method has some advantage over the following so-called Generalized Newton Method (GNM)

$$\dot{p} = -X'(p)^{-1}X(p)$$

since it, through sign reversal, can pass certain singular points without coming to a halt. The GNM, however, is of potential interest for designing more potent price mechanisms. Only this procedure admits local stability in general (see Saari and Simon 1978, 1103). The main work of Saari and Simon (1978) consists in investigating whether the informational content for so-called (locally) effective price mechanisms (LEPM) can be substantially lower than that of the GNM (which is also an LEPM).

The above GNM has two deficiencies. First, it requires knowledge of $X(p)$ and of all its partial derivatives $\partial X_i/\partial p_j$. Second, it has the unpleasant property that it reduces all excess demands monotonically along the adjustment path (leaving in particular all markets that are already in equilibrium in this position). It is therefore of great interest to ask whether there exist other types of locally effective price mechanisms that are more plausible from an economic point of view and need less information on the Jacobian of excess demand functions than the GNM.

The extended Walrasian tâtonnement dynamics (3.12), (3.13) may represent such a mechanism that also pays attention to adjustments on the side of production. It has been obtained from purely economic considerations: first, by taking seriously the original approach of Walras for a production economy and, second, by observing that the direction of change of the two excess function values should also affect the determination of the price and quantity reactions of such an economy. Moreover, system (3.12) (3.13) is surprisingly similar, from a formal point of view, to the GNM.

The dynamics (3.12), (3.13) has been reformulated as follows:

$$\dot{z} = \begin{bmatrix} \dot{p} \\ \dot{Y} \end{bmatrix} = (I - \gamma \cdot F'(z))^{-1}F(z), \qquad z = \begin{bmatrix} p \\ Y \end{bmatrix} \tag{3.A1}$$

where F denotes our function of section 3.4. We here assume a uniform parameter γ for the derivative control terms. Note that in order to have a globally well-defined mechanism we should make the parameter γ dependent on the excess function F, that is, on the particular economy, in such way that $(I - \gamma \cdot F'(z))^{-1}$ is always well defined for regular economies.

It is not difficult to show the relation of (A1) to the GNM and prove the local effectiveness of our mechanism by making use of certain definitions and results from Jordan 1983. According to Jordan, a GNM is an adjustment mechanism, in his case solely a price mechanism, of the following kind

$$\dot{z} = A(F(z), F'(z)), \qquad \det F'(z) \neq 0 \tag{3.A2}$$

where the function $A : \mathbb{R}^n \times \Omega \longrightarrow \mathbb{R}^n$ is continuously differentiable. Ω denotes the set of regular $n \times n$ matrices $M : \det M \neq 0$. System (3.A1) is of this type. However, process (3.A2) must be defined for all regular matrices $M = F'(z)$, a possible solution to this problem, which demands that γ must be made dependent on M in a smooth way. Furthermore, the definition of a GNM also demands that this method exhibit the general properties of a price mechanism as defined in Jordan 1983, 241. This in particular means that such a mechanism is considered as defined on a domain as large as possible.

With regard to our own approach (3.A1) we are now able to formulate the following proposition; for a proof, see Flaschel 1991:

Proposition 3.7

Define $\gamma(M)$ by $\|M^{-1}\| \cdot (1 + \epsilon)$ for all regular M by making use of a C^1 matrix norm $\| \cdots \|$ and an arbitrary $\epsilon > 0$.[36] Then the adjustment mechanism

$$\dot{z} = (I - \gamma(F'(z)))^{-1} F(z) \text{ if } \det(F'(z)) \neq 0, \text{ and } \dot{z} = F(z) \text{ otherwise}$$

is well defined and a GNM.

In view of the literature on Global Newton Methods this mechanism is therefore of a fairly "universal" nature.

4 Non-Neoclassical Variants of Dynamic Macroeconomics

4.1 Introduction

The macromodels of this chapter are by and large of non-neoclassical origin. We specifically study nonoptimizing variants originating in Keynesian or classical tradition. The models are low dimensional (two- or three-dimensional) so that they can be investigated analytically. The chapter remains introductory insofar as the macromodels are partial in nature and display prototype dynamics of a basically known type. We present and compare dynamical models of the product market, the monetary sector, the labor market, and of the interaction between the labor market and the market for goods. These dynamic models serve as expositions for the later parts of the book, specifically chapters 7–10 as well as chapters 11–12, where related three- or even higher dimensional macrodynamic systems are studied analytically or numerically.

The models studied here exhibit deviation-amplifying mechanisms particular to those studied in the Keynesian tradition. Keynesian macrodynamics attempts to explain fluctuations in output and employment by referring more to propagation mechanisms than to exogenous impulse dynamics (e.g., the Slutsky-Frisch tradition, see chapter 5). That is, the fluctuations are conceived of as being generated endogenously. What are studied are deviation-amplifying mechanisms resulting from strong accelerator effects, imperfect competition and markup pricing, wage and price flexibility, adaptive expectations mechanisms, or monetary factors. One can then construct macrodynamic models with propagation mechanisms strong enough to explain the sizable fluctuations in output and employment.

Since globally unstable systems are usually regarded as nonsensible formulations of macrodynamic systems, however, we also explore for those locally unstable models the forces that may eventually give rise to bounded fluctuations and so keep the system viable. We show that boundedness of fluctuations may stem from some directly imposed viability constraints, state–dependent reaction functions, derivative control (as discussed in chapters 2 and 3) or may be due to the existence of thresholds beyond which the dynamics change.

We begin our study with models that exhibit local instability, which may arise, for example, when certain adjustment speeds become too large. We elaborate on the famous knife-edge problem of the Harrodian real growth theory by employing an adaptive growth expectations mechanism as well as myopic perfect foresight.[1] We illustrate that such a knife-edge problem also exists in Cagan's monetary model (1956) with adaptive price expectations, that is, in a purely nominal context. We then demonstrate that in real and monetary models of this type, the fluctuations remain bounded if certain viability constraints are introduced. The use of viability constraints is discussed with respect to nonmonetary business cycle models such as the one by Kaldor (1940), as well as the Cagan (1956) monetary model. It is shown in particular that these models can produce so-called relaxation oscillations if the adjustment speed of certain equilibrating processes becomes very large.[2]

Subsequently, we discuss Goodwin's prototype classical growth cycle model (1967), introducing a nominal extension that includes a Phillips curve type labor market dynamic, a markup type price dynamic, and adaptive expectations or myopic perfect foresight. State-dependent reaction functions and derivative control are used as stabilizing devices when the steady state becomes unstable.

Finally, we explore the Rose (1967) model of supply side-driven Keynesian growth dynamics and contrast it with a demand side-oriented growth model of classical origin, both of which include a labor market. The Rose model, too, generates bounded fluctuations. They are obtained here through a wage mechanism where increasing nominal wage flexibility supports viability when the system departs too much from its steady state. To a certain degree this model is similar to a recent approach by Skott (1989), where persistent fluctuations again originate in the conflict over income distribution in a Wicksellian IS-framework. Here the supply reaction of firms is no longer determined solely by the growth rate of the capital stock.

The demand side oriented growth model that concludes this chapter poses more problems with respect to viability because the Harrodian type accelerator effects may prove too strong to ensure global stability. This indicates that multiplier-accelerator approaches to monetary growth may be difficult to analyze; they are in fact rarely treated in the literature on monetary growth. In this book the nominal analog of such an accelerator mechanism will receive extensive treatment in the context of complete Keynesian models of monetary growth in chapters 7–9, and from the perspective of a Keynes-Wicksell growth model in chapter 10. The analysis of demand-driven growth cycle models of a more elaborate type is taken up again in chapters 11 and 12.

Technically, the local dynamics in this chapter are examined by employing the Routh Hurwitz conditions as well as local bifurcation theory. This latter theory is presented in detail, including economic applications, for example in Lorenz 1993 and Tu 1994. From a more global point of view, we refer to the Poincaré-Bendixson theorem, which is thoroughly explained in Hirsch and Smale 1974. For example, Liapunov functions and relaxation oscillations deriving from constrained dynamical systems are also utilized to explore the global stability behavior.[3] Since these mathematical tools for the analysis of dynamical systems are well documented in the economic literature on such systems, we shall not go into a presentation of such techniques, but instead confine ourselves to visual and intuitive characterizations when using these tools.

4.2 Instability in Real and Monetary Models

We start this section by examining the product market and Harrod's (1973) growth model. This model type exhibits local instability or the well-known knife-edge growth problem due to quantity imbalances between the actual and expected capacity utilization rates of firms. The Harrod model is only one example of the whole class of so-called multiplier–accelerator models, but it is special in its focus on the interaction of growth and expectations dynamics. A simple discrete-time version of this model that makes Harrod's approach to growth dynamics particularly clear is given in Sen 1970.

To begin with our (continuous–time) reformulation of this model, let us denote with $S = sY$ the simple proportional savings function of growth theory and by

$$\widehat{I/K} = \beta_x(Y^e/K - (Y/K)^\star) \tag{4.1}$$

the net investment function of accelerator type to be employed.[4] It is posited that $I = S$, so that the goods market is always in equilibrium.

According to the multiplier theory the output of firms is thus determined by $Y = I/s$. We define

$x = Y/K$, output-capital ratio (utilization of capital)

$x^\star = (Y/K)^\star$, desired utilization, a constant

$g_k = I/K$, the growth rate of the capital stock

$x^e = Y^e/K$, the expected rate of capacity utilization

Furthermore, we posit an adaptive expectations mechanism with respect to sales expectations (see [4.3] below); its limit, $\beta_{x^e} = \infty$, is equivalent to myopic perfect foresight, that is, $x^e = x$.

From

$$g_k = I/K = S/K = sx \quad \text{and thus} \quad \hat{g}_k = \hat{x}$$

and the above investment function we get

$$\hat{g}_k = \beta_x(x^e - x^\star) = \hat{x}, \text{ or}$$

$$\dot{x} = \beta_x(x^e - x^\star)x \tag{4.2}$$

while the adaptive expectations mechanism reads

$$\dot{x}^e = \beta_{x^e}(x - x^e) \tag{4.3}$$

Equations (4.2) and (4.3) are a system of two autonomous differential equations in the variables x (actual capacity utilization) and x^e (expected capacity utilization), which combine a multiplier–accelerator approach with a simple sales expectations dynamics.

An equivalent representation in terms of growth rates and their dynamics is

$$\hat{g}_k = \beta_x(g_k^e - g_k^\star)/s$$

$$\dot{g}_k^e = \beta_{x^e}(g_k - g_k^e)$$

where $g_k^e = sY^e/K$, $g_k^\star = sY^\star/K$

The economically meaningful steady state ($\dot{x}^e = \dot{x} = 0$) of the above dynamics is given by

$$x = x^e = x^\star; \qquad g_k = g_k^e = g_k^\star = sx^\star$$

with $x^\star$ the given desired rate of capacity utilization. The rate $g_k^\star$ corresponds to so-called warranted rate of growth of Harrod-Domar models. The second stationary point of (4.2), (4.3) is meaningless: $x = 0 = x^e$.

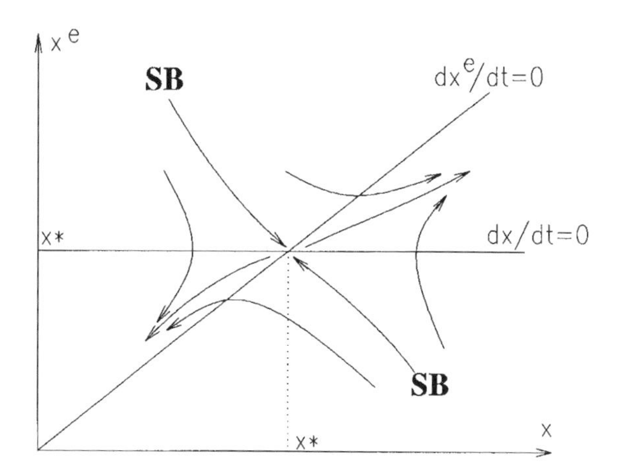

Figure 4.1
Harrodian growth under adaptive expectations

The local stability analysis with the Jacobian J (evaluated at the steady state) yields

$$J = \begin{bmatrix} 0 & \beta_x x^\star \\ \beta_{x^e} & -\beta_{x^e} \end{bmatrix} = \begin{bmatrix} 0 & + \\ + & - \end{bmatrix}$$

Since det $J < 0$ the steady state is a saddle point. The phase diagram of figure 4.1 depicts this situation in finer detail.

Except for the two stable branches (SB), all trajectories diverge eventually. The real sector is, therefore, characterized by a knife-edge situation created through the interaction of the multiplier-accelerator and the adaptive expectations mechanism. Are there meaningful economic mechanisms that contain these deviation-amplifying effects? In later writings Harrod recognizes some economic bounds for these unstable growth dynamics arising from some nonmonetary forces (Harrod 1973, chap. 3), but he has never formally built them into his model.

Let us also look at the perfect foresight case ($\beta_{x^e} = \infty$) with $x^e = x$ whereby the dynamics becomes one-dimensional:

$$dx/dt = \dot{x} = \beta_x (x - x^\star) x$$

Figure 4.2 illustrates unambiguously repelling forces of this case.

Local and global deviation-amplifying forces arise whenever the initial value of the rate of capacity utilization x is off $x^\star$. If x increases above the steady state, for example, x^e starts to increase as well. This

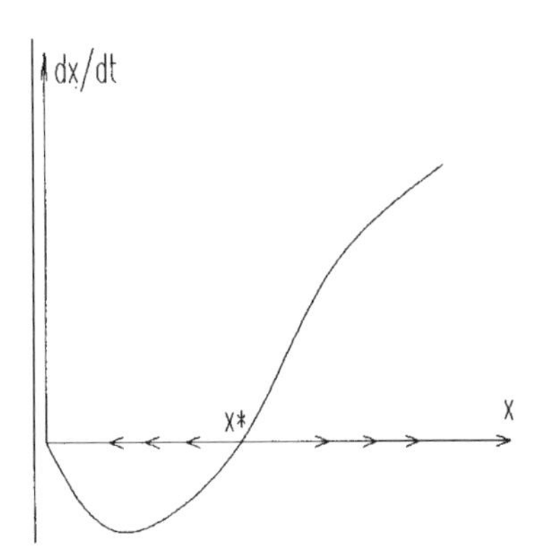

Figure 4.2
Harrodian growth under myopic perfect foresight

leads to further increases in x and x^e without bounds.[5] This unstable dynamic represents the simplest version of a knife-edge growth problem. Hicks (1950), among others, generated this type of instability by means of appropriate lags in the place of sales expectations and using certain ceilings and floors to obtain boundedness for this real dynamic. Goodwin (1951) assumed such thresholds solely for investment behavior and obtained viability, allowing for a wide range of asymmetries in the generated trade cycle pattern. In order to demonstrate viability for multiplier–accelerator models we shall, however, make use of the Kaldor trade cycle approach in the following section, which both is similar in spirit to the above approaches and allows for growth as in Hicks (1950). Furthermore, the Kaldor approach to a bounded dynamics can also be used to limit certain purely nominal instabilities. This questions the meaningfulness of the popular jump variable solution procedure that generally finds application in the presence of such instabilities.

It may also be asked whether there are monetary forces that may limit this unstable real dynamics. The first appealing idea is to add an LM schedule to the above IS-variant. In the present context we abstract from any price- and wage-level dynamics, that is, $\hat{p} = \hat{w} = 0$. This is compatible with changes in the money supply if a constant growth rate $\hat{M} = g_k^\star = sx^\star =$ const. is assumed. Wage and price dynamics will be discussed in later sections of this chapter when building models of the labor market. Here we shall consider only interest rate effects in their interaction with real economic growth.

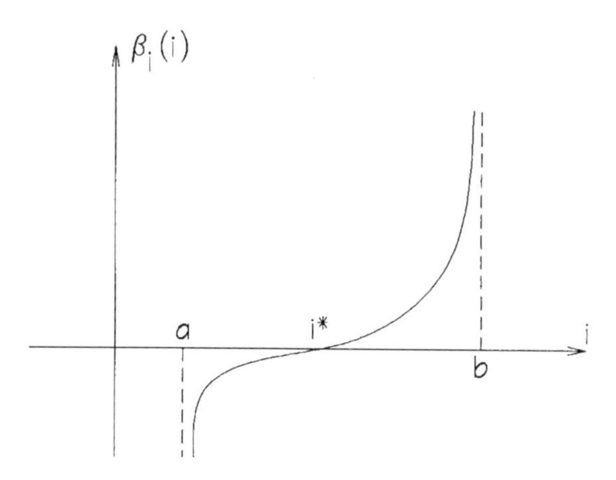

Figure 4.3
The interest rate effect in the investment function

We employ a simple linear money demand function for describing the interaction of real and monetary forces,

$$\text{LM}: \quad M = h_1 pY - h_2 pK(i - i^\star), \qquad h_i = \text{const.}, \; i = 1, 2$$

where the parameter $i^\star$ is the "natural" rate of interest. The money market is cleared in each instance of time. We enrich the product market dynamic by an interest rate effect in the following way:

$$\hat{x} = \hat{g}_k = \beta_x(x - x^\star) - \beta_i(i), \qquad \beta_i^{'} > 0$$

which says that investment now also depends (negatively) on the nominal = real rate of interest. We assume that the interest rate effect is larger, the larger the deviation of this rate from its natural level becomes, as it is shown in figure 4.3. We expect that the interest rate effect of this nonlinear shape will make the real dynamics a bounded one or will at least lead to turning points when the rate of capacity utilization departs by too much from its steady-state value.

With $m = M/(pK) = h_1 x - h_2(i - i^\star)$, the interest rate can be obtained as a function of the rate of capacity utilization and real balances per unit of capital as follows

$$i = i(x, m) = \frac{h_1 x - m}{h_2} + i^\star$$

Moreover, we get by the usual formulae for rates of growth calculations:

$$\hat{m} = \hat{M} - \hat{p} - \hat{K} = sx^\star - 0 - g_k, \text{ or}$$

$$\dot{m} = s(x^\star - x)m \tag{4.4}$$

This is to be coupled with the law of motion of real magnitudes

$$\hat{x} = \beta_x(x - x^\star) - \beta_i(i) \tag{4.5}$$

The inner steady state $\dot{m} = \dot{x} = 0$ is $i = i^\star$, $m^\star = h_1 x^\star$, and $x = x^\star$.

The Jacobian at the steady state is

$$J = \begin{bmatrix} (\beta_x - \beta_i'(i^\star)\frac{h_1}{h_2})x^\star & +(\beta_i'(i^\star)/h_2)x^\star \\ -sm^\star & 0 \end{bmatrix} = \begin{bmatrix} ? & + \\ - & 0 \end{bmatrix}$$

because we have for the partial derivatives of the function i

$$i_x = \frac{h_1}{h_2} > 0, \qquad i_m = -1/h_2 < 0$$

Harrodian local instability is obtained via trace $J > 0$ if and only if:

$$\beta_x > \beta_i'(i^\star)\frac{h_1}{h_2},$$

that is, the accelerator works with sufficient strength relative to the interest rate effect, since det $J > 0$ always. Moreover and more specifically, the Hopf bifurcation theorem can be applied with respect to the parameter β_x since purely imaginary roots arise at the parameter value $\beta_x^H = \beta_i'(i^\star)h_1/h_2$.[6] A loss of stability therefore occurs in a cyclical fashion at this value by way of a stability corridor, surrounded by an unstable limit cycle, that shrinks to zero (the so-called subcritical case) or by way of the birth of stable limit cycle that increases in amplitude (the supercritical case) when the bifurcation value β_x^H is crossed.[7] Finally, the instability will become locally monotone for large parameter values β_x, since the eigenvalues

$$\lambda_{1,2} = \text{trace}/2 \pm \sqrt{(\text{trace}/2)^2 - \det}$$

of the above Jacobian must then become real numbers. Thus, a large output reaction, β_x, to an imbalance between actual and desired output leads locally to either cyclical or monotonic instability. We have a phase diagram with the following isoclines:

$$\dot{x} = 0: \quad m = h_1 x + (i^\star - \beta_i^{-1}(\beta_x(x - x^\star)))h_2 \text{ and}$$

$$\dot{m} = 0: \quad x = x^\star$$

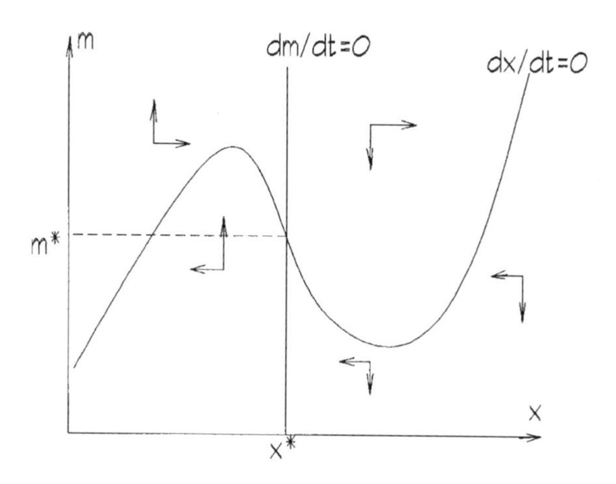

Figure 4.4
Phase plot of the Harrodian monetary growth dynamics

the details of which are shown in figure 4.4.

In sum, the interest rate effect can make Harrodian cumulative forces cyclical, but maybe not yet in a viable way. Nevertheless, there are turning points now. This is fairly obvious with respect to the existence of lower turning points and at least plausible for the upper ones, since an increase in x eventually must lead to a decrease in m owing to an interest rate i that would rise beyond any bound otherwise. Note that this is only one example of why cumulative instability may turn its direction. The viability of multiplier–accelerator growth dynamics is further investigated in section 6 of this chapter and—from a somewhat different angle—in the next section.

The monetary side has been extremely simplified in the above extension of the Harrod model:

$$\hat{M} = sx^{\star}, \qquad \hat{p} = \hat{w} = 0, \qquad \pi^{e} = 0$$

The model is therefore solely of a very preliminary nature. Subsequently, we shall show in a different context that the excluded $\hat{p}$, π^{e}-movements may exhibit a dynamic that is of a similar type as that of this extended Harrod model. This subsequent part will be of particular importance for chapters 7–10, where it is considered in much more detail and generality.

To demonstrate such a relationship between models of real growth and models of money and inflation, let us employ the inflation model by Cagan (1956) with $\bar{K}, \bar{Y}$ =const. in order to concentrate completely on the nominal side. Here we will allow the money market to be in disequilibrium, thus $L \neq M$. With the expected real rate of interest $i - \pi^e = i^{re}$ and output Y assumed as constant we have for the loglinear money demand function that is typically employed in this context:[8]

$$M^d = \bar{h} p \bar{Y} e^{\alpha i} = \bar{h} p \bar{Y} e^{\alpha(i^{re}+\pi^e)} \tag{4.6}$$

$$= \bar{h} \bar{Y} e^{\alpha(i^{re})} p e^{\alpha \pi^e}, \qquad \alpha < 0 \tag{4.7}$$

Slightly extending Goldman's (1972) generalization of the Cagan model and, furthermore, assuming $g_m = \hat{M}$ =const., we posit as theory of inflation

$$\hat{p} = \beta_p \ln(\frac{M}{M^d}) + \eta \pi^e + (1 - \eta) g_m \tag{4.8}$$

Prices are assumed to be driven by (the logarithm of) the excess supply in the money market and by the inflationary climate within which this excess supply is operating. This is again coupled with adaptive expectations, now of the rate of inflation[9]

$$\dot{\pi}^e = \beta_{\pi^e}(\hat{p} - \pi^e) \tag{4.9}$$

where again for the limit $\beta_{\pi^e} = \infty$ we have $\hat{p} = \pi^e$ (myopic perfect foresight). Note that the above disequilibrium approach to the determination of the rate of inflation is compatible with money-market equilibrium in the steady state, since the additional terms in this adjustment equation sum up to steady-state inflation in this case. Note furthermore that there are backward- as well as forward-looking aspects involved in this price level adjustment equation.

We assume $\bar{K} = 1$ and $h\bar{Y}e^{\alpha i^{re}} = 1$ for simplicity and make use of the new dynamic variable $m = ln(M/p)$ in the place of p in the investigation of the above laws of motion. This gives

$$\dot{m} = \widehat{lnM} - \widehat{lnp} = \hat{M} - \hat{p} = g_m - \pi^e$$

and thus the following linear system of differential equations

$$\dot{m} = g_m - \beta_p(m - ln(M^d/p)) - \eta\pi^e - (1 - \eta) g_m$$

$$= \eta g_m - \beta_p(m - \alpha\pi^e) - \eta\pi^e$$

$$= \beta_p(\alpha\pi^e - m) - \eta\pi^e + const. \tag{4.10}$$

$$\begin{aligned}\dot{\pi}^e &= \beta_{\pi^e}(\hat{p} - \pi^e)\\ &= \beta_{\pi^e}(g_m - \dot{m} - \pi^e)\\ &= \beta_{\pi^e}((1-\eta)g^m + \beta_p(m - \alpha\pi^e) - (1-\eta)\pi^e)\\ &= \beta_{\pi^e}(\beta_p m - ((1-\eta) + \beta_p\alpha)\pi^e) + const.) \end{aligned} \tag{4.11}$$

The steady state of the above system is $m^\star = \alpha\pi^{e\star}$, $\pi^{e\star} = \hat{p}^\star = g^m$. We thus get for the Jacobian J at the steady state

$$J = \begin{bmatrix} -\beta_p & \beta_p\alpha \\ \beta_p\beta_{\pi^e} & -\beta_{\pi^e}(\beta_p\alpha + (1-\eta)) \end{bmatrix} = \begin{bmatrix} - & - \\ + & ? \end{bmatrix}$$

and thus in particular $\det J = \beta_p(1-\eta)\beta_{\pi^e} > 0$ iff $\eta < 1$ holds.

The Hopf bifurcation theorem is again applicable, now for the parameter β_{π^e}, but only in the case where β_p is so large that $-\beta_p\alpha - (1-\eta) > 0$ is fulfilled ($\alpha < 0$),[10] that is, where the second component in the trace of J is positive. This Hopf bifurcation takes place at the parameter value

$$\beta^H_{\pi^e}\colon \beta^H_{\pi^e} = \beta_p/(-\beta_p\alpha - (1-\eta))$$

where trace $J = 0$ holds. Again, the loss of stability is of a cyclical nature when this bifurcation point is crossed, but now only of degenerate type since the dynamical system considered is linear. By the same argument we know that the system is globally asymptotically stable below this bifurcation point—as the extended Harrod growth model for a weak accelerator. For $\beta_{\pi^e} \to \infty$ and $-\beta_p\alpha > (1-\eta)$ again an unstable node arises, since $\det J > 0$ always and since $(\text{trace } J)^2/4 - \det J$ must become positive eventually.

The isoclines of the above dynamics are (for $\eta < 1$)

$$\dot{m} = 0: \quad m = \eta(g_m - \pi^e)/\beta_p + \alpha\pi^e$$

$$\dot{\pi}^e = 0: \quad m = (1-\eta)(\pi^e - g_m)/\beta_p + \alpha\pi^e$$

Let us assume $g_m = 0$ ($m^\star = \pi^{e\star} = 0$) for the following graphical exposition of the dynamics. As shown, the generally stable case[11] arises if $-\alpha < (1-\eta)/\beta_p$ holds, and it looks like figure 4.5a. By contrast, we have a potentially globally unstable case[12] if $\dot{\pi}^e$ is negatively sloped. An increase of β_{π^e} beyond $\beta^H_{\pi^e}$ produces this type of instability. Note that the isoclines depicted above do not depend on the parameter β_{π^e}; the above

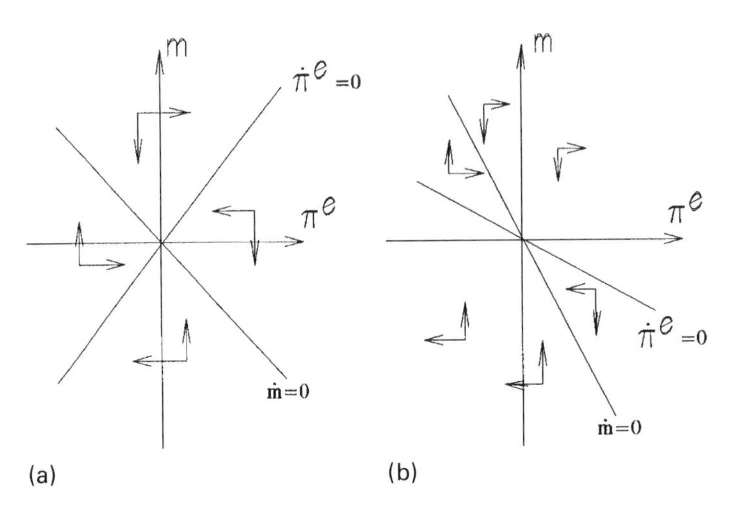

Figure 4.5
(*a*) Global stability and (*b*) a potential for global instability

phase diagrams thus cannot mirror the destabilization resulting from the adjustment speed of inflationary expectations.

As stated, the above Hopf bifurcation is always of a degenerate type; thus no limit cycle can arise. We have a stable node, stable spiral, unstable spiral, unstable node for β_{π^e} in the case where $\hat{p}_\pi > 1$ holds for this partial derivative of the equation that defines inflation. If prices are sufficiently flexible and inflationary expectations sufficiently fast, all trajectories are cyclically or monotonically explosive. We have a similar positive feedback, as in the Harrod model, however, now that inflation and its expectations take the place of actual and expected capacity utilization. As in the case of the Harrod model, no assumptions guaranteeing global viability are provided yet. Appropriate nonlinearities resulting in limit cycles are discussed in the following section.

Finally, we want to note that Sargent and Wallace's (1973) paper concentrates solely on the limit case of myopic perfect foresight $\pi^e = \hat{p}$ and on $\eta = 1$ ($g_m = 0$ in addition), which necessitates a money-market equilibrium. We then get a single linear differential equation for $q = \ln p$, $\dot{q} = (q - lnM)/(-\alpha)$, where $\alpha < 0$. We thus have purely explosive paths as in the simplest Harrod case with myopic perfect foresight. The solution of Sargent and Wallace (1973) to this instability problem is the well-known jump-variable technique. We shall see, however, that the case $\eta < 1$ and a plausible nonlinearity in the money demand function can give rise to quite different solutions than those resulting from the jump-variable technique. This will be motivated by means of the Kaldor trade cycle model in the following section whose basic viability-generating mechanism is then appropriately applied to the Cagan model of the present section. A more detailed study of this latter approach of taming an inflation-accelerating mechanism is pursued in section 9.6.

4.3 Boundedness in Real and Monetary Models

The Kaldor model (1940) is one of the early nonlinear business cycle models which, similarly to the Harrod model, exhibits local instability but global boundedness. As viability mechanism an investment function is conceived of that becomes bounded as income passes through certain thresholds. This idea is also employed in Goodwin's (1951) multiplier-accelerator approach to the trade cycle as well as in other variants of this model type. We concentrate here on Kaldor's approach since it, too, allows for an analog in the monetary sector as described by the Cagan model of the preceding section. This monetary analog will reappear in a different form in later chapters of the book.

The simple form of the Kaldor model (1940) reads

$$C = \bar{C} + cY, \qquad \bar{C} > 0, \ c \in (0,1), \qquad S = -\bar{C} + (1-c)Y$$

$$I = I(Y, K), \qquad I_Y > 0, \ I_K < 0$$

where I stands for net investment. Allowing now for goods-market disequilibrium and employing the dynamic multiplier in this situation gives

$$\dot{Y} = \beta_y(C + I - Y) = \beta_y(I - S) = \beta_y(I(Y, K) + \bar{C} - sY) \tag{4.12}$$

where $s = 1 - c$, which gives the first differential equation of the Kaldor model. The second differential equation is the accumulation equation

$$\dot{K} = I(Y, K) \tag{4.13}$$

where it is posited that net investment is always realized. Note that this model exhibits negative net investment and savings in the depressions. This can be remedied by a growth cycle reformulation of it that we shall briefly consider later on.

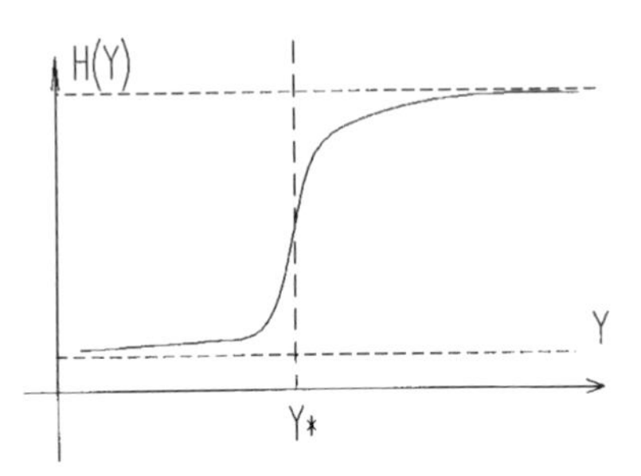

Figure 4.6
A Kaldorian nonlinear investment function

The isoclines of this system of differential equations are determined by:

$$\dot{Y} = 0: \quad sY = I(Y, K) + \bar{C}, \qquad \dot{K} = 0: \quad I(Y, K) = 0$$

We assume that equations (4.13)–(4.14) have a positive steady-state solution given by

$$Y^\star = \frac{1}{s}\bar{C} \tag{4.14}$$

$$I(\frac{1}{s}\bar{C}, K^\star) = 0 \tag{4.15}$$

If a solution to (4.15) exists it must be unique. An example is provided by the investment function $I(Y, K) = H(Y) - \alpha K$, $H' > 0$ which gives $K^\star = H(Y^\star)/\alpha$, $Y^\star = \bar{C}/s$.

The boundedness of investment may be illustrated by employing a function $H(Y)$ as shown in figure 4.6. where it is expressed that net investment is always positive if the capital stock—and thus αK—is sufficiently small, and investment eventually ceases to increase if income continuously increases. On this basis, the phase diagram of the above dynamical systems looks as in figure 4.7.

Chang and Smyth (1971) provide a somewhat more general model with specific assumptions on investment I and savings S such that the Poincaré-Bendixson theorem can be applied, guaranteeing the existence of a persistent cycle in the positive orthant of the (Y, K)-phase space. Varian (1979) reconsiders their model from the viewpoint of catastrophe theory.[13] A third perspective for an understanding of the

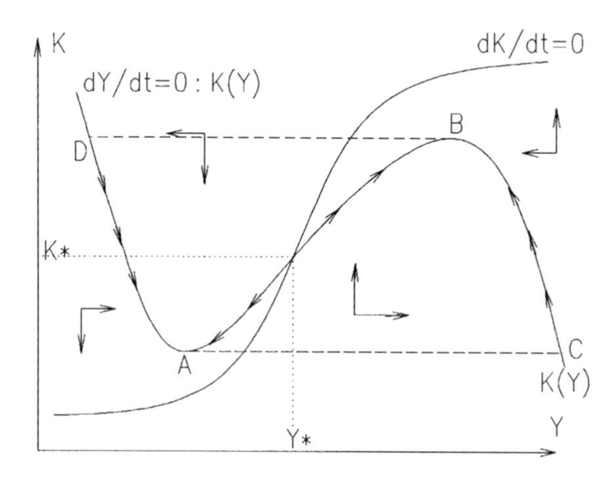

Figure 4.7
The phase portrait of the Kaldor trade cycle

trade cycle mechanism of the Kaldor (1940) model can be proposed as follows.

For this purpose we analyze the local stability properties of the steady state by means of the Jacobian of this system first. This gives

$$\det J = \det \begin{pmatrix} \beta_y(I_Y - s) & \beta_y I_K \\ I_Y & I_K \end{pmatrix} = \det \begin{pmatrix} -\beta_y s & 0 \\ I_Y & I_K \end{pmatrix} > 0 \text{ and}$$

$$\text{trace } J = \beta_y(I_Y - s) + I_K > 0$$

$$\text{iff } \beta_y > -I_K/(I_Y - s) \text{ and } I_Y > s(> 0)$$

which thus describes the case of local instability.

The above statement on instability is subsequently posited to hold. In fact, it denotes Kaldor's unstable dynamic multiplier based on an adjustment speed chosen sufficiently large. Write the dynamics (4.13), (4.14) as follows

$$\frac{1}{\beta_y}\dot{Y} = I(Y, K) + \bar{C} - sY \tag{4.16}$$

$$\dot{K} = I(Y, K) \tag{4.17}$$

To explore the dynamics of (4.16) and (4.17) for β_y sufficiently large, it may be of help to consider the following constrained system (the case $\beta_y = \infty$):

$$0 = I(Y, K) + \bar{C} - sY, \quad \text{i.e. } K(Y) \text{ as in Figure 4.7}$$

$$\dot{K} = I(Y, K) = sY(K) - \bar{C} \tag{4.18}$$

which replaces the two-dimensional dynamics (4.16) and (4.17) by a single dynamical equation (4.18) defined on the graph of $Y(K)$. Geometrically, this means that the dynamics are confined to the $\dot{Y} = 0$ curve in the former phase space for (Y, K).

Equation (4.18) implies that $\dot{K}$ is negative to the left of $Y^{\star} = \bar{C}/s$ and positive to its right, which gives rise to the adjustments along $\dot{Y} = 0$ as shown in Figure 4.7. For any starting point on $\dot{Y} = 0$ the state variable K therefore evolves to either point A or B. Owing to $sY - \bar{C} < 0$ or $sY - \bar{C} > 0$ at these points, they cannot be fixed points of the dynamics. Without the unconstrained system (4.16) and (4.17) it would be difficult to decide what happens when point A or B is reached. On the basis of (4.16) and (4.17) one may, however, reasonably assume that the rate of output Y changes discontinuously, jumping to points C or D in Figure 4.7, respectively (with a constant value of K during their jump). The dynamic is therefore characterized by so-called relaxation oscillations and gives rise to a perpetual cycle DACB, a limit limit cycle as it is called in Chiarella 1990.

The constrained system (4.18) is thus asymptotically related to an unconstrained system (4.16) and (4.17) of higher dimension, the so-called regularization of the constrained system.[14] It can be considered as a refinement of the constrained model. This refinement will produce limit cycles that are close to the limit limit cycle DACB if the parameter β_y (the speed of the dynamic multiplier) is sufficiently large.

In this simple geometrical way, we have developed an idea of the characteristics of the Kaldorian trade cycle (for β_y sufficiently large). Starting in point D, we can say that income Y is low there relative to the capital stock K and that disinvestment takes place slowly, while the dynamic multiplier keeps output close to the equilibrium output for each K: $I(Y, K) = sY - \bar{C}$. Because of the declining K we have an increasing $I(\cdot, K)$ and thus an increasing Y until the point A is reached, where $K = \underline{K}$ holds, still exhibiting a fairly low level of equilibrium output Y. There is, however, no further goods-market equilibrium of Y to the left of the steady level $Y^{\star}$ for values of K below A, yet there is a unique asymptotically stable equilibrium output at C for $\underline{K}$, which then attracts disequilibrium output Y at a very high speed (or instantaneously, if $\beta_y = \infty$ holds). The system then jumps from a state of depression at A to a state of boom at C. From then on, output is high relative to the capital stock K generated by moving from D to A. Net investment therefore becomes positive, and the capital stock starts to increase. These increases tend to diminish net investment, and the highest attained value of output Y starts to fall slowly from then on. The system moves upward in this way until point B is reached, where rapid income movement from high to low occurs – the exact opposite of the movement that led us from A to C.

The Kaldorian trade cycle therefore exhibits rapid upturns and downturns followed by very slow upturns and downturns that can be tailored to fairly different phase lengths and shapes of the cycle. This finding also holds true for all speeds β_y of goods-market adjustment with respect to investment and savings behavior as illustrated in the following equation

$$\beta_y > -I_K/(I_Y - S_Y), \qquad I_Y - S_Y > 0$$

(see Chang and Smyth 1971). Appropriate nonlinearities in the investment function through which investment behavior changes when income (and capital stock) pass through thresholds are an essential ingredient that keeps the explosive dynamics around the steady state within economically meaningful bounds and thus makes the system viable.

Observe that a discrete time version of the Kaldor model can generate chaos by a sufficient increase in the parameter β_y (see Dana and Malgrange 1984). This is because the dynamic multiplier that is highly stabilizing in the continuous time case is overstretched in the discrete time case. It is also worthwhile noting that Dana and Malgrange (1984) have extended the Kaldor model to a growing economy.

In a growth context Skott (1991a) shows that it is reasonable to assume that the investment function is homogeneous of degree one in output and the capital stock, that is, it is then of the form $I(Y, K) = KH(Y/K)$ where the function H is again of the type depicted in figure 4.6. Setting $\bar{C}$ equal to zero (as is usual in growth theory) then gives rise to

$$\hat{Y} = \beta_y(I(Y/K)/(Y/K) - s), \qquad \hat{K} = I(x), \text{ i.e.}$$

$$\dot{x} = x\beta_y(I(x) - sx) - I(x)x, \qquad x = Y/K$$

The dynamics reduces in this case to a one-dimensional one that for $I'(x^*) > s$ is explosive, at least locally, if the dynamic multiplier acts with sufficient strength. However, in the case of an investment function as in figure 4.6, there will again be two outward equilibria that are attracting so that the dynamic settles down at one of them. However, since the investment is not shifting in this situation, no further law of motion is present and thus no limit cycle behavior is possible. It follows that a second state variable seems to be needed to generalize the Kaldorian trade cycle to a model that allows for economic growth.

However, assuming an exogenously growth trend g for autonomous expenditures, as Dana and Malgrange (1984) do, is also sufficient to generalize the limit cycle of the stationary Kaldor economy to the case of a growing economy:

$$\dot{Y} = \beta_y(\bar{C}e^{gt} + cY + I(Y,K) - Y), \dot{K} = I(Y,K)$$

If we make use of the state variables $y = Ye^{-gt}, k = Ke^{-gt}$, this simple modification of the Kaldor model gives rise to[15]

$$\dot{y} = \beta_y(I(y,k) - sy + \bar{C}) - gy$$

$$\dot{k} = I(y,k) - gk$$

This model allows for a Kaldorian growth cycle in the same way as in the stationary case we have considered above (see Dana and Malgrange 1984 for the necessary assumptions and derivations).[16] We shall not go into this analysis here, since the original Kaldor trade cycle approach is already sufficient for our following purposes.

The above procedure—making the dynamics viable by means of an appropriate fold in one of the isoclines, on the basis of the shape of the investment function—can be applied to the unstable Cagan model of the preceding section as well. We will show here that its locally unstable cases will then also lead to economic viability intuitively demonstrated again by means of relaxation oscillations that here generate jumps of a quite different nature than those postulated by Sargent and Wallace (1973) in a purely log-linear context.

Where is, however, the appropriate economically meaningful nonlinearity in the above Cagan model that can bound its dynamic when explosiveness prevails around the steady state? We can refer to the wealth constraint or more directly to a money demand function of the following form in order to provide an example that answers this question:[17]

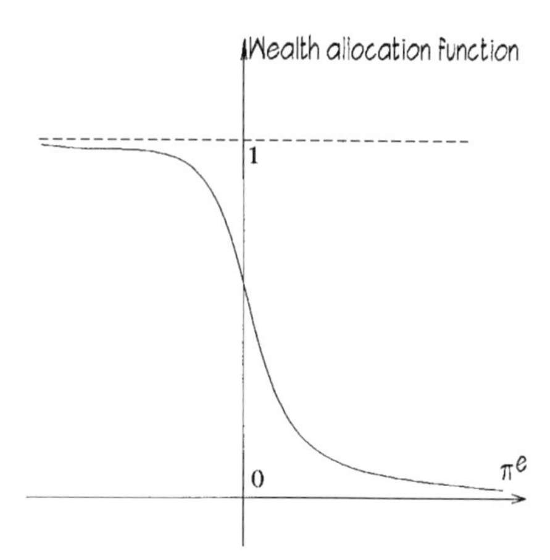

Figure 4.8
The nonlinear shape of the wealth allocation function

$$M^d/p = \bar{h}\bar{Y} + \bar{W}\tilde{\alpha}(\pi^e), \qquad \tilde{\alpha}' < 0$$

where $\bar{W}$ is real wealth, a constant, and $\bar{h}\bar{Y} = 1$ again by normalization, and where $\tilde{\alpha}(\pi^e)$ is a wealth allocation function of the shape as depicted in figure 4.8.

This functional form gives expression to the fact that portfolio shifts are always of a bounded nature. We expect that this functional form adds bounds to the dynamics of the Cagan model, since the parameter α of this model, that is, here the slope of the wealth allocation function, approaches zero far off the steady state.

Taking logarithms gives a function

$$\ln(M^d/p) = \ln(1 + \bar{W}\tilde{\alpha}(\pi^e)) = \alpha(\pi^e)$$

which has the same shape as $\tilde{\alpha}(\pi^e)$.[18] This function $\alpha(\pi^e)$ is to be used in the place of $\alpha\pi^e$ in the Cagan model of the preceding section, and it provides an immediate generalization of the dynamics there considered.

The differential equations are now (with $\eta < 1$):

$$\dot{m} = \beta_p(\alpha(\pi^e) - m) - \eta\pi^e + \eta g_m \tag{4.19}$$

$$\dot{\pi}^e = \beta_{\pi^e}(\beta_p(m - \alpha(\pi^e)) - (1 - \eta)\pi^e + (1 - \eta)g_m) \tag{4.20}$$

where again $m = \ln(M/p)$. The isoclines of these dynamics are:

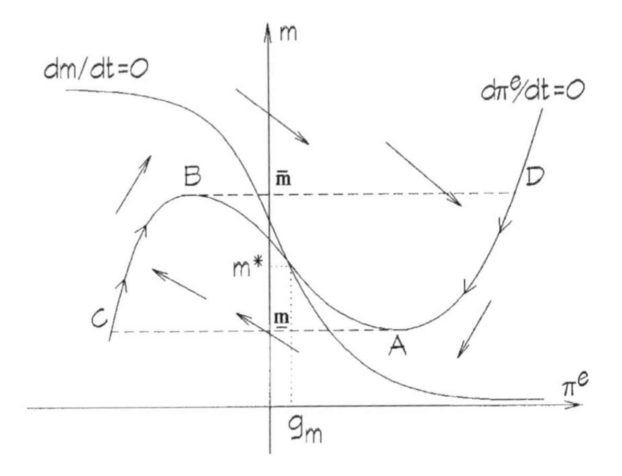

Figure 4.9
The nonlinear shape of the wealth allocation function

$$\dot{m} = 0: \quad m = \alpha(\pi^e) + \eta(g_m - \pi^e)/\beta_p$$

$$\dot{\pi}^e = 0: \quad m = \alpha(\pi^e) + (1 - \eta)(\pi^e - g_m)/\beta_p$$

and the steady state is determined by $\eta(g_m - \pi^{e\star}) = 1 - \eta(\pi^{e\star} - g_m)$, which gives $\pi^{e\star} = g_m$ and $\alpha(g_m) = m^\star$. Moreover, from $\dot{m} = 0$ we also have $\hat{p}^\star = g_m$. For $\eta = 0$, as in section 4.2, we have an unstable case if $-\alpha'(g_m) + 1/\beta_p > 0$ holds and if β_{π^e} is sufficiently large. The phase plot of such a situation looks as in figure 4.9. For very large β_{π^e}, as in the Kaldor model, we again obtain the relaxation oscillations that approach the limit limit cycle $A \to C \to B \to D$. But via Poincaré-Bendixson—as in Kaldor's model—limit cycles also appear under weaker conditions, that is, for significantly smaller values of β_{π^e}.

Sargent and Wallace (1973) only consider those dynamics with $\alpha(\pi^e) = \alpha\pi^e, \alpha < 0$, via a linear approximation, that is, close to the steady state (fig. 4.9). They conclude from the repelling forces surrounding this steady state that the system is purely explosive, which from a global perspective it is not, so that their agents may then be assumed to adopt the jump-variable technique, leading them back to the steady state when monetary disturbances occur. In the present extension there is no basis for such a methodology. The constrained system here is given by the perfect foresight assumption $\pi^e = \hat{p}$ leading—as in the Kaldor model—to a dynamic along the curve $\dot{\pi}^e = 0$: $m = m(\pi^e)$ in the above figure. Again this constrained system cannot predict what happens when points B and A are reached from below or from above, respectively, although it is already much more informative than the purely local instability analysis by Sargent and Wallace (1973).

Adaptive expectations, that is, (4.19) and (4.20), are one possible regularization of the constrained system, since these unconstrained and constrained systems are asymptotically related. This regularization[19] implies that perfect foresight is restored at $\bar{m}$ by a jump of π^e from B to D and at $\underline{m}$ by a jump of π^e from A to C. The nonlinear Cagan model (for $\eta < 1$) therefore implies quite a different jump-variable situation than is obtained in the literature from the extreme case $\eta = 1$, $\alpha(\pi^e) = \alpha\pi^e$, which under myopic perfect foresight reduces equation 4.19 to: $\dot{m} = m/(-\alpha) + g_m$. Such a model cannot be used for global analysis, which is implicitly involved when the conventional jump-variable technique is employed.

We conclude that the case of myopic perfect foresight must be treated in a different way than done so far in the literature (see also Chiarella 1990; Flaschel 1993; and Flaschel and Sethi 1995). The discussion of problems that are generated in deterministic dynamical macrosystems by the assumption of myopic perfect foresight are further investigated within an AD-AS growth framework in chapters 7–9. A concluding section in chapter 9 returns to the simple nonlinear Cagan inflation model just considered and further elaborates on our criticism of the conventional jump-variable technique used in this simple model of purely nominal relationships and their dynamics.

4.4 Classical Growth Dynamics and Viability

In this section the emphasis is shifted from the goods and money markets to the labor market including a wage-price sector for a growing economy. The classical prototype model of growth based on a labor market dynamic is the Goodwin (1967) growth cycle model, written in real terms. Goodwin (1972) also suggested a nominal version of this model that separates wage from price inflation. We draw on the work of Desai (1973) and Wolfstetter (1977) and employ this type of model as a starting point in this section.

Let us start with the following formulation of this model. The growth rate of the money wage is given by:

$$\hat{w} = \beta_w(e - \bar{e}) + \eta\pi^e \tag{4.21}$$

This is a nominal wage Phillips curve, here still linear and augmented with expected price inflation π^e when $\eta > 0$ holds. We have $\bar{e} \in (0, 1)$ where $1 - \bar{e}$ denotes the NAIRU unemployment rate. In addition, we posit a dynamic markup pricing where $v = wL/(pY)$ is the wage share.

$$\dot{p} = \beta_p \left[A\frac{wL}{Y} - p \right] \Rightarrow \hat{p} = \beta_p[Av - 1] \tag{4.22}$$

We assume for simplicity for the markup factor $A = 1 + \mu, \quad \mu > 0$ $Av^\star = 1$.[20] There is therefore no inflation in the steady state (see also Wolfstetter 1977 for a further justification of this assumption). We allow adaptive or perfect expectations as before.

$$\dot{\pi}^e = \beta_{\pi^e}(\hat{p} - \pi^e) \tag{4.23}$$

where $\beta_{\pi^e} \in [0, \infty]$.

Goodwin's accumulation equation reads on the basis of a linear technology with no technical change,[21] that is, on the basis of given input–output proportions $\bar{x} = Y/K$ =const., $\bar{y} = Y/L$ =const., and its assumption of Say's law in the simplest form possible $I \equiv S = (1 - v)Y$

$$\hat{K} = \bar{x}(1 - v)$$

where it is assumed with respect to savings propensities that $s_c = 1; s_w = 0$ holds. From the definitional equation $e = \frac{L}{L^s} = \frac{L}{Y}\frac{Y}{K}K\frac{1}{L^s}$ we get

$$\hat{e} = \hat{K} - n$$

Owing to fixed coefficients in production we have $\hat{\bar{y}} = \widehat{Y/L} = 0$, and $\hat{x} = \widehat{Y/K} = 0$. From the above we get:

$$\hat{v} = \hat{w} - \hat{p} - \hat{y} = \beta_w(e - \bar{e}) + \eta\pi^e - \beta_p[Av - 1] \tag{4.24}$$

$$\hat{e} = \bar{x}(1 - v) - n \tag{4.25}$$

$$\dot{\pi}^e = \beta_{\pi^e}(\beta_p[Av - 1] - \pi^e) \tag{4.26}$$

Three autonomous differential equations in the variables v, e, π^e, are obtained. In contrast to the original Goodwin model our nominal extension of this model includes actual price and price expectations dynamics.

The interior steady state solution is

$$v^\star = 1 - n/\bar{x}, \qquad e^\star = \bar{e}\ \pi^{e\star} = 0 = \hat{p}^\star \text{ since } Av^\star = 1$$

For the Jacobian J at the steady state we get with respect to the $\dot{v}$, $\dot{e}$, $\dot{\pi}^e$ equations:

$$J = \begin{bmatrix} -\beta_p A v^\star & \beta_w v^\star & \eta v^\star \\ -\bar{x} e^\star & 0 & 0 \\ \beta_{\pi^e}\beta_p A & 0 & -\beta_{\pi^e} \end{bmatrix}$$

We have trace $J < 0$, that is, in terms of the Routh Hurwitz conditions[22] for local asymptotic stability a first positive finding: $a_1 = -$ trace $J > 0$. Furthermore, the principal minors of this matrix fulfill:

$$J_1 = J_{22}J_{33} - J_{23}J_{32} = 0$$

$$J_2 = J_{11}J_{33} - J_{13}J_{31} = \beta_p A v^\star \beta_{\pi^e}(1-\eta) \gtreqless 0$$

$$J_3 = J_{11}J_{22} - J_{12}J_{21} = \bar{x} e^\star \beta_w v^\star > 0$$

Thus

$$a_2 = J_1 + J_2 + J_3 > 0 \quad \text{if } \eta \leq 1$$

or if the parameter β_w, that is, wage flexibility, is sufficiently high. Furthermore, we obviously have

$$\det J = -a_3 = -\bar{x} e^\star \beta_w v^\star \beta_{\pi^e} < 0$$

For the Routh-Hurwitz conditions of local asymptotic stability we finally need $b = a_1 a_2 - a_3 > 0$. Since the expressions that form det J are contained among the expressions that give (-trace J) ($J_2 + J_3$) and thus cancel each other in the calculation of b we get local asymptotic stability at least for all η with:

$$\eta < 1 + \frac{\bar{x} e^\star v^\star \beta_w}{(\beta_p A v^\star + \beta_{\pi^e})\beta_{\pi^e}} =: \eta^H$$

We add the following remark. There occurs Hopf bifurcation at η^H, that is, in particular, stability is lost in a cyclical fashion. This Hopf bifurcation can be shown to be of the trivial degenerate center type as it occurs in purely linear systems.

Furthermore, for the perfect foresight case $\beta_{\pi^e} \to \infty$, it follows that $\eta^H \to 1$. The same holds true for $\beta_p \to \infty$. An increase in β_{π^e}, β_p increases the instability range and an increase in β_w reduces it. This is a striking difference in the role price and wage flexibilities play in such classical framework.

For $\eta > 1$ it is also easy to determine the Hopf bifurcation point with respect to the adjustment speed of inflationary expectations. This point is given by the uniquely determined positive solution of a quadratic equation for β_{π^e}. The bifurcation from stability to instability is of the same type as before. In contrast to the Cagan model of section 4.2, however, it will exist only for parameter values $\eta > 1$.

To further study this system let us go to the limit case $\beta_{\pi^e} = \infty$: $\pi^e = \hat{p}$, which means myopic perfect foresight. The system then reduces to two differential equations:

$$\hat{v} = \beta_w(e - \bar{e}) - (1 - \eta)\beta_p[Av - 1] \tag{4.27}$$

$$\hat{e} = \bar{x}(1 - v) - n \tag{4.28}$$

The above suggests that $\eta^H = 1$ is now the bifurcation value that separates nonexplosive from explosive cyclical behavior by a center-type stability at $\eta = 1$. In fact, those two special cases $\pi^e = \hat{p}$ and $\eta = 1$ represent the original Goodwin (1967) growth cycle model where the employment-wage dynamics was only considered in real terms.

It is not difficult to prove this local assertion. Yet, more general—since of a global nature—and also easy to apply is a proof that employs a Liapunov-function for the dynamics (4.27)–(4.28) around its steady state $e^\star = \bar{e}$, $v^\star = 1 - n/\bar{x}$. The function

$$H(v, e) = \int_{e^\star}^{e} \beta_w(\tilde{e} - e^\star)/\tilde{e}\, d\tilde{e} - \int_{v^\star}^{v} (x(1 - \tilde{v}) - n)/\tilde{v}\, d\tilde{v}$$

defines such a Liapunov function. It has the following shape (see fig. 4.10) on the phase space for $(v, e) \in \mathbb{R}^2_+$. Its level surfaces are the Goodwin (1967) growth cycles that here result from choosing $\eta = 1$. The Liapunov function is zero at the steady. It is well defined and strictly positive elsewhere in the positive orthant $\mathbb{R}^2_+$. Moreover, its time derivative along the solution curves of the above dynamical system reads

$$\begin{aligned}\dot{H} &= H_v\dot{v} + H_e\dot{e}\\ &= -(\bar{x}(1 - v) - n)\hat{v} + \beta_w(e - \bar{e})\hat{e}\\ &= +(\bar{x}(1 - v) - n)(1 - \eta)\beta_p[Av - 1]\end{aligned}$$

which gives zero for $v = v^\star$. For $v \neq v^\star$ in contrast we get:

$$\dot{H}\begin{cases} < 0 & \text{if } \eta < 1\\ = 0 & \text{if } \eta = 1\\ > 0 & \text{if } \eta > 1\end{cases}$$

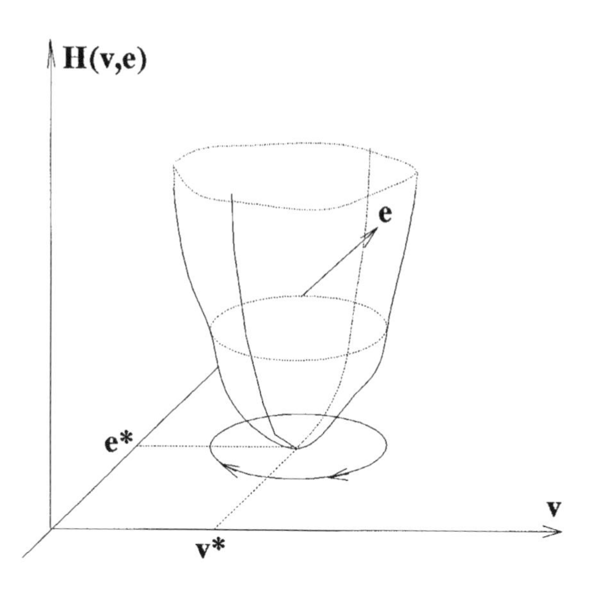

Figure 4.10
A Liapunov function for the myopic perfect foresight dynamics

since $x(1-v)-n$ and $Av-1$ are of different sign to the left and to the right of $v=v^\star$.

The theorem 2 of Hirsch and Smale (1974, 195) is applicable, since $\dot{H}=0 \Leftrightarrow v=v^\star$ (for $\eta \neq 1$). We thereby get

$$\eta \begin{cases} <1 & \text{a globally asymptotically stable dynamics in the invariant} \\ & \text{domain } \{(u,v) \in \mathbb{R}^2,\ u,v>0\} = \mathbb{R}^2_+ \\ >1 & \text{a totally unstable dynamics in this same invariant domain} \\ =1 & \text{all trajectories in } \mathbb{R}^2_+ \text{ are closed orbits, representing the} \\ & \text{original Goodwin growth cycles.} \end{cases}$$

These results are intuitively plausible since the sign of the derivative $\dot{H}$ simply expresses whether the trajectories of the dynamics in v, e-space are accompanied by declining or rising or constant magnitudes of their corresponding value $H(v,e)$ (see figure 4.10. Trajectories accompanied by a rising $H(v,e)$ for example must therefore be explosive.

The above approach, when restricted to myopic perfect foresight, gives a neat and simple generalization of Goodwin's (1967) classical growth cycle model of the dynamic interaction of the employment rate and income shares in the conflict about income distribution. With respect to the closed orbit shown in figure 4.10, as well as any other such orbit, this conflict about income distribution points inside and thus produces convergence to the steady state for parameter values $\eta < 1$ and outside, implying divergence, for $\eta > 1$.

Two problems might arise in such a situation. First, $(e, v) > (0, 0)$ holds automatically along the orbits of the model, but we also have to ensure that $(e, v,) \leq (1, 1)$ holds true. Second, the case $\eta > 1$ is not yet viable, that is, the dynamic is still incomplete, just as it is in the purely explosive multiplier-accelerator model. What, however, may determine outer bounds if economically implausible values are approached and thus instability prevails?

A possible solution for these problems is to use viability constraints as in Hicks's (1950) trade cycle model. We may posit

$$\hat{e} = \begin{cases} \bar{x}(1 - v) - n, & \text{if } e < 1 \text{ or } \dot{e} < 0 \\ 0, & \text{if } e = 1 \text{ and } \dot{e} > 0 \end{cases}$$

enforced by forced consumption of capitalists such that $s_c\bar{x}(1 - e) = n$ in the latter case. Here s_c is assumed as endogenous, since no worker will be found to operate additional machines.

In contrast, or in addition, we could assume state dependent reaction functions $\eta = \eta(v)$, $\beta_p = \beta_p(v)$ of the wage share v such that

$\eta(v^\star) > 1$ local instability, but $\eta(v) < 1$ if v close to 1

$\beta_p(v) = 0$ for $v \leq \underline{v} \leq v^\star$ [23]

$\beta_p(v) \to \infty$ as $v \to 1$ guaranteeing $\hat{v} < 0$ if v close to 1.

These assumptions state that sufficiently large wage shares—caused by local instability—will speed up inflation while at the same time the pressure from nominal wage increases is released. Furthermore, and for simplicity, the occurrence of deflation is restricted to a certain domain below the steady state. Assumptions of this kind give rise to a phase portrait of the type in figure 4.11. This solves not only the first but also the second problem, since $(0, 1) \times (0, 1]$ is made on invariant set by these assumptions, which cannot be left by any trajectory that starts in it. Furthermore, the steady state is unstable by the choice of the η and the β_p-function.

By the Poincaré-Bendixson theorem one can then demonstrate existence of a stable limit cycle in $(0, 1) \times (0, 1]$. This result is intuitively clear from figure 4.11, since the dynamics point outward at the steady state while the depicted box is at the same time an invariant set of the dynamics where the trajectories cannot escape from.

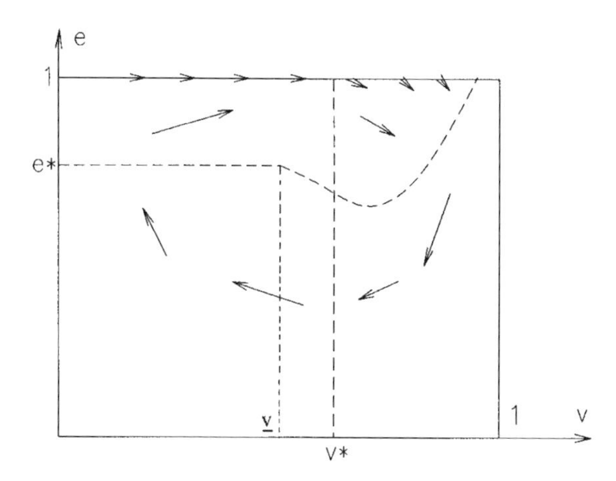

Figure 4.11
Viability constraints for the explosive classical growth cycle

In figure 4.11 we have limited ourselves to a sketch of possible bounds of the dynamics when the trajectories get close to $v = 1$ or to $e = 1$. As in chapter 3 we might, however, want a better construction, or a more reliable mechanism, in order to make such a system viable in a domain much smaller than the one allowed for by the above restrictions.

As in chapter 3 we may, therefore, introduce derivative control forces as another means to bound the repelling forces. We can write, for example,

$$\hat{v} = \beta_{w_1}(e - \bar{e}) + \beta_{w_2}\hat{e} - (1 - \eta)\beta_p[Av - 1]$$

$$\hat{e} = \bar{x}(1 - v) - n$$

by assuming that the money wage Phillips curve is also subject to derivative forces (as already observed by Phillips himself). Such a revision of the original dynamics implies as new autonomous dynamical system:

$$\hat{v} = \beta_{w_1}(e - \bar{e}) + \beta_{w_2}[\bar{x}(1 - v) - n] - (1 - \eta)\beta_p[Av - 1]$$

$$\hat{e} = \bar{x}(1 - v) - n$$

The same steady state as for (4.27)–(4.28) arises. We can also apply the same Liapunov-function H as before but have to replace β_w by β_{w_1} now.

$$\dot{H} = -[\bar{x}(1-v) - n]\hat{v} + \beta_{w_1}(e - \bar{e})\hat{e}$$
$$= -[\bar{x}(1-v) - n]\beta_{w_2}[\bar{x}(1-v) - n] + [\bar{x}(1-v) - n](1-\eta)\beta_p[Av - 1]$$
$$= 0 \quad \text{if } v = v^\star$$

If $v \neq v^\star$:

$$\dot{H} = -[\bar{x}(1-v) - n]^2[\beta_{w_2} + (1-\eta)\beta_p \frac{Av - 1}{\bar{x}(1-v) - n}]$$

With l' Hospital's rule we get

$$\frac{Av - 1}{\bar{x}(1-v) - n} \rightarrow -\frac{A}{\bar{x}} \quad \text{for } v \rightarrow v^\star$$

which means that the expression $\frac{Av-1}{\bar{x}(1-v)-n}$ is bounded on the interval $[0, 1]$:

$$\left| \frac{Av - 1}{\bar{x}(1-v) - n} \right| \leq c_1 \quad \text{on } [0, 1]$$

where c_1 is a positive constant. We thus have $\dot{H} < 0$ if $\beta_{w_2} > |1 - \eta|\beta_p c_1$ in the case where $\eta > 1$ holds. For $\eta \leq 1$ we always have $\dot{H} < 0$.

Theorem 2 of Hirsch and Smale (1974, 196) can again be applied and shows that the case $\eta > 1$ is then globally asymptotically stable in $\mathbb{R}^2_+$ if β_{w_2} is chosen as above. The intuitive explanation of this result is again obtained from the graph of the Liapunov function shown in figure 4.10. The above second problem of instability is thereby removed.

The first problem can now also be solved. Take the largest cycle of the original Goodwin (1967) model ($\eta = 1$, $\beta_{w_2} = 0$) that is contained in $[0, 1] \times [0, 1]$ (see fig. 4.12 and note that the boundary $v = 1$ may also determine the choice of this set.

There then exists $c_0 \in \mathbb{R}$ and that $H^{-1}(c_0) = \vartheta D$ for the boundary ϑD of the set $D = H^{-1}([0, c_0])$.[24] It is now easy to show that the set D is contained in the basin of attraction of the steady state $(v^\star, e^\star)$ since the derivatively controlled process points inward on D if β_{w_2} is chosen as above. Any trajectory that starts in D must therefore stay away from the boundary of the interval $[0, 1] \times [0, 1]$, that is, it describes a viable dynamics. Therefore, any $\eta > 1$ leads to a stable dynamics.

Finally, we want to introduce the following extension of the myopic perfect foresight model (4.27), (4.28):

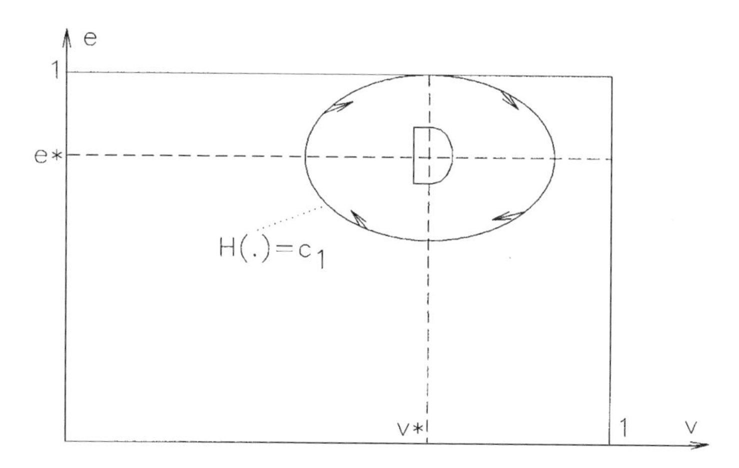

Figure 4.12
The largest economically feasible Goodwin growth cycle

$$\hat{v} = \beta_{w_1}(e - \bar{e}) + \beta_{w_2}(H(v, e))[\bar{x}(1 - v) - n] - (1 - \eta)\beta_p[Av - 1]$$

$$\hat{e} = \bar{x}(1 - v) - n$$

Here the term $\beta_{w_2}(H(v, e))$ is new and it is used to express that the parameter β_{w_2} becomes greater as the distance from the steady-state increases, measured for simplicity by the above Liapunov function H or by its level surfaces. Assuming furthermore that β_{w_2} is zero close to this steady state means that there are no derivative forces present near it. Coupled with $\eta > 1$ this implies that the steady state is locally unstable.

Assuming $\beta_{w_2}(c_1) > |1 - \eta|\beta_p c_1$ then implies that there exists a limit cycle in the interior of ϑD. This could again be proven by applying the Poincaré–Bendixson theorem.

If the instability caused by $\eta > 1$ dominates near the steady state and if the derivative control mechanism dominates the dynamics further away from it, we get a limit cycle in the Goodwin (1967) context, that is, on the basis of labor market dynamics alone. Those two forces turn the periodic motions of center type dynamics of the original Goodwin model into a persistent growth cycle.

As above shown in the Harrod model where wages are taken as constant, it is possible to tame the destabilizing accelerator effect by an interest rate effect arising from an LM schedule. Relaxation oscillations are found in the Kaldor trade cycle model where a sufficiently stable dynamic multiplier and a nonlinear investment function interact, giving rise to a limit cycle with fixed wages. In the Cagan model such relaxation oscillations arise because of an interaction of an unstable inflation multiplier $\hat{p}_\pi > 1$, fast inflationary expectations, and a nonlinear money demand function. In the latter case, a purely nominal dynamic arises. Finally, labor market dynamics with the above viability conditions or derivative controls can generate persistent growth fluctuations. At this stage, a further integration of the Harrod and Kaldor type product market dynamics, the Cagan type money market dynamics, and classical labor market dynamic appears as highly desirable. This integration will be achieved for the goods and labor markets from two different perspectives in the following sections. Fully integrated models, without accelerator effects, are studied in chapters 7–10 whereas capacity utilization problems are again viewed in chapters 11 and 12.

4.5 Supply-Driven Keynesian Growth Dynamics

In the subsequent model, based on Rose 1967, labor and goods markets interact dynamically. It is a simple presentation of the central idea of a Keynes-Wicksell employment cycle that rests on differing degrees of wage and price adjustment speeds. A more elaborate version of this growth cycle model, including a money market, a more general investment function and inflationary expectations, will be discussed in chapter 10.[25] General Keynes-Wicksell goods and money-market equilibrium variants, so-called AD-AS growth models, will be considered in chapters 8 and 9. A Cagan type instability mechanism is present in all these extensions, based on a theory of inflation pertaining to the product market now.

We posit a neoclassical production function $Y = F(K, L)$ with the usual properties, $w/p = F_L(K, L)$ for real wage, $S = sY$ in the Harrod model, and $I/K = h(r), h' > 0$ as investment function, with the rate of profit $r = (Y - (w/p)L)/K$ as its sole argument. Price inflation is given by $\hat{p} = \beta_p(I/K - S/K)$ that is, as a linear Wicksell price dynamic, and wage inflation by $\hat{w} = \beta_w(e), \beta_w' > 0$, a nonlinear Phillips curve. Following Rose,[26] capital stock growth $\hat{K} = S/K$ is determined by planned savings, and $\hat{L}^s = n =$ const. holds for natural population growth. The supply-side character of the model derives from its assumption that firms always operate at full capacity as determined by the marginal productivity theory of employment. Goods market disequilibria show up only by their impact on the rate of inflation and thus have no immediate effect on the volume of sales, aggregate income, and the savings plans based on it.

The version proposed by Rose (1967) employs a Solow-type growth model with a nominal Phillips curve ($\eta = 0$ now) and a Keynesian $C + I$ demand block that drives inflation and not output, as in the Kaldor model. Owing to the marginal productivity theory of employment in this approach a stable wage dynamic interacts with a Wicksellian price dynamic. These are the essentials of Rose's (1967) Keynes-Wicksell approach.[27]

The intensive form reads

$$x = f(l), \;\; x = Y/K, \;\; l = L/K, \;\; w = f'(l)$$

$$r = f(l) - f'(l)l = r(l), \;\; r'(l) = -f''(l)l < 0$$

$$\hat{\omega} = \hat{w} - \hat{p} = \beta_w(l/l^s) - \beta_p(h(r(l)) - sf(l))$$

The function $\omega = f'(l)$ can be inverted to obtain employment as a function of the real wage, ω:

$$l = (f')^{-1}(\omega) = l(\omega), \;\; l'(\omega) < 0$$

Labor supply, as a ratio to capital stock, is

$$l^s = L^s/K\colon \;\; \hat{l}^s = n - sf(l(\omega))$$

Note that $l = l(\omega), l'(\omega) < 0$ holds because of to the marginal productivity theory of employment. Rose chooses l^s, l as dynamic variables and obtains for the variable l

$$\hat{l} = l'(\omega)\dot{\omega}/l(\omega) = \epsilon(\omega)\hat{\omega}, \qquad \epsilon(\omega) = l'(\omega)\omega/l(\omega) < 0$$

The full dynamical system can be represented by two differential equations

$$\hat{l} \;= \epsilon(\omega(l))[\beta_w(l/l^s) - \beta_p(h(r(l)) - sf(l))] \tag{4.29}$$

$$\hat{l}^s = n - sf(l) \tag{4.30}$$

with $h(r(l)) - sf(l))$ abbreviated by $H(l)$ in the following.

The steady state $\dot{l}^s = \dot{l} = 0$ is given by

$$l^\star \; = f^{-1}(n/s), \;\; \omega^\star = f'(l^\star)$$

$$l^{s\star} = \frac{l^\star}{\beta_w^{-1}(\beta_p H(l^\star))}$$

Note that $H(l^\star) \neq 0$ holds true in general, that is, we have goods market disequilibrium and thus inflation also in the steady-state. This also

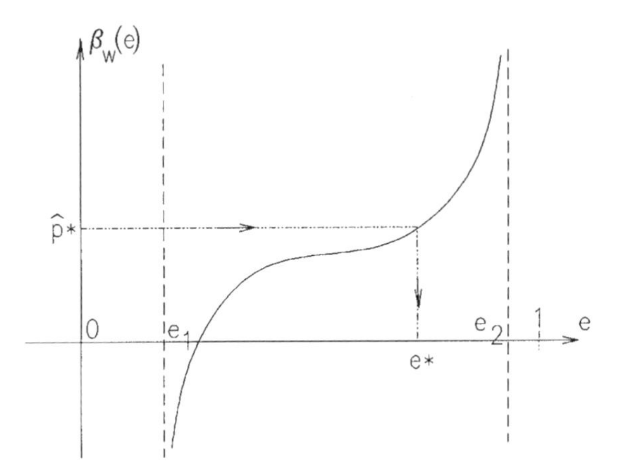

Figure 4.13
Increasing wage flexibility with increasing labor market disequilibrium

determines the steady-state wage inflation and thus the rate of employment by means of an appropriate choice of l^s. Increases in price adjustment speeds, β_p, thus increase steady state wage inflation and thus also the steady rate of employment (see figure 4.13).

As in Rose (1967) we assume for the Phillips curve $\beta_w(l/l^s)$ the shape $(e = l/l^s)$ (see figure 4.13). The denominator for the steady-state value of $l^{s\star}$ is thus well defined. The isoclines of the dynamics are

$$\dot{l}^s = 0: \quad l = l^\star$$

$$\dot{l} \ = 0: \quad l^s = \frac{l}{\beta_w^{-1}(\beta_p H(l))}$$

We have a denominator in this last expression that is always larger than $> e_1$.

Assume $h'(r^\star)r'(l^\star) > sf'(l^\star)(> 0)$, that is, investment is more responsive than saving to employment and thus to real wage changes near the steady state. Thus, $H'(l^\star) > 0$. The $\dot{l} = 0$ isocline is consequently negatively sloped near the steady state if the parameter β_p, that is, price flexibility, is sufficiently large.[28] Furthermore, the slope of this isocline approaches $1/e_i$ as the rate of employment approaches its lower or upper limit $e_i, i = 1, 2$. On the basis of these observations the following phase diagram can be established. We have the following Jacobian of the dynamics

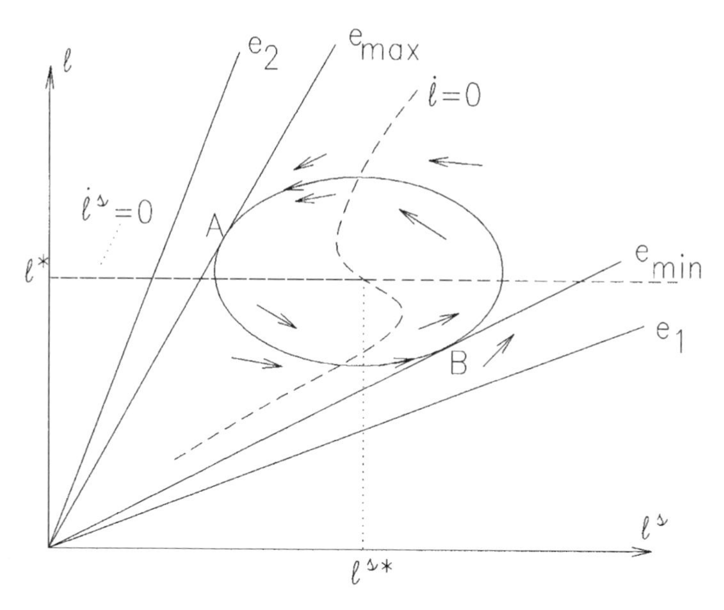

Figure 4.14
The Rose employment cycle in (l^s, l) space

$$J = \begin{bmatrix} 0 & -sf'(l^\star)l^{s\star} \\ -\epsilon^\star\beta'_w & \epsilon^\star[\beta'_w/l^{s\star} - \beta_p H'(l^\star)]l^\star \end{bmatrix}$$

where $J_{12} < 0$ and $J_{21} > 0$.

Assume $\beta'^\star_w$ small, that is, β_w is flat near the steady state and assume that

$$\beta_p > (\beta'^\star_w/l^{s\star})/H'(l^\star) > 0$$

A sufficiently large value for price flexibility relative to wage flexibility is chosen to ensure local instability. Because $\epsilon^\star < 0$ we then get trace $J > 0$. Moreover, we always have det $J > 0$, that is, the equilibrium is an unstable node or focus under these assumptions. On the basis of this local result, Rose (1967) then shows that the assumptions of the Poincaré-Bendixson theorem are all fulfilled, so that a stable limit cycle exists in the cone (see figure 4.14). This viability or boundedness result basically derives from the assumption that wages must become more flexible than prices far off the steady state owing to the assumed shape of the Phillips curve. This Keynes-Wicksell model strongly illustrates the role nominal rigidities play in a supply-driven Keynesian framework where capital is always fully employed.

To show this interaction in more detail, assume that the system is initially at its steady state $l^\star, l^{s\star}$ and is shocked by a real wage increase $\omega > \omega^\star$ implying $l < l^\star$. In place of $\hat{w}^\star = \hat{p}^\star$ we thereby get $\hat{w}^\star > \hat{w} > \hat{p}$, since price inflation reacts more strongly to the decrease in employment than wage inflation near the steady state. We thus get $(H'(l) > 0$, $l'(\omega) < 0)$:

$$\hat{\omega} = \beta_w(l(\omega)/l^s) - \beta_p(H(l(\omega))) > 0$$

near the steady state and a further increase in the real wage ω accompanied by a further decline in employment and output. This amplifying mechanism continues to work until stabilizing wage flexibility, $\beta_w(\cdot)$, has risen to such an extent that the monotonically destabilizing influence of price flexibility, β_p, is overcome. Persistent fluctuations in employment and the real wage are established as the result of these counteracting forces. The original Goodwin (1967) growth cycle model center-type dynamics are thus here made locally unstable via a Keynes-Wicksell demand pull inflation mechanism, but made globally stable via smooth factor substitution combined with ever increasing wage flexibility far off the steady state.

The Rose (1967) growth cycle version is quite different from the classical limit cycle model sketched at the end of the preceding section. Here we have $\eta = 0$ with respect to inflationary expectations and the inflation rate, $\hat{p}$, is driven by quantity imbalances on the product market, representing a cross-dual adjustment process as discussed in chapter 3. In the earlier classical growth cycle model, however, the inflation rate, $\hat{p}$, was driven by a markup price equation, following a dual-adjustment rule, and there was no substitution between capital and labor interacting with the above nonlinearity in the Phillips curve. Note here that the real part of the Rose model collapses into a Solow-Goodwin type model (see chap. 5) when perfect foresight $\eta = 1$ is assumed. Chapter 10 will consider a more refined and complete version of this Keynes-Wicksell type of dynamics under myopic perfect foresight and will stress the similarity of this generalized model type with conventional AD-AS growth models.

For an intuitively easier proof by the Poincaré-Bendixson theorem, an alternative formulation can be undertaken in terms of ω, l^s as dynamic variables.

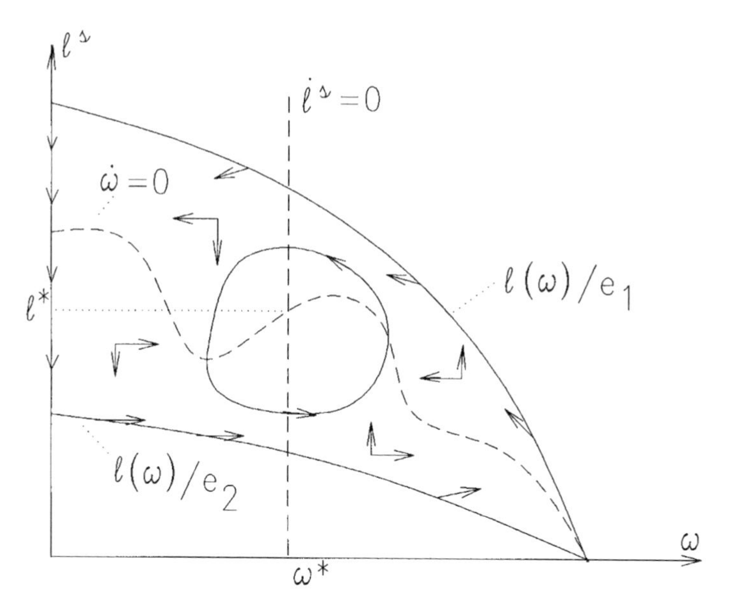

Figure 4.15
An alternative presentation of the Rose employment cycle

$$\hat{\omega} = \beta_w(l(\omega)/l^s) - \beta_p H(l(\omega))$$

$$\hat{l}^s = n - sf(l(\omega))$$

We obtain the steady state as before. The isoclines of this dynamics are

$$\dot{l} = 0: \quad \omega = \omega^*$$

$$\dot{\omega} = 0: \quad l^s = \frac{l(\omega)}{\beta_w^{-1}(\beta_p H(l(\omega)))}$$

and they imply the phase portrait of figure 4.15.

The application of the Poincaré-Bendixson theorem is fairly obvious, though a full mathematical proof involves some technical details.[29] An advantage of the presentation originally chosen by Rose is also that this phase plot allows for a visual representation of the rate of employment (as shown in figure 4.14) so that the turning points of economic activity (points A,B), as measured by the rate of employment, can be shown. The above figure, however, is closer in form to the generalization of this model-type in chapter 10.

4.6 Effective Demand in Classical Growth Dynamics

In the final section of this chapter, we introduce demand forces into the classical growth cycle model of section 4.4 that—in contrast to the employment cycle model just considered—now give rise to underutilization of capital as well as labor. This describes a situation that might be considered more Keynesian than the supply-driven wage-price dynamics previously shown. The following growth model builds on work of Wolfstetter (1982) and Flaschel (1993). It interrelates labor- and goods-market phenomena via classical cross-dual and Keynesian dual adjustment rules built around the multiplier process of income determination and the conflict over income distribution. More elaborate models of this type are considered in chapters 11 and 12. Related approaches have been introduced into the literature by Lance Taylor and others (see in particular L. Taylor 1991, and Dutt 1990).

We posit the following systems of classical and Keynesian building blocks.

1. Fixed proportions: $x^p = Y^p/K, y = Y/L =$ const., that is, $Y^p = x^p K$ and $L = Y/y$ as expressions for full capacity output Y^p and actual employment, on the basis of actual output Y;
2. Wage share dynamic: $\hat{v} = \beta_w(e - \bar{e}) - (1 - \eta)\beta_p[Av - 1]$ as in section 4.4 derived from a money wage Phillips curve and a delayed markup pricing mechanism;
3. Extreme classical savings habits ($0 = s_w, s_c = 1$): $S/K = x(1 - v), x = Y/K$ as in section 4.4;
4. Capacity-oriented investment behavior: $I/K = \beta_k(x/x^p - \bar{x}^c) + n$, $\bar{x}^c \in (0, 1)$ the given desired rate of capacity utilization and n the trend growth rate;
5. Goods-market equilibrium: $I = S$, which now determines actual output, x, and thereby employment, l, per unit of capital.

The differences to the Rose model should be obvious and are quite significant. Short-run output and employment equilibrium are no longer determined by the marginal productivity principle, but by Keynesian effective demand, which in per unit of capital terms is calculated as follows:

$$x = \frac{(\beta_k \bar{x}^c - n)x^p}{\beta_k - (1 - v)x^p} = x(v)$$

Keynesian effective demand Y and the actual rate of capacity utilization thus depends in the present context solely on the state of income distribution, measured by the wage share that is now a state variable of the model. We assume in the following, $\beta_k > (1 - v_{min})x^p =$ maximum profit rate at full utilization of capacity, and thus get a positive denominator in $x(v)$. This should imply for reasonable values of $\bar{x}^c, n$ that the numerator in the above fraction is positive as well, so that $x(v) > 0$ holds unambiguously.[30]

Besides the above law of motion for the wage share v we have a second differential equation, for the rate of employment e, as in the Goodwin model, which is now derived as follows:

$$\hat{e} = \hat{L} - n = \hat{Y} - n = \widehat{Y/Y^p} + \hat{Y}^p - n$$

$$= \widehat{(Y/K)/(Y^p/K)} + \hat{K} - n = \hat{K} + \hat{x} - n$$

$$= x(v)(1-v) - \{\frac{(\beta_k \bar{x}^c - n)(x^p)^2}{(\beta_k - (1-v)x^p)^2}/x(v)\}\dot{v} - n$$

$$= x(v)(1-v) - \frac{vx^p}{\beta_k - (1-v)x^p}\hat{v} - n, \quad \text{that is,}$$

$$\hat{e} = x(v)(1-v) - \frac{vx^p}{\beta_k - (1-v)x^p}[\beta_w(e - \bar{e}) - (1-\eta)\beta_p(Av - 1)] - n \tag{4.31}$$

where $\frac{vx^p}{\beta_k - (1-v)x^p} = \frac{vx^p}{(\beta_k \bar{x}^c - n)x^p}x(v)$ holds. Moreover, from the above we have

$$\hat{v} = \beta_w(e - \bar{e}) - (1-\eta)\beta_p[Av - 1] \tag{4.32}$$

where, as in section 4.4, $Av^\star = 1$ is assumed. Here now there are no nonlinear reaction functions postulated. The nonlinearities that are present naturally derive from the definition of savings per unit of capital and the product market equilibrium condition, including its implications for $\hat{x}$.

The steady state, $e^\star = \bar{e}, x^\star = \bar{x}^c, v^\star = 1 - n/y^p$ is uniquely determined in $\mathbb{R}^2_+$. The isoclines of the dynamics are

$$\hat{v} = 0: \quad e = \bar{e}(1-\eta)(\beta_p/\beta_w)[Av - 1]$$

$$\hat{e} = 0: \quad e = \bar{e}\frac{1}{\beta_w}[(1-\eta)\beta_p[Av - 1] + \frac{\beta_k(x(v)/x^p - \bar{x}^c)[\beta_k - (1-v)x^p]]}{vx^p}$$

We get the Jacobian

$$J = \begin{bmatrix} -(1-\eta)\beta_p A v^\star & \beta_w v^\star \\ (\beta_k x'(v^\star)/x^p - (1-\eta)\beta_p A \frac{v^\star x^p}{\beta_k - (1-v^\star)x^p})e^\star & -\frac{\beta_w v^\star x^p e^\star}{\beta_k - (1-v^\star)x^p} \end{bmatrix}$$

and therefrom

$$\det J = -\beta_w v^\star \beta_k x'(v^\star)/x^p > 0, \qquad x' < 0$$

$$\text{trace } J = -[(1-\eta)\beta_p A v^\star + \frac{\beta_w x^p v^\star e^\star}{\beta_k - (1-v^\star)x^p}]$$

In the Jacobian J, $\eta \leq 1$ acts as an additional stabilizer, although now, however, through demand effects. In the Goodwin model, $\eta^H = 1$ is the bifurcation value. In the present case there is a bifurcation value:

$$\eta^H = \frac{\beta_w x^p v^\star e^\star}{\beta_p A v^\star(\beta_k - (1-v^\star)x^p)} + 1 > 1,$$

where stability gets lost in a cyclical fashion owing to det > 0 and trace $J = 0$.

Here η^H increases as β_w increases, or β_p, β_k or the markup factor A decrease. Hopf bifurcation can again be demonstrated, but it suffices here to note that it is again not possible to determine analytically whether the Hopf bifurcation is of a supercritical or a subcritical nature.[31] Both cases are possible: a shrinking corridor or the generation of a stable limit cycle that bounds the instability. Simulations indicate a subcritical bifurcation, however, that is, a shrinking stability corridor as the bifurcation point is approached from below. The $\eta > 1$ instability thus is, within a certain corridor around the steady state, not effective until η becomes larger than η^H. Figure 4.16 provides a numerical example for such a subcritical bifurcation.[32]

If this growth cycle model is made viable along the lines suggested in section 4.4, the numerical example in figure 4.16 will imply that there exists a second stable limit cycle surrounding the unstable one that arises farther out due to arguments of Poincaré-Bendixson type. The behavior of the economy is thus shock-dependent for appropriate parameter values of η either convergent to the steady state in a cyclical manner or exhibiting persistent fluctuations around it.

Before we had $g_k = I/K = \beta_k(x/x^p - \bar{x}^c) + n$. In that case no accelerating investment appeared, but rather stabilizing effects arose. This investment function is a special case of an investment function employed by Wolfstetter (1982, 387) in the same context. He proposed the form:

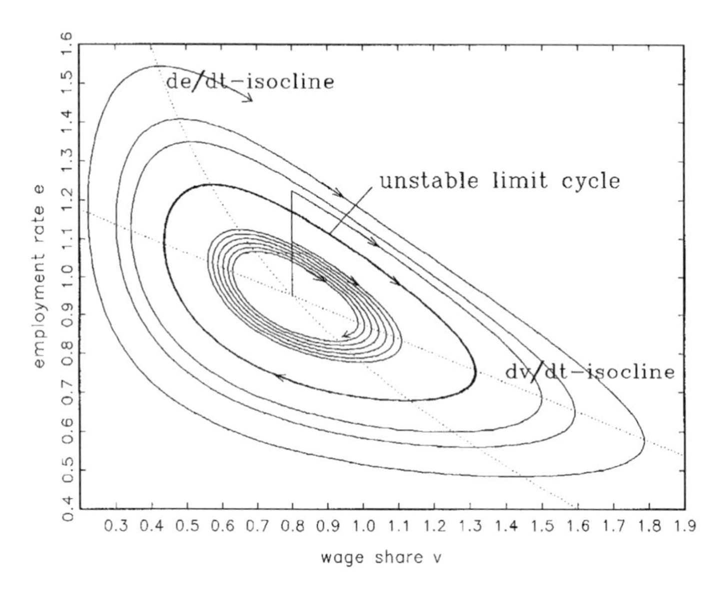

Figure 4.16
An unstable limit cycle in a demand determined growth cycle model

$$\hat{K} = I/K = \frac{\beta}{D+\beta}[\beta_k(x/x^p - \bar{x}^c) + n], \quad \text{that is,}$$

$$\widehat{I/K} = \beta[\beta_k(x/x^p - \bar{x}^c) + n - I/K]$$

In the above case we had $\beta \to \infty$, representing instantaneous adjustment, which was stabilizing. Now, the first term inside the brackets represents the desired and the second term the actual growth rate of capital stock. We thus now have a lagged adjustment of capital stock growth to its desired value. Therefore, three dynamical equations now appear with the first two the same as before:

$$\hat{v} = \beta_w(e - \bar{e}) - (1 - \eta)\beta_p[Av - 1] \tag{4.33}$$

$$\hat{e} = x(1 - v) - n + \hat{x} \tag{4.34}$$

Via product market equilibrium $I = S$ we now get in addition

$$x(1 - v) = \frac{\beta}{D+\beta}[\beta_k(x/x^p - \bar{x}^c) + n] \quad \text{or}$$

$$\dot{x}(1 - v) = x\dot{v} - \beta x(1 - v) + \beta[\beta_k(x/x^p - \bar{x}_c) + n] \tag{4.35}$$

A dynamic relation between x, v, instead of $x(v)$, as before, arises. Complicated feedbacks will now change the dynamics considerably. This new formulation of classical growth dynamics represents an extreme type of instability, which has been analyzed in detail in Flaschel 1993, chapter 4. This is one example of how a delayed adjustment may lead us back to the Harrodian instability of warranted growth.

A simpler example of Harrodian accelerator instability in the framework of classical growth cycles can be given by employing still another variant of the above investment functions. As always we have goods-market equilibrium in the form $g_k = I/K = S/K = x(1-v)$. For investment per unit of capital we now assume, in correspondence to section 4.2 on Harrodian growth dynamics

$$\hat{g}_k = \beta_k(x/x^p - \bar{x}^c)$$

Together with

$$\hat{v} = \beta_w(e - \bar{e}) - (1-\eta)\beta_p[Av - 1]$$

$$\hat{e} = \hat{x} + \hat{K} - n = g_k - n + \hat{g}_k + \hat{v}\frac{v}{1-v}$$

we then have

$$\hat{g}_k = \beta_k(\frac{g_k}{1-v}/x^p - \bar{x}^c) \tag{4.36}$$

We here have a differential equation system in the state variables v, e, g_k. The steady state of those dynamics are the same as before. We now obtain the following Jacobian as far as its diagonal elements are concerned

$$J = \begin{bmatrix} -(1-\eta)\beta_p A v^\star & *** & *** \\ *** & \frac{v^\star}{1-v^\star}\beta_w e^\star & *** \\ *** & *** & \beta_k/((1-v^\star)x^p) \end{bmatrix}$$

where J_{11} may be negative or positive depending on the parameter η and where $J_{22} > 0$ and $J_{33} > 0$. The case $\eta \geq 1$ is now always unstable. For $\eta < 1$ there are opposing forces at work, since increasing β_p has a stabilizing effect, while increasing β_w, β_k supports instability. The trace of J now shows various sources for instability in a very straightforward way.

Finally, we want to stress that a proper integration of a Goodwin growth cycle with the multiplier-accelerator model and the study of the dynamics arising from it is still an open problem and should be addressed by future research. Our intention here is solely to indicate how Harrodian instability may show up in the context of the conflict over income distribution. Accelerator type investment functions are now rarely considered in the literature in models of real or monetary growth and will not be employed in the remaining chapters of this book. Here, profitability-driven investment behavior—in generalization of the one considered in the preceding section—will generally be assumed. An exception appears in chapter 12, however, where capacity-utilization effects show up in the assumed investment function. Therefore, an important source of instability is generally missing in the investigations of the macrodynamical systems introduced in the sequel.

4.7 Some Conclusions

This chapter has focused on nonoptimizing versions of models of growth and fluctuations that arose in Keynesian or classical traditions. We have studied deviation-amplifying mechanisms as well as forces that may create a boundedness of macro fluctuations. To some extent, this parallels the methodology employed in chapter 3.

In the context of elementary descriptive type macroeconomic models we reviewed and compared in particular the dynamics of real and monetary variants. We demonstrated that deviation-amplifying mechanism operating locally can exhibit boundedness of fluctuations if certain contracting forces or stabilizing factors are introduced far off the steady state. We also showed that such forces may arise from viability constraints, state-dependent reaction functions, thresholds in the dynamics, and derivative controls. Another important conclusion of this chapter is that propagation mechanisms, not impulse dynamics, effectively give rise to sizable fluctuations in output, employment, and nominal variables.

Although the original models and mechanisms studied here are still elementary, none fully integrate labor, product, and money-market dynamics—their analysis will be of use in more complex settings later on when we study models of monetary growth of the conventional Keynesian or newer fully demand-constrained types in chapters 8–10 and 11–12. Table 4.1 provides a brief survey of what has been studied in the various sections of this chapter and how this material relates to

Table 4.1
A survey of models of real and monetary growth

Model Type / Market	Goods	Money	Labor	Reference
Harrod	X			Sec. 2 (Demand-Determined Growth)
Kaldor	X			Sec. 3 (Demand-Determined Cycles)
Cagan		X		Secs. 2, 3 (Inflation-Accelerator)
Goodwin			X	Sec. 4 (Full Capacity Growth)
Rose	X		X	Sec. 5 (Full Capacity Growth)
Harrod/Goodwin	X		X	Sec. 6 (Demand-Determined Growth)
Keynes/Wicksell	X	X	X	Chap. 10 (Full Capacity Growth)
AD-AS Growth	X	X	X	Chaps. 8, 9 (Full Capacity Growth)
IS-LM Growth 1	X	X	X	Chaps. 8, 9 (Demand-Determined Growth)
IS-LM Growth 2	X	X	X	Chaps. 11, 12 (Demand-Determined Growth)

complete models of monetary growth investigated in later parts of this book.

The letter *X* is used in table 4.1 to characterize which markets are present in each case. The table shows in particular an important dividing line between those models that rest on full capacity growth and those that exhibit an under- or overutilized capital stock in the course of the business or growth cycle. The latter models, in fact variants of a multiplier–accelerator type, also show an interesting similarity to the dynamics arising in the monetary part of macromodels, as has been shown from a local as well as a global perspective.

5 Neoclassical Variants of Dynamic Macroeconomics

5.1 Introduction

Different variants of growth theories have been employed as a basis for dynamic macroeconomics. Neoclassical models of real growth of market-clearing type originate in Solow's seminal contribution (Solow 1956), although, as we will show, the Solow model itself does not require market clearing.

Solow's article originally intended to question, on the one hand, the "fundamental opposition of warranted and natural growth rates," g_k^* and n, of the Harrodian goods-market approach, and on the other hand, the knife-edge property of the warranted growth path (see sections 4.2 and 4.4). According to Solow, both results were due to the critical assumption that production takes place under conditions of fixed proportions. It is now known that this claim is not generally true,[1] but that it is rather the assumption of an accelerator type independent investment function that is primarily responsible for Harrod's two problems. Yet, the continuing importance of the Solow model as a basis for a theory of real economic growth does not depend on its failure to provide a critique of Harrod–Domar growth theory. Its significance instead rests on the fact that it represents the simplest approach to supply-driven economic growth that allows for factor substitution. We will show that the Solow model can also be a substantive part of monetary macro models exhibiting labor- or goods-market disequilibrium problems,[2] although more frequently it has been used for market-clearing models of dynamic macroeconomics.

We begin this chapter by briefly describing the real growth Solow model and by discussing descriptive and optimizing versions of neoclassical growth theory. We explore steady-state properties and the out-of-steady-state dynamics for low-dimensional models. We will not touch upon neoclassical growth models with complex dynamics.[3]

The original Solow model is a one-good descriptive model. The transitional path to the steady state is reduced to only one law of motion and is thus monotone. A first extension to be considered pertains to augmenting the Solow model by a real wage dynamic, most conveniently in the form of an ordinary Phillips curve. This procedure incorporates classical features in a neoclassical growth model (see section 4.4). The model behavior is characterized by fluctuations in output and employment where the elasticity of factor substitution is sufficiently low. Nevertheless, these fluctuations are dissipating, giving rise to long–run convergence of the steady state.

In a second type of extension we deal with the intertemporal version of the Solow model, still for a one–good model. However, we will leave aside overlapping generations models that are covered in Azariadis 1993. In the intertemporal market-clearing models there will be growth of per capita income and consumption at the steady state arising from labor augmenting exogenous technical progress. In the original Solow model at the steady state there is no growth of income or consumption per capita.[4]

In stochastic growth models the rate of technical change is made stochastic given by a sequence of technology shocks. A version of this type is employed in equilibrium business cycle or real business cycle (RBC) theory in macroeconomics, which pursues the Slutsky-Frisch methodology of the impulse-propagation mechanism. Capital is fully utilized, and households face the labor-leisure choice so that there is only voluntary unemployment. The time series properties of such a model will be explored with respect to the question of whether it can explain the variability of actual macroeconomic data.

In the next step we discuss models of endogenous technical change. The Solow model predicts that per capita income will converge for countries with the same savings rate and rate of population growth. Accordingly, cross-country growth rates of countries are predicted to negatively covary with their initial level of income. Differences in the steady state growth rates are due solely to differences in exogenous rates of technical change. By contrast, in recent models with endogenous technical change growth is generated endogenously by either learning by doing, externalities, and increasing returns (Lucas 1988; Romer 1986a), or the accumulation of human and knowledge capital

(Lucas 1988; Romer 1990). Per capita income and consumption grow at the steady state but the income shares are fixed.

Finally, we indicate how money and finance is considered in the context of growth models. Although there are numerous monetary growth models, growth models primarily abstract from the problem of finance. Some kind of irrelevance of the financial side of the accumulation process is usually presumed.[5] One frequently supposes perfect capital markets, as suggested by the Modigliani and Miller theorem (1958), which means that the real decisions are separated from the finance ones. We will show that the second state equation of an endogenous growth model representing human capital (or the stock of knowledge) can, in principle, be replaced by a state equation representing the evolution of finance. When such a modeling procedure is adopted and sufficient cross-effects to the return function are admitted, the evolution of finance will be relevant for the steady-state path and the out-of-steady state dynamics.

The study of the transitional dynamics of intertemporal models is fraught with difficulty. So, if clear-cut analytical results are no longer obtainable, one usually resorts to numerical simulations on the basis of approximation techniques or a dynamic programming algorithm, which we will leave aside here.[6]

5.2 The Solow Version and the Labor Market

We begin with a brief recapitulation of Solow's seminal contribution to real economic growth. The Solow model can be obtained as a limit case of a classical growth cycle model as considered in section 4.4 by positing an infinitely fast adjustment speed for the real wage.

Instead of a given capital-labor ratio, as in the model shown in section 4.4, Solow (1956) employs a neoclassical macroeconomic production function $Y = F(K, L)$ with two factors of production, capital K and labor L. The usual assumptions on this production function $F(K, L)$ are posited to hold. Dividing by employment L it can be transformed into the following intensive form:

$$y = Y/L = F(K/L, 1) = F(k, 1) =: f(k) \tag{5.1}$$

where $f'(\cdot) > 0$, $f''(\cdot) < 0$, $f'(0) = \infty$ and $f'(\infty) = 0$ as well as $f(0) = 0$ and $f(\infty) = \infty$.

The fundamental differential equation of Solow's model can be introduced from a pure supply side perspective and is based on market clearing on the labor and product markets. It remains only to specify how the factors K and $L^s = L$ develop over time,

$$\hat{L}^s = \hat{L} = n > 0 \tag{5.2}$$

$$\dot{K} = I \equiv S = sY \tag{5.3}$$

Labor demand, L, and labor supply, L^s, coincide, and $S = sY$ is the simple savings function of the Harrod model of the previous chapter. The supposition of $I \equiv S$ means that there is no investment function proper.

On the labor market the equilibrium (for any given K) is described at each moment in time by the marginal productivity principle

$$F_L(K, L^s) = \omega = w/p$$

with ω being the real wage rate. Employing the intensive formulation, $k = K/L$, then gives

$$f(k) - f'(k)k = \omega \tag{5.4}$$

where $f'(k)$, the marginal product of capital, equals the rate of return on capital r. The macroeconomic neoclassical theory of income distribution thus holds at each point in time.

Decomposing the ratio $k = K/L$ into growth rates gives

$$\hat{k} = \hat{K} - \hat{L} = sY/K - n$$

$$= s(Y/L)(L/K) - n$$

$$= sf(k)/k - n$$

hence

$$\dot{k} = sf(k) - nk \tag{5.5}$$

Both the capital stock and employment are increasing according to a supply principle (one endogenous and one exogenous) because of their full employment. Equation (5.5) is already Solow's fundamental dynamic equation of neoclassical growth theory. The assumptions on the production function imply a unique steady-state equilibrium,

$$n/s = f(k^\star)/k^\star$$

The stationary point k^* is globally asymptotically stable in the domain of positive real numbers, since $\dot{k} > 0$ holds to the left of $k^\star$ and $\dot{k} < 0$ to its right.

An alternative description of the Solow growth path is obtained by normalizing the real variables by K instead of by L. Defining $l = L/K$, the counterpart of equation (5.5) is

$$\hat{l} = n - s\tilde{f}(l) \tag{5.6}$$

with $\tilde{f}(l) := F(1, l) = F(1, l/K) = Y/K$. It will be convenient to employ this form of the fundamental growth equation later in chapters 8–10.

Returning to (5.5), we point out that the Solow approach may be enriched by permitting disequilibrium on the labor market. A real wage Phillips curve of the form $\hat{\omega} = h(L/L^s)$, with $h' > 0$, can be established by the assumption of an expectations-augmented money wage Phillips curve when coupled with the assumption of myopic perfect foresight (section 4.4). Inserting $k = K/L$ and $k^s = K/L^s$ into this Phillips curve gives rise to the following law of motion of the new state variable ω,

$$\hat{\omega} = h(k^s/k) \tag{5.7}$$

Moreover, similar to what occurs in (5.5) we obtain $\hat{k}^s = sf(k)/k - n$.

Equation (5.4) formulates a firm relationship between the real wage rate, ω, and the actual capital intensity k. Since the left-hand side of (5.4) is strictly increasing in k, the derivative being $-f''(k)$, $k > 0$, k may be expressed as a function of ω. That is, we have $k = k(\omega)$ and capital is substituted for labor as the real wage rises, $k'(\omega) > 0$. The economy can thus be described by two differential equations in the variables ω and k^s,

$$\hat{\omega} = h(k^s/k(\omega)) \tag{5.8}$$

$$\hat{k}^s = sf(k(\omega))/k(\omega) - n \tag{5.9}$$

Denoting the right-hand side by $f^1 = f^1(\omega, k^2)$ and $f^2 = f^2(\omega)$, we know that at the steady state (where $k = k^s$)

$$f^1_{k^s} = h'/k^s > 0, \qquad f^1_\omega = -h'k'/k^s < 0, \qquad f^2_\omega = -sk'\omega/(k^s)^2 < 0$$

holds for the partial derivatives of this system so that the Jacobian reads,

$$J = \begin{pmatrix} f^1_\omega \omega & f^1_{k^s}\omega \\ f^2_\omega k^s & 0 \end{pmatrix} = \begin{pmatrix} - & + \\ - & 0 \end{pmatrix}$$

It follows from the sign pattern that this model, too, is locally asymptotically stable ($\det J > 0$, trace $J < 0$). Cyclical behavior is obtained if $4 \det J > (\text{ trace } J)^2$, that is, if

$$h'k'\omega/k^s = h'\epsilon(\omega) < 4s\omega/k^s$$

This condition holds true if the Phillips curve is sufficiently flat ($h' \approx 0$) or if the elasticity of substitution $\epsilon(\omega)$ is sufficiently small, that is, the technology is close to the case of fixed proportions in production as in the Goodwin growth cycle model. This extended version of the Solow model can, therefore, be viewed as a labor market–oriented neoclassical accumulation theory on the one hand, or as a classical growth model with substitution properties instead of a fixed–coefficient technology on the other hand, where the resulting degree of freedom is closed by the marginal productivity theory of employment.

A global stability analysis can again be carried out by means of a suitably chosen Liapunov function. To this end let e denote the employment rate, $e = L/L^s = k^s/k$. Its rate of change is given by

$$\begin{aligned}\widehat{e} &= \widehat{k^s} - \hat{k} \\ &= sf(k(\omega))/k(\omega) - n - k'(\omega)\dot{\omega}/k(\omega) \\ &= \frac{-k'(\omega)\omega}{k(\omega)}\hat{\omega} + \frac{sf(k(\omega))}{k(\omega)} - n \\ &= -\epsilon(\omega)h(e) + \frac{sf(k(\omega))}{k(\omega)} - n\end{aligned}$$

where $k(\omega), \epsilon(\omega)$ as introduced above. Abbreviate $g(\omega) = sf(k(\omega))/k(\omega) - n$ and with respect to the steady state values e^* and ω^* define:

$$H(\omega, e) = \int_{e^*}^{e} \frac{h(x)}{x} dx - \int_{\omega^*}^{\omega} \frac{g(y)}{y} dy$$

This function H is well defined on the positive orthant of ω and e and strictly positive—except at the steady state, where it is zero. Furthermore,

$$\begin{aligned}\dot{H} &= \frac{h(e)}{e}\dot{e} - \frac{g(\omega)}{\omega}\dot{\omega} \\ &= h(e)\widehat{e} - g(\omega)\hat{\omega} \\ &= h(e)(-\epsilon(\omega)\hat{\omega} + g(\omega)) - g(\omega)h(e) \\ &= -\epsilon(\omega)h(e)^2\end{aligned}$$

Since $\epsilon(\omega) > 0$ the last expression is ≤ 0 and $= 0$ iff $e = e^\star$.

Since the set where this derivative of the Liapunov function vanishes, given by $e = e^\star$, does not contain an entire orbit of the dynamics (up to the point of rest) it follows from Hirsch and Smale 1976 (196) that the basin of attraction of the steady state is equal to the positive orthant. In other words, the steady state is globally asymptotically stable in this domain.

The original Solow model of capital accumulation with its full employment equilibrium can be viewed as a special case of the above augmented-growth model when a vertical Phillips curve is assumed (at the natural rate of employment $e^* = 1$). The Solow model thereby eliminates labor market problems and consequently exhibits only a monotonic convergence of the capital stock-labor ratio toward its steady-state value. This special situation is the point of the departure for the modifications and extensions of neoclassical growth theory considered in the remainder of this chapter. By contrast, the Solow model with unemployment will become an important building block in chapter 8, chapter 9 in AD-AS growth models, and in chapter 10 in Keynes-Wicksell monetary growth models.

5.3 The Intertemporal Version of the Solow Model

In addition to the fact that the Solow model does not exhibit per capita growth of income at the steady state, the savings rate is, as in the Harrod-Domar growth theory, fixed customarily or socially. Optimal-growth models attempt to explain the savings rate and thus the path of capital accumulation endogenously by parameters characterizing the intertemporal choice of agents. Modern optimal-growth models building on representative agents, specifications of preferences of intertemporally optimizing agents, and rational expectations originate in the work of Uzawa (1965, 1969), Shell (1966, 1976), and Cass (1965); see also that of Blanchard and Fischer (1989, chap. 2) and Stokey and Lucas (1989, chap. 4). In the present chapter we first discuss a one-capital-good version with Harrod-neutral technical change that is given exogenously at a constant rate. Product as well as labor markets are continuously clearing, that is, capital is fully utilized and labor fully employed (with labor inelastically supplied).[7]

Employing a Cobb-Douglas production function in intensive form but assuming labor-augmented technical change, we normalize by labor expressed in efficiency units,

$$L(t) = L_o \exp((n + \mu)t)$$

where n is the population growth rate and μ the exogenous growth rate of technical change. We accordingly define $k(t) = K(t)/L(t)$ and, with respect to consumption, $c(t) = C(t)/L(t)$. We omit the time index t. If we take the case of constant returns to scale, with α the labor share and $\beta = 1 - \alpha$, the capital share in income, the Cobb-Douglas production function in intensive form reads $y = k^{\beta}$, with $y = Y/L$. From $\hat{k} = \hat{K} - \hat{L}$ we obtain

$$\hat{k} = (k^{\beta} - c)/k - (n + \mu), \text{ or}$$

$$\dot{k} = k^{\beta} - c - (n + \mu)k \tag{5.10}$$

To ease the calculations, let the consumer's preference be specified as a utility function with constant elasticity preference, $U(c) = (c^{1-\eta} - 1)/(1 - \eta)$, with c the flow of consumption goods, $\eta \in (0, \infty)$ the coefficient of relative risk aversion and ρ characterizing the time preference.[8]

The one-good optimal growth model of Solow type in terms of efficiency labor reads

$$\max_{c} \int_0^{\infty} e^{-\rho t}(c^{1-\eta} - 1)/(1 - \eta)\, dt \tag{5.11}$$

s.t. (5.10).

Employing Pontryagin's maximum principle, the current value Hamiltonian[9] has one control variable c, one state variable k, and one co-state variable θ, with a capital stock, k_0, given at $t = 0$.

$$H = H(c, k, \theta) = U(c) + \theta(k^{\beta} - c - (n + \mu)k) \tag{5.12}$$

The co-state variable, θ, represents the shadow price of capital. Using the current value Hamiltonian, from the necessary conditions for optimality, we obtain

$$c^{-\eta} = \theta \tag{5.13}$$

$$\dot{\theta} = \rho\theta - \partial H/\partial k \tag{5.14}$$

Equation (5.13) is obtained from setting $H_c = 0$.

The two-dimensional differential equation system for the out-of-steady-state dynamics with the associated transversality condition reads,

$$\dot{k} = k^{\beta} - c - (n + \mu)k \tag{5.15}$$

$$\dot{\theta} = (\rho - \beta k^{\beta-1} + n + \mu)\theta \tag{5.16}$$

$$\lim_{t\to\infty} e^{-\rho t}\theta k = 0 \tag{5.17}$$

where the last equation represents the transversality condition. Note that $\theta^{-\frac{1}{\eta}}$, obtainable from (5.13), can be substituted in place of c in (5.15). The steady-state values of the above system can easily be computed by setting the left-hand side of (5.15), (5.16) to zero and solving for $k^{\star}$, $\theta^{\star}$, which are constants at the steady state.

Moreover, since the growth rate of the co-state variable is zero at the steady state the marginal product of capital is

$$\beta k^{\beta-1} = \rho + n + \mu \tag{5.18}$$

The dynamics of such a system are typically characterized by saddle point stability. The optimal solution of system (5.15)–(5.16) is to jump with the optimal control $c(t)$ to the stable branch of the saddle path. This is required by the transversality condition that prevents the trajectories from becoming explosive. The transversality condition, in fact, is a superimposed non-explosiveness condition. Such systems are then always asymptotically stable starting at the stable branch, and the out-of-steady-state dynamics for $k(t)$ follows a monotone path back to the equilibrium.[10]

Before extending the original Solow model further, we want to spell out the determinants of the steady-state growth rate and the savings rate. Given the population growth rate n, the growth rate of per capita consumption and capital stock is simply given by μ. This follows from (5.10).[11] The savings rate is in the Lucas version given by

$$s = \frac{\beta(\mu + n)}{\rho + \eta\mu} \tag{5.19}$$

The latter equation[12] shows the parameters determining the savings rate. The savings rate is not exogenously given by custom or tradition but endogenously determined by the preference and technology parameters entering equation (5.19).

Since the optimal trajectories converge to the steady state, Lucas directly assumes that the economy is already close to the path of balanced growth (Lucas 1988, sect. 2). In this way he is able to give some estimates of the parameters of the intertemporal version of the Solow model. Utilizing the work by Denison (1961) on U.S. growth from 1909 to 1957, he suggests $n = 1.3\%$, $\mu + n = 2.7\%$, $s = 10\%$, and $\beta = 0.25$. By virtue of (5.19) the two parameters characterizing consumers' preferences are found to be related by

$$\rho + 0.014\eta = 0.0675$$

The parameters are obtained only from averaging actual data representing constant ratios of macroeconomic variables.

Although the parameters are not uniquely identified,[13] the Lucas approach to empirical growth, compared to the original Solow model, has the advantage that the above parameters may be helpful in identifying differentials in growth rates and levels of per capita income across countries; for an exercise of this type see Lucas 1988, section 3.

5.4 Stochastic Growth and Equilibrium Business Cycles

The growth model of Solow type has recently been extended to stochastic growth and labor supply as a choice variable in the framework of intertemporal utility maximization. It can here be dealt with as a stochastic version of the model of the previous section. Such a version has become the prototype model in the equilibrium business cycle (RBC) theory, which attempts to encompass both growth and fluctuations. It is now often viewed as a basic model of dynamic macroeconomics.

Although the optimal trajectories exhibit a tendency toward the steady state, in the tradition of the Slutsky-Frisch methodology these paths are, however, stochastically perturbed by a sequence of technology shocks. Frequently, by employing serially correlated shocks, an impulse-propagation mechanism is designed to generate macro fluctuations of business cycle frequency.

RBC models with the above characteristics originate in the work by Kydland and Prescott (1982), Long and Plosser (1983), Prescott (1986), and King, Plosser, and Rebelo (1988a, b). A recent survey on applications to different areas in macroeconomics is given in Cooley 1995. The following elaboration builds on Chow (1993), who stays close to the Solow framework. Since the stochastic growth model is simpler to describe in a setting of discrete market periods we subsequently discuss a discrete-time version of an equilibrium business cycle model.

Let us first employ the intensive form of section 5.2. With Harrod-neutral technical progress the per capita Cobb-Douglas production function is

$$y_t = k_t^{1-\alpha}(A_t h_t)^{\alpha} \tag{5.20}$$

where A_t denotes the efficiency of work effort per capita and h_t the hours worked per capita.[14] The total factor productivity—the Solow residual—can be obtained from (5.20) by taking logs and rearranging the equation,

$$\alpha \ln(A_t) = \ln(y_t) - [(1-\alpha)\ln(k_t) + \alpha \ln(h_t)] \tag{5.21}$$

With regard to households, in the baseline RBC model often a time separable log-linear utility function in consumption c and leisure $1-l$ is employed where l is the fraction devoted to work effort. Thus, l and h are related by $\overline{h}l = h$ where $\overline{h}$ are the total hours available

$$U(c_t, l_t) = \ln(c_t) + \theta \ln(1 - l_t) \tag{5.22}$$

This specification of the utility function is simpler than in the previous section but includes two choice variables. The stochastic optimization problem of the representative consumer reads,

$$\max_{c,1-l} = E \sum_{t=0}^{\infty} \beta^t U(c_t, l_t) \tag{5.23}$$

s.t.

$$x_{t+1} = \gamma + x_t + \epsilon_t \tag{5.24}$$

$$k_{t+1} = (1-\delta)k_t + k_t{}^{1-\alpha}\exp(\alpha x_t)h_t^{\alpha} - c_t \tag{5.25}$$

Hereby we have assumed a depreciation rate of the capital stock of δ and β denotes the discount factor. Equation (5.24) represents a random walk where $x_t = \ln A_t$, possibly with a drift, γ, and ϵ_t, the sequence of technology shocks. Equation (5.25) describes the evolution of the capital stock. Note that $A_t^{\alpha} = \exp(\alpha x_t)$. Moreover, E represents expectations conditioned by the information at time t and $U(c_t, l_t)$ the above utility function. In feedback form, in general, the choice variables, constituting the optimal solution, are nonlinear functions of the state variables.

$$(c_t, l_t) = G(x_t, k_t) \tag{5.26}$$

where (c_t, l_t) are, however, only implicitly determined. Because of these analytical difficulties, linearization techniques are usually employed to study the time-series properties of output, investment, consumption, labor effort, real wage, and employment (for a survey of those techniques see Taylor and Uhlig 1990). Generally, the solution depends on the above five deep parameters, $\varphi = (\alpha, \beta, \theta, \delta, \gamma)$.

An important part of the evaluation of RBC models is to show the extent to which they can match the time series generated from the model with actual macroeconomic time-series data of an economy. Researchers often calibrate their models such that their trajectories exhibit summary statistics similar to data in the real world. Reference is made in particular to serial correlation, volatility (measured as standard deviation), and cross-correlation to output. However, setting the parameters $\varphi = (\alpha, \beta, \theta, \delta, \gamma)$ free hand is usually only partly successful. It typically turns out that some of the model time series do match actual macroeconomic time series, whereas other series, for example, the sequence of real wage and employment, are far from sufficient in replicating actual time-series data (see Prescott 1986; Hansen 1988; King, Plosser, and Rebelo 1988b; Christiano and Eichenbaum 1992).

There are also more sophisticated econometric estimation strategies available that permit one to obtain parameters through statistical estimation techniques.[15]

As aforementioned, the equilibrium view builds on the Slutsky-Frisch tradition of stochastic dynamic macroeconomic models, that is, fluctuations are assumed to be a result of an impulse-propagation mechanism originating in a sequence of randomly occurring shocks—technology shocks. The theory then usually claims it can explain the variability of macroeconomic time-series data. Actually, however, those claims are at best only partially fulfilled for current RBC models. Two shortcomings are particularly disturbing.

First, equilibrium business cycle models have to demonstrate the existence of unemployment as a result of labor-leisure trade-off. Empirically, the real wage fluctuates only mildly in the business cycle however. In order to obtain realistic movements in unemployment, the model has to postulate a rather high elasticity of labor supply to changes in real wages. This postulate is strongly at variance with estimations from actual macroeconomic time series data (see Summers 1986; see also Mankiw 1989). In fact, the "available empirical evidence suggests only a minimal response of labor to transitory wage changes." (Summers 1986, 176); for a further criticism, see Stadler 1994.

Second, the stochastic high-frequency technology shocks do not appear to be a realistic assumption. Technological shocks are usually of low frequency, as Schumpeter pointed out long ago. The high-frequency movements of the Solow-residual appear to be determined by other factors, for example, variations in demand and labor hoarding, locally increasing returns to scale and externalities.[16] The Solow-residual does not appear an adequate measure of technology shocks.

In general, the propagation mechanisms inherent in current equilibrium business cycle models are too weak to explain macro fluctuations. In our view, equilibrium business cycle models in their present form do not fare well when compared to Keynesian disequilibrium models in explaining employment and output fluctuations.

5.5 Endogenous Technical Change and Growth

The task of making technical change endogenous in a Solow-type optimal growth model has been taken up by endogenous growth theory, which has recently been employed as another approach to dynamic macroeconomics. The basic framework for this new development was provided by Uzawa's theory of intertemporal capital accumulation (Uzawa 1965).[17] The standard models are deterministic and exhibit saddle point stability, as does the model in section 5.3. These are market-clearing models too, although labor supply is generally assumed to be inelastic, that is, labor effort is not a choice variable. Several different versions of endogenous growth models have now emerged.

One such version (Romer 1986a; Lucas 1988) relies on learning by doing, externalities, and increasing returns. Along the line of Arrow 1962a, it is posited that industrywide spillover effects of production activities enhance the stock of knowledge. The knowledge, resulting from experience, represents positive externalities of a private firm. The increase of the industrywide stock of knowledge produces increasing returns to scale for all firms and thus for the aggregate production function. The accumulated experience is then represented either by the industrywide stock of physical capital (Romer 1986a) or human capital (Lucas 1988, sect. 4). Learning patterns may also be related to past investment, so that more recent investment may give rise to stronger impact on the stock of experience (see Young 1993 and Greiner and Semmler 1994, 1996).

In contrast to these model types where the accumulation of knowledge is a by-product of production activities, a second major type of model assumes that endogenous growth is brought about by the intentional use of resources for the creation of human capital (Lucas 1988, sect. 4). In Lucas, there is a stock of human capital, in addition to accumulated experience, that is being created through investment in human capital.[18] This stock enters the production of human capital and the aggregate production function. Persistent per capita growth is therefore feasible because of the unlimited growth of human capital. Sufficient support for this fact is that the production function of human capital is nondecreasing.

A slightly different version of the intentional production of knowledge capital is developed in Romer 1990 and also in Grossman and Helpman 1991 that can be called R&D models of endogenous growth. Here, the stock of human capital is fixed but a stock of knowledge, representing designs, is created through R&D effort that exhibits nondecreasing returns. This type of model also relates back to a work by Arrow (1962b) that had already extensively discussed the informational problems involved when resources are intentionally used for inventions. The results of inventive investments, that is, the innovations produced, Arrow argued, exhibit properties of a partially excludable and nonrival (public) good. The innovations are partially excludable since they are created by intentional actions of profit-seeking private agents. At the same time they are nonrival since knowledge can be used over and over again to create new knowledge.

More specifically, what is considered as an engine of economic growth in Romer 1990 and Grossman and Helpman 1991 are inventive investments in new varieties or qualities of capital goods that are partially excludable and nonrival. If the activity generating varieties or qualities of capital goods—stimulated by market incentives—exhibits nondecreasing returns to the number of varieties and qualities, persistent endogenous growth is feasible even when there are diminishing returns to each type of capital. In fact, the spillovers from existing R&D activities generate nondecreasing returns to investment in R&D. This keeps firms investing resources in R&D and thereby increasing the stock of knowledge at a constant rate. What drives growth is the fact that the stock of knowledge is growing without limits as a product of R&D investment.

Formally, in both the Lucas and the Romer versions of endogenous growth there are two state and two control variables involved. In Lucas (1988), the two state variables are the stock of physical capital and human capital, whereas consumption and the time allocated to the development of human capital are the control variables. In Romer 1990 the two state variables are physical capital and a stock of knowledge, whereas the control variables are consumption and the proportion of human capital employed in research.[19]

The above new variants of growth models make it feasible that income and consumption per capita grow at a positive rate that is endogenously generated. At the steady state the growth rate of the capital stock is equal to the growth rate of consumption per capita when a constant population is presumed (Romer 1990), or it exceeds the growth rate of consumption per capita when a growing population is posited (Lucas 1988).

In either case, the marginal product of capital exceeds the interest rate in the Romer and Lucas models, and at the steady state the important macroeconomic ratios, for example, capital-output ratio, savings rate, and so on, are constant. In this respect the theory of endogenous growth mirrors the stylized facts that the non-neoclassical tradition has pointed out in numerous contributions to growth (see for example, Kaldor 1961 and Kaldor and Mirrlees 1962).[20]

Since both the Lucas and the Romer models exhibit growth at the steady state the problem arises of whether the integral in the consumer's preferences is finite—a requirement for a solution to exist.[21] For endogenous growth models the existence of solutions is secured if one puts a restriction on the discount rate. The restriction, in general, is that

$$\rho > n + g(1 - \eta) \tag{5.27}$$

where ρ is the discount rate, g the growth rate, and η the coefficient of relative risk aversion appearing in the utility function; for details of a proof, see Romer 1986b.

Since the Lucas and the Romer models are very similar they exhibit the same difficulty in studying the out-of-steady-state dynamics of the variables. Both authors concede that owing to the dimension of their systems, the dynamics are not easily studied (see Lucas 1988, 25 and Romer 1990, 97).

To study the steady-state and the out-of-steady-state dynamics of the endogenous growth models, Pontryagin's maximum principle and the associated Hamiltonian function again provide an important tool. Yet, stability properties of systems with a state space dimension higher than two are difficult to analyze, since, with the Hamiltonian approach, the dimension of the system increases beyond the number of variables that can conveniently be studied analytically. Often Hopf bifurcation theory is invoked that at least allows one to locally study the dynamics of the system (see Dockner and Feichtinger 1991).

The continuous-time version of a typical endogenous growth model with two state variables and two control variables,[22] for example, the model by Romer (1990), reads as follows

$$\max_{C,H_A} \int_0^\infty e^{-\rho t}(C^{1-\eta} - 1)/(1-\eta)\, dt \tag{5.28}$$

s.t.

$$\dot{K} = \bar{\eta}^{(\alpha+\beta-1)} A^{\alpha+\beta} H_Y^\alpha L^\beta K^{1-\alpha-\beta} - C \tag{5.29}$$

$$\dot{A} = \delta H_A A \tag{5.30}$$

The consumer exhibits a utility function with constant elasticity preference $U(C) = (C^{1-\eta} - 1)/(1-\eta)$ with C, the flow of consumption goods, $\eta \in (0, \infty)$, the coefficient of relative risk aversion, ρ the time preference, and δ and $\bar{\eta}$ are constants.

Technical change is endogenized through the increase of the variety of capital goods. Innovations are created through intentional private investment in R&D, resulting, for example, in the Romer model, in the production of a stock of knowledge (designs).

The resource that has to be committed to innovations is a portion of human capital H_A with the constraint $\bar{H} = H_A + H_Y$ where $\bar{H}$ is fixed. Thus, besides C the second control variable in the above system is H_A. In the research sector competitive firms create designs A at a rate as formulated in (5.30). The accumulated stock of knowledge, A, serves as (partially excludable) nonrival input in the creation of new knowledge. The producers of the varieties of capital goods have to pay an R&D fee for designs when supplying the varieties of producer durables[23] that are employed jointly with labor input L and human capital H_Y into the production of final goods. Total labor L is also taken to be fixed.

The capital stock K is related to the varieties of durable goods used in the production of final output by $K = \bar{\eta} \sum_{i=1}^{\infty} x_i$ where x_i now denotes the input used by a firm. The production function for the final goods exhibits constant returns to varieties. If we treat the index i as continuous variable, the sum can be replaced by an integral so that the final output as the first expression in the equation for the evolution of the physical capital stock is

$$\begin{aligned} Y(A, H_y, L, x) &= H_y^\alpha L^\beta \int_0^\infty x(i)^{1-\alpha-\beta} di \\ &= \bar{\eta}^{\alpha+\beta-1} A^{\alpha+\beta} H_Y^\alpha L^\beta K^{1-\alpha-\beta} \end{aligned}$$

Since in the Romer version population growth is zero it requires for the integral of the consumer's utility function to be finite. This is true if the following relation holds

$$\rho > (1 - \eta)g$$

The current value Hamiltonian of the above problem reads as follows

$$H = (C^{1-\eta})/(1-\eta) + \lambda[\bar{\eta}^{\alpha+\beta-1}A^{\alpha+\beta}(\bar{H} - H_A)^{\alpha}L^{\beta}K^{1-\alpha-\beta} - C] + \mu\delta H_A A \tag{5.31}$$

Employing the Hamiltonian the necessary conditions for optimality provide the following system

$$\max_{C,H_A} H \tag{5.32}$$

$$\dot{\lambda} = \rho\lambda - \frac{\partial H}{\partial K} \tag{5.33}$$

$$\dot{\mu} = \rho\mu - \frac{\partial H}{\partial A} \tag{5.34}$$

$$\lim_{t\to\infty} \lambda e^{-\rho t} K = 0 \tag{5.35}$$

$$\lim_{t\to\infty} \mu e^{-\rho t} A = 0 \tag{5.36}$$

The latter two conditions represent the transversality conditions. Note that here λ and μ are the co-state variables.

The first order conditions for (5.32) ($\frac{\partial H}{\partial C} = 0$, $\frac{\partial H}{\partial H_A} = 0$) give the following results

$$C^{-\eta} = \lambda \tag{5.37}$$

$$\bar{\eta}^{\alpha+\beta-1}A^{\alpha+\beta}(\bar{H} - H_A)^{\alpha}L^{\beta}K^{1-\alpha-\beta} = (\bar{H} - H_A)\frac{\delta\mu}{\alpha\lambda}A \tag{5.38}$$

Equations (5.29)–(5.30) and (5.32)–(5.34) together with the transversality conditions (5.35)–(5.36) determine the optimal path of the variables K, A, C, H_A, λ, and μ. One can define the balanced growth equilibrium as the solution of the set of equations derived from the above Hamiltonian that satisfy the conditions[24]

$$\dot{\mu}/\mu = \dot{\lambda}/\lambda \quad \text{and} \quad \dot{C}/C = \dot{A}/A$$

Furthermore, we have,

$$C/Y = 1 - \dot{K}/Y = 1 - (\dot{K}/K)(K/Y)$$

$$g = \dot{C}/C = \dot{Y}/Y = \dot{K}/K = \dot{A}/A = \delta H_A$$

In the Romer model the growth rate of consumption is equal to the growth rate of the capital stock. The growth rate of population is taken as zero. Also, at the steady state the shadow price of the capital stock K, $\dot{\lambda}/\lambda$, declines at a constant rate. So we have $\dot{\lambda}/\lambda = -\eta g$.

From the above equations it can be derived that the steady state growth rate is given by

$$g = \frac{\delta \bar{H} - \phi\rho}{\phi\eta + (1 - \phi)} \tag{5.39}$$

where $\phi = \alpha/(\alpha + \beta)$.[25]

The steady-state properties are defined by the parameters entering eq. (5.39). As one can observe from (5.39) the stock of human capital $\bar{H}$, the fraction δ (impacting the growth of the stock of designs $\dot{A}/A$), the increase in patience (a lower discount rate) and an increase in the rate of intertemporal substitution (captured by a decrease in η) will positively affect the growth rate g.

With regard to taxes or subsidies from the above model it follows that—since the decision to invest in physical capital is decoupled from the decision to invest in research—a policy that encourages the accumulation of physical capital K is not necessarily accompanied by an investment in research and thus by a speeding up of growth. In contrast, a subsidy of human capital, $\bar{H}$, and of the research sector has the effect of increasing the growth rate. Romer then suggests that gains from trade arise when there is an integration, not into an economy "with a large number of people but rather into one with a large amount of human capital" (Romer 1990, 98). The features of the new growth theory are quite appealing since the welfare properties of the steady-state solution of the model appear to give quite transparent rules for welfare-enhancing policies.

An analytical treatment of the out-of-steady-state dynamics is given in Asada, Semmler and Novak 1994, where it is shown that, as in the one-capital-good intertemporal model, the steady state is also a saddle point.[26] The trajectories of K and A are asymptotically stable and monotonically approaching the balanced growth path if the control variables, C, H_A, are properly chosen at $t = 0$. This at least holds if the production function in the human capital good sector is of the form in (5.30). If physical capital is also employed in the production of knowledge capital the properties of the model are not well known. As shown by Caballe and Santos (1993) the similar dynamic properties hold for the basic Lucas (1988) model. The result there holds, at least if no physical capital is used in the production of human capital.[27]

The Lucas (1988) as well as the Romer (1990) models have initiated a number of empirical studies that employ proxies for human or knowledge capital to explain differences in growth rates.[28] For regions within a country where the same preference and technology parameters are assumed to prevail, conditional convergence is predicted. The growth rate of real per capita GDP should tend to be inversely related to the initial real per capita GDP (see Barro and Sala-i-Martin 1992, 1995). Since growth rates across countries are predicted to be higher with greater investment in human or knowledge capital, convergence should be feasible—a negative relation between the growth rate and the starting position of the country—after holding constant the proxies for the variables distinguishing the countries.[29] These tests are, however, based on the hypothesis that real economies are close to the steady state "most of the time" and if not, the economies are assumed to monotonically converge toward its steady state growth path.[30]

In general, however, a note of caution might be added pertaining to empirical convergence studies and the economic policy conclusions. If the model is more complex, for example, if physical capital is also employed in the production of human capital and knowledge capital, or if increasing returns, learning-by-doing effects, or complementarities between inputs exist, the dynamic properties are not well known. Moreover, if there are multiple steady states or indeterminacy of equilibria, empirical studies may not be well grounded.[31]

5.6 Growth, Money, and Finance

The final class of dynamic macromodels we will discuss here originates in the studies of growth and money, and growth and finance.

We will not address the variants on growth and money introduced by Tobin (1965) that were based on a Harrod-Domar model and then turned into an intertemporal model with infinite horizon by Sidrauski (1967) or into overlapping generations models (see, for example, Azariadis 1993). An extensive survey on nonoptimizing and optimizing variants of growth and money is given in Orphanides and Solow 1990. The nonoptimizing models of monetary growth will also extensively be discussed later in chapters 8–10. Here, we will focus briefly on intertemporal model variants with credit market borrowing and external finance of economic agents.[32]

For standard optimal growth models it can be shown that finance is irrelevant for the decisions of the economic agents. Thus, the separation theorem holds, according to which optimal decisions can be separated from finance decisions, and consequently, the solution properties of the intertemporal growth model do not change. In general, this appears as a common feature in prototype infinite horizon optimal growth models where either the firms' optimal investment or households consumption flows are the control variable and the capital stock is the state variable. Since finance—finance of firms' investment or households' finance of expenditure—can, because of the separation theorem, be regarded as nonessential, the standard models permit one to disregard an explicit specification of the evolution of the external finance-capital structure in the case of firms and debt in the case of households.

To exemplify those results let us focus on a prototype model of the firm. A standard model—allowing, however, for convex adjustment cost—may be employed. An adequate formulation of this standard model is given in Uzawa 1969. It reads as follows. Let the firm maximize its present value

$$\max_{g} \int_0^{\infty} e^{-\rho t}(r - \phi(g))K dt \tag{5.40}$$

s.t.

$$\dot{K}/K = g \tag{5.41}$$

$$0 = \phi(g)K - S_f - \dot{E}p^e \tag{5.42}$$

where r is the rate of return on capital, $\phi(g)$ the resources that have to be committed for the growth rate of capital stock, g, S_f denotes retained earnings of firms, and $\dot{E}$ and p^e the change of equity and the price of equity respectively. Whereas equation (5.41) denotes the growth of (infinitely lasting) capital stock, equation (5.42) represents the budget constraint of the firm.[33]

Along the line of Modigliani and Miller 1958 it then can be demonstrated that neither the type of equity finance (finance through retained earnings or the issue of new equity) nor the capital structure, measured for example by the debt-asset ratio, if debt finance is allowed for, matter for the value of the firm and its optimal investment program (see also Blanchard and Fischer 1989, section 6.3).

Formally, it is not too difficult to allow debt finance in the above model, in addition to equity finance. Investment is then financed by internal funds (retained earnings), and external finance (equity and debt finance). In this case the equation (5.42) has to be altered to

$$\dot{D} = \phi(g)K + iD - S_f - \dot{E}p^e; \tag{5.43}$$

where D is the current debt of the firms and i the interest rate.[34] Here, then, with no cross-effects between the stock of debt and the present value of the firm, the Modigliani-Miller theorem holds true, and a second dynamic equation depicting the evolution of finance is irrelevant for the accumulation path.[35]

Equivalent results hold in models where the household's utility is maximized over time. Then the expression under the integral (5.40) would be replaced by a utility function. Formally (see for example, Blanchard and Fischer 1989, section 2.4), a system with two state variables representing the evolution of capital stock and a debt equation—similar to the one shown in (5.43)—can be introduced, now, however, depicting the household's evolution of debt (see Blanchard and Fischer 1989, 58). Here too, then, if debt has no impact on consumption or investment behaviors, finance is irrelevant for optimal consumption, investment, and output paths, and for the system dynamics one can disregard the evolution of debt as long as the transversality or nonexplosiveness condition is not violated. The solution is then the same as for the one-capital-good model (see Blanchard and Fischer 1989, 63).[36]

In contrast, however, to such models, recent theories on capital markets and growth have initiated a change of perspective and overturned the above stated position of the irrelevance of finance for growth.[37] It was in particular the theory of incomplete capital markets that explored the relevance of asymmetric information and (costly) state verification for finance and investment behavior of firms. Those theories have the implication that the separation theorem does not hold. More specifically, three major results can be demonstrated to hold:

- Asymmetric information between borrowers and lenders and costly state verification lead to a cost premium that firms must pay for external finance;

- The wedge between the cost of internal and external finance (resulting from risk cost) is an increasing function of firms' leverage;[38]
- The firms' optimal investment negatively covaries with the risk cost arising from the leverage of firms.

Those results imply that there are cross-effects between the financial structure of the firms and their market evaluation. Those results, however, are presented mostly in the context of one-period models.[39] In an intertemporal model a reasonable way to introduce a cross-effect between the stock of debt and valuation of the firm is to admit a risk cost—reflecting the marginal risk of bankruptcy[40]—entering the integral (5.40) and possibly the finance equation (5.43).[41]

In order to apply such considerations from one-period models with incomplete capital markets to an intertemporal growth model the following specification has been suggested by Asada and Semmler (1995) where, however, equity finance is disregarded.[42]

The model, including a debt equation, reads,

$$\max_{u,g,s_f} \int_0^\infty e^{-\rho t}[(p(u)-c)u-\phi_1(g)-\phi_2(d)]K\,dt \tag{5.44}$$

s.t.

$$\dot{K} = gK \tag{5.45}$$

$$\dot{d} = \phi(g) - [\{p(u)-c\}u - id]s_f - gd,\ d_0 > 0 \tag{5.46}$$

where

$$\phi_1(0)=0,\ \phi_1'(g)>0,\ \phi_1'(0)=1,\ \phi_1''(g)>0,\ \phi_1'''(g)=0$$

$$\phi_2(0)=0,\ \phi_2'(d)>0,\ \phi_2''(d)>0,\ \phi_2'''(d)=0$$

Hereby, given the price for capital goods, set equal to 1, p stands for the product price with the price determined by an inverse demand function, u the utilization of capacity x/K, c the constant unit cost, s_f the retention ratio, and d the debt-asset ratio (D/K). The equation (5.46) is then obtained from the identity $\dot{d} = \dot{D}/K - gd$. Moreover, $\phi_1(\cdot)$ denotes the investment cost (including adjustment costs) and $\phi_2(\cdot)$ a convex risk cost for the borrower arising from firm's leverage. The interest payment in the debt equation (5.46) can also be made a convex function of the debt-asset ratio.

The function $\phi_2(\cdot)$ is supposed to capture the impact of high leverage and risk cost on the firm's value, where bankruptcy cost is a sign-preserving function of the debt-asset ratio. In the context of an intertemporal growth model this is equivalent to stating that capital markets are imperfect.

In Asada and Semmler 1995 the analysis of a model such as (5.44)-(5.46) with appropriate transversality conditions is given in three steps: First, the steady state is computed through the use of the Hamiltonian function associated with the above intertemporal optimization problem. Second, a study of local dynamics and the possibility of periodic solutions is pursued through the use of the Hopf bifurcation theorem. Third, the global dynamics are studied through the use of the dynamic programming algorithm as presented in Semmler 1995. The results can be briefly summarized as follows:

- For the intertemporal growth model where the evolution of finance appears in a second-state equation, the growth rate of the capital stock and the steady-state debt-asset ratio are not easily derived in an analytical form since they are implicitly given by a higher-order nonlinear system of equations. A computer study, however, has shown that, similar to the endogenous growth models, a positive growth rate can arise; here, however, it is due to the inverse demand function, that is, the demand being sufficiently inelastic and thereby producing a sufficiently large derived optimal markup. A sufficiently large markup also allows the rate of return on capital to exceed the discount rate.
- Although there are multiple steady states, the computer results show that at relevant economic equilibria the optimal growth rate of the capital stock is negatively related to the discount rate, the interest rate, the unit cost, and the impact of financial risk on the value of the firm captured in $\phi_2(\cdot)$. A change of any of those parameters alters the steady-state growth rate and the debt-asset ratio. These steady-state properties are interesting insofar as they imply empirical predictions for the optimal investment and leverage policies of firms.[43]
- The cross-effects between the leverage and the present value of the firm also admit periodic solutions for the growth rate of capital stock, the debt-asset ratio, and the utilization of capacity. The latter feature is proved by employing the Hopf bifurcation analysis for the Hamiltonian associated with the above system (5.44)–(5.46). Here, too, a dynamic programming algorithm again proves to be a useful tool for the demonstration of the global features of the optimal paths—its amplitude and frequency.

5.7 Concluding Remarks

Recent standard models of neoclassical dynamic macroeconomics originate in Solow's contribution to economic growth. Those are commonly represented by elegant and analytically tractable models exhibiting simple dynamic properties. The Solow model predicts monotone convergence to the steady state whenever the capital stock is displaced from its steady-state value. This appears to also hold for the one- and two- capital-goods intertemporal variants originating in the work of Cass (1965), Uzawa (1965, 1969), Lucas (1988), and Romer (1990). These variants are saddle path stable where the transversality condition, superimposed nonexplosiveness, forces the trajectories always to jump to the stable branch of the saddle path. The latter variant, the two-capital-goods version may, however, change its dynamic properties if one admits more general production functions, in particular for the production of human capital or knowledge capital, learning-by-doing effects, and complementaries between inputs.

In all of those variants of equilibrium macro models, capital is fully utilized and labor markets are always cleared. In variants where labor is elastically supplied and employment is a choice variable, for example, in equilibrium business cycle models, implausible time series properties arise with respect to labor market time series. This assertion holds at least for the standard version employed as dynamic macromodel.[44]

We want to note, however, that there are optimizing versions for which periodic or more complex solution paths are admissible. Such paths are likely to arise in intertemporal models as soon as the state space becomes two-dimensional and there are sufficient cross-effects[45] between the state space variables, or between state space variables and return function. These models, however, have not been successfully confronted with actual time series data and thus must still demonstrate their usefulness in explaining the variability of actual macroeconomic time series.[46]

Next, we turn to nonoptimizing monetary models originating in the Keynesian nonmarket-clearing tradition where no jumps to stable paths occur, but instead gradual disequilibrium adjustments take place.

II

Price Flexibility, Nominal Rigidity, and Macrodynamics

We start our study on monetary macromodels and the nominal-real interaction by focusing on the short and medium run. Although the models will thus still be partial in nature, they permit us to study the role of price flexibility or nominal rigidity. In fact, traditionally the Walrasian versus Keynesian perspectives were associated with the position they take on the question of whether flexibility of nominal wages and prices ensure macroeconomic stability and lead to full employment. Macroeconomists in the Walrasian tradition view price flexibility as stabilizing, whereas new Keynesians work with models of nominal rigidity. Yet, as Tobin has pointed out on several occasions, neither Keynes or Keynesian theory rely on nominal rigidity, nor is there any a priori reason to expect that the equilibria necessarily be stabilized by (nearly) perfect flexibility of nominal wages and prices.

The Tobin position is explored in chapters 6 and 7 by means of models where labor, product, and money markets respond with either price or quantity adjustments to disequilibrium. To begin with, chapter 6 is a rather short-run model, that is, all expectations are fixed. In this context, stability prospects are not universal but quite favorable. Chapter 7 covers the medium run and introduces endogenous inflationary expectations, of the adaptive expectations as well as the myopic perfect foresight type (the use of the often despised adaptive expectations is defended in sections 7.2 and 7.3). Our most important point is that these economies give rise to results that may jeopardize the common stability optimism.[1]

At the risk of some oversimplification, the stability conditions may be characterized by saying that fast reactions in expectations to changes in inflation, and fast adjustments of nominal prices and wages, tend to be destabilizing. Conversely, price inflexibilities turn out to act as a stabilizer. This position is in stark contrast to the assumptions and results of the new Keynesian theory, which holds the view that aggregate fluctuations are generated by nominal rigidities (though as yet no truly dynamic macromodels have been formulated from which this kind of instability endogenously emerges).

To keep the dynamics as transparent as possible, the model variants of chapters 6 and 7 are stationary, and other complicating factors such as capital accumulation, more ambitious expectations formation mechanisms, or the dynamics of income distribution are as well neglected. These topics will be taken up subsequently in parts III and IV of the book.

6 Wage Flexibility and Stability in the Short Run

6.1 Introduction

In the neoclassical synthesis, Keynesian economics is characterized by the absence of the labor market equilibrium condition. Correspondingly, the money wage rate is regarded as being exogenously given and contemporaneously unaffected by changes in the other variables in the model. Full employment of labor is consequently not automatic, and over the period considered, the volume of output can be influenced by monetary and fiscal policies. The only role of the labor supply schedule is to help determine the unemployment rate. By contrast, in the classical model nominal wages are also fully flexible and the labor supply curve is combined with a market-clearing condition. In this way full employment is guaranteed, and fiscal and monetary variables have no impact on output and employment within the given period, though they may influence their growth rates (cf. Sargent 1987, 50ff).

The present chapter[1] reconsiders the discussion of disequilibrium processes in the neoclassical synthesis and fills a lacuna regarding the role of the money wage rate. On the one hand, there are many Keynesian theorists who contend that the assumption of rigid money wages is not as central in Keynes's work as one is made to believe in the textbook literature. The assumption is only a polar case of what was really essential to Keynes, namely, that wages do not completely and instantaneously clear the labor market. In fact, chapter 19 of the *General Theory* is devoted to a study of various effects from "Changes in Money Wages." This analysis is important since it directs attention to possibly destabilizing mechanisms that are connected with highly flexible nominal wages.

The arguments made in this section of the *General Theory* bring us to a second point: The discussion makes allusion to dynamic feedback effects. A dynamic analysis is also required for a closer study of the classical equilibrium positions. As Sargent (1987, 29) writes, "It is important to verify . . . that there is a tendency to return to them if the system is displaced from them. Otherwise the comparative static exercises we have performed are of little practical interest." However, if for an investigation of the system's stability properties, one refers to Patinkin 1965, a most influential book at the time of its publication, one will be disappointed. The stability issue is dealt with in chapter 11, but under the assumption of an always-equilibrated labor market (258, 261).[2] The same conceptual limitation is even found in a more recent common textbook, such as the one by Sargent (1987, section 1.7), though it is not stated explicitly. At least at the textbook level, therefore, wage dynamics is neglected not only in Keynesian but also in classical economics.

We seek to contrast classical and Keynesian economics under a dynamic perspective by means of the adjustment processes that we consider typical for them. Along with output, prices, and the rate of interest, money wages are also flexible in both types of economies. The general framework is that of a short period within an IS-LM system, which means that all real and financial assets remain fixed and expectations do not change. The behavioral functions involved are taken from Sargent 1987, chapters 1 and 2. Money demand derives from the notion of liquidity preference. With regard to the short-term profit maximization of firms, the first fundamental postulate of the classical theory is supposed to apply in which the real wage is always equal to the marginal product of labor. It is well known that Keynes also accepted this supposition.

In this context, we see the essential distinction between a classical and a Keynesian economy in the role of the goods market. In the classical economy, excess demand for goods governs the adjustments of price levels, which may be called a Walrasian type of adjustment, whereas in the Keynesian economy the direct impact of goods market disequilibrium is on output. This specification has an important consequence for the interpretation of the marginal productivity principle. In the first case, the money wage rate and the price level are predetermined variables, and the real wage determines the volume of output. In the Keynesian case causality is reversed: it is the money wage rate and output that are predetermined, and the marginal productivity principle serves to determine price levels. Both dynamic systems have the same equilibrium position, and the problem we investigate is that of local asymptotic stability with respect to either of the two processes.

We know from Sargent 1987, section 1.7 that the Walrasian adjustments are stable if nominal wages were to adjust instantaneously, such that the full-employment real wage prevails in every instant of time. Hence, we ask whether the stability result carries over if money wages are driven directly by excess demand on the labor market, where in general, the real wage will deviate from its full employment level. To anticipate our findings, we will answer in the affirmative. In chapter 2 of his book Sargent puts forward a "Keynesian" adjustment process. The Walrasian adjustment rule on the goods market is maintained, however, and the only "Keynesian" feature is the fixed money wage. In contrast, we hold the view that the hypothesis of quantity adjustments is more appropriate to capture the basic Keynesian ideas. In the corresponding model it turns out that the question of whether quantity adjustments, too, entail stability can be answered with a qualified "yes"—provided that wages are not too flexible. If they are, the system may exhibit a tendency toward explosive cyclical behavior, the possibility of which was not even noticed by Keynes himself. One must nevertheless bear in mind that these results pertain to the short period.

The organization of the chapter is simple: section 6.2 presents the Walrasian adjustment process; section 6.3 deals with the Keynesian case; and section 6.4 contains some concluding remarks. The mathematical proofs of the two stability theorems provided in section 6.2 and 6.3 are given in the appendix.

6.2 The Walrasian Adjustment Process

The following magnitudes are held constant within the time horizon considered: the real capital stock $\bar{K}$ with its rate of depreciation δ, money supply $\bar{M}$, real tax collections $\bar{T}$, and the expected rate of inflation π^e. Endogenous variables are real output Y, the nominal interest rate i, the price level p, and the money wage rate w. $F = F(L, K)$ is a neoclassical production function exhibiting the standard properties of its partial derivatives, $F_L > 0$, $F_{LL} < 0$, $F_K > 0$, $F_{KL} > 0$. Four behavioral functions are common to both the Walrasian and the Keynesian adjustment process. These are: (1) The labor supply function,

$$L^s = L^s(w/p), \qquad dL^s/d(w/p) > 0$$

(2) The consumption function with a simplified notion of real disposable income, the real interest rate, and the price level as arguments,

$$C = C(Y - \bar{T} - \delta\bar{K}, i - \pi^e, p), \qquad 0 < C_Y < 1, \; C_i \leq 0, \; C_p \leq 0$$

Financial assets being fixed, C_p represents the Pigou effect. C may include real government demand as well as the (constant) replacement investment. (3) The (net) investment function, which is essentially based on Tobin's q (see Sargent 1987, chap. 1),

$$I = I(F_K - \delta - (i - \pi^e)), \qquad I' > 0$$

(4) The demand function for real balances,

$$M^d/p = f_m(Y, i), \qquad f_{mY} > 0, \quad f_{mi} < 0$$

In the Walrasian system, firms are price takers, and the role of the marginal productivity principle $w/p = F_L(L, \bar{K})$ is to determine the demand for labor $L = L_c$. That is,

$$L_c = L_c(w/p)$$

(the index c, for *classical*, is introduced to distinguish this labor demand function from the Keynesian one in the next section). Of course, L_c is downward sloping. The corresponding supply of goods is

$$Y^s = Y^s(w/p) = F(L_c(w/p), \bar{K})$$

As for consumption and money demand, we have to decide on the entering income variable. Real gross profits (before tax) from optimal production are $Y^s - (w/p)L_c$, while wages desired by workers amount to $(w/p)L^s$. Together this implies that total gross income relevant for "notional" demands deviates from goods supply by $(w/p)(L_c - L^s)$. It could be assumed, however, that actual employment, even if it exceeds supply, is always determined by the present flow of production $Y = Y^s$.[3] Consequently, workers make their plans on the basis of the wage bill $(w/p)L_c$, and aggregate income of households is just equal to Y^s. Not the least because notional excess demand requires intermediation of an artifact such as the auctioneer, or otherwise rationing schemes would have to be introduced, it is the latter hypothesis that will be adopted in the following. For the stability result itself, this specification is inessential.

On this background, the components of gross demand on the goods market sum up to

$$\begin{aligned} Y^d &= Y^d(p, i, w) \\ &= C[Y^s(w/p) - \bar{T} - \delta\bar{K}, i - \pi^e, p] + I[F_K(L_c(w/p), \bar{K}) - \delta - (i - \pi^e)] \end{aligned}$$

so that the excess demand function reads

$$E_1 = E_1(p, i, w) := Y^d(p, i, w) - Y^s(w/p)$$

Subscript 1 may stand for the goods market, subscript 2 for financial markets, and subscript 3 for the labor market. Excess demand for real balances is given by

$$E_2 = E_2(p, i, w) := f_m[Y^s(w/p), i] - \bar{M}/p$$

and the excess demand for labor by

$$E_3 = E_3(p, w) := L_c(w/p) - L^s(w/p)$$

From the Walrasian point of view, equilibrium on the goods market is brought about by price variations. With regard to the money and the labor market, the rate of interest and the money wage rate, respectively, are supposed to take care of market clearing. Adjustments of p, i, and w will certainly be in the direction of the corresponding excess demands. To be precise, all this has to be interpreted as taking place in the so-called ultra short-run. In continuous time, we have the following system of differential equations,

$$\dot{p} = \alpha_p E_1(p, i, w) \tag{6.1}$$

$$di/dt = \alpha_i E_2(p, i, w) \tag{6.2}$$

$$\dot{w} = \alpha_w E_3(p, w) \tag{6.3}$$

where the αs are positive parameters indicating the speed of adjustment. Like Sargent (1987, 21), we do not bother about existence problems and simply assume that a unique and economically meaningful triple $(p^\star, i^\star, w^\star)$ exists at which the RHS of system (6.1)–(6.3) vanishes. Obviously, such a point represents a full employment equilibrium position.

To present a handy stability proposition it is convenient to introduce the following assumption (CI) on a limited responsiveness of consumption and investment expenditures. It is a slight extension of the usual supposition that the marginal propensity to consume out of income fall short of unity. In fact, it is tantamount to assuming a negative slope of the IS-curve in the next section when investment is also (indirectly) dependent on the present level of production, *via* the marginal product of capital. As is stated in the ensuing theorem, this concept is sufficient to guarantee stability—irrespective of the relative speeds of adjustments on the three markets. The proof of the theorem reveals that assumption (CI) is not a necessary condition, but since a downward-sloping IS-curve is a common device a formulation of further refinements does not seem worthwhile.

Assumption 6.1 (CI) With respect to evaluations at the equilibrium $(p^\star, i^\star, w^\star)$, reactions C_Y and I' are so moderate that $C_Y + I'F_{KL}/F_L < 1$.

Theorem 6.1 Let assumption (CI) apply. Then the equilibrium point $(p^\star, i^\star, w^\star)$ of the Walrasian adjustment process (6.1)–(6.3) is locally asymptotically stable.

The two adjustment processes that are put forward by Sargent (1987) can be viewed as special cases of system (6.1)–(6.3). That is, they represent two polar cases of the speed of adjustment, α_w, of the money wage rate. It has already been mentioned in the introduction that in chap. 1 Sargent follows Patinkin's suggestion to assume that equilibrium has already been reached on the labor market and is not disturbed by what is happening on the other markets. Hence, output and employment do not need to change anymore (this assumption is not explicitly stated by Sargent but can be inferred from his evaluation of the Jacobian matrix). Nominal prices and wages are still allowed to vary. Writing $\omega^\star = w^\star/p^\star$ for the equilibrium real wage, we note they are strictly linked by the relationship $w = \omega^\star p$. Denoting equilibrium output by $Y^\star = Y^s(\omega^\star)$, we describe the adjustments on the remaining two markets by[4]

$$\dot{p} = \alpha_p[Y^d(p, i, \omega^\star p) - Y^\star] \tag{6.4}$$

$$di/dt = \alpha_i[f_m(Y^\star, i) - \bar{M}/p] \tag{6.5}$$

From the proof of theorem 6.1 it is easily seen that this process satisfies the stability conditions of the Jacobian to have a positive determinant and a negative trace (cf. also Sargent 1987, 30). In shorthand notation, the characteristic point distinguishing (6.4), (6.5) from process (6.1)–(6.3) may be designated $\alpha_w = \infty$.

Another extreme assumption is to put $\alpha_w = 0$. It means that the money wage is frozen at some value $w = \bar{w}$, while the rest of the modeling is preserved. Employment in the stationary point of the thus defined differential equations will, of course, deviate from the natural level if $\bar{w} \neq w^\star$. However, this is of no importance for the stability issue. Process (6.1)–(6.3) under the assumption $\alpha_w = 0$ is presented in Sargent 1987, chap. 2) as a "Keynesian" adjustment process. Yet, we have already expressed our view that it is the principle of quantity adjustments on the goods market that is the most distinctive Keynesian feature.

Assumptions like $\alpha_w = 0$ or $\alpha_w = \infty$ reflect a concept of a hierarchy of markets. In particular, $\alpha_w = \infty$ is a convenient device to represent the idea that adjustments on the labor market occur significantly faster than those on the other markets. But can this be considered a reasonable approximation of what is observed in the real world? If in reality there are markets that are (almost) instantaneously clearing, then this is true for financial markets. It follows that if, for reasons of simplification, attention is restricted to two-dimensional dynamic processes, it would be much more meaningful to postulate fast adjustments of the interest rate so as to maintain continuous equilibrium on the money market, while the groping of prices as well as wages for their equilibrium values is much slower. Denoting by $\rho = \rho(p, w)$ the function of the interest rate that causes E_2 to vanish for all (p, w), we would thus obtain

$$\dot{p} = \alpha_p E_1(p, \rho(p, w), w) \tag{6.6}$$

$$\dot{w} = \alpha_w E_3(p, w) \tag{6.7}$$

as an alternative to the adjustments considered by the textbooks. It is a routine mathematical exercise to verify that under assumption (CI) this process, too, is locally asymptotically stable.[5]

Turning back to process (6.1)–(6.3), we know of one other example in the literature which in a comparable context includes adjustments of money wages at a positive but finite speed. This is done by Smithin and Tu (1987), and they get a similar stability result. The main conceptual difference is that they dispense with liquidity preference. Instead, interest rates adjust to clear the market for loanable funds. Apart from that, the behavioral functions are much simpler. Specifically gross demand for goods is (negatively) dependent on the price level alone. This feature implies that the disequilibrium dynamics in p and w are decoupled from the interest rate, that is, financial markets are a mere appendix to the real economy.

6.3 The Keynesian Adjustment Process

The main difference to the Walrasian adjustment process (6.1)–(6.3) is to reverse causality in the marginal productivity equation and to postulate quantity adjustments on the goods market. To begin with the latter, we note present production is predetermined in any "ultra short-run" period and, in the next period seeks to adjust to the observed level of demand. Labor demand $L = L_k$ is thus given by inverting the mapping $L \mapsto Y = F(L, \bar{K})$ (the index k stands for "Keynesian"),

$$L_k = L_k(Y) = F^{-1}(Y; \bar{K})$$

As in the preceding section it is assumed that L_k is always realized so that it coincides with actual employment, and that demand originating with workers' households is based on actual wages rather than on their desired income. So it is current real output that is to enter as the income variable into the functions of consumption and money demand.

In the present framework the marginal productivity principle constitutes a price-setting rule for firms, with respect to given wages and output,

$$p = w/F_L(L_k(Y), \bar{K})$$

p is the aggregate supply price and clearly increases both with output and with money wages.[6] Since the functional relationships have changed, another letter, X, may be used to distinguish this section's functions of excess demand. They are determined as follows,

$$X_1 = X_1(Y, i, w) := C[Y - \bar{T} - \delta\bar{K}, i - \pi^e, w/F_L(L_k(Y), \bar{K})] + I[F_K(L_k(Y), \bar{K}) - \delta - (i - \pi^e)] - Y$$

$$X_2 = X_2(Y, i, w) := f_m(Y, i) - \bar{M}/p = f_m(Y, i) - F_L(L_k(Y), \bar{K})\bar{M}/w$$

$$X_3 = X_3(Y) := L_k(Y) - L^s(w/p) = L_k(Y) - L^s[F_L(L_k(Y), \bar{K})]$$

Correspondingly, the dynamical adjustments in output, the rate of interest, and money wages are represented by

$$\dot{Y} = \beta_Y X_1(Y, i, w) \tag{6.8}$$

$$di/dt = \beta_i X_2(Y, i, w) \tag{6.9}$$

$$\dot{w} = \beta_w X_3(Y) \tag{6.10}$$

where the speeds of adjustment are here denoted by the β-coefficients. This process is an obvious generalization of the occasional discussions of the IS-LM apparatus in macroeconomic textbooks that consider the special case $p =$ constant and $\beta_w = 0$. The economy of process (6.8)–(6.10) has the same full employment equilibrium position as process

(6.1)–(6.3). That is, if we take the stationary point $(p^\star, i^\star, w^\star)$ of (6.1)–(6.3) and put $Y^\star = Y^s(w^\star/p^\star)$, then $(Y^\star, i^\star, w^\star)$ establishes an equilibrium of system (6.8)–(6.10). Assumption (CI) is again helpful to obtain a definite result concerning its stability properties. However, in this economy it is no longer sufficient to ensure that the equilibrium is attracting. This rather hinges on the relative speeds of adjustments.

Theorem 6.2 Let Assumption (CI) apply. Then, dependent on the various reaction intensities in the behavioral functions, there exist three positive numbers H_1, H_2, H_3 such that the equilibrium point $(Y^\star, i^\star, w^\star)$ of system (6.8)–(6.10) is locally asymptotically stable if

$$\beta_w[1 - (1 + (\beta_Y/\beta_i)H_2)H_3|C_p|] \;<\; (\beta_i + \beta_Y H_2)H_1$$

The equilibrium is unstable if the inequality sign is reversed.

The Pigou effect $C_p \leq 0$ is stabilizing, insofar as an increase in the modulus of C_p reduces the left-hand side of the stability condition. Apart from that, there is no other reaction parameter of the behavioral functions (labor supply and consumption, investment, money demand) that can unambiguously be identified as fostering instability tendencies. The main argument can already be verified without going into the computational details of the mathematical proof. In fact, we have the following sign pattern of the Jacobian matrix J (evaluated at the equilibrium),[7]

$$J = \begin{bmatrix} - & - & - \\ + & - & + \\ + & 0 & 0 \end{bmatrix}$$

Clearly, the autofeedbacks in the main diagonal are nonpositive. It is also immediately seen that the 2×2 submatrix in the upper-left corner has a negative trace and a positive determinant. This means that the partial IS-LM dynamics with a frozen wage rate (but instantaneously adjusting price level) is stable. By the same token, the partial process with the rate of interest held fixed likewise proves to be stable. In addition, the determinant of J itself is negative, as it must be for the stability of the full system. The complete analysis makes use of the Routh-Hurwitz conditions. The necessary and sufficient conditions for all eigenvalues of J to have negative real parts are

$$A_1 = -\text{trace } J > 0 \qquad A_2 = J_1 + J_2 + J_3 > 0$$

$$A_3 = -\det J > 0 \qquad B = A_1 A_2 - A_3 > 0$$

(J_i denotes the i-th principal minor, i.e., the determinant of the 2×2 submatrix that is obtained after deleting the i-th row and i-th column.) It is easily checked that the first three inequalities are always fulfilled. That is, so far all feedback effects have the "correct" sign (for stability). The existence and position of the two zero entries, however, cause $J_1 = 0$. Owing to this phenomenon, B can turn negative, which happens if the condition on the adjustment speeds given in the theorem is violated. We have elaborated on this line of reasoning in order to show that if instability arises, all feedback mechanisms are involved and interact with each other.[8]

The basic result of theorem 6.2 states that overly flexible money wages are devastating for the stability of the economy (presupposing that the Pigou effect is not so strong as to let the coefficient of β_w fall below zero). This seems to square with the negative evaluation of this issue that Keynes arrived at in chapter 19 of the *General Theory* (see 270ff). However, a caveat is in order here. For the problem as such, Keynes argues that "the reduction in money-wages will have no lasting tendency to increase employment except by virtue of its repercussion either on the propensity to consume for the community as a whole, or on the schedule of the marginal efficiencies of capital, or on the rate of interest" (262). When we recall that changes in the marginal efficiency of capital are tantamount to changes in the state of long-term expectations (which has been supposed to be given in the present framework), then we realize that only the third factor is captured by process (6.8)–(6.10). But in Keynes's analysis this one is recognized as a stabilizing mechanism:

> The reduction in the wages-bill, accompanied by some reduction in prices and in money-incomes generally, will diminish the need for cash for income and business purposes; and it will therefore reduce *pro tanto* the schedule of liquidity-preference for the community as a whole. *Cet. par.* this will reduce the rate of interest and thus prove favorable to investment (263).

In the present setup this is reflected by $\partial X_2/\partial w > 0$ and $\partial X_1/\partial i < 0$ (see the matrix J). Hence, a decreasing money wage puts a downward pressure on the interest rate, which in its turn increases excess demand on the goods market and, thus, output and employment. Keynes indeed views this mechanism as the only relevant argument in favor of a (high) flexibility of money wages. Provided that the quantity of money is virtually fixed, he summarizes, "[i]t is, therefore, on the effect of a falling wage- and price-level on the demand for money that those who believe in the self-adjusting quality of the economic system must rest the weight of their argument" (266. As is well known, this mechanism is now called the Keynes effect).

It follows that the potential instability result put forward in theorem 6.2 is even in a certain contradiction to the conclusions reached by Keynes himself. The reason is that he considered the first-round effects, so to speak. To see what can happen in the subsequent rounds, let us study the dynamic evolution of the economy by means of an IS-LM diagram. Figure 6.1 shows the (Y, i)-plane with an IS- and LM-curve.[9] The former is downward sloping by virtue of assumption (CI), the latter clearly has a positive slope. Underlying is the nominal wage rate $w = w^\star$, so that the point of intersection represents the full employment equilibrium. If w remained fixed, the movements of output and the rate of interest would be in the direction as indicated by the arrows in the four regions I, II, III, IV (and the equilibrium would be stable as observed above). In region I the economy moves south-west, since $di/dt < 0$ above the LM-curve and $\dot{Y} < 0$ above the IS-curve (which is readily inferred from the sign pattern of the matrix J), and so forth. Generally, there seems to be a tendency toward counterclockwise spirals, although the equilibrium might also be approached directly from within one region.

To ease the exposition of the dynamics with flexible wages, let us neglect the Pigou effect in the consumption function and suppose $C_p = 0$. This implies that the IS-curve is not affected by changes in the money wage rate. As concerns the LM-curve, application of the Implicit Function Theorem to the equation $X_2 = 0$ gives a positive partial derivative of the LM-interest rate with respect to changes in w,

$$\partial i_{LM}/\partial w = -[\partial X_2/\partial w]/[\partial X_2/\partial i] > 0$$

Hence, the LM-curve moves upwards (downwards) as the money wage increases (decreases), and the regions I–IV shift correspondingly. The locus of LM-equilibria is therefore drawn as a dashed line in figure 6.1.

Consider a state with unemployment and also a high rate of interest, that is, $Y < Y^\star$ and $i > i^\star$. The money wage may be at $w = w^\star$, though this is not essential to the argument. Specifically, let (Y, i) be contained in region I, at point A, for example. Accordingly, output, employment, and the rate of interest are falling, as is the money wage rate ($X_3 = X_3(Y) < 0$ since $dX_3/dY > 0$). The latter means that the LM-curve gradually shifts downward. If w declines sufficiently fast, the distance

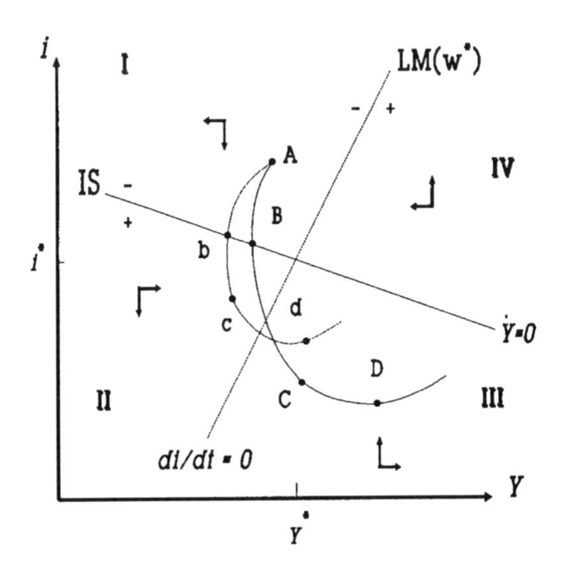

Figure 6.1
Phase diagram of process (6.8)–(6.10) in IS-LM space

to (Y, i) increases, which speeds up the fall in i. At point B or b, respectively, the economy crosses the IS-curve (an explanation of the difference between the solid and dotted trajectory in figure 6.1 follows). The movement into region II signifies the beginning of the recovery. The rise in output then setting in diminishes the excess supply of labor. The fall in money wages decelerates until the wages finally reach a lower turning point when $X_3 = 0$. This may occur at point C or c. Subsequently $X_3 > 0$ and the wage rate rises. This ends the downward movement of the LM-curve and causes it to shift backward in north-east direction. Now LM and (Y, i) move toward each other, and they must meet at some point, D or d. The LM-curve continues its upward movement and (Y, i) comes to lie below it, in region III. The rate of interest has passed a trough value, and both it and output are rising. The ensuing dynamics are (qualitatively) symmetrical to the chain of events after point A.

As depicted in figure 6.1, the solid trajectory may spiral outward while the oscillations of the dotted trajectory may be damped. This is due to the assumption in the first case of a much faster speed of adjustment β_w. The effect of the faster fall of money wages from point A on, and consequently of the faster fall of the price level, is a much stronger rise in the real value of the money supply. This is tantamount to a faster decrease in the excess demand for real balances and, thus, to a stronger fall in the rate of interest. The evolution from point A to D or d, respectively, could be described as a phase of stabilization. The main mechanism at work is the same as the one recognized by Keynes as the only stabilizing force that could be of any significance to the classical stance on flexible wages.

Comparing the two trajectories and stopping at points D and d, one might have the impression that the higher flexibility in money wages has been more efficient in stabilizing the economy and bringing output back to its natural level $Y^\star$. However, if we keep track of the future course of events after these first three rounds, it could turn out that the more flexible wages have done their job too well: not only might they have caused an overshooting phenomenon, but the overshooting might also be so strong that the resulting fluctuations around the equilibrium become larger and larger. Thus, our dynamic analysis has revealed that even within the case that Keynes thought to be most favorable to the postulated "self-adjusting quality of the economic system" based on flexible money wages, destabilizing and oscillation-amplifying tendencies can be detected.

The possibly destabilizing tendency should nevertheless not be overinterpreted. The main reason for instability, still within the model's narrow framework, is a notion of a hierarchy of markets. If it is accepted that adjustments on financial markets take place much faster and more efficiently than on the other markets—especially the labor market—then we are entitled to view the equilibrium position of process (6.8)–(6.10) as being asymptotically stable (at least locally so). It suffices to observe that the stability condition of Theorem 6.2 is satisfied as β_i tends to infinity. Incidentally, the same holds true for a high responsiveness to goods market disequilibrium (β_Y large).

6.4 Conclusion

The purpose of the present chapter has been to point out the incompleteness of the dynamic adjustment processes that are typically considered within the neoclassical synthesis and to close this gap by adding the appropriate adjustment equation for money wages. Both Walrasian and Keynesian variants have been distinguished. They are characterized by price and quantity adjustments, respectively, on the goods market, which at the same time implies a different direction of causality in the relationship between real wages and the marginal product of labor. Though the resulting systems of differential equations are three-dimensional, a local stability analysis could be undertaken. It turned out that the full employment equilibrium in the Walrasian economy is always locally asymptotically stable. By contrast, in the Keynesian case this equilibrium can be unstable if money wages are sufficiently flexible relative to the adjustments of output and the rate of interest. Stability is nevertheless ensured if money wages respond sufficiently sluggishly to labor market disequilibrium. In particular, it follows that if adjustments to the interest rate are perceived as being considerably faster than those to wages, then local stability can safely be regarded in the Keynesian economy as the prevailing normal case in this short-run model of full employment positions.

It should finally be emphasized that all these results rest on the assumption that the state of the long-term expectations is given and fixed. Dropping this hypothesis and introducing, in the first instance, the expected rate of inflation as another dynamic variable may easily give rise to additional destabilizing feedback effects. These mechanisms will be considered in the following chapters.

6.5 Mathematical Appendix

Proof of Theorem 6.1 If we write $E_{jz} = \partial X_j/\partial z$ $(j = 1, 2, 3, z = p, i, w)$, the Jacobian J of the RHS of (6.1)–(6.3) reads

$$J = \begin{bmatrix} \alpha_p E_{1p} & \alpha_p E_{1i} & \alpha_p E_{1w} \\ \alpha_i E_{2p} & \alpha_i E_{2i} & \alpha_i E_{2w} \\ \alpha_p E_{3p} & 0 & \alpha_w E_{3w} \end{bmatrix}$$

(it goes without saying that all evaluations are at equilibrium values). To compute the entries, observe first that labor demand $L_c = L_c(w/p)$ is determined by the equation $w/p = F_L(L_c, \bar{K})$, so that its derivative is $L_c' = 1/F_{LL} < 0$. Furthermore, $dY^s/(w/p) = F_L L_c' < 0$. Abbreviating $\omega := w/p$ we then obtain (omitting the star symbol),

$$E_{1w} = -[(1 - C_Y)F_L - I'F_{KL}]L_c'/p > 0 \qquad E_{1p} = -\omega E_{1w} + C_p < 0$$

$$E_{2w} = f_{mY} F_L L_c'/p < 0 \qquad E_{2p} = -\omega E_{2w} + \bar{M}/p^2 > 0$$

$$E_{3w} = (L_c' - L^{s'})/p < 0 \qquad E_{3p} = -\omega E_{3w} > 0$$

$$E_{1i} = C_i - I' < 0 \qquad E_{2i} = f_{mi} < 0$$

The first inequality derives from assumption *(CI)*. The Routh-Hurwitz conditions, which are necessary and sufficient for all eigenvalues of J to have negative real parts, are given by

$$A_1 = -\text{ trace } J > 0 \qquad A_2 = J_1 + J_2 + J_3 > 0$$

$$A_3 = -\text{ det } J > 0 \qquad B = A_1 A_2 - A_3 > 0$$

where J_i $(i = 1, 2, 3)$ denotes the second-order principal minors of J, that is, the determinants of the matrices that are obtained by deleting the i-th row and the i-th column. It is readily checked that the first three inequalities are satisfied. In particular, $J_1 > 0$, $J_2 \geq 0$, $J_3 > 0$. The sign of B can be estimated as follows:

$$\begin{aligned} B &= A_1 A_2 - A_3 \\ &= (\alpha_p |E_{1p}| + \alpha_i |f_{mi}| + \alpha_w |E_{3w}|)(J_1 + J_2 + J_3) \\ &\quad + \alpha_i J_2 f_{mi} - \alpha_i \alpha_p \alpha_w (C_i - I') E_{3w} \bar{M}/p^2 \\ &> -\alpha_i J_2 f_{mi} + \alpha_w |E_{3w}| J_3 + \alpha_i J_2 f_{mi} + \alpha_i \alpha_p \alpha_w (C_i - I')|E_{3w}|\bar{M}/p^2 \\ &= \alpha_w |E_{3w}| \alpha_i \alpha_p \big[(\omega E_{1w} - C_p)|f_{mi}| - (C_i - I')(-\omega E_{2w} + \bar{M}/p^2)\big] \\ &\quad + \alpha_i \alpha_p \alpha_w (C_i - I')|E_{3w}|\bar{M}/p^2 \\ &= \alpha_i \alpha_p \alpha_w |E_{3w}| \big[(\omega E_{1w} - C_p)|f_{mi}| + \omega |C_i - I'||E_{2w}|\big] > 0 \end{aligned}$$

q.e.d.

Proof of Theorem 6.2 Since $L_k'(Y) = 1/F_L$, the price level $p = w/F_L$ $(L_k(Y), \bar{K})$ has derivatives $\partial p/\partial Y = -wF_{LL}L_k'/F_L^2 = -pF_{LL}/F_L^2 > 0$ and $\partial p/\partial w = 1/F_L > 0$. The partial derivatives of the excess demand functions are then computed as

$$X_{1Y} = -[(1 - C_Y) - I'F_{KL}/F_L] - p|F_{LL}||C_p|/F_L^2 < 0$$

$$X_{2Y} = f_{mY} + \bar{M}|F_{LL}|/(wF_L) > 0$$

$$X_{3Y} = (1 + |F_{LL}|L^{s'})/F_L > 0$$

$$X_{1i} = C_i - I' < 0 \qquad X_{1w} = -|C_p|/F_L \leq 0$$

$$X_{2i} = f_{mi} < 0 \qquad X_{2w} = \bar{M}/(pw) > 0$$

$$X_{3i} = 0 \qquad X_{3w} = 0$$

Defining

$d_1 := X_{3Y}/F_L \geq 0$

$d_2 := X_{1Y}X_{2i} - X_{1i}X_{2Y} > 0$

$d_3 := -X_{3Y}(X_{1i}X_{2w} - X_{1w}X_{2i}) > 0$

the simple Routh-Hurwitz terms turn out to be given by

$A_1 = \beta_Y|X_{1Y}| + \beta_i|X_{2i}| > 0$

$A_2 = \beta_Y(\beta_w d_1|C_p| + \beta_i d_2) > 0$

$A_3 = \beta_Y\beta_i\beta_w d_3 > 0$

The critical condition derives from the composite term B. Defining

$H_1 := d_2|f_{mi}|/d_3 > 0 \qquad H_2 := X_{1Y}/f_{mi} > 0$

$H_3 := d_1|f_{mi}|/d_3 > 0 \qquad H_4 := H_3(1 + H_2\beta_Y/\beta_i) > 0$

the term B can be arranged as

$$B = A_1A_2 - A_3 = \beta_Y\beta_i d_3[-\beta_w(1 - H_4|C_p|) + H_1(1 + H_2\beta_Y)]$$

Since $B > 0$ ($B < 0$) is sufficient for stability (instability), this completes the proof of the theorem.

q.e.d.

7 Price Flexibility and Instability in the Medium Run

7.1 Introduction

Keynesian economics is often said to be founded on wage (and possibly also price) rigidities. Correspondingly, these "imperfections" are taken as the primary cause for unemployment. Tobin especially has shown that this is not generally true. So in a well-known article (Tobin 1975), he incorporates dynamic adjustments of money wages and the price level into a simple macroeconomic framework. Specifically, in combination with adjustments of inflationary expectations, they constitute a dynamic process whose stability properties are then to be investigated. It turns out that under certain conditions the full employment equilibrium may well be unstable. Tobin's conclusion (1989, 18) in this regard is:

> I regarded my article [i.e., Tobin 1975] as supporting Keynes's intuition that price and wage flexibility are bad for real stability. I wanted to shake the profession off its conventional interpretation of Keynesian economics, according to which unemployment arises only because of a dubious assertion of wage and price rigidity. I wanted to recall and reinforce the second strand of Keynes's argument, according to which unemployment is attributable to inadequate real demand, a deficiency that flexibility will not remedy.

In this chapter we reconsider the stability issue in Tobin's approach. Our main concern is that in Tobin's specification, wage and price dynamics are virtually indistinguishable. This implies that the parameter that reflects the degree of price flexibility plays no role in the central instability condition. In order to pave the way for a more detailed discussion of the consequences of wage and price flexibility, we here put forward separate adjustment equations for the two variables. In essence, we shall find that highly flexible prices, and also (to some extent) highly flexible money wages, are indeed destabilizing. A side-effect of our treatment is that now the supposition of inflationary myopic perfect foresight is no longer precluded from the analysis, as was the case in Tobin's original specification.

When in this and the following chapters expectations about inflation evolve endogenously, we work for the most part with adaptive expectations. We are aware that after the intellectual triumph of the rational expectations hypothesis, this has become something of a heresy. The next two sections are laid out to justify our procedure. In section 7.2, a number of empirical and theoretical arguments are collected that demonstrate that adaptive expectations are less imprudent than usually stated. Section 7.3 is more specific. After indicating that adaptive expectations may approximate predictions from more sophisticated linear regression models, we focus on extrapolative regression forecasts and establish a close relationship between the two. Subsequently, both forecasting methods are subjected to the test of predicting a stochastically perturbed sine wave. The arrangement of this little simulation experiment favors the systematic forecast errors, but we wish to illustrate that for many purposes they may nevertheless be deemed to be tolerable. It should be pointed out that in all these discussions adaptive expectations are essentially meant to be one-period-ahead forecasts. The alternative interpretation—that adaptive expectations refer to a time average of the variable to be forecasted over a longer time horizon—is taken up later, in section 11.5.

In section 7.4 we return to our stability issue. After elucidating the main stabilizing and destabilizing feedback mechanisms, the central building blocks of the Tobin (1975) model are considered and our modification of the wage-price dynamics is introduced. We also point out similarities between Tobin's model and a monetary growth model advanced by Sargent (1987, chap. 5). Section 7.5 presents a local stability analysis of the full model under adaptive expectations of inflation. Section 7.6 deals with the case of myopic perfect foresight. Apart from the wider acceptance of this hypothesis, it clarifies that imperfect expectations alone are not to blame for the instability results. Section 7.7 contains some concluding remarks. The proofs of the mathematical propositions are relegated to an appendix.

Before going into the specifics, we should note that there has recently been a debate in the literature on the issue of whether increased price flexibility is stabilizing or destabilizing (two central contributions are DeLong and Summers 1986b, and Gray and Kandil 1991). This discussion, however, focuses on a different problem. What is studied, in connection with staggered wage contracts and an accompanying rational expectations hypothesis, is the relationship between the variance of the cyclical component of real output and some parameter(s) characterizing the flexibility of prices and wages. The fluctuations themselves are generated by exogenous stochastic shocks, whereas asymptotic stability is not called into question if exogenous stochastic shocks are absent.

7.2 In Defense of Adaptive Expectations

It has been indicated in the introduction that in the following chapters we will, for the most part, assume that expectations about the future rate of price inflation are formed adaptively. Myopic perfect foresight is then included as the limiting case. To discuss this principle on a general level, let $x = x(t)$ be a dynamic variable and $x^e(t)$ its expected value. The rule of adaptive expectations says that x^e is revised upward, but only partially so, if the actual value of x exceeds the value that has been currently expected. Correspondingly, the revision is downward if $x < x^e$. In continuous time, the basic version of adaptive expectations is described by

$$\dot{x}^e = \beta_x (x - x^e) \tag{7.1}$$

β_x is a positive constant which is called the speed of adjustment, while $1/\beta_x$ indicates the adjustment lag. A simple reasoning is that if the right-hand side of (7.1) happened to remain constant during the adjustment process, then it would take exactly $1/\beta_x$ time units for the solution of this hypothetical differential equation to close the initial gap between x and x^e. Another view on β_x is given in the next section.

To be more precise about the meaning of the variable x^e, the general concept is that $x^e(t)$ is the value of x which, at time t, is expected to prevail at some future date, or over some future period (maybe as a time average). The usual interpretation, however, refers to the immediate future. That is, expectations are told to be formed at the beginning of the short period, and x^e is the expected value of x over the rest of this period. In a continuous-time framework, the period is, in fact, infinitesimally short. Myopic perfect foresight then means that $x^e(t) = x(t)$ for all t. Under the assumption of smooth time paths this identity is obtained as the limiting case when the parameter β_x tends to infinity. To point out the conceptual equivalence of, so to speak, infinitely fast adaptive expectations and myopic perfect foresight, we will occasionally write $\beta_x = \infty$ for this situation.

In discrete time where the "short period" is of definite length $h > 0$, expectations are formed at time t, and x_t^e is the predicted value of x for the ensuing time interval $(t, t+h)$. The updating of expectations here reads

$$x_{t+h}^e = x_t^e + h\beta_x(x_t - x_t^e) = h\beta_x x_t + (1 - h\beta_x)x_t^e \tag{7.2}$$

Naturally, equation (7.1) is obtained if h shrinks to zero. With a fixed positive number h, the discrete-time adjustment process is meaningful only if the adjustment lag $1/\beta_x$ does not fall short of the period length h, so that in this setting the possibility of identifying myopic perfect foresight with $\beta_x = \infty$ breaks down. This is an additional reason why it is useful to conduct the analysis in continuous time.

Equations (7.1) and (7.2) implicitly assume that the variable x exhibits no long-run trend. We might mention in passing, though it will not be relevant in this book, that they can be easily embedded in a growth context. It is then appropriate to include a growth rate $g^\star$, which represents the perceived trend of long-run growth. (7.1) and (7.2) are thus modified to

$$\dot{x}^e = g^\star x^e + \beta_x(x - x^e) \tag{7.3}$$

$$x_{t+h}^e = (1 + hg^\star)x_t^e + h\beta_x(x_t - x_t^e) \tag{7.4}$$

Value $g^\star$ may be a constant or itself be governed by (slow) adjustments of, for example, the adaptive expectations type.

Although the notion of x^e as one-period-ahead forecasts is predominant in macroeconomics, it should be taken with some care. In section 11.5 we call into question whether this point of view is really so meaningful, at least with respect to the economies in this book whose steady-state position is locally unstable. (A short hint is also given at the end of the next section.) In the meantime the usual interpretation may do, which in particular has the advantage that the polar case $\beta_x = \infty$ can be identified with the seemingly more rational concept of myopic perfect foresight.

Adaptive expectations involve systematic forecast errors over time. The principle is often criticized for this reason and rejected outright as a modeling device, especially when measured against the outcome of rational expectations. In the next paragraphs we argue that adaptive expectations may be better than they are made out to be.

The first issue is the behavior of actual human beings and the question of whether it is compatible with the rational expectations hypothesis. Although we are conscious that it is an unresolved methodological issue whether direct testing of the rational expectations hypothesis is a suitable and worthwhile activity, we nevertheless share the view that a theory that is said to be based on microfoundations should survive empirical testing at the level of individual units (cf. Lovell 1986, 110f). By contrast, if one follows the "instrumentalist" methodological statement that "the only real test [of the RE hypothesis] . . . is whether theories involving rationality explain observed phenomena any better than alternative theories" (Muth 1961, 330), then this should also mean that rational expectations cannot a priori claim exclusiveness.

There is ample evidence from psychological experiments that denies that forecast errors, as implied by rational expectations, are unbiased. For example, Alpert and Raiffa (1982) report of experimental subjects tending to be *overconfident*, which makes them take on more risk. *Overreaction* was found by Tversky and Kahneman (1982); in making inferences, too little weight was put on base rates and too much on new information. Andreassen and Kraus (1988) observed that individuals tend to *extrapolate* past time series, which could lead them to *chase trends*. Further references to psychological evidence on systematic judgment errors made by experimental subjects may be taken from De Long et al. 1991, 5. Concentrating on the field of cognitive and social psychology, Earl (1990) develops a survey that "suggest[s] to mainstream economists that there are gains to be had from seeking help from psychology" (718; for a short discussion of still existing misperceptions about inflation, see 747).

The phenomenon of judgment biases is not confined to laboratory studies of nonexperts. Overly optimistic forecasts and general overreaction on the part of professional investors on financial markets was extensively studied by De Bondt and Thaler (1985, 1987, 1990). Likewise, extrapolation is a key feature of popular stock market models, as shown in Shiller 1990, 1991. A similar approach with respect to predictions of the exchange rate is pursued by Frankel and Froot (1986). A particular sort of systematic error is the subject of a study by Saunders (1993). He determines that the weather in New York City has a long history of significant correlation with major Wall Street stock indexes, an effect that also appears to be robust with respect to a variety of market "anomalies."

Also, macroeconomic time series that are far less volatile than the movements on stock and foreign exchange markets involve serious difficulties. Even the many statisticians who have long been working on the problem of seasonal adjustments of GNP, M1, and other economic indicators have not learned enough from prior experience to achieve rational forecasts: the official preliminary data on these magnitudes turn out to deviate in a systematic manner from the revised time series that eventually appear (Lovell 1986, 118f). In sum, the empirical evidence is sufficiently strong to allow us to conclude that expectations are rich and varied phenomena that are not adequately captured by the concept of rational expectations.

A great deal of empirical research has been specifically devoted to the formation of inflationary expectations. The availability of data on such forecasts is certainly an important reason for the extensive nature of these studies. In particular the financial journalist J. A. Livingston has conducted a semiannual survey in the United States since 1947 in which respondents from a variety of occupations have given their wage and price predictions.[1] Confining oneself to the concept that present and past realizations of the price inflation rate $\hat{p}$ are the only determinants of inflationary expectations π^e, one tests a most elementary approach

$$\pi^e_{t+1} = \alpha_o + \alpha_1 \pi^e_t + \alpha_2 \hat{p}_t \qquad (\alpha_o, \alpha_1, \alpha_2 = \text{const})$$

Clearly, if $h = 1$, $\pi^e_{t+1} = x^e_{t+1}$, $\alpha_o = 0$, $\alpha_2 = \beta_x$, $\alpha_1 = 1 - \beta_x$ in (7.2), the two equations would be equivalent.

Employing this model to explain the Livingston and other data has typically produced insignificant estimates of α_o and estimates of α_1 and α_2 that sum to unity (see, for example, Turnovsky 1970 and Lahiri 1976). On the basis of the Livingston data, Figlewski and Wachtel (1981) conclude that the hypothesis of rational expectations "does not appear to provide an adequate explanation of actual inflation expectations in the post-war period" (4) and determine that an adaptive expectations model best describes the price expectations formation process. However, their study permits the expectations to vary across individuals and time. An experimental study by Williams (1987), which utilized repetitive-stationary market environments, indicates that the market dynamics "leading to a rational equilibrium" (16) are likely to be governed by an adaptive process that is inconsistent with Muthian rationality.[2]

If we limit the discussion to aggregate forecasts, a simple juxtaposition of the results from Turnovsky (1970) and Lahiri (1976) already suggests that a rigid adaptive expectations scheme may be a useful starting point, but the estimates do not seem very reliable in detail.[3] Jacobs and Jones (1980) present a multilevel adaptive expectations scheme that provides for expectations in inflation rate trends and distinguishes transitory price level shifts from permanent ones. Simulation of this model between the years 1947 and 1975 replicates the expectations adjustment process closely; the adaptation coefficients display remarkable stability over long periods of quite different inflation experience. To give a concrete figure, when fitted to the Livingston survey data the model explains 89 percent of the variation in expected inflation rates for thirteen-month forecasts, with two-thirds of the residuals lying under .5 annual per cent (276).

Taking for granted that one cannot dismiss as peripheral the experimental and empirical results that contradict the rational expectations hypothesis in general and suggest the use of (modified and extended) adaptive expectations mechanisms in particular, we must reconsider whether adaptive expectations are really as imprudent as they are often asserted to be. Here, the basic assumptions of the concept of rational expectations have to be recalled: economic agents utilize efficiently whatever information is available; and in addition, the information that is actually available to them is also sufficient to permit them to form their expectations as if they know the structure of the whole economic process itself (to within a set of additive white-noise disturbances). Even if this availability assumption is fulfilled, the information needed easily becomes so complex that it may be doubtful whether agents can entirely cope with the problem of correctly interpreting it. There still remains the problem of whether agents are capable of handling the bulk of information and transforming it into the objectively unbiased conditional expectations of the time series to be predicted.

Nevertheless, for the sake of the argument let us accept the assumptions about the availability and use of information, but not the accompanying assumption that acquiring and processing all the data is costless. The existence of such a cost, however, which may be called an optimization cost, has far-reaching theoretical consequences. If optimization is costly, and if cheaper, suboptimal expectations-formation procedures are available, the decisionmaker is faced with the problem of whether to optimize. There would be no difficulties if this choice could itself be made optimally, with full knowledge of the costs and benefits involved, but typically these factors are *not* known in advance. Hence, in order to determine the ideal degree of optimizing, a larger optimization problem that will have its own optimization cost must be solved. It is easy to see that attempts of this kind to fold optimization cost into a conventional optimization problem will inevitably be caught in an infinite regress (cf. Conlisk 1988, 214f).

In our view, the most appropriate theoretical approach in this situation is to start with behavioral heterogeneity of agents and admit optimizers, who must pay a cost, as well as nonoptimizers, who adopt less expensive rule-of-thumb behavior. Then, within a fully specified dynamic setting, suppose that the group performing better in the recent past wins some converts from the other group. This shift allows the population composition to evolve endogenously under the evolutionary pressure of differential payoffs. The basic question is: will one group, for example, the nonoptimizers, be totally competed away, or is there scope for coexistence even in the long run? A problem of this kind was first addressed by Conlisk (1980); his model provides an example in which naive agents can indeed survive. The result is not confined to the specific economy considered there. Isolating some of the most important mechanisms involved, the analysis in Franke and Sethi 1995 shows that naive expectations (simple adaptive expectations as in equation (7.2)) survive under very general conditions. It may also be noted that this approach of evolutionary dynamics argues not only against rational expectations, but also against the paradigm of the representative agent.

Moving away from these stylized thought experiments and closer to reality, we may negate altogether the existence of agents who are sufficiently competent to always react optimally (i.e., optimally if optimization cost were neglected). Instead, there are several groups of agents with different forecasting procedures, whose cost increases with the degree of sophistication. The forecasting competitions conducted by Makridakis et al. (1984) also yielded a considerable evolutionary fitness of rule-of-thumb behavior under these circumstances. In these tournaments, straightforward and informationally undemanding adaptive forecasting methods regularly outperformed more complicated and informationally demanding techniques.

Models of adaptive expectations use past observations of the variable to be forecasted as their only "input." Whether disregarding additional sources of information is inefficient depends not only on the cost of collecting and processing other data, but also on the cost of *selecting* data relevant to the specific forecasting problem. This cost may be considerable if there is an overload of information or if there are competing working hypotheses. Again, the benefits of such a data selection process are unknown in advance. In the case of inflationary expectations there is some evidence that it might not be worthwhile to make this investment. A necessary condition for the utilization of nonnegligible cost information sets to increase forecasting accuracy is that such sets serve as leading indicators. In order for a time series to qualify as a leading indicator it must "cause" inflation as defined by Granger. Examining measures of monetary and fiscal policy (the growth rates of monetary aggregates and the high-employment budget surplus, respectively), Feige and Pearce (1976) find that the incremental information contained in these measures is not useful for predicting inflation when information contained in past inflation rates has already been efficiently exploited (506). They conclude that "an economically rational agent would not employ these series to help him forecast inflation" (518).

With respect to procedures less technical than the Box-Jenkins methodology employed by Feige and Pearce, let us recall the enhanced adaptive expectations model by Jacobs and Jones (1980), whose results rely exclusively on observations of past prices. Mullineux (1980) and Noble and Fields (1982) report that the Livingston (and other) forecast data are informationally efficient in the sense that forecasts are uncorrelated with a set of pertinent past information.[4]

The adaptive expectations hypothesis was put forward originally as a plausible rule for updating and revising expectations in the light of recently observed errors. It nevertheless does not need to conflict with optimizing behavior. Perhaps the best-known fact, established by Muth (1960), is that adaptive expectations in equation (7.2) are optimal in the sense of yielding minimum mean-square prediction errors if the variable to be forecast follows a stochastic process that has an integrated autoregressive moving average representation ARIMA(0,1,1). There are other examples of such a statistical optimality property,[5] but it clearly does not hold in general.

A second and more important characteristic of adaptive expectations is that they may be compatible with Bayesian learning. An illuminating example is provided by Lawson (1980). He supposes that the variable in question is composed of a normal or permanent component, where agents believe that it remains constant or has just undergone a step change, and a transitory noise term with zero as expected value. Using simple conditional probability theory one can then express the predicted value of the variable as the adaptive expectations formula

(7.2). The speed of adjustment, however, is endogenous and may vary over time (see 307). Lawson then works out that his model conforms with the empirical evidence (312–316).[6] Another contribution in this direction is made by Caskey (1985). He reconsiders the Livingston expectations data and assumes that this panel followed Bayes's Rule in updating their beliefs (where the observations include the prices as well as other variables), and that it believed the underlying parameters of the inflation process were constant over the estimation period. Under these conditions reasonable initial beliefs can be found such that the outcome of the thus defined Bayesian process is fairly close to the Livingston forecasts. If we take into account that the Livingston data may alternatively be explained by adaptive expectations mechanisms, Caskey's result also shows that the principle of adaptive expectations may be quite consistent with optimal forecasting behavior of Bayesian type.

7.3 Adaptive Expectations and Extrapolative Regression Forecasts

The Bayesian updating procedures that have been discussed in the previous section are based on the notion that agents believe they live in a stationary stochastic environment. If they do not trust this assumption or consider the lag lengths involved to be too long, they may act as many econometricians in practical work do. That is, they may think the best they can do is to employ a linear model that relates the variable to be forecast to a vector of predetermined variables, and then form the corresponding minimum variance expectations. Friedman (1979, 34–37) demonstrates that the predictions derived from these least-squares estimations are similar in form to the familiar rule of adaptive expectations, in particular, if old observations are discounted or a rolling sample period is adopted. The result of optimal least-squares learning therefore provides further evidence that the adaptive model may be a useful approximation of more sophisticated procedures. Friedman also mentions that the least-squares estimator of the slope parameters is the Bayes estimator when there is no prior information about these parameter values. Moreover, if economic agents apply a quadratic loss function to prediction errors, their use of least-squares estimations is fully consistent with the spirit of rational expectations (30 n. 5).

There are many empirical studies that obtain significant explanations of inflationary expectations such as the Livingston data by regressing them on lagged values of actual inflation and a couple of other predetermined variables. We have already pointed out, however, that these expectations can be satisfactorily explained by elementary adaptive mechanisms. As a side result, Friedman's analysis helps to elucidate why the explanatory power of the simple approach is not much worse than that of the more advanced procedures. Consciously or not, application of the former implies approximation of the latter. The accuracy of the approximation depends, of course, on the concrete specifications.

Recent literature has shown that there are many variants of least-squares learning mechanisms, that is, algorithms of how agents revise their perceptions of the law of motion of decision variables. A representative survey is Sargent 1993. Here it is also seen, however, that the presently available algorithms still struggle with the problems arising from nonlinearities and multiple equilibria. So in the rest of this section we content ourselves with considering more closely one of the most elementary least-squares forecast procedures.

A straightforward estimations approach is to extrapolate past observations of the variable x. Agents may try this approach first and search for a better alternative only if the losses resulting from the forecast errors appear to be too heavy in relation to the presumed costs and benefits of searching for or selecting a more extensive model. If these extrapolative regression forecasts have an underlying constant rolling sample period, then the finer details of their relationship to simple adaptive expectations can be spelled out. Consider a discrete-time framework and let h be the length of the adjustment period, with T the length of the sample period. Suppose that, at the end of period $[t, t+h)$, agents fit a straight line through the last $1 + T/h$ logarithmic values of x (logarithms allow a proper handling of long-run exponential growth in linear models). The formal regression equation is

$$\ln x_\tau = \alpha_{t,o} + \alpha_{t,1} \cdot \tau, \qquad \tau = t - T, \ldots, t - h, t$$

With $a_{t,o}$ the estimated intercept and $a_{t,1}$ the slope, the one-period-ahead forecast, denoted by x^r_{t+h}, is given by

$$\ln x^r_{t+h} = a_{t,o} + a_{t,1} \cdot (t + h) \tag{7.5}$$

A constant rolling sample period means that one period before, at the end of period $[t, t+h)$, the same regression was performed on the basis of observations $x_{t-T-h}, \ldots, x_{t-2h}, x_{t-h}$. It gave rise to x^r_t, the one-period-ahead forecast for period $[t, t+h)$. The corresponding slope coefficient being $a_{t-h,1}$, it is shown in Franke (1992b) that the old and the new forecast are connected by the approximate equation

$$\ln x^r_{t+h} \approx \ln x^r_t + h a_{t-h,1} + \frac{4h}{T+h}[\ln x_t - \ln x^r_t]$$

This formula provides an updating rule which bears some similarity to the adaptive expectations equation (7.4), with a constant speed of adjustment $4/(T+h)$ and an endogenous term $a_{t-h,1}$. Since the latter estimates the present growth trend of x, extrapolative regression forecasts can be conveniently incorporated in small macrodynamic models if $a_{t-h,1}$ in the above equation is now replaced with a (possibly constant) rate of perceived long-run growth, $g^\star$. If we also use the approximation properties of the logarithmic function,[7] this yields the following adaptive mechanism

$$x^r_{t+h} \approx x^r_t + h g^\star x^r_t + \frac{4h}{T+h}(x_t - x^r_t) \tag{7.6}$$

Going to the limit, $h \to 0$, the continuous-time formulation reads

$$\dot{x}^r \approx g^\star x^r + (4/T)(x - x^r) \tag{7.7}$$

The correspondence to equations (7.3) and (7.4) is obvious. Hence, the adaptive expectations formula may alternatively be viewed as approximately representing the one-period ahead extrapolative forecasts that are obtained from linear regressions of x on time with a constant rolling sample period T. In continuous time, the speed of adjustment β_x is then linked to T by the equation

$$\beta_x = \begin{cases} 4/T & \text{in continuous time,} \\ 4/(T+h) & \text{in discrete time} \end{cases} \tag{7.8}$$

This interpretation of the adjustment speed is also helpful in assessing the numerical values that will be assigned to β_x in the computer simulations later on. Clearly, β_x rises when in the regression approach more of the older observations of x are discarded as misleading and so the length of the rolling sample period decreases.

Whether agents really regard the imperfections associated with the methods of adaptive expectations or extrapolative regression forecasts as tolerable will depend on the particular applications. In order to get an impression of the order of magnitude of the forecast errors, we put the rules (7.2) and (7.5) to the test of a little simulation experiment. Let x, the series to be predicted, favor systematic forecast errors in that it

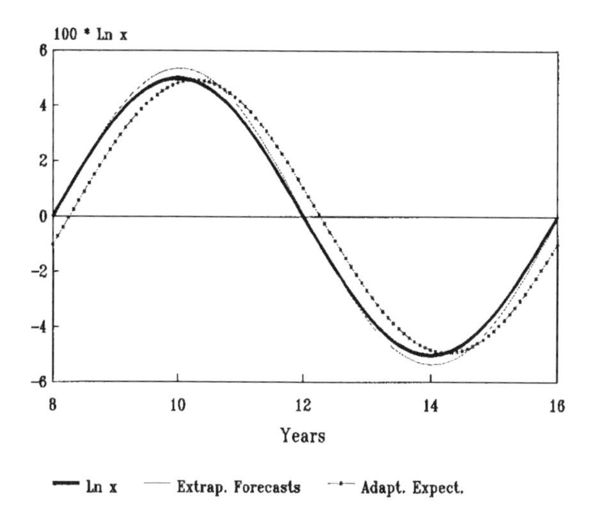

Figure 7.1
Extrapolative forecasts and adaptive expectations: deterministic case

oscillates in a rather regular way. Algebraically, let $\ln x$ be a trendless sine wave perturbed by serially correlated random shocks,

$$\ln x_t = \alpha \ sin(\phi t) + u_t$$

$$u_t = \rho u_{t-h} + \varepsilon_t$$

where the disturbances ε_t are drawn from a normal distribution with zero mean and standard deviation σ. The parameter values are as follows:

$$\alpha = 5/100 \qquad \rho = 0.75 \qquad \phi = 2\pi/8 \qquad h = 1/12 \qquad T = 1 \qquad g^\star = 0$$

That is, we have a monthly series with an amplitude of ± 5 percent, an average cycle period of eight years, and relatively high autocorrelation in the random shocks, while the length of the sample period is one year. By virtue of (7.8), the corresponding value of β_x is $\beta_x = 4/(T+h) = 3.69$. Setting the initial value of x^e equal to the first regression forecast x^r and allowing for a transition period of a full cycle, we see that figure 7.1 is a representative example of the evolution of the regression forecasts and the adaptive expectations if x is a purely deterministic sine wave. In figure 7.2 the motion of x is stochastic, the standard deviation of the random perturbations being one-fifth of the amplitude of x, that is, $\sigma = 2/100$.

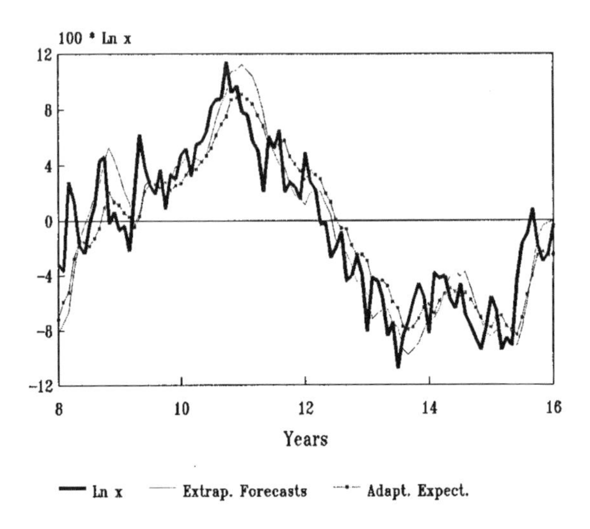

Figure 7.2
Extrapolative forecasts and adaptive expectations: stochastic case ($\sigma = 2/100$)

Figure 7.1 plainly displays the weaknesses of the two naive forecasting methods. Adaptive expectations are chasing the series, catching up shortly after the turning points, and then chasing it again. In contrast, the regression forecasts overpredict the series near the turning points. Though these deviations are systematic, they are limited in size. Figure 7.2 indicates that with random shocks imposed on the oscillations, the shortcomings are less severe and the differences between the two procedures tend to be washed out.

Table 7.1 presents some quantitative results for different degrees of the stochastic noise. The standard deviation of the error terms covers the range from $\sigma = 0$, the deterministic case, to $\sigma = 5/100$, where the noise begins to dominate the cyclical pattern of x. One realization of the stochastic disturbances is sufficient to gain the basic insights. (The seed of the sequences of the pseudo-random numbers from which the ε_t were derived was the same for each σ.)

Naturally, the root mean-square prediction error exceeds the standard deviation of the shocks, but the difference is not too large. Regression forecasts show smaller prediction errors than adaptive expectations when the series x is smooth; adaptive expectations yield comparatively better forecasts when the noise level of the series increases.

The Durbin-Watson coefficients in table 7.1 measure the extent of systematic prediction errors with respect to first-order serial correlation.[8]

Table 7.1
Root mean-square prediction error with respect to $\ln x_t (\times 100)$ and Durbin-Watson statistic of prediction errors (in parentheses)

	Standard deviation σ of the ε_t-shocks (times 100)				
	0.0	0.5	1.0	2.0	5.0
Regression Forecasts	0.26 (0.00)	0.76 (0.69)	1.44 (0.77)	2.83 (0.79)	7.04 (0.80)
Adaptive Expectations	0.72 (0.01)	0.97 (0.39)	1.42 (0.72)	2.50 (0.93)	5.93 (1.03)

They indicate strong positive autocorrelation for low values of σ. At higher values of σ, adaptive expectations display somewhat less autocorrelation than the regression forecasts, though it is still significant. In many applications economic agents may nevertheless regard the forecast errors as tolerable, or expect only minor improvements from other forecast methods. More important, a model builder may be willing to accept these errors in formulating and investigating small and tractable macrodynamic models of the economy as a first approximation to the "true" processes of expectations formation; and he or she may do this in a deterministic framework as an approximation to a stochastic setting, where the bias in the forecasts would be less annoying.

The source of the most severe prediction errors in the example is that the (major) peaks and troughs of x are recognized too late. Now, if agents are aware that they live in a cyclical environment and the variable x, say, has increased for some time above "normal," then it will seem more likely to them that the series is about to peak. If agents stuck to the rigid rule of adaptive expectations, they would miss this turning point and overestimate the series in the first stage of the downturn then setting in. In a great deal of decision problems, especially those with irreversibilities, overshooting will be more costly in such a situation than a possible underestimation. Hence, agents may hesitate near the (suspected) turning points and adjust their expectations more slowly.

As an elementary improvement of adaptive expectations in a cyclical framework, this consideration of return-to-normal expectations suggests to introduce a variable speed of adjustment β_x in the following way: (1) Assume fast adjustments after agents can be sure that a (major) turning point has been passed and let the adjustment speed be maintained over the ensuing evolution of x as long as the values of the variable are not regarded as "too extreme." (2) Reduce the adjustment speed if x comes closer to "normal" turning point values (which have been experienced in the past). This enhancement of adaptive expectations becomes even more meaningful when a longer time horizon of expectations than the one-period-ahead forecasts are taken into account, which, though usually neglected, is an important conceptual issue of its own. As mentioned above we postpone this discussion to section 11.5, where we will see that such a modification of adaptive inflationary expectations is also capable of containing the otherwise divergent cyclical forces. In this and the next chapters, however, the speed of adjustment is fixed and the reader may still adopt the interpretation of x^e (i.e., $x^e = \pi^e$, the expected rate of inflation) as referring to the next period (which is infinitesimally small). Thus, high speeds of adjustment, $\beta_x \to \infty$, can be viewed as approaching the case of myopic perfect foresight. The macroeconomic implications of this rationality concept will be contrasted several times with slow adjustments of expectations.

7.4 Basic Features of the Tobin and the Sargent Model

In the Tobin (1975) model, two main feedback loops, whose theoretical significance goes far beyond the particular specifications adopted there, can be identified. The first chain of feedback effects has the Keynes effect as its basic ingredient; the second relies on the Mundell effect.[9] According to the Keynes effect, a falling price level raises real money balances, decreases the nominal rate of interest on the bond market, and increases investment expenditures. The subsequent rise in production and thus employment has a positive impact on money wages. When output prices are directly or indirectly linked to the wage bill, the price level moves upward, too.[10] A similar argument applies to changes of the price level, that is, to the rate of inflation. In sum, we have a negative feedback loop in inflation, which acts as a stabilizer. For easier reference let us call the intermediate chain of reactions from rising/falling output to rising/falling inflation, the output-inflation feedback.

In essence, this mechanism was already pointed out by Keynes in chapter 19 of his *General Theory*, which is devoted to a discussion of "Changes in Money Wages." As is well known, Keynes was very skeptical in this chapter about the beneficial effects of flexible wages. The mechanism of the later so-called Keynes effect is indeed the only one he recognized as being of any significance to the classical stance of flexible wages (Keynes 1936, 266).

By contrast, the Mundell effect contributes to a destabilization. It rests on the notion that investment is dependent on the real rate of interest. Changes in anticipated price inflation consequently drive a wedge between the nominal interest rate, which clears the money market, and the real interest rate, which determines the demand for goods. If the rate of inflation is falling and causes expectations about future inflation to be revised downward, investment will be negatively affected and there is a contractionary effect on output. Through the same channels as those sketched earlier, inflation will then be further reduced (or deflation will accelerate). Thus, a positive feedback loop will be activated. In particular, the destabilizing effect will be stronger and therefore tend to outweigh the stabilizing Keynes effect, the faster expected inflation adjusts to actual inflation. The overall impact of fast money wage and price adjustments, however, is less clear since they are constituent parts of the output-inflation feedback that underlies both the Keynes and the Mundell effect.

Tobin (1975) makes his point by means of an elementary model consisting of the dynamic multiplier process, a natural rate-based Phillips curve for price inflation, and the standard form of an adaptive mechanism of inflationary expectations. This so-called Wicksell-Keynes-Phillips (WKP) model has, therefore, three dynamic variables, whose evolution is governed by three differential equations. These are output Y, the price level p, and the expected rate of inflation π^e. Let Y^d_p, Y^d_π denote the partial derivatives of aggregate demand with respect to p and π^e, and let β_π represent the speed at which π^e adjust to $\hat{p} = \dot{p}/p$ (a caret over a variable denotes its growth rate). Then the stabilizing influence of the Keynes effect (the partial derivative of Y^d with respect to the price level, $Y^d_p < 0$), and the destabilizing influence of the Mundell effect (the partial derivative of Y^d with respect to expected inflation, $Y^d_\pi > 0$), as well as of the adjustment speed β_π are neatly reflected in one of the necessary conditions for local stability (ibid., 199),

$$\beta_\pi Y^d_\pi < -pY^d_p \tag{7.9}$$

In particular, it is immediately seen that the equilibrium is unstable if, in the presence of a positive Mundell effect, adaptive expectations are close to the case of myopic perfect foresight, that is, if β_π

is large. Note that instability can prevail irrespective of the parameters characterizing the adjustments on the goods and the labor market.[11]

Considering the model in greater detail, we should like to point out Tobin's assumption that product and labor markets are condensed in one sector, so that the wage and price dynamics are virtually indistinguishable. Conceptually, it is money wages that, in a Phillips curve–like manner, are meant to respond to output and employment. The specification of this law nevertheless refers to changes in the price level,

$$\hat{p} = \dot{p}/p = \beta_p(Y - \bar{Y}) + \pi^e \tag{7.10}$$

($\bar{Y}$ being the exogenously given "natural" output that corresponds to the level of full, or normal employment $\bar{L}$). The use of (7.10) can be justified by the straightforward pricing rule of a constant markup over wage unit costs, which firms are supposed to follow in every instant of time.[12] The interpretation given by Tobin, however, cannot be maintained. He postulates (ibid., 198) that prices are determined by marginal variable costs, that is, $p = w/F_L$ (w is the money wage rate, F the production function, F_L its partial derivative with respect to labor). The reason for rejecting this background story is that it would imply

$$\hat{p} = \hat{w} - (F_{LL}/F_L) \cdot \dot{L} \tag{7.11}$$

which differs from the price Phillips curve (7.10) by the accelerating term

$$-(F_{LL}/F_L)\dot{L} > 0$$

More important than this interpretational aspect, in our view, is a certain asymmetric treatment of prices and wages. On the one hand, nominal wages are supposed to react with some lag to excess labor supply, which, using the above "Okun gap" $Y - \bar{Y}$, we may provisionally write down as

$$\hat{w} = \beta_w(Y - \bar{Y}) + \pi^e, \qquad 0 < \beta_w < \infty \tag{7.12}$$

See Tobin 1975, 198. Prices by contrast are thought to be perfectly flexible and to adjust instantaneously such as to satisfy the marginal productivity equation (or some similar principle).[13] This device precludes deeper insights into the different consequences for stability of high or low speeds of wage *as well as* price adjustments, an issue Tobin has been concerned with in various verbal discussions (Tobin 1975, 1980, 1989).

In the present context it seems to be more natural to put price and wage adjustments on an equal footing. If we include the marginal productivity principle alluded to by Tobin, this means that prices adjust to marginal wage cost at a finite speed β_p, so that $\dot{p} = \beta_p(w/F_L - p)$ or[14]

$$\hat{p} = \beta_p(w/(pF_L) - 1), \qquad 0 < \beta_p < \infty \tag{7.13}$$

After thus setting the stage, it is interesting to compare Tobin's (1975) approach with a monetary growth model developed by Sargent in his macroeconomic textbook (Sargent 1987, chap. 5). He designs it with a view to demonstrating some of the hypotheses or assertions that were advanced by Milton Friedman in his 1968 presidential address to the ASSA. The most fundamental assertion is, of course, that of the asymptotic stability of the steady state (in the absence of stochastic perturbations). Sargent's analysis of his dynamic process, however, is incomplete in that he assumes, but does not prove, asymptotic stability. As a matter of fact, it is shown in Franke 1992a that his stability optimism is generally unwarranted: the system changes from being locally convergent to locally divergent if the adaptive expectations of inflation become sufficiently fast.

Although it has not been noticed in the reception of the two models by Sargent and Tobin, there is a close conceptual relationship between them once we abstract from growth and the capacity effect of fixed investment in Sargent's model. Apart from an explicit representation of the LM-part and the components of aggregate demand, the differences are the following:

- Sargent adopts an expectations-augmented wage Phillips curve (with the employment rate as its main argument).
- He explicitly incorporates the marginal productivity principle to determine the price level.
- He works with an IS-equation, that is, the multiplier is supposed to work out with infinite speed.

The third point should be of minor importance since Tobin's critical stability condition (7.9) makes no reference to the goods market and the efficiency of the multiplier. The first two points are the direct formalization of Tobin's verbal presentation. Seen from this perspective, the Sargent model's potential instability may no longer come as a surprise. Although the mathematical treatment is quite involved,[15] the basic stability and instability arguments are the same as those in Tobin's model.

It follows from this discussion that our modification (7.12) and (7.13) of the wage-price dynamics can also be viewed as a direct generalization of the Sargent model.[16] In the next section these two adjustment equations are combined with the other elements of the two models, where our specification will be somewhat closer to Sargent's than to Tobin's approach.

7.5 The Case of Adaptive Expectations

Abstracting from growth and the endogenous evolution of fixed capital, we wish to investigate a model that can be formulated in terms of the level variables. Correspondingly, let the capital stock $K = \bar{K}$ and the volume of full, or normal, employment $L = \bar{L}$ be given (L may be thought of as actual working hours and $\bar{L}$ as the total of normal working hours at full employment of the labor force, so that a possible situation $L > \bar{L}$ signifies overtime-work). Since we likewise neglect inflation in the long run, the money supply may be exogenously fixed at $M = \bar{M}$. Letting i denote the nominal rate of interest and δ the rate of capital depreciation, we then describe the model by the following set of short-run equilibrium conditions and dynamic adjustment rules,

$$Y = C(Y) + I(Y - wL/p - \delta\bar{K} - (i - \pi^e)\bar{K}), \quad 0 < C' < 1, I' > 0 \tag{7.14}$$

$$\bar{M} = pf_m(Y, i), \quad f_{mY} > 0, \quad f_{mi} < 0 \tag{7.15}$$

$$Y = F(L, \bar{K}) \tag{7.16}$$

$$\hat{w} = \beta_w(L/\bar{L} - 1) + \pi^e, \quad 0 < \beta_w < \infty \tag{7.17}$$

$$\hat{p} = \beta_p(w/(pF_L) - 1), \quad 0 < \beta_p < \infty \tag{7.18}$$

$$\dot{\pi}^e = \beta_\pi(\hat{p} - \pi^e), \quad 0 < \beta_\pi < \infty \tag{7.19}$$

Equations (7.14) and (7.15) assume continuous clearing of the goods and money markets. They constitute the IS-LM part of the model, where the temporary equilibrium is brought about by variations in output Y and the interest rate i. Nothing has to be said on consumption demand $C = C(Y)$ (which here includes government expenditures plus the constant replacement investment) and the demand for real balances $f_m = f_m(Y, i)$. When deciding on investment, firms compare their rate of profit $(pY - wL - \delta\bar{K})/p\bar{K}$ with the alternative real rate of return on bond holding, $i - \pi^e$.[17] On usual Keynesian grounds, the marginal propensity to consume is supposed to fall short of unity.[18] By inverting the production function, the demand for labor is determined by equation (7.16). It is assumed that firms are not rationed in this respect.

At this point we address a peculiarity in the practice of macroeconomic modeling. In this and many other models only one type of expectations is considered, namely, expectations about future inflation. More often than not, these expectations turn out to be crucial for the dynamic behavior. In the present model the influence of inflationary expectations is mainly attributable to their entering in the investment function. But note that in (7.14) the expected rate of inflation is combined with the nominal interest rate and the rate of profit, where the latter two are taken at their current values. If one has the notion that investment expenditures basically depend on one variable, the differential between profit and real interest rates, and if here expectations have an important role to play, would it then not be more consistent to assume that expectations are formed with respect to the *entire* expression $Y - wL/p - \delta\bar{K} - (i - \hat{p})\bar{K}$, and not only with respect to price inflation $\hat{p}$ alone? It is astounding that, to our knowledge, such an elementary conceptual issue is nowhere discussed in the literature. Since an alternative specification of expectations in the investment function is too unfamiliar, we join the habit of focusing on expected inflation and leave the investigation of other concepts for future research.

Equations (7.17)–(7.19) represent the dynamic part, where linear adjustments are fully sufficient for our limited purpose of studying local stability. Equation (7.18) rewrites (7.13) in the previous section, equation (7.17) directly follows Sargent and replaces the Okun gap in (7.12) with the deviations of the employment rate from its normal level. Equation (7.19) finally formulates the conventional adaptive expectations of inflation. This hypothesis is employed both in Tobin 1975 and Sargent 1987, section 5.1. In sum, equations (7.14)–(7.19) can easily be viewed as a modification of the Sargent model: the latter is simplified by removing growth and the capacity effect of net investment, and it is generalized by allowing for a finite speed at which firms seek to adjust product prices to marginal variable costs (going to the limit, $\beta_p \to \infty$, would reestablish the Sargent model).[19]

The dynamic variables of system (7.14)–(7.19) are the real wage rate $\omega := w/p$, the price level p, and expected inflation π^e. They determine the IS-LM equilibria of $Y = Y(\omega, p, \pi^e)$ and $i = i(\omega, p, \pi^e)$. It is a routine exercise to verify the following reaction pattern in the partial derivatives, which can of course be explained by the usual textbook stories,

$$Y_\omega < 0 \qquad Y_p < 0 \qquad Y_\pi > 0$$

$$i_\omega < 0 \qquad i_p > 0 \qquad i_\pi > 0$$

It may also be mentioned that $Y_\pi = |Y_\omega|$. Next, define

$$\phi = \phi(\omega, p, \pi^e) := 1/F_L(L(\omega, p, \pi^e))$$

as the reciprocal of the marginal product of labor when $L = L(\omega, p, \pi^e)$ is the volume of employment associated with the IS-LM output. Clearly, L and ϕ respond in the same way to changes in ω, p and π^e as the production level Y. If we subtract (7.18) from (7.17), the dynamics are then compactly represented by the three differential equations

$$\dot{\omega} = \beta_w \omega[L(\omega, p, \pi^e)/\bar{L} - 1] + \pi^e - \beta_p[\omega\phi(\omega, p, \pi^e) - 1] \tag{7.20}$$

$$\dot{p} = \beta_p p[\omega\phi(\omega, p, \pi^e) - 1] \tag{7.21}$$

$$\dot{\pi}^e = \beta_\pi[\beta_p(\omega\phi(\omega, p, \pi^e) - 1) - \pi^e] \tag{7.22}$$

Under standard assumptions, process (7.20)–(7.22) has a unique stationary point $(\omega^\star, p^\star, \pi^\star)$. It is given by $\pi^\star = 0$, $\omega^\star = F_L(\bar{L}, \bar{K})$, $L^\star = \bar{L}$, $Y^\star = F(\bar{L}, \bar{K})$. The steady-state rate of interest $i^\star$ can subsequently be derived from the IS-equation (7.14) and $p^\star$ from the LM-equation (7.15) (which, however, is only a purely formal procedure).

It was pointed out above that the present system, unlike Tobin's model, allows us to study the dynamics of real wages. To do this in a pure form, put the Mundell effect to rest and suppose that the expected rate of inflation stays at a constant level. If employment is below normal, $L < \bar{L}$, the downward money wage reactions in (7.17) tend to improve profitability in the investment function and to carry the economy back to equilibrium. But goods prices may persistently go down, too. They might even undo the good by falling more rapidly, so that the real wage rate *increases* and the decline in output continues. Such perverse real wage effects are possible if three conditions are satisfied: (1) Money wages are more sticky than prices, that is, the adjustment speed β_w is small relative to β_p. (2) In order for Y to fall in response to an increase in real wages, the Keynes effect on output (the modulus of Y_p) must be weak relative to the direct impact of real wages on output (the modulus of Y_ω). (3) Besides falling at all, output must also fall sufficiently fast. The reason is that p only decreases if the rising real wage rate w/p in equation (7.18) is dominated by the rising marginal product of labor F_L. The precise conditions for this to happen are given in Proposition 7.1.

Proposition 7.1 Consider system (7.20), (7.21) with $\pi^e = 0$ and define $A := -1 + (\omega|Y_\omega| - p|Y_p|)|F_{LL}|/F_L^2$. Then the equilibrium is repelling with respect to this partial process if

$$A > 0 \quad \text{and} \quad \beta_p/\beta_w > |Y_\omega|/A$$

It is locally asymptotically stable if $A \leq 0$ or, in case of $A > 0$, if the second inequality is reversed.

We have thus identified a set of conditions on the system's parameters, though they appear somewhat special, under which fast price adjustments and slow wage adjustments turn out to destabilizing.[20] This is a first difference to the original Tobin model where one would always obtain stability if expectations π^e are frozen at zero (cf. Tobin 1975, 200). With $A \leq 0$, by contrast, unemployment is always associated with a falling real wage rate steering the economy back to equilibrium. In the following, we consider this mechanism to be the normal case. For short, it may be called the (stabilizing) real wage effect.

Returning to the general model ($\beta_\pi > 0$) and examining the Routh-Hurwitz conditions with respect to the Jacobian matrix of process (7.20)–(7.22), we can characterize local stability or instability in several ways. For simplicity, only ceteris paribus variations of one reaction parameter at a time are taken into account.[21]

Proposition 7.2

1. A necessary condition for local asymptotic stability of the stationary state of process (7.20)–(7.22) is the inequality

$$\beta_\pi Y_\pi < p|Y_p| + (\beta_\pi/\beta_w)(|F_{LL}|/F_L)p|Y_p| + (\beta_\pi/\beta_p)\omega|Y_\omega|$$

2. The equilibrium is locally asymptotically stable either if (i) β_p is sufficiently small, or if (ii) the expression A defined in Proposition 7.1 is nonpositive, $\beta_p < B := \omega F_L/(|Y_\omega|\,|F_{LL}|)$ and β_w is sufficiently small, or if (iii) $A \leq 0$ and β_π is sufficiently small.

3. The equilibrium is unstable either if (i) $\beta_p > B$ and β_π is sufficiently large, or if (ii) $\beta_\pi > -AB$ and β_p is sufficiently large, or if (iii) $p|Y_p| + (\beta_\pi/\beta_p)\omega|Y_\omega| < \beta_\pi Y_\pi$ and β_w is sufficiently large.

The necessary condition in part 1 of the proposition is presented as the counterpart of Tobin's critical condition (7.9). It makes clear that in the extended model, the price and wage adjustment speeds β_p and β_w too have a bearing on stability. In particular, the equilibrium may now be locally stable even if inequality (7.9) (adjusted to the IS-LM temporary equilibrium framework) is violated, that is, even if $\beta_\pi Y_\pi > -pY_p$. This corresponds to the fact that the Keynes and Mundell effect are now complemented by a real wage effect.

The feedback loops discussed in the preceding section that are constituted by the Keynes and Mundell effect are both weakened if somewhere in the output-inflation feedback there is a sluggish reaction. Most evidently in the benchmark case where $\beta_p = 0$ and the price levels remains fixed, the Mundell effect dies down as the rate of expected inflation approaches zero in equation (7.19). Practically, we are back in the situation of proposition 7.1, where the Keynes effect plays no role either. The economy converges to its equilibrium position since falling money wages here automatically mean a falling real wage rate, and the real wage effect can fully work out. This elementary argument shows that strong inertia in goods prices are very favorable for stability, which is the first statement of part 2 of proposition 7.2. Hesitant adaptive expectations of inflation, second, have a similar effect to the one they have in the Tobin model. The Keynes effect takes over and stability is ensured, at least if the other possibility of destabilization previously discussed, that is, a positive term A, does not apply.

Third, both the Keynes effect and the Mundell effect lose their strength if the wage adjustments in (7.17) are slow. It may thus appear that the relative strength of the Keynes and Mundell effect are decisive for stability and β_w plays a subordinate role. The mathematical analysis, however, reveals that with $A \leq 0$ and if, in addition, prices exhibit a bounded degree of flexibility, we have an economy where sufficiently sluggish wages are capable of bringing about stability. This property may be contrasted with the adverse effects of sticky wages under the circumstances of proposition 7.1 above.

The significance of the upper bound B on the price adjustment speed β_p in proposition 7.2.2 is more clearly brought out by the first statement in part 3. It says that if $\beta_p > B$, then the Mundell effect becomes the dominant destabilizing feedback loop if adaptive expectations are fast enough. In particular, the equilibrium will be unstable if inflationary expectations are so "rational" as to approximate myopic perfect foresight, $\beta_\pi \to \infty$. Note that there are no perverse real wage movements: if π^e is close to $\hat{p}$ then equation (7.17) implies a falling real wage rate if $L/\bar{L} < 1$. Thus, the expectations dynamics also marginalizes the real wage effect.

An increase in β_p, however, speeds up reactions in both the Keynes and the Mundell feedback loop. Nevertheless, if the adjustment speed of adaptive expectations exceeds a certain lower bound, the reactions in the Mundell loop run faster than in the feedback loop set up by the Keynes effect. Consequently, a higher degree of price flexibility, in the sense that firms seek to close the gap between marginal cost and current prices more rapidly, has a strongly destabilizing effect. The impact of highly flexible wages is similar. The last statement in proposition 7.2.3 asserts that a sufficiently fast wage adjustment speed β_w destabilizes the equilibrium, provided that both of the reaction coefficients β_p and β_π are not too low. The condition $p|Y_p| + (\beta_\pi/\beta_p)\omega|Y_\omega| < \beta_\pi Y_\pi$ could be interpreted as expressing the idea that the real wage effect weighted by β_π/β_p and the Keynes effect are jointly weaker than the Mundell effect.[22]

The mathematical stability analysis can be exploited a bit further to demonstrate a tendency of the economy to exhibit oscillatory motions. Consider, for example, a rising price adjustment speed β_p and let β_p^H denote a benchmark value at which the dynamics changes from being locally convergent to locally divergent. When β_p passes β_p^H, some eigenvalue of the Jacobian J of (7.20)–(7.22) crosses the imaginary axis in the complex plane. Since the proof of proposition 7.1 shows that the determinant of J is always negative, it is not a real eigenvalue but a pair of conjugate complex eigenvalues. This phenomenon is the key condition for a Hopf bifurcation to occur (therefore the superscript H). For a certain range of parameter values of β_p close to β_p^H, this analytical tool allows us to establish the existence of strictly periodic orbits. That is, the loss of stability that we find as firms adjust prices faster to their marginal wage costs is associated with the emergence of persistent but bounded cyclical variations in the variables of system (7.20)–(7.22). A similar reasoning applies if β_π is chosen as a bifurcation parameter.[23]

Before we state the Hopf bifurcation result, proposition 7.3 provides a condition that guarantees the uniqueness of β_p^H, that is, it rules out a "reswitching" of local stability as β_p varies from zero to infinity.

Proposition 7.3 Suppose, with regard to the definition of A and B in propositions 7.1 and 7.2 respectively, that the reaction coefficients β_w and β_π satisfy

$$\beta_w < |F_{LL}|p|Y_p|/\omega|Y_\omega|, \qquad \beta_\pi > -AB$$

that is, money wages are sufficiently sluggish and adaptive expectations are sufficiently fast. Then there exists a benchmark value β_p^H of the price adjustment speed such that the equilibrium of system (7.20)–(7.22) is locally asymptotically stable if $\beta_p < \beta_p^H$, and it is unstable if $\beta_p > \beta_p^H$. Furthermore, there exists a function $\varepsilon \mapsto \beta_p(\varepsilon)$ with the following property:

1. for all sufficiently small $\varepsilon > 0$ there is a nondegenerate periodic orbit generated by system (7.20)–(7.22) with respect to $\beta_p = \beta_p(\varepsilon)$;
2. $\beta_p(\varepsilon) \to \beta_p^H$ and the corresponding periodic orbits collapse to the stationary point of that system as $\varepsilon \to 0$.

It has to be noted, however, that the theorem contains no information as to whether the periodic orbits are repelling or attracting. Mathematical conditions exist to tell which case prevails. Unfortunately, they depend on higher-order nonlinear terms in the Taylor expansion of the right-hand side of (7.20)–(7.22) and are so complicated that they would not be accessible to economic interpretation. The proposition is also essentially local in its nature, and we do not know exactly what happens to the periodic orbits when the deviations of a rising β_p from the bifurcation value β_p^H get larger. So, Proposition 7.3 provides a first step to study the oscillatory tendencies inherent in our economy, but it cannot take the place of a careful inquiry into the global dynamics.[24]

Tobin (1975, 200) has claimed that the case $\beta_\pi = 0$ is always stable, whereas the other extreme, $\beta_\pi = \infty$ (that is, $\pi^e = \hat{p}$), is necessarily unstable. It has already been shown that the first claim need not be true in the present economy. Of more interest, however, is the second conjecture (which cannot be proved within the Tobin model itself since according to (7.10), this supposition would fix actual output at its full employment level). The case of myopic perfect foresight of inflation is the subject of the next section, where an extended model of the Tobin variety will also be considered.

7.6 The Case of Myopic Perfect Foresight

In this section an infinite adjustment speed of inflationary expectations, $\beta_\pi = \infty$, is assumed, which is tantamount to the supposition $\pi^e = \hat{p}$. In the IS-equation (7.14) π^e, therefore, has to be replaced with the actual rate of inflation $\hat{p}$ as it has been given by equation (7.18),

$\hat{p} = \beta_p(w/(pF_L(L, \bar{K})) - 1)$. This means that output, employment, and current inflation are determined simultaneously from the goods market equilibrium condition, whereas in the adaptive expectations (AE) economy the IS-LM volume of employment has been determined independently of $\hat{p}$ (and π^e was historically given). To formalize the clearing of goods and financial markets and the concurrent price formation under perfect foresight (PF) of inflation, let $L = L(Y)$ be the inverse production function, that is, the inverse of the mapping $L \mapsto F(L, \bar{K})$, and define[25]

$$\phi = \phi(Y) := 1/F_L(L(Y), \bar{K})$$

Obviously, $L' = dL/dY > 0$ and $\phi' = d\phi/dY > 0$. With respect to a given price level p and a given real wage rate ω, the temporary equilibrium part is then represented by

$$Y = C(Y) + I[Y - \omega L(Y) - \delta\bar{K} - i\bar{K} + \beta_p(\omega\phi(Y) - 1)\bar{K}] \tag{7.23}$$

$$\bar{M} = pf_m(Y, i) \tag{7.24}$$

It should be pointed out that the Mundell effect can now no longer be considered under the usual ceteris paribus assumption. It is, however, incorporated in the feedback effects that give rise to the impact multiplier Y_p and, in this sense, is combined with the Keynes effect. In fact, the "Mundell term" $\pi^e = \hat{p} = \beta_p(\omega\phi(Y) - 1)$ provides another channel for output Y to enter the investment function. Since inflation is positively related to output, the *overall* marginal propensity to spend out of current income will exceed unity if the price adjustment speed β_p is sufficiently high. Correspondingly, the thus defined IS-curve may have a positive slope and be even steeper than the LM-curve. It is easily verified that this would change the familiar negative sign of Y_p. In such a situation the Mundell effect may be said to dominate the Keynes effect.

The sign of Y_p has an important bearing on the stability of the adjustment process of ω and p. Denoting the temporary equilibrium output by $Y = Y(\omega, p)$, the differential equations read

$$\dot{\omega} = \beta_w\omega[L(Y(\omega, p))/\bar{L} - 1] \tag{7.25}$$

$$\dot{p} = \beta_p p[\omega\phi(Y(\omega, p)) - 1] \tag{7.26}$$

In comparison to the economy with adaptive expectations in equations (7.20)–(7.22), the present dynamic system not only saves the state variable π^e, but the equation for the real wage is also much simpler (owing to $\pi^e = \hat{p}$, we have a real wage Phillips curve in (7.17)). The main results of the IS-LM analysis and the local behavior of (7.25), (7.26) are collected in Proposition 7.4.

Proposition 7.4 Let $\beta_o = B$ be defined as in proposition 7.2.2 and put $\beta_1 := w\bar{L}/p\bar{K}$. Then the following statements hold.

1. If $\beta_p < \beta_o$ the combined Keynes-Mundell effect causes $Y_p < 0$ for the output solution of (7.23), (7.24), while $Y_p > 0$ if $\beta_p > \beta_o$.
2. The equilibrium point of process (7.25), (7.26) is locally asymptotically stable if $\beta_p < \min\{\beta_o, \beta_1\}$, and it is a saddle point if $\beta_p > \beta_o$.
3. Assuming $\beta_1 < \beta_p < \beta_o$, the equilibrium is also locally asymptotically stable if β_w is sufficiently small, and locally repelling if β_w is sufficiently large.
4. If $\beta_1 < \beta_o$ then, with respect to variations of β_p, the system undergoes a Hopf bifurcation at $\beta_p = \beta_1$.

It should be noted that the benchmark value β_1 equals the product of the wage share times the output-capital ratio in equilibrium. The proposition shows that dominance of the Mundell effect over the Keynes effect, as specified by $Y_p > 0$, is sufficient to destabilize the economy, whereas the dominance of the Keynes effect, $Y_p < 0$, definitely favors stability. These phenomena are connected with the price adjustment speed β_p. The myopic PF economy shares with the AE economy the property of a locally asymptotically stable equilibrium, provided that price adjustments are sufficiently sluggish. It is unstable if β_p exceeds the benchmark value $\beta_o = B$ that has already played a crucial role in proposition 7.2. It should also be noted that the decisive condition $Y_p < 0$ amounts to $\partial Y/\partial M > 0$, that is, expansionary monetary policy works as expected. It follows that monetary policy is efficient if the economy is stable—it may not be needed then—and it is counterproductive if instability prevails.

Despite the close analogy to proposition 7.2.2 and 7.2.3 there is, however, a difference when the system switches from stability to instability under variations of β_p. In the AE economy such a structural change always gives rise to a Hopf bifurcation (not only under the conditions of proposition 7.3) and its periodic motions. In the present case, this happens only if $\beta_o > \beta_1$; the bifurcation is of a different type if $\beta_o < \beta_1$.

Contrary to Tobin's view we conclude the important result that even a PF economy can be stable—if price reactions are not so fast that they eliminate a discrepancy between price and marginal wage costs.[26] Compared to proposition 7.2, the role of the wage adjustment speed β_w is somewhat more limited. Sufficiently sluggish wages may still be stabilizing and sufficiently flexible money wages destabilizing, but this requires the expression β_1 to fall short of β_o and β_p to be contained in the interval (β_1, β_o).

Let us return to Tobin's (1975) original formulation and employ a dynamic multiplier, but now within a setting of delayed price adjustments and myopic perfect foresight of inflation.[27] With respect to a finite output adjustment speed $\beta_Y > 0$, the evolution of the economy is described by

$$\dot{Y} = \beta_Y\{C(Y) + I[Y - \omega L(Y) - \delta \bar{K} - i\bar{K} + \beta_p(\omega\phi(Y) - 1)\bar{K}] - Y\} \quad (7.27)$$

$$\dot{\omega} = \beta_w \omega[L(Y)/\bar{L} - 1] \quad (7.28)$$

$$\dot{p} = \beta_p p[\omega\phi(Y) - 1] \quad (7.29)$$

where $i = i(Y, p)$ is the LM-rate of interest determined by (7.24). Proposition 7.5 shows that the previous stability and instability properties of the parameters β_p and β_w are essentially maintained. The new adjustment coefficient β_Y has no bearing on stability if β_p exceeds the same threshold value as in proposition 7.4. By contrast, the stabilizing effect of low price adjustment speeds can be destroyed by sufficiently slow reactions of producers to excess demand or supply. Incidentally, the same is possible in Tobin's (1975) model (cf. the proof of proposition 7.5). Apart from that, system (7.27)–(7.29) again widens the scope for the Hopf bifurcation.

Proposition 7.5 Making reference to β_o and β_1 defined in proposition 7.4, the following statements hold.

1. The equilibrium point of process (7.27)–(7.29) is locally asymptotically stable if β_p is sufficiently small, whereas it is unstable if $\beta_p > \beta_o$.

2. With respect to a given price adjustment speed $\beta_p < \beta_o$, local asymptotic stability prevails if β_w is sufficiently small. Large values of β_w destabilize the equilibrium (at least) if $\beta_1 < \beta_p < \beta_o$.

3. With respect to a given $\beta_p < \min\{\beta_o, \beta_1\}$, the equilibrium is locally asymptotically stable if β_Y is sufficiently large, but it becomes unstable if β_Y is small.

4. Whenever upon variations of β_p the system switches from stability to instability, a Hopf bifurcation occurs.

Lastly, a remark should be added concerning the low adjustment speeds β_Y. If one wants to pinpoint a focal reason for economic instability in the efforts of firms to smooth production, as expressed by low values of β_Y, then goods market equilibrium must be taken more seriously. If rationing schemes are neglected as being of minor significance at the macro level, inventories and their feedback effects on the rest of the system have to be introduced. Since Metzler's discussion of inventory cycles it is known that then, the interplay between gross demand, output, and desired and actual inventory investment may generate new destabilizing forces.[28]

7.7 Conclusion

Starting out from what turned out to be closely related macrodynamic models of Tobin (1975) and Sargent (1987, chap. 5), several variants of these two prototype economies have been considered. Our central modification concerned the formation of goods prices. The assumption that they instantaneously adjust to the marginal wage costs was dropped and replaced with the behavioral rule that in each market period firms seek to only partially close the gap between actual prices and marginal costs. The most notable versions are summarized in table 7.2, where the differences between the models are expressed in terms of the adjustment speeds β_x, $x = w, p, \pi, Y$. Finite coefficients are indicated by the symbol itself, while the prevalence of an equilibrium condition is designated by the infinity sign. $\beta_p = \infty$ means that prices are continuously equal to marginal costs, $\beta_\pi = \infty$ signifies myopic perfect foresight of inflation ($\pi^e = \hat{p}$), and $\beta_Y = \infty$ stands for IS-equilibrium. β_w refers to the wage Phillips curve.[29] Model 1 was treated as our basic case in section 7.5, Models 2 and 3 were presented in section 7.6. Analysis of the variant where all four adjustment speeds are of finite order was bypassed here because of its higher complexity, although we expressed our belief that it would not add anything essentially new to the other stability findings (cf. n. 27).

Our primary finding is that the "imperfections" of price adjustments have a significant stabilizing potential, at least as far as the local stability of the equilibrium position is concerned. A sufficient degree of price stickiness in models 1, 2, and 3 can always achieve local asymptotic stability. The basic reason for these results is that the stabilizing Keynes effect, usually in conjunction with the real wage effect, keeps the destabilizing Mundell effect down. Wage adjustments, by contrast, are less forceful: they may have the same property over a limited range of the

Table 7.2
Variants of Tobin-Sargent models

	Tobin	Sargent	Model 1	Model 2	Model 3	Model 4
$\dot{Y}$	β_Y	∞	∞	∞	β_Y	β_Y
$\hat{w}$	β_w	β_w	β_w	β_w	β_w	β_w
$\hat{p}$	∞	∞	β_p	β_p	β_p	β_p
$\dot{\pi}$	β_π	β_π	β_π	∞	∞	β_π

price adjustment speed, but not generally so. Destabilization, however, can be brought about by highly flexible prices and fast adjustments of expected inflation toward the current rate of inflation. Above certain threshold values of the reaction coefficients, either feature is sufficient to make the Mundell effect dominate over the Keynes effect. Again, money wages share this property only over a limited set of parameters. These characteristics also provide a better understanding of the above-mentioned destabilization tendencies found in the models by Tobin and Sargent, with their infinitely fast price adjustments.

The fact that the modifications across all three model variants leave the results regarding the price adjustment speed basically unaffected leads us to expect that our characterization of the impact of price flexibility on dynamic stability may prove to be fairly robust under further modifications and generalizations of the present modeling framework. At the least, this aspect of the macroeconomic consequences of the price-setting behavior of firms should not be neglected when discussing the likely effects of high or low price flexibility.

7.8 Appendix: Mathematical Proofs

Proof of Proposition 7.1 Assuming for notational simplicity that the levels $\bar{L}$ and $\bar{K}$ are normalized at unity, the Jacobian of the full process (7.20)–(7.22) with $\beta_\pi > 0$, evaluated at the equilibrium point, is given by

$$\begin{bmatrix} \omega[\beta_w L_\omega - \beta_p(\phi + \omega\phi_\omega)] & \omega(\beta_w L_p - \beta_p \omega \phi_p) & \omega(1 + \beta_w L_\pi - \beta_p \omega \phi_\pi) \\ \beta_p p(\phi + \omega\phi_\omega) & \beta_p p \omega \phi_p & \beta_p p \omega \phi_\pi \\ \beta_\pi \beta_p(\phi + \omega\phi_\omega) & \beta_\pi \beta_p \omega \phi_p & \beta_\pi(\beta_p \omega \phi_\pi - 1) \end{bmatrix}$$

In the calculations to follow here and in the proof of the next propositions, repeated use is made of the relationships $L_x = Y_x/F_L = Y_x/\omega$ and $\phi_x = \gamma Y_x/\omega$, where $\gamma := |F_{LL}|/F_L^2$ and $x = \omega, p, \pi$. One furthermore has

$Y_\pi = -Y_\omega = |Y_\omega|$. For later use in the proof of Proposition 7.4 we also note that $|Y_\omega| = |f_{mi}|I'/[I' f_{mY} + |f_{mi}|(1 - C')]$.

Under the circumstances of proposition 7.1, the upper-left 2×2 submatrix of J has to be considered. Denote it by $\tilde{J}$. Then det $\tilde{J} = \beta_w \beta_p p|L_p| > 0$, while the trace of $\tilde{J}$ can be reformulated as trace$\tilde{J} = -\beta_w|Y_\omega| + \beta_p A$. The equilibrium is locally asymptotically stable (repelling) if this expression is negative (positive).

q.e.d.

Proof of Proposition 7.2 Computing the Routh-Hurwitz terms of the Jacobian J established in the previous proof yields

$$\begin{aligned} a_1 &= -\text{ trace } J \\ &= \beta_w \omega |L_\omega| + \beta_p \omega(\phi - \omega|\phi_\omega| + p|\phi_p|) + \beta_\pi(1 - \beta_p \omega \phi_\pi) \\ &= \beta_w |Y_\omega| - \beta_p A + \beta_\pi(1 - \beta_p \omega \phi_\pi) \end{aligned}$$

$$a_2 = J_1 + J_2 + J_3 = \beta_\pi \beta_p p \omega |\phi_p| + \beta_w \beta_\pi \omega(|L_\omega| - \beta_p \phi L_\pi) + \beta_w \beta_p p |L_p|$$

$$a_3 = -\text{ det } J = \beta_\pi \beta_p \beta_w p |L_p|$$

$$b \; = a_1 a_2 - a_3$$

(to calculate the determinant, factorize ω, p, β_π and then subtract the second row from the third). The necessary and sufficient conditions for all eigenvalues of J to have negative real parts are

$$a_1 > 0, \qquad a_2 > 0, \qquad a_3 > 0, \qquad b > 0$$

The condition in part 1 of the proposition follows from multiplying the condition $a_2 > 0$ by $F_L/\beta_w\beta_p$ and rearranging the resulting terms appropriately.

Turning to part 2, a_1 and a_2 are positive and bounded away from zero for β_p sufficiently small. Term a_3 is always positive and tends to zero a $\beta_p \to 0$. Thus, the Routh-Hurwitz conditions are satisfied if β_p is small enough. Next, note that $1 - \beta_p \omega \phi_\pi > 0$ is equivalent to $\beta_p < 1/(\omega \phi_\pi) = \omega F_L/(|Y_\omega|\,|F_{LL}|) = B$. It follows that a_1 is positive and bounded away from zero for all $\beta_w > 0$ if $A \leq 0$ and $\beta_p < B$. Since a_2 has the same property and $a_3 \to 0$ as $\beta_w \to 0$, the Routh-Hurwitz conditions are fulfilled if β_w is small enough. The argument that they are also fulfilled if $A \leq 0$ and β_π is sufficiently small, is very similar. As regards part 3, consider the definition of B and conclude that, with $\beta_p > B$, the last term in a_1 tends to $-\infty$ as $\beta_\pi \to \infty$, so that $a_1 < 0$ eventually. Factorizing β_p in a_1, we easily check that the same holds true if $\beta_p \to \infty$, provided that $-A - \beta_\pi \omega \phi_\pi < 0$. But the latter inequality is equivalent to $\beta_\pi > -AB$. To show that large values of β_w may be destabilizing too, rewrite $a_2 = \beta_\pi \beta_p p\omega|\phi_p| + \beta_w[\beta_p p|L_p| + \beta_\pi \omega|L_\omega| - \beta_p \beta_\pi L_\pi]$ and note that the last condition in the proposition, $p|Y_p|/\beta_\pi + \omega|Y_\omega|/\beta_p < Y_\pi$, is equivalent to a negative square bracket. This completes the proof.

q.e.d.

Proof of Proposition 7.3 Using the relationships for L_x and ϕ_x that were pointed out above, we easily verify that the first condition implies $\beta_p \beta_\pi [p\omega|\phi_p| - \beta_w \omega \phi L_\pi] > 0$ in a_2, and the second $\beta_p[-A - \beta_\pi \omega \phi_\pi] < 0$ in a_1. Hence, a_2 is linearly increasing, and a_1 linearly decreasing in β_p (actually, the condition on β_w is stronger than necessary to obtain this result). Moreover, a_3 is linearly increasing in β_p, so that b is a quadratic function of this parameter. Since the quadratic term has a negative coefficient, and it has already been established that $b > 0$ when $\beta_p = 0$, the function $b = b(\beta_p)$ has exactly one positive root β_p^H. The value of $a_3 > 0$ implies that the product $a_1 a_2$ is positive at this point. Term a_2 must here be positive too, since we know that a_1 is positive for all $\beta_p > 0$. From this we can conclude that all Routh-Hurwitz terms a_1, a_2, a_3, b are positive if $0 < \beta_p < \beta_p^H$, which completes the proof of the first part of the proposition.

As concerns the Hopf bifurcation, it has already been observed in the text that the Jacobian has two purely imaginary eigenvalues at β_p^H. The other conditions for the dynamics to undergo a Hopf bifurcation with respect to variations of β_p are: (a) the equilibrium is independent of β_p; (b) the functions on the RHS of (7.20)–(7.22) are continuously differentiable; (c) the Jacobian is continuous; (d) for all β_p near but not equal to β_p^H, no eigenvalue has zero real part (cf. Theorem A in Alexander and Yorke 1978, 263–66). Conditions (a)–(c) are obvious, whereas (d) follows from Orlando's formula for the eigenvalues λ_i (see Gantmacher 1959, 233), which here reads $b = (\lambda_1 + \lambda_2)(\lambda_2 + \lambda_3)(\lambda_1 + \lambda_3)$, and the fact that β_p^H is a (locally) unique root of $b = b(\beta_p)$.

q.e.d.

Proof of Proposition 7.4 The comparative-static exercise for (7.23), (7.24) yields $Y_\omega = |f_{mi}|I'(\beta_p/\omega - 1)/\Omega$ and $Y_p = -I'\bar{M}/p^2\Omega$, where $\Omega := |f_{mi}|(1 - C' - \beta_p I'|F_{LL}|/F_L^2) + f_{mY} I'$. Utilizing the explicit formula for Y_ω in the adaptive expectations economy given in the proof of Proposition 7.1, and recalling the definition of $B = \omega F_L/(|Y_\omega|\,|F_{LL}|)$, we see that the statements $\Omega < 0$, $Y_p > 0$, and $\beta_p > B = \beta_o$ are equivalent. This proves part 1.

To study the stability of system (7.25), (7.26) consider the Jacobian

$$J = \begin{bmatrix} \beta_w \omega L' Y_\omega & \beta_w \omega L' Y_p \\ \beta_p p(\phi + \omega \phi' Y_\omega) & \beta_p p \omega \phi' Y_p \end{bmatrix}$$

The determinant is given by $\det J = -\beta_w \beta_p p \phi Y_p$. Thus, $\det J < 0$ if $\beta_p > \beta_o$, which implies saddle point instability, and $\det J > 0$ if $\beta_p < \beta_o$. Turning to the trace of J in the latter case $\beta_p < \beta_o$, we observe that $Y_\omega < 0$ and so trace $J < 0$ if $\beta_p < \omega = w\bar{L}/p\bar{K} = \beta_1$. With $\beta_1 < \beta_p < \beta_o$, in contrast, we have $Y_\omega > 0$. It follows that the trace is negative (positive) if β_w is small (large) enough (while $\det J$ is still positive). The technical details of establishing the Hopf bifurcation in part 4 are analogous to those in Proposition 7.3 (they are actually simpler).

q.e.d.

Proof of Proposition 7.5 The Jacobian of the dynamics (7.27)–(7.29) is given by

$$J = \begin{bmatrix} -\beta_Y(1 - C' + i_Y I' - \beta_p \omega \phi' I') & -\beta_Y i_p I' & \beta_Y I'(\beta_p/\omega - 1) \\ \beta_p p \omega \phi' & 0 & \beta_p p \phi \\ \beta_w \omega L' & 0 & 0 \end{bmatrix}$$

We note in passing that the matrix has the same structure as the Jacobian obtained in the original Tobin model (Tobin 1975, 199, equation (3.3.)). Taking account of the LM-derivative $i_Y = f_{mY}/|f_{mi}|$, we see the Routh-Hurwitz terms are:

$$a_1 = \beta_Y(1 - C' - \beta_p I'|F_{LL}|/F_L^2 + f_{mY} I'/|f_{mi}|) = \beta_Y \tilde{a}_1$$

$$a_2 = \beta_Y I'(-\beta_w(\beta_p/\omega - 1) + \beta_p p \omega \phi' i_p) = \beta_Y \tilde{a}_2$$

$$a_3 = \beta_Y \beta_w \beta_p p i_p L' I' = \beta_Y \beta_w \beta_p \tilde{a}_3$$

$$b = \beta_Y(\beta_Y \tilde{a}_1 \tilde{a}_2 - \beta_w \beta_p \tilde{a}_3)$$

On the basis of the computations in the proof of proposition 7.4 the following conclusions can now be drawn. Whereas a_3 is always positive (by virtue of $i_p > 0$), a_1 is negative (positive) if $\beta_p > \beta_0$ ($\beta_p < \beta_o$). Since $\beta_p/\omega - 1$ is positive (negative) if $\beta_p > \beta_1$ ($\beta_p < \beta_1$), a_2 is negative if $\beta_p > \beta_1$ and β_w is sufficiently large. These observations prove the instability statements with respect to variations of β_p and β_w.

Suppose next that $\tilde{a}_1 > 0$ as well as $\tilde{a}_2 > 0$ (which, in particular, is ensured by $\beta_p < \beta_o$, $\beta_p < \beta_1$). Then $b > 0$ if β_p tends to zero ($\tilde{a}_1$ and $\tilde{a}_2$ are bounded away from zero then) or if β_Y is sufficiently large. On the other hand, b turns negative if β_Y gets small. Finally, the Routh-Hurwitz conditions are also satisfied if $\beta_p < \beta_o$ and β_w is so small that $\tilde{a}_2 > 0$ and, subsequently, $b > 0$.

The proof of part 4 is practically the same as that for proposition 7.3.

q.e.d.

III

AD-AS and IS-LM Models of Monetary Growth

The investigation of wage-price dynamics and price expectations dynamics is continued in this part of the book. We concentrate here on inflation and expectations examining how they can be, and how they have been, introduced and treated in monetary Keynesian-type growth models.

Expectations dynamics in macromodels with forward-looking agents were studied widely in the 1970s, and microeconomic foundations for small macro models with optimizing representative agents and efficient markets have been discussed extensively in the economic literature in this context. On the basis of those partial models, inferences were then made with respect to the effectiveness of monetary policy. What we want to address, however, is the problem of how price and expectations dynamics can be formulated consistently in full-fledged Keynesian macrodynamic growth models, where labor, product, and money markets dynamically interact and not all of them are continuously clearing. Our perspective is that these models are capable of producing *endogenous* cyclical behavior, whereas in much modern business cycle theory the fluctuations are generated by suitable exogenous random shocks. Certainly, this alternative Keynesian paradigm may also have a bearing on the effectiveness of monetary policy. This issue may be pursued later, after our models and their typical behavior have been sufficiently studied.

The model variants we discuss in the following sections are based on the Tobinian model from the previous chapter. We begin with an AD–AS growth version of the economy and employ it to study how the interactions among the above mentioned three major markets are affected by (1) adaptive expectations of price inflation, (2) myopic perfect foresight, and (3) multiperiod-ahead forecast on the basis of regression equations. We also indicate that in past treatments of similar economies errors have been made that gave rise to serious inconsistencies. More specifically, we point out an incomplete analysis of the dynamic properties of such models, various inconsistencies concerning their continuous-time and discrete-time formulations, and an illegitimate separation of the nominal from the real side.

After identifying these problems, we propose to resolve them by formulating an IS-LM growth dynamic, by which (in comparison to the AD–AS version) we mean that goods prices are not perfectly flexible but adjust with some delay, such that firms are not always on their supply curve. Persistent macroeconomic fluctuations of business cycle frequency can then be demonstrated to emerge even in such standard

Keynesian growth models under adaptive expectations as well as under myopic perfect foresight. Making use of computer simulations, we can additionally integrate some recently discussed learning algorithms into this model type. One might argue that the presented model versions are not microfounded and are not built on first principles of intertemporal optimization (which, however, would pose serious problems once agents realize that they have only limited forecast abilities). However, our consistent formulations of fully specified IS-LM growth models, with various procedures to form expectations, have their own merits by permitting new and fruitful insights into important macroeconomic feedback mechanisms.

In the next chapter, we evaluate the continuous-time and discrete-time versions of a textbook model by Sargent (1987) under the assumption of myopic perfect foresight, where competitive pricing and the marginal productivity theory still prevail. We reveal that this variant of a "Keynesian dynamics" creates more problems than it helps to solve. Subsequently, those standard assumptions are relaxed, and a markup pricing rule based on normal cost, together with a more elaborate money wage determination, are introduced.

By employing an extended Phillips curve, we show in this context that inside-the-firm employment, measured by the deviation of work hours from normal work hours, and outside the firm employment, measured by the deviation of the rate of employment from its natural level, interact in the formation of money wages and give rise to an adjustment pattern where Keynesian aggregate demand is transmitted into wage and employment changes with only a time delay. In this version—owing to the modified pricing rule—it also turns out that the real wage moves proyclically, a phenomenon in line with, or at least not in contradiction to, empirical stylized facts.

Usually, macroeconomic textbooks first introduce the simple adaptive expectations mechanism and then "improve" on the theory by addressing the case of perfect foresight—often simultaneously modifying other building blocks of the model, such as the degree of wage flexibility (see, e.g., Sargent 1987). We intentionally reverse this order and begin in chapter 8 with the perfect foresight version, arguing that this represents an inconsistent model in an AD-AS growth context but not in an IS-LM growth context with gradual price and wage adjustments, where myopic perfect foresight does not give rise to significant differences when compared with a fast adaptive expectations mechanism.

8 Keynesian Growth Dynamics, Perfect Foresight, and Viability

8.1 Introduction

Perfect foresight versions of macrodynamic models have become popular since the 1970s, through the writings of Lucas (1972), Sargent and Wallace (1973, 1975), and many others. Their original criticism was aimed at Keynesian AD-AS economics[1] where economic agents do not appear to optimize or to make efficient use of information available to them. Though the first applications of perfect foresight models (see Sargent 1987, chap. 5 and its references) were undertaken with respect to the Phillips curve, as a Keynesian macroeconomic building block to determine the interaction between unemployment and price dynamics, perfect foresight models were soon applied to other markets, such as product or financial markets. The application of perfect foresight models to the labor market did, however, seem to have particularly devastating consequences for stabilization policy. As in long-run adaptive expectation models, in the context of perfect foresight models money neutrality appeared to deprive monetary policy of all its expansionary effects, even in the short run. In extreme versions of perfect foresight models such as those proposed in Sargent and Wallace 1973 and Sargent 1987, chapter 5 this holds true regardless of whether monetary shocks are anticipated or unanticipated. As we demonstrate below, it turns out that short-run neutrality of monetary surprise shocks result from the model's strong dichotomy: The nominal side of the model is completely separated from the real side under perfect foresight. Through infinitely fast price and wage jumps monetary shocks will thus have nominal but no real effects.

In contrast, the monetarist position was that monetary policy matters. In the monetarist view monetary surprise shocks have real effects because monetary policy in its perception initiates price as well as quantity adjustments. In addition, in Lucas's (1972) imperfect information model, agents have only local knowledge of the price change, resulting from a change in money supply. The model thus entails effects on real variables when monetary surprise shocks occur. Most of the ensuing positions more or less pursued the perspective that unanticipated monetary policy is effective in inducing output and employment fluctuations. If no "market institutions" (Stiglitz 1990) can be conceived of to allow for such price jumps[2] and if the empirical evidence speaks overwhelmingly for slow price adjustments—compared to quantity adjustments—then the Sargent-Wallace version of perfect foresight will not be convincing.

Subsequently, the assumption that prices are set one period in advance so that an imbalance in the product market cannot be removed by a price adjustment became the core empirical proposition in theoretical models justifying real effects of monetary surprise shocks. Later papers by Lucas (see, e.g., Lucas 1989 and also Woodford 1990a) correctly claim that if prices are changed slowly as, for example, when buyers appear sequentially on the market and producers sequentially change their capacity too, then monetary surprise shocks do indeed matter. Unanticipated monetary shocks have also real effects in the context of recent variants of the "real business cycle theory" where unanticipated monetary events are typically predicted to induce fluctuations in output, investment, and employment.[3] This effect happens even more emphatically if prices and wages are sticky (cf. Blanchard and Fischer 1989, chap. 8), a position demonstrated and strongly defended by the new Keynesians.[4] Thus, in recent times, the majority in the economic profession has accepted the view that monetary surprise shocks do affect real variables. In addition, as shown in models where prices and wages are set a period in advance, systematic monetary policy, that is, anticipated monetary policy, matters (see Fischer 1977; Phelps and Taylor 1977; and recently Woodford 1996).

Despite these developments, the Sargent-Wallace propositions on the effects of monetary policy are nevertheless important and should be further investigated. Such efforts are in particular important since they reveal that there are major unresolved problems in AD-AS growth models concerning the treatment of monetary shocks and price and wage reactions in such integrated growth models to which solutions still must be found.[5] In contrast to these various aspects of the debate among Keynesians, monetarists, and new classical economists, the subsequent analysis will focus on the dynamic analysis of a complete Keynesian AD-AS monetary growth model (Sargent 1987, chap. 5). As for inflationary expectations, the effects of sudden (un)anticipated changes in the money supply, via open-market operations, are analyzed for the case of perfect foresight. From this case Sargent derives the following results: There is strict neutrality of money if the change in monetary policy is not foreseen, and there are price reactions, which precede action, when it is foreseen and which guarantee strict neutrality of money at the time where the shock in the money supply actually occurs.

Our main object in the following pages[6] is to demonstrate that there is no room for such neutrality propositions under perfect foresight in a truly complete and consistent Keynesian monetary growth model. These propositions are only obtained when the AD-AS growth model is modified to establish the classical version of the neoclassical synthesis, by assuming that money wages as well as the price level are perfectly flexible. The route that allows the price level, in line with money wages, to adjust only with finite speed—which is also a modifying assumption with respect to the conventional AD-AS monetary growth model—reestablishes the Keynesian (demand-constrained) nature of the model. We thereby show that the real choice is between infinitely fast price adjustments in contrast to only finitely fast price reactions on the goods and factor markets of the economy when specifying complete models of monetary growth (of the classical or the Keynesian type), whereas the mixed situations of AD-AS type—as the one we begin with in the next section—must be considered inconsistent.[7] The details for such a conclusion are presented in the next two sections. The following sections introduce an IS-LM growth modification of this AD-AS growth model with gradual wage and price adjustments that is internally consistent and that leads to similar cyclical growth patterns under perfect foresight as well as adaptive expectations.

8.2 RE Propositions in Fully Specified AD-AS Growth Models: A Reconsideration

In the following sections, we shall investigate the perfect foresight variant of a conventional Keynesian AD-AS monetary growth model. We demonstrate that its properties are neither well understood nor simple to analyze. The model is founded on standard assumptions of Keynesian economics and on a Wicksellian investment function as far as the formulation of its temporary equilibrium subsystem is concerned. These temporary equilibrium positions are then used as a basis for the model's laws of motion. In this way, a simple but complete picture of a monetary economy is constructed and then employed for a study of economic evolution.

The forces responsible for evolution in such a context are given by

- a standard money wage Phillips curve based on labor market conditions and the expected rate of inflation,
- alternative assumptions concerning inflationary expectations, and
- the usual macroeconomic formulation of the process of capital accumulation $\dot{K} = I$, and of labor force growth $\dot{L}^s = nL^s$.

Sargent (1987, chap. 5) makes use of such an AD-AS growth model to formalize "the relationships among the various hypotheses advanced in Milton Friedman's AEA presidential address (1968)." In particular he claims that this model will

- give rise to Keynesian short- and medium-run features if expectations are formed adaptively, but
- give rise to neoclassical neutrality assertions in the long run, often with stagflationary effects in between, *and*
- imply classical neutrality even in the short run if short-run expectations are rational (i.e., here, of the myopic perfect foresight type).

Therefore, despite the choice of a seemingly conventional model of Keynesian dynamics with sluggish wage adjustment, he suggests that such a model must give rise to mainly classical conclusions in the end. Figures 8.1a,b serve to provide a preliminary illustration and explanation of these assertions:

Figure 8.1a, the case of adaptive expectations, shows that a sudden increase in the money supply will have both expansionary and inflationary short-run effects that give rise to a cyclical movement in the medium run. In the long run, the original steady-state position is again approached, that is, the initial monetary shock will eventually become purely nominal. By contrast, figure 8.1b, which illustrates the case of myopic perfect foresight, shows that a monetary shock will have no real consequences even from the start: the Solowian steady-state val-

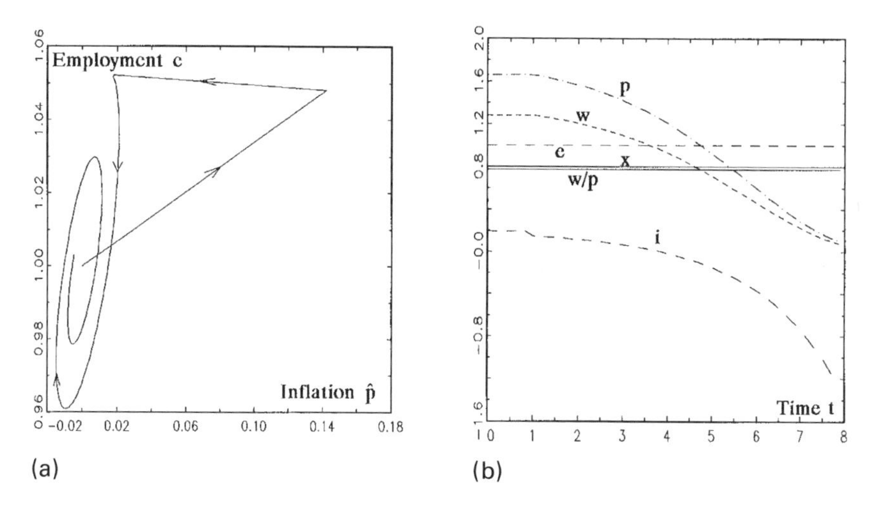

Figure 8.1
The effects of a monetary shock for(a) adaptively formed expectations and (b) for myopic perfect foresight

ues remain fixed under open market operations in such a regime of myopic perfect foresight. Instead, there will be a purely nominal deflationary spiral, including a falling nominal rate of interest. In view of such a peculiar situation, where wages and prices are assumed to be historically given or predetermined when the open market operation occurs, Sargent (1987, chaps. 1 and 5) then argues that economic agents will be aware of this special type of a nominal instability of the steady state. They will then choose an immediate adjustment of the nominal magnitudes by means of a model-consistent forward-looking price formation rule that will keep them on the steady state in all respects under the present circumstances, that is, prices and wages will jump in line with the money supply shock, producing thereby short-run neutrality of monetary shocks.

In the next chapter we will show that the assertion on the case of adaptive expectations is not correct in general, since it will allow for explosive cycles for a variety of parameter constellations. Mechanisms that keep the resulting dynamics within economically reasonable bounds must therefore be added to the model in order to make it truly a complete model of monetary growth. However, the resulting complete model of a business cycle no longer implies classical neutrality as claimed. Instead, this revised model will generate *persistent employment cycles* with the money supply acting only on average as an inflation ceiling.

In the present chapter we shall critically examine the other assertion of Sargent (1987, chap. 5): the strict neutrality of money in the short run under myopic perfect foresight. We will do this in section 8.3 by first pointing out a number of weaknesses in his approach. These weaknesses imply that the model must be modified to give it a structure that is not sensitive to minor changes in the specification of its time structure. In section 8.4 we shall propose an IS-LM modification of Sargent's model by which its problematic features can be overcome. There we will also show that myopic perfect foresight will give rise to cyclical behavior. Myopic perfect foresight, therefore, no longer represents an assumption with totally new implications, in contrast to Sargent's (1987, chap. 5) treatment of it. Yet, similar to the case of adaptive expectations, the modified model will not yet be viable in general. It, too, must be completed by adding forces to it that keep its dynamics within economically reasonable bounds. Such "viability considerations" will be introduced in section 8.5.

The conclusion of the chapter is that assuming myopic perfect foresight in consistently specified IS-LM growth models represents a convenient assumption that allows to reduce by one the order of the considered dynamics. This is obtained by eliminating the biased error terms from its adaptive expectations variant. Assuming myopic perfect foresight thus does not change the dynamics of a well-formulated Keynesian IS-LM monetary growth model in the radical fashion, as it is asserted by Sargent. Instead, the results of the perfect foresight assumption will mirror the behavior of the adaptive expectations case with its typical cyclical features; this mirroring increases, the faster the adaptive expectations mechanism becomes. Modifying Sargent's problematic AD-AS model of monetary growth in this way will eventually lead us to a monetary model of the growth cycle for a considerable range of its parameter values. A by-product of this result is that the conventional AD-AS growth models do not represent consistent *Keynesian* models of monetary growth despite their use of seemingly standard tools of Keynesian macroeconomics.[8]

We start from the continuous-time model of Keynesian AD-AS growth dynamics of Sargent (1987, chap. 5). This model is given by the following set of equations:

$$Y = F(K, L) \tag{8.1}$$

$$w/p = F_L(K, L) \tag{8.2}$$

$$C = c_h(Y - T^n - \delta K), \qquad 0 < c_h, \delta < 1 \tag{8.3}$$

$$I/K = i_f((F_K(K, L) - \delta) - (i - \pi^e)) + n, \qquad i_f > 0 \tag{8.4}$$

$$Y = C + I + \delta K + G \tag{8.5}$$

$$M = pYf_m(i), \qquad f_m^{'}(i) < 0 \tag{8.6}$$

$$\hat{M} = g_m = \text{ const} \tag{8.7}$$

$$\hat{w} = \beta_w(L/L^s) + \pi^e, \qquad \beta_w(1) = 0, \; \beta_w^{'} > 0 \tag{8.8}$$

$$\dot{\pi}^e = \beta_{\pi^e}(\hat{p} - \pi^e), \qquad 0 < \beta_{\pi^e} \leq \infty \tag{8.9}$$

$$\hat{L}^s = n = \text{ const} \tag{8.10}$$

$$\hat{K} = i_f((F_K(K, L) - \delta) - (i - \pi^e)) + n \tag{8.11}$$

The symbols of this model and most of the assumptions underlying it have been introduced before.[9] The model exhibits a neoclassical production function (8.1); the "marginal productivity theory of employment" (8.2); a simple consumption function (8.3); a particular form of investment behavior (8.4); and the textbook form of the liquidity preference function (8.6). Goods market equilibrium is given by (8.5) and money market equilibrium by (8.6). A money wage Phillips curve (8.8); the adjustment mechanism (8.9) for expected inflation; and the equations for factor growth (8.10),(8.11), together with the growth rate of the money stock (8.7) finally constitute the dynamic part of this growth model. We remark that the "limit case" of myopic perfect foresight of this model—which will be our focus of interest in the following—is represented above by $\beta_{\pi^e} = \infty$, which is to be viewed to give rise to: $\pi^e = \hat{p}_+$; that is, short-run inflationary expectations are then always equal to the right-hand logarithmic derivative of the price level p. The endogenous variables of the model are: output and income Y, the capital stock K, employment L, labor supply L^s, the nominal wage w, the price level p, consumption C, investment I, the nominal rate of interest i, the expected rate of inflation π^e, taxes net of interest T^n, government expenditure G, and money supply M. Following Sargent, we shall assume for the variables T^n and G that their per capital values, θ, γ, stay constant over time.

There is one remark necessary with respect to a subdivision of the endogenous variables into static and dynamic ones. Dynamically endogenous variables are those whose time derivative, but not the variable itself, is considered as endogenous, that is, instantaneously determined at each point in time. It is consequently assumed in the above model that the change in money wages is determined at each moment t (by the rate of employment $e = L/L^s$), while the money wage itself is considered as given or predetermined for each t. It is important to note that the price level p is considered as a statically endogenous variable, in sharp contrast to the treatment of the wage level w just considered.

To allow for the existence of steady states Sargent (1987) assumes—as shown above—that the functions F, C, I, M^d exhibit appropriate homogeneity properties. Dividing by K (or pK) and using for the resulting ratios lower case letters in the place of capital ones, we obtain the following intensive form of this AD-AS growth model:

$$x = f(l) \tag{8.12}$$

$$w/p = f'(l) \tag{8.13}$$

$$c = c_h(y - \theta - \delta) \tag{8.14}$$

$$g_k = i_f(f(l) - \omega l - \delta - (i - \pi^e)) + n \tag{8.15}$$

$$x = c + g_k + \delta + \gamma \tag{8.16}$$

$$m = x f_m(i) \tag{8.17}$$

$$\hat{m} = g_m - g_k - \hat{p} \tag{8.18}$$

$$\hat{w} = \beta_w(l/l^s) + \pi^e \tag{8.19}$$

$$\dot{\pi}^e = \beta_{\pi^e}(\hat{p} - \pi^e) \tag{8.20}$$

$$\hat{l}^s = n - g_k \tag{8.21}$$

Given initial conditions $w(t_0), \pi^e(t_0), K(t_0)$, the above model will generate, under suitable assumptions, time paths for the dynamically endogenous variables w, π^e, K, since the statically endogenous variables x, l, p, i can all be expressed as functions of these dynamic variables by means of the implicit function theorem. Assuming, in addition, $\hat{M} = g_m = n = \hat{L}^s$ and choosing appropriate initial conditions allows in particular for a full-employment steady-state evolution with

$$\hat{w} = \pi^e = \hat{p} = 0, \qquad \hat{K} = \hat{L} = \hat{Y} = n$$

With regard to such reference paths Sargent (1987, 122ff) describes in mainly verbal terms possible effects when such a steady state is disturbed at some moment $t > t_0$ by a once-and-for-all jump in money supply M [engineered via an open-market operation that leaves $\hat{M}$ unaltered]. He then claims for the case of adaptive expectations formation that "though this model is clearly Keynesian in its momentary or point-in-time behavior, its steady state or long-run properties are 'classical' in the sense that real variables are unaffected by the money supply." No formal proof of this assertion is, however, given in Sargent's text, but only verbal and graphical arguments that seem to suggest this result as well as the possibility of a damped cyclical movement back to the steady state are presented. As argued above, this assertion is in general not true (see chapter 9).

For the "limit case" of an infinitely fast adjustment of expectations, that is, for myopic perfect foresight, Sargent (1987, 125ff.) furthermore obtains the following two results that drastically differ from the situation he claims to hold for finite adjustment speeds, that is, for adaptive expectations:

1. *Short-run neutrality* An unexpected jump in the money supply M (that leaves $\hat{M}_+$ unchanged) implies an instantaneous jump in prices p and wages w *and* leaves all other variables unaffected.

2. *Hyper-anticipation* A jump in M of the above type which is expected at time t to occur at time $t + \Delta t$, $\Delta t > 0$ is already reflected in all values of the price level $p(s)$, $s \geq t$, such that neutrality prevails from $t + \Delta t$ onwards.

There are two features accompanying these assertions for which Sargent—and the literature in general—offer no good economic explanation or full justification, at least in the context of an integrated AD-AS Keynesian monetary growth model. These features are:

1. the variable w, which was *assumed* to be statically exogenous in the case $\beta_{\pi^e} < \infty$, is now able to perform jumps, that is, has become a statically endogenous variable now;

2. the methodology of the adaptive expectations case of solving a macrodynamic system by means of historically given initial conditions now gives way to a solution procedure that in general assumes knowledge of the whole future growth path of the above nonlinear growth model.

We shall see in section 8.3 of this chapter that Sargent's mathematical manipulations of the above AD-AS growth model by which he determines its dynamics in the case of myopic perfect foresight are far from being compelling. In contrast to Sargent's procedure, which extends the above type of myopic perfect foresight to (hyper-)perfect foresight over an infinite horizon in order to allow for an asymptotically stable reaction to a shock in the money supply, we shall show in section 8.4 (under appropriate assumptions) that the case of myopic perfect foresight can be solved in a Keynesian environment in the conventional way by means of historically given values such that no significant difference to the case of adaptive expectations will in fact be observed. This result is accompanied by the conclusion that AD-AS growth models have to be replaced by IS-LM growth models, where a gradual adjustment of price and wage levels occurs, in order to become consistent Keynesian models of monetary growth.

8.3 Hyperperfect Foresight: An Exceptional Case in an Exceptional Environment

In order to allow for a thorough discussion of Sargent's results, we need a discrete-time formulation of the above continuous model, which we shall present here in a nutshell. Let us denote by h the length of the period of the "Hicksian week" underlying this reformulation to which the instantaneous flows L, and so on must then be applied to obtain the levels of employment, and so forth for the period h. The six equations that determine the six statically endogenous variables

$L_t = Lh, C_t = Ch, I_t = Ih, Y_t = Yh, i_t = ih$ and p_t

are then determined by the following discrete-time equations:[10]

$$Y_t = hK_t^a L_t^{1-a} \tag{8.22}$$

$$w_t/p_t = h(1-a)(K_t/L_t)^a \tag{8.23}$$

$$C_t = c_h(Y_t - T_t^n - h\delta K_t), \qquad T_t^n = h\theta K_t \tag{8.24}$$

$$I_t = i_f(ha(L_t/K_t)^{1-a} - h\delta - (i_t - \pi_t^e))K_t + hnK_t \tag{8.25}$$

$$Y_t = C_t + I_t + h\delta K_t + G_t, \qquad G_t = h\gamma K_t \tag{8.26}$$

$$hM_t = p_t Y_t \exp(-bi_t/h) \tag{8.27}$$

Note here that we have employed in these equations and for the numerical investigations that follow the special functions that Sargent (1987, chap. 5) makes use of in his presentation of the model. Note, furthermore, that the continuous-time model determines the "flows" among the model's variables per time-unit in a unique fashion, that is, the rates $C_t/h, I_t/h, Y_t/h, i_t/h$ and also p_t are already well determined by the continuous-time approach. The discrete-time variables—with the exception of the price level p_t—consequently should vary in proportion to h, if such a variation of the institutional setup, that is, of the length of the Hicksian week of our model, is considered as economically sensible.

In addition to the above determination of the statically endogenous variables, we have for the dynamically endogenous variables $K_{t+h}, \pi_t^e, w_{t+h}$ [11] the following dynamical laws:

$$\frac{K_{t+h} - K_t}{K_t} = i_f(ha(L_t/K_t)^{1-a} - h\delta - (i_t - \pi_t^e)) + hn \tag{8.28}$$

$$\pi_t^e = \pi_{t-h}^e + h\beta_{\pi^e}\left(\frac{p_t - p_{t-h}}{p_{t-h}} - \pi_{t-h}^e\right), \qquad \beta_{\pi^e} < \infty \tag{8.29}$$

$$\frac{w_{t+h} - w_t}{w_t} = h\ln(L_t/L_t^s) + \pi_t^e \tag{8.30}$$

They are to be supplemented by

$$\frac{M_{t+h} - M_t}{M_t} = hn, \qquad \frac{L_{t+h}^s - L_t^s}{L_t^s} = hn. \tag{8.31}$$

This model is the proper discrete-time analog as far as Sargent's treatment of the case of adaptive expectations is concerned. The following will, however, show that it will not give rise to his case of myopic perfect foresight simply by assuming $\beta_{\pi^e} = \infty$ (or $1/\beta_{\pi^e} = 0$), as in the continuous-time model.

We have briefly described in section 8.2 two consequences of an isolated open market operation dM asserted by Sargent when myopic perfect foresight $\pi^e = \hat{p}_+$ replaces the adaptive expectations mechanism $\dot{\pi}_+^e = \beta_{\pi^e}(\hat{p}_- - \pi^e)$.[12] We shall supply now some arguments for and against these assertions by reconsidering them in different versions of a discrete-time analog to the given continuous-time model. This will shed some light on the reasons that are responsible for the asserted dramatic change in the model's behavior—from a Keynesian demand side model to a Solowian supply side approach when myopic perfect foresight is substituted for adaptive expectations.

In order to obtain the basic discrete-time version for the myopic perfect foresight case $\pi^e = \hat{p}_+$, we have to insert the identity $\pi_t^e = (p_{t+h} - p_t)/p_t$ into the discrete model of the preceding section and to remove the adaptive mechanism from it. This gives rise to the following (condensed) set of equations (M_t, L_t^s, L_t as before, and $h = 1$ for simplicity from now on):[13]

$$x_t = c_h(x_t - \theta - \delta) + i_f(ax_t - \delta - i_t + \frac{p_{t+1} - p_t}{p_t}) + n + \delta + \gamma \tag{8.32}$$

$$m_t = x_t \exp(-bi_t) \tag{8.33}$$

$$p_t = w_t x_t^{\frac{a}{1-a}}/(1-a) \tag{8.34}$$

$$\frac{K_{t+1} - K_t}{K_t} = i_f(ax_t - \delta - i_t + \frac{p_{t+1} - p_t}{p_t}) + n \tag{8.35}$$

$$\frac{w_{t+1} - w_t}{w_t} = \ln(e_t) + \frac{p_{t+1} - p_t}{p_t}, \qquad e_t = L_t/L_t^s \tag{8.36}$$

A first and well-known observation for such a perfect foresight approach is that the model will now exhibit one more variable than it has equations. It can only determine p_{t+1} on the assumption that p_t is given or vice versa. The first situation of a given p_t is generally used to investigate whether the model exhibits saddle point behavior with a uniquely determined stable path. This is indeed the situation that Sargent finds to hold true in the continuous-time case. In his continuous-time model it is, however, difficult to understand completely the then employed mathematical manipulations of the model with respect to their economic content and justification, as the following will make clear.

In this model, the above degree of freedom is used in a way that gives rise (1) on the real side to a Solowian growth model that is augmented by a real wage Phillips curve[14] and (2) on the side of nominal magnitudes to a determination of the price dynamics (including interest and nominal wage determination). The latter exercises no influence on the real side of the model and, furthermore, is totally unstable. Since individuals are assumed to shy away from the consequences of such an instability, they are therefore assumed to react to monetary shocks such that a certain terminal condition for the price dynamics is always guaranteed. Discontinuous open market operations at time t will thus, and according to Sargent's solution of the continuous-time model, lead to jumps (or—if foreseen—even earlier jumps) in prices and wages such that AD-AS equilibrium is always guaranteed and such that inflation converges back to zero—if there is inflation at all. The real side is completely unaffected by such open market operations, since it has become independent from the AD–part of the model by the assumed smooth reaction of the real wage—owing to the modified Phillips curve that now directly determines the change in the real wage rate.

Yet, this continuous analysis does not, and cannot, integrate point-in-time jumps dp of prices caused by point-in-time jumps in the money supply dM into its notion of inflation, and therefore, it simply assumes that the real wage will react continuously, while the nominal wage is now grouped among the statically endogenous variables in order to allow it to jump in line with the price level p. One may wonder whether this change in the formal setup of the model—which by no means is an obvious consequence of the myopic perfect foresight assumption $\pi^e = \hat{p}_+$—is really compelling or whether there exist alternative respecifications of the model that allow for different dynamics. In this regard the above specification of a discrete-time version may be viewed as providing such an alternative, since it does not make use of a real wage Phillips curve right from the start.

It is indeed possible to obtain from the above discrete-time version a model that is capable of reflecting Sargent's solution procedure as it was sketched above. This model now makes explicit use of the variable ω (the real wage) and—for simplicity also—of k^s (capital per head of the labor force), and it is obtained from the above basic discrete-time approach by employing the following approximate relationships

$$\frac{\omega_{t+1} - \omega_t}{\omega_t} \sim \frac{w_{t+1} - w_t}{w_t} - \frac{p_{t+1} - p_t}{p_t} \tag{8.37}$$

$$\frac{k^s_{t+1} - k^s_t}{k^s_t} \sim \frac{K_{t+1} - K_t}{K_t} - \frac{L^s_{t+1} - L^s_t}{L^s_t}. \tag{8.38}$$

assuming that their use will not change the dynamics of our initial approach qualitatively.[15] If this assumption is justified, then the basic discrete-time model will behave in the manner that has been described above (following Sargent), since it can then be replaced by the following set of equations, to be called the real-wage approximation in the following:

$$\frac{\omega_{t+1}-\omega_t}{\omega_t} = \ln(l_t k_t^s), \qquad k_t^s = K_t/L_t^s, \qquad l_t = (\frac{\omega_t}{1-a})^{-1/a} \tag{8.39}$$

$$\frac{k_{t+1}^s - k_t^s}{k_t^s} = x_t - c_h(x_t - \theta - \delta) - n - \delta - \gamma, \qquad x_t = l_t^{1-a} \tag{8.40}$$

$$m_t = x_t \exp(-bi_t) \tag{8.41}$$

$$x_t = c_h(x_t - \theta - \delta) + i_f(ax_t - \delta - (i_t - \frac{p_{t+1}-p_t}{p_t})) + n + \delta + \gamma \tag{8.42}$$

Note that we have used in the first dynamic law the marginal productivity assumption (8.2) to replace l_t by ω_t. By means of this substitution we also obtain in discrete-time by the above approximation a Solowian supply side dynamics including a real wage Phillips curve that determines ω and k^s (and x) in complete independence from the rest of the model. Keynesian effective demand no longer has any influence on the dynamics of the real part of the model in such a situation.

It is not difficult to describe the reasons that are responsible for such a result. Given the current value of the capital stock, marginal productivity theory determines employment on the basis of the current real wage. The resulting employment then in turn determines the change in the real wage through the Phillips curve relationship, while the capital stock is changing in line with the savings that flow from the income generated by the current level of employment. Accumulation is thus driven by savings as in the original Solow model, independently of any forces responsible for goods and money-markets equilibrium.

Yet, we have an independent investment demand function in this model and thus the Keynesian problem of how investment and savings are equalized. Savings is already determined—as seen—by the present output (income) and thus is no longer free to adjust in a Keynesian manner toward an equality with investment plans. Therefore, in the given situation, investment has to adjust. And it does so in the following way. First, the interest rate is determined through money-market equilibrium, since marginal cost prices and output are already fixed. Inserting this result into the goods market equation leaves only one variable to be determined, that is, the new rate of inflation or the future price level p_{t+1}. Taking for granted that this variable will indeed generate IS-equilibrium thus gives rise to the following dynamic equation for the nominal side of the above model:[16]

$$\begin{aligned}\frac{p_{t+1}-p_t}{p_t} &= i_t - ax_t + \delta + \frac{x_t - c_h(x_t-\theta-\delta)-n-\delta-\gamma}{i_f} \\ &= \frac{\ln p_t + \ln x_t + \ln k_t^s L_t^s - \ln M_t}{b} - ax_t + \delta \\ &\quad + \frac{x_t - c_h(x_t-\theta-\delta)-n-\delta-\gamma}{i_f} \\ &= \frac{\ln p_t}{b} - \frac{\ln M_t}{b} + A_t,\ A_t = [\text{autonomous terms}] \qquad (*)\end{aligned}$$

This is[17] the discrete-time analog of the equation that Sargent employs for the nominal part of his model in order to demonstrate his two theorems on (un-) anticipated monetary shocks.

Equation $(*)$ may, in a first attempt, be solved by means of historically given (initial) conditions: At time t where the jump ΔM in the money supply occurs it is only the rate of interest that can respond immediately and in the opposite direction—since prices and wages are given from the past. On the basis of its reaction it is then possible to determine p_{t+1} and $w_{t+1} = \omega_{t+1}p_{t+1}$ by the above formula for the price dynamics. Note here that the real wage does not change by assumption, so that the real part of the model will stay at its steady-state values (A_t = const). Yet, changing, that is, here, falling[18] prices, feed back into the money market and will there lead to a further decline in the rate of interest, and so on. The result is the perpetual deflation that is shown in figure 8.2a.

And, figure 8.2b shows, the case of an expansion in government expenditures will also lead to such a deflationary spiral. This is due to the fact that the only immediate effect of such expenditures is to crowd out investment, which is achieved by a deflationary impulse (on p_{t+1}). The resulting spiral is then again due to the subsequent, positively correlated reactions of the rate of interest and the price level (the so-called Gibson paradox as it is called in Sargent 1973a).

If we replace the above equation $(*)$ by its continuous-time limit,[19] this dynamic equation for $p(t)$ can be easily solved and gives rise to the following explicit expression (see Sargent 1987, chap. 5):

$$\ln p(t) =$$

$$\int_t^\infty \exp(-s/b)(\ln M(s)/b - A(s))ds \cdot \exp(t/b) + \text{const} \cdot \exp(t/b) \quad (8.43)$$

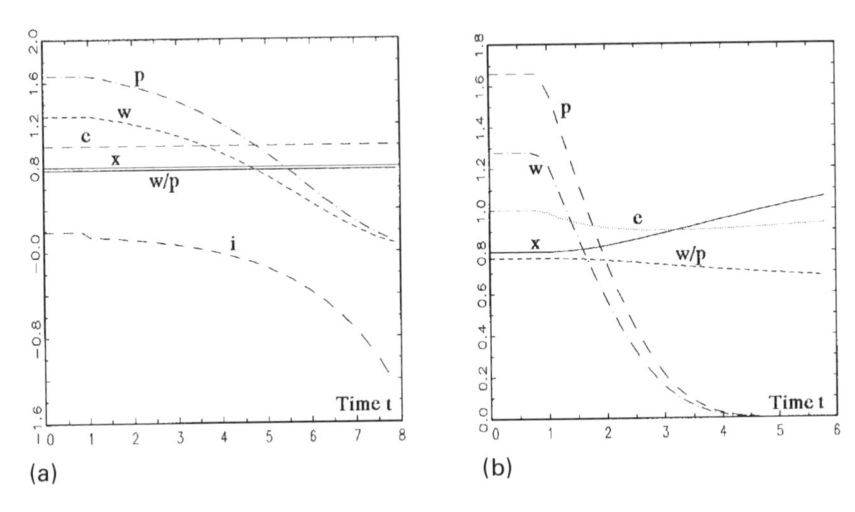

Figure 8.2
Sargent's case of myopic perfect foresight with initial conditions solely. (*a*) monetary policy, (*b*) fiscal policy

for all $t \in \mathbb{R}$. This equation provides the analytical basis for the two theorems on monetary shocks we have considered in section 8.2—if the explosive term *const* $\exp(t/b)$ is excluded from consideration by the usual stability arguments of such approaches, as we have sketched them in section 8.2. However, removing the second term from the above price equation clearly implies that we are now considering some sort of *hyperperfect foresight*, since this amounts to the choice of a terminal condition. By this method, *the whole future* of the world is now involved in the determination of the current price level $p(t)$. This is much more demanding than only myopic perfect foresight $\pi^e = \hat{p}_+$ at each moment of time—which in principle demands only that p_{t+1} must be determined in a way such that investment will fill the predetermined demand gap on the market for goods. Yet, since individuals are now assumed to insist on a convergent solution for the price level p_t, a case of hyperperfect foresight is implied.

In discrete-time one can restate the first of Sargent's propositions in the following way:[20]

1. *Short-run neutrality* An unexpected increase in the money supply M_t solely implies a corresponding jump in prices p_t and wages w_t and leaves all other variables unaffected.

This proposition is easily demonstrated in continuous time by means of the following formula: For the implied change $p'(t)$ in the price level $p(t)$ induced by an unforeseen point-in-time increase $\phi M(t)$ (or $\ln M(t) + \ln \phi$) at time t ($\phi > 1$) we get:

$$\ln p'(t) - \ln p(t) = \int_t^{\infty} \exp(-s/b)(\ln \phi/b)ds \cdot \exp(t/b)$$

$$= b\exp(-t/b)(\ln \phi/b)\exp(t/b) = \ln \phi$$

and $\ln p'(s) = \ln p(s)$ for $s > t$.[21]

Yet, this jump in prices by the factor ϕ proved to follow the jump in the money supply dM is—in contrast to this continuous-time case—in discrete-time necessarily part of the definition of the rate of inflation.[22] The following interpretation of the term "not anticipated" has therefore to be adopted for the discrete-time analog of the continuous-time model.

Up to point $t-1$ everything has been steady, that is, in particular $p_{t-1} = p_{t-2} = \ldots$. At time t, however, we necessarily get $\frac{p_t - p_{t-1}}{p_{t-1}} = \frac{w_t - w_{t-1}}{w_{t-1}} > 0$ and after that point these rates will again be zero—if the above neutrality assertion indeed holds true in the discrete-time case. Wage earners will suffer no loss by this sudden and temporary change in the inflation rate because they are fully compensated by the assumed reaction of their nominal wage $w_t = \omega_t p_t$ (cf. the above *approximate discrete-time approach*). But bond holders and investors have been deceived—since they by assumption do not react to this temporary change in the real rate of interest. The term "not anticipated" thus refers solely to these two types of economic agents and is defined by a modification of their perceived rate of inflation $\frac{p^e_{t+1} - p_t}{p_t}$ $(= 0)$, which, when entered into the investment function, then guarantees that the interest rate can remain constant in the case of such monetary shocks.

The short-run neutrality result therefore ultimately rests on *asymmetric information*: whereas investors can be surprised by monetary policy (and must therefore be characterized as having some weaker form of hyperperfect foresight), wage earners can never be deceived (they have true hyper-perfect foresight), since real wages have to stay constant (whenever there is a jump in the money supply) in order to allow for such short-run neutrality. Note that this conclusion is not possible in the continuous-time case, since the point-in-time consequences dp of monetary shocks dM^s are there not integrated into the actual rate of inflation and therefore also do not matter in the Phillips curve in this continuous-time case. This fact is the basis of Sargent's (1987, 20) statement, "Notice that the anticipated rate of inflation, which is assumed to be unanimously held, . . . " Such a statement is, however, not possible in a discrete-time specification of the economic background of the continuous-time model. This shows that continuous-time versions should be conceived as mathematical approximations to fully specified discrete-time models. Continuous-time models may ease their mathematical discussion—but as we have just seen—not their interpretation.

If one, by contrast, assumes that perfect foresight holds for investors as well, then the rate of interest must respond in the above situation already at time $t-1$ to the now correctly expected rate of inflation $(p_t - p_{t-1})/p_{t-1}$. The economy will thus respond to the assumed shock in t already at time $t-1$ (due to the unanimously perceived change in the real rate of interest), that is, there will be a price effect in $t-1$ to which it already has to react in $t-2$, and so on. We then consequently get nominal effects back to $-\infty$ (unless there is again a point-in-time t_0 where investors do not have such perfect foresight with regard to the immediately following actual rate of inflation). This provides the explanation for the second proposition of section 8.2, which can now be restated in the following form:

2. *Hyper-anticipation* All future changes in the money supply M are reflected in all past values of the price level p_t if perfect foresight of the kind $\pi_t^e = \frac{p_{t+1} - p_t}{p_t}$ holds true at all points-in-time in the determination of the real rate of interest used for investment decisions.

Removing seemingly minor anticipation errors from the model thus has dramatic consequences for the model's behavior. In our view, the basic reason for such an occurrence lies in the fact that the model becomes basically an *overdetermined* one in the case of myopic perfect foresight, since the level of employment is then determined by the level of effective demand and a given real wage at one and the same time—if the rate of inflation is given. Yet, since this rate is in fact still to be determined, it can be used to solve this overdetermination by removing the theory of effective demand from the model. This solution to a contradiction between the marginal productivity employment schedule, a fairly narrow theory of effective demand and a real wage Phillips curve (i.e., a perfect indexation of wages), however, is not the only way out of the observed overdetermined structure. It is well known, for example, that the employed form of marginal productivity relationship is not confirmed by facts. Quantities and real wages do not move in the countercyclical fashion that is implied by such an approach. The necessary degree of freedom and the solution to the above conflict may thus also be found in a more flexible theory of prices—away from their narrow and strict dependence on marginal wage costs.

The second proposition above is again easily demonstrated in continuous time: For the change in the price level $p(t)$, and in the level of wages $w(t)$, we get for $t \in [t_0, t_1]$ by the above formula for the price level $p(t)$ in the case of a jump in the money supply $M(t_1)$ at time t_1 by a factor ϕ foreseen at time t_0:

$$\begin{aligned}\ln p'(t) - \ln p(t) &= \int_{t_1}^{\infty} \exp(-s/b) dM(s) ds \cdot \exp(t/b) \\ &= b \exp(-t_1/b)(\ln \phi/b) \exp(t/b) \\ &= \ln \phi \exp((t - t_1)/b)\end{aligned}$$

and $\ln \phi$ thereafter. The change in the money supply is therefore already reflected in all earlier values (if there is no first t_0 of the above kind with regard to investment decisions).

There may, however, also exist a situation where investors never anticipate the rate of inflation for the next period correctly. To provide a brief sketch of such a possibility, let us assume for simplicity that the expected component of the money supply is characterized by the steady rate of growth n, but that unexpected monetary shocks will hit the economy in each of its market points $\ldots, t-1, t, t+1, \ldots$. Investors will thus expect no inflation at all, whereas wage earners are—by assumption—always fully informed about the true amount of price inflation or deflation. The future real rate of interest will then never be correctly perceived by investors—since they dislike adaptive expectations formation and thus never look back to observe the jumps dp in the current price level p. The myopic perfect foresight assumption $\pi^e = \hat{p}_+$ of the continuous-time approach will then never be applicable to the discrete-time case. It is to be replaced by $\pi^e = 0$ in the above example. Myopic perfect foresight can in such a situation no longer be defined independently of the perceived future money supply path—by referring only to price expressions.

We conclude that the above approach to price level changes, which solely concerns the determination of the real rate of interest if the approximate discrete-time model is a valid approximation, has no longer any objective meaning in such situations, since it only regulates the imagination of investors in a way that makes them able to find out that hypothetical rate of price change, or that fictitious future price level p_{t+1}, that will just induce them to invest the amount necessary to close the predetermined demand gap $x_t - c_h(x_t - \theta - \delta) - n - \delta - \gamma$ at each moment of time t. The strict quantity theory of money is then true in a straightforward manner whenever there is a change in the money supply that is not foreseen by investors.

But, do we really need the above hypothetical and complex forecasting mechanism of investors—which fully incorporates the complete steady or unsteady future of the process of capital accumulation, but not all monetary shocks—in order to obtain the conclusion that investment is equated to savings at each moment of time? Or should we not better conclude that something must be wrong with this model, since the change in its behavior is too implausible when we go from adaptive expectations to the case of myopic perfect foresight?

The above discussion clearly shows that the discrete-time model has priority over the continuous-time one, since a thorough interpretation of the structure of the model and an explanation of its implications is only possible in discrete-time. Reformulating the continuous version by means of a period model with a given period length h also clarifies another important point for the continuous time model, that is, the question of the *frequency of discontinuous open market operations* that Sargent's approach allows for. Since the continuous-time model represents only a mathematical "approximation" of the fully specified discrete-time economic model it is, of course, an immediate consequence that the above open market operations can only occur at $\ldots, t-1, t, t+1, \ldots$. There is thus no need to reflect the problem that a continuous-time approach that allows for discontinuous changes in the money supply should allow for such operations at each point-in-time. A given "h-economy" is the true interpretive background of such continuous-time models leaving as question solely whether the magnitude of h is such that the continuous version will indeed provide some first information on the given h-economy.

We have seen above that there is a discrete-time model that partially approximates our basic discrete version and that may justify the change in the choice of the continuous variables of the continuous-time approach (w_t, K_t in the case of adaptive expectations and ω_t, K_t for myopic perfect foresight). The question arises whether this change in the continuity assumptions for the continuous-time framework also provides a good representation of our basic discrete-time approach, that is, whether the real wage approximation we have used above is an admissible one with regard to the analysis of its dynamics. Simulating (8.32)–(8.36) in the same way as its real wage reformulation (8.39)–(8.42) gives—as a first impression—by and large again the above figures 8.2a,b so that this approximation may indeed be a valid one. In the case of monetary policy, this is not very astonishing, since it is easy to see that results then must even be identical for the above two discrete-time versions. The chain of events is in such a case practically the same as that described above for the real wage approximation, up to the fact that we now have to calculate the real wage according to the formula [23]

$$\hat{\omega}_t = \frac{\hat{w}_t - \hat{p}_t}{1 + \hat{p}_t}$$

to really see whether it will remain unchanged. This formula once again gives rise to purely nominal reactions (deflation) if a monetary shock disturbs the steady state and if stability is again investigated by means of historically given initial conditions.

In the case of fiscal policy numerical simulations at least exemplify that the instability result depicted above may be nearly the same. It is nevertheless an unsettled question here whether the real wage Phillips curve implicit in the discrete-time version

$$\hat{\omega}_t = \frac{\ln(e_t)}{1 + \hat{p}_t}$$

may not lead to a different dynamics in comparison to its approximation

$$\hat{\omega}_t = \ln(e_t)$$

studied above—since this minor change in the form of the real wage Phillips curve implicit in the model may be sufficient to allow for a significant departure from the strict dichotomy exploited above to show Sargent's propositions. Only if this can be proved not to be true is the switch in continuity conditions that takes place in Sargent's treatment of adaptive expectations in contrast to perfect anticipations really justified. Beside this problem, however, the forecasting method that is used for calculating the evolution of the price level in our basic discrete-time model should be derived from this correctly specified model and not from its real wage approximation.[24]

This simple fact creates the following additional problem: in order to solve the real part of the model we need an historically given real wage at $t = t_o$, for example. Yet, in our basic discrete-time version we at first know only the given nominal wage, since the price level is determined endogenously. If Sargent's above forecasting method for the price level is indeed valid, it can of course be applied to any given situation of a stable dynamics of the model's real part to calculate the nominal values that must accompany it. The result, however, feeds back on the initial conditions used to determine the employed real dynamics. We consequently encounter the additional difficulty that the real part is no longer independent from the nominal part, but that both parts have to be solved simultaneously in order to make the determination of p_{t_o} consistent with the real dynamics. Thus, although the solution to the basic discrete model may be similar to its real wage approximation when historically given values are used throughout, the switch to Sargent's hyperperfect foresight case may nevertheless be much more complicated because of the dependence that now exists between the determination of the price level, the nominal wage, and the real wage at the time t_o where an unanticipated change occurs, if $e_{t_o} \neq 1$ and thus $\hat{\omega}_{t_o} \neq 0$ holds true. This situation thus demands the solution of a continuum of Solowian adjustment paths toward the steady state in order to determine (hopefully) that particular path that generates a price level that is—on the basis of the implied level of wages—compatible with the choice of the initial conditions that govern the evolution of the Solowian adjustment path used for the calculation of the price level. Life therefore becomes much harder for economic agents if "earthquakes" hit the economy than in the case of the economy's steady-state evolution with only monetary disturbances. Summing up, we can formulate the following list of arguments against Sargent's approach to myopic perfect foresight by comparing full-fledged Keynesian AD-AS models in discrete time (DTM) and in continuous time (CTM):

- DTMs have logical priority over CTMs in the case of a problematic comparison between the two (since they are more specific and reliable with regard to economic content).
- The considered CTM is incorrect in its treatment of the consequences of discontinuous jumps in the money supply.
- Short-run neutrality can be shown to be true in a correctly specified discrete version of the CTM with a money wage Phillips curve, but only if extremely asymmetric information is allowed for.

- DTMs reveal that myopic perfect foresight for all agents and all times is not a sensible procedure.
- DTMs determine the set of points-in-time in the CTM where the money stock can perform jumps.
- DTMs shows that it may be difficult to provide a simple expression for the assumption of perfect foresight.
- The existence of qualitatively distinct DTMs for the same CTM in certain situations questions the meaningfulness of the dichotomy present in the employed CTM.
- Our basic DTM shows that hyperperfect foresight is a very difficult analytical task in the case of unsteady economic change.

Further, yet less specific points of critique of the present approach to a complete model of monetary growth are

- The model incorporates into its solution the whole future of at least the real magnitudes of a Solow growth model with unemployment for the current value of the price level. In our view this is too hypothetical a completion of the assumption of myopic perfect foresight: $\pi^e = \hat{p}_+$.
- The model is much too dependent on the existence of an explicit solution to a certain type of difference or differential equations and is thus fairly "linear" in its views of the world.
- The model has to assume extreme, and costless, computation capabilities of economic agents in situations of unsteady growth.
- The model—like many other Keynesian models—employs an implausible mix of Walrasian price taking and Keynesian rationing assumptions.

In light of all these aspects, in the next section we propose a modification of this inconsistent AD-AS monetary growth model. The modification moves us toward an IS-LM growth model with less-than-infinite adjustment speeds for prices as well as wages that will generalize the basically cyclical nature of the adaptive expectations case to the case of perfect foresight. This will be done by allowing for a looser connection between price and quantity movements and by incorporating a structural equation for current inflation. This equation allows agents to form an "educated guess" by means of the structure and the parameter values of the model, shown here in the simplest possible fashion, without the need to incorporate the whole future of the world into their computations. Furthermore, CTM and DTM approaches are generally equivalent in this proposed modification—if the length of the period h does not become implausibly large—so that the problems considered in this section are of no relevance in these modifications.

8.4 Myopic Perfect Foresight and Cyclical IS-LM Growth

The starting point for our modification of the model in section 8.3 is the observation that it employs too radical a difference between the reaction speeds of prices and wages, infinite versus finite, in the continuous-time version, and immediate in contrast to h-dependent (and β-dependent) in the case of discrete time. The twofold assumption of an immediate and full reaction of prices to changes in marginal wage costs is problematic both from a theoretical as well as from an empirical point of view.[25] Particularly under conditions of a modern economy, where prices are generally set, at least by large firms, on the basis of normal costs of operation and where quantities are adjusted primarily in the short run to meet discrepancies between supply and demand, it is highly implausible that the marginal cost rule (8.2) will be binding with regard to the evolution of the price level p_t at each moment of time. Instead, the inequality

$$p_t \geq p_c := \frac{w_t}{h(1-a)(K_t/L_t)^a}$$

will hold true only in general. This implies that the theory of the price level or of the rate of inflation has still to be formulated.

In order to close this gap, we shall make use of the following simple idea which, of course, represents only a first step in the construction of a complete and consistent prototype model of Keynesian monetary growth.

Instead of equation (8.2) of section 8.2 we now assume the following rule for price level **changes:**

$$\frac{p_{t+h} - p_t}{h} = \beta_p \left[(1+\mu) \frac{w_t L_t}{K_t^a L_t^{1-a}} - p_t \right], \qquad \mu > 0 \tag{8.44}$$

Marked–up current unit wage costs—at the normal level of operation and with a mark-up factor $1+\mu$—in comparison to actual prices determine here the rate of change in the price level per unit of calendar time (a year, say). Essential is that price adjustment—just as wage adjustment—is now lagged with regard to the current quantity reactions, that is, the two nominal magnitudes w_t, p_t are now both h-dependent (and adjustment-speed dependent) in their reaction to exogenous shocks. This removes the problematic asymmetry we have noted above and allows for a partially independent development of prices and quantities over time and thus for Keynesian theory of employment even in the case of myopic perfect foresight. Making use of (8.44) in place of (8.2) has the additional advantage that empirical conditions can be met in a more plausible way.[26]

This equation can be reformulated as follows:

$$\frac{p_{t+h} - p_t}{p_t h} = \beta_p \left[(1+\mu) \frac{w_t L_t}{p_t K_t^a L_t^{1-a}} - 1 \right] = \beta_p \left[(1+\mu)\omega_t l_t^a - 1 \right]$$

which states that the real wage and employment per unit of capital $l_t = l_t^s e_t$ are the decisive variables that govern the evolution of the rate of inflation per unit of time. It is important to note here that this new rule for price determination also implies a change in the investment function (8.4) of section 8.2, since the real net rate of return on capital per unit of time is now given by $x_t - \delta - \omega_t l_t$ instead of by the expression $ax_t - \delta = F_K - \delta$.

In addition to the above and for reasons of simplicity, we shall allow for further changes of the model of sections 8.2 and 8.3 which turn its IS-LM substructure into a linear one that can be solved explicitly in a simple way. In the light of the existence of two basic motives for money demand, the particular choice (8.6) of this demand function does not look very convincing, as these two motives have to be combined in an additive, not in a multiplicative way, and since one of them, the speculative motive, is related to stocks and not to flows. Furthermore, linear relationships on the goods market are, for reasons of simplicity and symmetry, now supplemented by linear relationships on the money market.

These observations suggest the following simple form of an LM equation

$$M_t = f_m^1 p_t Y_t + (f_m^{2a} - f_m^{2b} i_t) p_t K_t$$

which allows in the simplest way possible for an explicit system of difference equations, as we shall see in the following. A second change in the equations of the model is implied by the observation that the

$\ln(e_t)$-component of the Phillips curve (8.8) of Sargent's model exhibits the wrong type of curvature with regard to empirical results on such curves. Yet, instead of using a mirror image of this curve with regard to the 45° line, we shall for reasons of simplicity replace it, too, by a linear relationship, that is,

$$\frac{w_{t+h} - w_t}{w_t h} = \beta_w(e_t - 1) + \pi_t^e$$

Moreover, we now propose a modification of Sargent's model that represents an important step in the description of the adjustment mechanisms of actual economies. We shall assume in the following that employment L_t is not immediately adjusted to the level L_t^* that is induced by effective demand, but that short-run variations in work time (here without impact effects on the wage costs of employment) are used to satisfy this level of demand.

This means that equation (8.1) is now used to determine the work–time L_t^* of the employed L_t for any state of effective demand Y_t by

$$Y_t = hK_t^a(L_t^*)^{1-a}$$

whereas actual employment is adjusted toward this short–run level of over– or underemployment by means of

$$\frac{e_{t+h} - e_t}{h} = \beta_e(e_t^* - e_t), \qquad e_t^* = \frac{L_t^*}{L_t^s}, \qquad e_t = \frac{L_t}{L_t^s}$$

It is obvious that the utilization rate e^* should play a role in the above Phillips curve. This can be done by including the following term into this equation:

$$+\beta_w^*(e_t^* - e_t)$$

which represents the delayed wage effect of over- or undertime work. Note here that pricing decisions have been based on L_t and not on L_t^*, that is, they are related solely to the normal or intended level of operation of the firm.

This proposal concludes the set of modifications we make with regard to Sargent's original Keynesian model of monetary growth. Our next task will be to collect these equations and to show that they imply a well-defined and explicit system of difference equations and also of differential equations, when transformed back to continuous time.

As IS and LM equations we get from the proposed modifications the two intensive form equations:

$$x_t \stackrel{\text{IS}}{=} c_h(x_t - \theta - \delta) + i_f\left(x_t - \omega_t e_t l_t^s - \delta - (i_t - \hat{p}_t)\right) + \delta + n + \gamma \qquad (8.45)$$

$$m_t \stackrel{\text{LM}}{=} f_m^1 x_t + f_m^{2a} - f_m^{2b} i_t \qquad (8.46)$$

The second equation can be solved for i_t, which gives

$$i_t = \frac{f_m^1 x_t + f_m^{2a} - m_t}{f_m^{2b}}$$

This expression inserted into the first equation gives rise to the following expression for the output-capital ratio x_t:

$$x_t = \frac{i_f\left(\beta_p((1+\mu)\omega_t(e_t l_t^s)^a - 1) + \frac{m_t - f_m^{2a}}{f_m^{2b}} - \delta - \omega_t e_t l_t^s\right) + \delta + n + \gamma - c_h(\theta + \delta)}{1 - c_h - i_f\left(1 - f_m^1/f_m^{2b}\right)} \qquad (8.47)$$

This expression determines x_t as a function of the statically exogenous variables ω, l^s, e, m. We *assume* that the denominator of this expression is positive, which, for example, is ensured if the marginal propensity to spend out of income is < 1. Note that the partial derivatives of the x_t-function with respect to ω, l^s, e, m are then all positive if β_p is sufficiently large, while the first three are negative if this parameter is small. The assumption of perfect foresight therefore influences these derivatives in different ways, depending on the adjustment speed of the price level p. Equation (8.47) can then be used to remove the equilibrium variable x_t from the formulation of the dynamics of this modified system, making it an autonomous system thereby.

Transferred back to continuous time we therefore end up with the following autonomous dynamical model for the four variables ω, l^s, m, e:[27]

$$\hat{\omega} = \beta_w(e - 1) + \beta_w^*(e^* - e), \qquad e^* = x^{1/(1-a)}/l^s \qquad (8.48)$$

$$\hat{l}^s = n - s_h(x - \delta - \theta) + \gamma - \theta, \qquad s_h = 1 - c_h \qquad (8.49)$$

$$\hat{m} = n - s_h(x - \delta - \theta) + \gamma - \theta - \beta_p((1+\mu)\omega(el^s)^a - 1) \qquad (8.50)$$

$$\dot{e} = \beta_e(e^* - e) \qquad (8.51)$$

where the variable x is determined as shown above and where $e^* = x^{1/(1-a)}/l^s$ represents the actual employment of the employed labor force.[28] This is the four-dimensional nonlinear dynamics of Keynesian IS-LM growth with gradual wage and price adjustment that we shall contrast with the AD-AS growth model in the remainder of this chapter and in the following chapter. Note that the nonlinearities present in the model are solely due to its growth rate formulae, the employed Cobb-Douglas production function, and certain products that arise in a natural way from the formulation of such models.

Proposition 8.1 The steady state of the dynamics (8.48)–(8.51) is given by ($n = g_m$ as usual):

$$\omega^\star = 1/((1+\mu)(l^{s\star})^a)$$

$$l^{s\star} = l^\star = (x^\star)^{\frac{1}{1-a}}$$

$$m^\star = f_m^1 x^\star + f_m^{2a} - f_m^{2b} i^\star$$

$$e^\star = (e^*)^\star = 1$$

where $x^\star$ is given by $\delta + \theta + \frac{n+\gamma-\theta}{s_h}$ and $i^\star$ by $x^\star - \delta - \omega^\star l^{s\star}$.

Proposition 8.2 Consider the Jacobian J (the linear part) of the dynamics (8.48)–(8.51) at the steady state. The determinant of this $4 \star 4$-matrix: det J, is always positive.

It follows that the system can only lose or gain asymptotic stability by way of a Hopf bifurcation (if its eigenvalues cross the imaginary axis with positive speed as it is the case here).

Proof Exploiting the many linear dependencies involved in the above dynamical system and its Jacobian, we can easily show that its determinant can be reduced to the following qualitative form:

$$\begin{pmatrix} 0 & 0 & 0 & + \\ 0 & 0 & - & 0 \\ - & 0 & 0 & 0 \\ 0 & - & 0 & 0 \end{pmatrix}$$

which gives a positive expression for det J.

q.e.d.

We assert without proof that the steady state of the dynamics is locally asymptotically stable when the adjustment speeds β_e, β_p of employment and prices are chosen sufficiently small and the parameter β_w^* sufficiently large. This can be shown by freezing the employment dynamics at the steady state, via the choice $\beta_e = 0$, and by investigating the local stability of the remaining dynamics by means of the Routh-Hurwitz theorem. An alternative procedure with similar results is given by freezing the wage dynamics at its steady-state value and choosing the parameter β_e sufficiently large. We therefore can expect that the system will allow for a variety of Hopf bifurcation situations, depending on the parameter that is being varied.

The following numerical calculations of Hopf bifurcation loci illustrate and qualify these assertions further:[29]

The curves in figure 8.3 represent the loci where a Hopf bifurcation takes place, that is, where a (first) pair of conjugate complex eigenvalues crosses the imaginary axis whereby the system loses its local asymptotic stability. This can happen in three different ways, by way of a supercritical Hopf bifurcation, where a stable limit cycle is born "at" the bifurcation point; by way of a subcritical Hopf bifurcation, where a corridor of local asymptotic stability and an unstable limit cycles disappears when the bifurcation point is crossed; or by a degenerate Hopf bifurcation, where purely implosive behavior may change into a purely explosive one (without the appearance or disappearance of a limit cycle). The type of Hopf bifurcation that occurs is shown in figure 8.3 (supercritical Hopf bifurcations solely). Note that figure 8.3 shows in addition that wage and price flexibility are bad for economic stability, as is a rise in the markup factor $1 + \mu$, and that a more flexible employment policy of firms is good for it. The above limit cycle result is further illustrated in the following phase plots of the dynamics where the above parameter set applies—up to the choice of the parameter β_p, which is chosen here in the domain of local instability (equal to 1). We note that this type of stability, a persistent or stable oscillation in the four dynamical variables, may be turned into purely explosive behavior if the parameter β_p is chosen sufficiently large. This shows that the employed dynamics do not represent a viable economy under all, and even under reasonable, circumstances. Furthermore, even if the dynamics are bounded, the amplitude of the cycle may be too large from an economic point of view (see fig. 8.4). Further nonlinearities may therefore be necessary in order to tailor the dynamics in view of the empirical magnitudes of the considered variables. The next section will return to this question of economic viability.

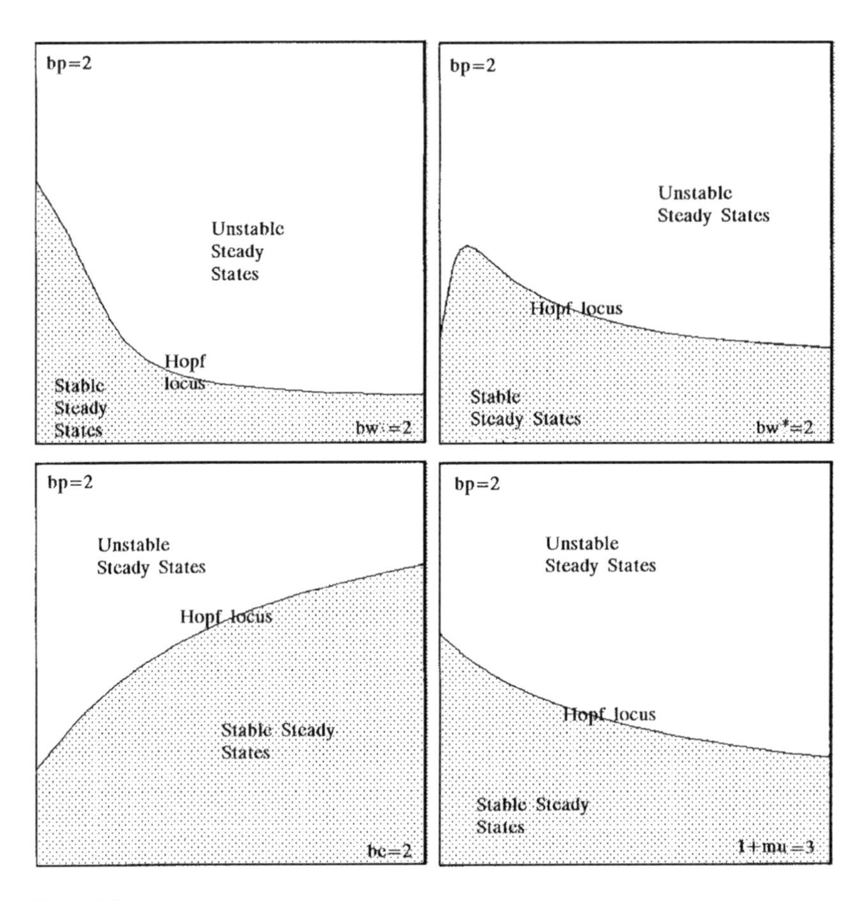

Figure 8.3
Hopf bifurcation curves, stable limit cycles, and stable corridors ($bw = \beta_w$, etc.)

Note that figure 8.4 shows a real wage movement that is by and large procyclical. The interaction of the price level—broadly speaking, the inverse of real cash balances per capital—with the rate of employment exhibits overshooting episodes of stagflationary type. Note also that the amplitudes generated via a change in the parameter β_p may be considered as too large and too sensitive in their dependence on this parameter. This suggests that further nonlinearities must be added to these dynamics to tailor them from the global point of view (see the next section).

In sum, the conflict over income distribution as expressed by the parameters β_w, β_w^*, β_p and $1 + \mu$ appears to exercise a significant influence on the behavior of the model. Yet, it is by no means clear at present

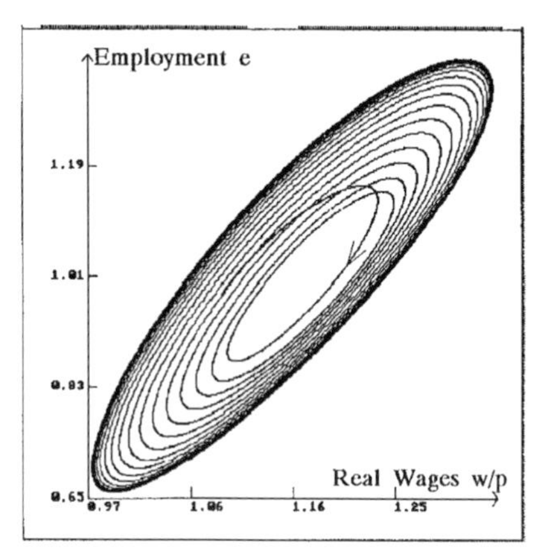

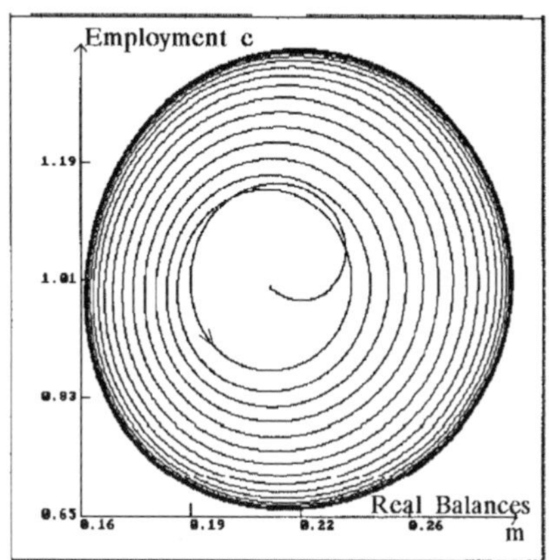

Figure 8.4
Stable limit cycles via supercritical Hopf bifurcations

whether the above typical shape of the generated cycle is due mainly to this conflict.

Before concluding this section let us finally stress that economic reaction—with regard to open market operations—can no longer precede action in this version of a monetary growth model with perfect foresight (as was the case in section 8.3), since the system is now always solved in the conventional way, by means of historically given initial conditions, in an economically meaningful way on the basis of a gradual adjustment of both wages and prices.

8.5 IS-LM Growth Dynamics and Viability

The numerical investigations of the preceding section—as well as many other investigations—show that the above model has to be developed further in order also to handle the situations where it will generate limit cycles that are too large, from an economic point of view, or even total instability. In our view it is in such cases simply not completely specified, since it does not yet contain the forces that come into being when the distance from steady-state income distribution and from the "normal" rate of employment become too large. Thus, instead of studying the present model further by means of simulations, as with the above model, we will continue our investigation by introducing the concept of "viability" for such a macro-model and by introducing some viability mechanisms that when appropriately combined—it is hoped—allow for general viability. Note that this is not an easy task since the dynamics are already of dimension four.

A dynamic macro-model will be called *weakly viable* if all of its prices (including the rate of interest i) and all of its quantities (including disposable income: $Y - T^n - \delta K$) remain positive in the course of the evolution of its dynamics *and if*, in addition,

1. the share of wages $\omega L/Y$ stays in the open interval $(0, 1)$, and
2. the rate of employment e does not increase beyond a given magnitude, the maximum rate of employment e_{max} of the model.[30]

Such a model will be called *viable under a purely Keynesian regime* or purely demand constrained if we furthermore have along its trajectories (for a reasonable range of initial conditions):

$$e < e_{max} \quad \text{and} \quad p > p_c = \frac{w}{F_L(K, L)}$$

where F_L denotes the marginal productivity of labor.

We shall be concerned only with viability in the purely Keynesian context in the following, that is, we will not deal with the extreme form of a regime of so-called repressed inflation ($e = e_{max}$). There is, however, a lower limit for any type of price-setting behavior that is given by the textbook price level p_c of perfect competition. Setting prices below this level in fact means that firms are accepting losses at the current rate of employment. For values of p equal to or lower than p_c we therefore enter the so-called classical regime, which would again demand a reflection and reformulation of the present structure of the model. These two modifications of the purely Keynesian dynamics will remain excluded from our following considerations by assumption. Note, furthermore, that the above side-condition on the level of prices implies for the real wages rate ω:

$$\omega(el^s)^a < 1 - a$$

that is, it guarantees the basic condition of profitability for a capitalistic economy in a stricter way than it has been demanded for the case of a weakly viable economy. Note, also, that the growth rate of the capital stock, $i(\cdot) + n$, should not fall below the minimum rate compatible with the assumed fixed rate of depreciation, that is, not below $-\delta$. We do not care about such an occurrence in the following, however.

Of basic interest here is to collect and test simple forms of additional reaction patterns that may be capable of generating Keynesian viability for the resulting dynamic model, that is, one which will guarantee more than $1 - a$ as profit share and prevent the labor market from becoming totally exhausted. Since the above model exhibits four dynamical laws this is by no means an easy task. In fact, there exist a variety of proposals that at first look fairly convincing but that too often fail when tested by means of computer simulations.

A candidate for a viability mechanism is a modification of the dynamic laws of section 8.5 that attempts to incorporate economically motivated nonlinearities into these laws such that the upper bound $e_{max}(= 1.3$, for example) or $v = \omega L/Y = 1 - a$ will not become effective. As in the original Goodwin (1967) growth cycle model, with its two dynamic laws for the rate of employment e and the share of wages v, the problem thus posed is to find viability mechanisms that will keep these central economic variables away from certain upper economic bounds. In the two-dimensional dynamics of the Goodwin model this task is in principle easily solved, since even one nonlinearity may then already be sufficient to achieve this aim. Yet, our system is four-dimensional, and it exhibits only two variables that—due to our characterization of "viability"—have to be bounded from above. The question, then, is whether this can be achieved by means of solely two candidates for viability mechanisms, as we shall attempt to exemplify in the following, or whether further nonlinearities—not immediately related to the employment decision or the conflict over income distribution—are necessary to accomplish this goal.

The other conditions for (weak) viability do not create difficulties similar to this endogenous consideration of such upper bounds. This is due to the fact that many dynamic economic laws are—and must be—formulated in terms of growth rates. Their variables thus can at best approach zero, but cannot reach this value in finite time (in continuous-time models). In the above model this guarantees in principle that p, w, ω, and K will stay positive if they start positive. There thus remains disposable income $Y - T^n - \delta K$ (and thus consumption) and the rate of interest i to be considered.

We have already noted above that the formulation of investment behavior must integrate the fact that gross investment cannot become negative. Such an extension of the investment function used so far then immediately implies that gross national product (and thus also employment) must be positive throughout if the following side condition is fulfilled: $G - c(T^n + \delta K) > 0$ or $\gamma - c(\theta + \delta) > 0$.[31] In the same way, the slightly stronger condition $G - T^n - \delta K > 0$ will then guarantee that disposable income will also remain positive throughout.

It is obvious that a similar reasoning can be applied in the case of the rate of interest, that is, the shape of the money demand curve can surely be reformulated in such a way that this rate will be positive throughout. This is not true, of course, for the linear form introduced in the preceding section. Yet, an appropriate modification of this functional form is not difficult, but will be left out here, since we want to concentrate on the above two basic upper bounds for our economic dynamics. The other viability conditions will here be taken care of by the choice of appropriate initial conditions for the various simulation runs.

There are two basic mechanisms—one for the employment barrier and one for the distributional conflict—that we shall investigate in the remainder of this section:[32]

1. a reduction of investment projects in the neighborhood of absolute full employment as represented by e_{max}; and

2. increasing inflationary pressure when the share of profits is approaching the value a from above, combined with a decrease in the accelerator term π^e in the wage adjustment equation.[33]

These two types of behavior can be integrated into the present model, for example, in the following simple way: Let $i_f(\cdot)$, $\beta_p(\cdot)$, and $\eta(\cdot)$ denote functions of the rate of employment $e = l/l^s = x^{1/(1-a)}/l^s$ or the wage share $v = \omega l^a = \omega(el^s)^a$, which are of the shape seen on the interval $(0, e_{max})$ and $(0, 1-a)$, respectively in figure 8.5.

The function to the left will be used in the following simulation to incorporate the effect that gross investment will fall to $(n + \delta)K$ when the full employment barrier is approached.[34] And the two functions to the right will be used to incorporate into the model that (1) the adjustment toward mark-up prices will be the stronger, the closer the share of wages comes to the maximum "competitive" share $1 - a$ where prices are equal to marginal wage costs, and that (2) wage claims do not fully incorporate the rate of inflation in situations where the share of wages is already exceptionally high (and less importantly: they incorporate more than this rate in the opposite case).

Integrating these additional adjustment features into the model of the preceding section leads to its following reformulation:

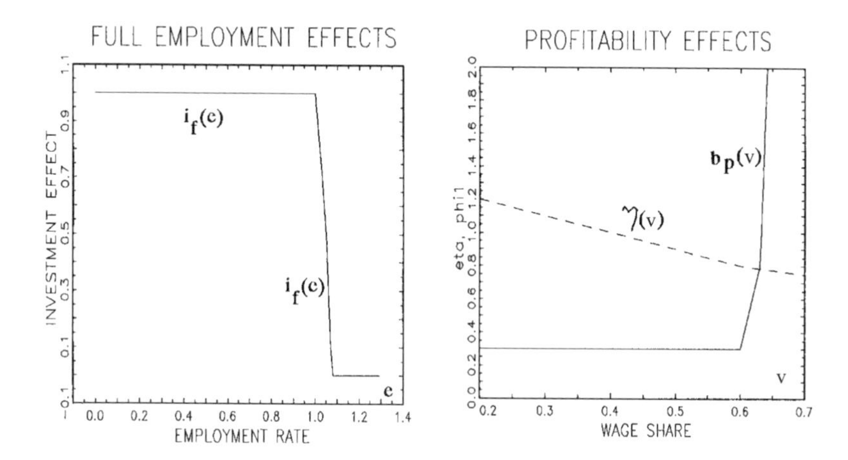

Figure 8.5
Simple adjustment functions for situations of full employment and low profitability ($b_p = \beta_p$)

$$\hat{\omega} = \beta_w(e-1) + \beta_w^*(x^{1/(1-a)}/l^s - e) + \eta(\omega(el^s)^a)\beta_p(\omega(el^s)^a)((1+\mu)\omega(el^s)^a - 1)$$

$$\hat{l}^s = n - s_h(x - \delta - \theta) + \gamma - \theta, \qquad s_h = 1 - c_h$$

$$\hat{m} = n - s_h(x - \delta - \theta) + \gamma - \theta - \beta_p(\omega(el^s)^a)((1+\mu)\omega(el^s)^a - 1)$$

$$\dot{e} = \beta_e(x^{1/(1-a)}/l^s - e)$$

where the value of output per unit of capital is again given by (8.47) with a "parameter" i_f that now depends on the state variable e as shown above.

Simulating the model with only the distributional nonlinearity in effect does not appear to improve its stability properties significantly. Yet, applying the other or both of the above outward forces is indeed sufficient to stabilize the model in its formerly unstable parameter region, that is, over a broader range of parameters values, as the typical simulation run in figure 8.6 exemplifies ($1 + \mu = 2$ now).[35]

This figure clearly shows the importance of the full employment or investment ceiling in stabilizing the above dynamical system of dimension four. The influence of the distributional barrier is not obvious, since this barrier may interact with the demand side of the model in an

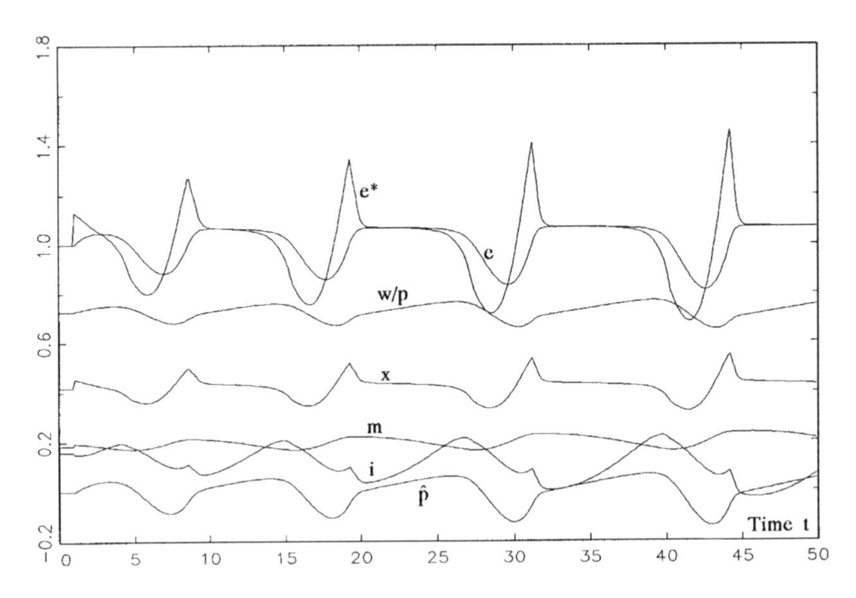

Figure 8.6
Stabilizing explosive cyclical growth through endogenous ceilings for employment and the share of wages

unstabilizing way. It is associated with a very transitory kind of stagflationary process: employment slowly declines after a phase of rapid growth in conjunction with rising inflation and rising real wages, until a point is reached after which decreasing employment is accompanied by improving profitability.

This time-series presentation furthermore reveals various comovements between variables, such as a procyclical movement of real wages, a comovement of the interest rate and the price level ($p \sim 1/m$),[36] a comovement of the rate of inflation and the level of economic activity over a considerable period of time, and so forth. It is remarkable here that the above model generates the asymmetrical three-phase structure for its business cycle (rapid growth, trend growth, and recession) that was found to be typical in the empirical literature in the sixties.[37] Note that we make use in this section solely of ceilings, not of floors, in order to generate viability for the dynamics of the model. This might explain the asymmetric shape of the business cycle. Floors may be introduced via investment behavior and via downwardly rigid wages and prices, and will lead to the opposite asymmetry then. Finally, be aware of the role played during peaks in effective demand by overtime work, mirrored by the movement in e^* in contrast to the behavior of e, which in fact allows the economy to function fairly smoothly despite abrupt changes in the demand for goods.

The above discussion provides only an example of the model's behavior in the presence of ceilings for macroeconomic activity, here full employment and a lack of profitability.[38] Further refinements of the model will, of course, be needed in order to allow for a better match of the time series obtained and actual macroeconomic time series.

Nevertheless, the above illustrates soundly the role of possible candidates for economic viability for a relatively complicated set of macrodynamic laws. Furthermore it shows that local knowledge—as it is contained in the Jacobian of this system at the steady state—is quite secondary for the final cyclical behavior of the model, that is, local bifurcation analysis is of extremely limited use here. Investment habits and the conflict over income distribution in situations far away from the steady state shape a considerable portion of the cycle. Finally, myopic perfect foresight is only a handy assumption here which allows a reduction of the order of the considered dynamics, but which does not lead to significant—or even dramatic—changes in the implied dynamics (see also the next chapter). Thus, there is no problem in assuming such perfect foresight in order to remove from the model minor discrepancies between some variables.

We conclude this section with a simulation of the above nonlinear monetary growth model in a simple and partially stochastic environment where it is assumed that the two adjustment speeds β_w^* and β_e that are related to the overtime work situation within firms are subject to uniformly distributed stochastic shocks.

Figure 8.7 shows that the stable limit cycle underlying the last figure then gives rise to a broad limit corridor within which the dynamics take place after some transitory period ($1 + \mu = 1.25$ again). The deterministic part is therefore still dominant—in contrast to "real business cycle" models that are built around an asymptotically stable point attractor of their deterministic part (see chapter 5). Yet, once endogenous persistent fluctuations are involved, the question of whether it is the deterministic or the stochastic part of the model that by and large shapes the cycle cannot be avoided.

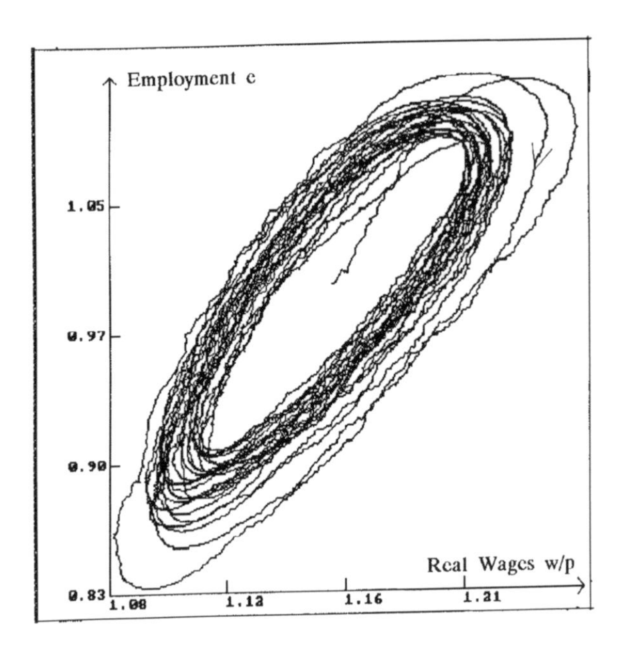

Figure 8.7
Cyclical viability in a stochastic environment

8.6 Concluding Remarks

We have reconsidered in this chapter a complete Keynesian prototype model of monetary growth and have shown that it does not behave in an economically meaningful way if inflationary expectations are of the myopic perfect foresight type. The basic reason for this result is that a contradiction arises between the Keynesian theory of effective demand and the assumption that prices are governed by marginal wage costs. This contradiction may be solved as in Sargent (1987, chap. 5) by means of a variable in the aggregate demand function that has still to be determined and that is adjusted such that aggregate demand equals aggregate supply. But we have also seen that this solution is not convincing: it creates more problems than it helps to solve.

In our view, a proper solution to the above contradiction can be found only if the theory of the price level is reformulated to take into account that it is not sensible in a Keynesian model—which should allow for rationing of firms—to assume that firms are price-takers, as in Walrasian general equilibrium theory, and always on their supply schedule. If, however, prices are set by firms, it is far from obvious that they are indeed instantaneously set equal to marginal wage costs.

In the second part of the chapter we have therefore used as an example a simple rule for price setting in order to show that the assumption of myopic perfect foresight will then no longer create dramatic changes in the model's behavior. Our finding now is that this revised Keynesian prototype model gives rise to very typical cyclical patterns, which are fairly independent from the functional forms of its behavioral relationships *and* which are characteristic for adaptive as well as for perfect inflationary expectation schemes, as will be seen in the next chapter. The difference between these two types of expectations is fairly exaggerated in the literature on rational expectations, since this literature concentrates primarily on stochastically disturbed point attractors of (log)linear flexprice models. This literature has failed to consider, however, the relevance of its assumptions in Keynesian models of monetary growth with gradual price adjustments and with bounded persistent fluctuations already in the deterministic part of the model.

9 Adaptive Expectations or Myopic Perfect Foresight: The Wrong Alternative

9.1 Introduction

In this chapter[1] we continue our investigation of Sargent's (1987) AD-AS growth model, which was examined in the previous chapter regarding its behavior under myopic perfect foresight. We concluded that the model's exceptional behavior with regard to correct anticipations of the short-run rate of inflation is based on logical flaws in the model's structure. These flaws deprive the model and its implications of economic content. By an appropriate modification, primarily to the model's price sector, we showed that one can also achieve quite standard results regarding the evolution of the price level in a regime of myopic perfect foresight. The resulting model could again be solved in an economically meaningful way via historically given price data from each point in time onward showing cyclical behavior of a stable or unstable (explosive) nature in general. In the latter case we used additional stabilizers to keep the explosive dynamics within economically meaningful bounds.

By means of the AD-AS growth model we could thus demonstrate in chapter 8 various weaknesses in the monetarist application and interpretation of such models and the inapplicability of the conventional "rational expectations" *solution methodology* in a Keynesian setup. Nevertheless, we have not yet considered the basic reason for the "rational expectations" dichotomy that results in such a model. In this chapter we attempt to solve this problem by reconsidering the AD-AS growth model from the perspective of adaptive expectations and their relationship to their mathematical limit, myopic perfect foresight.

We introduce a discrete-time version of this model of Keynesian dynamics with adaptive expectations in section 9.2. In particular, it will be seen that some equations in such a version are not uniquely determined by the given continuous-time model briefly reviewed below; one rather has to choose from a variety of possibilities. The consequences of this type of choice will also be considered. In section 9.3 we demonstrate that it is not true that the adaptive expectations variant of the model will be asymptotically stable for reasonable ranges of parameter values—in contrast to the assumption stated by Sargent (1987, chap. 5). We perform this task by means of numerical simulations and a theorem taken from Franke (1992a). Monetary shocks thus do not necessarily give rise to (neo-)classical neutrality results in the long run. As in investigations of neoclassical models of monetary growth under adaptive expectations,[2] the AD-AS growth model will also tend toward global instability if the parameter that governs the speed of the adjustment of expectations becomes even moderately large. This shows that we do not yet have an economic model at our disposal that can be considered as satisfactory.

Our analysis of the main cause of this result will demonstrate the following points:

1. By using the modified Keynesian dynamics with delayed price adjustment introduced in section 8.4, we show in sections 9.4 and 9.5 that the above instability result will come about only in such a modified model (where the myopic perfect foresight case can be meaningfully solved by means of historically given initial conditions) if it is assumed that the price level is adjusted toward its target level with sufficient speed. This result is similar to one we obtained in chapter 7 for marginal cost pricing and in a medium-run context.

2. It can be shown by means of the Jacobian of these dynamical systems that the close relationship between adaptive expectations and myopic perfect foresight (for a fast adjustment of the former) must get lost if there is a *fast* adjustment of the price level toward its target. This is again close to results obtained in chapter 7 for the medium run.

3. The degree of flexibility in goods prices is the decisive element that makes both the case of fast adaptive as well as perfect expectations look odd, if this flexibility becomes too large. This is because a fast price adjustment coupled with fast adaptive expectations will make the model both extremely explosive and implausible.

4. These results suggest that the origin of the "rational expectations" *methodology*—that is, the paper of Sargent and Wallace (1973)—should

be considered anew, which we do in section 9.6. We again make use of large but finite reaction speeds of prices, as well as finite but fast adaptive adjustments of expectations, to understand more fully the double limit of an infinitely fast price adjustment and correct inflationary expectations. We show that Sargent and Wallace's methodology is erroneous, since it uses a fairly partial and linear approach solely in order to justify the choice of a particular global solution for the price dynamics considered in their paper.

In section 9.6 we reinvestigate the most basic of all myopic perfect foresight models to show how to handle the case where myopic perfect foresight differs significantly from fast adaptive expectations and to make this difference disappear. The introduction of a straightforward nonlinearity into this simple model of money and growth will demonstrate that the case of myopic perfect foresight has been solved implausibly in the literature owing to the linear or local perspectives employed. From a global perspective the local explosiveness of the steady state of such models is not at all a problem if the adjustment speed of the price level remains finite.

In an appendix to this chapter we finally supply a variant of the Sargent (1987, chap. 5) model where prices are forecast in a much more refined way on the basis of past information. The stability properties of such a model with forecasted prices will differ significantly from the adaptive expectations case and its perfect foresight limit. This assertion is, however, exemplified solely by means of numerical simulations.

In sum, this chapter attempts to show that a well-defined, that is, viable Keynesian IS-LM growth model with gradual price adjustments does not give rise to monetarist assertions on the effects of (un)anticipated monetary policy by means of the Sargent and Wallace (1973) methodology of price level manipulations. On the one hand, establishing viability for such models removes from them the strange and contrasting results of small versus no errors in inflationary expectations and, on the other hand, it supports the old-Keynesian view that more sluggish prices enhance the stability of models of monetary growth.

It is worth stressing that this and the preceding chapter are not built on a theory of nominal rigidities as it is used in the context of new Keynesian economics. The new Keynesians maintain that nominal price and wage rigidities are necessary to enable nominal macroeconomic shocks to affect real variables. Considerable research effort has heretofore been undertaken to develop a theory of nominal rigidities as a basis for macroeconomics. By contrast, there are positions such as Tobin's (see chapter 7) maintaining that Keynesian models of macro fluctuations should not be based on such wage and price rigidities,[3] but rather must demonstrate the existence of such fluctuations even if wages and prices are very flexible.[4] The fundamental issue of macroeconomics then becomes the speed of adjustment processes in market economies, or as Tobin puts it: "existence, reliability, and speed of adjustments by which a market economy maintains or restores economy-wide equilibrium" (Tobin 1989,2). According to this view the research effort should be directed toward viable dynamic models of macro fluctuations that allow for various degrees of price and wage flexibility.

Taken from the preceding chapter, the continuous-time model of Keynesian dynamics on which Sargent's (1987, chap. 5) analysis of the classical consequences of monetary policy in a regime of adaptive expectations (AE) or myopic perfect foresight (MPF) is based is given by the following set of equations, now directly in intensive form:[5]

$$x = l^{1-a} \tag{9.1}$$

$$w/p = (1-a)l^{-a} \tag{9.2}$$

$$c = c_h(x - \theta - \delta) \tag{9.3}$$

$$g_k = i_f(ax - \delta - (i - \pi^e)) + n \tag{9.4}$$

$$x = c + g_k + \delta + \gamma \tag{9.5}$$

$$m = x\exp(-bi) \tag{9.6}$$

$$\hat{m} = g_m - g_k - \hat{p} \tag{9.7}$$

$$\hat{w} = \ln(l/l^s) + \pi^e \tag{9.8}$$

$$\dot{\pi}^e = \beta_{\pi^e}(\hat{p} - \pi^e) \tag{9.9}$$

$$\hat{l}^s = n - g_k = -i_f(ax - \delta - (i - \pi^e)) \tag{9.10}$$

Assuming for all that follows $g_m = \hat{M} = n = \hat{L}^s$ gives rise to a (unique) full-employment steady state of the model of the form $\hat{w} = \pi^e = \hat{p} = 0$, $\hat{K} = \hat{L} = \hat{Y} = n$. With regard to such a reference path Sargent (1987, 122ff) describes possible dynamic effects when such a steady state is disturbed at some moment $t > t_0$ by a *once-and-for-all jump in money supply M*. For the case of adaptive expectations formation (AE) he claims that "though this model is clearly Keynesian in its momentary or point-in-time behavior, its steady state or long-run properties are 'classical' in the sense that real variables are unaffected by the money supply." Verbal and graphical arguments are presented that seem to suggest this result as well as the possibility for a damped cyclical movement with stagflationary episodes. In Sargent's words the "model thus has implicit in it, depending on the particular parameter values, a theory of the business cycle." We show in section 9.3, however, that his claim on (or assumption of) the asymptotic stability of the steady state of this model will be wrong if the adaptive expectations mechanism works with sufficient speed, which need not be very high. As a result the model will exhibit business cycles for most of its parameter values, but often with an increasing cycle amplitude. As in Hicks's (1950) multiplier-accelerator approach to the theory of the business cycle, the model thus needs completion, for example, by means of ceilings or floors, in order to provide a theory of the business cycle that can be considered economically complete.

We have considered Sargent's treatment of the alternative case of myopic perfect foresight (MPF) in chapter 8 in great detail. Though mathematically MPF represents the limit of adaptive expectations, Sargent's treatment of perfect foresight leads to extremely different results in comparison to the above, as we have seen in the preceding chapter. This surprisingly different behavior of the model under myopic perfect foresight is used in Sargent (1987, chap. 5) to derive monetarist theorems on (un)anticipated shocks in the money supply, here in the context of a seemingly complete Keynesian AD-AS growth model. Earlier proofs of such results[6] are not difficult to understand regarding the assumptions that are responsible for such theorems in these cases, since they make use of a Lucas supply function and therefore basically assume a vertical supply schedule in combination with the standard negatively sloped aggregate demand function in the derivation of these propositions. In such a situation it is understandable that conventional Keynesian conclusions on fiscal and monetary policy can be invalid and may be replaced by monetarist ones on the strict neutrality of money (and on total crowding out), as far the deterministic part of such models is concerned. However, in the Sargent 1987, chapter 5 model this is far from obvious, since the model is close to the textbook model of AD-AS growth, where wages are sluggishly revised according to the state of the labor market and the prevailing (expected) rate of inflation. The neutrality of money in the strict sense thus should be impossible in such a case. Yet, Sargent 1987, chapter 5 "proves" this neutrality.

A simple rejection of his "proof" could point to the fact that Sargent—after running through a series of computations—simply assumes that prices *and* wages are both fully flexible, so that the model becomes the classical variant of the neoclassical synthesis of the Keynesian model (for which this neutrality result is well known—again because of the assumption of a vertical supply schedule).[7] Yet, such an answer is too simple, since it rejects only the specific solution procedure of Sargent in the case of perfect foresight. A more thorough analysis must instead address the reason(s) for the strange dichotomizing behavior of the AD-AS growth model in the presence of myopic perfect foresight—independently of Sargent's particular flexprice solution built upon this dichotomy.

The answer—as shown in the following discussion continuing the arguments put forward in the previous chapter—will be that Keynes's (1936, 5ff) critique of the classical postulate number II (as he called it) cannot be considered sufficient to remove all basic logical flaws from a Keynesian alternative to the classical model. The reason for this insufficiency is that postulate number I (the equality of the real wage with the marginal product of labor) is also in fact incompatible with a Keynesian theory of producers that are constrained by effective demand. This will be demonstrated in the following discussion by showing that the flexibility of prices that fully reflect marginal wage costs establishes a mechanism in a Keynesian model of effective demand (and growth) that makes it extremely nonviable, as this creates a latent conflict between two concurrent principles of the employment level determination.

Therefore, the proper answer to the problematic dichotomy of the AD-AS growth model under perfect foresight is not that money wages should be manipulated implicitly to make them react as they do in the classical variant of the Keynesian model of the neoclassical synthesis; it is instead that wages *and* prices must be assumed to be *sufficiently inflexible* in their reaction to certain imbalances—independent of the particular law that governs their dynamics—if the economy is to be expected to be stable in its short-run equilibrium position as well as in its medium- and long-run dynamics. The classical postulate number I is a problem, not so much with respect to the price level theory it contains, but with regard to the extreme degree of price flexibility it assumes.

In sum, this chapter demonstrates by way of the IS-LM growth model introduced in section 8.4 that full-fledged Keynesian models of monetary growth will not give rise to monetarist results of the Sargent and Wallace type unless they are supplemented by a neoclassical full employment aggregate supply schedule as in Sargent 1973b and Sargent and Wallace 1975 and are based on prices and wages that are fully flexible. They instead provide a non-neoclassical theory of the business cycle if their possibly unstable behavior is kept within economically meaningful bounds by means of appropriate economic delimiters far off the steady state. The extent of wage and price flexibility and economic viability are the real issues of Keynesian monetary growth dynamics and not the choice between adaptive expectations and myopic perfect foresight, which is shown to be of minor importance in properly reformulated IS-LM growth models.

9.2 The AD-AS Growth Model in Discrete Time

We have already observed in the preceding chapter that it is not straightforward to provide a discrete-time version of Sargent's (1987, chap. 5) model of "Keynesian Dynamics." There indeed exist several choices from an economic point of view with different static as well as dynamic properties in the case of an adaptive formation of expectations, too.

In order to obtain for this model a first and in fact our basic version for discrete time, we postulate that the nominal rate of interest should then be statically endogenous, too (as in the continuous-time version) and that (by the same reasoning) the real rate of interest should be determined at each point-in-time t on the basis of statically exogenous (given) expectations on the inflation rate that are also to be used in the formulation of the Phillips curve. These assumptions imply that the model is structured with respect to its dynamic feedbacks in the same way as its continuous-time predecessor, and they give rise to the following discrete-time formulation of this Keynesian monetary growth model.

We denote again by h the length of the "Hicksian week" underlying the discrete-time model. The six equations that determine the six statically endogenous variables[8]

$$l_t = l, \ c_t = c, \ g_{kt} = g_k, \ x_t = x, \ i_t = ih \text{ and } p_t = p \ \ (\text{but } w_t = wh)$$

are—under the above assumptions—determined by the following equations:

$$x_t = l_t^{1-a} \tag{9.11}$$

$$p_t = \frac{w_t/h}{(1-a)l_t^{-a}} \tag{9.12}$$

$$c_t = c_h(x_t - \theta - \delta) \tag{9.13}$$

$$g_{kt} = i_f(al_t^{1-a} - \delta - (i_t - \pi_{t-h}^e)/h) + n \tag{9.14}$$

$$x_t = c_t + g_{kt} + \delta + \gamma \tag{9.15}$$

$$m_t = x_t \exp(-b(i_t/h)) \tag{9.16}$$

Note that this intensive formulation of the model determines the statically endogenous variable as in the continuous–time version in a unique fashion. Note also that the above discrete model, as well as its continuous-time analog, determine the rate of interest *per unit of calendar time,* since h-variations should not imply a change in the portfolio decision of wealth owners if all other conditions remain unchanged (h the period for interest payments).

Labor L_t is paid ex post (in t), and it produces by means of the capital stock K_t in the time interval $(t-h, t]$ the output Y_t for the market point t. This output increases in proportion to the length of the period of production h, which implies a similar relationship for the marginal products of labor and capital. This treatment of the length of the period h becomes important when variations of h are to be considered.

In addition to the above determination of the statically endogenous variables, we have for the dynamically endogenous variables[9] w_{t+h}, K_{t+h}, π_t^e now the following dynamical laws (which determine their future evolution solely on the basis of the past and the present temporary equilibrium values):[10]

$$\frac{w_{t+h} - w_t}{w_t} = h \ln(l_t/l_t^s) + \pi_{t-h}^e \tag{9.17}$$

$$\frac{l_{t+h}^s - l_t^s}{l_t^s} = i_f(ax_t h - \delta h - (i_t - \pi_{t-h}^e)) \tag{9.18}$$

$$\pi_t^e - \pi_{t-h}^e = \beta_{\pi^e} h \left(\frac{p_t - p_{t-h}}{p_{t-h}} - \pi_{t-h}^e \right) \tag{9.19}$$

Using π_t^e in place of π_{t-h}^e in the investment function or in the Phillips curve (or in both, as in Sargent 1973a) does not—under certain stability conditions—modify the dynamics very much (see the following section). Note, however, that they will alter the feedback structure of the model since in such cases the current update of inflationary expectations has already to be used in the determination of temporary equilibrium—or in the Phillips curve—in contrast to the procedure that applies in continuous time (see section 8.1). The above discrete-time model in fact is the only discrete-time version of the AD-AS growth model which, on the one hand, preserves the simultaneous IS-LM-determination of output, employment, interest and (via AS) prices, and which, on the other hand, relies on given results with regard to the dynamic variables w, l^s, π^e.

The above dynamic model requires the solution of its AD-AS part at each step of iteration. This AD-AS part is given by:

$$x_t = c_h(x_t - \theta - \delta) + i_f(ax_t - \delta - (i_t - \pi^e_{t-h})/h) + n + \delta + \gamma \tag{9.20}$$

$$m_t = x_t \exp(-b(i_t/h)) \tag{9.21}$$

where

$$p_t = (w_t/h)l_t^a/(1-a), \quad l_t = x_t^{\frac{1}{1-a}} \quad \text{and}$$

$$m_t = (M/L^s)l^s/p_t, \quad (M/L^s) \text{ given by initial conditions.}$$

The above equations can be uniquely solved for x_t, l_t, p_t, m_t and i_t for any given θ and γ in direct correspondence to Sargent's continuous-time version of these equations.

Inserting the results into (9.17) - (9.19) we get an autonomous system of difference equations in the variables w, l^s, π^e. This is the dynamic-period model we shall mainly consider in our following simulations of the AD-AS growth model under adaptive expectations.

There exist, however, at least two meaningful alternatives to this discrete-time version that concern the formulation of the investment function and the Phillips curve of the above model. In *a first modification* of the above we may assume that the nominal yield of bonds of period $t-h$ is fixed in $t-h$ in advance and not a result of the trading in the bond market at time t. This is economically more plausible and compares even better with the definition of profits (as the result of past capital accumulation) that was used above. It implies the following form for the employed investment function:

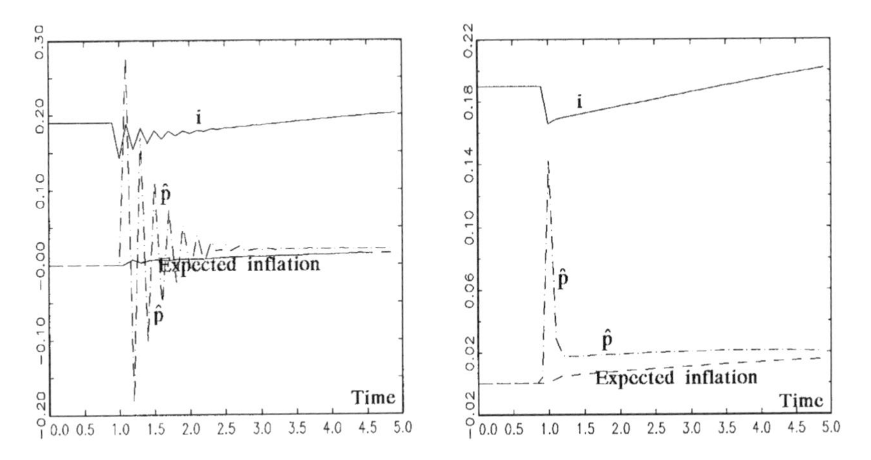

Figure 9.1
A comparison of two different period versions of the AD-AS growth dynamics

$$i_f(ax_t - \delta - (i_{t-h} - \pi^e_{t-h})/h) + n$$

which—when used in the equilibrium part of the model—now gives rise to a sequential solution for the IS-LM subsystem. Goods-market equilibrium can now be determined independently of money-market equilibrium in each moment of time t leading to a solution x_t on the basis of which the new rate of interest i_t—needed only for the subsequent period—can then be determined by means of the LM-equation. This discrete version of Sargent's model consequently gives rise to an explicit system of difference equations, since x_t and i_t can now be written as simple functions of the dynamically endogenous variables and can thus be removed from the final presentation of these difference equations. This advantage in the formal treatment of the model is, however, accompanied by its disadvantage to react more "stiffly" to shocks in its numerical solutions (see figure 9.1 on the left).

The origin of the difference to our basic discrete-time model can be easily described. When the steady state is disturbed by an open market operation—a point-in-time jump in the money supply—it is now only the rate of interest that can react immediately and that therefore carries the whole burden of this adjustment. This leads to its overshooting, which is then reversed in the subsequent period, and so forth. If the resulting adjustment process is asymptotically stable, this overreaction will eventually disappear—as shown above. Yet, if—as in our subsequent analysis—the steady state is no longer an attractor, even small initial shocks will lead to a pronounced overreaction of the interest rate after some time and will thus induce dynamics that are fairly different—much more explosive—than those of the other discrete-time versions of the originally continuous-time model. This version is therefore not a good representation of the AD-AS growth model, despite the fact that it only differs from the other period versions by a seemingly small deviation in the determination of the rate of interest that is used for investment planning.

The insufficient correspondence between discrete- and continuous-time dynamics is again removed if the following *second alternative* to our basic discrete version is considered. The investment function here reads

$$i_f(ax_t - \delta - (i_t - \pi_t^e)/h) + n$$

and thus compares the proceeds of past capital accumulation with the real rate of interest that is expected for the immediate future, to be based on:

$$\pi_t^e = \pi_{t-h}^e + \beta_{\pi^e} h \left(\frac{p_t - p_{t-h}}{p_t} - \pi_{t-h}^e \right)$$

These updated expectations are used also in the Phillips curve for the determination of money wage rate changes.

This representation of the original model may be considered as even more convincing from an economic point of view, since p_t and thus $(p_t - p_{t-h})/p_{t-h}$ should be viewed as being known at time t, which implies that π_{t-h}^e is not too sensible a choice for representing inflationary expectations at time t. In this approach, the IS-LM part is again fully interdependent and has to be extended by equation (9.19) in order to allow for the determination of a temporary equilibrium solution in terms of past values. The implied dynamics are, however, close to the dynamics of our basic model. The approach thus represents only an interpretive alternative to the discrete-time model that we have considered at length above (but has the disadvantage that its equilibrium feedback structure differs from the original continuous-time approach).

These two alternatives to our choice of a discrete-time representation of the Sargent model will, however, be largely neglected in our following analysis of this model of monetary growth. They have served here to indicate that the mapping between discrete- and continuous-time formulations runs from the former to the latter as far as uniqueness and economic interpretations are concerned. Continuous-time formulations can ease the mathematics (as is well known), but they do this at the cost of a less clear-cut economic background of the analyzed dynamics.

9.3 A Numerical Analysis of the AE Case

Following conventional economic procedures, we have indexed the expected rate of inflation in equations (9.17)–(9.19) by $t-h$. From a mathematical point of view the index t is, however, equally admissible and leads to the following form of the basic discrete-time AD-AS growth model:

$$w_{t+h} = w_t + w_t\left(h\ln(l_t/l_t^s) + \pi_t^e\right)$$

$$l_{t+h}^s = l_t^s + l_t^s[i_f(ax_t h - \delta h - (i_t - \pi_t^e))]$$

$$\pi_{t+h}^e = \pi_t^e + \beta_{\pi^e} h\left(\frac{p_t - p_{t-h}}{p_{t-h}} - \pi_t^e\right)$$

The values of x_t, i_t are now given by the solution of

$$0 = x_t - c_h(x_t - \theta - \delta) - i_f(ax_t - \delta - (i_t - \pi_t^e)/h) - n - \delta - \gamma$$

$$0 = m_t - x_t\exp(-bi_t/h)$$

and l_t, p_t, m_t are determined as in the preceding section.

The above reformulation of the basic-period version shows that this version is obtained by applying the simple Euler approximation from the set of numerical methods available for simulating continuous-time dynamical systems[11] to the continuous-time AD-AS growth model, with the provision that at each step of this iteration a specific nonlinear system for the temporary equilibrium variables x_t, l_t, i_t, p_t, m_t has to be solved in addition. We thereby have arrived at a period model that is at the same time economically meaningful and mathematically justified in the light of its continuous-time "original."

In order also to simulate the two alternative discrete-time formulations discussed in the preceding section, one can employ in the first case the following sequential solution of the IS-LM equilibrium part:

$$x_t = (\gamma + n + \delta - c_h(\theta + \delta) - i_f(\delta + (i_{t-h} - \pi_{t-h}^e)/h)/(1 - c_h - ai_f)$$

$$i_t = h(\ln(x_t) - \ln(m_t))/b.$$

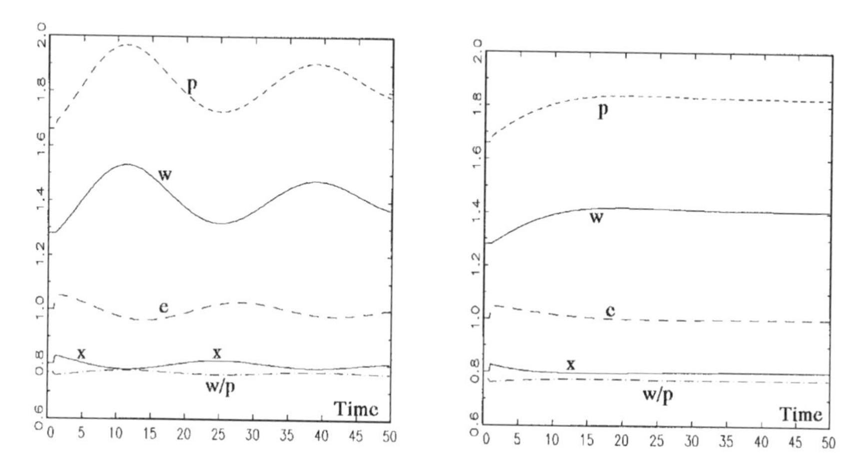

Figure 9.2
The case of a stable stagflation cycle ($\beta_{\pi^e} = .3$, left). The Sargent (1973a) case of strong asymptotic stability ($\beta_{\pi^e} = 0$, right)

This means that a solution routine for nonlinear equation systems becomes redundant here, which considerably simplifies the iteration procedure.

In the case of the second alternative discrete-time version, the dynamic law

$$\pi^e_{t+h} = \pi^e_t + h\beta_{\pi^e}\left(\frac{p_t - p_{t-h}}{p_{t-h}} - \pi^e_t\right)$$

has to be inserted into the IS-LM part of the model in order to allow for its solution in terms of the dynamically endogenous variables, including π^e_{t+h}. Returning to our basic formulation of a period version of AD-AS growth model, we get for the parameter values

$$c_h = .7, \quad \delta = .05, \quad \gamma = \theta = .65, \quad g_m = n = .03, \quad b = 2,$$

$$i_f = .25, \quad \beta_w = .3, \quad \beta_{\pi^e} = .3, \quad a = .3, \quad M/L^s = 1.25$$

and a 10 percent shock of the monetary base at time $t = 1$ the damped fluctuations shown in figure 9.1

This can be compared with the case $\beta_{\pi^e} = 0$, which can be proved to be locally asymptotically stable[12] and which is discussed at length in Sargent (1987, chap. 5).[13]

Increasing β_{π^e} to .7, 1, . . . (cf. the following figures), however, increases the cyclical nature of this model of monetary growth considerably, so that its amplitude in fact becomes undamped (from $\sim .7$

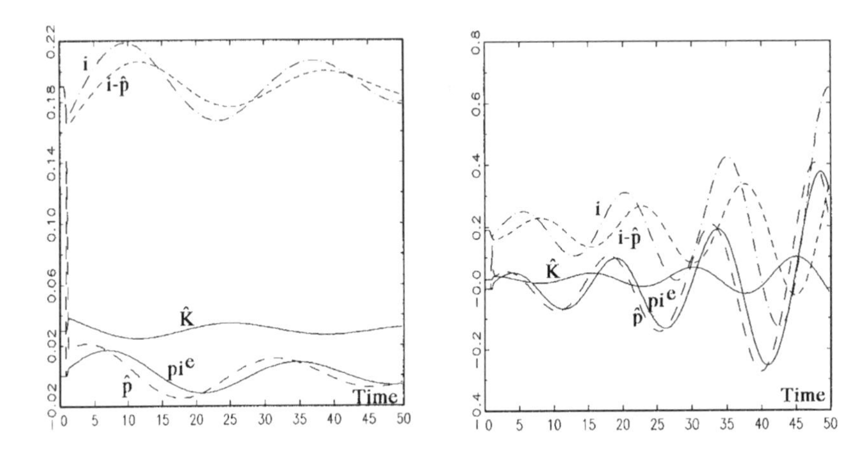

Figure 9.3
Stable and unstable situations under adaptive expectations ($pi^e = \pi^e$). Left hand side: $\beta_{\pi^e} = .3$; Right hand side: $\beta_{\pi^e} = 1(pi^e = \pi^e)$

onward). This result shows that Sargent's (1987, 124) general claim that this model behaves "classically" in the long run must be rejected as false.

Adaptively formed inflationary expectations that react with sufficient strength with regard to past errors thus represent one important possibility to get cyclical fluctuations with increasing amplitude in this growth model of AD-AS type. Such a result is not too unexpected in the light of the literature on neoclassical models of monetary growth with adaptive expectations (see for example the paper by Benhabib and Miyao [1981]). The consequences of such an instability in a fairly conventional AD-AS growth model, however, have not yet been thoroughly investigated—in particular not in the light of the problems we have enumerated for the limit case of myopic perfect foresight. We shall see in the remainder of the chapter that attempts to turn the above situation into an economically viable one will in the end imply that the striking contrast between the adaptive and the perfect expectations case completely disappears from such a model. Not having noticed that the employed model will not yet be an economically meaningful one for adaptive expectations that are close to perfect foresight, we are consequently not astonished that Sargent's treatment of the limit case of perfect foresight is erroneous in its handling of the resulting saddle point situation.

The above depicted situation of total instability is typical for such models of monetary growth and has been investigated analytically in

Franke 1992a for the continuous-time case. This is not an easy task, since the nonlinear AD-AS block of the model implies that the system of differential equations to be considered is an implicit one. Under certain conditions it is shown in his paper that the steady state of this Keynesian model is locally asymptotically stable if the reaction coefficient β_{π^e} is chosen sufficiently small, and that it is locally unstable for all β_{π^e} sufficiently large, with a Hopf bifurcation (and also an ill-defined situation) occurring in between. We conjecture from the above typical simulations that this local instability is not bounded in the large—at least for β_{π^e} sufficiently high. This implies that the viability of the model is severely in question. Yet, viability—or boundedness—of the dynamics of a macro-model is the most basic requirement that one should make for such a model unless it is explicitly characterized as being of only a partial nature.

We conclude that the model of sections 9.1 and 9.2 has to be modified significantly in order to fulfill this most basic requirement for a complete macro model. Following section 8.4, we shall make use in the following section of such a modification, an IS-LM growth model with both sluggish wage and price dynamics, in order to show that the above problems can be overcome by such an approach.

9.4 AE and MPF I: Cases of No Difference

We have seen in sections 9.1–3 that the AD-AS growth model in general demands the investigation of a mixed algebraic equations/difference equations system, since it is based on equilibrium conditions as well as on laws of motion, both of a nonlinear type. Adding to this complexity of the model, one of the variables that is determined by its equilibrium part, that is, the price level p, is also used in derivative form, that is, as rate of inflation $\hat{p}$, in the formulation of the dynamics of the model, in the case of adaptive expectations, and even in its equilibrium part in the case of perfect foresight (cf. the preceding chapter). This derivative use of a statically endogenous variable gives rise to a complicated feedback structure between the temporary equilibrium part of the model and its dynamical laws.

We have also seen in the preceding chapter that there are a variety of reasons which suggest that the theory of the price level and of its rate of change is not yet well formulated in this AD-AS approach to economic growth. We therefore propose, as in the previous chapter, to replace the implicit (and contradictory) theory of inflation of the AD-AS growth model with the following explicit approach to the determination of the rate of price level changes in such models of monetary growth:

$$p_{t+h} = p_t + \beta_p h \left[(1+\mu) \frac{w_t L_t}{K_t^a L_t^{1-a}} - p_t \right], \qquad 1+\mu > 1 \tag{9.22}$$

Marked-up normal[14] unit wage costs, employing a mark-up factor $1+\mu$, compared to actual prices determine here the rate of change in the price level in the interval $[t, t-h]$. We stress again that it is also possible to use marginal wage–cost instead of the above average cost.[15] Essential is that price adjustment—just as wage adjustment—is now lagged with regard to current quantity reactions, that is, this nominal magnitude is now also h-dependent in the strength of its reaction to exogenous shocks. This removes the problematic asymmetry between wage and price adjustment we have considered at length in the preceding chapter and allows for a partially independent evolution of prices and quantities over time, and thus for a Keynesian theory of employment even in the case of myopic perfect foresight.

Reformulating the above price dynamics again for continuous time as $\hat{p} = \beta_p[(1+\mu)\omega l^a - 1]$ and revising the IS-LM growth model of section 8.4 to allow for adaptive expectations in the place of perfect foresight gives rise to the following five-dimensional dynamics:

$$\hat{\omega} = \beta_w(e-1) + \beta_w^*(e^* - e) + \pi^e - \beta_p((1+\mu)\omega(el^s)^a - 1) \tag{9.23}$$

$$\hat{l}^s = n - s_h(x - \delta - \theta) + \gamma - \theta, \qquad s_h = 1 - c_h \tag{9.24}$$

$$\hat{m} = n - s_h(x - \delta - \theta) + \gamma - \theta - \beta_p((1+\mu)\omega(el^s)^a - 1) \tag{9.25}$$

$$\dot{e} = \beta_e(e^* - e) \tag{9.26}$$

$$\dot{\pi}^e = \beta_{\pi^e}(\beta_p((1+\mu)\omega(el^s)^a - 1) - \pi^e) \tag{9.27}$$

where x is given by the solution to the IS-LM equations:

$$x = \frac{i_f \left(\pi^e + \frac{m - f_m^{2a}}{f_m^{2b}} - \delta - \omega el^s \right) + \delta + n + \gamma - c_h(\theta + \delta)}{1 - c_h - i_f\left(1 - f_m^1 / f_m^{2b}\right)} \tag{9.28}$$

and e^* by $x^{1/(1-a)}/l^s$. This is the adaptive expectations equivalent to the Keynesian growth model with perfect foresight of section 8.4. Note again that this model employs a sluggish adjustment of the labor force of firms in view of their actual employment and a theory of the rate of inflation that rests on the normal, not on the actual employment of this labor force. Note also that the partial derivatives of the function x are now unambiguously negative for ω, l^s, e and positive for m, π^e. The latter two partial derivatives represent the so-called Keynes and Mundell effects.

Proposition 9.1 The steady state of the dynamics (9.23)–(9.27) is given—as in the case of perfect foresight—by:

$$\omega^\star = 1/((1+\mu)(l^{s\star})^a)$$

$$l^{s\star} = l^\star = (x^\star)^{\frac{1}{1-a}}$$

$$m^\star = f_m^1 x^\star + f_m^{2a} - f_m^{2b} i^\star$$

$$e^\star = (e^*)^\star = 1 \qquad \text{and}$$

$$(\pi^e)^\star = 0$$

where $x^\star$ is again given by $\delta + \theta + \frac{n+\gamma-\theta}{s_h}$ and $i^\star$ by $x^\star - \delta - \omega^\star l^{s\star}$.

Proposition 9.2 Consider the Jacobian J (the linear part) of the dynamics (9.23)–(9.27) at the steady state. The determinant of this $5 \star 5$-matrix: $\det J$, is always negative.

It follows again that the system can only lose or gain asymptotic stability by way of a so-called Hopf bifurcation if its eigenvalues cross the imaginary axis with positive speed (as it is the case here).

Proof Exploiting the many linear dependencies involved in the above dynamical system and its Jacobian, we find it again easy to show that its determinant can be reduced to the following qualitative form:

$$\begin{pmatrix} 0 & 0 & 0 & + & 0 \\ 0 & 0 & - & 0 & 0 \\ - & 0 & 0 & 0 & 0 \\ 0 & - & 0 & 0 & 0 \\ 0 & 0 & 0 & 0 & - \end{pmatrix}$$

which gives a negative expression for $\det J$.

q.e.d.

In the same way it can be shown that the determinant of the linear part of the four-dimensional dynamics—where $\beta_{\pi^e} = 0, \pi^e = (\pi^e)^\star = 0$ is assumed for the new variable π^e of the model—is positive.

Proposition 9.3 Assume that the state variables e, π^e are fixed at their steady state values ($\beta_e, \beta_{\pi^e} = 0$). Then: The steady state of the subdynamics (9.23)–(9.25) is locally asymptotically stable if the parameter β_w^* is chosen sufficiently high and the parameter β_p sufficiently small.

Proof As in the case of the larger dynamical systems just considered it is straightforward to show that the determinant[16] of the linear part or the Jacobian of these subdynamics are always negative. However, the second entry in the trace of this Jacobian is positive, while the other two are negative. The parameter β_w^* in the first entry of its trace must therefore be chosen sufficiently large, until it and the third term dominate the positive sign of the second entry and thus enforce that $a_1 = -$ trace J gets positive. The principal minors of the Jacobian (which form the coefficient a_2 in the Routh-Hurwitz stability criterion), furthermore, are easily shown to be zero and one positive if the parameter β_p is set equal to 0, that is, their sum a_2 is positive for all β_p sufficiently small. There remains to prove the condition

$$a_1 a_2 - a_3 = -\text{ trace } J \cdot a_2 + \det J > 0$$

of the Routh-Hurwitz conditions for local asymptotic stability. Here again, the parameter β_w^* must be chosen sufficiently large to guarantee that this expression becomes positive. To see this, one need only note that the expression $a_1 a_2$ is a quadratic function of this parameter while a_3 depends on it only linearly.

q.e.d.

Corollary 9.1 Assume that the parameters $\beta_p, \beta_e, \beta_{\pi^e}$ are chosen sufficiently small and β_w^* sufficiently large. Then: The steady state of the dynamics (9.23)–(9.27) is locally asymptotically stable.

Proof Choose the parameters β_w^*, β_p as in the preceding proof for the three-dimensional dynamics, that is, the eigenvalues of this subsystem all have negative real parts. Since the four-dimensional system (where β_{π^e} is still zero) exhibits a positive determinant of its Jacobian, a small, but positive parameter β_e must give rise to four eigenvalues with negative real parts, owing to the continuity of the eigenvalues with respect to their dependence on the Jacobian J. This argument can then be repeated for small changes in the parameter β_{π^e}, which make it positive.

q.e.d.

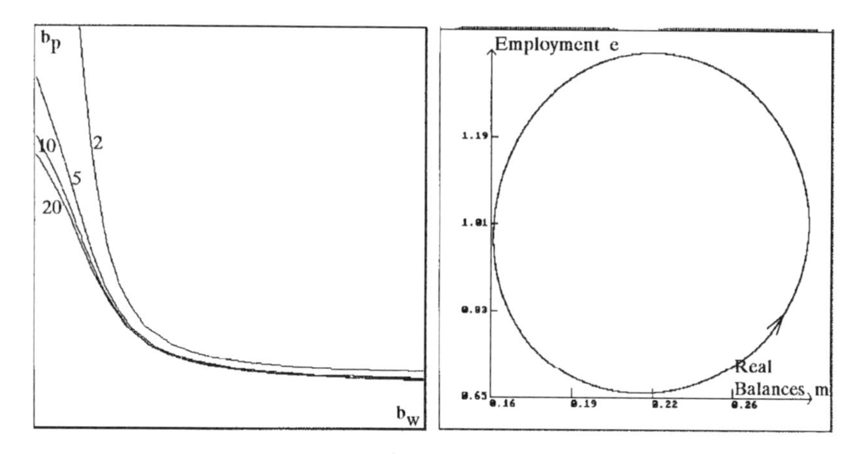

Figure 9.4
Hopf loci and limit cycles under fast adaptive expectations ($b_p = \beta_p$)

Remark We want to remark that the system with β_{π^e} equal to zero is stable for a broad range of its remaining parameters. Situations where instability can be proved will be considered in the next section.

Simulating this model for low adjustment speeds of the inflationary mechanism ($\beta_p \leq 1$, $\beta_w = 0.2$, for example) and for low or high adjustment speeds of the adaptively formed inflationary expectations gives rise to damped cycles that are not much changed when the speed of adjustment of expectations is high and rising. The dynamics are thus basically the same for perfect foresight and fast adaptive expectations in such cases, and a sufficient increase in the parameter β_{π^e} of the adaptive expectations mechanism in particular makes the difference between the actual and the expected rate of inflation nearly invisible. These observations also hold true in the case where the price adjustment speed is already so high that the steady state is unstable and "surrounded" by a stable limit cycle, as in figure 9.4 (right-hand side, $\beta_{\pi^e} = 100$!). In this case the shown limit cycle is generated via a supercritical Hopf bifurcation with respect to the parameter β_p. It is growing larger as the parameter β_{π^e} is increased and is approaching the limit cycle of the perfect foresight case shown in figure 8.4.[17]

A sufficiently low degree of price flexibility therefore guarantees that a crucial difference between (fast) adaptive expectations and myopic perfect foresight—much stressed in the literature—cannot be detected for a Keynesian model of IS-LM growth, as the one considered in this section. This is also mirrored in figure to the left in figure 9.4, which gives the Hopf bifurcation loci of the dynamics in (β_w, β_p)-space for rising parameter values β_{π^e}. These curves converge to the Hopf locus of the perfect foresight case shown in the first picture of figure 8.4 as the parameter β_{π^e} is approaching infinity—at least if, as figure 9.4 shows, the adjustment speed of the price level is not too high.

These—as well as other—numerical investigations of the model suggest that the assumption of myopic perfect foresight will not create problems as long as it is assumed that the model is sufficiently sluggish in its adjustment of prices, since they will then only generate a dynamics that is very close to the case of fast adaptive inflationary expectations. They furthermore tentatively suggest that the viability of the model that is generated by a sufficiently sluggish adjustment of prices p may be of central importance for any equivalence assertion on fast adaptive and myopic perfect foresight expectations. And they also imply that the viability considerations made in section 8.5 for the case of myopic perfect foresight will be applicable to the case of adaptively formed expectations as well and will enforce viability here, too. There is, in fact, not much difference then between the simulations shown in the preceding chapter and the repetition of these simulations for the adaptive expectations case which, because of this reason, are not repeated here.

Finally, these simulations of a modified IS-LM growth model of monetary growth also suggest a way by which the instability of the Keynesian AD-AS dynamics model we discussed in section 9.4 may be overcome—namely by assuming a sufficiently sluggish price adjustment here, too—now with respect to marginal wage cost, of course. Assuming the following equation for dynamic price formation in the place of equation (9.2) in an otherwise unchanged model (9.1)–(9.10):

$$\dot{p} = \beta_p(w/F_L - p), \quad \text{i.e. in our case, } \hat{p} = \beta_p(\omega l^a/(1-a) - 1) \qquad (9.29)$$

indeed gives rise to simulation results that are qualitatively close to the ones of our modified IS-LM growth model. We have investigated such a modification of the AD-AS approach in a medium-run context in chapter 7.

All this will change in the case of a price level that is very flexible in its adjustment toward the desired price level, as the following section will show—at least in the case where employment e reacts sensitively with respect to output changes.

9.5 AE and MPF II: Why Can There Be a Difference?

We shall now determine a typical situation where the global instability observed in section 9.3 for the AD-AS growth model can be shown by analytical reasoning for this growth model (as formulated in section 9.1), as well as our modification of it in section 9.4. We shall do this first for our reformulation of the AD-AS growth model as IS-LM growth model with finite adjustment speeds for wages and prices.

A first and negative finding with respect to instability, is the following:

Lemma 9.1 Consider the Jacobian J (the linear part) of the dynamics (9.23)–(9.27) at the steady state. The trace of this $5 \star 5$-matrix: det J is negative if the adjustment parameter β_w^* (or β_p or β_e or β_{π^e}) is chosen sufficiently large.

Remark This lemma implies that the Routh-Hurwitz stability condition $a_1 = -\text{trace } J$ is always fulfilled if the dynamics are based on sufficiently flexible adjustment processes.

Proof It is easy to check that it is only the second dynamical law that is based on a positive autofeedback mechanism ($\dot{l}^s_{l^s} > 0$). Yet, this partial derivative does not include any of the adjustment speeds of the model whereas (some of) the other depends on the above parameters. They can therefore be used to make the trace of the Jacobian negative.

q.e.d.

Lemma 9.2 Given the Jacobian J of the dynamics (9.23)–(9.27) at the steady state. The submatrix $J(e, \pi^e)$ of this $5 \star 5$-matrix given by the subsystem defined by the variables e, π^e reads:

$$\begin{pmatrix} \beta_e(e_e^* - 1) & \beta_e e_{\pi^e}^* \\ \beta_{\pi^e}\beta_p a(1+\mu)\omega l^s (el^s)^{a-1} & -\beta_{\pi^e} \end{pmatrix}.$$

The determinant of this matrix is negative for all price adjustment speeds β_p sufficiently high.

Remark The proof of this lemma is straightforward if one notes that the partial derivative e_e^* is negative and $e_{\pi^e}^*$ positive. Note here also that the sign of this determinant does not depend on the size of the parameters β_e, β_{π^e}. This determinant is one summation component of the Routh-Hurwitz coefficient a_2—which is the sum of all ten principal minors of dimension 2 of the matrix J. The isolated interaction between the rate of employment e and the expected rate of inflation π^e is therefore contributing to instability (leading to $a_2 < 0$) of the whole dynamical system. The basis of this destabilizing mechanism is a positive Mundell effect of π^e on demand x and thereby on employment e, which is here combined with a positive effect of employment e on inflation $\hat{p}$ and thus back on inflationary expectations π^e.

Proposition 9.4 For all adjustment speeds β_p, β_e sufficiently high there exists a parameter value $\beta^o_{\pi^e}$, such that for all adjustment speeds of inflationary expectations β_{π^e} larger than this value we have: $a_2 < 0$, that is, the dynamics are not locally asymptotically stable then.

Remark We thus know that sufficiently high adjustment speeds of prices, employment, and inflationary expectations will—at least in certain combinations—overthrow the local asymptotic stability of the five-dimensional dynamics (9.23)–(9.27) that may exist, according to the corollary of the preceding section for low values of these adjustment speeds. If stability gets lost in this way, it must be by way of a Hopf bifurcation, as the preceding section has shown. It is therefore not necessarily the case that there will be purely explosive cycles once this condition has been hurt. Numerical investigations, however, show that the dynamics becomes nonviable if the parameter β_{π^e} is chosen sufficiently large in the above situation.

Proof Choose the parameter value β_p as in lemma 9.1. We note that the parameters β_e, β_{π^e} are jointly involved only with respect to the principal minor $J(e, \pi^e)$ we have considered in lemma 9.1. The parameter β_e can therefore be chosen such that the principal minors that depend on the parameter β_{π^e} are dominated by this minor and thus can be made negative in sum by choosing the parameter β_e sufficiently large. Since the parameter β_{π^e} is a joint factor of all these minors and does not appear in the other ones, the sum of all these $2 * 2$ minors must become negative for all β_{π^e} chosen sufficiently large.

q.e.d.

Remark Note that the coefficient a_2 can be driven toward $-\infty$ in the way described in the above proof.

We have, however, not yet shown that the original AD-AS growth model will give rise qualitatively to the same type of instability as the IS-LM growth model we have just considered. In order to show this we shall make use of the dynamic equation (9.29) of section 9.4 instead of its static counterpart (9.2), that is, infinitely flexible prices p. We get as resulting dynamics for the AD-AS growth model under this modification of system (9.1)–(9.10) the following system of differential equations:[18]

$$\hat{p} = \beta_p(w/(pf'(l)) - 1) \tag{9.30}$$

$$\hat{w} = \ln(l/l^s) + \pi^e \tag{9.31}$$

$$\dot{\pi}^e = \beta_{\pi^e}(\beta_p(w/(pf'(l)) - 1) - \pi^e) \tag{9.32}$$

$$\hat{l}^s = n - s_h(f(l) - \theta - \delta) + \gamma - \theta \tag{9.33}$$

where we now use the general expression $f(l)$ in the place of l^{1-a} and $f'(l)$ in the place of l^{-a}, that is, a general neoclassical production function in intensive form in the place of the Cobb-Douglas production function used for our numerical investigations. The statically endogenous variables l and i employed in this dynamics have to be determined from the equation system [see eqs. (9.3)–(9.6), (9.1) in section 9.1]:[19]

$$f(l) = c_h(f(l) - \theta - \delta) + i_f(f(l) - (w/p)l - \delta - (i - \pi^e)) + \delta + n + \gamma,$$

$$\bar{d}l^s = pm^d(l, i) = pf(l)\exp(-bi).$$

where $\bar{d} = M/L^s$ is a constant that is given by initial conditions.

This system is now analyzed with regard to its stability properties for variations of the parameters β_p, β_{π^e}.[20]

Making use of the conventional Keynesian assumption on the marginal propensity to spend $Y_Y^d < 1$ (see also Sargent 1987, 54), which is here given when the condition $(1 - c_h - i_f)f' + i_f w/p > 0$ holds true, we see that the comparative–static evaluation of the above two equations gives rise to

$$\begin{pmatrix} (1 - c_h - i_f)f' + i_f w/p & i_f \\ pm_l^d & pm_i^d \end{pmatrix} \begin{pmatrix} dl \\ di \end{pmatrix}$$

$$= \begin{pmatrix} i_f wl/p^2 & -i_f l/p & i_f & 0 \\ -m^d & 0 & 0 & \bar{d} \end{pmatrix} \begin{pmatrix} dp \\ dw \\ d\pi^e \\ dl^s \end{pmatrix}$$

This implies the following sign pattern for the dependence of the statically endogenous variables on the dynamically endogenous ones (the sign structure of the partial derivatives of the implicitly defined functions for l and i):

$$l = l(\underset{?}{p}, \underset{-}{w}, \underset{+}{\pi^e}, \underset{+}{l^s}), \qquad i = (\underset{+}{p}, \underset{-}{w}, \underset{+}{\pi^e}, \underset{-}{l^s}) \tag{9.34}$$

By means of the implicitly defined function l the equations of system (9.30)–(9.33) can thus be characterized as follows:

$$\hat{p} = H^1(\underset{?}{p}, \underset{?}{w}, \underset{+}{\pi^e}, \underset{+}{l^s}) \tag{9.35}$$

$$\hat{w} = H^2(\underset{?}{p}, \underset{-}{w}, \underset{+}{\pi^e}, \underset{?}{l^s}) \tag{9.36}$$

$$\dot{\pi}^e = H^3(\underset{?}{p}, \underset{?}{w}, \underset{+}{\pi^e}, \underset{+}{l^s}) \tag{9.37}$$

$$\hat{l}^s = H^4(\underset{?}{p}, \underset{+}{w}, \underset{-}{\pi^e}, \underset{-}{l^s}) \tag{9.38}$$

Note that we have used the standard properties $f' > 0$, $f'' < 0$ of the neoclassical production function f in this determination of the signs of the partial derivatives of the functions $H^1, \ldots, H^4$ and that the characterization " + " of $H^3_{\pi^e}$ will be true only *for sufficiently large values of the adjustment parameter* β_p. This, however, is a meaningful restriction, since we want to reconsider the AD-AS case $\beta_p = \infty$. The meaning of this side condition is easily understood in the light of the above discussion of the instability of the IS-LM growth model (see lemma 9.2). Owing to $\beta_e = \infty$ in the present case, the potentially destabilizing feature $H^3_{\pi^e} > 0$ of the model now occurs in the trace of the Jacobian instead of in the minors of dimension two and is thus visible in a more direct way. Note, furthermore, that both employment l and inflation $\hat{p}$ depend positively on the expected rate of inflation—because of the assumed investment behavior and because of rising marginal wage costs in production. This positive dependence of inflation on expected inflation is the essential element in the following (in)stability investigation. It is now easy to provide again a typical example of why the steady state of the above dynamical system will be unstable for fast adaptive expectations. We have already noted that a suitably large choice of the parameter β_p will imply that the time rate of change of inflationary expectations will depend positively on the level of inflationary expectations, that is, the expected rate of inflation will be subject to centrifugal forces then—similar to the rate of growth in the Harrod model and closely related to the Cagan model we have considered in chapter 4. In contrast to standard formulations of Harrod's knife-edge situation, we have here, however, that this positive dependence does not work in isolation but is embedded in a four-dimensional dynamics that may (or may not) be capable of turning this partial instability into overall stability, for example, by sufficiently negative other elements in the trace of the Jacobian of the above model. Exactly this is prevented, however, when the parameter β_{π^e} becomes sufficiently large, on the basis of a given β_p that is chosen in the above way. In this way the trace of the Jacobian of the system can always be made positive, which according to the Routh-Hurwitz theorem implies the instability of the above model.[21]

A sufficiently fast adjustment of inflationary expectations on the basis of a sufficiently strong adjustment toward the rule of marginal cost pricing thus makes the above partial knife-edge situation in the expectations mechanism a total one, with a trace of the Jacobian as large as desired, and creates the strongly explosive type of behavior we have investigated numerically in section 9.3 (see also figure 9.5). This is an interesting price-sector analog to the steady growth instability observed in the Harrod model—though one that works in a more roundabout way. And it shows that the original Sargent (1987, chap. 5) approach to the discussion of adaptive vs. perfect expectations is highly problematic and incomplete in an essential way, since it does not pay any attention to these destabilizing forces of the adaptive expectations case.

Forces that attempt to limit the explosive behavior of this model and thus aim at making it a viable model may be introduced again in the way they were formulated in section 8.5, there with the aim of making the modified IS-LM growth model of this section a viable one in the presence of myopic perfect foresight. In this way the following improved viability situation can, for example, be established for the above unstable situation of the AD-AS growth model.

Figure 9.5 again exemplifies that the once-and-for-all disturbances of the steady state by open market operations as they are investigated in Sargent 1987, chapter 5 need not at all lead back to these steady-state

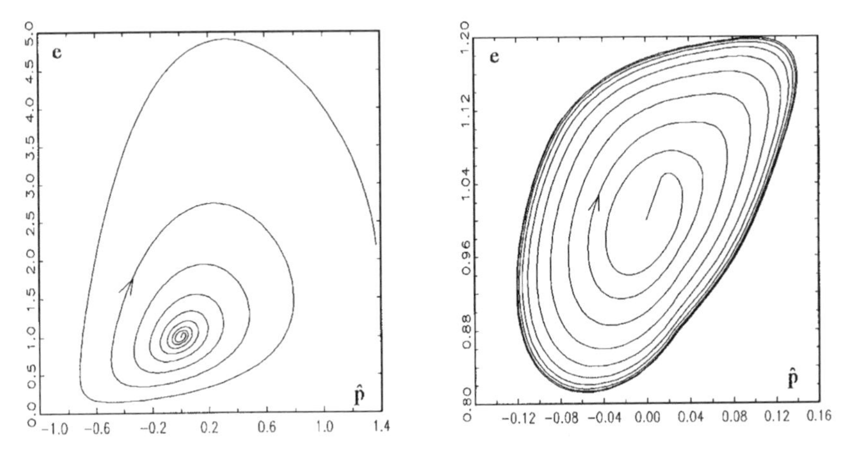

Figure 9.5
Viability constraints (right) for the AD-AS growth model (left)

paths. It thereby is understandable why Sargent (1987, 119) is forced to note: "Assuming that the system is dynamically stable, . . . the final effect of the once-and-for-all jump in M, once the system has returned to its steady-state, is to leave all real variables unaltered and to increase the price level and money wage proportionately with the money supply." The above stability analysis, however, shows that Sargent's claim that his Keynesian dynamics has "classical" long-run properties will in fact be true only in a version of the above model where prices are sufficiently sluggish and were the long run may thus be of a very long-run nature. In general, however, there holds the conclusion that assumptions on behavioral functions that enforce *steady states* to react neutrally to changes in money supply need not establish monetarist results for the dynamics of such Keynesian models.

Worse than that, however, is the fact that the above model cannot be stabilized by any means when prices are sufficiently flexible and when adaptive expectations tend to become perfect. There is no sensible limit to this model in the present form when the parameter β_{π^e} approaches the limit case of myopic perfect foresight.

We conclude that Sargent's limit case of myopic perfect foresight is built on a structure that is not economically meaningful and, mathematically seen, is structurally unstable. The analytical results that can be obtained from such a limit case are highly artificial and are thus not

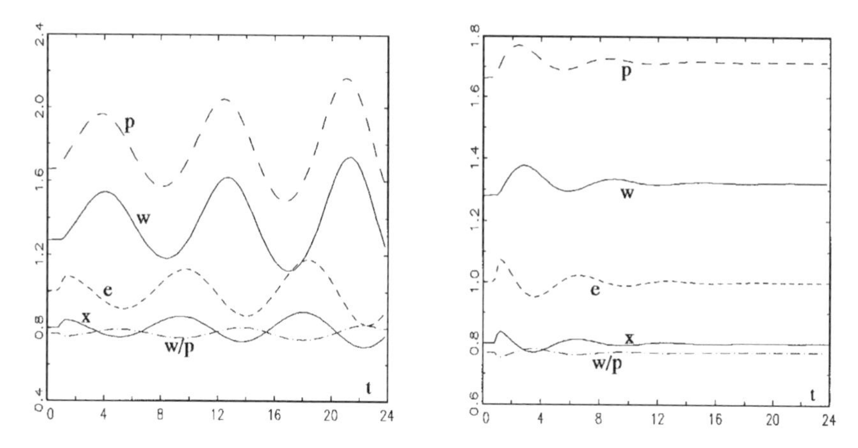

Figure 9.6
Monetary policy rule (right) to combat the explosive cycle (left) of the AD-AS growth model

representative of the relationship that in general exists between the case of adaptive expectations and that of myopic perfect foresight.

In the light of the instability phenomenon we have analyzed above it is interesting to ask whether there exist policy rules that are capable of removing the (explosive) cycle from the above dynamics. Since the price sector of the economy is responsible for this instability, a counter-cyclical monetary policy may be adequate and will be briefly investigated. We assume with regard to the growth rate of the money supply the following adjustment rule:

$$\hat{M} = n - \beta_m \pi^e, \qquad \beta_m > 0$$

which says that the so-far-constant growth rate of the money supply will be modified inversely to the discrepancy that exists between the currently expected rate of inflation and its steady-state rate, which is zero. This rule indeed allows the removal of both the instability and the cycle from the above dynamics, if the parameter β_m is chosen with care, that is, in some reasonable interval, for example, $\beta_m = .2$ in the simulation in figure 9.6. We only note, but do not show here, that the above rule is capable of suppressing the observed problematic behavior in the trace of the Jacobian of the above dynamical systems.

Summarizing the results of this chapter and the preceding one, we can state that the reason for the striking contrast between adaptive and perfect inflationary expectations is simply due to the fact that this type of Keynesian dynamics becomes an extremely unstable one for high adjustment speeds of the price level p toward its target value, if in addition, adaptive expectations are very fast and thus approach their limit case of myopic perfect foresight. The generally hidden unstable feedback mechanism of expected inflation onto its rate of change in the case of a flexible adjustment of prices is then revealed in a drastic way and eventually driven to the extreme of an infinitely large positive element in the trace of the Jacobian. Conceivable consequences of this fact are that assuming directly myopic perfect foresight and perfectly flexible prices, as in the AD-AS growth model, may lead either to an ill-defined dynamic model or to a model that reflects the extremely explosive nature of its adaptive companion model in a dichotomizing way—that is, by disrupture in its formerly integrated economic structure. The latter case is characteristic for the AD-AS growth model of the textbook literature.

We thus end up with the conclusion that flexible prices ($\beta_p \to \infty$) incorporate the germ of hyperinflation into otherwise fairly standard models of IS-LM growth that will completely destroy the structure or the viability of the model if fast adjusting expectations speed up this inflationary mechanism sufficiently. Hence, in order to get an economy that will fulfill the basic requirement of viability or reproducibility, at least over a certain period of time, a necessary condition is that prices react sufficiently sluggishly with respect to any imbalance to their target level. If such an assumption is made, the contrast that is generally observed between models with (fast) adaptive, as against correct, expectations will disappear from such models.

9.6 AE and MPF III: The Basic Fallacy

This chapter would not be complete if we did not examine the basic contribution of Sargent and Wallace (1973) that provided the basis for all later analysis of the saddlepath (in)stability phenomenon of perfect foresight models. Our analysis—which will rationalize jumps in certain variables in a natural way, but which will refute Sargent and Wallace's specific solution to this problem—owes its ideas to Chiarella (1990, chap. 7). The analysis will present them in a different way from Chiarella's and stays close to the dynamic variables that are used by Sargent and Wallace (1973). This section continues the analysis of local instability and of resulting relaxation oscillations of the Cagan model that we have presented in chapter 4.

We have seen there that—from a mathematical as well as an economic point of view—a natural generalization of the simple Cagan model employed by Sargent and Wallace (1973) in their analysis of the dynamic (in)stability of models of monetary growth is given by the following two-dimensional dynamic model:

$$\dot{\pi}^e = \beta_{\pi^e}(\beta_p(m - \alpha(\pi^e)) - (1-\eta)\pi^e) \tag{9.39}$$

$$\dot{m} = \beta_p(\alpha(\pi^e) - m) - \eta\pi^e \tag{9.40}$$

In this model, the symbol m denotes again the log of the real money supply M/p (see chapter 4 for further details). We assume for simplicity that the growth rate of the money supply is zero so that only isolated changes in this supply will be considered. The time derivative $\dot{m}$ is thus the negative of the rate of inflation $\hat{p}$. For the function α we furthermore assume the following concrete shape $\alpha(\pi^e) = atan(-a\pi^e)/\pi + 0.5$,[22] which is of the form utilized in chapter 4, figures 4.8/4.9. The model is therefore a special case of the generalized Cagan model we have investigated there which, nevertheless, mirrors all properties of the more general approach. Sargent and Wallace (1973), however, consider an extreme limit case of this model, namely, the case where β_{π^e}, β_p are both infinite and $\alpha(\pi^e) = -a\pi^e/\pi + .5$, that is, a linear function of π^e with the slope of the above nonlinear function at the steady state. Their restricted model therefore considers perfect flexibility of prices and expectations in a neighborhood solely of the steady state. The steady state of the above model is given by $\dot{m} = \dot{\pi}^e = 0$, which implies $(\pi^e)^\star = 0$ and $m^\star = .5$. The Jacobian of the system (9.39), (9.40) is given by:

$$J = \begin{pmatrix} -\beta_{\pi^e}(1-\eta+\beta_p\alpha'(\pi^e)) & \beta_{\pi^e}\beta_p \\ \beta_p\alpha'(\pi^e) - \eta & -\beta_p \end{pmatrix}$$

This gives at the steady state (where $\alpha'((\pi^e)^\star) = -a/\pi$ holds):

$$\text{trace } J = -\beta_p + \beta_{\pi^e}(\beta_p a/\pi - (1-\eta))$$

$$\det J = \beta_p\beta_{\pi^e} > 0$$

The above dynamics will therefore exhibit a Hopf bifurcation at

$$\beta_{\pi^e}^H = \frac{\beta_p}{\beta_p a/\pi - (1-\eta)} = \frac{1}{a/\pi - (1-\eta)/\beta_p}$$

This Hopf locus is of the following shape and it implies—as shown in

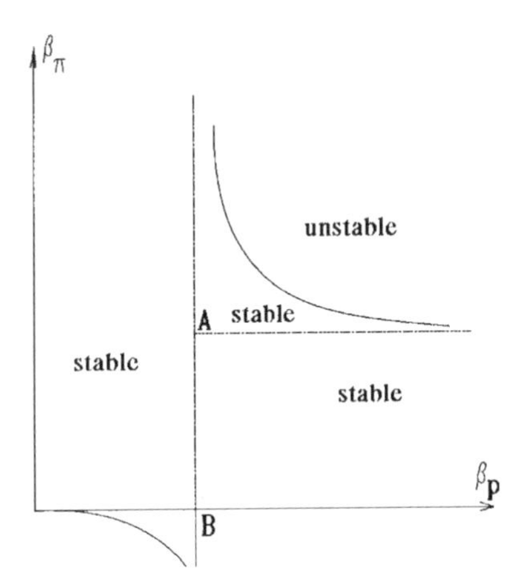

Figure 9.7
The Hopf locus for the extended Cagan model ($A = \pi/a$, $B = \pi(1-\eta/a)$

this figure—locally asymptotically stable steady states to the left of the point $B = \beta_p^o = \pi(1-\eta)/a$ and (to the right of it) unstable steady state for inflationary expectations that are sufficiently fast.

Price adjustment speeds below the value β_p^o will again allow the conclusion that fast adaptive expectations and myopic perfect foresight generate very similar dynamics, whereas price adjustment speeds above this value will imply the opposite conclusion. The degree of price flexibility is therefore again crucial for the local asymptotic stability of the model under fast adaptive expectations. For sufficiently flexible prices, the steady state of the dynamics loses its stability in a cyclical fashion when the speed of adjustment of inflationary expectations is increased beyond a value larger than π/a. Numerical simulations of these dynamics will show below that the loss of stability is accompanied by the birth of a stable limit cycle, that is, the Hopf bifurcation is of supercritical type.

Sargent and Wallace's (1973) paper now has the following restricted view with respect to the above: on the one hand, it considers only the double limit case $\beta_p, \beta_{\pi^e} = \infty$, and on the other hand, it does so solely from a local perspective, assuming thereby that $\alpha'(0)$ characterizes the shape of the money demand function not only near the steady state, but also for all other values of inflationary expectations π^e. On the basis of these assumptions the above dynamic system gives rise to the following single linear differential equation:

$$\dot{m} = \frac{\pi(m - 0.05)}{a}$$

since we then have money–market equilibrium $m = \alpha(\pi^e)$ and perfect foresight $\dot{p} = \pi^e = -\dot{m}$ throughout. This differential equation is the basis of Sargent and Wallace's analysis of jumps in the price level variable p, or here: in the variable m, which these authors offer as the solution to the obvious instability problem of such a fundamental model of monetary growth.

It is obvious that this linear approach to dynamic (in)stability is very restrictive and that we should investigate its validity anew from the broader perspective of the model (9.39), (9.40), in particular, since the local aspect it contains may conflict with the global aspect of Sargent and Wallace's proposal of an economically meaningful stable solution path for the above monetary dynamics.

In order to discuss the instability problem of Sargent and Wallace from this broader perspective we return to the two-dimensional dynamics and assume that the parameter β_p has been chosen such that $\beta_p > B$ holds true and that β_{π^e} is large enough to imply trace $J > 0$ on the basis of this choice. For any given value of the price adjustment parameter β_p, we have already shown in chapter 4 that the assumed nonlinearity in the money demand function will always guarantee the existence of a stable limit cycle in π^e, m-space, which makes the locally explosive dynamics globally viable. Furthermore, assuming faster and faster inflationary expectations will not change the form of this limit cycle significantly, but will only make the adjustments in the horizontal direction faster and faster, thereby leading to relaxation oscillations in the end. Hence, in the limit case of myopic perfect foresight, the dynamics can be assumed to be constrained to the $\dot{m} = 0$ isocline as shown in figure 9.8 with periodically occurring horizontal jumps in inflationary expectations from A to B and from C to D.

This viable dynamics is of the same type as that of the Kaldor business cycle model and its "relaxation oscillations" (see chapter 4).[23] If the adjustment speed β_{π^e} increases for a given β_p, there will be convergence of the stable limit cycle of the corresponding dynamics toward the above depicted perfect foresight path $\dot{\pi}^e = 0$ and the limit limit cycle it generates. On the left-hand side of this figure we have $\pi^e \sim \dot{p} < 0$ and therefore a shrinking level of prices, that is, a rising value of m. Yet, in this deflationary area, prices cannot fall below a value p_{min} represented above by $\bar{m}$, which means that deflation must find an end there.

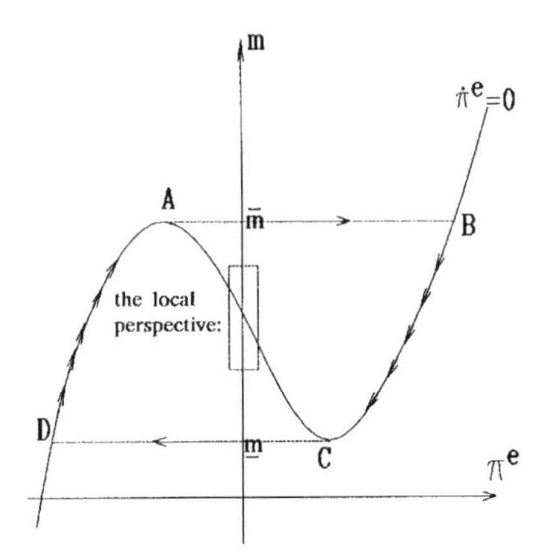

Figure 9.8
Relaxation oscillations for a given adjustment speed of the price level

There then exists, for this value of p and m, a stable equilibrium point for the expectations mechanism in the inflationary area on the right-hand side of figure 9.8. If β_{π^e} is infinite (large), there will consequently be a (nearly) immediate increase in inflationary expectations toward this new attracting point. Thereafter, we have inflation at a rate that is slowly falling, that is, the price level will increase, m will fall, and $\dot{p}$ and π^e will fall during this phase of the dynamic process. Again, this comes to an end at $p = p_{max}$, which corresponds to $\underline{m}$ in figure 9.8, and the rapid transitory process just described is now working in the opposite direction. We therefore get a stable, uniquely determined, limit cycle from these dynamics, which sometimes show slow movements in prices and their (expected) rate of change and which at other times give rise to sudden and sharp changes in the expected rate of inflation π^e, whereby the preceding direction of price changes becomes reversed.

Note that the above dynamics imply that π^e must be considered as the jump variable for a fast, but finite adjustment of prices p and the limit case of myopic perfect foresight $\beta_{\pi^e} = \infty$—and not the price level p as it is suggested in Sargent and Wallace 1973. Note also that figure 9.8 shows recurrent endogenous "jumps"—which are independent from any (further) shock in the money supply process—once the dynamics have left the steady state.

Sargent and Wallace (1973, 1045) explain their choice of a stable adjustment of prices in their local framework and their otherwise purely explosive dynamics by stating, "We assume that the public expects that,

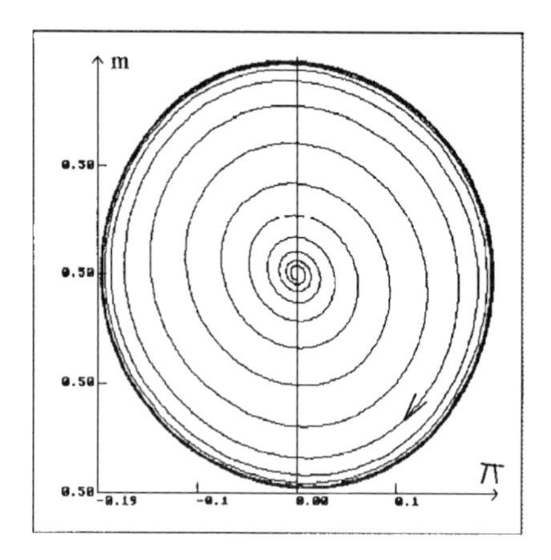

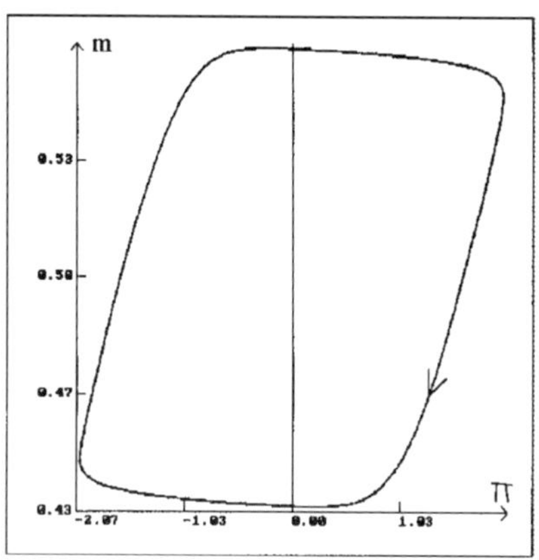

Figure 9.9
The limit cycle of the two-dimensional dynamics for $\beta_{\pi^e} = 1000$ and increasing price adjustment speeds ($\beta_p = 3.18, 5$, and $a = 1, \eta = 0$)

if M^{24} were to be constant over time, a process of ever-accelerating inflation or deflation would eventually come to an end, if only in the very remote future." There is, however, nothing in the above more general situation that could make this sentence applicable to it, since deflationary and inflationary periods are here limited; are, in addition, of a decelerating and not of an accelerating nature, and interchange each other at regular time intervals. We conclude that the dynamics we have analyzed above are the correct description of the economics behind the Sargent and Wallace "limit limit" case $\beta_{\pi^e} = \infty, \beta_p = \infty$. At some adjustment speeds, jumps in expectations or in the rate of change of prices can indeed be observed in it, but they are endogenous features of dynamics that work in the conventional way, and they do not lead us back to the steady state.

In Sargent and Wallace 1973 we have not only perfect foresight, but also an instantaneous adjustment of the price level toward market equilibrium. Increasing the adjustment speed of the price level in our two-dimensional dynamics shows in this regard that the limit cycle generated by the dynamics grows larger and larger in its amplitude—as figure 9.9 exemplifies. The relaxation oscillations therefore can be increased in amplitude without limit in this way.

With regard to figure 9.8 this simply means that the projection of the points D and B onto the π^e-line will approach $-\infty$ and $+\infty$ as β_p goes to infinity. Viewed from such limit procedures, the end result therefore

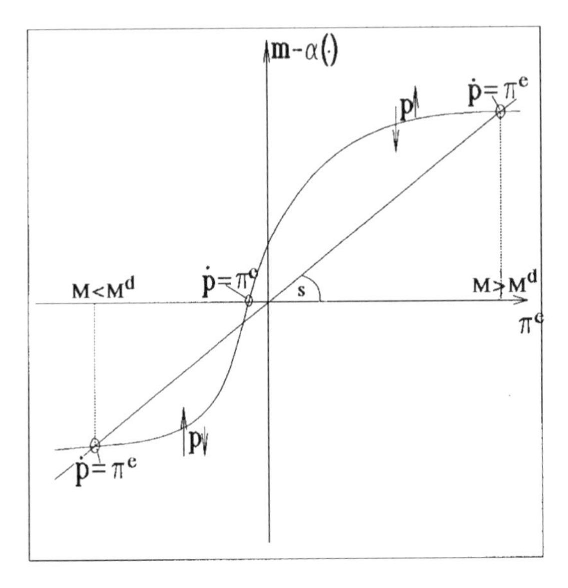

Figure 9.10
A Kaldorian representation of the Cagan model under myopic perfect foresight ($s-(1-\eta)/\beta_p$)

simply is a "limit limit limit cycle" ($+\infty \to -\infty \to +\infty$, etc.) where the decelerating parts of inflation or deflation have now been removed from sight. In view of such an extreme type of limit cycle dynamics, it is, however, very questionable whether β_p should indeed be allowed to approach infinity.

We therefore have it that models of monetary growth may be unstable with respect to their steady state, but that this instability does not prevent their conventional solution by means of a predetermined variable p—if these models include the nonlinear economic forces that must come about far off the steady state and that make them viable. This basic idea can also be summarized by making use of Kaldor's original and—as far as the mathematics is concerned—naive presentation of relaxation oscillations (see again chapter 4).

Figure 9.10 shows three perfect foresight equilibria,[25] two stable and one unstable as far as, for example, adaptively formed expectations are concerned. In the stable equilibrium on the right of the figure we have an excess supply of money and thus inflation, which attempts to reduce and indeed succeeds in reducing this excess supply. This is accomplished by shifting the nonlinear excess supply curve $m-\alpha(\pi^e)$ downward, which moves the inflationary point of perfect foresight to the left toward less inflation. This process continues until a point is reached where the upper stable perfect foresight position coincides with the unstable perfect foresight point—and then disappears completely as the downward shift of the excess function continues. There is, then, only one perfect foresight equilibrium to the left, which, for example, is rapidly approached under fast adaptive expectations. Thereafter, perfect foresight prevails again, but now at a point where there is excess demand for money, which starts a deflationary process. This process reduces again the disequilibrium on the money market by now shifting the curve $m - \alpha(\pi^e)$ upward. If it could continue without limit, the price dynamics would again make the money market disequilibrium disappear. Yet, once again, there is now a negative rate of inflation where the perfect foresight point responsible for the deflation disappears and gives way to a single perfect foresight equilibrium, again on the right and with a positive rate of inflation.

Money market disequilibrium dynamics—here of an extremely simple type—allows perfect foresight points consequently to move in time so that disequilibria are reduced, inflation or deflation is declining, and there is no need or scope for letting the price level jump. The price level here functions as the relatively slow variable that is predetermined at each moment of time and that adjusts in the direction of the above excess supply. The fast variable is quite naturally the expected rate of inflation that (nearly) instantaneously adjusts whenever there is a need for change in the relevant perfect foresight regime. A very fast, though not necessarily infinitely fast, mechanism is thus assumed that quickly reestablishes correct anticipations whenever they have gotten lost and that creates a perfect foresight price level dynamics of the kind

$$(1 - \eta)\dot{m} - \beta_p\alpha(-\dot{m}) = -\beta_p m$$

which is stable at the rate of inflation or deflation the expectational mechanism has led it to, since $1 - \eta + \beta_p\alpha' > 0$ holds at these points.

Furthermore, we once again see that the Sargent and Wallace assumption of $\beta_p \to \infty$ will move the above two stable expectational equilibrium points to $\pm\infty$ and will eventually make the above analysis invisible. By thus removing two important equilibria from their model, Sargent and Wallace (1973) end up with a proposal for their price level dynamics that—though motivated by global considerations—is based illegitimately on local analysis. The model thus depends heavily on the assumption of linearity and is inadequate from any more global view on the properties of the money demand function.

Assuming infinite adjustment speeds on one market in an attempt to reduce dynamical models by one dimension may thus lead to erroneous conclusions with respect to the proper dynamical structure that must be assumed to hold for the reduced order system.

9.7 Appendix: Forecasted Price Changes and Adaptive Learning

Recent models attempt to approximate rational expectations by ARMA processes where, in the dynamic model forecasted (lagged), endogenous variables appear. These models are neither adaptive expectations nor perfect foresight versions of expectations formation, but are rather based on the postulate that agents, by making efficient use of the information available, forecast endogenous variables. This idea can be integrated into the formulation of a dynamic model where prices are forecast from lagged endogenous variables and where the thereby generated expected prices enter as one- (or n) period-ahead price forecast in the dynamic model. In simple versions of such type the solutions and stability properties can be explored analytically. Those have been studied by Taylor (1980a); Bray (1982); Marcet and Sargent (1988, 1989); and Evans and Honkapohja (1988, 1990). This section will explore such a type of expectations formation for a price dynamic and its respective influence on the stability properties of an AD-AS growth model.

In a model such as that introduced in section 9.1 a forecast rate of price change can be obtained by forming a price predictor based on the efficient use of information available up to period t. Technically, in each period a regression on lagged price change is run to obtain an efficient price forecast for next period's price change. In this way, in the IS-equation, expected price change, entering the investment function, is based not on an adaptive version of price change such as eq. (9.9) but on a predicted price change $E_t\hat{p}_{t+1}$. The expected price change is also employed for the capital accumulation equation and the wage dynamics.

In a subprogram added to our simulation program expected price changes for period $t+1$ were generated as follows

$$E_t\hat{p}_{t+1} = \beta_o + \beta_1\hat{p}_t + \beta_2\hat{p}_{t-1}$$

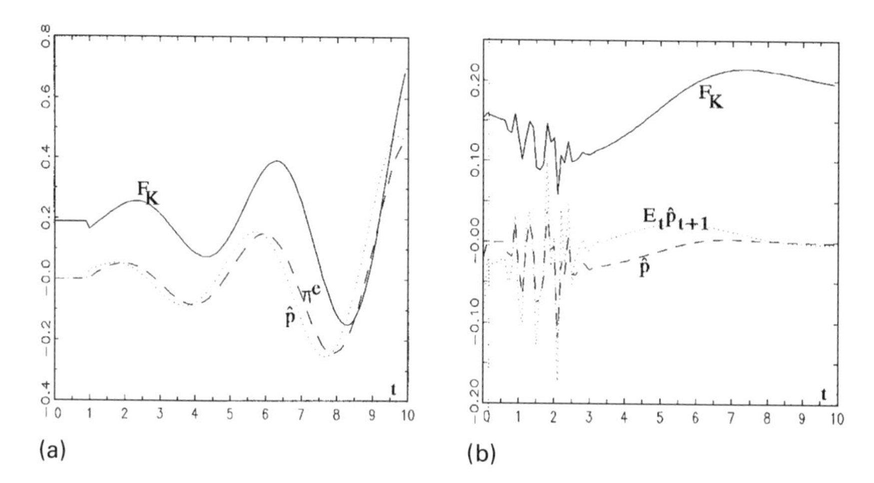

Figure 9.11
(*a*) dynamics with adaptive expectations ($\beta_{\pi^e} = 1$; $h = .4$), and (*b*) with forecasted price change ($h = .4$)

where the coefficients $\beta_o, \beta_1, \beta_2$ for the prediction form of next period's price change are obtained from an AR(2) process such as

$$\hat{p}_t = \beta_o + \beta_1 \hat{p}_{t-1} + \beta_2 \hat{p}_{t-2} + \epsilon_t$$

starting with arbitrary initial values for $\hat{p}_{t-2}, \hat{p}_{t-1}, \hat{p}_t$ (see below for a more detailed discussion).

The simulation result for the adaptive version with $\beta_{\pi^e} = 1$ is depicted in figure 9.11a. The simulation for the version with a price forecast is shown in figure 9.11.

As observable, for $\beta_{\pi^e} = 1$, the macrodynamic model is unstable. As can also be observed from figure 9.11 the system dynamics become stabilized when the adaptive price formation is replaced by an expectations formation based on forecast price change.

As shown by recent literature, for simpler models, also analytically, such processes of recursively revising the regression coefficients β_i according to new incoming information is stable if certain restrictions on the recursive mechanism are fulfilled. The stability properties of such models of least-square learning of future endogenous variables are discussed in Evans and Honkapohja 1988, 1990; Marcet and Sargent 1988, 1989; and Sargent 1993. Neither does our stability result, however, necessarily follow from this literature—since in our case a large number of variables of our dynamic system have an indirect impact on the price expectations formation—nor do we expect that our result holds in general (in the context of related models). In the context of our specific model it appears to show, however, that though the adaptive expectations version destabilizes the systems' dynamics, our proxy for a rational expectations version (forecasted price change) does not destabilize the macrodynamic model. The trajectories converge instead, though still in a cyclical manner. We could thus here exemplify that the stability properties of a dynamic system with future (expected) variables is likely to change when the mechanism of expectations formation changes.[26] In the context of the here employed type of expectations formation, monetary shocks indeed have transitory real effects, dissipating, however, over time when the trajectories converge toward the steady-state values of the system.

Adaptive Learning of the Expected Price Change

Forecast with Constant Coefficients

A one- (or n) period-ahead forecast of the change of the price level with constant coefficients can be obtained by a univariate process. A linear forecasting model with constant coefficients in autoregressive form with, for example, two lags (and leaving aside the constant term), can be written as

$$\hat{p}_t = \beta_1 \hat{p}_{t-1} + \beta_2 \hat{p}_{t-2} + \epsilon_t$$

In general, for n lags and for the disturbance term $E(\epsilon_t/I_t) = 0$ with I_t the information set at period t, we have[27]

$$z_t = Az_{t-1} + C\epsilon_t, \tag{9.41}$$

with staggered variables $z_t = (\hat{p}_t, \hat{p}_{t-1}, \hat{p}_{t-2}, \ldots, \hat{p}_{t-n})'$,

$$A = \begin{bmatrix} \beta_1 & \beta_2 & \beta_3 & \cdots & \beta_n \\ 1 & 0 & 0 & \cdots & 0 \\ 0 & 1 & 0 & \cdots & 0 \\ \vdots & \vdots & \vdots & \vdots & \vdots \\ 0 & 0 & 0 & 0 & 0 \end{bmatrix}$$

and $C = (1\ 0\ 0\ 0\ \cdots\ 0)'$.

The expected next period value of z is

$$E(z_{t+1}/I_t) = Az_t \tag{9.42}$$

With

$$z_{t+1} = Az_t + C\epsilon_{t+1} \tag{9.43}$$

the one step ahead forecast error is

$$z_{t+1} - E(z_{t+1}/I_t) = C\epsilon_{t+1}$$

Using (9.43) repeatedly, we obtain a moving average representation such as

$$z_t = Az_{t-1} + C\epsilon_t = A^2 z_{t-1} + AC\epsilon_{t-1} + C\epsilon_t$$

$$= \sum_{\tau=0}^{t-1} A^\tau C\epsilon_{t-\tau} + A^t z_o \tag{9.44}$$

The moving average representation for (9.44) j steps shifted forward in time is

$$z_{t+j} = \sum_{s=0}^{j-1} A^s C\epsilon_{t+j-s} + A^j z_o$$

and the j step ahead prediction is

$$E_t z_{t+j} = A^j z_t$$

with $j = 1$ for the one-step-ahead forecast as used in the first part of this appendix.

Forecast with Least-Square Learning

Note, however, that in the first part of this appendix in our repeatedly used forecast of the price change the information set is changing in each step. In our model of this part agents are learning adaptively the price change by regressing a variable with its lagged endogenous variable when new information is provided through the past data of the dynamic system. To forecast the price change, we have employed an AR(2) process where, recursively, the β-coefficients are revised when the information set is expanded. This is a specification of the recursive least-square learning procedure proposed by Ljung and Soederstroem (1987) and Ljung (1987). The law of motion of the β-coefficients (with β a vector) in terms of a differential equation system should be

$$\dot{\beta} = T(\beta) - \beta \tag{9.45}$$

with T an operator on β. For certain restrictions on such a (least-square) learning mechanism, Marcet and Sargent (1989), by building on the work of Ljung and Soederstroem (1987), demonstrate that the process (9.45) converges. Note that in this procedure there can be different weights attached to the information of different time periods. One might also conceive of a forecast that moves forward with a fixed window size of the information set. In addition, different groups of agents may utilize a different information set or forecasting algorithm. In general, however, there are restrictions to be imposed to keep the algorithm converging (for details, see Ljung 1987, 314). Without restrictions on the algorithm, convergence problems may arise (Grandmont 1990). In addition, multiple equilibria may cause further problems in the convergence process (cf. Evans and Honkapohja 1990).

Note also that in our context a proof of convergence of the recursive mechanism does not seem to be feasible since the price change predictor interacts with a higher-dimensional system and since the predictor introduces, through lags, additional dimensions into the dynamic system. Therefore, only simulation results could be provided.

IV

Supply and Demand Side Models of Keynesian Growth Dynamics

In the framework of the neoclassical synthesis, business cycles are viewed as being driven from the supply side. Specifically, unemployment on the labor market prevails, whereas the capital stock is supposed to be always fully utilized. In chapter 10, we follow this tradition by maintaining this assumption as well as that of competitive pricing or the marginal productivity theory. For purposes of labeling, it may be said that we discuss a general Keynes-Wicksell variant of the conventional AD-AS monetary growth model considered in chapter 8. This type of modeling originates in the work of Stein and Rose. A central feature of their models is that they admit an imbalance in the product market, that is, investment and saving may not match and price changes are determined by this excess demand of goods. The theoretical flavor is that the marginal productivity theory of employment can be designed to coexist with a Keynesian coordination problem between saving and investment decisions.

Our specification of the interaction of labor, product, and money markets, which also builds on chapter 4, results in a three-dimensional dynamic system. The three state variables are the real wage, factor intensity, and real balances. Although similar models have already been formulated, as we mentioned earlier, the stability properties have as yet not been fully investigated in this literature. Such a local stability analysis is resumed in chapter 10, which yields that in these economies both asymptotic stability and instability also may be obtained. A succinct verbal characterization of the main stability conditions should look quite familiar by now. The full employment equilibrium may become unstable if prices move sufficiently fast, while sluggish price adjustments ensure stability. It is furthermore shown that the loss of stability, occurring when the speed of price adjustments increases beyond a critical bifurcation value, is associated with imaginary eigenvalues. This finding indeed reveals a potential for cyclical behavior, although the fluctuations themselves are counterfactual in some respects, as discussed below.

In chapter 11, our perspective changes from the supply side to the demand side. We still include the interaction of the money, labor, and product markets, but the model to be constructed now moves away from the neoclassical production function, competitive pricing, and marginal principles. To capture some elements of oligopolistic pricing, we assume that prices are determined by a markup on unit labor costs, where, however, the markup itself is subjected to dynamic adjustments. The basic idea of the adjustment rule that we employ here goes back to the work of Kalecki. Certainly, changes in income distribution are intimately related to these variations of the markup. The other building blocks are well known; in particular, an expectations-augmented Phillips curve and adaptive expectations of inflation. After a number of suitable transformations the model is again three-dimensional. We provide a local stability analysis, but even more than in the prior sections our main interest is with the global dynamics. To contain the centrifugal forces we decided to introduce a modification of the standard adaptive expectations rule. The system then typically exhibits persistent and bounded oscillations of the state variables. Moreover, limit cycles can be detected that, at least under our functional specifications, seem to be unique.

In addition, the model can be reasonably well calibrated so that the resulting macroeconomic time series conform with actual time series data. There are no inconsistencies regarding the cycle period, the amplitude of the fluctuations, and the succession of turning points for the major macro variables, and numerically, the variables also behave quite satisfactorily. In particular, labor productivity and the real wage rate move nearly procyclically. Economic activity and inflation, however, display loops of a kind that have already been pointed out by Phillips. In these respects the demand-driven model of chapter 11 is superior to the supply driven model and its theory of inflation studied in chapter 10, whose behavior is totally at odds with the basic empirical facts concerning productivity and real wages.

10 Supply Side Keynesianism and the Classical Growth Cycle

10.1 Introduction

In this chapter,[1] we explore the local stability features and the potential for cyclical growth of monetary growth models of the Keynes-Wicksell type as they were studied in the seventies and early eighties. These models were introduced into macrodynamic analysis by Rose (1966, 1967, 1969) and Stein (1966, 1969, 1970, 1971) with the intent to discuss Keynesian aspects of monetary growth, contrasting their implications with neoclassical Tobin type (1965) models of monetary growth. Newer types of growth models with Wicksellian features have been provided by Stein (1982), Marglin (1984, chapter 20), Skott (1989), and Rose (1990).[2]

The central feature distinguishing Keynes-Wicksell models from neoclassical ones was the assumption of an independent investment function based on rate of return differentials, which was lacking in Tobin-type models. This investment function was used in combination with a standard saving function to determine the rate of inflation by the relative extent of goods market disequilibrium.

Fischer (1972) added expected inflation to this theory, both for consistency and to provide an expression for the inflationary climate in which the excess demand for goods was operating at each point in time. His contribution, in particular, removed one questionable feature from early Keynes-Wicksell models, which to this point permitted steady-state inflation only in the presence of excess demand for goods. Viewed from today's perspective, this model type can be characterized as an AD-AS model that allows for labor and goods market disequilibrium and their inflationary consequences, the latter in a Wicksellian manner.[3]

In the generalized form in which it will be presented here, this model type provides a background interpretation to the textbook model of Sargent (1987, chap. 5) and other authors on Keynesian AD-AS growth dynamics that we addressed in the first sections of chapter 8 and chapter 9. The general model of monetary growth dynamics to be considered in this chapter can thus be used as a disequilibrium interpretation of the conventional equilibrium AD-AS growth dynamics. It reveals once more and even more strikingly that this growth dynamics is based on a supply side-based view of Keynesian dynamics that will be contrasted with a demand-side view in the next chapter. The present chapter therefore helps in understanding what has really been achieved in the orthodox analysis of Keynesian growth dynamics, the Keynesian variant of the so-called neoclassical synthesis.

The framework of a Keynes-Wicksell monetary growth model was used by Stein (1982) to characterize the distinguishing features of monetarist, Keynesian, and new classical economics, and its limiting AD-AS case—as already considered in various places of this book—was utilized by Sargent (1987, chap. 5) to give formal expression to hypotheses of Milton Friedman. Attention was thereby shifted toward the treatment of inflationary expectations and their implications in such a context when they are adaptive, or of the myopic perfect foresight type (as in Sargent's model), or asymptotically rational (as in Stein's model). One defect of these two related model types, however, is that they do not offer a convincing and complete analysis of the dynamics they introduce. This is true for Sargent's (1987, chap. 5) treatment of adaptive expectations and of myopic perfect foresight. Here, only the inflationary expectations schemes with no and with infinitely fast adjustments of expectations are discussed to some extent. The same is true for Stein's (1982) monetary growth model where a general three-dimensional dynamical model is introduced, but not treated analytically in this generality.

The present chapter provides a stability analysis as well as numerical simulations for a general model of a Keynes-Wicksell type by extending and elaborating a version introduced in chapter 8 of Flaschel 1993. We here build on the earlier Wicksellian approach toward a theory of the rate of inflation by assuming a finite adjustment behavior of prices in reaction to goods market disequilibrium and the inflationary climate that may surround it. Allowing for goods market disequilibrium in a growth context implies that one has to decide whether capital accumulation is driven by intended investment or by saving plans, or by some combination or modification of each. In this chapter we make use of a solution to this problem that follows the approaches of the seventies, that is, we simply assume that actual capital accumulation is given by some weighted average of investment and saving plans. If we view this approach from the more modern perspective of neo-Keynesian regime-switching analysis, it is not difficult to point to disadvantages of such an approach in contrast to a full consideration of spillover effects of market disequilibria. The justification for maintaining the earlier approach to this type of disequilibrium growth theory is that we want to stay close to the Keynes-Wicksell models of the seventies in order to discuss and understand their stability implications to a fuller extent. In addition, we want to investigate the theory of the business cycle they give rise to, particularly by means of numerical simulations. As was pointed out previously, the results obtained will also be characteristic for the AD-AS growth models of today's textbook literature.

Throughout the present chapter we address the limit case of myopic perfect foresight with respect to the cost push term in the money wage Phillips curve (see chap. 8). Furthermore, we simplify our treatment of inflationary expectations in the price formation rule by assuming an extreme form of Stein's asymptotically rational expectations. Using this reformulation of a Keynes-Wicksell prototype model, which we introduce in the next section, we subsequently analyze the local stability properties in section 10.3. Section 10.4 concentrates on the polar case where capital accumulation is driven by saving. We show that this case can be considered an interpretation of the still more extreme limit case of Sargent's (1987, chap. 5) Keynes-Friedman model of monetary growth, where prices adjust with infinite speed and where the goods market is continuously in equilibrium. The neoclassical dichotomy, which Sargent found prevails in this type of Keynesian dynamics when adaptive expectations give way to myopic perfect foresight, is present for all values of price adjustment speeds since the real part of the model always consists of a growth cycle model[4] (with Solowian features) of a Goodwin (1967) or Rose (1967) type that is globally asymptotically stable. This is augmented by a theory of the rate of inflation that is based on deviations of the rate of investment from the rate of saving.

Section 10.5 considers the alternative case of capital stock growth determined by investment, not saving plans. We again investigate the local stability properties, adding a number of details to what has already been discovered for the more general case of a weighted average of saving and investment governing the growth of fixed capital. This case is interesting since it represents a macrosynthesis of the Goodwin/Marx profit squeeze growth cycle model and the classical/Marxian characterization of the process of equalizing rates of return (here on physical capital and financial assets), supplemented by a specific form of the law of demand on the market for labor, as well as on the market for goods. The model in this section, therefore, can be conceptualized as providing a basically complete model of the classical business cycle with independent saving and investment functions and a Keynesian market for money and other financial assets. It synthesizes the Goodwin-type (1967) growth cycle processes we considered in chapter 4 with the Walrasian price-quantity adjustments considered in chapter 3, where, however, the capital stock and nominal wages were considered as given.

A first appendix to this chapter compares our dynamic results with results that can be derived for Stein's (1982) general model. We shall find that stability occurs in this latter approach when we assume a reaction of the excess demand for goods with respect to changes in the real wage that is just the opposite of the condition needed for the stability of our Keynes-Wicksell model of monetary growth. A second appendix provides proofs for the propositions of this chapter.

10.2 A General Keynes-Wicksell Model of Monetary Growth

The following model generalizes the dynamic textbook model of Sargent (1987, chap. 5) to a form as it was common in the discussion of so-called Keynes-Wicksell models that occurred mainly in the seventies (see e.g., Stein 1971; Fischer 1972; and Boggess 1983). A brief survey of such models that starts from early work of Rose and Stein is given in Orphanides and Solow 1990, 234–36. The basic new feature of this model type in comparison to the textbook model considered in the first sections of chapters 8 and 9 is that it provides us with an explicit theory of inflation (of Wicksellian type). This theory of inflation is also present in modern textbook treatments of goods market disequilibrium (see Sargent 1987, chap. 2; Barro 1990a, 532), though the implications it may give rise to in a monetary growth context are nowhere analyzed.

The equations of the model are the following:

$$Y = F(K, L) \tag{10.1}$$

$$\omega = F_L, \qquad \omega = w/p \tag{10.2}$$

$$C = c_h(Y - \delta_1 K - T^n), \qquad c_h \in (0, 1) \tag{10.3}$$

$$I/K = i_f((F_K - \delta) - (i - \pi^e)) + n, \qquad \delta = \delta_1 + \delta_2, \ i_f > 0 \tag{10.4}$$

$$S = Y - \delta K - C - G \qquad [\neq I \text{ in general}] \tag{10.5}$$

$$M = pYf_m(i), \qquad f_m^{'} < 0 \tag{10.6}$$

$$\widehat{M} = g_m = \text{const} \tag{10.7}$$

$$\widehat{w} = \beta_w(L/L^s - 1) + \pi^e, \qquad \beta_w > 0 \tag{10.8}$$

$$\widehat{p} = \beta_p((I - S)/K) + g_m - n, \qquad \beta_p > 0 \tag{10.9}$$

$$\pi^e = \hat{p} \tag{10.10}$$

$$\widehat{K} = \beta_k I/K + (1 - \beta_k)S/K, \qquad 0 \leq \beta_k \leq 1 \tag{10.11}$$

$$\widehat{L^s} = n = \text{const} \tag{10.12}$$

$$\dot{Z} = \delta_2 K + \beta_k(I - S) \tag{10.13}$$

The first equation provides again a standard neoclassical production F. Labor input L is determined by the real wage ω in the second equation by equating the latter with the marginal product of labor F_L, that is, Keynes's classical postulate number 1 holds, and it provides a theory of employment here. The consumption function C is based on the simple concept of disposable income $Y_D = Y - \delta K - T^n$ (T^n = lump-sum taxes net of interest, and δ the sum of the depreciation and the inventory rate [see below]). The investment function is typical for models of the Keynes-Wicksell type. It states that deviations from trend growth are caused by discrepancies between the net marginal product of capital (the rate of profit r) and the real rate of return on bonds (with equities assumed as perfect substitutes of bonds; see Sargent 1987, chap. 1 for details). Equation (10.5) describes saving and goods-market disequilibrium, whereas equation (10.6) gives a simple form of money-market equilibrium (which generalizes the equation that is used in Sargent 1987, chap. 5). This IS-LM (dis)equilibrium part of the model is definitely a simple one, but it is not our main concern here, which is the now following dynamic part of the model. Nevertheless, the IS-LM part is of a prototype nature, and it can be expected that not many of its usual modifications will radically modify the conclusion on cyclical growth we derive in the following—as long as the dynamic part (10.7)–(10.12) remains as it is formulated here.

Equation (10.8) describes the standard money wage Phillips curve based on deviations of the rate of employment L/L^s from the natural one ($=1$) augmented by expectations π^e of the rate of inflation in the usual additive way. Equation (10.9) adds to the Wicksellian part of the model (10.4) a Wicksellian price adjustment equation $\widehat{p} = \dot{p}/p$, here based on per capital excess demand in the market for goods and on the long-run rate of inflation $g_m - n$,[5] the inflationary climate that surrounds this price formation rule near the steady state.[6] We stress that this expression for the inflationary climate is of quite a different type than the cost-push term π^e in the money-wage equation (10.8) which in this version of the model is based on perfect anticipations (10.10).

Equation (10.11) is again typical for Keynes-Wicksell models that are based on goods-market disequilibrium (see, e.g. Fischer 1972), for which one has to decide whether the growth of the capital stock is driven by investment I or by total saving $S = S_p + S_g$ or by some combination of both. Private saving S_p is given by $Y - \delta K - T^n - C$, and government saving S_g by $T^n - G$, where T^n represents (lump-sum) real taxes net of interest. The two limit cases $\beta_k = 0 : \dot{K} = S; \beta_k = 1 : \dot{K} = I$ of equation (10.11) will be of particular importance in the following. Equation (10.12) gives the simple dynamics of labor supply of conventional growth models. Equation (10.13) finally has been added for consistency reasons, but is—in the present model—of no importance for the considered dynamics. It calculates the inventory changes present in the model on the assumption that $\delta_2 K$ describes the voluntary inventory changes of firms living in a growing economy. To these voluntary inventory changes we have to add those caused by goods market disequilibrium and by our description of the actual growth rate (10.11) of the capital stock, that is, those unsold goods that are not added (involuntarily) to the capital stock of firms. Inventory changes are of purely passive nature in this model. Note that the side condition that inventories Z cannot become negative should be checked in all global investigations of the model in the cases where $\beta_k > 0$ holds.

The statically endogenous variables of the model are L, Y, C, S, I and i, where the first four are basically determined through the marginal productivity postulate (10.2) and the nominal rate of interest i by the LM-equation (10.6). The dynamically endogenous variables are w, p, K and M, L^s, while all others are data or parameters of the model. The ratios $\gamma = G/K$ and $\theta = T^n/K$ are—as in chapters 8, and 9—assumed to be given magnitudes so that strictly speaking, government expenditures G and taxes net of interest T^n are also endogenous variables of the model.

The Sargent (1987, chap. 5) model can be obtained from the above by assuming $I = S$ ($\beta_p = \infty$). This makes the size of β_k irrelevant for the dynamics of the model and is achieved by making the rate of inflation an equilibrating variable—which adjusts investment toward predetermined saving!

The above model is easily reduced to per capita form ($c = C/K$, etc.) by employing the intensive formulation of the production function: $x = f(l)$, $x = Y/K$, $l = L/K$, and $\omega = F_L(K, L) = f'(l)$, which gives $r(\omega) = F_K(K, L) - \delta = f(l) - f'(l)l - \delta$ as the net rate of profit of this approach. Its dynamics read in intensive form:

$$\widehat{\omega} = \beta_w(l/l^s - 1), \quad \omega = w/p \tag{10.14}$$

$$\widehat{l^s} = n - \beta_k[i_f(r - (i - \widehat{p})) + n] - (1 - \beta_k)[(1 - c_h)f(l) + c_h(\theta + \delta) - \delta - \gamma], \quad l^s = L^s/K \tag{10.15}$$

$$\widehat{m} = -\beta_p[i_f(r - (i - \widehat{p})) + n - (1 - c_h)f(l) - c_h(\theta + \delta) + \delta + \gamma], \quad m = M/(pL^s) \tag{10.16}$$

where $\widehat{p} = g_m - n - \widehat{m}$ and where this expression is to be inserted into eq. (10.16) in order to obtain an autonomous dynamical system in the three variables $\omega = w/p, l^s = L^s/K$, and $m = M/(pL^s)$.[7] This system is an autonomous one since the statically endogenous variables l, i can be substituted by means of the relationships

$$l = (f')^{-1}(\omega) = l(\omega), l' < 0$$

$$r = r(\omega) = f(l(\omega)) - \omega l(\omega) - \delta, r'(\omega) = -l(\omega)$$

$$i = f_m^{-1}(ml^s/f(l)) = i(\omega, l^s, m), i_1 < 0, i_2 < 0, i_3 < 0$$

With these relationships in mind the dynamics to be studied can be finally expressed as follows:

$$\widehat{\omega} = \beta_w(l/l^s - 1), \omega = \frac{w}{p} \tag{10.17}$$

$$\widehat{l^s} = -[\beta_k(i_f(r - i - \widehat{m}) + (1 - \beta_k)(1 - c_h)f(l)] + \text{const}, l^s = \frac{L^s}{K} \tag{10.18}$$

$$\widehat{m} = -\frac{\beta_p}{1 - \beta_p i_f}[i_f(r - i) - (1 - c_h)f(l)] + \text{const}, m = \frac{M}{pL^s} \tag{10.19}$$

10.3 Local Stability Analysis

The (interior) steady state of the dynamic model of section 10.2 is given by:

$$x^\star = f(l^\star) = \frac{n + \gamma + \delta - c_h(\delta + \theta)}{1 - c_h}$$

$$\omega^\star = f'(l^\star), r^\star = r(\omega^\star) = f(l^\star) - f'(l^\star)l^\star$$

$$i^\star = r^\star + (g_m - n)$$

$$l^{s\star} = l^\star$$

$$m^\star = f(l^\star) f_m(i^\star)/l^{s\star}$$

Note that the steady state is characterized by $I = S$, and $\widehat{p} = g_m - n$, so that account is taken of Fischer's (1972) criticism of earlier models of the Keynes-Wicksell type, which allowed for goods-market disequilibrium in the steady state.

The Jacobian of system (10.17) – (10.19) at the steady state reads:

$$J = \begin{pmatrix} \beta_w l'/l^s\omega & -\beta_w/l^s\omega & 0 \\ \hat{l}_1^s l^s & \beta_k i_f(i_2 + \widehat{m}_2)l^s & \beta_k i_f(i_3 + \widehat{m}_3)l^s \\ \widehat{m}_1 m & \widehat{m}_2 m & \widehat{m}_3 m \end{pmatrix}$$

where $\hat{l}_1^s$ is given by

$$-[\beta_k i_f(r' - i_1 - \widehat{m}_1) + (1 - \beta_k)(1 - c_h)f'l']$$

and

$$\widehat{m}_1 = \frac{1}{1/\beta_p - i_f}[(1 - c_h)f'l' - i_f(r' - i_1)]$$

$$\widehat{m}_2 = \frac{1}{1/\beta_p - i_f} i_f\, i_2, \qquad \widehat{m}_3 = \frac{1}{1/\beta_p - i_f} i_f\, i_3$$

Theorem 10.1 Assume (i) $\beta_p < 1/i_f$, (ii) $(1 - c_h)f'l' - i_f(r' - i_1) > 0$. Then the steady state of the dynamics (10.17) – (10.19) is locally asymptotically stable.

Proof See appendix 2 of this chapter.

Remarks

1. Under the assumed conditions we have stability for $\beta_p < 1/i_f$ and instability for $\beta_p > 1/i_f$ (det $J > 0$), while the system is ill defined for $\beta_p = 1/i_f$. This already shows that the case $\beta_p \geq 1/i_f$ should be treated with care. In fact, we will argue in the next section that it is not meaningful to allow for adjustment speeds β_p for which $\widehat{p}_{\pi^e} > 1$—the implication of $\beta_p > 1/i_f$—holds true (cf. eqs. (10.4), (10.9)).

2. The above theorem holds independently of the size of the $\beta_k' s$.

3. While condition (i) is simple to understand, the second condition in theorem 10.1 is an unusual one (from a Keynesian perspective) in its role as a *stability* condition, since it says that saving must be less sensitive to real wage (and thus income) variations than investment:

$$i_f(r' - i_1) < (1 - c_h) f' l' < 0$$

4. Numerical investigations of the dynamics suggest that the above sufficient conditions for local asymptotic stability are much stronger than is really necessary.

5. Since we have det $J < 0$ for $\beta_p < 1/i_f$ (see appendix 2), a loss of stability can occur in this range for the parameter β_p by means of a Hopf bifurcation solely, that is, in particular, it must happen in a cyclical fashion.

10.4 The Neoclassical Case: Savings and Monetary Growth

In Sargent 1987, chap. 5, the above model is considered in the special case where I = S ($\beta_p = \infty$) holds true, so that a choice between the two polar cases $\beta_k = 0$: $\dot{K} = S$ and $\beta_k = 1 : \dot{K} = I$ is irrelevant. The model is then employed by Sargent to formalize for students "the relationships among the various hypotheses advanced in Milton Friedman's AEA presidential address" (117). There in particular he shows for this model of Keynesian dynamics that it will become a purely "classical" one[8] (with neutral money) under perfect foresight $\pi^e = \widehat{p}$ (see chapter 8 for details).

We have considered in chapter 8 the flaws of the $I = S$ ($\beta_p = \infty$) approach to the neutrality of money, which has to assume infinitely flexible wages in order to really allow for such neutrality. By contrast, the Keynes-Wicksell goods market disequilibrium model of section 10.2

assumes less than perfectly flexible prices in addition to the less than perfectly flexible money wages, and it gives rise—when perfect foresight is assumed—to a real wage Phillips curve without any need to consider money wages as perfectly flexible from then on, as in Sargent 1987, chap. 5. There is here no room for short-run neutrality as in the conventional classical version of the neoclassical synthesis (see Sargent 1987, chap. 1). Nevertheless, this model is capable of reproducing the remaining part of Sargent's (1987, chap. 5) perfect foresight results in the border case $\beta_k = 0$ by giving rise to a synthesis, not so much of Keynes's and Friedman's hypotheses on short-, medium-, and long-run economic dynamics, but of the classical growth cycle approach of Goodwin with the neoclassical theory of capital accumulation of Solow. This will be demonstrated in the remainder of this section. The dominance of the supply side is particularly striking in this variant of the general Keynes-Wicksell monetary growth model, since the Keynesian components of the model here serve only to determine the nominal rate of interest and (on this basis) the rate of price inflation.

Theorem 10.2 Assume $\beta_k = 0$. Then: The steady state of the model (10.17)–(10.19) is globally asymptotically stable for all adjustment speeds $\beta_p < 1/i_f$.[9]

Proof See appendix 2 of this chapter.

Remarks

1. Besides providing insights into questions of global stability, the above implies that stability condition (*ii*) of theorem 10.1 is not necessary in the case $\beta_k = 0$. This can, of course, be obtained from the proof of theorem 10.1 if the extra information $J_{22} = J_{23} = 0$ is taken into account in it ($J_{21} = -(1 - c_h) f' l' l^s$).

2. In the opposite case $\beta_p > 1/i_f$, we get instead of the above a real sector that is again globally stable, but now coupled with a monetary dynamics that is totally unstable. We believe that this is not a sensible model of economic dynamics.

3. Under conditions of hyperinflation it may happen that β_p gets close to infinity (from a practical point of view). Yet, the discussion of hyperinflation demands significant modifications of the model. It thus remains excluded here.

4. The real part of the model will be the closer to Goodwin's (1967) original dynamics, the smaller the elasticity term $\varepsilon(\omega)$ used in the proof

of this theorem; it will be identical to Goodwin's center-type dynamics for $\varepsilon(\omega) \equiv 0$, that is, in the case of a fixed coefficient technology. By contrast, its dynamics will give rise to a monotonic adjustment to its steady state and thus to a Solowian type of dynamics if the elasticity term $\varepsilon(\omega)$ becomes sufficiently large. The choice of a classical growth cycle view vs. a neoclassical view on the pace of capital accumulation thus depends on factual elasticities of substitution between labor and capital.

5. We thus end up here with a model that exhibits a globally stable private sector, where money is but a veil, and where there is long-run as well as short-run neutrality of money if its influence on the level of planned, but not realized investment is left aside. This dichotomizing structure of the dynamics implies that the border case $\beta_k = 0$ is not a meaningful approach to monetary growth dynamics.

6. Rose (1967) gets instability of the steady state of his model via the goods market theory of the rate of inflation and the negative dependence of goods market disequilibrium on the real wage (see section 4.4). Yet, his instability mechanism is not present in the above dynamics, since the Phillips curve is now expectations augmented and since expectations have been based on perfect foresight. The Rose dynamics are thereby turned into stable dynamics here, despite many similarities of the above model to the Rose (1967) employment cycle model.

10.5 The Classical Case: Cross-Dual Monetary Growth Dynamics

Though others have also contributed significantly to the analysis of classical dynamics, the contribution of Richard Goodwin is of particular importance when it comes to a separate (or joint) analysis of classical dynamics on the macro as well as on the micro level. His basic macro contribution to the Marxian analysis of cyclical growth is well known and has been employed in modified form in section 10.4 already to show that the limit case $\beta_k = 0$ may exhibit a Marxian growth cycle pattern (with Solowian features). Less known are, however, his contributions to classical microdynamics, which, with a Walrasian flavor, began as early as 1953.[10] These microeconomic contributions have been reconsidered and extended in chapter 3 of this book.

These two applications of a *cross-dual* type of reaction pattern on the macro and on the micro level have meanwhile received an extensive treatment in the literature. Yet, there have been no thorough attempts to integrate the macroeconomic profit squeeze mechanism with the microeconomic process of equalizing profits rates, as it would be appropriate, at least from a classical perspective. This is to some extent also an important topic from a neoclassical perspective if, for example, the Solow model is reconsidered with sluggish real wage adjustment and more than only one rate of return.

In the light of this last observation, it may not appear very astonishing that the model of section 10.2 is capable of providing a synthesis of classical profit-squeeze mechanisms with processes of equalizing rates of return. Nevertheless, this finding is remarkable, since it comes about here as a by-product of the macroeconomics of the seventies and the investigation of so-called Keynes-Wicksell monetary growth models, and not as a conscious attempt of writers in the tradition of Smith, Ricardo, and Marx, which so far have not established a prototype monetary growth version of classical macro- and microdynamics. To demonstrate this, let us reconsider the model of section 10.2 for the case $\beta_k = 1$, that is, where investment and not saving determines the growth rate of the capital stock. We then have, on the one hand, that the rate of return differential

$$r - (i - \widehat{p}) = (F_K - \delta) - (i - \widehat{p})$$

governs the reaction of supply in its dependence on the growth of the capital stock. On the other hand, we have in these models the (elaborate) two laws of demand:

$$\widehat{w} = \beta_w(L/L^s - 1) + \pi_1^e, \qquad \widehat{p} = \beta_p((I - S)/K) + \pi_2^e$$

where the expected rates of inflation π_1^e, π_2^e have been determined by cost-push and self-reference considerations in section 10.2. We here have a macroeconomic model with two specifications of a profit-squeeze mechanism ($r(\omega), r' < 0$ and $r - (i - \hat{p})$) and at the same time a formulation of rate-of-return differentials that interact with demand and supply discrepancies, though here more of a macro- than of a microeconomic type.

The question now is whether these cross-dual adjustment processes are here combined in their known potential to create overshooting processes of cyclical growth or whether they may neutralize each other with respect to this unifying characteristic. The following theorem shows that there is—at present—no far-reaching answer to this question available. Furthermore, subsequent simulation studies of the model of section 10.2 (for $\beta_k = 1$) will show that it may not be the case that these cross-dual overshooting mechanisms will combine in such a way that this overshooting feature will be enhanced. Instead, two profit squeezes ($\omega, i - \widehat{p}$) in the place of only one (ω) may be capable of producing rapidly converging adjustments toward steady growth in place of an expected increase in economic instability and fluctuations.

Theorem 10.3 Assume $\beta_k = 1$ and $\beta_p < 1/i_f$. Then:

(1) The dynamics (10.17), (10.18), (10.19) is close to Goodwin's (1967) growth cycle model in the qualitative features of its real or (ω, l^s)–subsector if

- the situation in the money-market is close to the liquidity trap[11]
- the elasticity of substitution term $\varepsilon(\omega) = -\omega l'(\omega)/l$ is close to 0
- prices p react in a sufficiently sluggish way with respect to goods market disequilibrium (β_p sufficiently close to zero).

(2) The model will produce an asymptotically stable dynamics for all β_p which are sufficiently small, if $l'i_2 + i_1 - r' > 0$ holds.

(3) The condition

$$\underbrace{l'i_2}_{\alpha_1} + \underbrace{i_1 - r' + (1 - c_h)\omega l'}_{\alpha_2} > 0$$

is sufficient for $\begin{vmatrix} J_{11} & J_{12} \\ J_{21} & J_{22} \end{vmatrix} > 0$, that is, for the "stability" of the real sector of the model. A loss of stability of the complete dynamics (by increasing β_p) can then occur only in a cyclical manner, since all real eigenvalues must be negative in this situation.[12]

(4) The dynamics will be unstable for example if the following situation prevails:

- the value of i_f is sufficiently small
- the value of $\beta_p < 1/i_f$ is sufficiently large
- the value of $i \approx const$ (the liquidity trap prevails)

(5) If $l'i_2 - (r' - i_2) + \frac{1}{i_f}(1 - c_h)\omega l' > 0$ holds, the dynamics will be stable for all β_p sufficiently close to $1/i$ (from below).

Proof See appendix 2 of this chapter.

Remark This $I \neq S - LM$ monetary growth model—not unexpectedly—gives rise to nearly closed orbits around the steady state, as in Goodwin (1967), if the nominal rate of interest is pegged through money-market phenomena, if there are nearly fixed proportions in technology, and if the rate of inflation stays close to zero, owing to sluggish price responses to goods market disequilibrium. This statement is also true from a global point of view, giving rise to a model of cyclical growth around the "minimum" real rate of interest $i \approx i^\star - \hat{p}^\star$ instead of Goodwin's average rate of profit. In general, however, the model adds Solowian factor substitution, a Wicksellian inflationary process, and Keynesian interest rate phenomena to this core case of a growth cycle in an $I \neq S - LM$ context. Though the dominance of the supply side is less striking in this variant of the general Keynes-Wicksell monetary growth model compared to the one of the preceding section, the Keynesian components of the model still simply help to determine the nominal rate of interest and (on this basis) the rate of price inflation via goods market disequilibrium. Yet, the supply of new capital now also depends on money-market phenomena, that is, the dynamics are here fully integrated. Note, however, that firms are still assumed to always produce at their full capacity level, that is, their production is completely determined through the currently given supply of capital and the marginal productivity principle.

In contrast to the dichotomizing case $\beta_k = 0$ of the preceding section we have here a dynamic macroeconomic model that integrates classical ideas (Smith, Ricardo, Marx) with a Keynes-Wicksell synthesis and which supports the view that endogenous cyclical growth is the prime characteristic of the evolution of capitalistic economies, in particular, if sluggish price and wage adjustments are assumed. This is to some extent shown by the above and the following theorem. The power, and the defects, of this model for analyzing processes of cyclical growth become more visible, however, by means of the numerical simulations with which we shall close this section.

Theorem 10.4 Assume $\beta_k = 1$ and $\beta_p < 1/i_f$. Then: Any loss of the stability of the dynamics (10.17)–(10.19) occurs in a cyclical fashion, by way of a Hopf bifurcation with respect to the parameter under consideration.

Proof A straightforward consequence of det $J < 0$ (all eigenvalues $\lambda_i \neq 0, \ \ i = 1, 2, 3$), see appendix 2 of this chapter.

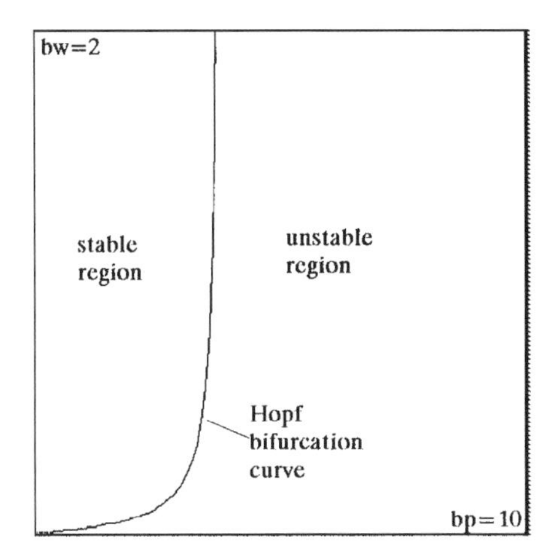

Figure 10.1
The Hopf bifurcation locus for wage and price adjustment speeds ($bw = \beta_w$, etc.)

Figure 10.1 provides a numerical illustration for this last theorem. It is based on the border case of a Cobb-Douglas production function $f(l) = l^{1-\alpha}$ (for which $\varepsilon = 1$ holds true). In this figure we consider the parameter space $(\beta_p, \beta_w) \in [0, 10] \cdot [0, 2]$ and show the curve where a Hopf bifurcation occurs when one of these two parameters is varied.[13] We can see from this figure that wage flexibility supports economic stability, while price flexibility is bad for it. Furthermore, except for very small values of the parameter β_w (≤ 0.047), the Hopf bifurcation that occurs is of subcritical type, that is, a corridor of local stability shrinks to zero as a bifurcation point on the shown curve is approached from the left.[14]

In the Cobb-Douglas case the conditions of theorem 3.4 for local instability read: $i_f < (1 - c_h)/\alpha$, $\beta_p \to 1/i_f$, and β_i sufficiently large. This in particular explains the choice of β_i in the above numerical illustration, and it suggests—as has been checked by further numerical investigations—that higher interest rate flexibility (a lower value of β_i) will significantly contribute to the local stability of the dynamics and enlarge the above stable domain rapidly. The Cobb-Douglas case therefore is predominantly locally asymptotically stable (for $\beta_p < 1/i_f$) if the value of β_i is chosen at a level significantly less extreme than that in figure 10.1.

The following phase plots serve to exemplify further the assertions provided by theorem 10.3. The first numerical example (the phase plot top-left) illustrates the assertion of theorem 10.3.1 (the Goodwin growth cycle subcase of the dynamics) which here, however—despite a very low degree of factor substitution[15]—exhibits already a considerable speed of convergence to the steady state.[16] Neglecting convergence, the shown interaction of the wage share $v = \omega l / l^s$ with the rate of employment $e = l / l^s$ is of the type suggested by the simple Goodwin approach to cyclical growth (cf. chapter 4).

Increasing in this situation the price adjustment parameter β_p step-by-step from 0.01 to 0.8 increases continuously the amplitude of the cycle in this first figure and decreases its period length until an explosive type of behavior comes about (as the top right-hand phase plot in fig. 10.2 shows, time horizon again 30 years). Note that this plot is still based on the situation of a liquidity trap ($i \approx i^\star$, $\beta_i = 200$ still).

Allowing some nominal interest rate flexibility in a next step ($\beta_i = 20$ bottom left, and $\beta_i = 10$ bottom right) does not further increase the instability in the top right figure, but instead gives rise to a more and more stable reaction pattern. The second profit-squeeze mechanism (based on the real rate of interest) thus does not add to the explosive and cyclical nature of the dynamics in the plot at top right. Note also, with respect to the last two phase plots shown, that some of the eigenvalues of this dynamics have a very small negative real part, which generates a nearly horizontal convergence back to the original steady state—given by the starting point of the vertical line—when the strong cyclical contractions caused by the other eigenvalues have reestablished full employment, but have not yet reestablished the steady share of wages in national income. Note that the time horizon of the last two phase plots is 500 years.

Similar results can also be achieved by increasing the elasticity of substitution in production: $\varepsilon = (1 + \eta)^{-1}$, that is, by means of a decreasing parameter η.

The simulations below show various phase plots of an employment/profitability cycle that could be interpreted as an overshooting profit squeeze mechanism, yet one that is not built on a firmer basis when we add nominal interest rate flexibility to it. Furthermore, there are two fairly counterfactual elements involved in this model of cyclical growth processes, as figure 10.3 shows.

The figure to the left shows that the early phase of recovery (here measured by the unemployment rate $1 - e$) is accompanied by a rising rate of inflation which, however, begins to fall again long before the employment peak is reached. The rate of inflation then continues to fall until the rate $1 - e$ reaches its normal (= average) level (from above).

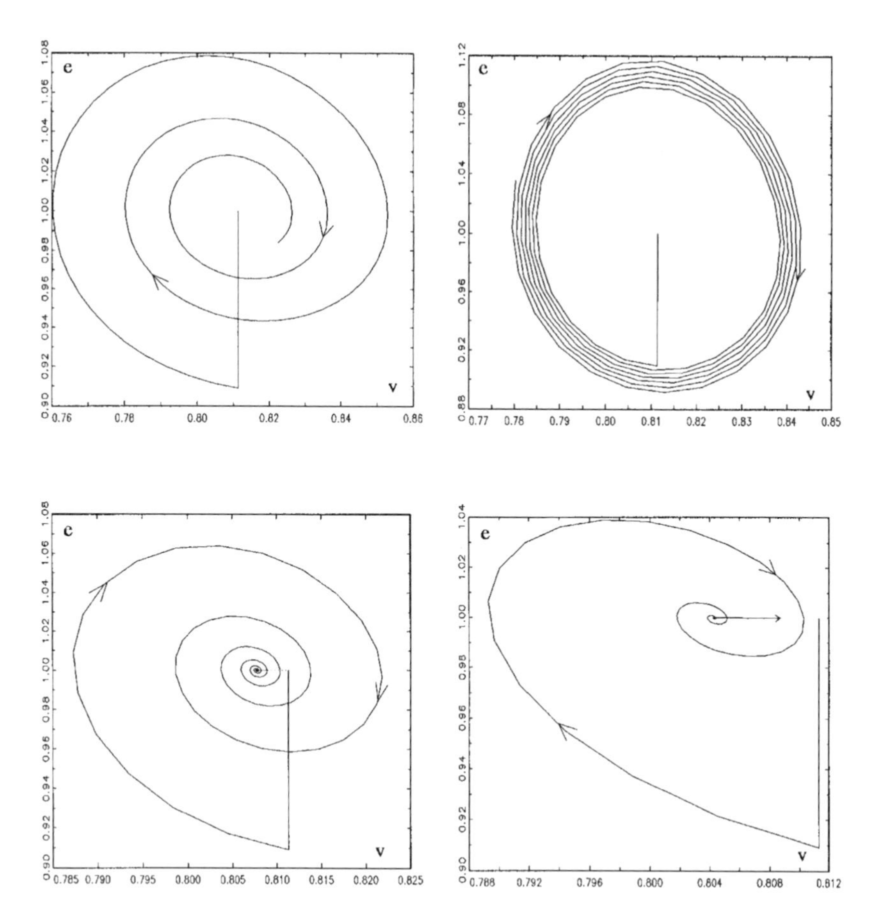

Figure 10.2
Subcases of the classical version of the Keynes-Wicksell model

From then on, the inflation rate starts rising again, though employment continues to fall, that is, the inflationary process is reversed toward a positive rate of inflation during the beginning of the depression and not in the late phase of the boom. This peculiar cyclical pattern is due to the Wicksellian nature of the price inflation mechanism (a demand-pull mechanism), and it is transmitted to money wage inflation through cost-push elements ($\pi^e = \widehat{p}$).

Yet, many empirical phase plots of this type—in particular those of the postwar period—show a clockwise, not counterclockwise motion. The theory of inflation and stagflation of this classically oriented

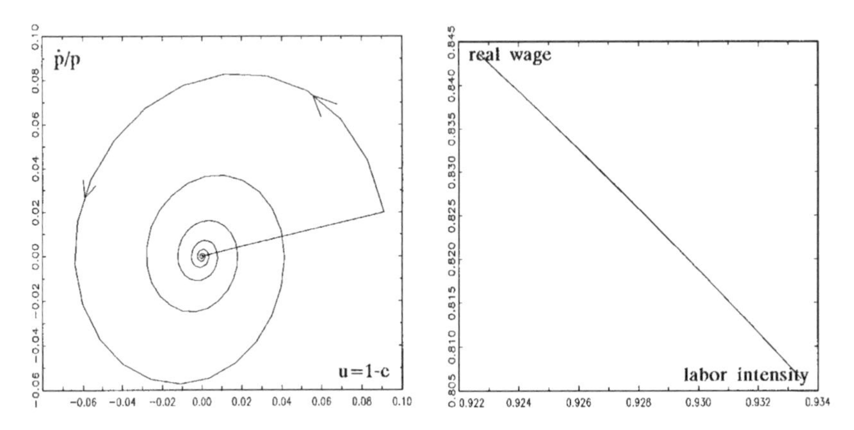

Figure 10.3
Left inflation and unemployment; right: the marginal productivity relationship

Keynes-Wicksell prototype model is thus at odds with stylized empirical facts. Furthermore, as is well known, the marginal productivity theory of employment utilized in this model type is not confirmed by empirical facts. The phase plot on the right-hand side of figure 10.3 is thus also of a counterfactual nature. We conclude that the Keynesian monetary growth model presented here must be modified to get its stylized patterns into closer contact with some stylized empirical facts.

10.6 Conclusions

In this chapter we have considered a generalization of Keynes-Wicksell prototype models and have stressed in particular their reinterpretation by means of classical cross-dual adjustment procedures. Important as this reformulation of Keynes-Wicksell approaches may be from the perspective of macrodynamic model-building history, however, this model does not provide us with a convincing synthesis of classical and *Keynesian* aspects of monetary growth, in particular because of the lack of Keynesian quantity adjustment mechanisms in this model variant. It is for this reason we have characterized this prototype model as a supply side version of Keynesian monetary growth dynamics.

Nevertheless, in this chapter we have shown that Keynes-Wicksell models of monetary growth exhibit interesting stability properties as well as classical cyclical features that are far from being sufficiently understood, especially concerning the implications of their use of classical cross-dual adjustment rules. The potential of this AD-AS disequilibrium variant of monetary growth to generate specific business cycle patterns is still largely unexplored and warrants detailed analytical and numerical investigation. This effort deserves attention independently of any attempt to establish more Keynesian versions of such Keynes-Wicksell models of inflation and growth.

10.7 Appendix 1: Stein (1982)

For his discussion of monetarist, Keynesian and new classical economics, Stein (1982) makes use of a general macrodynamical model (see his table 2.1 on p. 20) by which he intends to discriminate among the assumptions and the implications of these three important economic schools of thought. We shall reconsider in this appendix this dynamical model from the perspective of section 10.2 and shall also discuss its stability properties, which in general (i.e., in three dimensions) have not been investigated in Stein's book.

As in our model, Stein (1982, 20) starts from relationships of the kind

$$x = f(l), \omega = f'(l), r(l) = f(l) - f'(l)l - \delta$$

augmented by a technical progress factor $A(t)$ which we neglect for simplicity in the following. Instead of using $l = L/K$, however, he presents the above intensive form relationships in terms of l^s, makes use of a Cobb-Douglas function with respect to the determination of r, and represents the marginal productivity relationship $\omega = f'(l)$ as a not quite convincing linear approximation of it (see his eqs. (2.1) – (2.3)).

His equation (2.4) then provides a real wage Phillips curve that is based on the following money wage form:

$$\widehat{w} = -\beta_w(\overline{e} - e) + \pi^e \tag{10.20}$$

which is thus of the type considered in this chapter.[17] His equation (2.5) should read (because of the economic dimensions that are involved)

$$D \ln k = i_f(r - (i - \pi^e)), \qquad k = K/L^s$$

instead of using only Dk on its left-hand side; it is then identical in type to the investment function employed here in section 10.2. The theory of the nominal rate of interest used by him in equation (2.6) is more elaborate than our form $i = f_m^{-1}(l, l^s, m), l = l(\omega)$, since it refers to inflationary expectations and the per capita stock of bonds in addition. We shall neglect this extension in the following.

Next, his equation (2.7), which is considered as extremely important by Stein (21), gives price inflation as a function of wage inflation and the relative excess demand gap

$$\widehat{p} = \widehat{w} + \beta_p(\frac{I - S}{K}) \cdot k \tag{10.21}$$

where excess demand is made dependent on x, i, π^e, k, γ (as in our model in section 10.2[18]) and furthermore on $m = M/(pL^s)$, and again on the stock of bonds per capita. We again suppress these additions, which, however, are of importance when it comes to a discussion of the dynamics of the government budget constraint (which is not intended here [see, however, Stein 1982, section 5.3 in this regard]). Leaving such wealth effects aside allows us also to ignore the government budget constraints (2.9) and (2.11) of Stein (1982), that is, we here still employ the simple monetary policy rule $\widehat{M} = g_m =$ const , which again gives rise to $\widehat{m} = g_m - n - \widehat{p}$. Expectations are introduced by his equations (2.10a,b) and are of the form $\pi^e = \widehat{p}$ or $\dot{\pi}^e = \beta_{\pi^e}(g_m - n - \pi^e)$, that is, they are "rational" or "asymptotically rational."

Though presented in a very different way, Stein's (1982) model is thus fairly close to the model we have investigated here in section 10.5 in its interactions of a cross-dual type. Considering Stein's case of "rational expectations" first, we must however state that this variant of the model is "contradictory," as it implies two different laws of real wage movements:

$$\widehat{\omega} = -\beta_w(e - \overline{e}), \qquad \widehat{\omega} = -\beta_p(\frac{I - S}{K})$$

(see equations (10.20) and (10.21) above). This case is treated only by means of partial models in Stein's book so that the consequences of these equalities for the dynamics of this model of monetary growth are nowhere discussed.

The other case (of asymptotically rational expectations: ARE) $\dot{\pi}^e = \beta_{\pi^e}(g_m - n - \pi^e)$ is discussed in Stein 1982 in its limit form $\beta_{\pi^e} = \infty$, that is, $\pi^e = g_m - n$, which when inserted into the above model gives rise to the following two dynamic equations

$$\widehat{w} = -\beta_w(\overline{e} - e) + g_m - n, \qquad \widehat{\omega} = -\beta_p((I - S)/K)$$

which reverse the way that expectations were treated in the main part of this chapter. The classical model of section 10.5 is thereby reformulated in the following way (we use its elementary functional forms for simplicity) by making use of the dynamic variables $\omega = w/p, l^s = L^s/K$ and $\nu = M/(wL^s)$:

$$\widehat{\omega} = \beta_p((1-c_h)f(l) + c_h(\theta+\delta) - \delta - \gamma - i_f(r(\omega) - (i - \pi^e)) + n)$$

$$\widehat{l^s} = -i_f(r(\omega) - (i - \pi^e))$$

$$\widehat{\nu} = g_m - n - \beta_w(l/l^s - 1) - \pi^e = -\beta_w(l/l^s - 1)$$

where i is given by ($l = l(\omega), l' < 0$):

$$\nu l^s = (x/\omega) f_m(i), \text{ i.e.}$$

$$i = f_m^{-1}(\nu l^s \omega / f(l(\omega))) = i(\omega, l^s, \nu), \qquad i_1, i_2, i_3 < 0$$

The steady state of this model is the same as before. For the Jacobian of this dynamics at the steady state we here get:

$$J = \begin{pmatrix} \beta_p[(1-c_h)f'l' - i_f(r' - i_1)]\omega & \beta_p i_f\, i_2\omega & \beta_p i_f\, i_3\omega \\ -i_f(r' - i_1)l^s & i_f\, i_2 l^s & i_f\, i_3 l^s \\ -\beta_w l'/l^s\nu & \beta_w l(l^s)^{-2}\nu & 0 \end{pmatrix}$$

$$= \begin{pmatrix} J_{11} & - & - \\ J_{21} & - & - \\ + & + & 0 \end{pmatrix}$$

where J_{11} in particular is negative when assumption (*ii*) in theorem 10.1 is reversed.

Under this reversed assumption, we have $a_1 = -$ trace $J > 0$, $a_2 = J_1 + J_2 + J_3 > 0$ and $-a_3 = \det J = -J_{32}(J_{11}J_{23} - J_{13}J_{21}) = -\beta_w\nu\beta_p(1 - c_h)f'l'i_f i_3 < 0$. For the remaining Routh-Hurwitz condition $a_1a_2 - a_3 > 0$ we get, as in the proof of theorem 10.1:

$$a_1a_2 - a_3 > 0 \text{ if } J_{32}J_{13}J_{21} > 0 \text{ iff } (0 >)\, r' > i_1$$

since the other component of the determinant of J: $-J_{11}(J_{23}J_{32})$ is eliminated by one of the (all positive) products in the expression $a_1a_2 = -(J_{11} + J_{22} + J_{33})(J_1 + J_2 + J_3)$. Note here in addition that this last inequality will always hold if the parameter β_p is chosen at a level sufficiently small.

We thus find that the stability condition of Stein's model is the exact opposite of the corresponding stability condition—assumption (*ii*) in theorem 10.1—of the model in sections 10.2, 10.3 and 10.5. Furthermore, stability no longer depends here on the size of the parameter β_p (and β_w). This is due to Stein's ARE-assumption on expectations, which eliminates the real rate of interest effect (or Mundell effect) from aggregate demand and thereby increases the stability of the dynamics considerably.

Monetary growth cycles can be easily generated for the above model when $(1-c_h)f'l' - i_f(r'-i_1) > 0$ holds. Since the sign of this expression only influences the trace of J and $b = a_1a_2 - a_3$ (but cannot modify $a_2 > 0, a_3 = -\det J > 0$) it is easy to establish that the dynamics give rise to a Hopf bifurcation if the parameter β_p is made sufficiently large. This bifurcation value β_p^H is uniquely determined, since we have for $b(\beta_p) = a_1(\beta_p)a_2(\beta_p) - a_3(\beta_p)$ the functional form

$$b(\beta_p) = (\widetilde{a}_1\beta_p + a_1(0))(\widetilde{a}_2\beta_p + a_2(0)) - \widetilde{a}_3\beta_p$$

where $\widetilde{a}_1 \cdot \widetilde{a}_2 < 0$ and $b(0) = a_1(0)a_2(0) > 0$ must hold. This polynomial of degree two thus has exactly one positive root β_p^H, where cyclical adjustment gives way to a locally explosive cyclical pattern when β_p passes this parameter value from below.

Cyclical phenomena and instability are not discussed in Stein 1982 with respect to his general macrodynamic model. This means that one further "gospel"—besides the three he discusses in his book—is completely bypassed: the Marx/Cassel growth cycle model as it has been formalized by Goodwin (1967), Rose (1967), and others.

10.8 Appendix 2: Proofs of Theorems 10.1–10.3

Proof of Theorem 10.1 Let $\det(\lambda I - J) = \lambda^3 + a_1\lambda^2 + a_2\lambda + a_3 = \lambda^3 - (\text{trace } J)\lambda + a_2\lambda - \det J$ denote the characteristic polynomial of the Jacobian J (the coefficient a_2 is given by the sum $J_1 + J_2 + J_3$ of the principal minors of the matrix J). According to the Routh-Hurwitz stability criterion (see Brock and Malliaris 1989, 75, for example) we have to show that $a_1, a_2, a_3 > 0$ and $a_1a_2 - a_3 > 0$ holds true.

By assumption (i) we have the following sign structure of the Jacobian J

$$J = \begin{pmatrix} - & - & 0 \\ ? & - & - \\ ? & - & - \end{pmatrix}$$

since i_2, i_3, l' are all negative. This shows that $a_1 > 0$ holds.

For the determinant of the matrix J one gets under the same assumption, by noticing that the last principal minor of J:

$$J_1 = \begin{vmatrix} J_{22} & J_{23} \\ J_{32} & J_{33} \end{vmatrix}$$

is zero, the expression:

$$\begin{aligned}
\det J &= (-1)^{1+2}(-\beta_w l/(l^s)^2\omega) \begin{vmatrix} J_{21} & J_{23} \\ J_{31} & J_{33} \end{vmatrix} \\
&= \beta_w l/(l^s)^2\omega \begin{vmatrix} -(1-c_h)f'l'l^s & 0 \\ \widehat{m}_1 m & \widehat{m}_3 m \end{vmatrix} \\
&= -\beta_w\omega(1-c_h)f'l'i_f\, m i_3 \frac{1}{1/\beta_p - i_f} < 0
\end{aligned}$$

since

$$\begin{aligned}
J_{21} &= -\beta_k[i_f(r'-i_1) - (1-c_h)f'l' - i_f\widehat{m}_1]l^s - (1-c_h)f'l'l^s \\
&= -\beta_k \frac{1}{1-\beta_p i_f}[i_f(r'-i_1) - (1-c_h)f'l']l^s - (1-c_h)f'l'l^s \\
&= +(\beta_k/\beta_p)\widehat{m}_1 l^s - (1-c_h)f'l'l^s
\end{aligned}$$

and

$$J_{2j} = (\beta_k/\beta_p)\widehat{m}_j l^s,$$

due to $i_f(i_j + \widehat{m}_j) = \widehat{m}_j/\beta_p$ for $j = 2, 3$.

Assuming in addition condition (*ii*) gives for the sign structure of J the further result[19]

$$J = \begin{pmatrix} - & - & 0 \\ + & - & - \\ + & - & - \end{pmatrix}$$

from which we immediately obtain $a_2 > 0$, since the remaining two principal minors J_2, J_3 are both positive in this situation ($J_1 = 0$).

We have already shown above that $a_3 = -\det J$ equals

$$+J_{12}(J_{21}J_{33} - J_{23}J_{31}) = +J_{12}J_{21}J_{33} - J_{12}J_{23}J_{31}$$

The first of these two terms appears in $a_1a_2 = (-J_{11} - J_{22} - J_{33})(J_1 + J_2 + J_3)$ with the opposite sign and thus cancels out when $a_1a_2 - a_3$ is formed, while the remaining term $-J_{12}J_{23}J_{31}$ in a_3 is negative under the above sign structure of the Jacobian and thus cannot make $a_1a_2 - a_3$ negative ($a_1a_2 > 0$). This completes the proof of theorem 10.1.

q.e.d.

Proof of Theorem 10.2 The real part of this dynamics is here independent of its monetary part and given by:

$$\widehat{\omega} = \beta_w(l/l^s - 1), \qquad l = l(\omega), l' < 0$$

$$\widehat{l^s} = -(1 - c_h)f(l(\omega)) + \text{ const}$$

It can be reformulated in Goodwinlike terms by introducing the rate of employment as a new variable: $e = l/l^s$. This gives for the second equation by making use of the elasticity expression $\varepsilon(\omega) = -\omega l'(\omega)/l$:

$$\widehat{e} = \frac{l'(\omega)\dot{\omega}}{l} - \widehat{l^s} = -\varepsilon(\omega)\widehat{\omega} + (1 - c_h)f(l(\omega)) + \text{ const}$$

$$= -\varepsilon(\omega)\beta_w(e - 1) + (1 - c_h)f(l(\omega)) + \text{ const}$$

This, together with the equation $\widehat{\omega} = \beta_w(e - 1)$, is basically a Goodwinian reformulation of the real part this Keynes-Wicksell model.

Owing to its growth rate formulation, the dynamics $\widehat{\omega}, \widehat{e}$ exhibits $\mathbb{R}^2_+$ as an invariant set, that is, no trajectory of it that starts in the open set $\mathbb{R}^2_+$ can leave this set (the boundary of it is also an invariant set). We abbreviate by $g^1(\omega)$, $g^2(e)$ the two functions $-[(1 - c_h)f(l(\omega))/\omega + \text{ const}]$ and $\beta_w(e - 1)/e$ which are both well defined on $\mathbb{R}_+$. These functions give rise to the following Liapunov function $E : \mathbb{R}^2_+ \to \mathbb{R}$ for the above dynamics of the real part of the model:

$$E(\omega, e) = \int_{\omega^\star}^{\omega} g^1(x)dx + \int_{e^\star}^{e} g^2(y)dy$$

where $\omega^\star$, $e^\star(= 1)$ denote the steady-state values of the model (see section 10.3), that is,

$$g^1(\omega^\star) = 0, \qquad g^2(e^\star) = 0$$

Since both g^1 and g^2 are negative to the left of their steady-state value and positive to their right, we have for the function E: $E(\omega^\star, e^\star) = 0$ and $E(\omega, e) > 0$ otherwise. Furthermore,

$$\begin{aligned}\dot{E} &= E_1\dot{\omega} + E_2\dot{e} = g^1(\omega)\dot{\omega} + g^2(e)\dot{e} \\ &= -[(1-c_h)f(l(\omega)) + \text{ const }]\widehat{\omega} + \beta_w(e-1)\widehat{e} \\ &= -[(1-c_h)f(l(\omega)) + \text{ const }]\beta_w(e-1) \\ &\quad + \beta_w(e-1)[-\varepsilon(\omega)\beta_w(e-1) + (1-c_h)f(l(\omega)) + \text{ const }] \\ &= -\varepsilon(\omega)\beta_w^2(e-1)^2 < 0 \text{ if } e \neq e^\star = 1\end{aligned}$$

since $\varepsilon(\omega) = -\omega l'(\omega)/l$ is strictly positive. According to Beltrami (1987, 42) we thus get that the equilibrium $\omega^\star$, $e^\star$ of this dynamics is asymptotically stable in the sense of Liapunov, since the set $\dot{E} = 0$ contains no invariant subset other than the equilibrium itself.

Consider now an arbitrary point (ω, e) of $\mathbb{R}^2_+$. There exists $c > 0$, such that this point is contained in the subset $E^{-1}([0,c])$ of $\mathbb{R}^2_+$, which, owing to the above must be an invariant subset of $\mathbb{R}^2_+$ $(\dot{E} < 0)$ and which is a closed set. This set fulfills the conditions[20] of theorem 2 in Hirsch and Smale 1974, 196 on the basin of attraction B of the equilibrium point $(\omega^\star, e^\star)$, that is, we have $E^{-1}([0,c] \subset B)$. The point (ω, e) is thus attracted by $(\omega^\star, e^\star)$. This proves the global asymptotic stability of the real part of the model independently of any particular choice of adjustment speeds.

The (dependent) monetary dynamics of the model for $\beta_k = 0$ is given by

$$\begin{aligned}\widehat{m} &= -\frac{\beta_p}{1-\beta_p i_f}[i_f(r(\omega) - i(\omega, l^s, m) - (1-c_h)f(l(\omega)) + \text{ const }] \\ &= \frac{i_f}{1/\beta_p - i_f} f_m^{-1}(ml^s/f(l(\omega))) + q(\omega)\end{aligned}$$

which for $\beta_p < 1/i_f$ gives $\widehat{m}_m < 0$. This implies also asymptotic stability for these one-dimensional, nonautonomous dynamics.

q.e.d.

Proof of Theorem 10.3

1. In the case $\beta_k = 1$, the Jacobian of the dynamics (10.17) – (10.19) at the steady state is given by $(\beta = (1-\beta_p i_f)^{-1} > 0)$:

$$J = \begin{pmatrix} \beta_w l'/l^s\omega & -\beta_w l/(l^s)^2\omega & 0 \\ -i_f\beta(r' - i_1 - \beta_p(1-c_h)f'l')l^s & i_f\beta i_2 l^s & i_f\beta i_3 l^s \\ \beta_p\beta((1-c_h)f'l' - i_f(r' - i_1)) & \beta_p\beta i_f\, i_2 & \beta_p\beta i_f\, i_3 \end{pmatrix}$$

This Jacobian is close to

$$\begin{pmatrix} \beta_w l'/l^s\omega & -\beta_w l/(l^s)^2\omega & 0 \\ -i_f\beta r' & 0 & 0 \\ 0 & 0 & 0 \end{pmatrix}$$

in the assumed case (and negative). The above dynamics is consequently qualitatively close to the center type dynamics of the original Goodwin (1967) model in this case (see chapter 4).

2. The above Jacobian is in this case close to ($\det J < 0$ for $\beta_p \neq 0$!):

$$\begin{pmatrix} \beta_w l'/l^s\omega & -\beta_w l/(l^s)^2\omega & 0 \\ -i_f\beta(r' - i_1)l^s & i_f\beta i_2 l^s & i_f\beta i_3 l^s \\ 0 & 0 & 0 \end{pmatrix}$$

which gives for the principal minor J_3 of it ($l = l^s$ at the steady state):

$$\beta_w\omega i_f\beta(l'i_2 - (r' - i_1)) > 0 \text{ iff } l'i_2 - (r' - i_1) > 0$$

The roots of

$$\begin{pmatrix} J_{11} & J_{12} \\ J_{21} & J_{22} \end{pmatrix}$$

will thus have negative real parts exactly when this condition holds true and this extends to the situation of sufficiently small parameters β_p by continuity arguments.

3. For arbitrary β_p ($< 1/i_f$), we get for the principal minor J_3 just considered the following expression:

$$\beta_w\omega i_f\ \beta(l'i_2 - (r' - i_2) + \beta_p(1 - c_h)f'l')$$

that is, J_3 is positive if the stated condition holds ($\beta_p < 1/i_f$). From the proof of theorem 10.1 we already know that $J_2 > 0$, $J_1 = 0$, $\det J < 0$, trace $J < 0$ must hold true in addition ($\beta_p < 1/i_f$). The characteristic polynomial of J thus exhibits positive coefficients solely, which implies that all of its real roots must be negative (J is a so-called Hicksian matrix in this case). A loss of stability can therefore occur solely in a cyclical manner.

4. The minor J_3 is here approximately equal to $\beta_p(1 - c_h)f'l' - r'$ and thus can be made negative if β_p is sufficiently large (i_f sufficiently small), whereas J_2 is close to zero ($J_1 = 0$), that is, the coefficient a_2 of the characteristic polynomial will be negative in such a case.

5. Owing to

$$l'i_2 - (r' - i_1) - \beta_p(1 - c_h)f'l' > l'i_2 - (r' - i_1) - (1 - c_h)f'l'/i_f > 0$$

we have that a_2 (and, of course: a_1, a_3) have to be positive throughout, that is, only $a_1a_2 - a_3$ can become negative in this case. The coefficients of this expression are all linear functions of $\beta = (1 - \beta_p i_f)^{-1}$ (though their dependence on β_p is a nonlinear one). The positive sign of a_1a_2 will therefore dominate the negative one of $-a_3$ for β_p close to $1/i_f$ (β close to $+\infty$). This concludes the proof of theorem 10.3.

q.e.d.

11 Inflation, Distribution, and Cycles in a Keynesian Monetary Growth Model

11.1 Perspective of the Model

The model in this chapter[1] can be viewed as arising from two different motivations. On the one hand, it provides another modification of the macroeconomic Keynesian models that have been discussed in chapters 7–10. In contrast to the model of the preceding chapter and its limit case of infinitely fast adjusting prices considered in chapters 8 and 9, however, the emphasis is now again placed on demand-side effects so that the model is similar to the type introduced in the later sections of chapters 8 and 9. On the other hand, we again take up the classical approach to growth cycles dealt with in chapter 4 and reconsidered in section 10.5. This branch of economic theory sees the evolution of the economy as a continuous succession of booms and depressions that originate in the conflict over income distribution. Building blocks from these different traditions are combined, and the dynamics of the resulting model are then studied; our special interest here lies in their tendencies for cyclical behavior.

In short, the model may be labeled a Keynes-Goodwin model, where the IS(-LM) demand block is no longer used for a determination of the rate of inflation, as in the Keynes-Wicksell case of the previous chapter, but now determines—as it should in Keynesian theory—the rate of capacity utilization of firms (and the nominal rate of interest). In contrast to the four-dimensional IS-LM growth model considered in the later sections of chapters 8 and 9, labor-market effects and resulting adjustment processes are reformulated here to allow for a three-dimensional dynamical system. Central elements are a money wage Phillips curve, an adjustment rule for the price markup, and a law of motion for the evolution of the capital stock of firms.

Let us begin with a recapitulation of the main features of the models in the previous chapters. They are sufficiently general to address the most important relationships between the markets for goods, labor, and financial assets in an inflationary environment. Their structure can be characterized as either dynamic AD-AS or IS-LM models, the latter exhibiting a law of motion for the price level p. They incorporate a constant growth rate of money supply (in the growth versions), an expectations-augmented Phillips curve, and adaptive expectations or myopic perfect foresight of price inflation. It has been shown that the stability optimism expressed by Sargent (1987, section 5.1), for example, is generally unwarranted in these types of models. Actually, the speed at which the expected rate of inflation adjusts to current inflation turns out to be a key parameter, such that local stability prevails if it is sufficiently low, whereas higher reaction intensities, which are often associated with higher rationality, bring about destabilization. Moreover, the possibility of oscillatory behavior was observed. It was therefore concluded that this type of model is not very suitable for supporting the stability claims of monetarist theory, since it may instead inspire the modeling of self-sustaining economic cycles.

Our main criticism of the AD-AS growth models discussed so far concerns their price determination, that is, competitive pricing. On the basis of a production function with the standard properties, the price level is derived from the marginal productivity principle for labor, where the nominal wage rate is considered to be given in the short run. In the presence of persistent oscillatory behavior this implies countercyclical movements of the real wage. From the 1930s on there has been a long, still unsettled discussion on the empirical significance of this point. Here, it suffices to take seriously the initial finding by Dunlop (1938) that real wages, if anything, are procyclical rather than countercyclical, which, at least for the United States, has been largely confirmed by subsequent research (Blanchard and Fischer 1989, 17; see also the compilation by Mitchie [1987]). Apart from the question of real wages, one may feel uneasy about the fact that in these model types the assumption of a full utilization of the capital stock is explicitly or implicitly present—which gave rise to the characterization "Supply Side Keynesianism" in the preceding chapter.

These considerations suggest dropping the neoclassical competitive pricing and marginal productivity theory and adopting another approach for the formation of goods prices. A common alternative is the concept of markup pricing (on average cost). The markup rate is mostly assumed to be a given constant, then. We follow this simplification only with respect to the short run, but the markup may change from one period to another. Here, we go back to the work of Kalecki, from whose discussion of oligopolistic competition we extract an adjustment mechanism for the markup rate. In combination with a wage Phillips curve we can thus study truly *nominal* wage and price dynamics, which are based on better behavioral assumptions than those in either the AD-AS growth model or the Goodwin framework of Ch. 4 and its Keynes-Wicksell variant considered in section 10.5. The story of the other strand of economic theory, the classical growth cycle, runs basically as follows: The rate of return on capital is determined by the share of profits in national income. As derived from the notion of the industrial reserve army, however, the bargaining power of workers is inversely proportional to the rate of unemployment. Consider a phase of the cycle where the profit share is rising, and the rate of return on capital is also rising thus inducing an increase in investment. That is, the rate at which real capital accumulates is rising. The ensuing increase in production (relative to trend) reduces the rate of unemployment. So labor's bargaining strength improves, and workers can put through higher real wages (again relative to trend), which in turn raises the share of wages in national income. But this is to say that a reduction in the profit share as well as in the rate of return on capital obtains. At this stage we have the famous profit squeeze on investment. The corresponding decrease in capital growth leads to a slowdown in production and initiates a dynamic of descent into depression.

Besides neglecting the monetary and the government sector of the economy, the story of the feedback effects between distribution and employment rests on two simplifying suppositions: (1) a falling profit share implies a decline in the rate of return on capital, or the profit rate, for short; (2) an increase in the real wage rate (relative to its trend value) also increases the wage share. The statements are true if, as in Goodwin's prototype model and its many variants, two hypotheses are employed, namely, the capital-output ratio remains unchanged over the cycle, and labor productivity grows at a constant rate.

Now, both assumptions are known to be in stark contrast with what is observed as stylized facts. For one thing, the ratio of the flow of output to the capital stock is strongly correlated with proxies for capacity utilization, so that (besides the employment rate) the output-capital ratio may also be employed as a measure of economic activity. In a business cycle model, it should at any rate be treated as an endogenous variable. Since the profit rate stands in a positive relationship not only to the profit share but also to the output-capital ratio, dropping the assumption of a constant output-capital ratio directly affects the first supposition. Even if, as the expansion progresses, the profit share begins to fall, the rate of profit may continue to rise if the output-capital ratio keeps rising. The negative feedback effect from distribution (alone) may thus be too weak to reverse the upward motion of the economy.

As for the second supposition, it may be taken into account that the wage share is equal to the ratio of the real wage to labor productivity. The latter, however, also undergoes systematic variations over the cycle. It is actually one of the best-established facts in empirical studies of macroeconomic time series that the deviations of labor productivity from trend display a procyclical pattern. As a consequence, the positive effect on the wage share stemming from rising real wages in the expansion, or the negative effect on the profit share, will be partly compensated by the concomitant rise in labor productivity, and may even be overcompensated.

In addition to these two points, investment has to be considered more closely. If one wishes to incorporate Keynesian demand problems, an explicit investment function will have to be introduced. According to the classical tradition, the rate of profit is the main determinant of investment. In a richer model that includes financial assets, the profit rate has to be compared with the alternative rate of return, the (expected) real rate of interest. But this implies, for example, that a falling profit rate may be less severe for investment and, via the multiplier, for economic activity as a whole if this interest rate is falling, too. Also, much will depend on the underlying expectations about price inflation.

It follows from these observations that the working of the classical mechanism should be reconsidered in a more comprehensive model. In this chapter we start out from Sargent's AD-AS growth framework and its disequilibrium extension in the previous chapter, remove some questionable features, especially those regarding price setting on goods markets, and provide an explicit treatment of distribution. Furthermore, capacity utilization is made an endogenous variable.[2] The resulting model has the following features:[3]

1. Separation of investment and saving decisions;
2. Explicit consideration of interest-bearing financial asset;
3. Use of the rate of monetary expansion as a control variable;

4. Endogenous determination of the stock of capital that is growing over time;

5. Treatment of the inflation rate as an endogenous variable;

6. Adaptive formation of inflationary expectations;

7. Continuously clearing goods and financial markets, represented by the usual IS-LM temporary equilibrium conditions with the level of production and the rate of interest as the equilibrating variables;

8. Determination of the volume of employment by the output decisions of firms; this is generally different from the labor supply;

9. Nominal wages governed by an expectations-augmented Phillips curve;

10. Goods prices determined by a markup rule on average cost, where the markup rate itself is subject to a Kaleckian adjustment mechanism.

The model is formulated in such a way that it can be reduced to a system of three differential equations in three state variables. These are real balances relative to the capital stock, the markup rate, and the expected rate of inflation. At any point in time these state variables determine a temporary equilibrium solution of the output-capital ratio and the nominal rate of interest. All other variables of interest, such as in particular the profit rate and actual inflation, can be derived from them.

The study of this economy is concerned with the following points. First, an analysis of the local stability of the (unique) steady-state position is undertaken. It has already been mentioned that the adjustment speed of expected inflation plays a central role in Sargent's AD-AS growth model, where sluggish adjustments are stabilizing and fast adjustments are destabilizing. A result of this kind has a firm tradition in dynamic models of Keynesian or other inspiration. For instance, it holds true for the general Tobin models investigated by Hadjimichalakis (1971), Benhabib and Miyao (1981), Hayakawa (1984), or for the Tobin-Buiter model simulated by Smith (1980). The present model shares the same property, although in detail the mechanisms have been changed substantially.

In a second step, immanent cyclical tendencies can be identified. The mathematical instrument that can be utilized in this respect is the Hopf bifurcation theorem. At least for a limited range of parameter values, furthermore, it allows one to derive existence of periodic orbits, that is, of persistent and self-repeating oscillations of the state variables around the steady state.[4] Such an analysis, however, can be only a transitional stage. The theorem cannot reveal what happens for parameter values outside this range, or whether the steady state as well as the closed orbits arising from the Hopf bifurcation are unstable. Owing to the nonlinear nature of the model, a treatment of these global problems has to resort to computer simulations. If carefully designed, their significance need not be restricted to the special case under consideration but can also give some general insights.

These simulations suggest that, as specified, the economy always exhibits oscillatory motions. Concentrating on situations where they are continuously spiraling outward, we find the most obvious point to prevent the system from becoming economically meaningless is to modify the rule for adaptive expectations. The trajectories remain bounded if this device is made more flexible in the outer regions. With such a respecification, the steady state continues to be locally unstable, and persistent cycles emerge. These cycles, moreover, prove to be of a regular nature. After establishing this result, we can plot the most important variables against time, or against each other, and we can compare the outcome with stylized facts from empirical observations. In this way, the numerical simulations do not only serve illustrative purposes, they also provide a first validity test. As we mentioned in the general introduction, we hold the view that a certain degree of "realism," qualitative as well as quantitative, is a necessary component of the raison d'être of a macroeconomic business cycle model.

The remainder of the chapter is organized as follows. The next section sets up the formal model. New elements are the dynamic adjustments of the markup factor and a functional dependence of labor productivity on economic activity. A mathematical stability analysis is given in section 11.3. It includes a theorem on the existence of periodic orbits as the system undergoes a Hopf bifurcation. Section 11.4 illustrates the theoretical results by computer simulations. It also provides a sensitivity analysis and a description of the general cyclical pattern. Section 11.5 reconsiders the time horizon underlying the adaptive expectations. The discussion leads to a modification of the rigid mechanism, which amounts to an increased flexibility of the speed of adjustment. This device is subsequently applied to the original model in section 11.6. Computer simulations demonstrate that it is indeed capable of keeping the system within reasonable bounds and, in particular, it gives rise to unique and stable limit cycles. The characteristics of such a reference trajectory are compared with stylized facts from actual business cycles in the United States. Some concluding remarks are contained in section 11.7. The proofs of the mathematical propositions are given in a form that permits verification of the main arguments. The underlying computations are straightforward, though somewhat lengthy in detail. They are omitted for reasons of space but can be obtained from the authors upon request.

11.2 Formulation of the Model

For a growing economy, economic activity has to be measured as deviation from trend, or from "normal." To define the latter we introduce the notion of normal productive capacity, $Y^\star$. Current output, Y, may be below or above it. Presupposing Harrod-neutral technical progress, we determine $Y^\star$ by the capital stock, K, and a constant "normal" output-capital ratio, $x^\star$. The latter can be conceived of as "what firms on the average of boom and slump would regard as desirable" (Steindl [1952] 1976, $xiii$). With $Y^\star = x^\star K$ and $x = Y/K$ being the actual output-capital ratio, the trend deviations $Y/Y^\star$ can thus be expressed as $Y/Y^\star = x/x^\star$. Hence, total economic activity can be directly characterized by the output-capital ratio x. For this reason the terms *output-capital ratio* and *utilization* will be used interchangeably from now on.

In expounding the model, we begin with goods prices. They are determined by a markup μ on unit labor costs,

$$p = (1 + \mu)wL/Y \tag{11.1}$$

(w being the nominal wage rate, L the number of working hours). The magnitude μ is fixed in the short run but will vary from one adjustment period to another (see below). Of course, so does the share of wages in gross national income, only in the opposite direction, since $v = wL/pY = 1/(1 + \mu)$.

With a constant rate of capital depreciation, δ, the rate of return on capital is related to the markup rate and to utilization by the equation

$$r = (pY - wL - \delta pK)/pK = \mu x/(1 + \mu) - \delta \tag{11.2}$$

The central component of demand for goods will be (net) investment I. Remember that in Sargent's model, I is dependent on the difference between the marginal product of capital and the expected real rate of interest. Under the assumption that prices are determined by the marginal productivity principle for labor, it can easily be shown that the former coincides with the rate of profit.[5] Dropping neoclassical marginalism, we employ here the rate of profit directly. An investment function like (11.3) may also be traced back to Kalecki (1937b). It has been revived in a number of more recent studies by Taylor and O'Connell (1985), Taylor (1985), and Franke and Semmler (1989a). The expected real interest rate is defined as the difference between the current nominal rate of interest, i, and the expected rate of inflation, π^e. Accordingly, we have

$$I = f_I[r - (i - \pi^e)] \cdot K, \qquad f_I' > 0 \tag{11.3}$$

At this point a general remark concerning the two rates of return is in order. Though it is not essential for the formal analysis, in this as well as in the next chapter the rate of return on capital will be allowed to exceed the (real) interest rate even in a steady-state position (see the numerical specifications in section 11.4). When made explicit, this supposition was rejected in the previous sections, but it has already been demonstrated in section 5.4 that for endogenous growth models the marginal product of capital—or the rate of return on real capital for that matter—must be larger than the interest rate in the steady state. Moreover, within a framework of growth and finance it was shown in section 5.5 that, at certain parameter constellations, the same phenomenon can arise if the (optimal) markup is derived from a downward-sloping demand curve. Reference to the empirical work of Hall (1986) was made to justify such a pricing procedure. In addition, we want to note that the assumption of a profit rate in excess of the interest rate is very common in the Cambridge tradition of economic theory (it is, for example, a necessary criterion for implementing a technological innovation). Following the writings of Kalecki and others, we refer to the difference between profit rate and real interest rate and for convenience, from this point on, will call it simply the "risk premium."

In formulating consumption demand, we have the choice of distinguishing between consumption from wage and nonwage incomes and introducing different marginal propensities for capitalists and workers, or of following the Keynesian IS-modeling tradition, which largely disregards the impact of changes in distribution. We adopt the second approach in order to accentuate the fact that the destabilization effects we will encounter do not rest on the complications arising from a differentiation in consumption spending. By the same token, possible effects from underconsumption are not an issue. To keep the analysis simple, we also abstract from wealth effects. We (again) follow Sargent's (1987, section 5.1) specification and take consumption as a linear function of real disposable income alone, which is defined as output Y with taxes T and depreciation δK deducted (real tax collections T being net of transfers, where the latter include interest payments on the stock of government bonds [*ibid.*, section 1.3]).

Government policy is supposed to be neutral in the sense that taxes and government expenditures are proportional to the capital stock with factors θ and γ, respectively. Linking taxes to output would perhaps be more realistic, but a direct relationship of government spending to current output would possibly overemphasize the instantaneous multiplier effects. In total, denoting the average propensity to consume by c_h and dividing aggregate excess demand by the capital stock pK, we obtain the following IS-equation in intensive form:

$$f_I[\mu x/(1+\mu) - \delta - (i - \pi^e)] + c_h(x - \theta - \delta) + \delta + \gamma - x = 0 \qquad \text{(11.IS)}$$

To model the financial side of the economy, we adopt the textbook LM-framework, so that money and government bonds are the only financial assets (equities may be added as perfect substitutes). The money supply M is fully controlled by the central bank and does not change within the short period. The institutional details of the money supply mechanism are ignored. As another neutrality assumption for the government or the monetary authorities, M is supposed to grow at a constant rate, g_m, over time. Apart from the level of transactions, the demand for money depends on the current nominal rate of interest. By virtue of Walras's law and the autonomous monetary policy, the government budget restraint has no repercussion effects, and bonds can be treated as a residual (see Sargent 1987, section 1.2). Thus, portfolio equilibrium is described by

$$M = pY\, f_m(i), \qquad f_m' < 0 \qquad \text{(11.4)}$$

Defining $m = M/pK$ and dividing by pY yields the LM condition

$$f_m(i) - m/x = 0 \qquad \text{(11.LM)}$$

m, π^e, and μ are predetermined in the short run, so goods and financial markets are cleared by variations in x and i. Dependency of the IS-LM temporary equilibrium solution on m and π^e is fairly common. In the neoclassical synthesis, however, the role of distribution is seldom made explicit; it is dealt with only implicitly when, for example, nominal wages are fixed and a ceteris paribus increase of the price level is considered. Here distribution is directly reflected by the markup rate μ, which, as has been mentioned, is inversely related to the wage share.

The evolution of m, π^e, μ is governed by three differential equations. Consider first the changes in nominal wages. We assume that they can be represented by an expectations-augmented Phillips curve. Besides expected inflation π^e and (less often) productivity growth $\hat{y}$, wages are usually modeled as responding to the tightness of the labor market. Since, over the cycle, employment is highly correlated with total economic activity (see, e.g., figure C.2.5 in DeLong and Summers 1986a, 175), we here adopt utilization $x = Y/K$ as a proxy for the employment rate. Possible lags between turning points of employment and utilization are thus neglected, but this is outweighed by the advantage of saving one state variable.[6] Algebraically the Phillips curve is formulated as

$$\hat{w} = \hat{y} + \pi^e + f_w(x), \qquad f_w(x^\star) = 0, \;\; f_w' > 0 \tag{11.5}$$

It is seen that normal capacity utilization also serves as a reference in the wage-bargaining process, that is, the expected wage share is at rest ($\hat{w} - \pi^e - \hat{y} = 0$) when $x = x^\star$.

The price setting of firms is supposed to be adaptive. In the present model, however, it is not directly the price level that is adjusted but the markup rate. We postulate that its changes over time are related to the level of economic activity, as represented by x, and to its own level. It is notationally convenient to let such a function $f_\mu = f_\mu(x, \mu)$ refer to the growth rate of the markup factor $1+\mu$, that is,

$$\dot{\mu} = (1 + \mu) f_\mu(x, \mu) \tag{11.6}$$

where $f_{\mu x} = \partial f_\mu / \partial x < 0$, $f_{\mu\mu} = \partial f_\mu / \partial \mu < 0$.

The central issue in equation (11.6) is the influence of x (accordingly, in the numerical specifications later on $f_{\mu x}$ will be supposed to dominate $f_{\mu\mu}$). The main idea can be traced back to Kalecki. It starts out from the observation that in a recession, overheads are rising in relation to prime costs: "there will necessarily follow a 'squeeze of profits', unless the ratio of proceeds to prime costs is permitted to rise. As a result, there may arise a tacit agreement among firms of an industry to 'protect' profits, and consequently to increase prices in relation to unit prime costs" (Kalecki 1943, 50). Another reason for the reluctance of firms to reduce prices is their fear to unchain cutthroat competition (Kalecki 1939, 54), whereas the danger of new competitors may appear much lower in a recession. As for the opposite phase of the business cycle, Kalecki states that this "tendency for the degree of monopoly [which corresponds to the present markup rate μ] to rise in the slump . . . is reversed in the boom" (1943, 51). An argument here may be to deter new entry into the industry.[7]

The autofeedback in equation (11.6) expresses the notion of a target markup rate. If, with respect to a given level of utilization x, the present markup is considered too low, there may be some scope for an upward revision, that is, $f_\mu(x,\mu) > 0$. If, by contrast, μ is relatively high, firm managers may prefer to reduce it, $f_\mu(x,\mu) < 0$ (again, possibly, for reasons of entry deterrence). Taken together, these expressions imply the existence of a level $\mu = \mu(x)$ at which $f_\mu(x,\mu) = 0$. The assumptions on the partial derivatives make this target markup a decreasing function of x.

If $|f_{\mu\mu}|$ is small in comparison to $|f_{\mu x}|$, the direct consequence of equation (11.6) for the motions of the wage share $v = wL/pY$ is that it tends to rise in periods of high economic activity, $x > x^\star$, and to fall when utilization is below normal, $x < x^\star$. The same occurs in the Goodwin prototype model. But there it follows from the *real* wage Phillips curve (and the assumption of labor productivity to grow at a constant rate), whereas here it is the consequence of a hypothesis on price formation in oligopolistic industries (in essence, this has already been pointed out by Kalecki [1939, 54f]).

The Phillips curve (11.5) enters the picture in another place, namely, in the determination of current inflation. Upon logarithmic differentiation of the markup equation (11.1), one has $\hat{p} = \dot{\mu}/(1+\mu) + \hat{w} - \hat{y}$. Using (11.5) and (11.6), we obtain

$$\hat{p} = \pi^e + f_w(x) + f_\mu(x,\mu) \tag{11.7}$$

Equation (11.7) is a reduced form for price inflation, resulting from the (simultaneous) adjustments of nominal wages and the markup rate.

With respect to expected inflation, we maintain the simple hypothesis of adaptive expectations,

$$\dot{\pi}^e = \beta_\pi(\hat{p} - \pi^e) \tag{11.8}$$

where the parameter β_π gives the speed of adjustment. Working with adaptive expectations has been defended in sections 7.2 and 7.3. A flexibilization of the rigid rule in (11.8) is introduced in section 11.5 below.

We are now in a position to set up the differential equations for m, π^e, and μ. Equation (11.6) for $\dot{\mu}$ can be taken directly. As for $\dot{\pi}^e$, substitute (11.7) into (11.8), while with the supposition of a constant growth rate of money, g_m, $\dot{m}$ is obtained from $\hat{m} = \hat{M} - \hat{K} - \hat{p} = g_m - f_I[\cdots] - \hat{p}$ and equation (11.7). In sum, the system reads

$$\begin{aligned} \dot{m} &= m\{g_m - f_I[\mu x/(1+\mu) - \delta - (i - \pi^e)] - \pi^e - f_w(x) - f_\mu(x, \mu)\} \\ \dot{\pi}^e &= \beta_\pi[f_w(x) + f_\mu(x, \mu)] \qquad (11.9) \\ \dot{\mu} &= (1+\mu) f_\mu(x, \mu) \end{aligned}$$

where $x = x(m, \pi^e, \mu)$, $i = i(m, \pi^e, \mu)$ are the corresponding IS-LM solutions of utilization and the interest rate. Under some nonrestrictive assumptions, the latter are well-behaved functions, so that (11.9) constitutes a well-defined dynamical system.

Distribution in system (11.9) is represented by the wage share, that is, the inverse of the markup factor, $v = wL/pY = 1/(1+\mu)$. The other distributional variable, the real wage rate, is neither referred to nor can it be inferred from the other variables. In order to study its comovements with economic activity, it can be included in the model (as an appendix) if we add another relationship. Observe that the growth rate of real wages can be obtained by subtracting equation (11.7) from (11.5), but to this end the growth rate of labor productivity has to be determined (which otherwise has canceled out). It has already been pointed out as a well-established empirical regularity that the level of productivity $y = Y/L$ (not so much its growth rate) shows a significant positive correlation with utilization. A straightforward suggestion is to postulate a direct positive relationship between the ratio of y to its trend value $y^\star$, and the output-capital ratio x, that is,

$$y/y^\star = f_y(x), \quad \text{where } f_y(x^\star) = 1, \;\; f_y' > 0 \qquad (11.10)$$

The growth rate of trend productivity $y^\star$ may be an exogenous constant (though this will not matter). An empirical estimate justifying this approach is given in section 11.4.[8] Referring to equation (11.1) we see easily that the real wage after deflation by trend productivity, $\omega = (w/p)/y^\star$, is given by the formula

$$\omega = f_y(x)/(1+\mu) = v f_y(x) \qquad (11.11)$$

Equation (11.11) is a formal representation of the verbal statements above when discussing Goodwin's prototype growth cycle model. Notice that if system (11.9) really produces oscillatory behavior, the peaks and troughs of the real wage ω and the wage share v cannot coincide: these phase displacements result from the monotonicity of the function $f_y = f_y(x)$ and the observation that, by the very nature of equation (11.6), turning points of v and x will occur at different dates. More specifically, v will peak later than x. Hence, real wages will tend to move procyclically (unlike the countercyclical movements predicted by the neoclassical production function and the marginal productivity principle for labor), although they will lag somewhat behind utilization. More information on the extent of the lag and the size of the fluctuations can be provided by the computer simulations.

At the end of the section it may be mentioned that we have also set up a model where prices adjust directly to attain a target markup, with speed $\tilde{\beta}_p$, say. This price adjustment speed corresponds directly to the reaction coefficient β_p adopted in chapter 7, which measured the speed at which prices sought to adjust to marginal cost. Though there are some conceptual differences between the present model with its dynamic markup and the, so to speak, $\tilde{\beta}_p$-version, it turned out in the stability analysis that there are strong analogies in the computational details. In particular, under a slightly different assumption Theorem 11.1 and 11.2 below equally apply to the $\tilde{\beta}_p$-version. This remark shows that the dynamic properties of the Tobin-Sargent model type introduced in chapter 7 have a wide "radiation."

11.3 Local Analysis

A stationary point of system (11.9) constitutes a steady state of the economy. Demonstrating existence and uniqueness is a straightforward matter. Starting out from a given value of normal utilization, $x^\star$, it can be established in a number of successive steps.

1. The steady-state value $\mu^\star$ of the markup rate is obtained by setting $\dot{\mu} = 0$. That is, similar to the remark noted in the comment on equation (11.6), $\mu^\star$ is the solution of the implicit equation $f_\mu(x^\star, \mu) = 0$. It is unique since $\mu \mapsto f_\mu(x^\star, \mu)$ is a monotonic function.

2. Solving the IS-equation with $x = x^\star$ for f_I gives the long-run equilibrium rate of accumulation. Call it $g^\star$.

3. Substituting it in $\dot{m} = 0$ and taking account of $f_w = f_\mu = 0$ yields steady-state inflation, $\pi^\star = g_m - g^\star$.

4. The rate of interest derives from solving the implicit equation $f_I[\mu^\star x^\star/(1+\mu^\star) - \delta - (i - \pi^\star)] = g^\star$ for i. Uniqueness of $i = i^\star$ is implied by the monotonicity of f_I.

5. The ratio of real balances to the capital stock can now be computed from the LM-equation, $m^\star = x^\star f_m(i^\star)$.

We can, thus, consider the IS and LM curves. They are defined as the geometric locus of all pairs (x, i) that, with respect to m, π^e and μ given, simultaneously satisfy equations (IS) and (LM). At least in a vicinity of the steady state, existence and uniqueness of points of intersection are no problem. It is a routine matter to verify that the LM-curve slopes upward while a falling IS-curve is implied by Assumption 11.1. The impact reactions in the IS-LM temporary equilibria are summarized in the ensuing lemma.

Assumption 11.1 The average propensity to consume c_h falls short of unity and, evaluated at steady-state values, the responsiveness of fixed investment to changes in utilization is so restrained that

$$\partial f_I/\partial x = \mu^\star f_I'/(1+\mu^\star) < 1 - c_h$$

Lemma 11.1 Let Assumption 11.1 apply. Then for all m, π^e and μ close to the steady state a (locally) unique IS-LM solution $x = x(m, \pi^e, \mu)$ and $i = i(m, \pi^e, \mu)$ exists, with (continuous) partial derivatives

$$\begin{array}{lll} \partial x/\partial m > 0, & \partial x/\partial \pi^e > 0, & \partial x/\partial \mu > 0 \\ \partial i/\partial m < 0, & \partial i/\partial \pi^e > 0, & \partial i/\partial \mu > 0 \end{array}$$

In particular,

$$\partial x/\partial \mu = x v^2 \partial x/\partial \pi^e, \qquad \partial x/\partial m = (i/(m\eta_{m,i}))\partial x/\partial \pi^e$$

where $\eta_{m,i}$ is the modulus of the interest elasticity of money demand.

Changes in m and π^e have the familiar effects (the positive sign of $\partial x/\partial \pi^e$ reflects the Tobin effect in the investment function). As for the impact of distribution, observe that investment is the only function in the IS-LM equations in which the markup enters. It follows that a rise in the wage share v, which is tantamount to a falling μ, lowers the rate of return on capital and thus investment, so that there is a southwest shift in the IS-curve. Since the LM-curve remains unaffected, utilization

x and the interest rate i are both driven downward. However, this is only the usual ceteris paribus exercise. If, or when, production is really declining depends on the contemporaneous evolution of the other two variables m and π^e.

The formulas behind Lemma 11.1 are sufficient to set up the Jacobian matrix for the differential equations (11.9). It goes without saying that all evaluations to follow in this section refer to the steady state, so that the asterisk can be omitted. Local stability is studied by means of the Routh-Hurwitz conditions. Denoting the Jacobian by J and by J_1, J_2, J_3 its principal minors,[9] we have

i. $A_1 = -\text{ trace } J > 0$

ii. $A_2 = J_1 + J_2 + J_3 > 0$

iii. $A_3 = -\det J > 0$

iv. $B = A_1 A_2 - A_3 > 0$

which is necessary and sufficient for the eigenvalues of J to have negative real parts. Alternatively, the first or second inequality is implied by the remaining three (Gandolfo 1980, 250).

After the algebraic dust settles, the expressions for the A_i turn out to be as given by the next lemma. The way they are written puts special emphasis on the speed of adjustment of inflationary expectations, β_π. It is again our key parameter for stability.

Lemma 11.2 Suppose that assumption 11.1 holds. Then

$$A_1 = A_1(\beta_\pi) = D_1\beta_\pi + E_1$$

$$A_2 = A_2(\beta_\pi) = D_2\beta_\pi + E_2$$

$$A_3 = A_3(\beta_\pi) = D_3\beta_\pi$$

where

$$D_1 = (|f_{\mu x}| - f_w')\partial x/\partial \pi^e$$

$$D_2 = [-(1+\mu)|f_{\mu\mu}|f_w' + i(f_w' - |f_{\mu x}|)/\eta_{m,i}]\partial x/\partial \pi^e$$

$$D_3 = [i(1+\mu)|f_{\mu\mu}|f_w'/\eta_{m,i}]\partial x/\partial \pi^e > 0$$

$$E_1 = (1+\mu)|f_{\mu\mu}| + (i/\eta_{m,i})[1 - c_h + f_w' + (vx\eta_{m,i}/i - 1)|f_{\mu x}|]\partial x/\partial \pi^e$$

$$E_2 = [i(1+\mu)(1 - c_h + f_w')|f_{\mu\mu}|/\eta_{m,i}]\partial x/\partial \pi^e > 0$$

The stability analysis is particularly simple if the expression E_1 is positive. This can always be achieved by assuming a sufficiently low responsiveness to utilization in the markup adjustments, that is, $|f_{\mu x}|$ sufficiently small. From a practical point of view, however, such an assumption is unnecessary. With the numerical steady-state parameters employed in the computer simulations later on, one has $vx\eta_{m,i}/i = 2.81 > 1$, so that the coefficient of $|f_{\mu x}|$ in the definition of E_1 is positive. For this reason situations with $E_1 \leq 0$ will be neglected.

For low values of β_π, stability of the steady state can be verified immediately. Observe first that this entails $A_1(\beta_\pi) > 0$, $A_2(\beta_\pi) > 0$, $A_3(\beta_\pi) > 0$. Since A_1 and A_2 are positively bounded away from zero as $\beta_\pi \to 0$, whereas $A_3 \to 0$ in this case, $B = B(\beta_\pi)$ will be positive, too, if β_π is chosen small enough. All of the Routh-Hurwitz conditions are satisfied then. Without additional assumptions it can also be shown that high values of β_π bring about instability, and that, as β_π increases, there is no "reswitching" of stability. This holds irrespective of the sign of D_1 and D_2.

Theorem 11.1 Suppose that assumption 11.1 applies and that $E_1 > 0$ (E_1 as defined in lemma 11.2). Then there exists a positive critical value β_π^H of the speed of adjustment in adaptive expectations which entails that the steady state of system (11.9) is locally asymptotically stable if $0 < \beta_\pi < \beta_\pi^H$, whereas it is unstable if $\beta_\pi > \beta_\pi^H$.

Proof We distinguish by case. Suppose first that $D_1 < 0$. As β_π increases from zero, A_1 turns negative. Before that, however, $B = A_1A_2 - A_3$ changes sign from positive to negative (because $A_3 = D_3\beta_\pi$ becomes dominant). Let β_π^H be the corresponding root of $B(\beta_\pi)$.

Then, consider subcase 1*a*: $D_2 \geq 0$. This implies that a further increase in β_π cannot reverse the sign of B again. Otherwise, since $B < 0$ as β_π grows large, there would be two additional roots, which cannot possibly be brought about by a quadratic function. Hence condition (iv) is violated for $\beta_\pi > \beta_\pi^H$.

In subcase 1*b*: $D_2 < 0$, B is positive for large β_π. Let β_π^1, β_π^2 be the roots of A_1 and A_2, respectively. Clearly, they are positive. Also, $\beta_\pi^H < \min\{\beta_\pi^1, \beta_\pi^2\}$ and $B < 0$ for β_π in the interval between β_π^1 and β_π^2. Since B can have only two roots, $\beta_\pi > \beta_\pi^H$ implies either $B(\beta_\pi) < 0$ (violation of condition (iv)), or $\beta_\pi > \max\{\beta_\pi^1, \beta_\pi^2\}$ (which violates condition (i) and (ii)).

As for the second case, suppose that $D_1 \geq 0$. Observe that this implies

$D_2 \leq 0$. So, if A_2 approaches zero from above as β_π is rising, B will be falling too, and turn negative before. Again, call the corresponding root β_π^H. By the same argument as in subcase 1a above, the sign of B cannot change afterwards.

q.e.d.

The critical value β_π^H of the speed of adjustment in theorem 11.1 indicates the borderline case where the system changes from being locally convergent to locally divergent. It is, moreover, obvious that the Jacobian possesses a pair of purely imaginary eigenvalues at $\beta_\pi = \beta_\pi^H$ (otherwise $A_3 = -\det J$ would have to vanish). Hence, J has two conjugate complex eigenvalues for all β_π in a vicinity of β_π^H, and, at least close to the steady state, system (11.9) displays oscillatory motions. The fact that as β_π rises beyond β_π^H, the complex eigenvalues are crossing the imaginary axis in the complex plane, is the key condition for a Hopf bifurcation to occur (therefore the superscript H). It allows us to establish existence of periodic orbits for a certain range of parameters β_π close to β_π^H. That is, the loss of stability that we find as expectations adjust faster is associated with the emergence of persistent but bounded oscillations in the variables of system (11.9). Their amplitudes shrink to zero as these β_π approach β_π^H.

Theorem 11.2 Suppose that assumption 11.1 holds and that $E_1 > 0$. Then there exists a function $\varepsilon \mapsto \beta_\pi(\varepsilon)$ with the following property:

1. for all sufficiently small $\varepsilon > 0$, there is a nondegenerate periodic orbit generated by system (11.9) with respect to $\beta_\pi = \beta_\pi(\varepsilon)$;
2. $\beta_\pi(\varepsilon) \to \beta_\pi^H$ and the corresponding periodic orbits collapse to the stationary point of that system as $\varepsilon \to 0$ (β_π^H as determined in theorem 11.1).

Proof It suffices to verify the assumptions of theorem A in Alexander and Yorke 1978, 263–266. In the context of our model these are:

a. the equilibrium point of (11.9) is independent of β_π;

b. the functions on the RHS of (11.9) are continuously differentiable;

c. the Jacobian is continuous in β_π;

d. at $\beta_\pi = \beta_\pi^H$, the Jacobian is nonsingular and has a conjugate pair of complex eigenvalues;

e. for β_π near but not equal to β_π^H, no eigenvalue has zero real part.

Conditions (a)–(c) are obvious, whereas (d) and (e) have been demonstrated in the proof of Theorem 11.1.

q.e.d.

The limitations of the Hopf bifurcation results (together with references to the literature) have already been indicated in a remark on proposition 7.3 in chapter 7. We repeat the main points for convenience. In general, the closed orbits may arise on either side of β_π^H. The case in which $\beta_\pi(\varepsilon) < \beta_\pi^H$ is called a *subcritical* bifurcation: the asymptotic stability of $x^\star$ implies that the closed orbits are repelling. The case in which $\beta_\pi(\varepsilon) > \beta_\pi^H$ is called a *supercritical* bifurcation: because of the instability of $x^\star$ the closed orbits are attracting. Mathematical conditions exist telling if either of these two cases prevails. However, they involve derivatives up to the third order, which in most applications lack a reasonable economic interpretation. It may also be mentioned that a degenerate case would obtain if the dynamic system were linear; then the range of the $\beta_\pi(\varepsilon)$ would just be the single point β_π^H and, at that speed of adjustment, one would have a continuum of closed orbits in the phase space.

Theorem 11.2 is a local version of the Hopf bifurcation. Global information of a general, qualitative kind could be inferred from the theorem given in Alexander and Yorke 1978. There, the authors prove that the family of closed orbits arising from the Hopf bifurcation is connected in some topological sense. It follows that either this family contains members for β_π arbitrarily close to zero or for β_π tending to infinity, or it contains closed orbits that display an arbitrarily large period, or the closed orbits leave an economically meaningful region (as there are members that do not lie in any preassigned compact subset of $\mathbf{R}_+^3$). The remaining possibility that the closed orbits collapse to another stationary point distinct from $(m^\star, \pi^\star, \mu^\star)$ can be excluded here since the steady state was shown to be unique. All these statements, however, are too general for our purpose. For more specific information we have to make use of computer simulations.

11.4 Simulation Results for the Original Model

Numerical simulations to investigate the global dynamics of an economic system depend critically on the specification of the behavioral functions and the setting of the parameter values. As for the steady state the following values have been chosen (the underlying unit of time is one year). It is easily checked that they are mutually consistent.[10]

$x^\star = 1.50$	$\pi^\star = 3.00\%$	$m^\star = 0.225$	$\mu^\star = 33.3\%$
$v^\star = 0.75$	$i^\star = 8.00\%$	$g_m = 6.50\%$	$r^\star = 27.5\%$
$c_h = 0.80$	$\gamma = 0.375$	$g^\star = 3.50\%$	$\delta = 10.0\%$

$g^\star$ denotes the equilibrium rate of growth of real variables. $m^\star$ derives from $x^\star$ and from setting the reciprocal of the velocity of the circulation of money, $(M/pY)^\star = 0.15$. Government spending in relation to the national gross product is 25%. θ is residually determined by the IS-equation ($\theta = 0.1625$).

Except for the money demand function (where we follow Sargent 1987, section 5.2), we assume linearity. So, the investment function f_I, the money demand function f_m, the Phillips curve as defined by f_w, and the function f_μ determining the markup adjustments, have been specified as follows:

$$f_I = f_I[r - (i - \pi^e)] = g^\star + \beta_I[r - i + \pi^e - (r^\star - i^\star + \pi^\star)]$$

$$f_m = f_m(i) \qquad = \beta_{mY} \exp(-\beta_{mi} i)$$

$$f_w = f_w(x) \qquad = \beta_w (x - x^\star)/x^\star$$

$$f_\mu = f_\mu(x, \mu) \qquad = -\beta_{\mu x}(x - x^\star)/x^\star - \beta_{\mu\mu}(\mu - \mu^\star)/\mu^\star$$

The most important reaction parameter is β_π. In exploring the dynamics it was found that the main characteristics are not too sensitive to changes in the other coefficients. They have been fixed at the following values,

$$\beta_I = 0.50 \qquad \beta_w = 0.50 \qquad \beta_{\mu x} = 0.30 \qquad \beta_{\mu\mu} = 0.05$$

(notice the predominance of utilization effects in f_μ). On the basis of Goldfeld 1976 or the short compilation in Boorman 1976, 328–35 of empirical estimates of an interest rate elasticity in the demand for money, we have decided to set

$$\eta_{m,i} = 0.20$$

β_{mi} is subsequently determined from the definitional equation $\eta_{m,i} = |f_m'| i^\star / f_m = \beta_{mi} i^\star$, whereas the scaling factor β_{mY} is obtained from solving the LM-equation, $\beta_{mY} = 1/[(pY/M)^\star \exp(-\beta_{mi} i^\star)]$. As concerns the labor productivity function $f_y = f_y(x)$ in equation (11.10), which, we recall, is adopted only to study the comovements of real wages, we performed the simple regression

Table 11.1
Hopf bifurcation value of β_π resulting from isolated changes in selected reaction coefficients

Reaction	Changes in percent of reference values						
parameter	–50%	–25%	±0%	+25%	+50%	+100%	+200%
β_I	0.67	0.79	0.89	0.98	1.05	—	—
β_w	0.48	0.69	0.89	0.99	0.98	0.87	0.72
$\beta_{\mu x}$	0.93	0.99	0.89	0.71	0.56	0.38	0.23
$\beta_{\mu\mu}$	1.71	1.15	0.89	0.78	0.71	0.65	0.61
$\eta_{m,i}$	1.69	1.19	0.89	0.70	0.57	0.40	0.25

$$\ln(y/y^\star) = \alpha_y + \beta_y(x - x^\star)/x^\star$$

(U.S. quarterly data 1960:IV–1982:IV from Fair 1984 and Fair and Parke 1984). The value of α_y was not significantly different from zero, while $\beta_y = 0.411$ with $R^2 = 0.69$. Since also the peaks and troughs of $y/y^\star$ and $(x - x^\star)/x^\star$ are almost synchronous, we have adopted the specification

$$f_y = f_y(x) = \exp[\beta_y(x - x^\star)/x^\star], \qquad \beta_y = 0.40$$

After thus setting the stage, we can try selected values for the speed of adjustment β_π and compute the Routh-Hurwitz expressions (from the Jacobian of (11.9) or directly from lemma 11.2). The Hopf bifurcation value β_π^H, which can be found with the aid of a suitable iteration mechanism, turns out to be

$$\beta_\pi^H = 0.89305$$

This adjustment speed implies that if everything were frozen, it would take $1/\beta_\pi^H = 1.12$ years to correct a discrepancy between π^e and $\hat{p}$. Theorem 11.1 asserts that local stability prevails if this lag is longer, instability if it is shorter.

Before examining the dynamics, we insert a brief sensitivity analysis. Table 11.1 shows the impact on the bifurcation value β_π^H of variations in the reaction intensities in the investment function, the Phillips curve, the markup adjustments, and the money demand, as characterized by the parameters β_I, β_w, $\beta_{\mu x}$, $\beta_{\mu\mu}$, $\eta_{m,i}$, respectively. The response of β_π^H is limited with respect to the first two reaction parameters, as well as when $\beta_{\mu x}$ is declining and $\beta_{\mu\mu}$ is rising from the reference values. The impact is stronger for variations in the interest elasticity $\eta_{m,i}$, when $\beta_{\mu x}$ rises, and, perhaps somewhat surprisingly, when $\beta_{\mu\mu}$ is reduced (at $\beta_{\mu\mu}$ close to zero even $\beta_\pi^H = 2.69$ results). Parameter β_I plays a special role as regards the direction of the movements of β_π^H: it is the only parameter for which (large) increases do not lead to destabilization (by decreasing β_π^H; increasing β_I too much would violate assumption 11.1). Note that with respect to β_w the relationship is not monotonic. This suggests a caveat about premature conclusions of stabilizing or destabilizing effects of parameter changes in the behavioral functions. It may be added to these results that the responses of β_π^H are more moderate if the same exercise is carried out on the basis of $\beta_{\mu\mu}$ doubled.

When simulating the trajectories of the dynamic system, we follow principles similar to those in the chapters 8 and 9 and reformulate the model as a discrete-time sequential economy, where we keep track of all level variables. Composite variables like m are obtained from their definitions, not from a discrete-time counterpart of the first dynamic equation in the reduced system (11.9). The length of the market period (or the Hicksian "week") constitutes the step size h in the analogs to the time derivatives, which are usually taken forward. $\dot{K} = I$, for example, is captured by $K_{t+h} = K_t + hI_t$. Only the inflation rate entering the adaptive expectations mechanism in equation (11.8) is defined backwards as $\hat{p}_t = (p_t - p_{t-h})/hp_{t-h}$ (see also chapter 9). Term hI_t is the volume of investment over the week, from t to $t+h$, and the flow variables like I_t, Y_t, and so on are still measured per year, while p_t is the price per unit of the good that prevails during $[t, t+h)$.

Intuition says that the dynamic behavior of such a system becomes similar to that of the continuous-time formulation (11.9) if h is chosen small enough, and this is also fully confirmed in the present case.[11] For $h = 0.05$ years the trajectories behave as predicted by theorems 11.1 and 11.2 (only the bifurcation value is slightly affected). The stability and instability properties, furthermore, are not restricted to a vicinity of the steady state but carry over to practically the whole economically meaningful region. As a matter of fact, local and global dynamics look very much alike. In particular, at the Hopf bifurcation value there exists a continuous family of—approximately—closed orbits, which are growing in amplitude. In other words, we are close to the degenerate case mentioned in the remark on Theorem 11.2 where the mapping $\varepsilon \mapsto \beta_\pi(\varepsilon)$ is constant, that is, $\beta_\pi(\varepsilon) \approx \beta_\pi^H$ for all small ε. These phenomena are due to the fact that over the relevant range the nonlinearities in system (11.9) (which would not be eliminated by a linear money demand function) are very mild, so that with the above specifications, system (11.9) may be described as "quasi-linear" (cf. the remarks on Theorem 11.2). Periodic cycles must, therefore, be considered to be an exception in this economy. They are not even very realistic, since all these cycles exhibit a period of nearly 24 years (reducing the scale of utilization to a perhaps more familiar $x^\star = 0.50$, by the way, is of no great help).

Before thinking about a suitable modification of one or two building blocks of the model to improve its stabilizing forces, we must first understand the dynamics as they stand. The general cyclical pattern can be described as follows, beginning with what happens after utilization has reached a trough and is on the upturn. At that stage, both π^e and $\hat{p}$ are close to steady-state inflation. By contrast, the Kaleckian mechanism of equation (11.6) has raised the markup above normal, while $m = M/pK$ has fallen to a comparatively low level. The latter is in the first instance due to higher inflation in the preceding time.

The further evolution of x can be explained by the different effects that are exercised by the three state variables m, π^e and μ (recall from lemma 11.1 that $\partial x/\partial m$, $\partial x/\partial \pi^e$, $\partial x/\partial \mu$ are all positive). For a while the markup continues to rise but, owing to $\partial f_\mu/\partial \mu < 0$, the expression $f_\mu(x, \mu)$ in equation (11.6) eventually becomes negative, and μ begins to fall. Since $f_w(x) + f_\mu(x, \mu) < 0$ at that time, expected inflation is falling (see the second equation in (11.9)). The same holds true for current inflation $\hat{p}$ (see equation (11.7)). The ratio $m = M/pK$, by contrast, is rising because the money growth rate g_m exceeds the sum of the inflation and capital growth rates ($\hat{m} = \hat{M} - \hat{p} - \hat{K}$). Moreover, the positive effect upon x proves to dominate the negative effects coming from π^e and μ, so that utilization keeps on rising.

As the expansion progresses, f_w changes sign from negative to positive. Shortly after x has passed the level of normal utilization $x^\star$, this is sufficient to render $f_w + f_\mu$ positive. As a consequence, π^e attains a minimum and is then rising, an evolution which, through the Tobin effect, reinforces the growth in utilization.

The seeds of a recession are mainly contained in the acceleration of the growth of capital and prices. As current inflation approaches $\pi^\star$ (from below), the difference between the profit rate and the real interest rate has risen so high that $\hat{p} + f_I[r - (i - \pi^e)]$ catches up with g_m. This indicates the upper turning point of real balances $m = M/pK$ and causes them to fall. For a short time x continues to rise, but then the impact on x of the jointly falling m and μ dominates the positive influence of the rising π^e and initiates the contraction.

The pattern just described is quite independent of the precise speed of adjustment β_π (when it exceeds β_π^H). With increasing values of β_π, however, π^e as well as $\hat{p}$ can rise and fall faster, which has several quantitative effects: first the peak values of π^e and $\hat{p}$ increase and their trough values decrease. The increasing amplitude in inflation then gives rise to an increasing amplitude in M/pK. Owing to the faster motions of π^e, it also takes more time from the turning point of m until the ensuing turning point of x is reached—not very much, but the prolonged positive feedback effect on x also gives π^e an extra chance to grow (or decline) in the meantime. The increase in the amplitudes of m and π^e raises the amplitudes of x (as well as of μ). On the whole, beyond the threshold value β_π^H of the speed of adjustment, these phenomena generate a deviation-amplifying process or, when considered in the phase space, the trajectories are spiraling outwards. As mentioned above, these observations are not confined to a close neighborhood of the steady state; they hold true in a global sense. Besides, already at moderately increased values of β_π, the destabilizing forces are so strong that the variables soon tend to become economically meaningless.

Hence, we have to look for a stabilization mechanism that can take effect in the outer regions. If we do not invoke the government, this could mean nonlinearities in the behavioral functions f_I, f_m, f_w, or f_μ. Even at a speed of adjustment like, say, $\beta_\pi = 2$, however, it becomes difficult to check the explosive tendencies with plausible respecifications of this kind. It therefore appears more promising to turn directly to a reassessment of the formation of inflationary expectations.

11.5 A Modification of Adaptive Expectations

In this section a new aspect to the principle of adaptive expectations is discussed. One issue that is hardly ever mentioned in the macroeconomic literature is the question of the time horizon underlying these expectations, that is, what period do expectations about the rate of inflation refer to? In the introduction of adaptive expectations in section 7.2, we provisionally joined the usual interpretation that expectations are formed at the beginning of the (infinitesimally) short period (or at the end of the preceding period) and, with respect to inflation, π^e is the rate of inflation arising from the price level that is expected to prevail over the rest of this "period." Alternatively, however, $\pi^e(t)$ may be conceived of as a point estimation of some average inflation over a medium range of time, say, from t to $t+T$ (where the near future might be weighted more heavily). There is no general answer, but a discussion of which point of view is more meaningful must not neglect the kind of the decision problems using π^e.

In the first instance, the variable π^e enters into the determination of fixed investment in equation (11.3). Because of the long lifetime of capital goods and the irreversibility of investment, we should have quite a large T in this case.[12] Since, however, $\beta_\pi \rightarrow \infty$ is to mean that π^e tends to come close to current inflation, there is no particular reason why large values of β_π should claim priority in rationality; a good prediction of price changes over the next quarter or month will generally be of rather limited use for the evaluation of an investment project that reaches far into the future.

The other function employing π^e is the Phillips curve. Here, the time horizon derives from the assumption on the timing of wage settlements. If wages of the total labor force are renegotiated every short period (of length h), we have $T = h$.[13] A more realistic device is to hypothesize that wage settlements refer to only a segment of the labor force, for which it remains fixed for the next T years. The wage bargains that are taking place every adjustment period then refer to different segments, and w is an index of present and past wage settlements. This can easily be made more precise by employing certain uniformity assumptions so that, denoting by $w^s(t)$ the wage settlements at time t, the wage index $w(t)$ in continuous time is defined as

$$w(t) = (1/T)\int_{t-T}^{t} w^s(\tau)d\tau$$

Differentiating with respect to time leads to

$$\hat{w}(t) = (1/T)[w^s(t) - w^s(t-T)]/w(t)$$

This procedure makes the time horizon of the wage settlements explicit, which will be definitely shorter than a time horizon for investment decisions.[14] For concreteness, with respect to wage setting we might think of a time horizon of one or two years, whereas in the case of fixed investment inflationary expectations may extend over a period between, let us say, two to five years.[15]

It follows from these sketches that, in the investment function and in the Phillips curve, there are actually two different expected rates of inflation. If, like many other model builders, we continue to work with a uniform π^e, then of course this is due to the necessity of simplification, at least at the present stage of research. One might also feel it is expected inflation in the investment function that sets the pace, and feedback effects coming from a different rate of expected inflation in the Phillips curve are of secondary importance.

If it is acknowledged that the time horizon of expectations is definitely longer than the short period and, consequently, myopic perfect foresight loses its significance as a benchmark case, delayed adjustments like adaptive expectations may appear in a new light. A general analysis of this matter is conducted by Heiner (1988). He starts out from the notion of a gap between an agent's competence in the decision-making process and the difficulty in rightly interpreting information and selecting potential actions (even if information were complete). The stage is set by the assumption that the environment, which is exogenous to the individual agent and can be characterized by a single decision parameter, is initially in a period of relative stability. At some point in time the decision parameter starts shifting toward a new value that remains constant for another uncertain period before shifting again. This framework allows Heiner to be compatible with the analytical tools that are traditionally used to study optimal behavior. In particular, an optimal response exists that maximizes expected utility. The response itself might be "outward" behavior or "inward" subjective beliefs about probability or expectation variables (Heiner 1988, 270).

By contrast, an imperfect agent is a decisionmaker for whom there is a positive probability of missing the optimal response and of adjusting initially either too soon or in the wrong direction.[16] Heiner demonstrates that, in comparison to a perfectly optimizing agent, an imperfect agent needs to respond at a relatively slow rate or with a noticeable delay in order to control decision errors. In other words, the very attempt to respond soon after a parameter starts shifting without severely constraining the expected rate of response will actually reduce expected utility compared to not doing so (268). It follows that, given the explicit limitations imperfect agents are subjected to (rather than ruling them out by hypothesis), "behavioral rules (and the mechanisms needed to enforce them) can be viewed as fully rational even though they may prevent them from acting in the same manner as perfect agents would behave" (269).

Heiner's arguments provide a theoretical basis for inertial behavior in inflationary expectations, which, especially if a longer time horizon is involved, may also take the form of adaptive expectations. A specification of a constant speed of adjustment, however, is certainly not warranted. In this respect we may mention some empirical support of the fact that agents will not always revise their expectations in the same relation to the past observations of inflation. That is, they additionally have a conception of a rate of inflation which they regard as "normal" and to which they expect inflation to return if the current rates of inflation deviate too much from it. Incidentally, the value of normal inflation might shift over time. Kane and Malkiel (1976) establish that such return-to-normality elements play an important part in inflation forecasts.[17]

If one wishes to avoid introducing a completely new mechanism, return-to-normality may also be viewed as affecting the speed of adjustment of adaptive expectations in different stages of the inflationary process. Simply put, consider a situation with $\hat{p} > \pi^e$ that is characterized by an increasing π^e and accelerating prices, $d\hat{p}/dt > 0$. In addition, suppose that in the past, agents have learned that the upward motion of $\hat{p}$ tends to be reversed; the higher $\hat{p}$, the more likely this event seems to occur in the near future. If π^e were still increased at the same speed as before, it would later be found to be above current inflation, at a time when $\hat{p}$ is already on the downturn. With regard to the decisions about fixed investment, an overprediction would probably be more costly than a possible underestimation. It seems therefore reasonable to assume that, in order to reduce the risk of overprediction, the adjustments of π^e are more sluggish in the (suspected) late phase of the upswing of $\hat{p}$, or in the early phase of its downturn. Later, with $\hat{p}$ and π^e coming down again to medium values, adjustments in π^e might gain momentum.

Schmalensee 1976 represents an experimental study that makes a very similar point. He presented a total of twenty-three subjects with price observations from a nineteenth-century British wheat market and had them submit both point and interval forecasts of five-year averages of the price series. A central issue was the role of turning points in this series. The survey results obtained show that peaks and troughs were indeed "special" to the expectation formation process. Most important for our purpose, an adaptive expectations model was found to outperform an extrapolative expectations model with the response speed in the adaptive model tending to *fall* during turning points.

The slowdown of the adjustment speed may also be explained to some extent by Heiner's (1988) theoretical results. If in an upward motion of inflation we distinguish two regimes, a "normal" regime and a regime of excessively high inflation rates, then the transition from the first to the second regime corresponds to a decision parameter that begins to shift. Consequently, the initial response to this event will be adjustments in expected inflation that are less rapid than in the previous normal regime. Realistically, however, the environment as it is perceived by the agents is less stylized than in the clear distinction between an old and a new regime. This means that the change in the speed of adjustment will be more gradual than the analysis by Heiner might suggest. Apart from that, gradual changes of the adjustment speed will be obtained if the speed is interpreted as an average across heterogeneous agents.

On the basis of the above reasoning it would now be fairly easy to endogenize the adjustment speed of inflationary expectations, β_π, and make it a variable. Here, we prefer to work with a slightly different specification, which is, however, conceptually equivalent. Recall that in order to determine the change in expected inflation, the specification compares π^e to the current rate of inflation $\hat{p}$. That is, the latter serves as a reference. Our concept is that we allow for some flexibility in such a reference rate of inflation. Introducing the notation π_{ref}, we conceive of it as a *function* of current inflation, $\pi_{ref} = \pi_{ref}(\hat{p})$. In this way the rigid rule of adaptive expectations is generalized to

$$\dot{\pi}^e = \beta_\pi(\pi_{ref}(\hat{p}) - \pi^e) \tag{11.8'}$$

For simplicity, rising and falling inflation is treated symmetrically. We postulate that over a medium range of inflation π_{ref} still coincides with $\hat{p}$. Yet, when $\hat{p}$ has soared to higher levels the increase in the yardstick is faltering: $d\pi_{ref}(\hat{p})/d\hat{p} < 1$ then. Similar behavior occurs when inflation rates are considered to be low. For the simulations we specify π_{ref} as a piecewise linear function. Defining "medium inflation" as a symmetrical interval $I_\pi = [\pi^\star - d_\pi, \pi^\star + d_\pi]$ around steady-state inflation ($d_\pi > 0$) and supposing that the slope of π_{ref} outside this range is given by α_π ($0 \le \alpha_\pi < 1$), we have

$$\pi_{ref}(\hat{p}) = \begin{cases} \alpha_\pi \hat{p} + (1-\alpha_\pi)(\pi^\star + d_\pi)) & \text{if } \hat{p} > \pi^\star + d_\pi \\ \hat{p} & \text{if } |\hat{p} - \pi^\star| \le d_\pi \\ \alpha_\pi \hat{p} + (1-\alpha_\pi)(\pi^\star - d_\pi)) & \text{if } \hat{p} < \pi^\star - d_\pi \end{cases}$$

Note that if π^e as well as $\hat{p}$ turn out to remain bounded, these modified expectations might be described as partially (or qualitatively) self-fulfilling (otherwise, if the economy ran into hyperinflation, they would not be maintained). They differ from rational expectations, which are totally self-fulfilling, in a quantitative way.

The proposed flexibility of adaptive expectations is, of course, still a simple rule of thumb. The present framework, however, is already so complex that one may become skeptical if individual agents would really be able to develop a pertinent theory of the functioning of the economy and arrive at, or come close to, rational expectations. In particular, the influence that π^e exerts on $\hat{p}$ is only very indirect. It is channeled through a number of feedback effects that spread all over the economy. So, a reduction in π^e decreases utilization (via the Tobin effect) and lowers the increase in nominal wages (by way of the Phillips curve). After this works through, the rule of markup pricing puts a curb on inflation that is most clearly revealed by the reduced form of price inflation, equation (11.7). Nevertheless, this is only a ceteris paribus argument. At the same time the induced changes in utilization have an impact on capital growth and, thus, on m. Mediated by the financial markets, this impact in turn feeds back on x, which in turn feeds back directly on $\hat{p}$ but also on the markup factor μ, which is another source that modifies the speed in the price adjustments (see equation (11.7)). Keep in mind that generally these feedback chains may involve several nonlinearities. To conclude this short discussion, if the easing-off of inflationary expectations in the boom phase turns out to be followed by a falling rate of price inflation in the near future, then it is still an open question to what extent individual agents could ascribe this phenomenon to their specific expectation formation process. In other words, can they really be much smarter than, say, a naive econometrician who might obtain similar estimates by a more or less modified rule of adaptive expectations?

11.6 Simulation Results with Flexible Adaptive Expectations

The flexibilization of adaptive expectations has been specified in such a way that, replacing (11.8) with (11.8′), the equations of the original system are preserved as long as expected inflation does not deviate too much from the equilibrium inflation rate. Hence, the trajectories will continue to spiral outward in a vicinity of the steady state if $\beta_\pi > \beta_\pi^H$. Outside the inflation interval I_π, however, a mechanism is now built in which works as if β_π were decreased. We know that locally this would

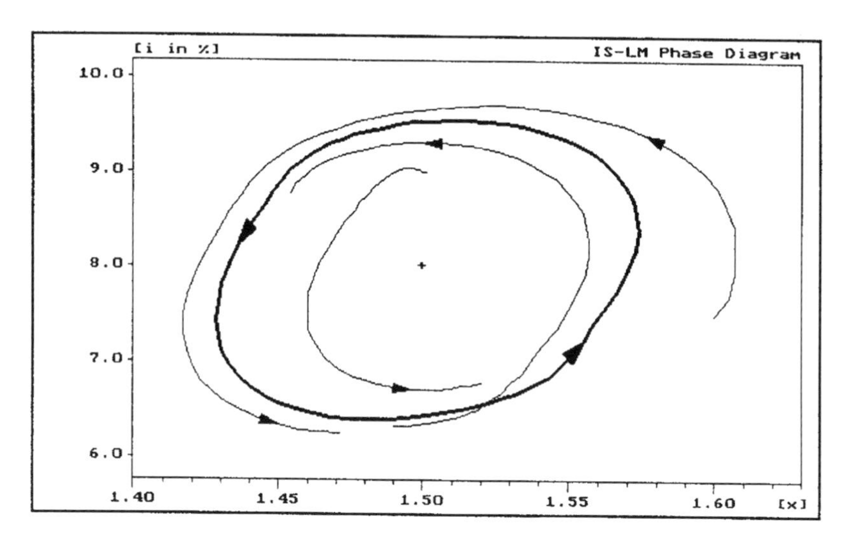

Figure 11.1
Interest rate i versus output-capital ratio x: Limit cycle and approaching trajectories

bend the spirals in the phase space inward, and we expect this property to carry over to the outer regions. As a consequence, persistent cyclical behavior should emerge.

In order to test the stabilization mechanism we adopt a particularly high value for β_π. In addition, the new parameters are set as follows,

$$\beta_\pi = 7.50 \qquad d_\pi = 1.20\% \qquad \alpha_\pi = 0.75$$

The simulation runs of this expanded dynamical system reveal that the simple idea of equation (11.8′) serves its purpose well. The trajectories display interesting properties: they no longer diverge but remain bounded and even approach a closed orbit. Moreover, from the many simulation runs we performed there is every reason to believe that such a limit cycle is uniquely determined. To understand this recall our observation in section 11.4 that within an economically meaningful region the original system (with equation (11.8)) is almost linear. Equation (11.8′) introduces one true nonlinearity: such that a key variable, which reflects the distance of the state variables from the steady state, is replaced with an S-shaped function of it. Seen from this perspective, the regular behavior should not be surprising. figure 11.1 illustrates the attraction of the limit cycle in the space suitable for IS-LM analysis, that is, in the (x, i)-plane.

Figure 11.2 and 11.3 plot the periodic motions of the main variables

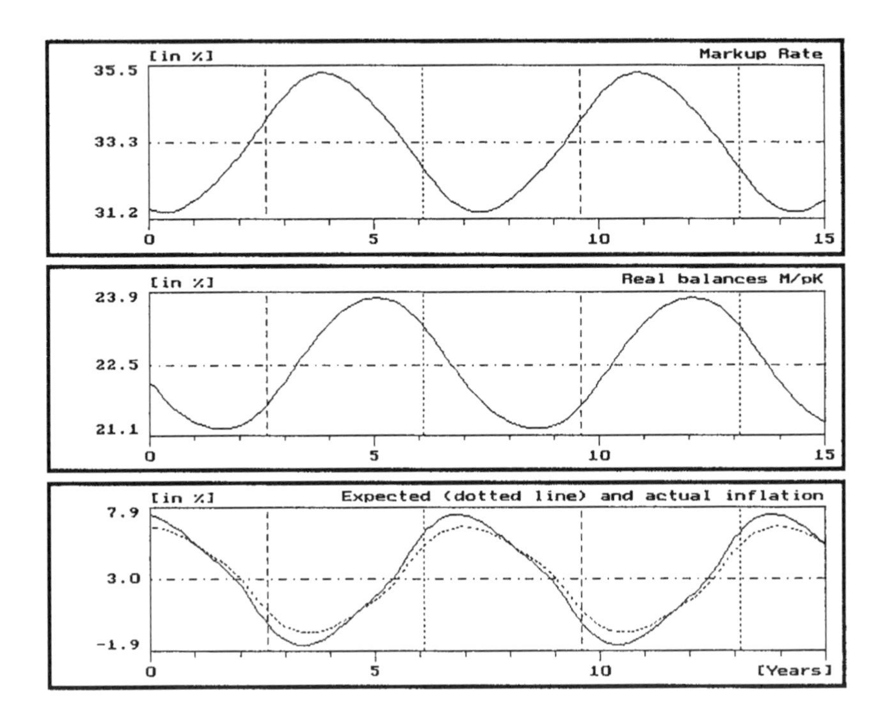

Figure 11.2
Time series of $\mu, m, \hat{p}$ and π^e arising from the limit cycle (Note: The vertical dashed lines indicate the troughs and peaks of the output-capital ratio [see also figure 11.3].)

against time. The calibration has succeeded insofar as the limit cycle exhibits a period of 7.0 years and the amplitudes of the single variables remain within a reasonable range (see also table 11.2), where the motions are nearly symmetrical. The third panel in figure 11.2 shows the working of the adjustment mechanism of inflationary expectations: π^e (slightly) leveling off as current inflation rises above $\pi^\star + d_\pi = 4.2\%$. After $\hat{p}$ has reached its peak, it takes 1.3 years until π^e exceeds $\hat{p}$ (from $t = 6.8$ until $t = 8.1$, for instance), but the differences between π^e and $\hat{p}$ are rather moderate (at the peak we have $\pi^e = 6.59\%$ versus $\hat{p} = 7.46\%$). Note also that, because of $x = x(m, \pi^e, \mu)$, the motions of x can be seen as resulting from "adding up" the motions of m, π^e, and μ.

As for the succession of the turning points of the different variables, figure 11.3 shows that, if we take the motions of x as defining the stages of the cycle, the real rate of interest is nearly countercyclical. Furthermore, there is a lead in (relative) real balances M/pK in figure 11.2 (nev-

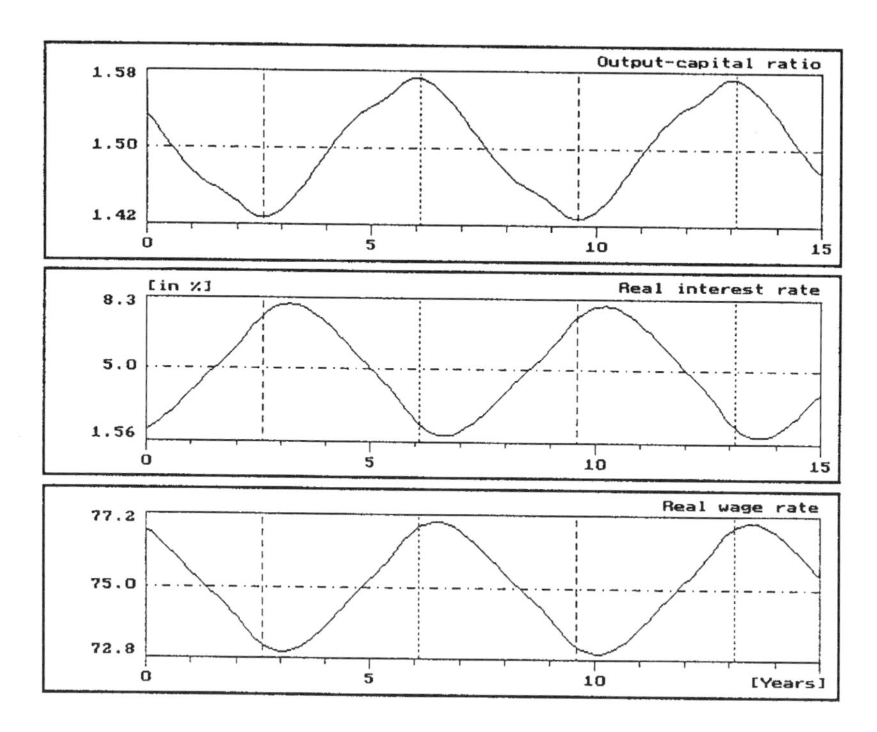

Figure 11.3
Time series of $x, i - \hat{p}$ and ω arising from the limit cycle

ertheless, it would of course be nonsensical to say that money "causes" output). Inflation, by contrast, is lagging. The substantial lag in μ or, what amounts to the same, in the wage share $v = wL/pY = 1/(1 + \mu)$, has already been inferred in the discussion of the markup adjustments of equation (11.6). The bottom panel of figure 11.3 also confirms our prediction about the behavior of real wages. It clarifies that the term $f_y(x)$ in equation (11.11): $\omega = vf_y(x)$, is dominating, so that the movements of the real wage rate are nearly procyclical, with only a short lag. The precise timing of the turning points of these and other variables is given in the last column of table 11.2.

It may be noted that in the late phase of the expansion of x, the falling markup dominates the positive effect of x in the definition of the rate of return on capital (see equation (11.2)) so that not only the profit share but also the rate of return on capital declines, and we have a profit squeeze. The expected real interest rate $i - \pi^e$, however, is falling faster (its motion is similar to $i - \hat{p}$ in figure 11.3). For this reason both the

Table 11.2
Amplitude and timing of turning points

Variable	Amplitude	Lag (+) or Lead (−) w.r. to x (in years)
x	1.50 ± 0.073	—
I/K	3.50% ± 1.46%	0.0
π^e	3.00% ± 3.64%	0.9
$\hat{p}$	3.00% ± 4.48%	0.8
m	22.50% ± 1.28%	−0.9
i	8.00% ± 1.58%	1.3
$i - \hat{p}$	5.00% ± 2.16%	(0.7)
v	75.00% ± 1.12%	1.3
ω	75.00 ± 2.02	0.4

Note: Numbers in parentheses refer to timing of trough in comparison with peak of x.

growth rate of capital and (via the multiplier) the rate of utilization are still rising, which shows that the effect of the profit squeeze is much more limited than it is in Goodwin's prototype model.

The data in table 11.2 can be compared with empirical observations of leads and lags. The evidence is ambiguous for some variables, but based on the quarterly time series for the United States 1960–1982 in Fair 1984 and Fair and Parke 1984 the following statements can be made:

1. In the United States, the oscillations of $x = Y/K$ around its trend $x^\star$ are highly correlated with capacity utilization or with the trend deviations of GNP. Contrary to the classification of the National Bureau of Economic Research, there is no significant asymmetry in the cycles of $x - x^\star$: expansions from trough to peak take about the same time as the contractions from peak to trough. With respect to GNP growth rates and GNP deviations from trend, the same point was made by DeLong and Summers (1986a). The latter series shows strong comovements with the trend deviations of the output-capital ratio. Also, the amplitudes of empirical and simulated $x - x^\star$ are of comparable size. By contrast, it is well known that the duration of the single cycles is subject to variations.[18]

2. The empirical growth rate of the capital stock, I/K, is markedly procyclical (with respect to x, that is), although with a lag of two or

three quarters. The latter could be explained by the lag of the gestation period, which of course is usually neglected in continuous-time macroeconomic modeling practice. In the present model, x and I/K move perfectly in line because of the simplifications in the other components of goods demand (cf. the IS-equation). The amplitude of I/K is acceptable.

3. When comparing the series of our M/pY or $m = M/pK$ with the corresponding trend deviations of M1, the differences are relatively minor. This is somewhat surprising since in reality M1 follows a less steady growth path than the money supply in the present model.

4. At least in the United States the detrended average real wage rate paid in the nonfinancial corporate business sector (including and excluding compensation for overtime work) shows a procyclical pattern, with a relatively low amplitude. The evolution of our $\omega = (w/p)/y^{\star}$ is compatible with this observation.

5. Empirical evidence of a typical cyclical pattern of the wage share is inconclusive, one possible interpretation being that there is a shift from a more countercyclical (with lags) to a more procyclical behavior. The peak and trough deviations from (the strong) trend are quite limited. This is also true for the present model. The loops of the wage share with respect to utilization, which are depicted in figure 11.4, are in close correspondence to the loops obtained in Goodwin type models (there, usually, the employment ratio is drawn against the wage share). It has, however, been discussed that the underlying mechanism is different.

6. Since the early times of the Phillips curve it has been recognized that inflation is not only related to the level of unemployment, but also to its time rate of change. Plotting inflation against unemployment, this gives rise to the so-called Phillips loops. If we take United States price inflation—sufficiently smoothed quarter-to-quarter inflation or four-quarter changes—adopt a suitable segmented linear trend, and plot the trend deviations against trend deviations of x, then clear and distinct counterclockwise loops are obtained. Figure 11.5 shows that for the limit cycle in our simulation run, a similar kind of behavior results, though the turning points of the two series might be somewhat close. Note that the amplitude of our instantaneous rate of inflation would be depressed when computing the above discrete-time statistical counterparts. In addition it should be pointed out that the counterclockwise Phillips loops of the rate of inflation imply more or

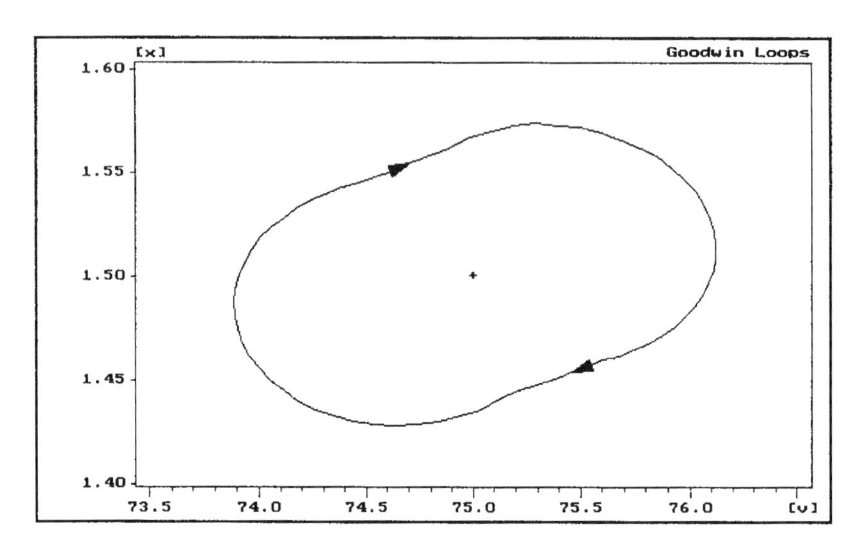

Figure 11.4
Output-capital ratio x versus wage share v on the limit cycle

less countercyclical (!) movements of the *level* of prices. This is spelled out in section 13.3, where empirical references are also given.

Experience with variations of the parameter values, finally, should be briefly reported. Most important, the qualitative nature of the preceding results is preserved, in particular the existence of an apparently unique and globally stable limit cycle. With respect to variations of the central adjustment parameter β_π, it turns out that a decrease prolongs the period of the cycle and diminishes the amplitudes of utilization as well as expected and current inflation. This is another facet of the stabilization forces it gives rise to. The impact on the amplitude of the other variables is negligible. Large variations in β_π may somewhat alter the shape of some of the loop patterns.

11.7 Conclusion

In the preceding sections a monetary growth model has been set up that, in direct and indirect ways, takes account of labor, goods, and financial markets. It explicitly treats income distribution, price setting of oligopolistic firms, and inflationary expectations. More specifically, a Kaleckian hypothesis on markup pricing and markup adjustments has been integrated into a Keynes-Wicksell modeling framework, thereby

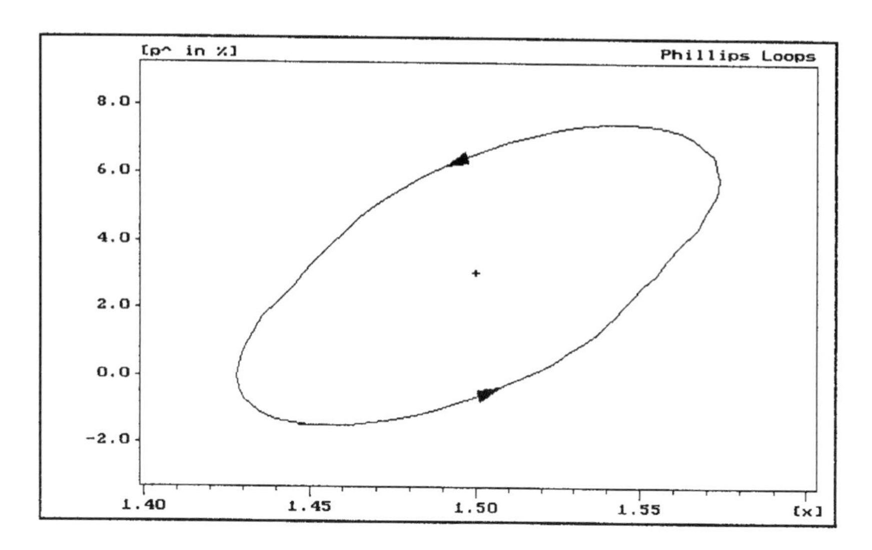

Figure 11.5
Rate of inflation $\hat{p}$ versus output-capital ratio x on the limit cycle

removing from it the Wicksellian theory of inflation. Local stability of the steady state can be characterized by the speed of adjustment, β_π, of adaptive expectations: a low responsiveness ensuring stability, faster reactions producing instability. At least close to some bifurcation value of β_π, tendencies for cyclical behavior and the existence of periodic orbits can be identified. Numerical simulations, however, show that they are only encountered over an extremely small range of β_π. With the specifications chosen, other values of β_π either bring about global stability of the steady state or trajectories that continuously spiral outward and soon leave an economically meaningful region.

Together with some theoretical and empirical evidence, the latter observation has led us to modify the rule of adaptive expectations and introduce some flexibility. Already, a simple respecification proves a sufficient check for the explosive oscillations. The outcome in the case of local instability (which by construction persists) is the existence of a seemingly unique and stable limit cycle in the three-dimensional state space. The periodic motions thus obtained can be compared with some stylized facts of the U.S. economy. Concerning the period of the cycle, the amplitude of fluctuations in the most important variables, and the succession of turning points, there are no significant inconsistencies and, if we take account of the low dimensionality, the variables behave quite satisfactorily. We consider these simulation results the most interesting feature of the present model. This, of course, does not rule out the possibility that similar results can be obtained by adopting different, and theoretically more ambitious building blocks.

As for improvements, in our opinion the most urgent one concerns expectations. As we pointed out in section 11.5, two distinct rates of expected inflation referring to different time horizons are involved. Furthermore, inflation is the only expectation variable that affects investment in the model, whereas it may be argued that in reality firms' investment decisions are influenced by a state of long-term expectations that, as hinted at in a remark on the investment function in section 7.5, encompasses more than the beliefs about future inflation. With regard to dynamic adjustments of such a new expectation variable, chapter 12 of the *General Theory* might be a stimulating source. This is one line of research pursued in the next chapter.

V

Finance, Long-Term Expectations, and Macro Fluctuations

In this last part of the book we explore the question of how financial factors and the financial-real interaction can be integrated into a macrodynamic model. In the previous chapters money and bonds were the only asset (possibly with equities as perfect substitutes for bonds in the background of the models), and the monetary-real interaction was studied with respect to the money market, inflation, expected inflation, and output. If we consider the Keynesian view on macrodynamics that financial markets also might contribute to destabilizing tendencies, this general idea should be more explicitly modeled in the context of Keynesian non-market-clearing models. There are, of course, numerous attempts to provide a microeconomic foundation of asset markets dynamics as well as of the fragility of financial intermediaries. We are, however, more concerned here with the macroeconomic implications; that is, the perspective of our approach is in the line of studies that pursues the question of how financial market fragility can impinge on real activity.

In order to focus our study, in chapter 12 we neglect the labor market and the price dynamics but address the financial market in specific detail. Besides money, equity of firms and bank loans to firms are included. The latter two assets provide an important additional link between the financial and real sector since they are needed to finance fixed investment. Following the Keynesian tradition, capital markets are viewed as imperfect. We also build on chapter 5 and the nonseparation theorem discussed there, that is, the conception that real decisions of firms cannot be separated from finance decisions.

At the center of our study are bank-dependent firms. We restrict ourselves to the modeling of some feedback effects between investment and the indebtedness of firms, and their impact on the stability of a macromodel. We will not elaborate on the feedback of the possible volatility of asset markets, for example, stock or foreign exchange markets on the macroeconomic times series data. The long-term trend in the capital structure is taken as given, so that the financial-real interaction can be dynamically studied from the point of view of flows. A key element in the model is our endogenization of Keynes's famous "animal spirits"; they enter firms' investment decisions and the demand of private households for the financial assets. The formulation of the dynamic adjustments of such a state of long-term expectations is based on modern views on asset markets, according to which the public opinion is influenced by objective factors (fundamentals) as well as by psychological factors, arising from group interactions of the economic agents and leading to overreactions.

Given those new elements, we are able to construct a very elementary model of the financial-real interaction that typically generates cyclical behavior. Under a more special (though not implausible) adjustment rule for the long-term expectations, the model may even exhibit what Leijonhufvud has called "corridor stability." This model, too, is calibrated to reflect reasonable steady-state values corresponding to certain ratios in the U.S. economy, and to reproduce business cycle properties of the amplitudes and turning points.

Finally, in chapter 13, we turn to the study of low-frequency movements in macroeconomic variables. In our context we are particularly interested in the capital structure. Our analysis builds on a differential equation for the evolution of the capital structure as represented by the debt-asset ratio of firms. The dynamics of this measure of indebtedness can be decomposed into variations of the rate of new borrowing, the growth rate of capital, and the rate of inflation (the influence of the latter, especially, should not be underestimated). Such a decomposition of the factors responsible for the development of the capital structure aids to understand its fluctuations in the postwar U.S. economy, particularly when the trend of the single components is changing. Generally, the effects of these trend movements are seen to dominate the effects of the business cycle fluctuations.

12 Finance, Expectations Dynamics, and Macro Fluctuations

12.1 Introduction

In the recent literature, an increasing number of approaches have been put forward that emphasize the role of financial factors and the financial-real interaction in the business cycle. Arising partly from a Keynesian tradition and partly from recent theories of imperfect capital markets, this development seeks to overcome the unfortunate separation of financial and real aggregate magnitudes in macrodynamic modeling and to allow for financial factors to exert propagating effects on macroeconomic disturbances. In addition, expectations are stressed as an important factor in determining asset-holding and investment decisions.

Before discussing our treatment of long-term expectations and presenting the economic model, we think it is worth emphasizing some general features of the role of financial markets for real economic activities. The traditional view is that, as we already discussed in section 5.5, finance does not matter for the value and the investment of the firm. There is—as reflected by the Modigliani-Miller theorem—no interdependence between the financial side and real economic activities. It is maintained that financial factors can be indicators of disturbances in the real sector, but financial disturbances and shifts in firms' risk are primarily results of real shocks that are generated by some exogenous random mechanism.[1] Consequently, the financial indicators contain information about only exogenous perturbations. Though it is agreed that the linkages between financial and real disturbances are undeniable, the latter are seen as dominant, and financial factors do not have independent deviation-amplifying effects. A monetarist view, in contrast, does allow for independent monetary or financial effects, but according to this school of thought they are the result of the variations in money supply (see Mishkin 1991).

These conventional views have recently been challenged by a large number of theoretical and empirical studies. Models in the Keynesian tradition[2] as well as recent theories of imperfect capital markets (imperfect information theory[3]) demonstrate the role of financial factors particularly for the propagation mechanism of business fluctuations. One line of reasoning is that asymmetric information between lenders and borrowers about future income may lead to credit rationing in which borrowers are arbitrarily denied loans (cf. Stiglitz and Weiss 1981). These liquidity constraints imply that current spending is dominantly determined by current income. Another approach maintains that investment and output are affected because imperfect information drives a significant wedge between the cost of internal and external finance (Bernanke and Gertler 1989, 1990; Mishkin 1991; Gertler, Hubbard, and Kashyap 1991; Myers and Majluf 1984). In the empirical literature, however, a great number of indicators for financial fragility of firms have been developed.[4] Among them are high debt-asset ratios, high interest payments on cash flows or low liquidity-asset ratios, the quick ratio, and so on, all conveying some information to lenders about the financial risk of firms. Frequently, it is argued financial fragility will show up in higher borrowing cost for firms, that is, in higher cost of external finance compared to internal finance. In this context interest rate spread between risky and safe bonds is often employed as a measure for financial risk, particularly in the business cycle (cf. Gertler, Hubbard, and Kashyap 1991, Mishkin 1991).[5]

In most of the models the increased financial fragility or risk is transmitted to output by postulating that the cost of external finance directly affects the volume of investment. In addition, investment demand is also instantly curtailed if credit constraints become effective. In the context of our present model, by contrast, financial risk—to be measured by the financial structure of firms, that is, by the debt-asset ratio—will not directly restrict investment. Its impact on investment and output is rather channeled through the profit expectations of firms. Indeed, the dynamics of our expectations variable will be at the heart of the cyclical behavior of the model.

More specifically, the connecting link between the real and financial sector in our economy is the financing of the firms' investment expenditures. Generally, there are three sources available to them: internal finance through retained earnings, external finance through equity issuance, and loans from commercial banks. The proportion of equity financing is considered to be given by a conventional rule; likewise with dividend pay-outs, so that internal finance is obtained by deducting them from profits (net of tax and interest payments). Once the level of investment has been determined, debt financing becomes the closure of the gap between predetermined levels of investment on one side of the investment-finance identity of firms, and equity financing and retained earnings on the other. That is, debt financing represents a residual.[6] As we mentioned earlier, this hierarchy in the financial structure of firms has been suggested recently in the literature on credit and financial constraints (cf. Stiglitz and Weiss 1981; Greenwald, Stiglitz, and Weiss 1984; Fazzari, Hubbard, and Petersen 1988), which stress that, as compared to debt financing, equity financing is both more difficult to obtain and more costly.

The remainder of the chapter is organized as follows. Section 12.2 contains a discussion of expectations about long-term profitability of investment projects and introduces the concept of what we called it, the state of confidence. We shall draw heavily on chapter 12 of Keynes's *General Theory*, especially as regards the forces governing the changes in this expectations variable. Section 12.3 presents the elements that are needed to formulate transactions on financial and goods markets in temporary equilibrium situations. These are characterized by IS and LM equations, which are further analyzed in section 12.4. Sections 12.5 and 12.6 are devoted to a study of the long-run dynamics of the model. A mathematical analysis is provided in section 12.5. Its central purpose is to point out the conditions for persistent cyclical behavior. Section 12.6 gives a quantitative characterization of the resulting trajectories by means of computer simulations. Section 12.7 contains concluding remarks. The main formulae to be computed for the proofs of the mathematical statements are collected in an appendix to this chapter. Lastly, we note that owing to the various simplifications adopted, in particular the freezing of inflation and distribution, the present model may better be viewed as a prelude to the subject at hand.

12.2 Investment and Long-Term Expectations

There are a large number of papers that attempt to provide a theory of how rational expectations agents learn the rational expectations equilibria. As has been shown by, for example, Woodford (1990) and Grandmont (1990), only if certain restrictions on the learning algorithm are imposed does the economy converge to a state where expectations turn out to be self-fulfilling.[7] Moreover, such an equilibrium is generally not uniquely determined. This critical direction is not pursued here. Our approach instead questions the narrow definition of rational behavior altogether.

A basic feature of the present model is that, within the short period and accomplished by the multiplier, the level of economic activity is essentially determined by the demand for capital goods. In formulating the investment function, two aspects are distinguished: a medium-run and a long-run aspect. The term "medium run" may refer to a period of, say, one to three years, while "long-run" in this context may refer to the lifetime of capital.[8] According to the medium-run aspect, investment responds to the pressure of demand. The reason, of course, is that firms strive for normal utilization of capacity; adjustments are partial. Thus, net investment may be specified as being positively related to the present level of the output-capital ratio, x (see the remark at the beginning of section 11.2). The long-run aspect is represented by a general "state of confidence," which we designate ρ. By the very name chosen it is obvious that investment rises with an increase in this expectations variable. In summary, the growth rate of capital is given by[9]

$$I/K = f_I(x, \rho), \qquad f_{Ix} = \partial f_I/\partial x \geq 0, \;\; f_{I\rho} = \partial f_I/\partial \rho > 0 \tag{12.1}$$

Note that we disregard the rate of interest as a direct determinant of investment expenditures; we justify this decision below. It will later be seen that the interest rate has an indirect influence on investment.

Dependence of I on x does not seem particularly problematic, so in the following we focus on the notion of the state of confidence. It has to be perceived against the background that capital goods are long lived and investment is virtually irreversible. This implies that investment is exposed not only to (normal) risk (which might be modeled by objective or subjective probability distributions), but rather a type of uncertainty is inflicted on investment in fixed capital that cannot be reduced to the risk calculus found in the economic textbooks, where the general evaluation of this "true" uncertainty is subject to substantial changes over the business cycle. For a formal analysis, we seek to capture this attitude of investors (or their "animal spirits") by our state of confidence ρ.[10]

Including an expectations variable in the investment function is highly compatible with Keynes's view on investment, although he usually refers to the (schedule of the) marginal efficiency of capital. On the one hand, this notion is based on current expectations as to the future yield of capital goods (Keynes 1936, 149). Given as they are "by the uncontrollable and disobedient psychology of the business world" (317), these expectations may be quite volatile. On the other hand, they are also dominant in the determination of investment, especially when compared to the influence of the interest rate: "[T]he market estimation of the marginal efficiency of capital may suffer such enormously wide fluctuations that it cannot be sufficiently offset by corresponding fluctuations in the rate of interest"—so as to secure a satisfactory rate of new investment (320). Hence, our specification of the investment function (12.1) can be seen to avoid the marginal efficiency of capital as a circuitous route and to give more immediate and direct prominence to a general "state of long-term expectations" (the title of chapter 12 of the *General Theory*).[11]

Of course, Keynes is not the only one who has emphasized the role of beliefs, confidence, and profit expectations for aggregate economic instability.[12] Even Kalecki, who in his early writings concentrates on the role of objective factors such as the time delay of the gestation period for investment goods as the main cause for macroeconomic fluctuations, published a version of his business cycle theory shortly after Keynes's *General Theory* had appeared that introduces prospective profits as an important determinant of investment expenditures (Kalecki 1937a, 86). He, too, points out the strong variations in this expectations variable over the business cycle.[13]

Now, turning to the factors causing our state of confidence to rise or fall, we recall that Keynes expresses strong skepticism that expectations are formed solely on the basis of the "most probable forecast" (Keynes 1936, 148). An evaluation of events, or potential events, that reach so far into the future as investment in real capital goods rests on rather shaky ground: "About these matters," Keynes writes at another place to clarify the basic issues of the *General Theory*, "there is no scientific basis on which to form any calculable probability whatever" (Keynes 1937, 114). Recognizing this irreducible uncertainty does not mean that theorizing has to turn to total irrationality or pure psychology.[14] What has to be noted is that Keynes's agents exhibit different *forms* of rationality, which depend upon circumstances (*ibid.*). So, posing the question, "[H]ow do we manage in such circumstances [of irreducible uncertainty] to behave in a manner which saves our faces as rational economic men?" Keynes responds that we employ "a variety of techniques," or "principles." He points out the following three as the most important. Since we see our modeling approach in this spirit we give the full citation.

(1) We assume that the present is a much more serviceable guide to the future than a candid examination of past experience would show it to have been hitherto. In other words we largely ignore the prospect of future changes about the actual character of which we know nothing.
(2) We assume that the *existing* state of opinion as expressed in prices and the character of existing output is based on a *correct* summing up of future prospects, so that we can accept it as such unless and until something new and relevant comes into the picture.
(3) Knowing that our own individual judgment is worthless, we endeavor to fall back on the judgment of the rest of the world which is perhaps better informed. That is, we endeavor to conform with the behavior of the majority or the average. The psychology of a society of individuals each of whom is endeavoring to copy the others leads to what we may strictly term a *conventional* judgment. (Keynes 1937, 114; Keynes's emphasis).

In greater detail, Keynes appears to hold the view that in the formation and revision of expectations, two mechanisms can be identified. Following Orléan (1990, 291) we may call them *self-reference* and *hetero-reference* (they may be represented by two types of investors; see below). Self-reference means a relationship strictly within a social group (a group of firms, or managers, for that matter) whereas, generally speaking, hetero-reference is concerned with the group's relationship to the environment, or with this group's state of opinion in its relationship to an external norm. Orléan illustrates the two notions by means of the famous example of the newspaper beauty contest in chapter 12 of the *General Theory*, where the readers "have to pick out the six prettiest faces from a hundred photographs, the prize being awarded to the competitor whose choice most nearly corresponds to the average preferences of the competitors as a whole; so that each competitor has to pick, not those faces which he himself finds prettiest, but those which he thinks likeliest to catch the fancy of the other competitors, all of whom are looking at the problem from the same point of view" (Keynes 1936, 156). This game exhibits essential characteristics of self-reference. They come out even more strongly when considering the corresponding game of hetero-reference. Here, the prettiest photographs are determined by a secret jury of experts, so that "beauty" is an exterior norm.

The notion of self-reference as an important aspect in economic decisions under radical uncertainty runs through the whole of chapter 12 of the *General Theory*. Keynes points out that in these situations agents are not very concerned with what an investment might be really worth; rather, under the influence of mass psychology, they devote their intelligences to anticipating what average opinion expects the average opinion to be (a judgment of the "third degree," as Keynes comments on its analogy, the beauty contest [156]). Thus, agents "fall back on what is, in truth, a *convention*" (152; Keynes's emphasis). Note that it is just rationality, both for "persons who have no special knowledge of the circumstances" (153) *and* for the expert professionals alike, that dictates going with the market rather than trying to follow one's own better instincts (154–58).[15]

Keynes develops his arguments mainly in the context of fully organized financial markets, in particular the stock market. In modified form the basic ideas may carry over to the general sentiment of entrepreneurs and firm managers who have to decide over the increase in the existing capital stock. Also, to some degree their state of confidence is certainly influenced by the bulls and bears on the stock market, and by the suspected future evolution of optimism and pessimism on the side of the potential demand for their products, although this needs to be worked out in greater detail.[16]

If the general phenomenon of forecasting the psychology of the market is taken for granted, then it is easily conceivable how waves of optimistic or pessimistic sentiment are generated, by means of a self-exciting, possibly accelerating mechanism.[17] A straightforward way to translate this into modeling language is to represent the working of self-reference by a positive feedback of the state of confidence ρ on itself. In our dynamic context, not the present level of ρ is to be determined, but its rate of change. So, we may assume that a low ρ induces a (further) fall in ρ, whereas if ρ is high, further improvements will be expected so that the time derivative of ρ is positive. We will not forget, however, that the speed at which this kind of adjustment occurs is likely to vary in the different stages of a cycle.

By contrast, the hetero-referential mechanism in the adjustments of the state of confidence takes account of the more "objective" factors—a norm or some economic fundamentals. They may reinforce or keep a curb on the "conventional" dynamics, or they may even reverse it.[18] So, in a wave of optimism, the rise of expectations may be damped if there are observations of some economic key variables that are not compatible with the current, still prevalent positive picture of the future. An increase in optimism will be especially damped if present profitability is in a less favorable range. A measure of profitability could be the rate of return on capital, r. Since potential investors always have the alternative of buying riskless government bonds, they will value the rate of return on capital against the real rate of interest, $i - \pi$, where $\pi = \hat{p}$ (i.e., in the present chapter inflation is taken to be current rather than expected). Accordingly, a more appropriate measure is the difference between these two rates of return, $\sigma = r - (i - \pi)$, which was called the "risk premium" in the previous chapter for ease of reference.[19]

Other fundamentals that may have some impact on the variations in the state of confidence are variables characterizing the financial structure of firms. Flow variables might be more pertinent (see chapter 13), but in the present framework it is more straightforward to refer to a ratio of stocks such as the debt-asset ratio $\lambda = \Lambda/pK$, which relates the volume of firms' loans outstanding, Λ, to the capital stock K valued at replacement costs p. A high value of this degree of indebtedness signals future financial risk and is thus supposed to exert a downward pressure on confidence. Summarizing the variables acting on ρ, we have

$$\dot{\rho} = f_\rho(\rho, \sigma, \lambda), \qquad f_{\rho\rho} \geq 0, \;\; f_{\rho\sigma} > 0, \;\; f_{\rho\lambda} \leq 0 \tag{12.2}$$

($f_{\rho z} = \partial f_\rho / \partial z$, $z = \rho, \sigma, \lambda$). The shape of this function for "extreme" values of the arguments will be discussed in finer detail when studying the global dynamics. Certain nonlinearities will then play a major role. For the time being, the general information given in (12.2) will suffice.

The two mechanisms governing the changes in long-term expectations could also be conceived of as being represented by two types of investors. In modern terms, one type can be called a feedback investor, or a noise trader.[20] These investors have less information and preferably follow the stories of success and failure. Attempting to "chase the trend," they are part of a self-referential mechanism.[21] The other type of investor gathers more specific information and undertakes sophisticated forecasts. Insofar as they process objective factors—the fundamentals when observable—they follow a hetero-referential mechanism.

In the theory of financial markets it is usually stated that changes in investor sentiment are fully countered by rational arbitrageurs. So the more naive investors are said to be competed away, or by learning the errors of their ways, they reform into perfectly rational traders. Shleifer and Summers (1990) provide several (brief) counterarguments suggesting that, although widespread, this conclusion is by no means self-evident. In particular, many situations are conceivable where informed traders do not find it useful to act against the market. Risk-taking feedback investors who simply extrapolate past experiences may even be more highly rewarded by the market than those investors who assume universal rationality. Under these circumstances, it seems rather more advantageous for the latter to vigorously observe public opinion and attempt to "stay ahead of the crowd." In this respect they, too, follow conventions and contribute to the positive feedback loop. However, they are more sensitive than the feedback investor to past experiences that an ongoing motion is eventually to be revised. Thus, the longer a boom or slump is under way, the more alert they become, and the greater is the weight they attach to the objective factors.

It should also be mentioned that arbitrage presupposes that there exist close substitutes of, say, overpriced assets. Even in financial markets these substitutes may not always be available (for example, in a phase when *all* bonds are overpriced); they will be much less available for investment in plant and equipment.

Other schools of thought stressing primarily the rationality of investors seem to consider these notions of expectations as old-fashioned, since they are not grounded in the methodological assumptions of optimizing agents and efficient forecasts of decision variables based on currently available information. Yet, in view of the discussion on expectations and beliefs about an uncertain future as, for example, put forward in Keynes, the expectations formation introduced by the rational expectations school should preferably be characterized as "extrapolative expectations," by which proxies for future values are obtained.[22] Also, as Lucas (1977, 7) has remarked, the rational expectations hypothesis and efficient market axioms simply do not apply in situations of (irreducible) uncertainty. Note that these objections against the rational expectations hypothesis are more fundamental than those discussed in sections 7.2 and 11.5.

Apart from these more or less theoretical considerations justifying the central role of the state of confidence and including the self-referential mechanism in the adjustment equation (12.2), the ample experimental and survey evidence that investors follow positive feedback strategies has already been pointed out in section 7.2.

Finally, we remark that investors' sentiment will have an impact on other economic variables as well, especially on the financial side. Our modeling approach accounts for this in a more indirect way. Yet, by doing so we are postulating, not primarily a volatility of confidence in financial markets, the disturbance of which may, or may not, be

Table 12.1
Balance sheet statement

Assets				Liabilities
		Central Bank		
High powered-money	H	:	D^c	Deposits of commercial banks (interest-free bank reserves)
		Commercial Banks		
Bank reserves	D^c	:	D^o	Interest-free deposits from the public
Loans to firms	Λ	:	D^i	Interest-bearing deposits from the public
		Firms		
Capital stock (valued at the demand price)	$p_k K$	:	Λ	Loans from commercial banks
		:	$p_e E$	Equity
		Public		
Deposits with commercial banks	D^o	:	W	Wealth
	D^i	:		
Equity	$p_e E$	:		

transmitted to the real side, but rather the interplay of the real and financial sector.

12.3 The IS-LM Configuration

Setting up the IS-LM part to model temporary equilibrium, let us first begin with the financial relationships. They can be best described by looking at the balance sheets represented in table 12.1. Four groups of agents are distinguished: the central bank, commercial banks, firms, and wealth holders or rentiers, or simply the public. The latter group excludes workers, who play a passive role in that they spend their wages instantaneously on consumption and do not own assets.

Firms are the main actors on the real and financial side of the economy. Term Y being total output, L employment, p the price level, w the wage rate, δ the rate of depreciation, and τ the tax rate on gross profits, firms' gross rate of return after tax is given by $r^g = (1-\tau)(pY - wL - \delta pK)/pK$ (the properties of the model are not affected if taxes are levied on profits net of interest payments). With $v = wL/pY$ the wage share and $x = Y/K$ the output-capital ratio, it can be written as

$$r^g = r^g(x) = (1 - \tau)[(1 - v)x - \delta] \quad (12.3)$$

Reference to v can be omitted since the wage share will be fixed in this chapter. If interest payments $i\Lambda$ are deducted (i the nominal rate of interest on bank loans and deposits alike), the net rate of return, denoted r, is obtained,

$$r = r^g(x) - i\lambda \quad (12.4)$$

The demand price of capital, p_k, depends negatively on the real rate of interest, $i - \pi$ (π the current rate of inflation), and positively on the gross rate of return and the state of confidence, ρ. It is very convenient to have ρ scaled in such a way that $r^g + \rho$ can be interpreted as an expected rate of profit, that is, it is expected as some average value over a longer time horizon (cf. the discussion in section 11.5). The demand price may then be specified as the capitalized value of expected earnings per unit of investment,[23]

$$p_k = (r^g + \rho)p/(i - \pi) \quad (12.5)$$

Term $p_k K$ gives the market value of the capital stock, as opposed to its replacement costs, pK. Thus p_k/p resembles Tobin's q. It may be noted, however, that even in a long-run equilibrium position, p_k/p may exceed unity (it definitely will in our numerical simulations). This point has been briefly discussed in section 11.2.

With respect to share prices, p_e, we assume that their formation is exclusively determined by the variables determining $p_k K$. Excess volatility or bubbles in the stock market are not included since they do not seem to be central for a basic model as the one developed here. Term E being the number of shares, the assumption reads

$$p_e E = p_k K - \Lambda \quad (12.6)$$

which is identical to the firms' balance sheet position.

Shares are bought by rentiers who plan to have their wealth split up into

$$p_e E = f_e W, \;\; D^o = f_d W, \;\; D^i = (1 - f_e - f_d)W, \;\; 0 < f_e, f_d, \;\; f_e + f_d < 1$$

where f_e is an increasing function of the difference between the two relevant prospective rates of return, $f_e = f_e(r + \rho - (i - \pi))$ and $f_e' = df_e/d(r + \rho - (i - \pi)) > 0$, while f_d may be any function (since it will be shortly eliminated).

Given the above relations, we are sufficiently equipped to derive an equation that characterizes clearing of all financial markets. Aggregating the balance sheets for the whole economy results in $W = H + p_k K$. Substituting $p_e E = f_e W$, we can rewrite equation (12.6) as $W = (p_k K - \Lambda)/f_e$. Defining $\phi = H/pK$, dividing the two equations by pK, equating them, and utilizing (12.4) and (12.5), we finally obtain the condition

$$f_e[r^g(x) - i\lambda + \rho - (i - \pi)] - [r^g(x) + \rho - \lambda(i - \pi)]/[r^g(x) + \rho + \phi(i - \pi)] = 0 \tag{12.LM}$$

Notice that this equation describes a stock equilibrium. Market clearing is thought to be brought about by variations of the nominal rate of interest. For these two reasons we have labeled the relationship an LM-equation. Values λ and ρ are given in every instance of time, while x is determined in the real goods markets (see below). The rate of inflation π will be supposed to be constant throughout, and ϕ is treated as a constant parameter standing for a neutral monetary policy (regarding the monetary base). It is worth mentioning that in this way the central bank, via D^c, imposes no restriction on the credit volume of commercial banks (see Franke and Semmler 1989, section 1.2, for a formula that explicitly refers to the credit multiplier). Since on the liability side of banks we have the deposits of the public, it follows that in this model money is fully endogenous.[24]

Turning to the real side of the economy, we note the planned rate of growth of the capital stock has already been introduced in the previous section as a function of utilization and the state of confidence (equation (12.1)). It is assumed that the corresponding volume of investment, I, can always be financed.

To obtain consumption demand, rentiers' households have to be considered. Their current flow of income consists of dividend payments from firms, plus interest payments, iD^i; plus profits from commercial banks, $i(\Lambda - D^i)$; plus capital gains, $\dot{p}_e E$. To keep the analysis simple, we suppose that the latter are completely added to the stock of wealth. As for dividends, we assume that firms retain a constant fraction s_f of their net profits and distribute $(1 - s_f)rpK$ to the shareholders. The public's propensity to consume out of the income thus specified is denoted by s_h. This is also assumed to be a constant magnitude[25] (certainly, $0 < s_f, s_h < 1$). Hence, together with consumption of wage earners, total consumption in monetary terms is given by $pC = wL + (1 - s_h)[(1 - s_f)r + i\lambda]pK$ (the complementary flow of savings increases the stocks of D^o, D^i, and p_eE, where the proportions are determined by the functions f_e and f_d above).

As a third point, we assume that, besides taxes on firms' profits, government expenditures are financed by the creation of base money, that is, $pG = \dot{H} + \tau(pY - wL - \delta pK)$.[26] Constancy of $\phi = H/pK$ implies $\hat{H} - \hat{p} - \hat{K} = 0$ or $\dot{H} = (\pi + I/K)H$, so that $pG = (\pi + f_I)\phi pK + \tau(pY - wL - \delta pK)$.

Finally, we postulate that all demands are satisfied. Clearing of real goods markets is tantamount to $wL + (1-\tau)(pY - wL - \delta pK) + \delta pK + \tau(pY - wL - \delta pK) = pY = pC + pI + \delta pK + pG$ (the first equality is only a convenient splitting up of pY). It is easily verified that, after dividing through by pK, this reduces to the following condition for zero excess demand:

$$f_I(x, \rho) + \phi[f_I(x, \rho) + \pi] - [s_h + (1 - s_h)s_f]r^g(x) + (1 - s_h)s_f i\lambda = 0 \qquad (12.\text{IS})$$

The equilibrating variable is the level of production or, in relative terms, utilization of capital, x. This is the reason for calling the condition an IS-equation.[27]

To sum up, predetermined values of the state of confidence, ρ, and the degree of indebtedness, λ, induce a temporary equilibrium that is characterized by equations (IS) and (LM) and brought about by simultaneous adjustments in the nominal rate of interest, i, and the output-capital ratio, x (all other magnitudes are constant parameters). Nevertheless, because of our treatment of financial variables, these equations differ considerably from the usual specifications in IS-LM modeling. Of course, changes in ρ and λ cause changes in the corresponding values of i and x. The motions of ρ and λ, in their turn, are governed by two differential equations, where the one for λ has still to be introduced. Before these dynamics can be studied, however, we have to analyze the comparative static properties of the temporary equilibria.

12.4 Analysis of Temporary Equilibria

In the following discussion it will be computationally more convenient to characterize the temporary equilibria, not by i and x, but by i and the net profit rate, r. To this end, we use (12.4) and rewrite the IS-LM equations as

$$f_e[r + \rho - (i - \pi)] - (r + \rho + \pi\lambda)/(r + \rho + i(\lambda + \phi) - \pi\phi) = 0 \qquad (12.7)$$

$$\pi\phi + (1 + \phi)f_I[x(i, r, \lambda), \rho] - s_o r - s_h i\lambda = 0 \qquad (12.8)$$

where $s_o := s_h + s_f - s_h s_f$ and a little rearrangement of (12.3) gives utilization

$$x = x(i, r, \lambda) = [r + i\lambda + (1 - \tau)\delta]/[(1 - \tau)(1 - v)] \tag{12.9}$$

Thus, our aim is to obtain the interest rate and the profit rate as functions of λ and ρ, $r = r(\lambda, \rho)$ and $i = i(\lambda, \rho)$, such that the two market-clearing equations (12.7) and (12.8) are identically fulfilled. This analysis is pursued in two steps. First, besides λ and ρ, r is also considered as given, and we look for an interest rate that establishes the LM-equation (12.7). As the solution depends on the sum of r and ρ, that is, the expected net profit rate, it may be designated as $i = j(\lambda, r + \rho)$. In the second step, a net profit rate r is sought with respect to a given pair (λ, ρ) such that putting $i = j(\lambda, r + \rho)$ satisfies the IS-condition (12.8). If this r is designated $r(\lambda, \rho)$ and, together with $i = i(\lambda, \rho) := j(\lambda, r(\lambda, \rho) + \rho)$, is inserted in (12.7) and (12.8), then by construction, both equations will be simultaneously fulfilled.

To guarantee existence and uniqueness of the LM-equilibria in the first step, Assumptions 12.1 and 12.2 are employed. They refer to the functional expression

$$\varepsilon(\lambda, r + \rho, i) := (r + \rho + \pi\lambda)/(r + \rho + i(\lambda + \phi) - \pi\phi)$$

Hence, with respect to λ and $r + \rho$ given, (12.7) is satisfied for those values of i at which the two functions $i \mapsto f_e[r + \rho - (i - \pi)]$ and $i \mapsto \varepsilon(\lambda, r + \rho, i)$ intersect. Note that at $i = 0$, $\varepsilon(\lambda, r + \rho, i) > 1 > f_e[r + \rho - (i - \pi)]$, so that the ε curve must somewhere exceed the f_e curve if a point of intersection is to exist. That is to say that over some range of interest rates, rentiers are sufficiently inclined to hold equities. By contrast, it will be reasonable to concede that this willingness appreciably declines if the expected rate of return from shares fell below the real interest rate. Formally, these suppositions read as follows.

Assumption 12.1

i. There exists a positive number $\alpha_r > \pi\phi$ such that for every $r + \rho > \alpha_r$ there is an interest rate $i > \pi$ entailing $f_e[r + \rho - (i - \pi)] > \varepsilon(\lambda, r + \rho, i)$.

ii. $f_e[r + \rho - (i - \pi)] = 0$ if $r + \rho < i - \pi$.

The features of assumption 12.1 are illustrated in figure 12.1. For $\lambda_1 > \lambda_2$, the curve $\varepsilon(\lambda_1, r + \rho, i)$ lies below (above) the curve $\varepsilon(\lambda_2, r + \rho, i)$ if $i > \pi$ $(i < \pi)$. Note, furthermore, that the f_e curves shift to the right

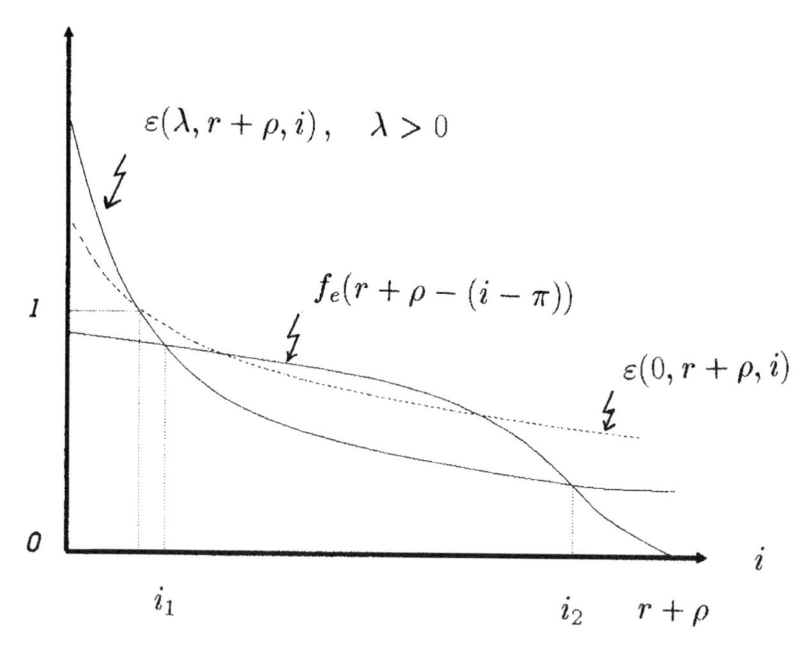

Figure 12.1
The LM-rate of interest

if $r + \rho$ increases; so the critical part of assumption 12.1(i) are low values of the expected profit rate $r + \rho$. Figure 12.1 shows that there are (at least) two values i_1 and i_2 bringing about equation (12.7). We decide to choose i_2 as the appropriate and economically meaningful LM-interest rate. One reason is that this choice corresponds to the stability condition for an ultra short-run process of disequilibrium adjustments on the asset markets.[28] The other reason is the implied signs of the comparative static results in lemma 12.1 (of course, the two reasons are closely connected by Samuelson's correspondence principle). The stipulation itself is written down in assumption 12.2.

Assumption 12.2 Let λ and $r + \rho$ be given, where $r + \rho > \alpha_r$ (cf. assumption 12.1). Then the LM-interest rate $i = j(\lambda, r + \rho)$ is taken as the greatest number i satisfying equation (12.7).

Lemma 12.1 Let assumptions 12.1 and 12.2 apply and let $i = j(\lambda, r + \rho)$ be the function of the LM-interest rate defined in assumption 12.2. Then $0 < i - \pi < r + \rho$ and

$$\partial j/\partial(r+\rho) = A_i/A_r > 1$$

$$\partial j/\partial\lambda = (i-\pi)(r+\rho-\pi\phi)/A_r > 0$$

where

$$A_r := A_o f_e' - (r+\rho+\pi\lambda)(\lambda+\phi) > 0$$

$$A_i := A_o f_e' - (i-\pi)(\lambda+\phi) > 0$$

$$A_o := (r+\rho+i(\lambda+\phi)-\pi\phi)^2$$

The proof is based on an application of the implicit function theorem to equation (12.7); the signs of A_i and A_r follow from the assumption that at $i = j(\lambda, r+\rho)$, the f_e-curve cuts the ε-curve from above. The impact reactions of the LM-interest rate are intuitively clear. A rise in the expected rate of profit tends to raise equity holding, so that shareholders would withdraw some of their deposits. Since Λ and D^c remain unchanged on their asset side, commercial banks have to offer a proportionately higher rate of interest if they want to avoid this reaction. This, however, is only a first-round effect. It is easily checked that the changes in $r+\rho$ and i reduce the demand price of capital, p_k, which in turn leads to a reduction in the equity price by equation (12.6) (the number of shares being fixed) and, thus, in the wealth of households. With the same splitting-up proportion of deposits and equities, there would be a fall in households' deposits. Banks have to prevent this by raising the interest rate a second time. The corresponding change in p_k disturbs the equilibrium on the stock market and opens up a new round of adjustments. In fact, this chain of events can be described as a multiplier process.

Things are a little different with respect to variations in indebtedness. If there is a ceteris paribus increase in the volume of loans Λ, banks may concede a higher interest rate to prompt an increase of deposits by the same amount. The resulting change in p_k is ambiguous, but if responsiveness in the equity-holding function is not too strong, the demand price of capital will rise. In this case the value of equities falls less than Λ increases and, in sum, total wealth of rentiers rises. At that stage there is some room for the banks to reduce the interest rate. Lemma 12.1 nevertheless shows that this kind of compensation is only partial: the interest rate that comes about when all financial markets have finally adjusted still exceeds the original one.

To take the second step, put

$$F(\lambda,\rho,r) := \pi\phi + (1+\phi) f_I[x(\lambda,r,j(\lambda,r+\rho)),\rho] \\ - s_o r - s_h j(\lambda,r+\rho)\lambda \tag{12.10}$$

On the basis of assumptions 12.1 and 12.2, the expression is well defined if $r > \alpha_r - \rho$. With respect to a given pair (λ, ρ), we are looking for a point r_o making the function $r \mapsto F(\lambda,\rho,r)$ vanish. The derivative is given by $\partial F/\partial r = -A_s/A_r$, where

$$A_s := A_h(A_r + \lambda A_i) + s_f(1-s_h)A_r$$

$$A_h := s_h - (1+\phi) f_{Ix}/[(1-\tau)(1-v)] \tag{12.11}$$

(A_i and A_r as defined in lemma 12.1, with i evaluated at $i = j(\lambda, r+\rho)$). Hence, such a r_o exists and is uniquely determined if $A_s > 0$ and if F is positive for sufficiently small r ($A_s > 0$ implies $F < 0$ for large r). This is ensured by the next assumption. For better readability, it is formulated slightly stronger than necessary.

Assumption 12.3

i. There exists an open interval D_ρ of the state of confidence around zero such that, with respect to the α_r of assumption 12.1 and the LM-function $i = j(\lambda, r+\rho)$ of assumption 12.2, $(1+\phi) f_I(0,\rho) > s_o(\alpha_r - \rho) - \pi\phi$

ii. $f_{Ix} < (1-\tau)(1-v)s_h/(1+\phi)$

Assumption 12.3(ii), which is equivalent to $A_h > 0$, limits the (instantaneous) multiplier effects of investment. Its role is similar to that of assumption 11.1 in the previous chapter (only that here the IS-curve is not made explicit). Assumption 12.3(i) on firms' willingness to invest is tantamount to $F(\lambda,\rho,r) > 0$ for all $\lambda \geq 0$ if $r + \rho$ is close to the α_r of assumption 12.1.

Lemma 12.2 Let assumptions 12.1–12.3 be satisfied. Then for every pair (λ,ρ), $0 < \lambda < 1$, $\rho \in D_\rho$, there exists a net profit rate r_o bringing about $F(\lambda,\rho,r_o) = 0$ (F defined by equation (12.10)). Term r_o is unique and $\partial F(\lambda,\rho,r_o)/\partial r < 0$.

As stated above, it now suffices to set $r(\lambda,\rho) = r_o$ with respect to the r_o of lemma 12.2 and define $i(\lambda,\rho) = j(\lambda, r(\lambda,\rho)+\rho)$. In this way the temporary equilibrium functions of r and i are obtained. The signs of all partial derivatives are determined if another assumption is added. The results are collected in theorem 12.1. It also includes information on the reactions of the differences between r and i, which will play a major role as stabilizing forces in the long-run dynamics.

Assumption 12.4

i. $f_{I\rho} > s_h \lambda A_i/((1+\phi)A_r)$

ii. $\eta_{e,\sigma} < (i-\pi)(r+\rho-i+\pi)[i(\lambda+\phi)A_h$
$+(r+\rho-\pi\phi)(s_f(1-s_h)+A_h)]/[iA_oA_hf_e]]$

where $\eta_{e,\sigma}$ is the elasticity of equity holding with respect to changes in the differentials of the two rates of returns, $\eta_{e,\sigma} = [r+\rho-(i-\pi)]f_e'/f_e$; A_h defined in (12.11), A_o, A_i and A_r in lemma 12.1.

Theorem 12.1 Under assumptions 12.1–12.3, there are two continuously differentiable real functions $i = i(\lambda, \rho)$ and $r = r(\lambda, \rho)$, defined on the set $(0,1) \times D_\rho$, that simultaneously satisfy equations (12.7) and (12.8). Moreover, $0 < i(\lambda, \rho) - \pi < r(\lambda, \rho) + \rho$ and $\partial r/\partial\lambda < 0$, $\partial i/\partial\rho > 0$. Assumption 12.4(i) guarantees $\partial r/\partial\rho > 0$ as well as $\partial r/\partial\rho - \partial i/\partial\rho < 0$, while $\partial i/\partial\lambda > 0$ if and only if $\eta_{e,\sigma}$ fulfills assumption 12.4(ii).

Of course, $\partial i/\partial\lambda > 0$ implies that the difference between r and i falls in response to an increase in λ, $\partial r/\partial\lambda - \partial i/\partial\lambda < 0$, whereas this latter inequality does not necessarily require $\partial i/\partial\lambda > 0$. With the parameter values employed in the numerical simulations later on, assumption 4(ii) becomes $\eta_{e,\sigma} < 0.524$. So the perhaps counterintuitive result $\partial i/\partial\lambda < 0$ that can occur when the financial sector is integrated with the real sector may not be too extraordinary (the mechanisms on the financial side, especially the feedback effects from changes in the demand price of capital, have been discussed in the remarks on lemma 12.1). Nevertheless, i gets closer to r, $\partial r/\partial\lambda - \partial i/\partial\lambda < 0$, at much higher elasticities (even at $\eta_{e,\sigma} = 10$ or $\eta_{e,\sigma} = 50$). In contrast, the reactions caused by a change in λ are relatively minor in comparison to the effects from a change in the state of confidence. In the cyclical dynamics it will, moreover, also turn out that the fluctuations in the debt-asset ratio are considerably weaker than those in ρ. We can, thus, preliminarily conclude that the stabilizing or destabilizing effects stemming from the variations of the state of confidence are dominant over those from the debt-asset ratio.

As for the significance of assumption 12.4(i) for the sign of $\partial r/\partial\rho$ and $\partial r/\partial\rho - \partial i/\partial\rho$, we note that, at least with our numerical specifications, the expression $a := s_h\lambda A_i/((1+\phi)A_r)$ is a decreasing function of the equity-holding elasticity $\eta_{e,\sigma}$. We obtain $a = 0.916$ for $\eta_{e,\sigma} = 0.30$ and $a = 0.091$ for $\eta_{e,\sigma} = 0.50$. Since f_I, the growth rate of the capital stock, and ρ, interpreted as the difference between the expected and the actual net rate of profit, both have the same dimension, it does not seem unreasonable to stipulate that $f_{I\rho}$ exceeds these benchmark values. However, the basic results of the global dynamics to be discussed in the next section are not dependent on this supposition.

12.5 Long-Run Dynamics

The rule governing the changes in the state of confidence has already been put forward in equation (12.2). To describe the evolution of the debt-asset ratio λ over time, we have to consider financing of investment. Firms have access to three sources: retained earnings, issuance of new share (at the ruling price p_e), and (net) borrowing from commercial banks. The proportions in which these sources are used are not derived from profit maximization. Indeed, it would be hard to do so. In a simple Modigliani-Miller world, the valuation of an individual firm is independent of its financial structure, and maximization gives no guidance as to the optimal retention ratio or debt issue. Outside this world, the valuation will be affected by financial decisions, but it is difficult to say exactly how, since conventional factors are likely to be very important in the determination of "prudent" finance (see also Skott 1991a, 386). Two of the key parameters will, therefore, be treated as constants. On the one hand, this concerns the retention ratio s_f. It is related to net profits and states that retained earnings amount to $s_f rpK$ (it has already been utilized above that $(1 - s_f)rpK$ is distributed to shareholders).[29] On the other hand, it is assumed that new shares are issued up to a constant fraction χ of total net investment. Lastly, as discussed in the introduction, firms are not quantity constrained in their borrowing, and accommodating variations in bank loans make up the difference between investment expenditures and the sum of retained earnings and new issues. This hypothesis is also consistent with the theory of a financing hierarchy of investment as discussed in section 5.5. Thus (with $I = \dot{K}$ = real investment), the finance equation of firms reads,

$$pI = s_f rpK + \chi pI + \dot{\Lambda}$$

where $\dot{\Lambda}$ is determined as a residual.[30] In relative terms, after dividing through by pK and taking account of the desired growth rate of the capital stock $f_I = f_I(x, \rho)$, the identity becomes

$$f_I(x,\rho) = s_f r + \chi f_I(x,\rho) + (\dot{\Lambda}/\Lambda)\cdot\lambda$$

Solving for the growth rate of loans and substituting it from the equation $\dot{\lambda}/\lambda = \dot{\Lambda}/\Lambda - \dot{p}/p - \dot{K}/K = \dot{\Lambda}/\Lambda - \pi - f_I$, leads to

$$\dot{\lambda} = (1-\chi-\lambda) f_I(x,\rho) - s_f r - \pi\lambda \tag{12.12}$$

Inserting the temporary equilibrium functions $i = i(\lambda,\rho)$ and $r = r(\lambda,\rho)$ in equations (12.2) and (12.12), we get a system of differential equations in the two variables λ and ρ,

$$\begin{aligned} \dot{\lambda} &= F_1(\lambda,\rho) \\ &= (1-\chi-\lambda) f_I[x(i(\lambda,\rho), r(\lambda,\rho),\lambda),\rho] - s_f r(\lambda,\rho) - \pi\lambda \qquad (12.13) \\ \dot{\rho} &= F_2(\lambda,\rho) = f_\rho[\rho, r(\lambda,\rho) - i(\lambda,\rho) + \pi, \lambda] \end{aligned}$$

The adjustment processes of the temporary equilibria in the real goods and financial markets have a direct impact on the state of confidence through the argument $r - (i-\pi)$ in the adjustment function $f_\rho(\cdot,\cdot,\cdot)$. In the first equation of (12.13), only the profit rate shows up explicitly. However, since it is determined simultaneously with the rate of interest, the evolution of the debt-asset ratio is directly influenced by current transactions on both sets of markets as well. In addition, both variables λ and ρ feed upon themselves, but cross-effects can also be recognized, directly and mediated through the temporary equilibrium functions $r(\lambda,\rho)$ and $i(\lambda,\rho)$. Aggravated by various nonlinearities, these effects make the differential equations (12.14) a fairly complex dynamical system.

In order to simplify the computations somewhat, we shall in the following neglect the influence of utilization on investment decisions. This is not essential; it mainly means that in writing down the formulae a positive *indirect* effect of ρ is omitted—the positive direct impact remains. If, furthermore, three not very restrictive assumptions limiting the level of the rate of interest are adopted, the partial derivatives of F_1 are unambiguously determined.

Assumption 12.5 The planned growth rate of the capital stock is independent of utilization x, that is, the investment function (12.1) is of the form $f_I = f_I(\rho)$. In addition, there exists a domain $D \subset (0,1)\times D_\rho$ (D_ρ from assumption 12.3) on which

(i) $\quad i(\lambda, \rho) < [\pi + f_I(\rho)]/s_h$

(ii) $i(\lambda, \rho) - \pi < [(\pi + f_I(\rho)](\lambda + \phi)(r + \rho + \pi\lambda)]/$

$$[(\pi + f_I(\rho)](\lambda + \phi) + s_f(r + \rho - \pi\phi)]$$

(iii) $\ i(\lambda, \rho)A_r < r(\lambda, \rho)A_i$

Lemma 12.3 Let Assumptions 12.1–12.3 and 12.5 be satisfied. Then

$\partial F_1(\lambda, \rho)/\partial\lambda < 0, \quad \partial F_1(\lambda, \rho)/\partial\rho > 0 \quad$ for all $(\lambda, \rho) \in D$.

The precise formulas for $\partial F_1/\partial\lambda$ and $\partial F_1/\partial\rho$ stated in the appendix show that the conditions (i)–(iii) in assumption 12.5 are by no means necessary for lemma 12.3 to hold true. Nonetheless, also the inequalities themselves seem quite acceptable. Since we know from lemma 12.1 that $A_i - A_r > [r + \rho - (i - \pi)](\lambda + \phi) > 0$, condition (iii) is fulfilled if $i < r$. Using the steady state parameters of the next section, we find condition (i) and (ii) become $i < 37.92\%$ and $i - \pi < 15.97\%$.

For the model to be economically meaningful it is required that there are pairs (λ, ρ) at which the motion of the debt-asset ratio is reversed, so that momentarily $\dot{\lambda} = F_1(\lambda, \rho) = 0$. Without loss of generality, it may be assumed that these pairs are contained in the domain D of assumption 12.5. Lemma 12.3 then implies that for all ρ there is exactly one λ bringing about $F_1(\lambda, \rho) = 0$, and that the resulting curve has a positive slope in the (ρ, λ) plane (ρ on the horizontal, λ on the vertical axis). That is, representing these values of λ as a function G_1 of ρ, $\lambda = G_1(\rho)$, and applying the implicit function theorem, we obtain

$$dG_1/d\rho = -(\partial F_1/\partial\rho)/(\partial F_1/\partial\lambda) > 0$$

where $\dot{\lambda} = 0$ if and only if $\lambda = G_1(\rho)$.

The picture is a little bit different for the function F_2 in the second equation in (12.13). In view of the discussion following theorem 12.1, we may safely work with the supposition that $\partial r/\partial\lambda - \partial i/\partial\lambda < 0$, so that

$$\partial F_2/\partial\lambda = f_{\rho\lambda} + f_{\rho\sigma} \cdot (\partial r/\partial\lambda - \partial i/\partial\lambda) < 0 \tag{12.14}$$

(recall $f_{\rho\lambda} \leq 0$, $f_{\rho\sigma} > 0$). Similar as above, we are interested in pairs (λ, ρ) causing the motions of the state of confidence to revise. According to (12.14), these λ are uniquely determined for all ρ. Hence, λ may be expressed as a function $\lambda = G_2(\rho)$ such that $\dot{\rho} = F_2(\lambda, \rho) = 0$ if and only if $\lambda = G_2(\rho)$. A point of intersection of the two curves G_1 and G_2

is a point of rest of system (12.13), that is, it constitutes a steady-state position of the economy. Besides its mere existence, we wish to exclude multiple equilibria (a condition entailing this follows from the ensuing discussion). The assumption that the state of confidence attains a zero value is added for reasons of consistency.

Assumption 12.6 There exists a unique pair $(\lambda^\star, \rho^\star)$ such that $F_1(\lambda^\star, \rho^\star) = F_2(\lambda^\star, \rho^\star) = 0$. Moreover, $\rho^\star = 0$.

Before going on, consider a situation in which $\rho^\star \neq 0$. Suppose first that such a steady state is repelling. Then $\rho^\star \neq 0$ might be irrelevant and the analysis of the global dynamics could run along lines similar to those below. By contrast, let us assume that the steady state is an attractor. This implies that after some time, r and ρ will practically cease to change. As a consequence, the expected net profit rate would persistently deviate from the realized one. Firms would not be satisfied with this discrepancy but would sooner or later revise their expectations, which in the formulation of the model means that the function $f_\rho(\cdot,\cdot,\cdot)$ is shifted. In this case, virtually a new dynamic process is set up; the steady-state values change and new motions are initiated. If the new $\rho^\star$ differs from zero, too, and the new stationary point $(\lambda^\star, \rho^\star)$ is again attracting, the procedure may be repeated, and so forth. Of course, the function $f_\rho(\cdot,\cdot,\cdot)$ or even another function might shift before the process gets near a rest point, or a limit cycle, for that matter. In fact, this seems to be the correct way to view what is actually happening in a dynamic economy. The significance of the supposition $\rho^\star = 0$ (and of the uniqueness assumption) is thus mainly that it serves to simplify the discussion of the long-run tendencies inherent in the economy.

After this short methodological note we can turn to the sign of the partial derivative of F_2 with respect to ρ. It reads

$$\partial F_2/\partial\rho = f_{\rho\rho} + f_{\rho\sigma} \cdot (\partial r/\partial\rho - \partial i/\partial\rho) \tag{12.15}$$

By virtue of Theorem 12.1, the second term tends to be negative. Whether $\partial F_2/\partial\rho$ is positive or not, therefore, depends on the relative strength of the autofeedback mechanism. However, the next theorem is concerned with the case of weak self-reference, which will be presented before we discuss the role of the autofeedback mechanism in finer detail.

Theorem 12.2 Let assumptions 12.1–12.3, 12.5, and 12.6 be satisfied and assume that, evaluated at the steady state $(\lambda^\star, \rho^\star)$, $\partial r/\partial\lambda - \partial i/\partial\lambda < 0$ as well as $f_{\rho\rho} + f_{\rho\sigma} \cdot (\partial r/\partial\rho - \partial i/\partial\rho) < 0$. Then the steady state $(\lambda^\star, \rho^\star)$ is locally asymptotically stable.

The proof is straightforward. Denote the Jacobian matrix of (12.13), evaluated at $(\lambda^\star, \rho^\star)$, by the letter Q. Its entries in the i-th row are $F_{i1} = \partial F_i/\partial\lambda$ and $F_{i2} = \partial F_i/\partial\rho$, respectively. $F_{11} < 0$, $F_{12} > 0$ by lemma 12.3, $F_{21} < 0$ by (12.14), and $F_{22} < 0$ in (12.15) by hypothesis. Hence, the determinant of Q is positive and the trace is negative, which is the sufficient and necessary condition for the eigenvalues of Q to have both negative real parts.

The argument also shows that the stability is preserved for $\partial F_2/\partial\rho = f_{\rho\rho} + f_{\rho\sigma} \cdot (\partial r/\partial\rho - \partial i/\partial\rho) > 0$, if the positivity is so moderate that trace Q and det Q do not change sign. Process (12.13), however, will become unstable if $\partial F_2/\partial\rho$ is sufficiently large or, in other words, if conventional forces (the self-referential mechanism) in the adjustments of the state of confidence (sufficiently) dominate the more objective influences (the hetero-referential mechanism). Furthermore, if the reaction coefficient $f_{\rho\rho}$ is very large then the instability is of the saddlepoint type (since det $Q < 0$). The steady state will be repelling if $f_{\rho\rho}$ is large enough to render trace $Q > 0$, but not too large, so that det Q is still positive. This scenario is the most remunerative one for us since it creates the possibility of persistent cyclical behavior.

To see this, observe that the slope of the isocline $\dot{\rho} = 0$ is positive, that is,

$$dG_2/d\rho = -(\partial F_2/\partial\rho)/(\partial F_2/\partial\lambda) > 0$$

for the function $\lambda = G_2(\rho)$ defined above. Taking account of the signs of the single partial derivatives, we easily check that the assumption det $Q > 0$ is equivalent to

$$dG_2/d\rho < dG_1/d\rho$$

near the steady state. An economy with these characteristics is illustrated in figure 12.2. Hence, in a vicinity of the steady state, these assumptions imply (directly) divergent motions or cause them to spiral outward. Can this go on forever? To answer this question, suppose that the state of confidence has been continuously rising (and with it economic activity or utilization x, through the rising growth rate of

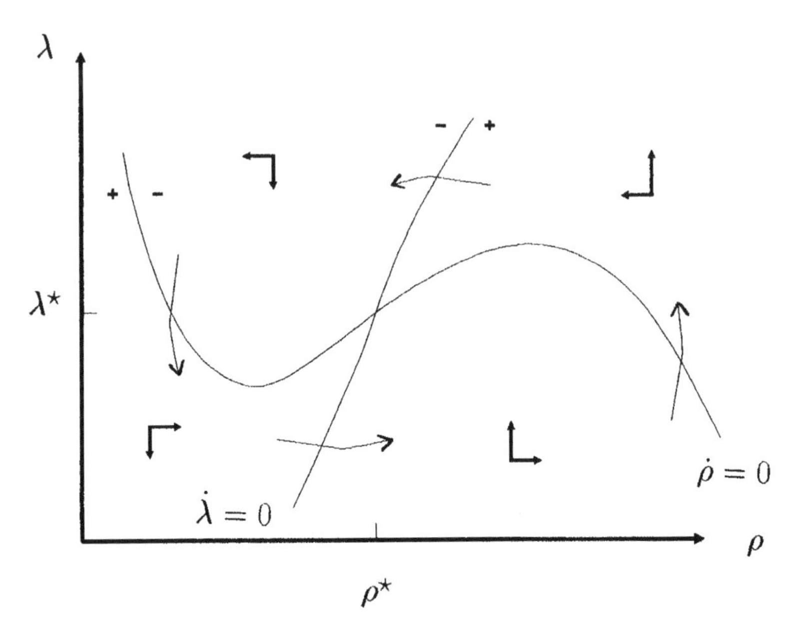

Figure 12.2
Phase diagram of process (12.13)

the capital stock $f_I(\rho)$). As mentioned in section 12.2 (and section 11.5 above), there will be agents that are aware of past experiences that an ongoing motion is eventually to be revised. In forming their expectations, they will accordingly tend to attribute an increasingly greater weight to the economic fundamentals. With respect to the adjustment function f_ρ, this means that the influence of the autofeedback gradually diminishes, implying that $\partial F_2/\partial\rho$ in equation (12.15) eventually becomes negative. The change in the sign of the partial derivative, in its turn, implies that at larger deviations of ρ from $\rho^\star$ the isocline $\dot{\rho} = 0$ is downward sloping, similar to what is depicted in figure 12.2. Hence, the state of confidence cannot increase indefinitely but must cross this isocline, after which it begins its decline. A corresponding reasoning applies when ρ is continuously falling. Figure 12.2 shows that the interplay and the shifting weights of the self-referential and the hetero-referential mechanism generate counterclockwise loops in the (ρ, λ)-plane.

Having thus identified the cyclical tendencies, we recognize it is quite another question whether these motions keep on perpetually spiraling outwards. With respect to Figure 12.2 it might be intuitively felt that this cannot occur if in the outer regions the slope of the $\dot{\rho} = 0$ isocline is sufficiently steep. This conjecture could indeed be confirmed by a mathematical analysis utilizing the Poincaré-Bendixson theorem. If some appropriate assumptions on the relative strength of the reaction intensities of the function f_ρ are added, the final result would be that every trajectory either itself is, or converges toward, a periodic orbit. We leave the details aside since they are rather technical and do not contribute much to the basic insights that have already been gained. Much more important, in our view, is the problem of whether this nice scenario has to be considered an extraordinary case, or it is consistent with economically meaningful steady-state parameter values and reaction intensities. This is the subject of the computer simulations in the next section, which can also provide some information on the quantitative relationships in this model.

12.6 Computer Simulations

To present the numerical specifications on which our simulation runs are based, we first introduce the steady-state parameters. In the first two columns of the following listing, the same values as those used in the previous chapter are employed; the others are not comparable.

$x^\star = 1.50$	$g^\star = 3.50\%$	$\lambda^\star = 0.30$	
$v = 0.75$	$\pi = 3.00\%$	$\rho^\star = 0.00\%$	$\chi = 0.20$
$\delta = 0.10$	$i^\star = 8.00\%$	$\tau = 20.0\%$	$\phi = 0.15$

($g^\star$ is the steady state growth rate of the real variables, the wage share v and the rate of inflation are denoted without a star symbol since they are held constant throughout; see section 11.4 for a justification of the value for the output-capital ratio). These parameters determine the values for $r^\star$, $f_e^\star$, and also s_f and s_h, as follows. Value $r^\star$ is given by (12.3) and (12.4).[31] Value $f_e^\star$, the fraction of private wealth held in equities, can then be computed from the LM-equation (12.7). To get the retention ratio s_f, we put $\dot{\lambda} = 0$ in the dynamic equation (12.12) and solve it for s_f. Subsequently, households' propensity to save, s_h, can be derived from the IS-equation (12.8) (putting $f_I^\star = g^\star$). In sum, one obtains

$r^\star = 19.60\%$	$f_e^\star = 90.11\%$	
$s_f = 4.34\%$	$s_h = 17.14\%$	$s_o = 20.73\%$

The high value of $f_e^\star$ can be put down to two reasons. On the one hand, only a limited number of financial assets is considered and, in particular, bonds are completely neglected. On the other hand, the value of $f_e^\star$ depends on the specification of the demand price for capital in equation (12.5), which, together with the value chosen for $x^\star$, results in a comparatively high ratio p_k/p. It is easily verified that a lower ratio would reduce $f_e^\star$. By contrast, the retention ratio s_f might appear too low. Here, one has to bear in mind that s_f is related to the profit rate. For example, if $a^\star$ denotes the steady-state proportion of undistributed profits in the financing of *net* investment, we have the equation $s_f r^\star pK = a^\star pI = a^\star g^\star pK$, or $s_f = g^\star a^\star / r^\star$. With a rough estimate like $a^\star \approx 0.30$, $g^\star a^\star \approx 0.01$, $r^\star \approx 0.20$, this gives $s_f \approx 0.05$.

Over an economically meaningful region, the investment and the equity holding function are specified linearly as

$$f_e = f_e(r + \rho - i + \pi) = \beta_{eo} + \beta_{e\sigma} \cdot (r + \rho - i + \pi)$$

$$f_I = f_I(\rho) \qquad\qquad = g^\star + \beta_{I\rho} \cdot (\rho - \rho^\star)$$

Given an elasticity of equity holding $\eta_{e,\sigma}$, the coefficients β_{eo} and $\beta_{e\sigma}$ are successively given by

$$\beta_{e\sigma} = \eta_{e,\sigma} f_e^\star / (r^\star - i^\star + \pi), \qquad \beta_{eo} = f_e^\star - \beta_{e\sigma} \cdot (r + \rho - i + \pi)$$

Numerically, we put

$$\eta_{e,\sigma} = 0.50 \qquad \beta_{I\rho} = 0.30$$

The value of $\eta_{e,\sigma}$ is somewhat higher than the interest elasticity of money demand of 0.20 in section 11.4, because we conceive of agents as being more responsive to the conditions of equity holding than of bond holding (responsiveness on the stock market, i.e., reshuffling of equities within a portfolio of a given size, is certainly much more volatile). Besides, higher values of $\eta_{e,\sigma}$ would be even more agreeable since the main effect would be a lower amplitude of the interest rate. To get a feeling for the implications of our parameter choice, we present the instantaneous temporary equilibrium reactions of the interest rate, the net rate of profit, and the difference between these two rates of return with respect to changes in λ and ρ. Table 12.2 additionally considers some alternatives for $\eta_{e,\sigma}$ and $\beta_{I\rho} = f_{I\rho}$.

The table also illustrates the statements of theorem 12.1. $\partial r/\partial\lambda$ is always negative, $\partial i/\partial\rho$ always positive. At $\eta_{e,\sigma} = 1.00$, $\partial i/\partial\lambda$ is negative since assumption 12.4(ii) is violated, at $\eta_{e,\sigma} = 0.30$ and $\beta_{I\rho} = 0.30$, $\partial r/\partial\rho$ is negative since assumption 12.4(i) is violated. By contrast, these con-

Table 12.2
Temporary equilibrium reactions

$\eta_{e,\sigma}$	0.50	0.50	0.30	0.30	1.00	1.00
$\beta_{I\rho}$	0.30	1.00	0.30	1.00	0.30	1.00
$\partial i/\partial\lambda$	0.01	0.01	0.22	0.22	−0.33	−0.33
$\partial r/\partial\lambda$	−0.07	−0.07	−0.12	−0.12	−0.58	−0.58
$\partial(r-i)/\partial\lambda$	−0.07	−0.07	−0.34	−0.34	−0.24	−0.24
$\partial i/\partial\rho$	3.60	8.85	8.98	22.06	2.63	6.46
$\partial r/\partial\rho$	0.77	3.35	−0.56	0.08	1.01	3.94
$\partial(r-i)/\partial\rho$	−2.83	−5.50	−9.54	−21.98	−1.62	−2.52

ditions affect the negativity of neither $\partial r/\partial\lambda - \partial i/\partial\lambda$ nor $\partial r/\partial\rho - \partial i/\partial\rho$. As already pointed out in the comment on theorem 12.1, the effects of variations in the debt-asset ratio are clearly seen to be almost negligible as compared to the variations in the state of confidence.

Before we turn to the specific simulations of the long-run dynamics, another unsatisfactory feature of the present model should be mentioned, namely, the fluctuations in the capital growth rate. Denoting it by g_k and rearranging the IS-equation (12.8), we have

$$g_k = [s_o r + s_h i\lambda - \pi\phi]/(1+\phi)$$

The variations in $s_h i\lambda$ and $\pi\phi$ are small relative to those in $s_o r$, so we may concentrate on the amplitude of $s_o r/(1+\phi)$. Recalling equations (12.3) and (12.4), we determine the amplitude of r mainly by the variations of the output-capital ratio. Realistically, the latter are not wider than 1.50 ± 0.10. This amplitude implies that the fluctuations of the net profit rate are in a range of something like $19.6\% \pm 2\%$. If we employ the above value for s_o, this means that the variations in g_k would be contained between $3.5\% \pm 0.4\%$. The empirical amplitude of the capital growth rate, by contrast, is at least 1% or 1.5% (with respect to the stated amplitude of x). A straightforward remedy to overcome this contradiction would be to drop the assumption of constant savings propensities, but we leave this aspect for future variants of the model. In calibrating the present simulations, we seek to achieve a realistic amplitude of the output-capital ratio and accept the distortions coming from the low amplitude of g_k.

To complete the model, we have to introduce the adjustment function f_ρ for the state of confidence. We assume linearity as regards the impact of the fundamentals λ and $r - (i - \pi)$, while the influence of ρ is to depend on its distance from $\rho^\star$. To ensure that the given steady-state parameters indeed constitute a stationary point of the dynamical system, we specify

$$\begin{aligned} f_\rho &= f_\rho(\rho, \sigma, \lambda) \\ &= \alpha_\rho(|\rho - \rho^\star|)\beta_{\rho\rho}(\rho - \rho^\star) + \beta_{\rho\sigma}(\sigma - \sigma^\star) - \beta_{\rho\lambda}(\lambda - \lambda^\star) \end{aligned}$$

where $\sigma = r - (i - \pi)$ is the risk premium and $\alpha_\rho(\cdot)$ is a piecewise linear function such that, with respect to a given reference value ρ_{ref},

$$\alpha_\rho = \begin{cases} \alpha_{\rho 1} & \text{if } |\rho - \rho^\star| = 0 \qquad\qquad \alpha_{\rho 1} = 0.20 \\ 1 & \text{if } |\rho - \rho^\star| = \rho_{ref} \\ \alpha_{\rho 2} & \text{if } |\rho - \rho^\star| = 2 \cdot \rho_{ref} \qquad \alpha_{\rho 2} = 0.20 \\ 0 & \text{if } |\rho - \rho^\star| \geq 4 \cdot \rho_{ref} \end{cases}$$

The three coefficients $\beta_{\rho\rho}, \beta_{\rho\sigma}, \beta_{\rho\lambda}$ obey

$$100 \cdot |\rho_{ref} - \rho^\star| \cdot \beta_{\rho\rho} = 1.00 \qquad \rho_{ref} = 0.50\%$$

$$100 \cdot |\sigma_{ref} - \sigma^\star| \cdot \beta_{\rho\sigma} = 0.50 \qquad \sigma_{ref} = r(\rho_{ref}, \lambda^\star) - i(\rho_{ref}, \lambda^\star) + \pi$$

$$100 \cdot |\lambda_{ref} - \lambda^\star| \cdot \beta_{\rho\lambda} = 0.50 \qquad \lambda_{ref} = 0.05$$

The value for $\beta_{\rho\rho}$ is so large that the steady state would be unstable if $\alpha_{\rho 1}$ were unity. The particular choice of $\alpha_{\rho 1} = 0.20$ makes it locally asymptotically stable. It could be said that at $|\rho - \rho^\star| = \rho_{ref}$, the self-referential mechanism dominates in the adjustments of ρ, whereas at $|\rho - \rho^\star| = 0$ as well as $|\rho - \rho^\star| \geq 2 \cdot \rho_{ref}$, the stabilizing influence of σ takes the lead. Correspondingly, in the first case the trajectories in the (λ, ρ) plane spiral outward; in the second case, they spiral inward. It follows that the stability of the steady state is not global. It is intuitively clear that there must be a watershed, a closed orbit such that all trajectories starting in its interior approach the steady state, and all trajectories that (close to it) start on the other side spiral away from it. Nevertheless, these latter motions cannot diverge forever since in the outer regions the centripetal forces gain the upper hand. So these trajectories converge to another closed orbit. This situation is illustrated by figure 12.3. The inner circle, which is repelling on both sides, represents, as Leijonhufvud (1973) has coined it, a case of "corridor stability." That is, small perturbations of the equilibrium values do not prevent the economy from converging back to its steady-state position, whereas after a stronger shock has occurred, the economy will never return to it.

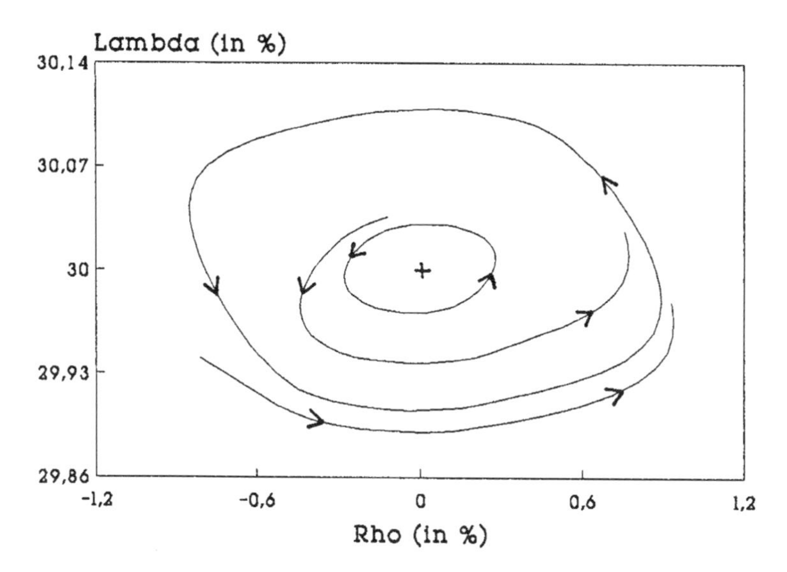

Figure 12.3
Numerical simulation of process (12.13)

The corridor phenomenon, however, is only a side aspect of the model, and there might be different opinions about the relative strength of the self-referential mechanism in economic constellations where all economic indicators are considered to be approximately normal. Conceptually more important for us is the outer limit cycle, which, except for the corridor, is globally attracting.[32]

The present calibration yields a cycle period of 6.20 years and a realistic amplitude of the output-capital ratio of ±0.081 around the steady-state value, which was our prior criterion (the inner limit cycle exhibits a wavelength of 5.80 years). Other characteristics of the limit cycle are listed in table 12.3. Since lags of −3.20 and 3.00 years indicate that the respective variables move nearly countercyclically, the only truly lagging variable is the debt-asset ratio. This is not surprising given the dominance of the impact effects of ρ in the partial derivatives of table 12.2.

The fluctuations are not completely symmetrical, that is, maximal positive and negative deviations from the steady-state values differ somewhat. For example, the highest value of the state of confidence is 0.895%; the lowest is −0.849%. table 12.3 gives the mean of the two values. The picture is similar for the other variables. As concerns the size of the amplitudes, two weak points of the model have already

Table 12.3
Characteristics of the stable limit cycle

Variable	Amplitude	Lag (+) or Lead (–) w.r.t. to x (in years)
x	1.50 ± 0.081	—
λ	30.00% ± 0.10%	1.9
ρ	0.00% ± 0.87%	0.0
g_k	3.50% ± 0.26%	0.0
i	8.00% ± 3.22%	0.0
r	19.60% ± 0.65%	−0.1
$r - i + \pi$	14.60% ± 2.57%	−3.2
IPR	10.91% ± 3.62%	0.0
DPR	1.36 ± 0.10	3.0

Note: g_k denotes the capital growth rate, IPR is the interest-profit ratio ($i\lambda/r^g$), DPR the debt-profit ratio (λ/r^g).

been indicated: the amplitude of the interest rate may be too high; the amplitude of the capital stock growth rate is much too low. At first sight, the fluctuations of the debt-asset ratio might also appear too narrow. At least within the present setup, however, they could hardly be any wider. This is one result of the discussion in the next chapter.

12.7 Conclusion

This chapter can be seen as standing in a long tradition of economic theory in which expectations were assigned a central role for the explanation of recurrent cyclical fluctuations of business activities. In the present model, however, the shifts in expectations are not considered a causal factor for macro-fluctuations; they are determined endogenously within the modeling framework. In addition, expectations are not condensed in predictions of the rate of inflation, as is most often the case in contemporary macroeconomic theory. They are rather supposed to represent a general business climate or, as we have called it, the general state of confidence. This variable plays an important part in the investment decisions of firms as well as in the asset-holding decisions of private households. The connecting link between the real and the financial sector is the financing of firms' investment, where three sources are available: internal finance through retained earnings, and external finance through equity issuance to households and loans from commercial banks. It follows that the effects of the expectational variable in this model work themselves out dynamically through the interdependence of the goods and financial markets.

Special reference was made to concepts expounded in chapter 12 of the *General Theory* with regard to the factors determining the changes in the state of confidence. The weights of these factors in the adjustment process of the state of confidence, however, were assumed to vary in the regions of the state space. This feature gives rise to different types of cyclical behavior, the most interesting case being the one generating limit cycles. The model can even exhibit the property of corridor stability, a term introduced by Leijonhufvud (1973). Given its low dimensionality, the model and the numerical calibration put forward here are on the whole quite satisfactory.

The next step that suggests future research is to drop the assumption of a fixed rate of inflation and a fixed wage share, and to attempt an integration of the model in the previous chapter into the present framework. In particular, expected inflation may lose its significance as the focal expectations variable in favor of the state of confidence. Another point is the modeling of the financial sector. In this chapter a proposal was made to maintain the basic philosophy of the conventional LM modeling, but to extend the narrow limits of the textbook specifications. To keep things as simple as possible, we accepted a number of other shortcomings: policy instruments such as government bonds or a reserve requirement ratio for deposits were neglected, and the credit market was still very rudimentary.[33]

If the issues that have just been discussed are addressed in building a more general macroeconomic model, then local, and all the more global, stability will probably no longer be analytically tractable. As a consequence one will have to rely on numerical simulations to study their long-run dynamics. The analytical results and the simulation experience in this and the previous chapters may provide a basis for such a greater and more ambitious research project.

12.8 Mathematical Appendix

Proof of Lemma 12.1 Define the function $f = f(\lambda, r + \rho, i) := f_e(r + \rho - i + \pi) - \varepsilon(\lambda, r + \rho, i)$. Term i is an LM-interest rate with respect to λ and $r + \rho$ given if $f(\lambda, r + \rho, i) = 0$. Evaluated at such points, the partial derivatives are

$$\partial f/\partial i = -f_e' + (r + \rho + \pi\lambda)(\lambda + \phi)/A_o = -A_r/A_o < 0$$

$$\partial f/\partial(r + \rho) = f_e' - (i - \pi)(\lambda + \phi)/A_o = A_i/A_o > 0$$

$$\partial f/\partial\lambda = (i - \pi)(r + \rho - \pi\phi)/A_o > 0$$

Employing the implicit function theorem gives

$$\partial j/\partial(r + \rho) = -[\partial f/\partial(r + \rho)]/[\partial f/\partial i] = A_i/A_r$$

$$\partial j/\partial(\lambda) = -[\partial f/\partial\lambda]/[\partial f/\partial i] = (i - \pi)(r + \rho - \pi\phi)/A_r$$

$A_i/A_r > 1$ since $i - \pi < r + \rho$ implies $A_i > A_r$. For further use we also note

$$\begin{aligned} 1 - \partial j/\partial(r + \rho) &= (A_r - A_i)/A_r \\ &= -(r + \rho - (i - \pi) + \pi\lambda)(\lambda + \phi)/A_r < 0 \end{aligned}$$

q.e.d.

Proof of Theorem 12.1 We begin with the partial derivatives of the function $F = F(\lambda, \rho, r)$ defined in equation (12.10). The value of $\partial F/\partial r = -A_s/A_r < 0$ has already been stated in the text (see (12.11) for the definition of A_s). After some elementary manipulations the other two derivatives can be written as

$$\partial F/\partial\rho = [A_1 f_{Iu} + (1 + \phi)A_r f_{I\rho} - s_h\lambda A_i]/A_r > 0$$

$$\partial F/\partial\lambda = -A_h[iA_r + \lambda(i - \pi)(r + \rho - \pi\phi)]/A_r < 0$$

where $A_1 := (1 + \phi)\lambda A_i/[(1 - \tau)(1 - v)] > 0$ and $A_h := s_h - (1 + \phi) f_{Iu}/[(1 - \tau)(1 - v)]$. The sign of $\partial F/\partial\rho$ is positive by, in particular, assumption 12.4(i), $\partial F/\partial\lambda$ is negative since $A_h > 0$ by assumption 12.3(ii). Applying the implicit function theorem to the equation $F(\lambda, \rho, r) = 0$ yields the partial derivatives of the IS-LM profit rate function $r = r(\lambda, \rho)$,

$$\partial r/\partial\rho = [A_1 f_{Ix} + (1 + \phi)A_r f_{I\rho} - s_h\lambda A_i]/A_s > 0$$

$$\partial r/\partial\lambda = -A_h[iA_r + \lambda(i - \pi)(r + \rho - \pi\phi)]/A_s < 0$$

To obtain the partial derivatives of the IS-LM interest rate we have to differentiate $j(\lambda, r(\lambda, \rho) + \rho)$. This leads to

$$\partial i/\partial\rho = [\partial j/\partial(r + \rho][\partial r/\partial\rho + 1]$$

$$\partial i/\partial\lambda = \partial j/\partial\lambda + [\partial j/\partial(r + \rho][\partial r/\partial\lambda]$$

$$=\big\{(i-\pi)(r+\rho-\pi\phi)[A_hA_r+\lambda A_hA_i+s_f(1-s_h)A_r-\lambda A_iA_h]$$

$$-\,iA_hA_iA_r\big\}/A_rA_s$$

$$=\{(i-\pi)[i(\lambda+\phi)A_h+(r+\rho-\pi\phi)(s_f(1-s_h)+A_h)]$$

$$-\,(iA_hA_of_e)\eta_{e,\sigma}/(r+\rho-i+\pi)\}/A_s$$

It is easily checked that $1+\partial r/\partial\rho>0$ even if assumption 12.4(ii) is not satisfied. In the computation of $\partial i/\partial\lambda$ use is made of the equality $A_s = A_h(A_r+\lambda A_i)+s_f(1-s_h)A_r$. Term $\partial i/\partial\lambda>0$ is equivalent to assumption 12.4(ii). Lastly, referring to the observation at the end of the proof of lemma 12.1, we find it obvious that

$$\partial r/\partial\rho-\partial i/\partial\rho=[1-\partial j/\partial(r+\rho)][\partial r/\partial\rho]-\partial j/\partial(r+\rho)<0$$

q.e.d.

Proof of Lemma 12.3 Defining

$$B_1 := s_o(\pi+f_I)-s_fs_hi$$

$$B_2 := (\pi+f_I)A_of_e'-(i-\pi)[(\pi+f_I)(\lambda+\phi)+s_f(r+\rho-\pi\phi)]$$

and taking account of the definition of A_i and of $f_{Iu}=0$, the partial derivatives of F_1 with respect to λ can be computed as

$$\partial F_1/\partial\lambda=-f_I-s_f(\partial r/\partial\lambda)-\pi$$

$$=\{-(\pi+f_I)A_s+s_fs_h[iA_r+\lambda(i-\pi)(r+\rho-\pi\phi)]\}/A_s$$

$$=-\{B_1A_r+s_h\lambda B_2\}/A_s$$

assumption 12.5(i) states that $B_1>0$ if s_f attains its maximal value $s_f=1$. Since B_1 is decreasing in s_f this ensures $B_1>0$ for all $0\le s_f\le 1$. assumption 12.5(ii) implies $B_2>(\pi+f_I)[A_of_e'-(r+\rho+\pi\lambda)(\lambda+\phi)]=A_r>0$. Thus, assumptions 12.5(i),(ii) guarantee $\partial F_1/\partial\lambda<0$.

As concerns the other derivative of F_1 with respect to ρ, it is convenient to make use of the following two equalities,

$$1+\phi=(s_or+s_hi\lambda-\pi\phi)/f_I,\qquad 1-\chi-\lambda=(s_fr+\pi\lambda)/f_I$$

The first one is equivalent to the IS-condition, the second holds true if $\dot{\lambda}=0$. We then obtain

$$\begin{aligned}\partial F_1/\partial\rho &= (1-\chi-\lambda)f_{I\rho} - s_f(\partial r/\partial\rho)\\ &= \big\{(f_{I\rho}/f_I)[(s_f r+\pi\lambda)(s_o A_r + s_h\lambda A_i) - s_f(s_o r + s_h i\lambda - \pi\phi)A_r]\\ &\quad + s_f s_h\lambda A_i\big\}/A_s\\ &= \big\{(f_{I\rho}/f_I)[(s_f s_h\lambda(rA_i - iA_r) + \pi\lambda A_s + s_f\pi\phi A_r] + s_f s_h\lambda A_i\big\}/A_s\end{aligned}$$

$\partial F_1/\partial\rho > 0$ if $rA_i - iA_r > 0$, where the latter inequality is equivalent to assumption 12.5(iii).

q.e.d.

13 Trends and Cycles in the Capital Structure

13.1 Introduction

In the previous chapters we attempted to explain the variability of macroeconomic variables in terms of nonmarket-clearing dynamic macroeconomic models with a primary interest in the business cycle characteristics. One might, however, argue that macroeconomic variables also exhibit clear trends or low-frequency movements. The state of confidence in chapter 12, for example, was seen by Keynes as a psychological variable that may as well be subject to the impact of some long-run forces. For various reasons, the same may be true for other variables such as the output-capital ratio, distributional shares, or monetary and financial key variables.

In this last chapter of the book, we extend our perspective from the business cycle to a longer time horizon. We focus on a macroeconomic variable that was particularly important in the context of Ch.12, namely the capital structure of firms. For simplicity this structure was represented by the debt-asset ratio, that is, the ratio of corporate debt to the stock of fixed capital.[1] We thus employ our dynamic methods to study the combined business cycle and trend variations in this magnitude. Our motivation is a preliminary inspection of empirical corporate debt asset-ratio time series: its evaluation displays less distinctively cyclical features, but is dominated by trend movements.[2] In the following sections we study the factors that are responsible for this phenomenon.

Before we go into the details of this discussion, it is worthwhile to survey some of the literature on the long-run determination of the financial structure of firms. Three distinguished approaches give some predictions on the long-term variation of the capital structure.

Arising from neoclassical financial theory, the first view assumes that the financial structure of firms tends to be optimal. Firms maximize the wealth of stockholders and decide to issue debt or equity according to the relative cost incurred in obtaining them (see, e.g., Auerbach 1979). Of vital importance is the famous Modigliani-Miller theorem, which states that the value of the firm and thus, investment, is independent of the choice of financial instruments. In this world of perfect information and certainty, the optimal capital structure is affected only by the tax structure (the latter acting upon the cost of capital; cf. Auerbach 1979; Fazzari, Hubbard, and Petersen 1988; the result might carry over to situations of pure risk, as opposed to ones of irreducible uncertainty). Faced with corporate profit taxes, a tax rate on dividends, and a capital gains tax, corporations can compute the cost of internal, equity, and debt finance and then choose the capital structure that minimizes the capital cost. If, for example, the capital gains tax is lower than the dividend tax (as was the case in the United States), internal finance would be less costly than equity finance. Deductible interest payments on debt, by contrast, might introduce a bias toward debt finance.[3] Moreover, as Feldstein, Green, and Sheskinski (1978, 64) have argued, the inflation rate can also skew the choice of financial instruments toward debt. Most of the statements, however, only hold upon the hypothesis of perfect capital markets. On the whole, this theory does not appear very convincing in demonstrating why firms extensively issue debt. Bernanke and Campbell (1988) remark that firms in different countries issue debt even if the above tax factors are not relevant.

A second view focuses on the relation between debt finance and financial risk. The literature on this position has been discussed in chapters 5 and 12. Recall that according to the theory of imperfect capital markets there is a hierarchy of cost of funds that can be sketched as follows: as a rule, internal finance is cheapest, though limited (Fazzari, Hubbard, and Petersen 1988). Equity issuance is, in principle, a method to spread risk, but firms cannot view the stock market as a perfect device for this purpose since issuing new equities typically gives a negative signal to holders of old shares. Furthermore, new issuance of equity dilutes old equity.[4] Equity finance is the most expensive financial instrument and the most constrained type of financing of firms' investments, whereas debt finance takes an intermediate position. On that account, one would predict for those firms the highest cost of external finance for which there is the least information on their economic performance.[5] Overall, this theory gauges that firms would engage predominantly in debt finance, and far less in equity finance, when internal funds are insufficient to finance planned investment.[6]

The third body of theory advances the hypothesis that debt finance is largely an expectationally driven phenomenon. This position is grounded in Keynes's view on the volatility of firms' state of confidence concerning their future cash flows (Keynes 1936, chaps. 5 and 12), but also in the earlier work by von Hayek and Hawtrey, where the ease and stringency of credit was seen to be intimately related to swings in beliefs and expectations.[7] More recently, a prominent role of expectations dynamics for credit expansion and contraction appears in Keynesian-oriented writings. This is especially true for Minsky's financial fragility hypothesis, where success in financial practices feeds confidence and a decline in confidence breeds pessimism. Movements in the debt-asset ratio may thus be correlated with fluctuations in economic activity. This hypothesis seems to be implicit in Minsky's theory when he writes, "acceptable financing techniques are not technologically constrained; they depend upon the subjective preferences and views of bankers and businessmen about prospects. . . . Success breeds a disregard of the possibility of failure; the absence of serious financial difficulties over a substantial period leads to the development of a euphoric economy in which increasing short-term financing of long-term positions becomes a normal way of life. As a previous financial crisis recedes in time, it is quite natural for central bankers, government officials, bankers, businessmen, and even economists to believe that a new era has arrived"(Minsky 1986, 213).

Resulting from audacious leverage strategies of firms, high growth rates of output may give rise to high growth rates in borrowing, with the reverse occurring as accumulation begins to falter.[8] On empirical grounds, we add that shifts in the financial structure, especially in the 1980s, are, at least in part, related to takeovers and financial reorganizations (see Bernanke and Campbell 1988).

The above theoretical positions may help to guide empirical studies on trends in corporate indebtedness, although unobservable expectation variables as well as specific institutional factors are likely to have an unmeasurable impact on the variations in the debt-asset ratio in different periods and over different countries. The approach taken here is more pragmatically oriented. In particular, it deliberately leaves aside the discussion on macroeconomic repercussion effects originating with risky debt finance and highly indebted firms, some of which have already been modeled in chapter 12. The method we propose is in effect to represent the capital structure by the debt-asset ratio and to decompose the movements of this ratio into their major components. In this context, our main concern is with the growth rate of real capital, new issuance of debt, and the rate of inflation.[9] To single out the main factors working on the debt-asset ratio, we consider hypothesized and stylized motions as well as empirically observed time series of these components. The results obtained in the corresponding scenarios may be related to the theoretical literature mentioned previously. It is also hoped that the insights gained in this way may help to more thoroughly study the underlying trends or low-frequency movements in the corporate financial structure that appeared to be puzzling.

The remainder of the chapter is structured as follows. In section 13.2 the general framework is introduced and the basic differential equation governing the evolution of the debt-asset ratio is derived. In sections 13.3 and 13.4 the dynamics of the debt-asset ratio are studied. The analysis is subdivided into various scenarios, according to what variables are held constant, fluctuate in a regular stylized way, or are directly given by their empirical counterparts. In section 13.3 the trend values of the variables involved are frozen, whereas in section 13.4 this assumption is relaxed. Section 13.5 delineates the chapter's conclusions. Empirical computations and demonstration of a mathematical stability proposition are relegated to the appendix.

13.2 A Simple Dynamic Approach

The central variables in this chapter, which all refer to nonfinancial corporate business, are real net investment, I; the real capital stock, K; loans of firms for investment purposes, Λ; the price deflator of capital goods, p; the debt-asset ratio, $\lambda = \Lambda/pK$; the rate of inflation of p, π; the growth rate of real capital, g (the index k may be safely omitted here); and the proportion of net investment that is financed by (net) borrowing, which we denote by β (adjustment speeds like β_π or β_p play no role in this chapter, so no confusion in the symbol β will arise). Trend or reference values of these variables are indicated by the star symbol (*). The time unit underlying the flow variables is one year.

Expressions like debt or borrowing exclusively relate to loans firms are raising to finance their net investment expenditures in fixed capital; replacement investment may be thought of as being paid from gross profits. We thus separate the process of firms' "real" growth from their (partly routine, partly speculative) activities in financial assets.

Our analysis starts out from the flow leverage ratio β. Net borrowing being given by $\dot{\Lambda}$, we have $\beta = \dot{\Lambda}/pI$. The growth rate of loans derives from $\hat{\Lambda} = \dot{\Lambda}/\Lambda = \beta pI/\Lambda = \beta(pI/pK)(pK/\Lambda) = \beta g/\lambda$, while by logarithmic differentiation, the growth rate of the debt-asset ratio λ can be decomposed into $\hat{\lambda} = \hat{\Lambda} - \hat{p} - \hat{K} = \hat{\Lambda} - \pi - g$. The evolution of λ is thus governed by

$$\dot{\lambda} = \beta g - \lambda(g + \pi) \tag{13.1}$$

This differential equation describes in what way the leverage ratio, capital growth, and inflation determine the changes in the debt-asset ratio. All these magnitudes vary over time. In the limited context of the present chapter, possible feedback effects between β, g, π, and λ are not discussed. That is, the motions of the first three variables are treated as being exogenously given, as pure functions of time. By the same token, an interest rate is not made explicit but may be lurking in the background. In a more or less direct manner, β in particular may be conceived of as being functionally dependent on it (among other things).

A first inspection of (13.1) reveals that the current level of λ has some self-stabilizing effect, as long as βg and $g + \pi$ are positive: high values of λ bring about a negative derivative, whereas at low values the term βg will be dominant such as to push λ upwards. If β, g and π remained constant we could compute an equilibrium value of λ. In the general case this concept evidently does no longer apply. Instead, the following generalization can be introduced. Suppose certain trend values of the exogenous variables are known, designated $\beta^\star$, $g^\star$ and $\pi^\star$. We then associate with this triple the debt-asset ratio that would cease moving if these constant trend values were adopted in (13.1). Denote this hypothetical value by $\lambda^\star$. Setting the right-hand side of equation (13.1) equal to zero, we determine it as

$$\lambda^\star = \beta^\star g^\star/(g^\star + \pi^\star) \tag{13.2}$$

Value $\lambda^\star$ will serve us as a reference value. Note that this stock measure of indebtedness coincides with the trend value of the flow leverage ratio $\beta^\star$ only if systematic inflation is absent; otherwise the measure is smaller.

Beyond the very definition, the economic significance of the reference value is not obvious when $\beta^\star$, $g^\star$, or $\pi^\star$ are shifting over time, since then

$\lambda^\star$ is also given to variations. More specifically, $\lambda^\star$ increases when $g^\star$ or $\beta^\star$ increases, and it is depressed by a rising trend in inflation. As for the order of magnitude, write $\eta_{\lambda,x}$ for the elasticity of $\lambda^\star$ with respect to $x^\star$ ($x^\star = g^\star, \pi^\star, \beta^\star$), i.e., $\eta_{\lambda,x} = (\partial\lambda^\star/\partial x^\star)x^\star/\lambda^\star$. It is easily verified that

$$\eta_{\lambda,g} = \pi^\star/(g^\star + \pi^\star), \qquad \eta_{\lambda,\pi} = -\pi^\star/(g^\star + \pi^\star), \qquad \eta_{\lambda,\beta} = 1 \tag{13.3}$$

Among all trend variables on the right-hand side of (13.2), $\beta^\star$ may be felt to be most prone to variations, whereas the trend capital growth rate is quite stable over time.[10] So, if an apparent trend in the debt-asset ratio is observed, one may, in the first instance, have a closer look at the behavior of the flow-leverage ratio over the same period. It will be argued below, however, that the trend in inflation must not be neglected, either. On the whole, the analysis in section 13.4 will show that the empirical long-term fluctuations of $\pi^\star$ and $\beta^\star$ have a considerable explanatory power for the motions, not only of $\lambda^\star$, but also of the actual ratio $\lambda = \lambda(t)$.

The concept of a reference value for debt dynamics is not new. An example of its application is a section in an article by Tobin where he studies "[T]he simple dynamics of [government] deficits and debt" (Tobin 1987, 207). He considers there the hypothetical situation in which movements of the ratio of total government debt to GNP would come to rest. In particular, the reference value of this ratio likewise decreases if, ceteris paribus, the trend rate of inflation increases.

13.3 The Dynamics of the Capital Structure: Constant Trend

It has already been mentioned that in studying the motions of the debt-asset ratio generated by the differential equation (13.1), we restrict ourselves to exogenously given time paths of β, g, and π. For these, we set up a number of scenarios. They differ by the variables held constant and by the assumed cyclical movements. At the initial stages, the latter are assumed to have the convenient shape of a sine wave. After these basic scenarios are understood, empirical time series can also be considered. We begin, however, with constant trend values of g, π, and β, so that $\lambda^\star$ also stays constant over time. The different scenarios are numbered consecutively through sections 13.3 and 13.4.

Scenario 13.1 In the case where all independent variables are constant: $\beta = \beta^\star$, $g = g^\star$, $\pi = \pi^\star$, equation (13.1) reduces to a simple linear differential equation with constant coefficients. If we start at time $t = 0$ from an initial debt-asset ratio $\lambda_o = \lambda(0)$, it is well known that its solution is given by

$$\lambda(t) = \lambda^\star + (\lambda_o - \lambda^\star)\exp[-(g^\star + \pi^\star)t] \tag{13.4}$$

($\exp[\ldots]$ being the exponential function and $\lambda^\star$ determined by (13.2)). Here, the general stability observation of the previous section substantiates to the (global) asymptotic stability of a single value of the debt-asset ratio, the constant reference value $\lambda^\star$ (the last term in (13.4) converges to zero as t tends to infinity). This elementary result is nevertheless only one part of the story. The next question to be asked is at which speed does convergence occur. By virtue of the strong assumptions, a general answer is readily available. However, it turns out to be not completely satisfactory since the adjustments toward equilibrium are quite slow.[11] This can be seen by computing the "half-time" τ, that is, the time needed to get halfway from λ_o to $\lambda^\star$. It is obtained by solving the equation $\exp[-(g^\star + \pi^\star)\tau] = 0.5$ for τ, leading to $\tau = -(\ln 0.5)/(g^\star + \pi^\star) \approx 0.693/(g^\star + \pi^\star)$ (notice that it is independent of the leverage ratio $\beta^\star$). So, with $g^\star = 4\%$, $\pi^\star = 4\%$, the half-time is 8.66 years. It is reduced to 6.93 years if inflation goes up 2% to $\pi^\star = 6\%$. Even in the latter case it still takes more than 20 years for the debt-asset ratio to bridge 9/10 of the original distance between λ and $\lambda^\star$.

What has just been found, namely, convergence, although at relatively low speed, will be met again in the examples below that are enriched by several oscillations. These will bring in some modifications, but the roots of the apparent prevalence of the general phenomenon have already been laid bare in the present, extremely simplified scenario.

Scenario 13.2 In this scenario regular oscillations of investment and inflation are introduced while the assumption of a constant leverage ratio $\beta = \beta^\star$ is maintained. In detail, suppose that

$$g = g(t) = g^\star + h_g(t), \qquad \pi = \pi(t) = \pi^\star + h_\pi(t) \tag{13.5}$$

where $g^\star$ and $\pi^\star$ are constant trend values of the capital growth rate and the rate of inflation, and $h_g(\cdot)$ and $h_\pi(\cdot)$ are periodic functions oscillating around the zero level with the same period T. In addition, deviations average out, that is,

$$\int_0^T h_g(\tau)d\tau = \int_0^T h_\pi(\tau)d\tau = 0 \tag{13.6}$$

We are by now accustomed to the thought of no stationary equilibrium of the debt-asset ratio to exist. Here, we will instead expect its role to be taken by a periodic function, which we hope will continue to be attractive. This conjecture can be mathematically confirmed. We expect a similar result to hold if β also exhibits regular fluctuations, but for simplicity we may leave it at the following statement (the proof is given in the appendix).

Proposition 13.1 Let hypotheses (13.5) and (13.6) apply, and let $\lambda(t; \lambda_o, t_o)$ be the solution of the differential equation (13.1) that starts out from λ_o at time t_o. Then for all $t_o \geq 0$ the sequence $\{\lambda(t_o + kT; \lambda_o, t_o)\}_{k\in\mathbf{N}}$ converges to a finite limit $\lambda_\infty = \lambda_\infty(t_o)$, which is independent of the initial value λ_o.

Thus, the periodic function that attracts all motions of the small dynamical system (13.1),(13.5),(13.6) is given by the application $t \mapsto \lambda_\infty(t)$. We call it the reference function, or the reference oscillations, of the debt-asset ratio. It will furthermore be expected that $\lambda_\infty(t)$ fluctuates around the reference value of equation (13.2), $\lambda^\star = g^\star\beta^\star/(g^\star + \pi^\star)$. A mathematical demonstration, however, seems to be extremely difficult, even in the elementary case when the deviations $h_g(t)$ and $h_\pi(t)$ are assumed to be sine waves. For our purpose it will suffice to consider a numerical example. It is all the more important when we wish to get some information about the succession of the turning points of λ relative to those of g. The significance of such a comparison derives from the fact that the fluctuations of $g = g(t)$ can be taken as a rough proxy for economic activity as a whole.[12] Certainly, also the speed of convergence is of great interest.

Two subcases are considered: in the first one, prices are steadily growing at a constant rate; in the other, the inflation rate, too, is subject to oscillations. For both cases let us set

$$T = 7 \qquad \beta^\star = 0.68 \qquad g^\star = 4\% \qquad \pi^\star = 6\% \tag{13.7}$$

Four percent approximates the mean of the empirical real growth rate of capital from 1960 to 1982.[13] This period encompasses three major trough-to-trough cycles, which explains our T. Also, the value of the leverage ratio is a (rounded) time average over the observation period (see below). Trend inflation, by contrast, may appear too high. Our motivation for fixing it at 6 percent derives from the little adjustment experiment that will be considered in a moment. Besides, the trend values chosen affect only the scale of the debt-asset ratio, not the pattern of its time paths. The two cases to be distinguished are now defined as follows.

Scenario 13.2a

$$g = g(t) = g^\star + 0.02 \cdot \sin(\omega t), \qquad \pi = \pi^\star = \text{const} \tag{13.8}$$

where $\omega = 2\pi/T$ (in this expression, π is the mathematical constant).

Scenario 13.2b In relating the variations of the inflation rate to those of the capital growth rate, we need a price theory. Here, we invoke the phenomenon of the Phillips loops mentioned at the end of section 11.6. In the plane with g on the horizontal, and π on the vertical axis, they yield counterclockwise cycles (at least after World War II and for more general concepts than the price level for investment goods). For simplicity, let us work with perfectly regular loops, which would come about if the time derivative of $\pi = \pi(t)$ is proportional to $g(t) - g^\star$. Since $-\cos$ is the integral of the sine function, this leads us to postulate

$$g = g(t) = g^\star + 0.02 \cdot \sin(\omega t), \qquad \pi = \pi(t) = \pi^\star - 0.02 \cdot \cos(\omega t) \tag{13.9}$$

where again $\omega = 2\pi/T$; the amplitude of the rate of inflation is $\pm 2\%$.

The bottom series of figure 13.1 show the reference oscillations of the debt-asset ratio in scenarios 13.2a and 13.2b. In both cases the amplitude around $\lambda^\star = 27.2\%$ is quite limited in size (indebtedness taken as a percentage ratio of capital pK). In scenario 13.2a, the trough and peak values are 26.28% and 28.10%, whereas the variations of inflation in scenario 13.2b bring about a slight increase in the amplitude, the turning points being 25.95% and 28.14%, respectively. It will be noted that the maximal deviations are not symmetrical. In general, there is a weak downward bias. Accordingly, the time average over a cycle in scenario 13.2a is $27.18\% < \lambda^\star$, in scenario 13.2b it further decreases to 27.04%. In the latter case the asymmetry can also be directly gathered from figure 13.1 (it would be aggravated with wider fluctuations in the rate of inflation).

The vertical lines in figure 13.1, which indicate the timing of the turning points of the capital growth rate, reveal a significant lag of λ. So, the debt-asset ratio continues to rise after g has passed its peak, although

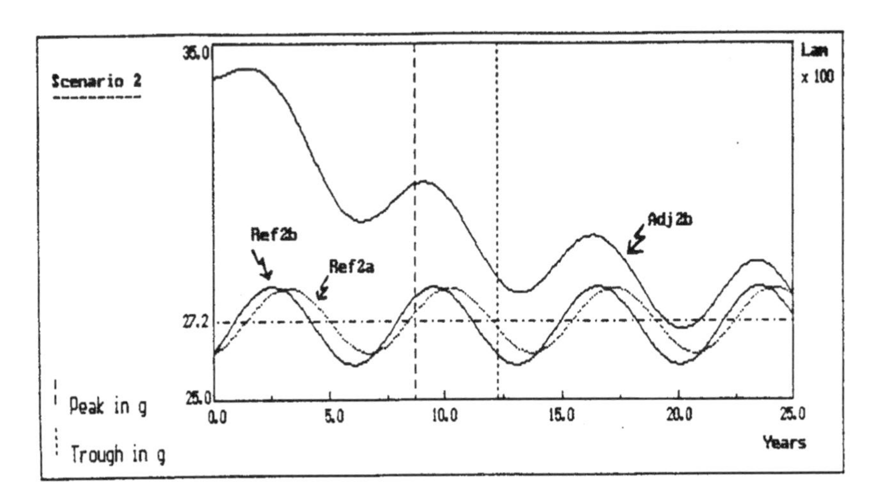

Figure 13.1
Motions of the debt-asset ratio (Lam = λ) in scenario 2. Ref2a (Ref2b): reference oscillations in scenario 2a (2b); Adj2b: adjustments from $\lambda_o = 34\%$ in scenario 2b

everything else, and in particular borrowing, has been "neutralized" (in scenario 13.2a even inflation). Such a lag has already been obtained in the model in chapter 12 (cf. figures 12.2 and 12.3 or Table 12.3 and recall that the state of confidence ρ and the capital growth rate were synchronous). It follows that a still rising debt-asset ratio at the beginning of a recession (as defined by the initial downturn phase of capital growth) does not necessarily point to a threat of financial distress that needs to be resolved by reduced net credit borrowing. An assessment like this should, therefore, be based on additional information from a flow measure of leverage or from an interest-coverage ratio. The finding also has a bearing on macroeconomic modeling that employs a stock measure of indebtedness to characterize financial tightness of firms: its entering into some of the behavioral functions may be analytically convenient, but direct and exclusive reference to it does not seem to be fully appropriate and should be modified at a later stage of research.[14]

In scenario 13.2a, λ is lagging approximately one and a half year behind g. The lag is shortened to one year in scenario 13.2b. The latter phenomenon is due to the countercyclical movements of the *level* of capital prices, relative to their trend, that is implied by equation (13.9). To verify the countercyclical pattern we only need to integrate the inflation rate,

$$\ln p(t) - \ln p(0) = \int_0^t \hat{p}(\tau)d\tau$$

$$= \int_0^t [\pi^\star - 0.02 \cdot \cos(\omega\tau)]d\tau$$

$$= \pi^\star t - 0.02 \cdot (1/\omega) \cdot \sin(\omega t) + 0$$

By virtue of (13.9) this equation is equivalent to

$$\ln p(t) = \ln p(0) + \pi^\star t - (1/\omega)(g(t) - g^\star) \quad (13.10)$$

Empirically, countercyclical prices are reported in, for example, Taylor 1980a, 112; Bils 1987, 851; and Backus and Kehoe 1992, 878ff. A detrended price deflator of capital goods is depicted in the top panel of figure 13.3.[15] If we take countercyclicality for granted, it follows that, in the phase of maximal capital growth, the relatively low price level indeed tends to raise $\lambda = \Lambda/pK$ somewhat in comparison to scenario 13.2a.

Attraction of the reference oscillations is illustrated by the upper series for scenario 13.2b. It starts out from $\lambda_o = 34\%$, which, for instance, is equal to the reference value $\lambda^\star = \beta^\star g^\star/(g^\star + \pi^\star)$ with $\pi^\star = 4\%$. If, at that level, the economy experiences a sudden jump of trend inflation from 4% to 6%, λ would follow the path given. We see, in particular, that again the adjustments take their time to work out. In this respect there is no difference from scenario 13.2a worth mentioning. In both cases the speed of convergence is even a little bit lower than in the nonoscillatory scenario 13.1.

The consequences of a sudden drop in the capital trend growth rate would be exactly the same (cf. equation (13.3)). However, a fall from $\lambda^\star = 34\%$ down to $\lambda^\star = 27.2\%$ with $\pi^\star$ fixed at 4% would require $g^\star$ to fall from 4% to 2.67%, a change that has to be regarded as being more radical than the 2% increase in $\pi^\star$ from 4% to 6%. Empirical results are cited in the next section.

Scenario 13.3 With respect to the assumed type of behavior of the exogenous variables in equation (13.1), this scenario is conceptually the same as the previous one. The difference is that the sine waves of investment and inflation are replaced with the trend deviations computed from empirical data. All series are quarterly observations. Reference is to the 22 years of the U.S. economy from 1960:4 to 1982:2, both quarters being lower turning points of the output-capital ratio.[16] We continue to

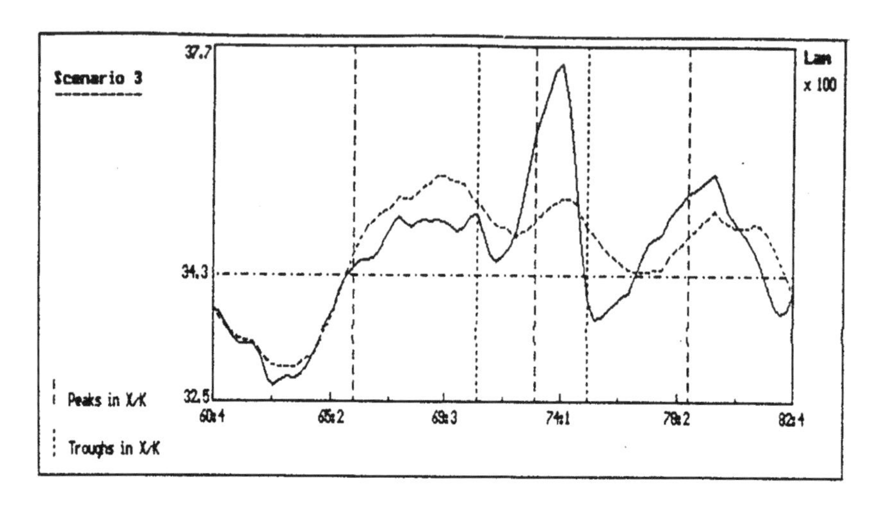

Figure 13.2
Motions of the debt-asset ratio (Lam = λ in scenario 3. Dotted line: scenario 3a; solid line: scenario 3b

assume constant trend values. Specifically, we put

$$\beta^{\star} = 0.68 \qquad g^{\star} = 4.08\% \qquad \pi^{\star} = 4\% \tag{13.11}$$

The corresponding reference value of the debt-asset ratio amounts to $\lambda^{\star} = 34.3\%$. The order of magnitude of $\beta^{\star}$ and $g^{\star}$ is already known from (13.7), $\pi^{\star}$ is deliberately chosen.

In complete analogy to scenario 13.2, we distinguish scenario 13.3a and 13.3b. In 13.3a simply $\pi(t) = \pi^{\star}$ is hypothesized. To establish scenario 13.3b, three steps are taken. First, the ragged quarter-to-quarter rates of inflation are slightly smoothed by a cubic moving average extending over five quarters.[17] Second, the (nonconstant) trend is determined. To capture the general increase of inflation in the seventies, the simple regression approach of a polynomial of third degree is employed (higher degrees are unnecessary). According to this method, the trend rate of capital price inflation steadily rises from 0.42% in 1960:4 to a maximum of 9.06% in 1977:3. The ensuing decline is faster, though in 1982:4 it is still at 5.9%.[18] Actual inflation, however, reaches its peak value in 1974:4 with 20.6%. The two series are graphically displayed in the middle window of figure 13.3.

Third, deviations from trend are calculated. Calling them $\psi(t)$, we finally set $\pi(t) = \pi^{\star} + \psi(t)$ in this scenario.

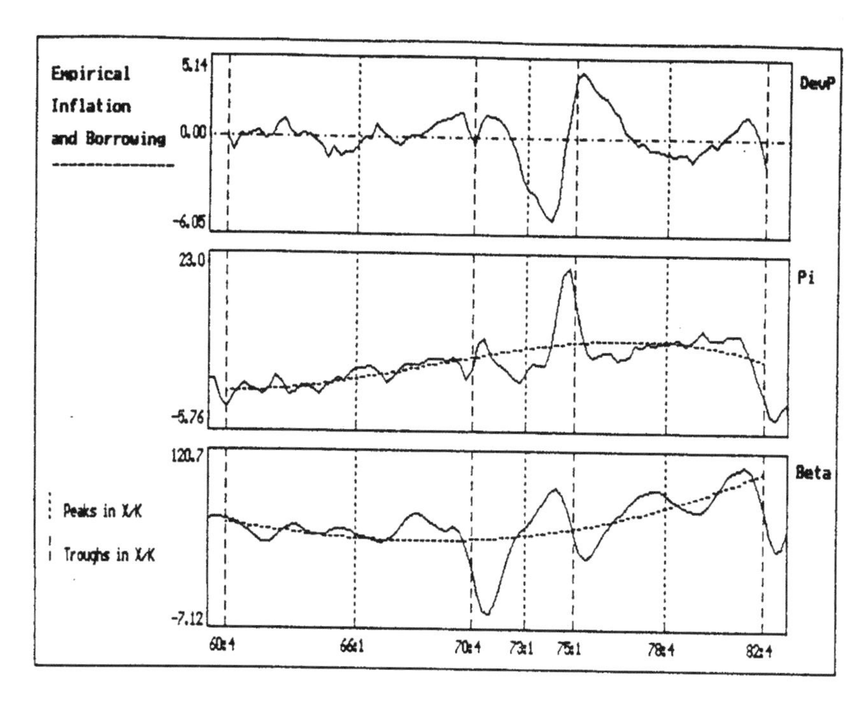

Figure 13.3
Empirical time series of inflation and borrowing. DevP: deviations of $100 \cdot \ln P$ from trend; Pi: rate of inflation π (in %) with trend line; Beta: leverage ratio β (in %) with trend line

On the basis of these inflation time series and another one of the real capital stock K, construction of the debt-asset ratio proceeds as follows. Time is running from $t = t_o = 60.75$ to $t = 82.75$, in steps of $\Delta t = 0.25$. To begin with capital prices, we normalize $p_o = p(t_o) = 1$ and iteratively compute

$$p(t + 0.25) = [1 + \pi(t)]^{1/4} p(t)$$

Net investment during period t in monetary terms is given by $p(t)[K(t + 0.25) - K(t)]$. After choosing an initial value λ_o slightly below $\lambda^\star$, namely, $\lambda_o = \lambda^\star - 0.5\%$, and putting $\Lambda(t_o) = \lambda_o p_o K(t_o)$, loans are determined by

$$\Lambda(t + 0.25) = \Lambda(t) + \beta^\star p(t)[K(t + 0.25) - K(t)] \tag{13.12}$$

It then remains to calculate

$$\lambda(t) = \Lambda(t)/p(t)K(t) \tag{13.13}$$

The time series of the debt-asset ratio for the two scenarios obtained in this way are depicted in figure 13.2. The phenomenon that appears from the mid-sixties on, that λ stays in both cases above $\lambda^\star$, has its origin in the shorter duration of the two cycles from 1970 to 1982 and the smaller amplitude of the capital growth rate, in comparison to the long and distinctive cycle over the sixties (of course, other things being equal, λ would eventually be attracted by $\lambda^\star$ and would fluctuate around it after a sufficient lapse of time). The succession of turning points relative to the peaks and troughs in economic activity, as characterized by the (detrended) output-capital ratio, is similar to the reference oscillations of figure 13.1. At least over the last two cycles this also holds for the earlier occurrence of the turning points in scenario 13.3b, with its price fluctuations. The high and low swings of this hypothetical λ in the first half of the seventies are caused by the extreme deviations of the inflation rate from its trend. With due delay they carry over to the level of prices, which is drawn in the upper panel of figure 13.3. From 1970 to 1982 the trend deviations are indeed broadly countercyclical, just as pointed out by equation (13.10) in scenario 13.2b.[19] Since variations in prices are much stronger than in the stock of loans, the high deviations of prices find their direct, mirror-imaged expression in the time series of λ.

A comparison of figures 13.2 and 13.3 thus shows the qualitative and quantitative impact of the oscillations in capital growth and inflation on the movements of the debt-asset ratio when we abstract from trend effects. They reveal the interplay of the cyclical features of g, π and λ. Information of this kind can be useful for evaluating the cyclical dynamics of a stock measure of leverage in macroeconomic models with the notion of an unstable steady-state equilibrium position.

13.4 The Dynamics of the Capital Structure: Trend Variations

Scenario 13.4 This scenario extends scenario 13.3 by dropping the hypothesis of a constant trend rate of inflation. Constancy of the leverage ratio $\beta = \beta^\star$ is preserved. We also keep on holding the trend rate of capital growth fixed, here as well as in the next section. The reason is that the long-term changes in $\pi^\star$ are much stronger than those of $g^\star$ (see scenario 13.3 and note 17), while their impact on $\lambda^\star$ is the same (cf. the elasticities in equation (13.3)).

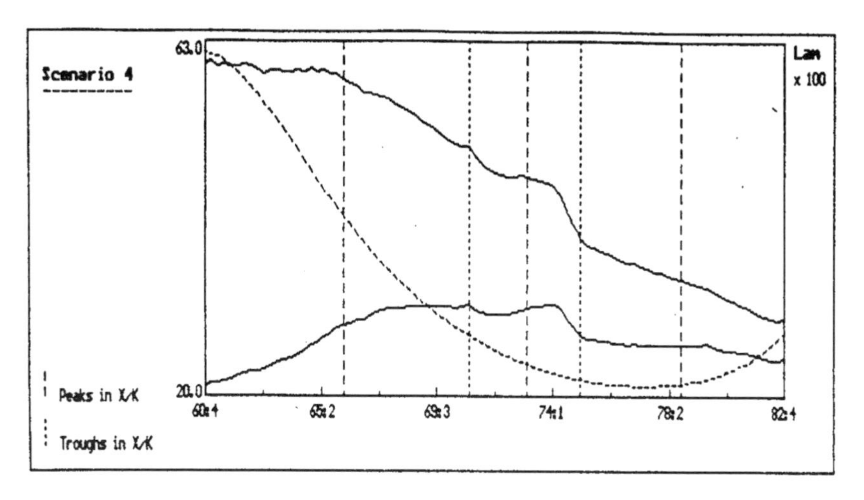

Figure 13.4
Motions of the debt-asset ratio (Lam = λ) in scenario 4 resulting from two distinct starting points (solid lines); the dashed line represents $\lambda^\star(t)$

In constructing loans by way of equation (13.12), here, the empirical capital prices can be used directly. Of course, λ is again obtained from equation (13.13). To understand the resulting time path, the reference value $\lambda^\star$ of equation (13.2) is of crucial importance. The present scenario is the first example where it is varying over time.The value $\pi^\star = \pi^\star(t)$ being the trend rate of inflation whose determination was described in scenario 13.3b, and $g^\star$ and $\beta^\star$ assuming the constant numerical values of equation (13.11), $\lambda^\star$ reads $\lambda^\star = \lambda^\star(t) = g^\star\beta^\star/[g^\star + \pi^\star(t)]$. This series is plotted as the dashed line in figure 13.4. It is an immediate reflection of the concave trend line of $\pi^\star(t)$ in figure 13.3, only the mirror image of it and on a different scale. It demonstrates the high sensitivity of the reference debt-asset ratio with respect to inflation. Owing to the low values of $\pi^\star$, it begins at 61.6% in 1960:4. The minimum is reached in 1977:3 with 21.1%. Falling inflation then raises it to 27.7% in 1982:4.

As for the initial value of λ in t_o = 1960:4, two polar cases are considered, $\lambda_o = 60\%$ and $\lambda_o = 21\%$ (21%, instead of the straighter 20%, only for graphical reasons). The outcome is shown by the solid lines in figure 13.4. Visually, some of the cyclical features of the previous two scenarios are still present, but, on the large scale given by the path of $\lambda^\star(t)$, they are clearly dominated by a trend phenomenon. We can recognize them in the middle cycle because of the extreme fluctuations of the inflation rate in this period. If they can be partly recognized in the first cycle, then this is due to the underlying marked upswing in the capital growth rate. Any cyclical remainders after 1975 seem almost completely washed out. The main is reason is that when λ begins to fall in 1979 in figure 13.2, this is now counteracted by the rising trend of inflation.

By contrast, the apparent trend behavior of $\lambda(t)$, as we may call it, is explained by the long-distance effect of the reference series $\lambda^\star(t)$ and thus, indirectly, by trend inflation. That is, $\lambda^\star$ is attractive, although it is no longer fixed. Furthermore, in accordance with the above examples, the corresponding adjustments are rather hesitating. The changes, over the medium-run, in this scenario's actual debt-asset ratio are consequently less dramatic than the ones in $\lambda^\star(t)$. By the same token, significant overshooting can also be observed. This means in particular that computing a statistical trend of $\lambda(t)$ and of the reference ratio $\lambda^\star(t)$ will give rise to two very distinct series. As for the former, it would probably be quite difficult to give a not-too-complicated rule for a continuous trend line such that the defined trend deviations resemble those in figure 13.2.

Scenario 13.5 It is now time to also have the leverage ratio β varying over the observation period. When using the statistical sources it has to be taken into account that, in the present context, funds are raised for the sole purpose of investment financing. In the appendix we describe a procedure of constructing such a hypothetical series. Owing to data restrictions, it is an annual one. To transform it to a quarterly series we apply a cubic moving average extending over nine quarters.[20] This is our empirical approximation for $\beta = \beta(t)$. It clearly turns out to be nonstationary in the long run. The corresponding trend series $\beta^\star(t)$, which has to be substituted in equation (13.2) to determine the now appropriate reference debt-asset ratio $\lambda^\star(t)$, is computed from a simple polynomial regression of third degree. Both series $\beta(t)$ and $\beta^\star(t)$ are displayed in the bottom window of figure 13.3.

The trend line $\beta^\star(t)$ declines from 68.4% in 1960:4 to roughly 55% in 1968 and 1969, and then steadily rises up to a level of even more than 100% at the end of the observation period (106% in 1982:4).[21] The diagram indicates that the upward motion continues thereafter. As alluded to in the introductory section, this might reflect credit expansion due to leverage buyout and financial reorganization of firms (at least, this factor is mentioned in a number of recent empirical studies). In particular, the two assumptions that are underlying our construction of $\beta(t)$ are now probably much too stylized to be compatible with these developments. For a first investigation of the debt-asset dynamics under trend variations in the leverage ratio, however, the present series may suffice.

With respect to deviations of $\beta(t)$ from the trend line, indications of a weak cyclical pattern can be recognized. Lower turning points of $\beta(t)$ occur shortly after the troughs in utilization, while the maxima are attained not too long before.[22] This feature might suggest a juxtaposition with (nominal) interest rates since they seem to exhibit a qualitatively similar behavior over the cycle, though with different lags. When we disregard the first half of the seventies (and, of course, the development after 1982), the amplitudes between the various ups and downs of β are not very different over the twenty years. Maximal deviations lie between 10 and 20 percentage points.

The impact of our estimated leverage ratio on the evolution of the debt-asset ratio is shown in figure 13.5. In comparing, first, the reference ratio $\lambda^\star(t)$ to that of figure 13.4 we see how the increase in the trend series $\beta^\star(t)$ (bottom panel of figure 13.3) from the mid-seventies on leads to a sharp rise in $\lambda^\star(t)$. The lower turning point of $\lambda^\star$ shifts accordingly backward in time. By contrast, the introduction of the variable leverage ratio has not essentially changed the long-term relationship between $\lambda^\star(t)$ and the actual ratio $\lambda(t)$ generated in this scenario. That is, $\lambda^\star(t)$ exerts the same kind of attraction, and the speed of convergence is about the same.

The starting points of the time paths of $\lambda(t)$ are identical in figures 13.4 and 13.5. The oscillations of $\beta(t)$ improve the cyclical features of $\lambda(t)$ considerably. This effect can be gathered from the dotted lines that have been obtained by replacing $\beta = \beta(t)$ with $\beta^\star = \beta^\star(t)$ in computing $\lambda(t)$. Again, however, there is probably no simple rule to construct a trend line of the two $\lambda(t)$ such that the resulting trend deviations would stand out as clearly as, say, the oscillations in figure 13.1. To sum up, despite the wider fluctuations in the leverage ratio over the business cycle, the trend phenomena continue to dominate the cycle characteristics.

13.5 Conclusion

To summarize our analysis of the debt dynamics of the differential equation (13.1), we point out the following results and suggestions. We hope they prove helpful in financial factor macrodynamic modeling.

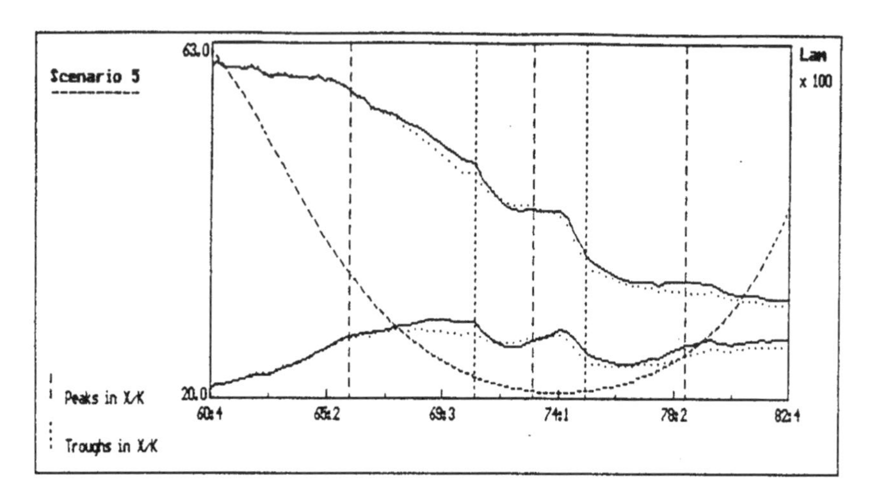

Figure 13.5
Motions of the debt-asset ratio (Lam = λ) in scenario 5 resulting from two distinct starting points (solid lines); underlying the dotted lines is $\beta^*(t)$, instead of $\beta(t)$; the dashed line represents $\lambda^*(t)$

The cyclical characteristics of the debt-asset ratio λ motions are best studied by freezing all trend variables at constant values and assuming regular oscillations in the rates of inflation π and capital growth g. The corresponding equilibrium notion of equation (13.1) is then not a single stationary point but an entire time path of reference oscillations around a constant reference value λ^*. In addition, if the actual leverage ratio is also fixed, $\beta = \beta^*$, it could be shown that they are attractive. Comparing the succession of turning points, we find that λ is still rising when the accumulation of capital begins to falter. Hence, what at first sight appears to be a threat of financial distress is no more than a direct consequence of the cyclical fluctuations in g and π. We conclude from this example that one has to be very careful in employing stock measures of indebtedness to characterize financial tightness of firms within a cyclical context.

If a macroeconomic model with the usual notion of a steady-state position introduces β^* as well as λ^* as parameters, or target values, in some of the behavioral functions, then it also has to take into consideration the systematic relationship between the stock and the flow measure of indebtedness as it is made explicit in equation (13.2). If the trend variables g^*, π^*, and/or β^* vary over time, they induce changes in the reference debt-asset ratio λ^*. Nevertheless, λ^* continues to be a now moving center of gravitation. As in the earlier simpler scenarios, however, the speed of convergence is rather low.

Empirically, changes in trend inflation had the strongest impact on $\lambda^\star$. Over the observation period they brought about variations of $\lambda^\star$ between 20 and 60 percent—with respect to a constant trend value of the leverage ratio $\beta^\star$. In reality, the latter also experienced significant changes. They carry over to $\lambda^\star$, but the extreme variations in $\lambda^\star$ originate in the trend inflation.

The fast changes in the reference value of the debt-asset ratio and its attractiveness imply that the cyclical features in the movements of the actual debt-asset ratio (in the respective scenarios) are dominated by some sort of trend behavior. Owing to the slow speed of convergence, however, the trend behavior is quite distinct from that of $\lambda^\star$. In particular, this easily gives rise to an overshooting phenomenon. Nevertheless, it should not be forgotten that in the end the long-term behavior of $\lambda(t)$ is explained by the time path of $\lambda^\star(t)$. Insofar as an increase in $\pi^\star$ diminishes $\lambda^\star$, and by virtue of its attractiveness the evolution of $\lambda^\star$ determines the long-term behavior of λ itself, high inflation rates exert a downward pressure on the debt-asset ratio. This contrasts what was expected in Feldstein, Green, and Sheshinski 1978. Now, it can be argued in greater detail that rising (decreasing) inflation causes the flow leverage ratio β to rise (fall), so that inflation has a positive effect on λ through this channel. A comparison of the trend series of π and β in figure 13.3, however, shows a lack of evidence for this mechanism. Similarly, a positive feedback of the trend growth rate of capital $g^\star$ on the leverage ratio is not supported, either, by our processing of the data. If anything, $g^\star$ rises in the sixties and falls in the seventies, whereas the opposite is true for $\beta^\star$.

The variable that appears to contribute most to a still visible cyclicity in λ is the leverage ratio β. This and the earlier result that β is a better characterization of the financing structure over the business cycle than λ itself, draws attention to the empirical fluctuations of β around its trend line, which shows weak indications of a certain regularity. Although possible tax effects were not taken into account, these ups and downs can hardly be attributed to the actual variations in the tax structure. In fact, in this respect there were more long-term trends in the postwar period (see Summers 1981, 79, table 2). Therefore, the position referring to the changes in the tax structure, as mentioned in the introduction, is evidently not appropriate for a theoretical explanation of the motions of the leverage ratio.[23]

The other two approaches seem more promising. With respect to (simple) macroeconomic modeling, considerations of the hierarchy of financial instruments may suggest a functional dependency of β upon some other system variables, while Minskian lines of reasoning may have to refer to a general state of confidence as determinant of the leverage ratio. This aside, model builders may wish to establish a close connection between the rate of interest and the leverage ratio; or between other important factors such as the interest-coverage ratio or acceptable debt-capacity. In our opinion, working on a synthesis of these elements is a fruitful perspective of future research. If these kinds of factors indeed turned out to be more or less linked to economic activity, or for that matter, to capital growth, and the interest rate also exhibited a "realistic" cyclical pattern, then such an approach would at least not contradict our reconstruction of the leverage ratio (see figure 13.3). Additional empirical work is needed to support this view, however. This work should preferably take place at more disaggregated levels.

In general we can conclude that, contrasted with the theoretical literature alluded to in the first section, which leaves us with a considerable ambiguity on the long-term determination of the capital structure, the pragmatic and more empirically oriented approach advanced in this chapter has an important advantage. It allows us to decompose the debt-asset ratio into cyclical as well as long-term components, both of which can be treated in a hypothetical, stylized way and subjected to empirical analysis. In addition, the method that we employed here for U.S. data can immediately be applied to other countries, which may raise new questions regarding the present results. Lastly, the method proposed here could even prove useful in studying other macroeconomic variables, for example, the evolution of household, government, or foreign debt.

13.6 Appendix

Construction of the Leverage Ratio β

The following annual time series are used. The first five are taken from B-92 of the Economic Report of the President (1988), the last one is from the Flow of Funds Accounts (1989), Tables 22–25.

GI	gross investment
D	depreciation
ΔF	change in financial assets
UP	domestic undistributed profits
ES	external sources
EI	equity issuance

Our starting point is the budget identity of firms,

$$\text{Uses} = GI + \Delta F = UP + D + ES = \text{Sources}$$

(where it is assumed that profits UP are net of interest payments). Writing NI for net investment in the following, $NI = GI - D$, defining $BOR =$ Borrowing $= ES - EI$, and subtracting $EI + D$ on both sides of the equation, one has

$$\Delta F + (NI - EI) = UP + BOR$$

We employ two assumptions. According to the first one, which is already indicated by the brackets, equities are exclusively issued for expansion of real capital. Thus, undistributed profits and borrowing have to cover the increase in financial assets and this finance gap of investment, $NI - EI$. For lack of more specific information, our second assumption says that this is done in equal proportions. That is, defining

$$\alpha := \Delta F/(UP + BOR)$$

we get

$$NI - EI = (1 - \alpha)(UP + BOR)$$

By construction, the fraction $1 - \alpha$ of total borrowing is used for investment finance. It therefore remains to put

$$\beta = (1 - \alpha)BOR/NI$$

Proof of the Stability Proposition in section 13.3 With respect to functions (13.5) and (13.6), write (13.1) as

$$\begin{aligned} \dot{\lambda} &= \beta^{\star}[g^{\star} + h_g(t)] - [g^{\star} + \pi^{\star} + h_g(t) + h_{\pi}(t)]\lambda(t) \\ &= b(t) \qquad\qquad\qquad + \ a(t)\lambda(t) \end{aligned}$$

The general solution of this linear differential equation, with respect to the initial condition $\lambda = \lambda_o$ at time $t = t_o$, is given by

$$\lambda(t;\lambda_o,t_o)=\exp\left(\int_{t_o}^{t}a(s)\,ds\right)\cdot\left[\lambda_o+\int_{t_o}^{t}b(s)\exp\left(-\int_{t_o}^{s}a(s)\,ds\right)\,ds\right]$$

Defining

$$A(s):=\int_0^s[h_g(u)+h_\pi(u)]\,du$$

we can write

$$\int_0^s a(u)\,du=-\int_0^s[(g^\star+\pi^\star)+h_g(u)+h_\pi(u)]\,du=-(g^\star+\pi^\star)s-A(s)$$

and

$$\lambda(t;\lambda_o,t_o)=\exp[-(g^\star+\pi^\star)t-A(t)]\cdot\left\{\lambda_o+\beta^\star g^\star\int_0^t\exp[(g^\star+\pi^\star)s+A(s)]\,ds\right.$$
$$\left.+\,\beta^\star\int_0^t h_g(s)\exp[(g^\star+\pi^\star)s+A(s)]\,ds\right\}$$

By virtue of equation (13.6), $A(\cdot)$ is a periodic function with period T. In particular, $A(kT)=0$ for all natural numbers k. Setting $t_o=0$, which can be done without loss of generality, we have

$$\lambda(kT;\lambda_o,0)=\exp[-(g^\star+\pi^\star)kT]\cdot\left\{\lambda_o+\beta^\star g^\star\int_0^{kT}\exp[(g^\star+\pi^\star)s+A(s)]\,ds\right.$$
$$\left.+\beta^\star\int_0^{kT}h_g(s)\exp[(g^\star+\pi^\star)s+A(s)]\,ds\right\}$$
$$=\exp[-(g^\star+\pi^\star)kT]\cdot[\lambda_o+B_1(kT)+B_2(kT)]$$

in obvious notation. Since $\exp[-(g^\star+\pi^\star)kT]\lambda_o\to 0$ as $k\to\infty$ (of course, independently of λ_o), we have to show that $\exp[-(g^\star+\pi^\star)kT]$ $B_1(kT)$ and $\exp[-(g^\star+\pi^\star)kT]B_2(kT)$ both converge to a finite limit. To this end, define

$$C:=\int_0^T\exp[(g^\star+\pi^\star)u+A(u)]\,du$$

and consider the expression

$$
\begin{aligned}
&(1/\beta^\star g^\star)\exp[-(g^\star+\pi^\star)kT]B_1(kT)\\
&\quad=\exp[-(g^\star+\pi^\star)kT]\int_0^{kT}\exp[(g^\star+\pi^\star)s+A(s)]\,ds\\
&\quad=\sum_{m=0}^{k-1}\exp[-(g^\star+\pi^\star)kT]\int_{mT}^{(m+1)T}\exp[(g^\star+\pi^\star)s+A(s)]\,ds\\
&\quad=\sum_{m=0}^{k-1}\exp[-(g^\star+\pi^\star)(k-m)T]\int_{mT}^{(m+1)T}\exp[(g^\star+\pi^\star)(s-mT)+A(s)]\,ds\\
&\quad=\sum_{m=0}^{k-1}\exp[-(g^\star+\pi^\star)(k-m)T]\int_0^{T}\exp[(g^\star+\pi^\star)u+A(u+mT)]\,du\\
&\quad=\sum_{m=0}^{k-1}\exp[-(g^\star+\pi^\star)(k-m)T]\int_0^{T}\exp[(g^\star+\pi^\star)u+A(u)]\,du\\
&\quad=C\cdot\sum_{m=0}^{k-1}e^{-(g^\star+\pi^\star)(k-m)T}
\end{aligned}
$$

(the fourth equality follows from a change of variables in the integral, the fifth since $A(\cdot)$ is periodic). It is seen that the constant C is multiplied by a geometric series $(a_1+a_2+\cdots+a_k)$ with members $a_n = e^{-n(g^\star+\pi^\star)T}$ and $a_n/a_{n-1}=e^{-(g^\star+\pi^\star)T}<1$. Hence, it is convergent, and the term $\exp[-(g^\star+\pi^\star)kT]B_1(kT)$ tends to a finite limit as $k\to\infty$. The argument for $\exp[-(g^\star+\pi^\star)kT]B_2(kT)$ reads exactly the same. We can thus conclude that, independently of λ_o, the sequence $\{\lambda(kT;\lambda_o,0)\}$ converges to a finite limit as $k\to\infty$, which completes the proof.

q.e.d.

14 Conclusions

Most of the work undertaken here represents aggregate analysis in the non-market-clearing disequilibrium tradition. Although macroeconomics has shifted toward intertemporal equilibrium models with strong assumptions on market clearing and information about future decision variables, our aggregate analysis, building on disequilibria in markets and adjustment mechanisms, stays in an (extended) IS-LM macroeconomics framework by integrating short-, medium- and long-run analysis of monetary economics in the tradition of Keynesian theory. Such perspective was pursued from the demand side by Tobin and by Stein, Rose, and Sargent from the supply side of Keynesian monetary macrodynamics.

To contrast our approach with market-clearing intertemporal models, we have included a chapter dealing with Ramsey optimal growth infinite horizon economics. It appears that those two frameworks, the temporary non-market-clearing disequilibrium analysis and the intertemporal approach of optimal growth, do not mix well. In fact, attempts to mix those two variants will create inconsistencies as when, for example, the AD-AS model with perfect foresight jump variable technique is used in place of an IS-LM framework, as also noted by Barro (1994). We have abstained from the Sargent-Wallace perfect foresight jump variable procedure in macromodels which results in money neutrality in the short as well in the long run. This jump variable technique has been employed in the study of the price level, prices in future markets, foreign exchange, and stock markets (see Turnosky 1995). We returned to gradual adjustments in prices and expectations by referring predominantly to the adaptive expectations formation mechanisms. By this method we hope to have reintroduced expectations into traditional macrodynamic models in a more plausible and consistent way.

Our work has extended the disequilibrium type of internally consistent macromodels to an analysis of fluctuating growth with or without mypoic perfect foresight (in chapters 8 and 9), and it has introduced and investigated new types of IS-LM growth models with emphasis on the labor and asset markets (chapters 11 and 12). These chapters in particular show that the IS-LM method is in fact of a very general type, meaning that goods and asset markets equilibria of various types can be investigated for gradually adjusting wages and prices in a growing economy. The outcome is frequently a theory of cyclical over- or underemployment of labor *and* capital services that generally does not converge to market-clearing values and the steady state.

In pursuing this perspective we have stressed sources of instability in monetary economies traditionally emphasized by Keynesian theory. Putting forward realistic models where instability is contained, however, requires us to work with a variety of nonlinear mechanisms. This view was adopted for nonmarket-clearing models regarding micro as well as macro adjustment mechanisms. This approach can help to explain strong propagation mechanisms of shocks and the variability of macroeconomic time series data.

We have applied standard tools from modern dynamic analysis to analytically study the dynamics, yet our book does not focus on tools but rather employs them to analyze particular issues and problems. Our dynamic macroeconomic systems are often of a higher order, so that the dynamics can be discussed only partially analytically and partially numerically. Dynamic macro analysis will increasingly need to rely on such an analytical/numerical approach. We hope that we have shown how to make such an approach useful.

Empirically, we have attempted to match the time series data from our dynamic models with the stylized facts mentioned in the introductory chapter. When doing so we have focused particularly on the behavior of the macroenomic variables over the business cycle. Besides long-run ratios, we have attempted to confront our models with data concerning frequency, if cycles occur, and amplitude and asymmetry in the movement of the variables. In the last two chapters we have also discussed high- and low-frequency movements, for example, with respect to the financial structure of firms. However, there is certainly still much work to be undertaken. In the above attempts we were successful only along some dimensions, not others. One also needs more sophisticated dynamic econometric methods to match the models' and the actual time series' data. Recent development in dynamic econometrics, alluded to in chapter 1, give us some hope to be more successful in this undertaking in the future.

We did not extensively discuss the government sector and fiscal and monetary policy. Certainly, chapters 6 and 7 on price flexibility and instability, and chapters 8 and 9 on an extended IS-LM framework with the wage-price and expectations dynamics, have implications for fiscal and monetary policies, but we did not elaborate specifically on those issues. The models in chapters 4 and 5 also have long-run implications for growth policies. Although we sporadically discussed government bonds we did not model budget deficits and government debt (though chapters 4 and 5 provide frameworks for a long-run perspective and chapters 8 and 9 for the medium-run business cycle perspective). Moreover, evolution of government debt can be empirically studied by employing the methodology presented in chapter 13. Finally, we want to note what the book has completely left aside. By pursuing nonmarket-clearing disequilibrium macroeconomics, we did not elaborate on the different Keynesian schools, in particular the rationing school. The latter has not really attempted to integrate growth in macromodels. Moreover, as known, various rationing schemes make the equilibria ambiguous.[1] We also abstained from issues in open economy macrodynamics, for example, modeling the relation between exchange rate, output, and prices. We also did not model in detail the financial sector with more than two assets and how it interacts with the real side including an IS framework. These examples are very useful extensions for future research. We are currently undertaking some work on these issues but have not included this material here.

Notes

Preface

1. It was Richard Day who brought to our attention that Walras's process of *tâtonnement* should actually be translated as "groping in the dark." Tâtonnement has its etymological origin, as does the German word "tasten," in the Latin word "taxare," later changed to "tastare," which means to search for something blindly.

Chapter 1

1. See Boldrin and Montrucchio 1986; Boldrin and Woodford 1990; and Boldrin 1994.

2. Imperfect markets (capital markets), learning mechanisms, and externalities may lead to nonlinear dynamics and chaotic motions with more realistic parameter sets (see Boldrin and Woodford 1990; Brock, Hsie, and LeBaron 1991). Thus, it generically appears to hold that only if the presumptions of concave return functions and convex technologies are abandoned, complex dynamics of the optimal trajectories are more likely to arise—although no optimal growth model with completely satisfying parametrization has been presented yet (see Boldrin 1994).

3. We would like to note that there are, of course, diverse traditions which are more or less viewed as Keynesian. Some of these views will not be discussed here, for example, the structuralist approach to macroeconomics (Taylor 1983; and Dutt 1990) or post-Keynesians (Minsky 1975, 1986). We hope that our characterizations are roughly correct, although we know that there may be exceptions to our description of essentials for a nonmarket-clearing approach. We also want to remark that subsequently we will primarily refer only to that type of work in the nonmarket-clearing tradition that has led to more formal studies of dynamic macroeconomics.

4. See, for example, Klein 1971; Fair 1984; Tobin 1994; and Mankiw 1990. Note that Keynesian disequilibrium nonmarket-clearing situations requiring price and/or quantity adjustments are also conceivable in the context of intertemporal models. (See Woodford 1994, 1996.)

5. See Canova 1992.

6. See, for example, Prescott 1986.

7. See Stadler (1994 for a survey of recent empirical evaluations of RBC models. Also models that rely on lags or costs of adjusting labor input are only partially successful. A careful investigation is provided by Cogley and Nason (1995).

8. See, for example, Blanchard and Fischer 1989, Ch.1.

9. We want to note, however, that we do not address the rationing school in Keynesian macroeconomics where predominantly quantities, not prices, adjust to bring about a temporary equilibrium with rationing (see, for example, Benassy 1986). This type of work has by and large not been applied to study dynamic macroeconomics for growing economies.

10. See the tradition of Rose (1990), Stein (1982), and Sargent (1987).

11. Barro remarks: "The AD curve reflects the underlying IS/LM model, and the key to this model is the presence of excess supply of goods and services . . . . In contrast, in the AS-AD model . . . the adjustment of the price level . . . eliminates the excess supply of goods . . . . Firms are, in particular, always able to sell whatever they wish at the going price level: they are not constrained by aggregate demand"(Barro 1994, 3).

12. This model is considered in a dynamic setup in chap. 6 of the book.

13. Note that the jump variable technique in the context of an IS-LM model is also applied in the Dornbusch (1976) exchange rate model and in Blanchard (1981) macroeconomic asset pricing model.

14. For a survey of nonlinear models in Keynesian economics, see Lorenz (1993).

15. See Day 1994, and for a macromodel, Day and Shafer 1987.

16. On the role of lags for chaos, see Medio 1991.

17. For presentations of those new methods, see Tong 1990, Granger and Teräsvirta 1993, and the papers by Mittnik, Mizrach, Potter, Rothman, and Sayers in Semmler 1994.

18. A second index designates a partial derivative with respect to the corresponding variable (thus, a double index does *not* represent cross-derivatives; they play no role in this book).

Chapter 2

1. See Tobin 1980, 1994; Mankiw 1990; Blanchard and Fischer 1989, chapters 8 and 9. Note that the problem of price and quantity adjustments may also arise in intertemporal models. See Woodford (1994, 1996).

2. There are three main approaches to the theory of price rigidity: (1) Prices are sluggishly adjusted because of suboptimal behavior of firms (Akerlof and Yellen 1985), (2) prices are changed in discrete steps because of adjustment cost; firms, for example, face menu cost when adjusting prices toward their optimal level (Ball, Mankiw, and Romer 1988), (3) firms choose to adjust quantities rather than price if there are imbalances in product markets because price adjustments may result in greater uncertainty concerning profit flows than quantity adjustments (Greenwald and Stiglitz 1988).

3. An extensive coverage of new Keynesians' views on this matter is provided in Blanchard and Fischer 1989, chaps. 7–9.

4. A verbal discussion can be found in Smith (1974, chap. 7), Ricardo (1951, chap. 4), Marx (1967, chap. 10), Walras (1977, chaps. 12 and 18) and Marshall (1947, chaps. 3 and 5).

5. See in particular Goodwin 1953; Morishima 1959, 1976, 1977.

6. In the book we will, however, leave aside the integral control.

7. See Morishima 1976, 1977.

8. See Hicks 1965, 82; and Kaldor 1985.

9. Though there is considerable doubt whether the above dual dynamics can really be found in Keynes's "General Theory," the Keynesian Revolution is usually associated with it, as Hicks (1965, 77) already mentions. Leijonhufvud (1968, 24) goes a step further than Hicks and suggests that the "General Theory" represents "a systematic analysis of the behavior of a system that reacts to disturbances through 'quantity adjustments' rather than through price-level or wage adjustments."

10. See Hicks 1965 and Kaldor 1985.

11. See, for example, Stein 1982 and Rose 1990.

12. For a further characterization of such cross-effects, see chap. 5.

13. Since price inflation can then be identified with wage inflation under these circumstances.

14. Where the price mechanism works with infinite speed.

Chapter 3

1. The material of this chapter is based on Flaschel 1991.

2. A more detailed treatment and analysis of this process, but one that is still based on partial equilibrium reasoning, can be found in Beckmann and Ryder 1969; see also Mas-Colell 1986, 64–67.

3. Note here that profits Π are neglected in Mas-Colell's (1986, 64) disequilibrium analysis. This contrasts the Arrow-Debreu general equilibrium model of a private ownership economy where the profits expected by firms are part of the budget perceived by households.

4. Note, however, that our stability results of section 3.3 below can also be applied to points of rest with $L''(Y^\star) < 0$ (which are no equilibria, since profits are at minimum here). These points of rest are of importance in the literature on public utilities and marginal cost pricing, but will not be considered in this chapter.

5. See Flaschel and Semmler 1987 for the classical roots of Walras' process of groping for production economies.

6. Which can be shown to be finite in number under simple additional conditions, cf. Dierker (1974, chaps. 1, 10) for details.

7. Which in this case is independent of adjustment speeds (D-stability).

8. In the case of $d_p > 0$, the second adjustment coefficient β_y must be chosen sufficiently large in order to obtain local asymptotic stability (if $L''(Y^\star) > 0$ holds true).

9. The dynamics are formulated in terms of gross outputs Y in this general case.

10. Note here, however, that one has to distinguish now between activity levels X and net outputs Y and that the *WA*-condition of proposition 1 is only "close" to the condition of 'NQD' that Mas-Colell actually employs.

11. The pure price adjustment process is—as we know—stable in the latter case.

12. $\det J = \beta_p \beta_y (1 - d'(p^\star) L''(Y^\star)) = \beta_p \beta_y (1 - d'(p^\star) \cdot c_2)$ is then always positive ($1/c_2 > d'(p^\star)$).

13. See, for example, Hirsch and Smale 1974 for a detailed presentation and proof of this theorem on closed orbits of planar vector fields.

14. The function is rotated around the middle steady state, if more than one equilibrium exists.

15. Parameter values are: $\beta_p = \beta_y = 1, c_2 = 0.77$ (figure to the left) and $c_2 = 0.5$ (figure to the right).

16. This limit cycle situation can also be used to study the case of a fast or even infinitely fast price dynamics, that is, β_p large. The above example then gives rise to nearly horizontal price adjustments whenever prices happen not to be close to the $Y = d(p)$-isocline. Except for such pretty fast traverses we consequently have it that the movement of prices and quantities is near to the $\dot{p} = 0$-isocline where the goods market is in equilibrium. Yet, due to price-cost differentials output keeps expanding (on the right-hand side of this isocline) and is contracting (on its left-hand side) until it reaches the critical point where the demand curve bends backwards (becomes positively sloped). The possibility of a right-hand respectively left-hand goods-market equilibrium then disappears, and there follows a rapid decrease respectively increase (or jump) of goods-market prices that restores goods-market equilibrium on the left respectively right part of the demand schedule. Such limiting cycles, so-called relaxation oscillations, are described in their details in Arrowsmith and Place 1982. Note that a very rapid adjustment of quantities does not give rise to similar observations.

17. See Wiggins 1990, section 3.1 for a detailed presentation of this theorem and its various subcases.

18. A stable limit cycle here collapses into a stable steady state as β_y is increased; see Wiggins 1990, 273ff. for a graphical representation of such a situation.

19. See again Wiggins 1990, fig. 3.1.11 for the graphical representation of such bifurcations.

20. See Wiggins 1990, 277 and Lux 1992, 189 for the involved calculations that imply the existence of a super- or subcritical Hopf bifurcation (which in general are complex).

21. The Debreu-Sonnenschein theorem states that the microeconomic axioms such as Walras's Law and continuity of demand functions do not put sufficient restrictions on market (excess) demand functions. Therefore, any market dynamics are admissible. For details see, for example, Dierker 1974; Mas-Colell 1985.

22. See Flaschel and Semmler 1987 for details.

23. See in particular Morishima 1977.

24. The adjustment speeds may, however, have an impact on the basins of attraction in the case of multiple equilibria.

25. The Walrasian, or classical, substructure is purely oscillatory because there are only purely imaginary eigenvalues.

26. The details of these assertions are worked out in Flaschel and Semmler 1988 and 1990 for dynamic Leontief input-output models.

27. Which could not be handled by the approach chosen in Flaschel and Semmler 1987 because of the choice of the Liapunov function there employed.

28. See Flaschel 1991, 19 for the general case of a multicommodity Walrasian economy with production.

29. Note here that the slope at points of rest in the lower part of figure 3.6 is given by $\frac{F'(p^*)}{1-\gamma F'(p^*)}$ which must be negative for each γ larger than $\frac{1}{F'(p^*)}$. This holds both for $F' < 0$ and $F' > 0$.

30. All propositions presented in the following hold also for multiproduct general equilibrium models as they are formulated in Mas-Colell 1986.

31. Note here that any finite set of equilibria can be made simultaneously stable in this way by choosing the parameters γ_i appropriately large.

32. Cf. Hirsch and Smale 1974, 193.

33. We know, however, of no reference where such a nonlocal type of Liapunov function is considered and where an exact proof for the mathematical part of this proposition is spelled out.

34. The demand function is now given by $d(p) = a_1 p + a_2$ and is chosen such that it runs through the equilibrium point $(13, 24.26)$ with slope .97. The other parameter values are again given by $\beta_p = \beta_y = 1, c_2 = .5$.

35. Since macrosystems are often based on growth rate formulations rather than on simple time derivatives, it is important to know that the assertions on derivative control also hold for such growth rate systems

$$\hat{z} = F(z) + <\gamma> \overbrace{F(z)}^{\cdot}.$$

This is easily demonstrated, since the transformation of the components of the vector z by means of $x = \ln(z)$ immediately gives rise to

$$\dot{x} = G(x) + <\gamma> \overbrace{G(x)}^{\cdot}$$

with the mapping G determined by $F \circ \exp$. This transformation of variables permits the same statements and proofs as in the case of simple time derivatives.

36. See, for example, Zurmühl 1964 for a list of such norms.

Chapter 4

1. The use of adaptive expectations scenarios is reconsidered and justified in section 7.2.

2. See Chiarella 1990 for an introduction into this type of viable dynamics and its application to the Cagan inflation theory.

3. See again Hirsch and Smale 1974 or Chiarella 1990, respectively.

4. See section 4.6 for modifications of this type of investment function.

5. Note that a sudden increase in expectations x^e above their steady-state value may be followed by slight decreases in expectations for some time, until the implied increases in the actual rate of capacity utilization reach this higher level of expected capacity utilization. From then on both rates will again increase in time without bounds.

6. The proof very much could follow Benhabib and Miyao 1981. In our case we have $n = 2$ and det $J > 0$.

7. Despite the nonlinearity in the influence of the interest rate on capacity growth, there may also exist a degenerate case where—as in linear systems—no limit cycle is present, but only closed orbits at the bifurcation value. Such a situation is, however, "of measure zero" relative to the occurrences of sub- or supercritical cases. Numerical examples of these latter types of bifurcations are shown in figures 3.2, 3.3 of the preceding and in figure 4.16.

8. This demand function also underlies the Sargent and Wallace (1973) model with its jump variable technique and is chosen for purposes of exposition solely. The Sargent and Wallace (1973) approach to money market dynamics is briefly discussed at the end of this section.

9. For a justification of our use of adaptive expectations with respect to the price level, see section 7.2.

10. Note that we have for the partial derivative $\hat{p}_{\pi^e} > 0$ in this case, that is, a positive feedback of the expected rate of inflation on actual inflation.

11. Where stability holds for all speeds of adjustment of inflationary expectations.

12. That is, a situation that becomes unstable when expectations are revised sufficiently fast.

13. These and other treatments of the Kaldor model are discussed in detail in Gabisch and Lorenz 1989.

14. See Arrowsmith and Place 1982 for details on this. See also Chiarella 1990.

15. $\dot{y} = \dot{Y}e^{-gt} - gy, \dot{k} = \dot{K}e^{-gt} - gk.$

16. Further multiplier-accelerator approaches will be considered in section 6 of this chapter.

17. With the real rate of interest again assumed as constant. Note that economically this money demand function is seen to be of a different type than the one employed in the preceding section. From the mathematical point of view it gives rise, however, to very similar expressions when expressed in logarithmic terms.

18. See also Chiarella 1990, 103–4, also with respect to the following.

19. And possibly also further alternative constructions of an unconstrained system.

20. μ, the markup rate, v^* the steady-state value of the wage share, see the following.

21. Technical change can subsequently be treated, for example, by assuming Harrod-

neutral technical progress, as in the original Goodwin model, or endogenous technical change along the lines of Kennedy-Weizsäcker, as in Shah and Desai 1980.

22. See, for example, Tu 1994 for details.

23. And $\beta_p > 0$ to the right of $\underline{v}$.

24. All Goodwin cycles are level surfaces of the function H.

25. Other types of growth models with Wicksellian features have been provided by Marglin (1984, chap. 20), by Skott (1989), and by Rose (1990). Space limitations, however, do not allow us to go into these more recent and more developed models of growth dynamics.

26. See chapter 10 for alternative cases.

27. Rose (1967) also includes interest rate effects in his model, but in a way that avoids a separate treatment of them (by means of a conventional LM-curve, for example).

28. The numerator of the derivative of this isocline at the steady state is given by $\beta_w^{-1}(\cdot) - l(\beta_w^{-1})'(\cdot)\beta_p H'(\cdot)$.

29. See Benassy 1986 for a situation of the same mathematical type.

30. The relevance of the effective demand constraint Y can then not be justified on grounds of the simple dynamic multiplier story.

31. Or by chance degenerate.

32. This simulation is based on the following parameters: $\beta_w = 1, \bar{e} = 0.95, \bar{x}^c = 0.9, n = 0.04, \eta = 1.3, \beta_p = 1, \beta_k = 0.5, y = 1/5$.

Chapter 5

1. See Flaschel 1993, chapter 3, where an approach by Nikaido is utilized to show Harrodian problems in the presence of smooth factor substitution.

2. These variants are considered in chapters 8 through 10.

3. In particular, we will not study Solow model discrete–time variants or models with strong nonlinearities and delayed reaction patterns, which originate with Day (1984). For a survey of nonoptimizing as well as optimizing versions of neoclassical growth giving possibly rise to complex dynamics, see Boldrin and Woodford 1990.

4. For an elaborate presentation of the original Solow model and early extensions, cf. Burmeister and Dobell 1970; for a reply to the Solow contribution emphasizing the role of income distribution for the path to the steady state, see Kaldor 1961. For a recent empirical study of an extended Solow model, see Mankiw, Romer, and Weil 1992.

5. Lucas (1988, 6), for example, views finance as unimportant to the process of growth.

6. For details of such algorithms, see Taylor and Uhlig 1990 and Semmler 1995.

7. The following version builds on Lucas's exposition of such a model; see Lucas 1988, sect. 2. The case when labor is elastically supplied is considered in the next section.

8. Note that in the case of a model where the variables are formulated in efficiency labor

the discount rate has to be modified so as to reflect the trend growth rate and population growth rate. We thus may write $\rho = \bar{\rho} - (n + \mu)$ where $\bar{\rho}$ is the discount rate; see also Blanchard 1983 and King, Plosser, and Rebelo 1988b.

9. For an exposition of those tools, see Carlson and Haurie 1987.

10. The local and global analysis of the stability properties of such a system with saddle point properties is similar to that in Blanchard and Fischer 1989, chapter 2, which the reader could consult for technical details.

11. Note that the other parameters, ρ and η, do not have an impact on the long-run growth rate, but only on the level of income per capita.

12. This is derived and further discussed by Lucas (1988, sect. 2), who, however, uses a production function of the type $Y(t) = A(t)K(t)^{1-\alpha}N(t)^{\alpha}$, where N denotes the number of persons employed, which is then reformulated in per capita variables.

13. Recently, as discussed in the next section, some statistical estimation procedures have been employed to test for parameters of intertemporal models, which also could be applied to the Lucas model; see remarks in the next section.

14. Note that we here again employ per capita variables.

15. A well-known procedure is the general method of moment estimate (GMM). Here, observed data are characterized by summary statistics such as the mean and variance. In parallel, a model based on a given parameter vector is employed. A distance function is then minimized so as to find a parameter vector, that is, a moment estimator, that minimizes the distance between the population and the sample moments. This procedure originates in the general method of moments (GMM) developed by Hansen (1982) and first empirically applied by Hansen and Singleton (1982); see also Semmler and Gong 1996 for a maximum likelihood (ML) procedure to estimate parameters of a RBC model.

16. For a discussion of labor hoarding, see Burnside, Eichenbaum, and Rebelo 1993.

17. Besides the paper by Uzawa (1965), the papers by Shell (1966, 1967) can also be considered important forerunners of Lucas's and Romer's versions of the endogenous growth theory.

18. Note that in the Lucas model externalities and learning are actually not needed to have persistent growth.

19. After Lucas and Romer had proposed their versions of a two-dimensional growth model a number of further studies have pursued this approach extensively, among them Barro and Sala-i-Martin 1991, 1992, 1995. In the framework of either the Lucas human capital model or the Romer-Grossman-Helpman version of R&D-driven growth models many studies also addressed the empirical question of convergence of per capita income across countries; see, for example, Barro and Sala-i-Martin 1991, 1992, 1995; and Mankiw, Romer, and Weil 1992. We will restrict our study to the original contributions.

20. Also in endogenous growth models a simple aggregate production function of the type $Y = aK, a > 0$ gives rise to persistent growth; see Barro and Sala-i-Martin 1995. Thus, a production function of fixed coefficients, as in the Harrod-Domar case where the marginal product is constant, will make growth feasible.

21. If the integral is infinite other techniques, for example, the overtaking criterion must

be employed to describe the behavior of the consumer; see Romer 1986b and Stokey and Lucas 1989, chapters 2-4.

22. We focus here on the model by Romer (1990), in particular on his version for a command economy; for a Romer version of the market economy, see Benhabib, Perli and Xie 1994; for a study of the dynamics of the Lucas version, see Benhabib and Perli 1994 and Caballe and Santos 1993. We represent the Romer model in level form, not normalized as in the previous sections. This way we can stay close to the main body of literature on this topic. The Romer as well as the Lucas models could be normalized by dividing all variables through by a growth trend; see Caballe and Santos 1993. One also can propose a slightly different way to obtain stationary equilibria, namely, by forming ratios of the state and co-state variables; see Asada, Semmler and Novak 1994.

23. In the Romer model it is assumed that only the producers of the varieties of durables produce noncompetitively and receive a rent on the new technologies.

24. For details of the derivations, see Asada, Novak and Semmler 1994.

25. Note that we have discussed here the version for a command economy. Since externalities are not fully captured in a market economy the growth rate for a market economy turns out to be smaller than defined by (5.39).

26. There it is also shown that saddle point stability is preserved even if the Romer model is slightly generalized.

27. These results do not appear to carry over to the case, however, when externalities through learning by doing are admitted; see, for example, Greiner and Semmler 1994, 1996, for a one-good model. For a more elaborate two-sector model, see Boldrin and Rustichini 1994; and Benhabib and Perli 1994.

28. In empirical work also proxies for government capital (Barro 1990b) are also used to explain endogenous growth.

29. See Barro and Sala-i-Martin 1992, 1995 and Mankiw, Romer, and Weil 1992, where some empirical success of this type of study is reported with respect to proxies of human capital.

30. See, in particular, Barro and Sala-i-Martin 1992, 3, where it is remarked that the steady state is "monotonically" approached. In their empirical study along the line of the original nonoptimizing Solow model, Mankiw, Romer, and Weil (1992) also assume a monotone path for the convergence process.

31. For further details on the latter problems, see Boldrin and Rustichini 1994; Benhabib and Perli 1994; and Benhabib, Perli, and Xie 1994.

32. See Blanchard and Fischer 1989, chapter 2 for an elaborate introduction to the problem of growth and finance in intertemporal models pertaining to households, firms, governments, or countries.

33. See Uzawa 1969, sect. 7, where only equity finance, as the only source of external finance, is admitted.

34. See Asada and Semmler 1995 for a growth version of this type of model.

35. For details; see Asada and Semmler 1995.

36. In Blanchard and Fischer 1989, chapter 2), an example for an open economy is also

given where external borrowing finances economic growth of a country. Here, too, as long as the transversality or nonexplosiveness condition is not violated finance does not matter for the optimal paths. One can, however, demonstrate, that in general, the nonexplosiveness condition can hold only in certain regions of the state space. This is shown in Semmler and Sieveking 1995, a result that appears to have been overlooked in many growth models with external finance.

37. This change of perspective is already notably visible in Azariadis 1993 where models of growth and finance in intertemporal models are treated—although there more from an overlapping generations perspective.

38. Usually, a hierarchy of financing behavior of the firm are derived from these considerations: desired investment is primarily financed by retained earnings; and, when exhausted, by debt; and lastly, by equity finance. See Myers 1984 and Fazzari, Hubbard, and Petersen 1988.

39. See, for example, the models by Bernanke and Gertler (1989) and Greenwald and Stiglitz (1987). In the latter version the marginal risk of bankruptcy depending on firms' indebtedness affects the stream of net profit.

40. Risk cost arising from the high leverage of firms most likely also increases the discount rate applied to the profit flows of firms.

41. The theory of incomplete capital markets admits such a cross-effect from the stock of debt to the present value of the firm. There are several types of literature along those lines. An early study on this matter can be found in Kalecki 1937b. Greenwald and Stiglitz (1986) make the (marginal) cost of bankruptcy explicitly dependent on the stock of debt. Also Myers, in a review article on this matter notes: "Costs of financial distress include the legal and administrative costs of bankruptcy, as well as the subtler agency, moral hazard, monitoring and contracting costs which erode firm value even if formal default is avoided" (Myers 1984, 581).

42. In models with the utility of consumption as the return function the negative effect of debt on intertemporal decisions can take the form of "disutility of debt." This road is taken in Blanchard 1983 for an open economy model. The impact of debt on the value of the firm, and thus the nonvalidity of the Modigliani-Miller theorem, is also stated by Blanchard and Fischer (1989, 288) without, however, their realizing that the dynamics of the model may change.

43. For empirical tests of investment functions for firms where finance is relevant, see Gertler, Hubbard, and Kashyap 1991 and Semmler and Franke 1995.

44. There are, of course, many attempts to extend the equilibrium business cycle model by incorporating new features and to make the model better match actual macroeconomic time series data (see Cooley 1995). Yet, basic implausibilities, such as large employment changes due to transitory wage changes, appear to remain unresolved.

45. For a more general analysis of the role of cross-effects in intertemporal models generating cycles, see Dockner and Feichtinger 1991. Note that already for classical micro as well as macro models the cross-effects give rise to periodic paths.

46. For an empirical evaluation of models giving rise to complex dynamics, see Boldrin 1994.

Introduction to Part II

1. The possibility of an unstable outcome might be reminiscent of the Harrodian multiplier-accelerator instability of warranted growth. Note, however, that the present case includes nominal interactions in addition to the purely real ones.

Chapter 6

1. An abridged version of this chapter is Flaschel and Franke 1996.

2. In a first step, unemployment is treated in chapter 13. At that stage of Patinkin's book, however, the references to the dynamic adjustments are missing.

3. The gap might be closed by extra shifts or overtime work, for example. Two reasons can be given why workers are willing to accept this: they consider this situation to be temporary, and at the same time, as will be postulated below, they already experience a rise in the wage rate.

4. The process as it is specified by Sargent is slightly more complicated since he uses a more ambitious definition of disposable income in the consumption function. It gives rise to a "flow Pigou effect" (in the wording of Tobin [1975, 197]), whereas the stock effect is absent.

5. Note that the signs of the partial derivatives of the LM-interest rate function are given by $\partial \rho / \partial p > 0$ and $\partial \rho / \partial w < 0$.

6. That Keynes had indeed this type of causality in mind may also be seen from the following quotation which is taken from chapter 19, "Changes in Money-Wages," of the *General Theory*: "[T]he price level will only change in the short period to the extent that changes in the volume of employment affect marginal prime costs" (Keynes 1936, 270).

7. Here C_p is assumed to be strictly negative, which gives the maximal number of nonzero elements of J. If $C_p = 0$ the (1,3) entry would be zero.

8. det $J \neq 0$ implies that upon variations of a suitable parameter, such as one of the adjustment speeds, two complex eigenvalues are crossing the imaginary axis when $B = 0$, that is, when equality holds in the stability condition of theorem 6.2. This is the typical situation for a Hopf bifurcation to occur, which signifies a certain tendency for the existence of periodic orbits (see proposition 7.3 for an application and a precise formulation). Here we leave further details aside, but the issue is indirectly reflected in the cyclical dynamics considered below.

9. Note here that the LM-curve shifts to the right as w decreases in the course of the adjustment process.

Chapter 7

1. For a detailed description see Turnovsky 1970; Turnovsky and Wachter 1972; Gibson 1972. Carlson (1977) pointed out that the Livingston data may be contaminated by measurement errors and, on the basis of this criticism, readjusted the series. Since then, the Carlson series is also frequently used in empirical research.

2. Additional evidence that the Livingston forecasts are not Muthian rational is given by Gramlich (1983) and, improving on a specification problem, Bryan and Gavin (1986). In another study, however, Schroeter and Smith (1986) conclude that while the Livingston CPI predictions are not rational, the PPI forecasts from this survey do pass rationality tests. Mullineux (1978) obtains that for the expected inflation series constructed by Carlson from the Livingston data, a weak form of Muthian rationality cannot be rejected.

3. See the substantial differences in the coefficients α_1 and α_2, which read $\alpha_1 = 0.226$, $\alpha_2 = 0.781$ over the period 1962 – 1969 in Turnovsky 1970, and $\alpha_1 = 0.534$, $\alpha_2 = 0.426$ over the period 1952 – 1970 in Lahiri 1976.

4. The latter characterization is taken from Williams 1987, 2, nz.

5. See the models developed by Taylor (1975) and Mussa (1975). There it is in particular the specific money supply process that implies that the optimal forecasts of the inflation rate are similar to an adaptive expectations assumption.

6. This refers to an augmented version of the model. It includes an incremental growth of inflation (i.e., trended inflation) that is supposed to follow a random walk. The author emphasizes that his model is similar to those that have long existed in control theory and the operations research literature.

7. Namely, $\ln x^r_{t+h} - \ln x^r_t = \ln(x^r_{t+h}/x^r_t) = \ln[1 + (x^r_{t+h} - x^r_t)/x^r_t] \approx (x^r_{t+h} - x^r_t)/x^r_t$, and similarly with $\ln x_t - \ln x^r_t$.

8. Values of the DW statistic in the neighborhood of 2 signify the absence of first-order autocorrelation. Smaller (larger) values reveal positive (negative) autocorrelation, the polar cases being DW = 0 and DW = 4, respectively.

9. Tobin speaks of price-level and price-change effects, respectively; cf. his recent article, Tobin 1992, 389. The Mundell effect also plays an important role in the abovementioned models of DeLong and Summers (1986b) and their successors.

10. Price determination by way of the marginal productivity principle for labor may provide a more indirect channel through which rising output translates into increasing prices. The price level is then inversely related to the marginal product of labor, which falls when employment rises. This effect also plays a role in the model specified below.

11. The destabilizing effect of high values of β_π was already pointed out by Cagan (1956). Inequality (7.9) is equivalent to one of the Routh-Hurwitz conditions. Thus, it is only necessary, not sufficient for asymptotic stability. Two of the four Routh-Hurwitz conditions are always satisfied, whereas the fourth may be violated even if (7.9) applies. In this sense the other parameters of the model may also have their bearing on stability.

12. Fluctuations in labor productivity are thereby neglected.

13. Equation (7.10) is a reduced form of price determination. So price reactions appear sluggish only in a certain formal way.

14. Following Fischer (1972) or Duguay and Rabeau (1988), expected inflation might also be added on the RHS of equation (7.13) (or a similar term; cf. Flaschel 1993, chap. 6, for several proposals in this regard). Such a specification of the price-setting behavior of firms would take account of the inflationary climate in which it takes place, and which at the same time it helps to sustain. Equation (7.13), by contrast, implies zero inflation in the steady state. Like as Boggess (1983), we assume that a possible self-reference of inflation on price level changes is based on this steady-state experience (in case of

instability, it might shine through as a time average). Mathematically, however, the issue is of secondary importance. Regardless of whether we include it, π^e in (7.13) does not essentially affect the stability propositions below.

15. It is not so much growth and the endogenous determination of the capital stock that greatly complicates the analysis, but the various repercussion effects when $\hat{p}$ in the equation representing adaptive expectations has to be expressed in terms of the other dynamic variables. Sargent has stopped his formal analysis just at this point.

16. Capacity effects and long-run growth are included in later chapters. The simple version is, however, sufficient to make our main points on the impact of low and high price flexibility on stability.

17. The investment function, which was also employed in the previous chapter, is a nonmarginalist version of Sargent's (1987, chap. 5) specification of investment as being dependent on $(F_K - \delta) - (i - \pi^e)$. When he assumes the marginal productivity principle for labor, the first bracket is identical with the average profit rate. The latter may, or may not, equal the real interest rate in long-run equilibrium; nothing in the stability analysis hinges on this.

18. Note that in an equilibrium state the marginal propensity to spend is simply given by C', since with $dL/dY = 1/F_L$ one has $dI/dY = I'(1 - w/(pF_L)) = 0$.

19. Groth (1988) investigates the stability properties of a related model where the expectations mechanism is of a combined adaptive–forward looking type (on the basis of a positive growth rate of the money supply). Apart from this extension and a somewhat peculiar treatment of taxes (tax levying is a residual in the government budget restraint), his model still suppresses money wages and works with the price Phillips curve (7.10). Groth's results provide further details on the importance of the Tobin condition (7.9) and its relationship to the Cagan (1956) instability condition for models of monetary growth. This analysis is continued in Groth 1992, where questions of global stability, corridor effects, and the existence of non-local limit cycles are also addressed.

20. Note that Y_ω outweighing Y_p would require a highly interest-elastic money demand function, since $|Y_\omega|/p|Y_p| = p|m_r|/\bar{M})$.

21. Some of the conditions in proposition 7.2 could be strengthened, but this would go at the expense of readability.

22. Observe that the condition in proposition 7.2(a) would be violated for large values of β_w, whereas it would be fulfilled if β_w is close to zero.

23. For an introduction to the Hopf bifurcation theorem see, for example, Gabisch and Lorenz 1989, chapter 4. The standard formulation of the theorem is Marsden and McCracken 1976, 65, 81, but referring to Alexander and Yorke 1978 in our proof of proposition 7.3 avoids some technical subtleties.

24. Since the dynamics are three dimensional, the convenient analytical device of the Poincaré-Bendixson theorem is no longer applicable. In the end one would, therefore, have to resort to numerical simulations. They will play a greater role in the subsequent chapters.

25. In order to confine notation the same symbol is used as in section 7.5. Note, however, the difference in the arguments of ϕ.

26. In this case there is no need to resort to the jump-variable technique that is adopted

by Sargent in chap. 5 of his textbook in order to cope with the immanent instability in the presence of $\beta_\pi = \infty$ and $\beta_p = \infty$ (it is, likewise, of saddle point type).

27. The case of adaptive expectations could also be extended in this way. Though the resulting system is four dimensional, a local stability analysis may not be impracticable since the Jacobian exhibits a number of zero entries. In the light of proposition 7.5 we do not expect to find anything essentially new, however.

28. A more recent treatment of this issue is provided in Franke and Lux 1993.

29. $\beta_p = \infty$ in the first column of table 7.2 must be interpreted as representing a constant markup over average (not marginal) wage costs, whereas the parameter β_p in equation (7.10) (which parallels Tobin's notation) originates with a wage Phillips curve. In accordance with our later notational practice, it may now be better substituted by β_w (see the discussion of (7.10)).

Chapter 8

1. The Keynesian textbook model of monetary growth with a perfectly flexible price level (or the Keynesian model variant of the so-called neoclassical synthesis) and the successor of monetary growth models of Keynes-Wicksell type. This monetary growth model has been analyzed in the literature only nascently (see Sargent 1987, chap. 5 and Turnovsky 1977 for examples). By contrast, simplified medium-run versions of this model type have been very popular in the analysis of inflation and stagflation (see here chapter 7 for a treatment of the full medium-run model).

2. As in the Wallace-Sargent case.

3. Cf. for example King 1990, where in a sticky price model, however, contrary to Keynesian positions, the interest rate is postulated to covary with the change in money supply. The latter position appears to have little support by empirical evidence, cf. Christiano and Eichenbaum 1992a.

4. The new Keynesian view on price rigidities and the effectiveness of monetary policy is best presented in Blanchard and Fischer 1989, chapter 8. See also the recent study by Woodford (1996), where it is also shown that, contrary to the Ricardian equivalence theorem, fiscal policy is effective when prices are sticky or gradually adjusting.

5. Barro (1994, 5) has recently expressed the view that the short-run AD-AS model is logically flawed "as usually presented because its assumption that the price level clears the goods market is inconsistent with the Keynesian underpinning of the aggregate-demand curve" and that it should be replaced by either a full market-clearing approach or by an IS-LM model with gradually adjusting prices and wages. The second part of this chapter contributes to the latter type of analysis from a medium- and long- run perspective.

6. See also Flaschel 1992 where subjects related to the ones considered in this chapter are investigated.

7. Compare again also Barro 1994.

8. The same observation has been made recently by Barro (1994) with respect to static AD-AS analysis.

9. See chapter 1 for the employed notation.

10. The expression hM_t in the last equation stands for the flow of services the stock of money supplies over the period h.

11. Note, here, that π_t^e is the expected rate of inflation corresponding to the future rate of inflation $(p_{t+h} - p_t)/p_t$.

12. The right- and left-hand derivatives are shown here to indicate the proper economic determination and interpretation of these rates of change. Since only isolated jumps in the money supply are analyzed, these specifications might be considered to be of no real importance for the numerics of the resulting dynamics. This, however, is not true, as we shall see in the following, since the present model is very sensitive with regard to a change in its forward- or backward-looking components.

13. Note, that the above discrete-time approach does not allow for a separate treatment of dp and $\hat{p}_+$, as in Sargent's continuous-time model, which in fact removes a logical flaw from this latter model.

14. This model is globally asymptotically stable (see section 10.5).

15. Using $\hat{}$ also in discrete-time for denoting forward-looking rates of growth, the exact formula, for example, for the real wage is: $\hat{\omega} = \hat{w} - \hat{p} - \hat{\omega}\hat{p}$.

16. Note that nominal wages are now simply given by $w_t = \omega_t p_t$ and that A_t=const. in the steady state.

17. Up to the integration of the discontinuous jumps dp of prices p into the definition of the discrete-time rate of inflation $\frac{p_{t+1}-p_t}{p_t}$ (i.e., the disappearance of dp as a separate entity besides $\hat{p}_+$).

18. Owing to the fact of a constant real rate of interest.

19. By using $\hat{p}_+$ in place of $\frac{p_{t+1}-p_t}{p_t}$.

20. Note that the side condition "that leaves $\hat{M}_+$ unchanged" of the continuous-time formulation does not make sense in the discrete-time version.

21. Note that the above result assumes a Ricardian fiscal policy regime, that is, there is no interaction of monetary and fiscal policy; on this point see Woodford 1994, 1996 and also Sargent 1986.

22. Since the change dp can and must be added to $\dot{p}_+$ when defining the rate of inflation $\hat{p}$ in discrete time.

23. Due to $\hat{w} = \hat{\omega} + \hat{p} + \hat{\omega}\hat{p}$ in discrete time.

24. The Phillips curve can be reduced to a real wage Phillips curve without any error term if $\hat{w} = \hat{p}$ and $e_t = 1$ holds true throughout. This situation is, however, not applicable in the case of a fiscal policy, owing to the real effects this policy has.

25. See Duguay and Rabeau 1988 for a numerical investigation of a model similar to the one here considered, where the adjustment speed of the price level toward the level of marginal wage costs is assumed as 0.5. See also Hall 1988 for a recent empirical investigation of the relationship between price and marginal costs in the U.S. industry.

26. Employing marginal wage cost in the place of average cost does not change the following dynamical model significantly.

27. Which owing to the above, is subject in particular to the side condition: $\omega < f'(l)$. Note, furthermore, that we here employ perfect foresight symmetrically in both the Phillips curve and the investment function without any analytical problems.

28. Normal employment being given by eL^s based an appropriate choice of the normal work-time unit.

29. The parameter values behind these computations are: $c_h = .7$; throughout $\delta = .05$; $g_m = n = .05$; $f_m^1 = .2$; $f_m^{2a} = .14$; $f_m^{2b} = .24$; $\gamma = \theta = .2$; $\beta_w = .2$; $\beta_w^* = .2$; $\beta_e = .5$; $i_f = .25$; $a = .3$; $1 + \mu = 1.25$ ($\beta_p = bp$, etc., in the following figures).

30. Which in the present approach is by definition larger than '1' (equal to 1.3 in the following numerical investigations).

31. Since any positive amount of gross investment will lead to excess demand and thus raise national product because of $c_h < 1$.

32. These two mechanisms can be related to approaches that derive from Goodwin's (1951) multiplier-accelerator mechanism and Goodwin's (1967) model of the conflict over income distribution.

33. Further stabilizing mechanisms may be obtained by assuming downward rigidity of wages or prices (or both), by making the parameter β_e dependent on e, and the like.

34. Note that we thus assume that some investment will take place even at full employment, which, however, is not essential for the following results.

35. Or in the case of a stable limit cycle with a smaller amplitude than in the unrestricted case.

36. The Gibson paradox, see Sargent 1973a.

37. See Evans 1969, 419, for example.

38. Which have here been used in a very strict manner.

Chapter 9

1. See also Flaschel 1994, where subjects related to the ones considered in this chapter are investigated.

2. See Benhabib and Miyao 1981 for an example.

3. In this respect Tobin remarks that "The New Keynesians have accepted the terms of the debate formulated by the anti-Keynesian New Classical counterrevolutionaries. Both sides of the contemporary debate misrepresent and exaggerate the role of price rigidities . . . in Keynesian macroeconomics" (Tobin 1989, 7).

4. As shown in chapter 6, it seems to also be the view of Keynes that even with wage and price flexibilities, periods of high unemployment will occur (cf. Keynes 1936, chapter 19).

5. We are now employing Sargent's special choice of the functional form of the technical and behavioral relationships of the model.

6. See Sargent 1973b and Sargent and Wallace 1975 for examples.

7. See Sargent 1987, chapter 1 for details.

8. Note that we use time indices only in the case of discrete time. Note also that we consider the variable $L_t = L$ underlying the intensive variable l_t as a stock variable (the number of employed persons), whereas $L_t h$ describes the services that are supplied by this work force during a period of length h. A similar interpretation applies to the stock of capital K_t and to the stock of money M_t and its services $M_t h$. A doubling of the period length under otherwise unchanged conditions increases both the services of $M_t h$ and the magnitude $Y_t h$ by the factor two and leaves all other variables in the original LM-equation invariant.

9. Note, here, that π_t^e corresponds to the future actual rate of inflation $(p_{t+h} - p_t)/p_t$. This means that we have to employ π_{t-h}^e in equations (9.14), (9.18) due to our assumptions on the discrete-time model. Of course, the use of initial dates $t - h$ to index rates of change (for example: $\hat{p}_{t-h} = (p_t - p_{t-h})/p_{t-h}$) is a pure matter of convention. The definition $\hat{p}_t = (p_t - p_{t-h})/p_t$ could have been used equally well. It would still better mirror the continuous-time indexation—without any significant change in formal content. By contrast, the discrete-time structure that is used in Sargent 1973a is not compatible with his 1987 continuous-time approach, though the case of adaptive expectations is treated there correctly by means of left-hand quotients $\hat{p}_-$ and not, as in Sargent 1987, chapter 5, by means of a right-hand time derivative.

10. $h\beta_{\pi^e} < 1$

11. See Hairer and Wanner 1987, 32, for example.

12. See Flaschel 1993, chapter 6.

13. Such a model gives the deterministic basis of Sargent's (1973a) stochastic approach toward an investigation of the so-called Gibson paradox.

14. L_t the currently employed labor force (see section 8.4).

15. For the Cobb-Douglas production function we then get $\left[(1+\mu)\frac{w_t l_t^a}{1-a} - p_t\right]$, replacing the above bracket, which is not very different from the above approach.

16. The term $-a_3$ of the Routh-Hurwitz conditions $a_1, a_2, a_3, a_1 a_2 - a_3 > 0$ for local asymptotic stability.

17. The parameter values for the left-hand picture are: $c_h = .7, \delta = n = g_m = .05, f_m^1 = .2, f_m^{2a} = .14, f_m^{2b} = .24, a = .3, \beta_w^* = .2, i_f = .25, \gamma = \theta = .2, \beta_e = .5, 1 + \mu = 1.25$ whereas we have assumed $\beta_w = .2, \beta_p = 1$ and $\beta_{\pi^e} = 100$ on the right-hand side in addition. The steady-state values of this numerical example are approximately given by: $\omega^\star = 1.16, l^{s\star} = 0.29, m^\star = 0.22, e^\star = 1, (\pi^e)^\star = 0$.

18. As in the IS-LM growth model we do not allow for a self-reference between the expected and the actual rate of price inflation in the following price adjustment equation (see, however, section 9.6 for such a case).

19. Note here that $f(l) - \omega l - \delta$ is now the correct measure for the actual rate of profit, and not $f(l) - f'(l)l - \delta$, as in the original AD-AS model (where $\beta_p = \infty$).

20. The adjustment of employment is immediate in this model type.

21. Of course, a complex structure such as (9.30)–(9.33) can exhibit a variety of other cases where the necessary and sufficient conditions of the Routh-Hurwitz criterion for asymptotic stability are violated. The above way can nevertheless be considered as the most typical one.

22. π^e inflationary expectations and π the number π.

23. In the Kaldor model the role of the parameter β_{π^e} is played by the adjustment speed β_Y of the dynamic multiplier process.

24. $= m$ in the original context.

25. Where $\pi^e = \dot{p} = \frac{\beta_p}{1-\eta}(m - \alpha(\pi^e))$ must hold.

26. As aforementioned the formulation of expected price change becomes particularly important if one is interested in the destabilizing effects of the price (and wage) dynamics on macrofluctuations as discussed in chapters 7 and 9.

27. For more details on the following, cf. Hansen and Sargent 1988.

Chapter 10

1. This chapter is an extended and modified version of Flaschel 1994a.

2. The approach chosen by Stein (1982) is closely related to the monetary growth model of this chapter and will be discussed in an appendix to it. Marglin (1984, chap. 20) considers an overdetermined real growth model where the conflict between investment and saving is resolved in a Wicksellian fashion. Skott (1989), by contrast, assumes perfectly flexible prices and IS-equilibrium. Finally, Rose (1990) allows for windfall profits during goods market adjustments and supplements this situation with an elaborate wage price sector.

3. See also Sargent 1987, section 2.2 and Barro 1990a, 532 for this type of inflation theory.

4. See chapter 4.

5. Note here that this rule refers only to the *prevailing* steady state of the economy. If such a steady state is disturbed by an increase in the rate of monetary expansion, one can use the above approach solely to test whether the new steady state is attracting or repelling if the motion of the economy is again already close to it.

6. See also Stein 1982, 20, 167 for its use in a Keynesian/Monetarist model with perfect foresight.

7. Note that we employ here a different definition of the real balances term m from the one used in the rest of this book.

8. In the sense of the neoclassical synthesis.

9. Note that there are no involuntary inventory changes in this limit case of the general model.

10. See his paper, "Static and Dynamic General Equilibrium models," reprinted in Goodwin 1983 and Goodwin 1989 for more classical reformulations of this approach to microdynamics.

11. The value of $i = i(\omega, l^s, m) \approx const.$

12. Note that the stronger condition $\alpha_2 > 0$ is equivalent to condition (ii) in theorem 10.2 in which case no loss of stability is possible.

13. Note here that the right-hand border of this interval gives exactly the locus where $\beta_p = 1/i_f$ holds true, where the dynamics of the Keynes-Wicksell model is ill defined.

Note, furthermore, that the limit case $\beta_k = 0$ of these dynamics is always globally asymptotically stable to the right of this border line.

14. In this example, we employ as function f_m in the money demand schedule the simple linear form $f_m(i) = 1 - \beta_i(i - i^\star)$, which provides us with the following explicit expression for the nominal rate of interest $i = i^\star + (x - ml^s)/(x\beta_i)$. Furthermore, the parameter values of this numerical example are: $c_h = .75$; $i_f = .1$; $\delta = .1$; $\gamma = \theta = .3$; $\alpha = .3$; $n = g_m = .05$; $\beta_i = 15$.

15. Described by a CES-production function $x = (a + (1-a)l^{-\eta})^{-1/\eta}$ with $a = 0.5$; $\eta = 19$ ($\varepsilon = 1/(1+\eta) = 0.025$).

16. The other parameter values are: $c_h = .9$; $\delta = .1$; $\gamma = \theta = .35$; $g_m = n = .05$; $i_f = 1$; $\beta_i = 200$ and $\beta_p = 0.01$; $\beta_w = 0.5$. The time horizon of this phase plot is 30 years.

17. Term $\bar{e}$ the "natural" rate of employment.

18. We suppress the factor k on the right-hand side of the above price equation in the following which is due only to the different intensive form that is employed by Stein.

19. See the above calculation of J_{21}.

20. $\dot{E} = 0$ does not contain an entire orbit of the dynamics other than the equilibrium itself.

Chapter 11

1. An abridged version of this chapter is Franke 1992c.

2. A first step in a similar direction has been undertaken by Asada, who incorporates a standard monetary sector in what he calls a Keynes-Goodwin model (Asada 1989, 145–49, 161–62). The present model can also be seen as a consequent development of this approach. To mention the main point, Asada's general formulation (still with the usual constant growth of productivity) allows for variable capacity utilization. However, in order to be in line with the Goodwin modeling tradition and to exploit some structural simplifications, he later decides to fall back on the assumption of full capacity utilization, which is tantamount to a constant output-capital ratio. In this way it is again price inflation that turns out to be determined by the IS temporary equilibrium condition, whereas in our model goods markets are cleared by quantity adjustments.

3. We recall that the first six items are also characteristics of Keynes-Wicksell models; cf. Stein 1982, 19–22, 163, 191; see chapter 10.

4. Among the works listed above, it was also successfully employed in Benhabib and Miyao 1981.

5. With a linearly homogeneous production function $Y = F(L, K)$ and $w/p = F_L$, one has $Y = F_L L + F_K K = (w/p)L + F_K K$ (the first equality from Euler's theorem). Hence $(pY - wL - \delta pK)/pK = F_K(L, K) - \delta$.

6. Another price that has to be paid for this simplification is that one cannot discuss if, or why, real variables grow in sympathy with the labor force over the long run. However, our simulations of other variants of Keynesian growth models suggest that the stability properties and the cyclical behavior of the economy may not change significantly if f_w in equation (11.5) is made dependent on the employment rate L/L^s and, say, $k^s := K/L^s$ is

introduced as a fourth-state variable (L^s being labor supply). For a theoretical analysis of the AD-AS growth model of chapter 9 along these lines see Franke 1992a.

7. See also the argument given in Steindl [1952] 1976, 17. Kalecki himself undertook an elementary empirical analysis, where the Polish and American time series he examined showed weak support of his theory (Kalecki 1939, 71; 1943, 57). A direct predecessor of equation (11.6) in macroeconomic theory can be found in the structuralist approach by Lance Taylor. He repeatedly works with the simpler specification $\dot{\mu} = \alpha(u - u^\star)$ (see Taylor 1983, 34; 1985, 390; 1989, 7).

8. In fact, equation (11.10) is closely related to Okun's law, which is usually formulated in growth rates.

9. J_i is the determinant of the 2×2 matrix that is obtained by deleting the i-th row and i-th column.

10. The value of the output-capital ratio may appear unusually high. It is based on empirical U.S. data for nonfinancial corporate business, taken from Fair 1984 and Fair and Parke 1984. Over the period from 1960 to 1980 the trend line of the corresponding ratio $x = Y/K$ showed a decline from 1.70 to 1.35 (roughly). The main explanation is the exclusion of the housing sector. Since income (rent R) from residential investment is minute relative to the corresponding huge stock of structures (S) and also does not seem to vary as systematically over the cycle as output in the manufacturing or service sector, the ratio R/S is not a very suitable component in the characterization of overall economic activity. Apart from that, residential investment is likely to depend on different factors than those included in the investment function (11.3), which was thought to apply to plant and equipment. For these reasons we prefer to ignore housing altogether in the present highly aggregated economy and to maintain a reference value $x = x^\star = 1.50$. The high value of the profit rate $r^\star$ is also due to this setting of $x^\star$, but note that taxes and other deductions from the proceeds of firms are here ignored.

11. For an investigation of the precise relationship between continuous-time systems and their one-step discretizations, with respect to Liapunov stable points or sets, see Kloeden and Lorenz 1986.

12. A short horizon would correspond to a neoclassical portfolio theory when there is no need to anticipate the rate of price increase over a longer term because the portfolio can be reshuffled at any time in the future. In fact, in neoclassical theory capital has been merely understood as material factors of production, with little attention paid to its fixity.

13. Observe that having introduced a rule determining the change in the markup rate, we are no longer free to replace π^e with the "rational" or myopically foreseen $\hat{p}$ in the Phillips curve. For in this case $\hat{p}$ would have to be substituted for π^e on the RHS of equation (11.7), which leaves $\hat{p}$ undetermined. At least this would change the modeling structure completely, just as in Sargent's AD-AS growth model in chaps. 8 and 9.

14. The concept of staggered wage contracts is known from its application in a certain branch of equilibrium business cycle models. Theorists like to adopt this approach (in a simple discrete-time setting) because with some suitable random shocks superimposed, the lags provide an easy means to generate serial correlation in output and prices. A most prominent early reference in this respect is J.B. Taylor 1980a,b.

15. This time span roughly corresponds to usual values of a payback time limit, within which an investment project is required to pay back the money advanced (see Blatt 1983, 279, 288). It is in itself a psychological variable.

16. The precise definition of an imperfect agent (Heiner 1988, 263f) is more technical and, in fact, somewhat weaker. The following comparison between perfect and imperfect agents rests on the supposition that similar adjustment costs apply to both of them (272).

17. Specifically, a crude return-to-normality model in which all other mechanisms were absent outperformed all versions of the error-learning models investigated.

18. From 1960 to 1982 there are three major trough-to-trough cycles, extending over 10, 4, and 8 years, roughly. In the model, the period of the limit cycle depends crucially on β_π (see below).

Chapter 12

1. This position is implicit in the real business cycle models, where, as shown in section 5.3, technological shocks have been favored as the main driving force.

2. Cf. Taylor and O'Connell 1985; Foley 1986, 1987; Day and Shafer 1985; Woodford 1986, 1988, 1989; Asada 1989; and Franke and Semmler 1989a.

3. For an excellent survey, cf. Gertler 1988.

4. For empirically oriented studies of the impact of financial factors on investment decisions, see early studies such as Meyer and Kuh 1957; Gurley and Shaw 1955. More recent work is by Fazzari, Hubbard, and Petersen (1988); Gertler, Hubbard, and Kashyap (1991); and also Semmler and Franke (1991).

5. Interest rate spread has recently also been used as a new leading indicator (see Stock and Watson 1989).

6. The above considerations would still apply if equity finance and retained earnings were more complicated functions of some economic key variables.

7. See Blume, Bray, and Easley 1982, for an introduction to the general problem.

8. With geometric depreciation at the constant rate δ (per year), lifetime of capital may be loosely defined as $1/\delta$ (years).

9. This type of investment function is also suggested by econometric evidence, where the role of our ρ is taken by a proxy for Tobin's q (see Abel and Blanchard 1986).

10. Blatt (1979, 1983) attempts to develop a framework of investment evaluation under uncertainty in which, in particular, the method of the payback time limit is not discarded outright as "perplexing, if not exasperating" (Eisner 1956, 8), but may find a certain theoretical explanation on the basis of more fundamental concepts. In Franke and Asada 1994 it is indicated in what way an investment function like (12.1) may be derived from the concepts put forward by Blatt, but here we do not dwell on this issue any further.

11. In order to avoid misunderstandings and in view of the methodological principle that "it is usual in complex systems to regard as the *causa causans* [principal force] that factor which is most prone to sudden and wide fluctuations" (Keynes 1937, 121), we may say that it would have been more consistent if Keynes himself had argued in terms of an investment function similar to equation (12.1) see also Blatt 1983, 291).

12. A good survey on the role of expectation and confidence in business cycle theories is given in Boyd and Blatt 1988. Primarily the asymmetry in the upturn and downturn of the

business cycle, that is, the sharp and sudden drop first in financial and then in real economic variables, seemed to be caused by the inherent instability of business confidence and sudden changes in the expectations about the future. This is an observation made by theorists in the nineteenth century (Mill and Marshall) and restated in the writings of Lavington (1921), Hawtrey (1950), and recently, Minsky (1975, chap.3).

13. Kalecki also draws attention to nonlinearities in the relationship between prospective profits and real variables over the cycle (*ibid.*,86–89).

14. Though it is a seemingly impossible project within the neoclassical framework (see O'Donnell 1990, 263f and his further references).

15. Formalizations of dynamic processes of imitation that lead from heterogeneous expectations to a more or less universal convention are endeavored, for example, by Harrison and Kreps (1978), or Orléan (1990). The role of social interaction for the formation of expectations and market volatility is also thoroughly studied in Shiller 1991.

16. In the *General Theory* we find statements like these: "[T]he entrepreneurs, who are directly responsible, will find it financially advantageous, and often unavoidable, to fall in with the ideas of the market, even though they themselves are better instructed" (Keynes 1936, 316, n. 1), and "[e]ven outside the field of finance, Americans are apt to be unduly interested in discovering what average opinion believes average opinion to be" (159).

17. In this respect there is an apparent similarity between Keynes and the recent sunspot theorists who have examined the possibility that, even in rational expectations models, prices and quantities may "fluctuate persistently under laissez-faire, if private economic units predicted that they will do so" (Grandmont and Malgrange 1987, 4). This may occur independently of shocks to fundamentals (taste and endowments and technology; see, e.g., Woodford 1986, 1988). It has to be noted, however, that in this school the process generating the fluctuations has (as yet) no firm basis: the waves essentially depend on the whims and fancies of economic agents, whereas the psychological process sketched by Keynes has an objective and institutional basis (Sen 1990). A (deterministic) process of the bulls and bears on the stock market that takes account of these features, and which under certain conditions exhibits chaotic dynamics, is developed in Day and Huang 1990 and Franke and Sethi 1993.

18. Here, a parallel might be drawn to the basic model of stock market fluctuations by Friedman and Laibson (1989). There the sequence of maximum likelihood estimates of expected returns of a representative agent's portfolio could be viewed as a stochastic process of self-reference (though it applies sophisticated statistical procedures). One of the discussants of the paper (J. Duesenberry) "argued for the importance of looking at 'fundamental' variables in addition to looking at the market's own behavior, suggesting that changes in investors' view about future inflation and interest rates and earnings are central to an explanation of market movements" (ibid., 185).

19. There, it entered the investment function directly (see the remarks on equation (12.3) in section 11.2).

20. See the review article by Shleifer and Summers (1990) on noise trader theory.

21. Only seldom do the proponents of the noise trader approach make explicit reference to Keynes. That this approach was nevertheless invented in chapter 12 of the *General Theory* has been pointed out by Piron (1991), who compares several focal quotations.

22. This is a suggestion by Nerlove (1984).

23. For simplification, equation (12.5) neglects the aspect that the denominator, too, should be an expected variable. Alternatively, it could be said that this is already captured by ρ. The formulation is borrowed from Taylor and O'Connell (1985).

24. Our method of analyzing the asset markets has eliminated households' liquidity preference, f_d. No further reference to it will be needed in the rest of the chapter, its role will be implicit only.

25. Mankiw and Zeldes (1992) have shown that a large fraction of the population is liquidity constrained and can only spend what they get. This observation may justify the simple savings function.

26. Also taxes on wages may be introduced. In the IS-equation below, however, this tax rate would cancel out again.

27. If it were to apply to a steady-state position, the equation could also be seen as a generalization of the Cambridge equation, $g - sr = 0$ in the usual notation. If we put $g = f_I$, $s = s_h$, $r = r^g$, (IS) reduces to it if all profits are distributed to households, $s_f = 0$, and there is no money, $\phi = 0$.

28. This is spelled out in Franke and Semmler 1989a, 48–50 in a slightly simpler setting. We admit, however, that it is debatable if this is a methodologically acceptable concept, even if it is a common argument in macroeconomic theory.

29. There is also some (older) empirical evidence that corporate managers tend to uphold the concept of a stable long-term payout ratio of realized profits (see Lintner 1956): Lintner found that historical payout ratios did not entirely conform to managers' stated policy, but tended to exhibit some smoothing behavior. (A comment on this article wonders if the simplicity of the results is not too good to be true).

30. A similar logic is employed in Skott 1991a, 383–386. There are of course other versions of financing regimes possible. One might, for example, assume that in a wider distance from the steady state, investment expenditures are constrained, namely, if firms (have to) maintain their dividend payments and equity-financing policy and banks set an upper limit to the growth rate of loans. Such a possibility in a critical stage of the business cycle may be reconsidered in future research.

31. Observe that r in chapter 11 is the *gross* rate of profit *before*, or without, tax.

32. In general there may be more than the two closed orbits in figure 12.3. The clear picture of this diagram is due to the fact that, over the economically relevant region, the building blocks of the model are almost linear—the only significant exception being our construction of the auto-feedback in f_ρ.

33. A financial sector that includes these elements is studied in Franke and Semmler 1994.

Chapter 13

1. In fact, this variable may to some extent be connected to swings in long-term expectations.

2. This appears to be true regardless of the measure of debt—as book value or market value (for data on market value of debt cf. Bernanke and Campbell 1988; for an attempt

to clarify why, as it is claimed, practical people consider debt ratios in terms of book rather than market values, cf. Myers 1977).

3. Cf. Bernanke and Campbell 1988 and their arguments opposing this view.

4. Fazzari, Hubbard, and Petersen (1988) introduce an equity premium required for equity issuance that springs from asymmetric information between firms and outsiders (see also Greenwald and Stiglitz 1987).

5. This is the argument of Fazzari, Hubbard, Petersen (1988). Large firms, in their hypothesis, resemble "full information firms" with easy access to capital markets, and "limited information firms" tend to be small firms with limited access to capital markets, so that they incur high cost of external finance.

6. In the theoretical literature three (additional) reasons are given for the prevalence of debt finance. According to the first, firms tend to choose debt finance because it is excessively costly to verify the state of firms (or impossible to distinguish the conditions of firms). The second argument refers to an incentive effect. Owners (or managers) of firms bear the full burden of the consequences of their decisions and "therefore make better decisions." Third, it is because of market incompleteness that "typical firms can raise funds more cheaply through debt than through equity," and the cost of borrowing depends on firms' net worth, that is, firms with larger net worth can borrow at lower cost (Bernanke and Campbell 1988, 89ff).

7. Cf. Boyd and Blatt 1988, which gives an excellent overview on the history of this position.

8. There are a number of theoretical studies that have attempted to model a "procyclical" and amplifying role of credit in macro models and where the expectational factors relating to the financial structure are considered in finer detail than in chapter 12 above—cf. Bernanke 1983; Skott 1991b; and Semmler and Sieveking 1993. Also to be mentioned here is the 1989 study by Bernanke and Gertler, who postulate a negative correlation of credit cost (agency cost to obtain credit) and net worth of firms. In addition, it should be noted that the quality of credit is usually inversely related to the ease of credit (cf. Bernanke and Campbell 1988, 23); for a more empirically oriented investigation of long-term swings in credit, see Kaufman 1986.

9. There are some similarities to the method by Tobin (1987), who studies the long-run trend in the government debt-income ratio.

10. Empirical observations are mentioned further below.

11. A similar result, within his framework, has been mentioned by Tobin (1987, 208).

12. Two remarks may be repeated here. Firstly, the sine waves are symmetrical motions, whereas the classification of the National Bureau of Economic Research of the U.S. business cycles yields much longer periods from trough to peak than from peak to trough. No systematic asymmetry, however, shows up if measures of capacity utilization, or trend deviations of the output-capital ratio or of the logarithm of GNP, are taken to define the stages of the cycle (see also Beveridge and Nelson 1981; DeLong and Summers 1986a). As a second point, the capital growth rate exhibits short lags with respect to, say, the output-capital ratio. On average, they amount to two or three quarters. This may be borne in mind when comparing the turning points of λ and g. In the empirical examples later on, explicit reference will be made to the turning points of the output-capital ratio.

13. These are our own computations on the basis of the quarterly U.S. data from Fair 1984

and Fair and Parke 1984. The exact value is 4.08 percent. Its exceeding the average growth rate of GNP or total output results in a rising trend of the capital coefficient.

14. Modeling examples using a stock measure are Foley 1986 and Jarsulic 1988, besides the previous chapter 12, of course.

15. We adopted a segmented linear trend with two break points in the NBER trough quarters in 1970 and 1975.

16. They do not essentially differ from the NBER trough quarters.

17. For the detailed formula see Kendall and Stuart 1968, 366–68.

18. By contrast, trend variations in real capital growth are much more moderate. If, for example, $g^{\star}(t)$ is computed as a quadratic trend line over the period 1960:4–1982:4, which proves sufficient, then in the two end-points we have $g^{\star} = 3.16\%$ and $g^{\star} = 3.04\%$, respectively, and the maximum is reached at 4.59% in 1971:3.

19. This phenomenon is even more clear-cut for output prices as a whole.

20. Cf. note 16 above. Extreme values of the annual data are moderately smoothed in this way.

21. There seem to be qualitative differences to a trend line that would result for the ratio of total net credit market borrowing over fixed investment. An indication thereof are the average values given in table 2 in Niggle 1989, 217.

22. The series of our $\beta(t)$ might also be compared with the leverage ratio of (total) credit market borrowing over capital expenditures in figure 1 in Niggle 1989, 209. The additional local minimum in 1980:2 seems to be related to the minor intermediate cycle in that period. The NBER classification yields a peak-trough-peak sequence of 1980:1–1980:3–1981:3.

23. It also seems doubtful if the long-term variations of $\beta^{\star}$ can be derived from this theory of an optimal capital structure.

Chapter 14

1. See Orphanides and Solow 1990.

References

Abel, A. B., and O. J. Blanchard. 1986. "The Present Value of Profits and Cyclical Movements in Investment." *Econometrica* 54: 249–73.

Akerlof, G. A., and J. Yellen. 1985. "A Near-Rational of Business Cycles with Wage and Price Inertia." *Quarterly Journal of Economics* 100, supp.: 823–38.

Alexander, J. C., and J. A.Yorke. 1978. "Global Bifurcations of Periodic Orbits." *American Journal of Mathematics* 100: 263–92.

Alpert, M., and H. Raiffa. 1982. "A Progress Report on the Training of Probability Assessors." In D. Kahneman, P. Slovic, and A. Tversky, eds., *Judgment under Uncertainty: Heuristics and Biases.* Cambridge: Cambridge University Press.

Andreassen, P., and S. Kraus. 1988. "Judgmental Prediction by Extrapolation." Cambridge: Harvard University. Mimeographed.

Aoki, M. 1977. "Dual Stability in a Cambridge-Type Model." *Review of Economic Studies* 44: 143–51.

Arrow, K. J. 1962a. "The Economic Implications of Learning by Doing." *Review of Economic Studies* 29: 155–74.

———. 1962b. "Economic Welfare and the Allocation of Resources for Innovation." In R. Nelson, ed., *The Rate and Direction of Inventive Activity: Economic and Social Factors.* Princeton: Princeton University Press.

Arrowsmith, D. K., and C. M. Place. 1982. *Ordinary Differential Equations.* London: Chapman and Hall.

Asada, T. 1989. "Monetary Stabilization Policy in a Keynes-Goodwin Model of the Growth Cycle." in W. Semmler, ed., *Financial Dynamics and Business Cycles,* 145-167. Armonk, N.Y.: Sharpe.

Asada, T., and W. Semmler. 1995. "Growth and Finance: An Intertemporal Model." *Journal of Macroeconomics* 17: 623–49.

Asada, T., W. Semmler, and A. Novak. 1994. "The Dynamics of Endogenous Growth and the Balanced Growth Equilibrium Models." Dept. of Stochastics, Operations Research and Computer Science, University of Vienna, working paper.

Auerbach, A. J. 1979. "Wealth Maximization and the Cost of Capital." *The Quarterly Journal of Economics* 93: 431–46.

Azariadis, C. 1993. *Intertemporal Macroeconomics*. Oxford: Blackwell Publishers.

Backus, D. K., and P. J. Kehoe. 1992. "International Evidence on the Historical Properties of Business Cycles." *American Economic Review* 82: 864–88.

Ball, L., N. G. Mankiw, and D. Romer. 1988. "The Keynesian Economics and the Output-Inflation Trade-off." Brookings Papers on Economic Activity, no. 1: 1–65.

Barro, R. J. 1990a. *Macroeconomics*. New York: John Wiley.

———. 1990b. "Government Spending in a Simple Model of Endogenous Growth." *Journal of Political Economy* 98: 5103–25.

———. 1994. "The Aggregate-Supply/Aggregate-Demand Model." *Eastern Economic Journal* 20: 1–6.

Barro, R. J. and X. Sala-i-Martin. 1991. "Convergence across States and Regions." *Brookings Papers on Economic Activity* 107–82.

———. 1992. "Convergence." *Journal of Political Economy* 100: 223–51.

———. 1995. *Economic Growth*. New York: McGraw-Hill.

Beckmann, M. J., and Ryder, H. E. 1969. "Simultaneous Price and Quantity Adjustment in a Single Market." *Econometrica* 37: 470–80.

Beltrami, E. 1987. *Mathematics for Dynamic Modeling*. New York: Academic Press.

Benassy, J. P. 1984. *The Economics of Market Disequilibrium*. New York: Academic Press.

Benassy, J. P. 1986a. *Macroeconomics: An Introduction to the Non-Walrasian Approach*. New York: Academic Press.

Benassy, J. P. 1986b. "A Non-Walrasian Model of the Business Cycle." In R. Day and G. Eliasson, eds., *The Dynamics of Market Economies*, 133–47. Amsterdam: North Holland.

Benhabib, J., ed. 1992. *Chaos and Cycles in Economic Equilibrium*. Princeton: Princeton University Press.

Benhabib, J., and T. Miyao. 1981. "Some New Results on the Dynamics of the Generalized Tobin Model." *International Economic Review* 22: 589–96.

Benhabib, J., and V. Perli. 1994. "Uniqueness and Indeterminacy: On the Dynamics of Endogenous Growth." *Journal of Economic Theory* 63: 113–42.

Benhabib, J., V. Perli, and D. Xie. 1994. "Monopolistic Competition, Interderminacy and Growth." *Ricerche Economiche* 48: 279–98.

Bernanke, B. S. 1983. "Nonmonetary Effects of Financial Crisis in the Propagation of the Great Depression." *American Economic Review* 73: 257–76.

Bernanke, B. S., and J. Y. Campbell. 1988. "Is There a Corporate Debt Crisis?" *Brookings Papers of Economic Activity*, no.1: 83–139.

Bernanke, B., and M. Gertler. 1989. "Agency Cost, Net Worth and Aggregate Fluctuations." *American Economic Review* 79: 14–32.

Bernanke, B. E., and M. Gertler. 1990 "Financial Fragility and Economic Performance." *Quarterly Journal of Economics* 55: 87–114.

Beveridge, S., and C. R. Nelson. 1981. "A New Approach to Decomposition of Economic Time Series into Permanent and Transitory Components with Particular Attention to Measurements of the 'Business Cycle'." *Journal of Monetary Economics* 7: 151–74.

Bils, M. 1987. "The Cyclical Behavior of Marginal Cost and Price." *American Economic Review* 77: 838–55.

Blanchard, O. 1981. "Output, the Stock Market and Interest Rate." *American Economic Review* 71: 132–43.

Blanchard, O. 1983. "Debt and the Current Account Deficit in Brazil." In P. A. Armella, R. Dornbusch, and M. Obstfeld, eds., *Financial Policies and the World Capital Market*. Chicago: University of Chicago Press.

Blanchard, O., and S. Fischer. 1989. *Lectures in Macroeconomics*. Cambridge: MIT Press.

Blatt, J. M. 1979. "Investment Evaluation under Uncertainty." *Financial Management* 8, no.2: 66–81.

Blatt, J. M. 1983. *Dynamic Economic Systems: A Post-Keynesian Approach.* Armonk, N.Y.: Sharpe.

Blume, L. E., M. Bray, and D. Easley. 1982. "Introduction to the Stability of Rational Expectations Equilibrium." *Journal of Economic Theory* 26: 313–17.

Boggess, T. E. 1983. "A Generalized Keynes-Wicksell Model with Variable Labor Force Growth." *Journal of Macroeconomics* 5: 197–209.

Boldrin, M. 1994. "Competitive Models and Endogenous Cycles: An Evaluation." In W. Semmler, ed., *Business Cycles: Theory and Empirical Methods*, 53–72 Boston: Kluwer Academic Publishers.

Boldrin, M., and L. Montrucchio. 1986. "On the Indeterminacy of Capital Accumulation Paths." *Journal of Economic Theory* 40: 26–39.

Boldrin, M., and Rustichini, A. 1994. "Growth and Indeterminacy in Dynamic Models with Externalities." *Econometrica* 62: 323–42.

Boldrin, M., and M. Woodford. 1990. "Equilibrium Models Displaying Endogenous Fluctuations and Chaos." *Journal of Monetary Economics* 25: 189–222.

Boorman, J. T. 1976. "The Evidence on the Demand for Money: Theoretical Formulations and Empirical Results." In T. M. Havrilesky and J. T. Boorman, eds., *Current Issues in Monetary Theory and Practice*, 315–60. Arlington Heights, Ill.: AHM Publishing Corp.

Boyd, I., and J. M. Blatt. 1988. *Investment, Confidence and Business Cycles*. New York: Springer.

Bray, M. 1982. "Learning, Estimation, and Stability of Rational Expectations." *Journal of Economic Theory* 26: 318–39.

Brock, W. A., and A. G. Malliaris. 1989. *Differential Equations, Stability and Chaos in Dynamic Economics.* Amsterdam: North Holland.

Brock, W. A., D. A. Hsie, and B. LeBaron. 1991. *Nonlinear Dynamics, Chaos and Instability*. Cambridge: The MIT Press.

Bryan, M. F., and W. T. Gavin. 1986. "Models of Inflation Expectations Formation: A

Comparison of Household and Economist Forecasts-Comment." *Journal of Money, Credit and Banking* 18: 539–44.

Burmeister, E., and R. Dobell. 1970. *Mathematical Theories of Economic Growth*. London: Macmillan.

Burnside, C., M. Eichenbaum, and S. Rebelo. 1993. "Labor Hoarding and the Business Cycle." *Journal of Political Economy* April, 101: 245–73.

Caballe, J., and M. S. Santos. 1993. "On Endogenous Growth with Physical Capital and Human Capital." *Journal of Political Economy* 101: 1042–67.

Cagan, P. 1956. "The Monetary Dynamics of Hyperinflation." In M. Friedman, ed., *Studies in the Quantity Theory of Money*, 25–117. Chicago: University of Chicago Press.

Canova, F. L. 1992. "Detrending and Business Cycle Facts." Dept. of Economics, Brown University, mimeo.

Carlson, J. A. 1977. "A Study of Price Forecasts." *Ann. Econ. and Soc. Measurement* 6: 27–56.

Carlson, D. A., and A. Haurie. 1987. *Infinite Horizon Optimal Control, Theory and Applications*. Heidelberg: Springer Verlag.

Caskey, J. 1985. "Modeling the Formation of Price Expectations: A Bayesian Approach." *American Economic Review* 75: 768–76.

Cass, D. 1965. "Optimum Growth and in an Aggregative Model of Capital Accumulation." *Review of Economic Studies* 32: 233–40.

Chang, W. W., and D. J. Smyth. 1971. "The Existence and Persistence of Cycles in a Non-Linear Model: Kaldor's 1940 Model Re-examined." *Review of Economic Studies* 38: 37–46.

Chiarella, C. 1990. *The Elements of a Nonlinear Theory of Economic Dynamics*. Berlin: Springer.

Chow, G. C. 1993. "Statistical Estimation and Testing of a Real Business Cycle Model." Princeton University, Econometric Research Program, Research Memorandum, no. 365.

Christiano, L. J., and M. Eichenbaum. 1992a. "Liquidity Effects and Monetary Transmission Mechanisms." *Federal Reserve Bank of Minneapolis, Staff Report*, 150.

Christiano, L. J., and M. Eichenbaum. 1992b. "Current Real Business Cycle Theories and Aggregate Labor Market Fluctuations." *American Economic Review* 82: 431–72.

Cogley, T., and J. M. Nason. 1995. "Output Dynamics in Real-Business-Cycle Models." *American Economic Review* 85: 492–511.

Conlisk, J. 1980. "Costly Optimizers versus Cheap Imitators." *Journal of Economic Behavior and Organization* 1: 275–93.

———. 1988. "Optimization Cost." *Journal of Economic Behavior and Organization* 9: 213–28.

Cooley, T., ed., 1995. *Frontiers of Business Cycle Research*. Princeton: Princeton University Press.

Dana, R. A., and P. Malgrange. 1984. "The Dynamics of a Discrete Version of a Growth Cycle Model." In J. Ancot, ed., *Analyzing the Structure of Macromodels*. The Hague: Nijhoff Publishing.

Day, R. H. 1982. "Irregular Growth Cycles." *American Economic Review* 72: 406–14.

———. 1984. "Irregular Growth Cycles." *American Economic Review* 72: 406–17.

———. 1994. *Complex Economic Dynamics*. vol. 1. Cambridge: The MIT Press.

Day, R. H., and W. Huang. 1990. "Bulls, Bears and Market Sheep." *Journal of Economic Behavior and Organization* 14: 299–329.

Day, R. H., and T. Y. Lin. 1991. "A Keynesian Business Cycle." In E. Nell and W. Semmler, eds., *Nicholas Kaldor and Mainstream Economics*. London: Macmillan.

Day, R. H., and W. Shafer. 1985. "Keynesian Chaos." *Journal of Macroeconomics* 7: 277–95.

———. 1987. "Ergodic Fluctuations in Deterministic Economic Models." *Journal of Economic Organization and Behavior* 2: 339–63.

De Bondt, W. F. M., and R. H. Thaler. 1985. "Does the Stock Market Overreact?" *Journal of Finance* 40: 793–808.

———. 1987. "Further Evidence on Investor Overreaction and Stock Market Seasonality." *Journal of Finance* 42: 557–81.

———. 1990. "Do Security Analysts Overreact?" *American Economic Review* 80, P.P.: 52–57.

DeLong, J. B., and L. H. Summers. 1986a. "Are Business Cycles Symmetrical?" In R. J. Gordon, ed., *The American Business Cycle: Continuity and Change*, 166–79. Chicago: University of Chicago Press.

———. 1986b. "Is Increased Price Flexibility Stabilizing?" *American Economic Review* 76: 1031–44.

De Long, J. B., A. Schleifer, L. H. Summers, and R. J. Waldman. 1991. "The Survival of Noise Traders on Financial Markets." *Journal of Business* 64: 1–19.

De Long, J. T. 1938. "The Movement of Real and Money Wage Rates." *The Economic Journal* 48: 413–34.

Denison, E. F. 1961. "Sources of Economic Growth in the United States and the Alternative before us, Supplement Paper 13." Committee for Economic Development, New York.

Desai, M. 1973. "Growth Cycles and Inflation in a Model of the Class Struggle." *Journal of Economic Theory* 6: 572–45.

Dierker, E. 1974. *Topological Methods in Walrasian Economics*. Heidelberg, New York: Springer.

Dieudonné, J. 1960. *Foundations of Modern Analysis*. New York: Academic Press.

Dockner, E., and G. Feichtinger. 1991. "On the Optimality of Limit Cycles in the Dynamic Economic Systems." *Journal of Economics* 53: 31–50.

Dornbusch, R. 1976. "Expectations and Exchange Rated Dynamics." *Journal of Political Economy* 84: 1161–77.

Duguay, P., and Y. Rabeau. 1988. "A Simulation Model of Macroeconomic Effects of Deficit." *Journal of Macroeconomics* 10: 538–64.

Duménil G., and D. Lévy. 1987. "The Dynamics of Competition: A Restoration of the Classical Analysis." *Cambridge Journal of Economics* 11: 133–64.

Dunlop, J. T. 1938. "The Movement of Real and Money Wage Rates." *The Economic Journal* 48: 413–34.

Dutt, A. 1990. *Growth, Distribution, and Uneven Development*. Cambridge: Cambridge University Press.

Earl, P. E. 1990. "Economics and Psychology: A Survey." *Economic Journal* 100: 718–55.

Economic Report of the President. 1984, 1988. Washington, D.C.: United States Government Printing Office.

Eisner, R. 1956. *Determinants of Capital Expenditures (an Interview Study)*. Urbana: University of Illinois Press.

Evans, G. W., and S. Honkapohja. 1988. "On the Robustness of Bubbles in Linear RE Models." Technical Report no. 539, Economic Series, Stanford University.

———. 1990. "Learning, Convergence, and Stability with Multiple Rational Expectations Equilibria." London School of Economics. Mimeographed.

Evans, M. K. 1969. *Macroeconomic Activity*. New York: Harper & Row.

Fair, F. C. 1984. *Specification, Estimation, and Analysis of Macroeconomic Models*. Cambridge: Harvard University Press.

Fair, F. C., and W. Parke. 1984. "The Tape of the Fair-Parke Program and the Fair US Model." New Haven: Yale University. Mimeographed.

Fazzari, S., R. G. Hubbard, and B. C. Petersen 1988. "Financing Constraints and Corporate Investment." *Brookings Papers of Economic Activity*, no.1, 141–95.

Feige, E. L., and D. K. Pearce. 1976. "Economically Rational Expectations: Are Innovations of the Rate of Inflation Independent of Innovations in Measures of Monetary and Fiscal Policy?" *Journal of Political Economy* 84: 499–522.

Feldstein, M., J. Green, and E. Sheshinski. 1978, "Inflation and Taxes in a Growing Economy with Debt and Equity Finance." *Journal of Political Economy* 86: S53–S70.

Figlewski, S., and P. Wachtel. 1981. "The Formation of Inflationary Expectations." *Review of Economics and Statistics* 63: 1–10.

Fischer, S. 1972. "Keynes-Wicksell and Neoclassical Models of Money and Growth." *American Economic Review* 62: 880–90.

———. 1977. "Long-term Contracts, Rational Expectations, and the Optimal Money Supply Rule." *Journal of Political Economy* 85: 191–205.

Flaschel, P. 1990. "Cross-dual Dynamics, Derivative Control, and Global Stability: A Neoclassical Presentation of a Classical Theme." *Political Economy* 6: 73–92.

———. 1991. "Stability–Independent of Economic Structure? A Prototype Analysis." *Structural Change and Economic Dynamics* 2: 9–35.

———. 1992. "A Keynes-Wicksell Model of the 'Growth Cycle'. The Myopic Perfect Foresight Case." In G. Feichtinger, ed., *Dynamic Economic Models and Optimal Control. Proceedings of the Fourth Viennese Workshop on Dynamic Economic Models and Optimal Control*, 467–89. Amsterdam: North Holland.

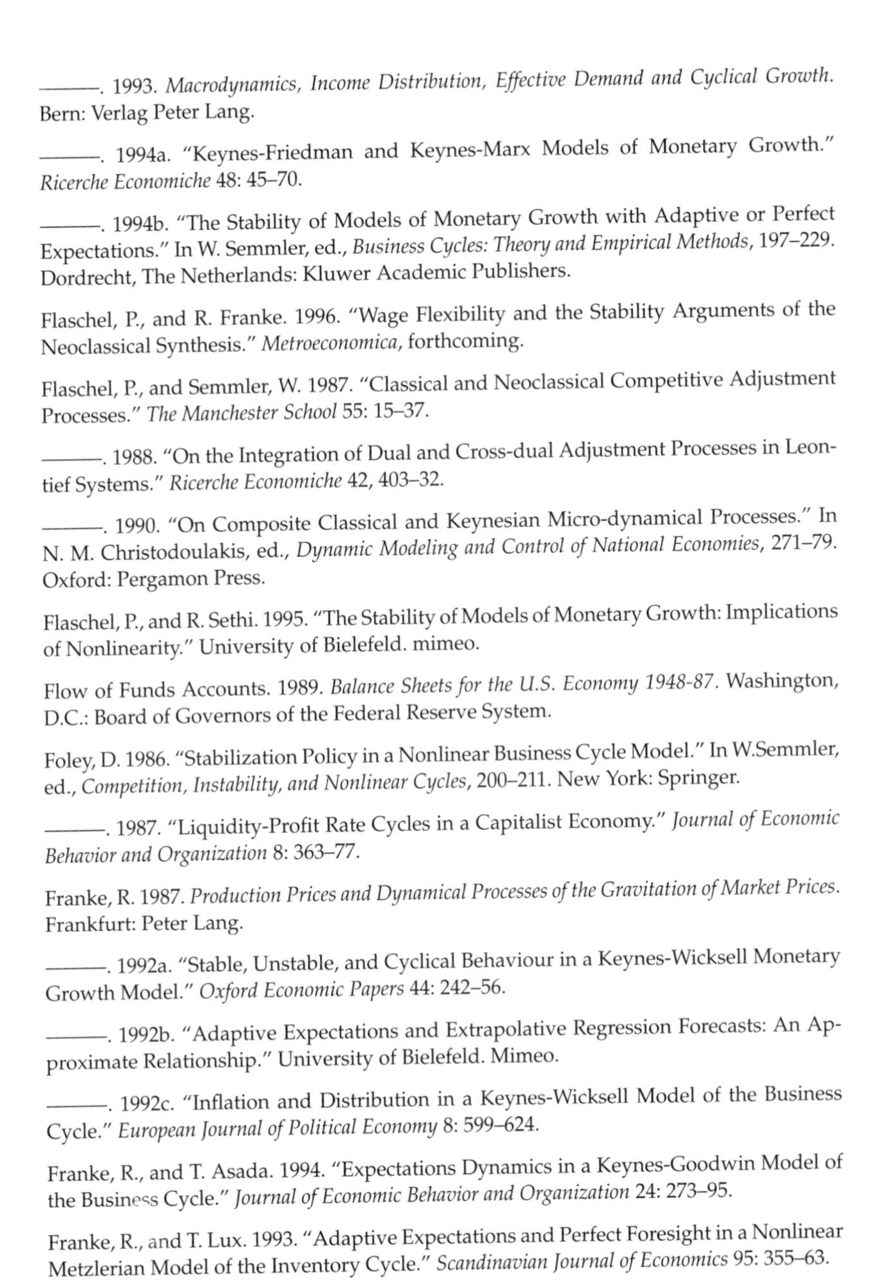

———. 1993. *Macrodynamics, Income Distribution, Effective Demand and Cyclical Growth.* Bern: Verlag Peter Lang.

———. 1994a. "Keynes-Friedman and Keynes-Marx Models of Monetary Growth." *Ricerche Economiche* 48: 45–70.

———. 1994b. "The Stability of Models of Monetary Growth with Adaptive or Perfect Expectations." In W. Semmler, ed., *Business Cycles: Theory and Empirical Methods,* 197–229. Dordrecht, The Netherlands: Kluwer Academic Publishers.

Flaschel, P., and R. Franke. 1996. "Wage Flexibility and the Stability Arguments of the Neoclassical Synthesis." *Metroeconomica,* forthcoming.

Flaschel, P., and Semmler, W. 1987. "Classical and Neoclassical Competitive Adjustment Processes." *The Manchester School* 55: 15–37.

———. 1988. "On the Integration of Dual and Cross-dual Adjustment Processes in Leontief Systems." *Ricerche Economiche* 42, 403–32.

———. 1990. "On Composite Classical and Keynesian Micro-dynamical Processes." In N. M. Christodoulakis, ed., *Dynamic Modeling and Control of National Economies,* 271–79. Oxford: Pergamon Press.

Flaschel, P., and R. Sethi. 1995. "The Stability of Models of Monetary Growth: Implications of Nonlinearity." University of Bielefeld. mimeo.

Flow of Funds Accounts. 1989. *Balance Sheets for the U.S. Economy 1948-87.* Washington, D.C.: Board of Governors of the Federal Reserve System.

Foley, D. 1986. "Stabilization Policy in a Nonlinear Business Cycle Model." In W.Semmler, ed., *Competition, Instability, and Nonlinear Cycles,* 200–211. New York: Springer.

———. 1987. "Liquidity-Profit Rate Cycles in a Capitalist Economy." *Journal of Economic Behavior and Organization* 8: 363–77.

Franke, R. 1987. *Production Prices and Dynamical Processes of the Gravitation of Market Prices.* Frankfurt: Peter Lang.

———. 1992a. "Stable, Unstable, and Cyclical Behaviour in a Keynes-Wicksell Monetary Growth Model." *Oxford Economic Papers* 44: 242–56.

———. 1992b. "Adaptive Expectations and Extrapolative Regression Forecasts: An Approximate Relationship." University of Bielefeld. Mimeo.

———. 1992c. "Inflation and Distribution in a Keynes-Wicksell Model of the Business Cycle." *European Journal of Political Economy* 8: 599–624.

Franke, R., and T. Asada. 1994. "Expectations Dynamics in a Keynes-Goodwin Model of the Business Cycle." *Journal of Economic Behavior and Organization* 24: 273–95.

Franke, R., and T. Lux. 1993. "Adaptive Expectations and Perfect Foresight in a Nonlinear Metzlerian Model of the Inventory Cycle." *Scandinavian Journal of Economics* 95: 355–63.

Franke, R., and W. Semmler. 1989. "Debt Financing of Firms, Stability, and Cycles in a Macroeconomic Growth Model." In W. Semmler, ed., *Financial Dynamics and Business Cycles,* 38–64. Armonk, N.Y.: Sharpe.

———. 1994. "Bond Rate, Loan Rate and Tobin's q in a Temporary Equilibrium Model of the Financial Sector." New School for Social Research, New York, Dept. of Economics. Mimeo.

Franke, R., and R. Sethi. 1993. "Cautious Trend-seeking and Complex Asset Price Dynamics." University of Bielefeld, Dept. of Economics. Mimeo.

———. 1995. "Behavioural Heterogeneity under Evolutionary Pressure: Macroeconomic Implications of Costly Optimisation." *Economic Journal* 105: 583–600.

Frankel, J. A., and K. A. Froot. 1986. "The Dollar as an Irrational Speculative Bubble: The Tale of Fundamentalists and Chartists." *Marcus Wallenberg Papers on International Finance* 1: 27–55.

Friedman, B. M. 1979. "Optimal Expectations and the Extreme Information Assumptions of 'Rational Expectations' Macromodels." *Journal of Monetary Economics* 5: 23–41.

Friedman, B. J., and D. I. Laibson. 1989. "Economic Implications of Extraordinary Movements in Stock Prices." *Brookings Papers on Economic Activity*, no.2: 137–89.

Friedman, M. 1968. "The Role of Monetary Policy." *American Economic Review* 58: 1–17.

Frisch, R. 1933. "Propagation Problems and Impulse Problems in Dynamic Economics." In *Economic Essays in Honor of Gustav Cassel*. London: Allen and Unwin, 171–205.

Gabisch, G., and H. W. Lorenz. 1989. *Business Cycle Theory: A Survey of Methods and Concepts*. 2nd ed. Berlin: Springer.

Gandolfo, G. 1980. *Economic Dynamics: Methods and Models*. Amsterdam: North-Holland.

———. 1985. *Economic Dynamics: Methods and Models*. 2nd ed. Amsterdam: North Holland.

Gantmacher, F. R. 1959. *Applications of the Theory of Matrices*. New York: Interscience Publishers.

Gertler, M. 1988. "Financial Structure and Aggregate Economic Activity." *Journal of Money, Credit and Banking* 20: 559–88.

Gertler, M., R. G. Hubbard, and A. Kashyap. 1991. "Interest Rate Spreads, Credit Constraints, and Investment: An Empirical Investigation." In R. G. Hubbard, ed., *Financial Markets and Financial Crises*. Chicago: The University of Chicago Press.

Gibson, W. E. 1972. "Interest Rates and Inflationary Expectations." *American Economic Review* 62: 854–65.

Goldfeld, S. 1976. "The Case of the Missing Money." *Brookings Papers on Economic Activity*, no.3: 683–739.

Goldman, S. M. 1972. "Hyperinflation and the Rate of Growth in Money Supply." *Journal of Economic Theory* 5: 250–57.

Goodwin, R. M. 1951. "The Non-linear Accelerator and the Persistence of Business Cycles." *Econometrica* 19: 1–17.

———. [1953] 1983. "Static and Dynamic General Equilibrium Models." In R. M. Goodwin, *Essays in Linear Economic Structures*. London: Macmillan.

———. 1967. "A Growth Cycle." In C. H. Feinstein, ed., *Socialism Capitalism and Growth*. Cambridge: Cambridge University Press.

———. 1972. "A Growth Cycle." In E. K. Hunt and J. G. Schwartz, eds., *A Critique of Economic Theory*, 442–49. Harmondsworth: Penguin Books.

———. 1983. *Essays in Linear Economic Structures*. London: Macmillan.

———. 1989. *Essays in Nonlinear Economic Dynamics*. Bern: Peter Lang.

Goodwin, R. M., and L. F. Punzo. 1987. *The Dynamics of a Capitalist Economy*. Cambridge: Polity Press.

Gramlich, E. M. 1983. "Models of Inflation Expectations Formation: A Comparison of Household and Economist Forecasts." *Journal of Money, Credit and Banking* 15: 155–73.

Grandmont J.-M. 1988. *Nonlinear Economic Dynamics*. Boston: Academic Press.

———. 1990. "Economic Dynamics with Learning: Some Instability Examples." CEPREMAP. Mimeo.

Grandmont, J.-M., and P. Malgrange. 1987. "Introduction." In J. M. Grandmont and P. Malgrange, eds., *Nonlinear Economic Dynamics*. Orlando: Academic Press.

Granger, C. W. J., and T. Teräsvirta. 1993. *Modelling Nonlinear Economic Relations* Oxford: Oxford University Press.

Gray, J. A., and M. Kandil. 1991. "Is Price Flexibility Stabilizing? A Broader Perspective." *Journal of Money, Credit, and Banking* 23: 1–12.

Greenwald, B., and J. E. Stiglitz. 1986. "Imperfect Information, Finance Constraints, and Business Fluctuations." In M. Kohn and S. C. Tsiang, eds., *Finance Constraints, Expectations, and Macroeconomics*, 103–40. Oxford: Clarendon Press.

———. 1987. "Keynesian, New Keynesian and New Classical Economics." *Oxford Economic Papers* 39, 119–32.

———. 1988. "Financial Markets Imperfections and Business Cycles." *NBER Working Papers*, no. 2494.

———. 1989. "A Theory of Price Rigidities: Adjustment under Uncertainty." *American Economic Review* 79: 364–70.

Greenwald, B. C., J. E. Stiglitz, and A. Weiss. 1984. "Informational Imperfections in the Capital Market and Macroeconomic Fluctuations." *American Economic Review* 74: 194–200.

Greiner, A., and W. Semmler. 1994. "Endogenous Technical Change Through Investment and Learning." discussion paper, University of Augsburg.

———. 1995. "Multiple Steady States, Indeterminacy and Cycles in a Basic Model of Endogenous Growth." *Journal of Economics* 63, 1: 79–99.

Grossman, G., and E. Helpman. 1991. *Innovation and Growth in the Global Economy*. Cambridge: The MIT Press.

Groth, C. 1988. "IS-LM Dynamics and the Hypothesis of Combined Adaptive–Forward Looking Expectations." In P. Flaschel and M. Krüger, eds., *Recent Approaches to Economic Dynamics*, 251–65. Bern: Peter Lang.

———. 1992. "Some Unfamiliar Dynamics of a Familiar Macro Model: A Note." *Journal of Economics* 58: 293–305.

Guckenheimer, J., and P. Holmes. 1983. *Nonlinear Oscillations, Dynamical Systems and Bifurcations of Vector Fields*. Heidelberg: Springer.

Gurley, J. G., and E. S. Shaw. 1955. "Financial Aspects of Economic Development." *American Economic Review* 45: 515–38.

Hadjimichalakis, M. G. 1971. "Money, Expectations, and Dynamics—An Alternative View." *International Economic Review* 12: 381–402.

Hahn, F. 1982. "Stability." In K. Arrow and M. D. Intrilligator, eds., *Handbook of Mathematical Economics*. Amsterdam: North-Holland.

Hairer, E., and G. Wanner. 1987. *Solving Ordinary Differential Equations I. Nonstiff Problems*. Berlin: Springer.

Hall, R. 1986. "Market Structure and Macroeconomic Fluctuations." *Brooking Papers on Economic Activity*, no.2: 285–322.

Hall, R. 1988. "The Relation between Price and Marginal Costs in the U.S. Industry." *Journal of Political Economy* 96: 921–47.

Hansen, G. H. 1988. "Technical Progress and Aggregate Fluctuations." University of California, Los Angeles. Mimeo.

Hansen, L. P. 1982. "Large Sample Properties of Generalized Methods of Moments Estimators." *Econometrica* 50: 1029–54.

Hansen, L. P., and T. Sargent. 1988. "Recursive Linear Models of Dynamic Economies." Hoover Institute, Stanford University. Mimeo.

Hansen, L. P., and K. J. Singleton. 1982. "Generalized Instrument Variables Estimation of Nonlinear Rational Expectations Models." *Econometrica* 50: 1268–86.

Harrison, J. M., and D. M. Kreps. 1978. "Speculative Investor Behavior in a Stock Market with Heterogeneous Expectations." *Quarterly Journal of Economics* 92: 323–36.

Harrod, R. F. 1948. *Towards a Dynamic Economics*. London: Macmillan.

Hawtrey, R. G. [1926] 1950. "The Trade Cycle." In American Economic Association, ed., *Readings in Business Cycle Theories*. London: Allen and Unwin.

Hayakawa, H. 1984. "A Dynamic Generalization of the Tobin Model." *Journal of Economic Dynamics and Control* 7: 209–31.

Heiner, R. A. 1988. "The Necessity of Delaying Economic Adjustment." *Journal of Economic Behavior and Organization* 10: 255–86.

Hicks, J. 1939. *Value and Capital*. Oxford: Oxford University Press.

———. 1950. *A Contribution to the Theory of the Trade Cycle*. Oxford: Oxford University Press.

———. 1965. *Capital and Growth*. Oxford: Oxford University Press.

Hirsch, M., and S. Smale. 1974. *Differential Equations, Dynamical Systems and Linear Algebra*. London: Academic Press.

Jacobs, R. L., and R. A. Jones. 1980. "Price Expectations in the United States." *American Economic Review* 70: 269–77.

Jarsulic, M. 1988. "Financial Instability and Income Distribution." *Journal of Economic Issues* 22: 545–53.

Jordan, J. S. 1983. "Locally Stable Price Mechanisms." *Journal of Mathematical Economics* 10: 235–59.

Jorgenson, D. W. 1960. "The Dual Stability Theorem." *Econometrica* 28, (4), 892–99.

Kaldor, N. 1940. "A Model of the Trade Cycle." *Economic Journal* 50: 78–92.

———. 1961. "Capital Accumulation and Economic Growth." In F. A. Lutz and D. C. Hague, eds., *The Theory of Capital*. London: Macmillan.

———. 1985. *Economics without Equilibrium*. New York: M. E. Sharpe.

Kaldor, N., and J. A. Mirrlees. 1962) "A New Model of Economic Growth." *Review of Economic Studies* 29: 174–92.

Kalecki, M. 1937a. "A Theory of the Business Cycle." *Review of Economic Studies* 4: 77–97.

———. 1937b. "The Principle of Increasing Risk." *Economica* 4: 441–47.

———. 1939. "Money and Real Wages." Reprint of the Polish booklet in M. Kalecki 1966. *Studies in the Theory of Business Cycles*, 40–71. Warsaw and Oxford: Polish Scientific Publishers and Basil Blackwell.

———. 1943. "Costs and Prices." Final version printed in M.Kalecki (1971. *Selected Essays on the Dynamics of the Capitalist Economy 1933–1972*, 43–61. Cambridge: Cambridge University Press.

Kane, E. J., and B. G. Malkiel. 1976. "Autoregressive and Non-autoregressive Elements in Cross-section Forecasts of Inflation." *Econometrica* 44: 1–16.

Kaufman, H. 1986. "Debt: The Threat to Economic and Financial Instability." In *Debt, Financial Stability, and Public Policy*, 15–26. Kansas City: Federal Reserve Bank of Kansas City.

Kendall, M. G., and A. Stuart. 1968. *The Advanced Theory of Statistics, Vol.3: Design and Analysis, and Time Series*. London: C. Griffin.

Keynes, J. M. 1936. *The General Theory of Employment, Interest and Money*. London: Macmillan.

———. 1937. "The General Theory of Employment." *Quarterly Journal of Economics* 51: 209–23.

King, R. 1990. "Money and Business Cycles." University of Rochester. Mimeo.

King, R. G., C. I. Plosser, and S. T. Rebelo. 1988a. "Production, Growth and Business Cycles I: The Basic Neo-classical Model." *Journal of Monetary Economics* 21: 195–232.

———. 1988b. "Production, Growth and Business Cycles II: New Directions." *Journal of Monetary Economics* 21: 309–41.

Klein, L. R. 1971. "Forecasting and Policy Evaluation using Large Scale Econometric Models: The State of the Art." In M. Intriligator, ed., *Frontiers of Quantitative Economics*. Amsterdam: North-Holland.

Kloeden, P. E., and J. Lorenz. 1986. "Stable Attracting Sets in Dynamical Systems and in their one-step Discretizations." *SIAM Journal of Numerical Analysis* 23: 986–95.

Kose, T. 1956. "Solutions of Saddle Value Problems by Differential Equations." *Econometrica* 24: 59–70.

Kydland, F. E., and E. F. Prescott. 1982. "Time to Build and Aggregate Fluctuation." *Econometric* 50: 1345–70.

Lahiri, K. 1976. "Inflationary Expectations: Their Formation and Interest Rate Effects." *American Economic Review* 66: 124–31.

Lavington, F. 1921. *The English Capital Market*. London: Methuen.

Lawson, T. 1980. "Adaptive Expectations and Uncertainty." *Review of Economic Studies* 47: 305–20.

Lee, B. S., and B. F. Ingram. 1991. "Simulation Estimation of Time-Series Models." *Journal of Econometrics* 47: 197–05.

Leijonhufvud, A. 1968. *On Keynesian Economics and the Economics of Keynes*. Oxford: Oxford University Press.

———. 1973. "Effective Demand Failures." *Swedish Journal of Economics* 75: 27–48.

Lintner, J. 1956. "Distribution of Incomes of Corporations Among Dividends, Retained Earnings and Taxes." *American Economic Review* 46: P.P.: 97–113.

Ljung, L. 1987. *System Identification*. Englewood Cliffs, N.J.: Prentice Hall.

Ljung, L., and T. Soederstroem. 1987. *Theory and Practice of Recursive Identification*. Cambridge, MA: MIT Press.

Long, J. B., and C. I. Plosser. 1983. "Real Business Cycle." *Journal of Political Economy* 91: 39–69.

Lorenz, H.-W. 1993. *Nonlinear Dynamical Economics and Chaotic Motion*. 2nd ed. Berlin: Springer Verlag.

Lovell, M. C. 1986. "Tests of the Rational Expectations Hypothesis." *American Economic Review* 76: 110–24.

Lucas, R.E. 1972. "Expectations and the Neutrality of Money." *Journal of Economic Theory* 4: 103–24.

———. 1977. "Understanding Business Cycles" in K. Brunner and A. M. Meltzer, eds., *Stabilization of the Domestic and International Economy*, 7–29. Amsterdam: North-Holland.

———. 1988. "On the Mechanics of Economic Growth." *Journal of Monetary Economics* 22: 3–42.

———. 1989. "The Effects of Monetary Shocks When Prices are set in Advance." University of Chicago. Mimeo.

———. 1990. "Supply Side Economics: An Analytical Review." *Oxford Economic Papers* 22: 3–42.

Lux, T. 1992. "A Note on the Stability of Endogenous Cycles in Diamond's Model of Search and Barter." *Journal of Economics* 56: 185–96.

Makridakis, S., A. Andersen, R. Carbon, R. Fildes, M. Hibon, R. Lewandowski, J. Newton, and R. Winkler, eds. 1984. *The Forecasting Accuracy of Major Time Series Methods*. New York: John Wiley.

Mankiw, G. D. 1989. "Real Business Cycles: A New Keynesian Perspective." *Journal of Economic Perspectives* 3: 79–91.

Mankiw, N. G. 1990. "A Quick Refresher Course in Macroeconomics." *Journal of Economic Literature* (December) 28: 1645–60.

Mankiw, N. G., Romer, and D. N. Weil. 1992. "A Contribution to the Empirics of Economic Growth." *Quarterly Journal of Economics*. 107, (2): 407–37.

Mankiw, N. B., and S. P. Zeldes. 1992. "The Consumption of Stockholders and Non-Stockholders." *Journal of Financial Economics* 29: 97–112.

Marcet, A., and T. Sargent. 1988. "The Fate of Systems with Adaptive Expectations." *American Economic Review* 78, P.P.: 168–72.

———. 1989. "Convergence of Least Squares Learning Mechanisms in Self-referencing Linear Stochastic Models. *Journal of Economic Theory* 48: 337–68.

Marglin, S. 1984. *Growth, Distribution, and Prices*. Cambridge, MA: Harvard University Press.

Marsden, J. E., and M. McCracken. 1976. *The Hopf Bifurcation and Its Applications*. New York: Springer.

Marshall, A. 1947. *Principles of Economics*. London: Macmillan.

Marx K. 1967. *Capital*. Vol. 3. New York: International Publishers.

Mas-Colell, A. 1985. *The Theory of General Economic Equilibrium. A Differentiable Approach*. Cambridge, UK: Cambridge University Press.

———. 1986. "Notes on Price and Quantity Tâtonnement Dynamics." In H. Sonnenschein, ed., *Models of Economic Dynamics*, 49–68. Heidelberg, New York: Springer.

McCallum, B. T. 1989. *Monetary Economics: Theory and Policy*. New York: Macmillan.

Medio, A. 1991. "Continuous-time Models of Chaos in Economics." *Journal of Economic Behavior and Organization* 16: 133–51.

Meyer, J. R., and E. Kuh. 1957. *The Investment Decision*. Cambridge, MA: Harvard University Press.

Meyrs, S. F., and N. S. M. Jajluf. 1984. "Corporate Financing and Investment Decisions when Firms have Information that Investors do not have." *Journal of Financial Economics* 13: 187–222.

Minsky, H. P. 1975. *John Maynard Keynes*. New York: Columbia University Press.

———. 1986 *Stabilizing an Unstable Economy*. New Haven: Yale University Press.

Mishkin, F. 1991. "Asymmetric Information and Financial Crices: A Hisotrical Perspective." In R. G. Hubbard, ed., *Financial Market and Financial Crises*, 69–108. Chicago: The University of Chicago Press.

Mitchie, J. 1987. *Wages in the Business Cycle*. London: F. Pinter.

Modigliani, F., and M. Miller. 1958. "The Cost of Capital, Corporate Finance and the Theory of Investment." *The American Economic Review* 53: 261–97.

Montrucchio, L. 1992. "Dynamical Systems that Solve Continuous-Time Concave Optimization Problems: Anything Goes." In J. Benhabib, ed., *Chaos and Cycles in Economic Equilibrium*. Princeton: Princeton University Press.

Morishima, M. 1959. "A Reconsideration of the Walras-Cassel-Leontief Models of General Equilibrium." In, K. Arrow, ed., *Mathematical Social Sciences*. Stanford: Stanford University Press.

———. 1976. *The Economic Theory of Modern Society*. Cambridge, UK: Cambridge University Press.

———. 1977. *Walras' Economics*. Cambridge, UK: Cambridge University Press.

Mullineux, D. J. 1978. "On Testing for Rationality: Another Look at the Livingston Expectations Data." *Journal of Political Economy* 86: 329–36.

———. 1980. "Inflation Expectations and Money Growth in the United States." *American Economic Review* 70: 149–61.

Mussa, M. 1975. "Adaptive and Regressive Expectations in a Rational Model of the Inflationary Process." *Journal of Monetary Economics* 1: 423–42.

Muth, J. F. 1960. "Optimal Properties of Exponentially Weighted Forecasts." *Journal of the American Statistical Association* 55: 299–306.

Muth, J.F. 1961. "Rational Expectations and the Theory of Price Movements." *Econometrica* 29: 315–35.

Myers, S. C. 1977. "Determinants of Corporate Borrowing." *Journal of Financial Economics* 5: 147–75.

———. 1984. "The Capital Structure Puzzle." *The Journal of Finance* 34: 575–92.

Nerlove, M. 1984. "Expectations, Plans, and Realizations in Theory and Practice." *Econometrica* 51: 1251–81.

Niggle, C. J. 1989. "The Cyclical Behavior of Corporate Financial Ratios and Minsky's Financial Instability Hypothesis." In W. Semmler, ed., *Financial Dynamics and Business Cycles*, 203–20. Armonk, N.Y.: Sharpe.

Noble, N. R., and T. W. Fields . 1982. "Testing the Rationality of Inflation Expectations Derived from Survey Data: A Structure-based Approach." *Southern Economic Journal* 49: 361–73.

O'Donnell, R. 1990. "An Overview of Probability Expectations, Uncertainty and Rationality in Keynes's Conceptual Framework." *Review of Political Economy* 2: 253–66.

Orléan, A. 1990. "Contagion Mimétiques et Bulles Spéculatives." In J. Cartelier, ed., *La Formation des Grandeurs Économiques*, 285–321. Paris: PUF.

Orphanides, A., and R. Solow. 1990. "Money, Inflation and Growth." In F. Hahn, ed., *Handbook of Monetary Economics*. Amsterdam: North Holland.

Patinkin, D. 1965. *Money, Interest, and Prices*. 2nd ed. New York: Harper and Row.

Phelps, E. S., and J. B. Taylor. 1977. "Stabilizing Power of Monetary Policy under Rational Expectations." *Journal of Political Economy* 85: 163–90.

Piron, R. 1991. "Keynes as a Noise Trader." *Journal of Economic Perspectives* 5: 215–17.

Prescott, E. C. 1986. "Theory ahead of Business Cycle Measurement." *Quarterly Review*, Federal Reserve Bank of Minneapolis, 10.

Ramsey, J. B. 1988. "Economic and Financial Data as Nonlinear Processes." In G. P. Dwyer and R. W. Hafer, eds., *The Stock Market: Bubbles, Volatility, and Chaos*. Boston: Kluwer Academic Publishers.

Ricardo, D. 1951. *Principles of Political Economy and Taxation*. Cambridge, UK: Cambridge University Press.

Romer, P. 1986a. "Increasing Returns and Long-Run Growth." *Journal of Political Economy* 94: 1002–37.

———. 1986b. "Cake Eating, Chattering, and Jumps: Existence for Variational Problems." *Econometrica* 54: 897–908.

———. 1990. "Endogenous Technical Change." *Journal of Political Economy* 89: 71–103.

Rose, H. 1966. "Unemployment in a Theory of Growth." *International Economic Review* 7: 260–82.

———. 1967. "On the Nonlinear Theory of the Employment Cycle." *Review of Economic Studies* 153–73.

———. 1969. "Real and Monetary Factors in the Business Cycle." *Journal of Money, Credit and Banking* 1: 138–52.

———. 1990. *Macroeconomic Dynamics. A Marshallian Synthesis*. Cambridge, MA: Basil Blackwell.

Saari, D. G., and C. P. Simon. 1978. "Effective Price Mechanisms." *Econometrica* 46: 1097–1125.

Samuelson, P. 1947. *Foundations of Economic Analysis*. New York: J. Wiley.

Sargent, T. 1973a. "Interest Rate and Prices in the Long Run: A Study of the Gibson Paradox. *Journal of Money, Credit, and Banking* 5: 385–49.

———. 1973b. "Rational Expectations, the Real Rate of Interest, and the Natural Rate of Unemployment." *Brookings Papers on Economic Activity* 429–72.

———. 1986. *Rational Expectations and Inflation*. New York: Harper & Row.

———. 1987. *Macroeconomic Theory*. 2nd ed. New York: Academic Press.

———. 1993. *Bounded Rationality and Macroeconomics*. Oxford: Clarendon Press.

Sargent, T., and N. Wallace. 1973. "The Stability of Models of Money and Growth with Perfect Foresight." *Econometrica* 41: 1043–48.

———. 1975. "'Rational' Expectations, the Optimal Monetary Instrument, and the Optimal Money Supply Rule." *Journal of Political Economy* 83: 241–54.

Saunders, E. M. Jr. 1993. "Stock Prices and Wall Street Weather." *American Economic Review* 83: 1337–45.

Schinasi, G. J. 1982. "Fluctuations in a Dynamic, Intermediate-Run IS-LM Model: Applications of the Poincare-Bendixson Theorem." *Journal of Economic Theory* 28: 365–75.

Schmalensee, R. 1976. "An Experimental Study of Expectation Formation." *Econometrica* 44: 17–41.

Schroeter, J. R., and S. L. Smith. 1986. "A Reexamination of the Rationality of the Livingston Price Expectations." *Journal of Money, Credit and Banking* 18: 237–46.

Semmler, W. 1995. "Solving Nonlinear Dynamic Models by Iterative Dynamic Programming." *Computational Economics* 8: 127–54.

Semmler, W. ed., 1989. *Financial Dynamics and Business Cycles*. Armonk, N.Y.: M. E. Sharpe.

———ed., 1994. *Business Cycles: Theory and Empirical Methods*. Boston: Kluwer Academic Publishers.

Semmler, W., and R. Franke. 1995. "The Financial-Real Interaction and Investment in the Business Cycle." In E. Nell and G. Deleplace, eds., *Money in Motion* London: Macmillan.

Semmler, W., and G. Gong. 1994. "Estimating and Evaluating Equilibrium Business Cycle Models." Paper prepared for the Conference on "Nonlinear Dynamic Phenomena in Economic and Financial Markets," Sydney, Australia, December.

———. 1996. "Estimating Parameters of Real Business Cycle Models." *Journal of Economic Behavior and Organization* forthcoming.

Semmler, W., and M. Sieveking. 1993. "Nonlinear Liquidity Growth Dynamics with Corridor Stability." *Journal of Economic Behavior and Organization* 22: 189–208.

———. 1995. "External Finance and Critical Foreign Debt." New School for Social Research, working paper no. 52.

Sen, A. 1970. "Introduction." In A. Sen, ed., *Growth Economics*, 9–40. Harmondsworth, UK: Penguin Books.

Sen, K. K. 1990. "The Sunspot Theorists and Keynes." *Journal of Post Keynesian Economics* 12: 564–71.

Shah, A., and M. Desai. 1981. "Growth Cycles with Induced Technical Change." *The Economic Journal* 91: 1006–10.

Shell, K. 1966. "Toward a Theory of Inventive Activities and Capital Accumulation." *A.E.R. Papers and Proc.* (May): 62–68.

Shell, K. 1967. "A Model of Inventive Activity and Capital Accumulation." In K. Shell, ed., *Essays on the Theory of Optimal Growth*. Cambridge: The MIT Press.

Shiller, R. J. 1990. "Speculative Prices and Popular Models." *Journal of Economic Perspectives* 4, no.2: 55–66.

———. 1991. *Market Volatility*. Cambridge, MA: The MIT Press.

Shleifer, A., and L. H. Summers. 1990. "The Noise Trader Approach to Finance." *Journal of Economic Perspectives* 4, no.2: 19–33.

Sidrauski, M. 1967. "Rational Choice and Patterns of Economic Growth in a Monetary Economy." *American Economic Review* 57: 534–44.

Skott, P. 1989. *Conflict and Effective Demand in Economic Growth*. Cambridge, UK: Cambridge University Press.

———. 1991a. "Cyclical Growth in a Kaldorian model." In E. J. Nell and W. Semmler, eds., *Nicholas Kaldor and Mainstream Economics*, 379–94. London: Macmillan.

———. 1991b. "Financial Innovation, Deregulation and Minsky Cycles." University of Aarhus. Mimeo.

Slutsky, E. 1937. "The Summation of Random Causes as the Source of Cyclical Processes." *Econometrica* 5: 105–46.

Smale, S. 1976. "Exchange Processes with Price Adjustment." *Journal of Mathematical Economics* 3: 211–26.

Smith, A. 1974. *The Wealth of Nations*. Middlesex, UK: Penguin.

Smith, G. 1980. "A Dynamic IS-LM Simulation Model." *Applied Economics* 12: 131–327.

Smithin, J. N., and P. N. Tu. 1987. "Disequilibrium Adjustment in a 'Classical' Macroeconomic Model: A Note." *Zeitschrift für Nationalökonomie* 47: 207–13.

Solow, R. M. 1956. "A Contribution to the Theory of Economic Growth." *Quarterly Journal of Economics* (February): 65–94.

Stadler, G. W. 1994. "Real Business Cycles." *Journal of Economic Literature* 32: 1750–83.

Stein, J. 1966. "Money and Capacity Growth." *Journal of Political Economy* 74: 451–65.

———. 1969. "Neoclassical and Keynes-Wicksell Monetary Growth Models." *Journal of Money, Credit and Banking* 1, 153–71.

———. 1970. "Monetary Growth Theory in Perspective." *American Economic Review* 60: 85–106.

———. 1971. *Money and Capacity Growth*. New York: Columbia University Press.

———. 1982. *Monetarist, Keynesian and New Classical Economics*. Oxford: Basil Blackwell.

Steindl, J. [1952] 1976. *Maturity and Stagnation in American Capitalism*. Reprint with a new introduction, New York: Monthly Review Press.

Stiglitz, J. E. 1990. "Symposium on Bubbles." *Journal of Economic Perspectives* 4: 13–17.

Stiglitz, J. E., and A. Weiss. 1981. "Credit Rationing in Markets with Imperfect Information." *American Economic Review* 71: 393–410.

Stock, J. H., and M. W. Watson. 1989. "New Indexes of Coincident and Leading Economic Indicators." In O. J. Blanchard and S. Fischer, eds., NBER *Macroeconomics Annual*. Cambridge, MA: The MIT Press.

Stokey, N. L., and R. E. Lucas. 1989. *Recursive Methods in Economics*. Cambridge, MA: Harvard University Press.

Summers, L. H. 1981. "Taxation and Corporate Investment: A q-Theory Approach." *Brookings Papers on Economic Activity*, no.1: 68–127.

———. 1986. "Some Skeptical Observations on Real Business Cycle Theory." *Quarterly Review*, Federal Reserve Bank of Minneapolis, 10.

Taylor, J. B. 1975. "Monetary Policy during a Transition to Rational Expectations." *Journal of Political Economy* 83: 1009–21.

———. 1979. "Staggered Wage Setting in a Macro Model." *American Economic Review* 69: 108–11.

———. 1980a. "Output and Price Stability. An International Comparison." *Journal of Economic Dynamics and Control* 2: 109–32.

———. 1980b. "Aggregate Dynamics and Staggered Contracts." *Journal of Political Economy* 88: 1–23.

Taylor, J. B., and H. Uhlig. 1990. "Solving Nonlinear Stochastic Growth Models: A Comparison of Alternative Solution Methods." *Journal of Business and Economic Statistics* 8, (January): 1–17.

Taylor, L. 1983. *Structuralist Macroeconomics*. New York: Basic Books.

———. 1985. "A Stagnationist Model of Economic Growth." *Cambridge Journal of Economics* 9: 383–403.

———. 1989. *Stabilization and Growth in Developing Countries: A Structuralist Approach*. Chur: Harwood Academic Publishers.

———. 1991. *Income Distribution, Inflation, and Growth*. Cambridge, MA.: MIT Press.

Taylor, L., and S. O'Connell. 1985. "A Minsky Crisis." *Quarterly Journal of Economics* 100: 871–86.

Tobin, J. 1965. "Money and Economic Growth." *Econometrica* 33: 671–84.

———. 1975. "Keynesian Models of Recession and Depression." *American Economic Review* 65: 195–202.

———. 1980): *Asset Accumulation and Economic Activity*. Oxford: Basil Blackwell.

———. (1987) "Unemployment, Interest, Deficits, and Money." In J. Tobin, *Policies for Prosperity. Essays in a Keynesian Mode*, 189–214. Brighton, UK: Wheatsheaf.

———. 1989. "Price Flexibility and Full Employment. The Debate Then and Now." Yale University. Mimeo.

———. 1992. "An Old Keynesian Counterattacks." *Eastern Economic Journal* 18: 387–400.

———. 1994. "Price Flexibility and Output Stability: An Old Keynesian View." In W. Semmler, ed., *Business Cycles: Theory and Empirical Methods*. Boston: Kluwer Academic Publishers.

Tong, H. 1990. *Nonlinear Time Series. A Dynamical System Approach*. Oxford: Oxford University Press.

Tu, P. 1994. *Dynamical Systems*. Berlin: Springer Verlag.

Turnovsky, S. J. 1970. "Empirical Evidence of the Formation of Price Expectations." *Journal of the American Statistical Association* 65: 1441–54.

———. 1977. *Macroeconomic Analysis and Stabilization Policies*. Cambridge, UK: Cambridge University Press.

———. 1995. *Methods of Macroeconomic Dynamics*. Cambridge: The MIT Press.

Turnovsky, S. J., and M. L. Wachter. 1972. "A Test of the 'Expectations Hypothesis' Using Directly Observed Wage and Price Expectations." *Review of Economic Statistics* 54: 47–54.

Tversky, A., and D. Kahneman. 1982. "Evidental Impact of Base Rates." In D. Kahneman *et al.* eds., *Judgment under Uncertainty: Heuristics and Biases.* Cambridge, UK: Cambridge University Press.

Uzawa, H. 1965. "Optimal Technical Change in an Aggregative Model of Economic Growth." *International Economic Review* 6: 18–31.

———. 1969. "Time Preference and the Penrose Effect in a Two Class Model of Economic Growth." *Journal of Political Economy* 77: 628–52.

Varian, H. R. 1977. "A Remark on the Boundary Restrictions in the Global Newton Method." *Journal of Mathematical Economics* 4: 127–30.

———. 1979. "Catastrophe Theory and Business Cycle." *Economic Inquiry* 17: 14–28.

Walker, D. A. 1987. "Walras's Theories of Tâtonnement." *Journal of Political Economy* 95: 758–74.

Walras, L. 1977. *Elements of Pure Economics*. Fairfield: Kelley Press.

Wiggins, S. 1990. *Introduction to Applied Nonlinear Dynamical Systems and Chaos.* Heidelberg: Springer Verlag.

Williams, A. W. 1987. "The Formation of Price Forecasts in Experimental Markets." *Journal of Money, Credit and Banking* 19: 1–18.

Wolff, E. N. 1989. "Trends in Aggregate Household Wealth in the U.S. 1900–83." *The Review of Income and Wealth* 35: 1–29.

Wolfstetter, E. 1977. *Wert, Profitrate und Beschäftigung*. Frankfurt a.M.: Campus Verlag.

———. 1982. "Fiscal Policy and the Classical Growth Cycle." *Zeitschrift für Nationalökonomie* 42: 375–93.

Woodford, M. 1986. "Stationary Sunspot Equilibria in a Finance Constraint Economy." *Journal of Economic Theory* 40: 128–37.

———. 1988. "Expectation, Finance and Aggregate Instability." In M. Kohn and S. C. Tsiang, eds., *Finance Constraints, Expectations, and Macroeconomics*. Oxford: Oxford University Press; 150–79.

———. 1989. "Finance, Instability and Cycles." In W. Semmler, ed., *Financial Dynamics and Business Cycles*, 18–37. Armonk, N.Y.: Sharpe.

Woodford, M. 1990a. "Optimal Monetary Policy in an Economy with Sequential Service of Buyers." University of Chicago. Mimeo.

Woodford, M. 1990. "Learning to Believe in Sunspots." *Econometrica* 58: 277–307.

———. 1994. "Price Level Determinacy without Control of Monetary Aggregate." University of Chicago. Mimeo.

———. 1996. "Control of the Public Debt: a Requirement for Price Stability?" NBER working paper, no. 5684. Cambridge: National Bureau of Economic Research.

Yong, A. 1993. "Invention and Bounded Learning by Doing." *Journal of Political Economy* 101: 443–72.

Zurmühl, R. 1964. *Matrizen*. Heidelberg: Springer.

Index

Accelerator, 63, 68
Accumulation, 109, 190, 200, 206, 273, 281, 375, 390
AD-AS growth model(s), 189–196, 248–249
  in discrete time, 233–238
  intensive formulation, 194, 234
  Keynes-Wicksell variant, 269
Adaptive expectations
  and AD-AS growth model, 195
  and Bayesian learning, 155
  and extrapolative regression forecasts, 156–162
  defense of, 149–156
  modification of, 321–326
  vs. myopic perfect foresight, 150, 227–264
  and Sargent model, 165
Adaptive learning, 262–266
Adjustment mechanisms
  of actual economies, 212
  macroeconomic, 27–31
  microeconomic, 23–27
Agent
  imperfect, 323
  perfectly optimizing, 323
Animal spirits, 337, 342
Anticipated price inflation, 163
AR(2)-process, 263, 265
ARMA-processes, 262
Asymmetric information, 123, 208, 340
Asymptotically rational expectations, 273, 290
Autocorrelation in random shocks, 159
Autonomous expenditures, 78
Axiom of revealed preferences, 35, 38
Backward-looking aspects, in price adjustment, 70
Balanced growth equilibrium, 119
Bank loans. *See* Loans
Bankruptcy cost, 125
Bargaining power of workers, 301
Base money, 351
Basin of attraction
  and cross-dual dynamics, 43
  and derivative control, 51
  and extended Solow model, 109
  and Goodwin model, 88
Bayesian learning, 155
Bifurcation. *See also* Hopf bifurcation
  subcritical, 41–42, 98, 216, 316
  supercritical, 41–42, 216, 245, 316
Bond market, 162
Boundedness
  of goods demand, 40
  of investment, 74
  of market fluctuations, 43, 48, 57
  in real and monetary models, 73–81
Budget
  constraint of the firm, 122
  identity of firms, 393
Business cycle(s). *See also* Growth cycle; Limit cycle; Orbit
  classical, 274
  equilibrium, 112–115
  and finance, 340, 342–343
  and IS-LM growth, 222
  and Keynesian dynamics, 231
  and Keynesian monetary growth, 304
  and Keynes-Wicksell models, 273

Cagan, P., 70
Cagan model, 70, 78–79, 81, 251

Cagan model, *(cont.)*
  generalization, 255
Capacity utilization, 63–65, 67, 97, 101, 299, 301–302, 308, 330
  desired rate of, 64, 96
Capital accumulation, 109, 190, 206, 273, 281
Capital stock
  and debt-asset ratio, 346
  decision about increase, 345
  depreciation rate of, 113
  empirical growth rate, 330
  evolution of, 118, 123, 299
  growth of, 90, 99, 111, 117, 125, 273, 276, 282
  and Keynesian growth dynamics, 193
  market value of, 349
  planned growth rate, 358
  shadow price of, 120
  and Solow model, 106
  as state variable, 110, 122
  under-/overutilized, 102
Capital structure, 373–374, 376
  dynamics, 378–389
Ceilings for macroeconomic activity, 223
Center type stability, 84
Central bank, 348, 350
Chaos, 77
Classical business cycle, 274. *See also* Business cycle; Growth cycle
Classical growth dynamics, 81–90
Classical regime, 218
Classical savings habits, 96
Cobb-Douglas production function, 109, 214, 285
  intensive form, 110
  per capita, 112
Commercial banks, 348, 350, 354, 357, 369
Competitive pricing, 300
Composite price and quantity adjustment, 47–48, 57
Constant returns to varieties, 118
Constant rolling sample period, 157–158
Consumption
  demand, 134, 138, 306, 350
  and disposable income, 307
  function, 133, 193, 275
  growth rate of, 120
  per capita, 117
Control
  derivative, 48–57, 87
  proportional, 36, 48–57
Corridor (of local) stability, 216, 338, 366, 369
Cost premium, 123
Cost push term, 273
Credit rationing, 340
Cross-dual dynamics, 24–25, 44, 46–50, 55
Cross-dual monetary growth dynamics, 281–288
Current value Hamiltonian, 110, 119
Cutthroat competition, 309
Cyclical fluctuations, increasing amplitude, 240
Cyclical IS-LM growth, 210–217

Damped cycles, 245
Debreu-Sonnenschein theorem, 43, 58
Debt-asset ratio, 124, 346, 356–359, 373, 375–377. *See also* Capital structure
Debt finance, 123, 341, 374–375
Deflationary spiral, 191, 201
Degenerate Hopf bifurcation, 216
Demand pull
  inflation, 94
  mechanism, 287
Deposits, 354
Desired rate of capacity utilization, 64, 96
Deviation-amplifying
  effects, 65
  process, 321
Dichotomy of AD-AS growth model, 232
Discontinuous changes in money supply, 206
Discrete-time formulation
  of AD-AS growth model, 196
  of Keynesian monetary growth model, 233
Disequilibrium interpretation of AD-AS growth dynamics, 272
Distribution, 307–308, 310, 312
Distributional barrier, 221
Dividends, 350
Dual adjustment process, 44, 46–48
Dual dynamics, 25
Durbin-Watson coefficients, 160
Dynamic multiplier
  and Kaldor model, 73, 75–77
  and Tobin model, 163, 175
Dynamically endogenous variables, 194, 197, 250

Economic activity
and debt-asset ratio, 375
as deviation from trend, 305
and employment, 308
peaks and troughs, 386
and price setting, 308
turning points of, 95
Educated guess, 209
Effective demand
and employment, 212
in AD-AS growth model, 204
in classical growth dynamics, 96–101
Efficiency units, 109
Efficient price forecast, 262
Elasticity of substitution, 108, 286
Employment
actual, 212, 214, 242
decreasing, 222
full, 106, 131, 135, 138, 144, 166, 223
and labor demand, 138
and marginal productivity theory, 90–91, 108, 193, 200, 269, 288
normal, 164, 166, 217
peak, 286
and production, 134
rate of, 92, 108, 167, 194, 216, 276, 286
and utilization, 308
volume of, 168, 303
Endogenous growth, 115–121, 284
Endogenous technical change, 115–121
Entry deterrence, 309
Equilibrium
business cycle, 112–115
full-employment, 109, 135, 138, 144, 269
general, 35
goods market, 96, 100, 193, 236
interior, 36, 44, 50
money market, 193, 200, 236, 257, 275
portfolio, 307
unstable, 39
Equity
financing, 341, 374
price, 122, 354
Euler approximation, 238
Excess demand, 135, 138, 276, 290
Excess supply, 260
Expectations
adaptive, 64, 70, 81–82, 149–156, 166–172, 321–326
asymptotically rational, 273, 290
minimum variance, 156
rational, 150–153, 189–196, 227–228, 273, 290, 341
Expected rate of inflation, 133, 144, 167, 193, 204, 250, 258, 261, 282
External finance, 122–123, 340, 368, 374
Extrapolative regression forecasts, 156–162

Feedback loops
in Sargent/Tobin model, 170
in Tobin model, 162
Finance
external, 122–123, 340, 368, 374
internal, 340–341, 368, 374
Financial assets, 307
Financial fragility of firms, 340
Financial markets, 137, 339, 347–348, 350, 354, 358
Financial risk and debt finance, 374
Financing hierarchy of investment, 357
Fixed coefficients in production, 82
Fixed proportions in technology, 284
Flexibility in money wages, 143
Forecast
error(s), 148, 150, 158, 161, 265
with constant coefficients, 264
Forward-looking aspects, in price adjustment, 70
Frequency of discontinuous open market operations, 206
Full employment barrier, 220
Full employment equilibrium
and Keynesian adjustment process, 138, 144
and Keynesian growth dynamics, 269
and Solow model, 109
and Walrasian adjustment process, 135, 144
Full employment steady state, 194, 230
Fundamental dynamic equation of neoclassical growth theory, 106

General equilibrium, 35
Generalized Newton method, 59
Gibson paradox, 201
Global Newton method, 58
Goods market disequilibrium, 73, 271–272, 276, 281, 283–284
Goods market equilibrium
and AD-AS growth model, 193, 236
and classical growth dynamics, 96, 100
Goodwin, R. M., 81–82, 281, 284

Goodwin's center-type dynamics, 281
Goodwin model, 82, 219
Government expenditure(s), 193, 201, 276, 307, 351
Growth
  endogenous, 115–121
  IS-LM, 210–224
  monetary, 183–225, 274–288
  and money and finance, 121–125
  real, 105–109
  stochastic, 112–115
Growth cycle
  classical, 271–297
  and Goodwin model, 84, 89, 219, 285, 311
  and Kaldor model, 78
  and Rose model, 94
  and Stein's model, 292

H-economy, 206
Hamiltonian, 110, 117, 119
Harrod-neutral technical progress, 112, 305
Harrod, R. F., 29, 63, 65
Heterogeneity of agents, 154
Hetero-reference, 344
Hicksian matrix, 296
Hicksian week, 196–197, 233, 319
Hierarchy of markets, 137, 143
Hopf bifurcation. *See also* Bifurcation
  degenerate, 216, 319
  and generalized Cagan model, 255
  and Goodwin model, 83
  and Hamiltonian, 125
  and IS-LM growth, 214, 215
  and Keynes-Goodwin model, 315–316
  and Keynesian growth model, 243
  and Keynes-Wicksell growth model, 284–285
  and modified Tobin model, 175
  and Sargent/Tobin model, 171, 174, 179
  and Stein's model, 292
  theorem, 41, 45, 68, 71
Human capital, 115, 116, 118, 120
Hyperanticipation, 195, 204
Hyperinflation, 254, 280
Hyperperfect foresight, 196–210

Imbalance in the product market, 269
Imperfect capital markets, 340
Imperfect information, 340
Implicit function theorem, 141, 194, 354, 359, 370
Impulse propagation mechanism, 104, 112, 114
Income distribution, conflict over, 85–86, 101, 216, 223, 299
Incomplete capital markets, 123–124
Inflation
  and Cagan model, 70, 72
  dependence on expected inflation, 250
  expected rate of, 133, 144, 167, 193, 204, 250, 258, 261, 282
  and leverage ratio, 391
  medium, 325
  and Mundell effect, 163
  repressed, 218
  and Rose model, 92
  and share of wages, 220
  of Wicksellian type, 274
Inflationary climate, 276
Inflationary expectations, 152, 156, 163, 167, 237, 248, 251, 256–258, 303, 325, 328
Inflationary pressure, 220
Information set, 265–266
Input-output analysis, 47
Instability
  in AD-AS dynamics, 240, 247
  in AD-AS growth model, 251
  in Cagan model, 71
  and financial sector, 361
  in Goodwin model, 84, 86, 89
  in Harrodian growth, 66, 68–69
  in Kaldor model, 75
  in Keynes-Goodwin model, 333
  in Keynes-Wicksell model, 279
  and price flexibility, 147–176
  in real and monetary models, 63–73
  in Rose model, 93
Interest rate, 123, 125, 137, 140, 163, 222
Interest rate effects, 66
Internal funds, 123
Inventory changes, 276
Investment
  behavior, 96, 101, 193, 219,
  and finance, 368, 376
  irreversibility of, 322
  in Keynes-Goodwin model, 305
  and long-run expectations, 341–348
  and Mundell effect, 163
  and output-capital ratio, 342

and price-quantity adjustment, 47
and rate of profit, 166
Investment function
and AD-AS growth model, 235, 237
and expectations, 343
and Harrod model, 63
independent, 103, 271
and inflationary expectations, 167
and Kaldor model, 74, 77–78
of Keynes-Wicksell type, 275
and output, 173
and Rose model, 90
Wicksellian, 190
IS-condition, 352, 371
IS-curve, 135, 141–142, 173, 312, 355
IS-equation, 168, 307, 363, 365
IS-LM
dynamics, 139
equations, 351
equilibria, 167, 312
and financial markets, 307, 348
growth, 210, 214, 217, 398
interest rate, 370
method, 398
output, 168
part of generalized Sargent model, 166
profit rate function, 370
solution of utilization and interest rate, 310
subsystem, 236
temporary equilibrium conditions, 303
volume of employment, 173

Jump(s)
in money supply, 195, 201, 203, 205, 208, 230, 236
in price level, 257
in prices and wages, 199, 202
Jump variable technique, 80, 81, 397

Kaldor, N., 73
Kaldor model, 73
Kalecki, M., 301, 308
Keynes effect, 141, 162–163, 168, 170–171, 173–174, 177, 243
Keynes-Goodwin model, 299
Keynes-Wicksell
approach, 91
model, 271, 274–279
Keynesian adjustment processes, 44–48, 137–143
Keynesian growth dynamics, 187–224
supply driven, 90–95, 271–288
Keynesian growth model
with adaptive expectations, 242
with perfect foresight, 212
Keynesian IS-LM growth, 214
Knife-edge growth, 63, 66

Labor force growth, 190. *See also* Population growth
Labor market, 105–109
disequilibrium, 107
and growth, 81
Labor productivity, 301–302, 310
Labor supply function, 133
Lack of profitability, 223
Lagged adjustment of capital stock, 99
Least-square estimations, 156
Least-square learning, 265
Leverage
of firms, 124
ratio, 377, 388–389, 391–395
Liapunov-function, 52–54, 84, 87, 89, 108–109, 294
Limit limit cycle
and Cagan model, 80
and generalized Cagan model, 257
and Kaldor model, 76
Limit cycle. *See also* Business cycle; Growth cycle; Orbit
and AD-AS growth, 258–259
and Cagan model, 80
and cross-dual dynamics, 41–42
and derivative control, 55
and financial sector, 360, 367
and Goodwin model, 86, 89
and Harrodian growth, 68
and IS-LM growth, 216
and Kaldor model, 76
and Keynes-Goodwin model, 327–328, 331–333
and Rose model, 93
stable, 216, 223, 245, 257
Linear technology, 82
Liquidity preference function, 193
Liquidity trap, 283, 286
LM-curve, 141–142, 173, 312
LM-equation, 168, 211, 276, 312, 350, 352, 363
LM-interest rate, 353–354
LM-schedule, 66

Loans, 341, 354, 357, 376–377, 387
Locally effective price mechanisms, 59
Long run, 342
Lucas, R., E. 115–116, 121, 188, 347
Lucas supply function, 231
Lump-sum taxes, 275

Marginal cost function, 39, 40
Marginal productivity
  principle, 106, 134, 138, 165, 284, 300, 305
  theory, 90–91, 108, 193, 200, 269, 288
Marginal propensity to consume, 135, 166–167
Marginal risk of bankruptcy, 124
Market
  adjustments and Newton method, 58–60
  mechanisms, 33–57
Markup
  factor, 210, 216, 242, 308, 310
  pricing, 82, 300
Marxian analysis of cyclical growth, 281
Mas-Colell, A., 35–36, 38–39, 41, 45–46
Medium run 147, 342
Modigliani-Miller theorem, 105, 123, 339, 374
Monetary policy
  countercyclical, 253
  effectiveness, 174
  rule, 290
Monetary shock, 190, 202, 207
Money
  endogenous, 350
  and growth and finance, 121–125
  market, 70
  neutrality of, 192, 231, 279
  quantity theory of, 206
  supply, 166, 193, 195, 202, 204, 253, 255, 307
  wage, decreasing, 140
Money demand function
  linear, 67
  loglinear, 70
  nonlinear, 257, 317
Money market disequilibrium, 261
Money market equilibrium
  and AD-AS growth model, 193, 200, 236
  and generalized Cagan model, 257
  and Keynes-Wicksell model, 275
Money stock, 193
Moving average, 265
Multi-goods case, 47
Multiplier-accelerator model, 63, 101
Multiproduct economies, 49
Multisectoral economy, 38
Mundell effect, 162–163, 168, 170–171, 173–174, 177, 243, 248
Myopic perfect foresight
  and adaptive expectations, 150, 227–264
  and AD-AS growth model, 195–210
  and Cagan model, 70, 81
  and classical growth dynamics, 84
  and cyclical IS-LM growth, 210–217
  and sales expectations, 64
  and Sargent/Tobin model, 172–176

NAIRU, 82
Natural output, 164
Natural rate of interest, 67
Neoclassical accumulation theory, 108
Neoclassical synthesis, 232, 269, 280, 307
Neutrality of money, 192, 231, 279
Newton method
  generalized, 59
  global, 58
Noise trader, 346
Nonlinearities
  and classical growth dynamics, 97
  in Keynesian IS-LM growth, 214
  and viability, 219
Normal distribution, 159
Normal employment, 164
Normal level of operation, 210
Normal productive capacity, 305
Notional demands, 134
Numéraire, 35

Okun gap, 164, 167
Oligopolistic competition, 301
One-step-ahead forecast, 265
Open market operations, 251
  discontinuous, 199, 206
  and jump in money supply, 195
  and myopic perfect foresight, 191
Optimal control, 111
Optimal growth models, 109
Optimal trajectories, 111–112
Optimization cost, 153–154
Orbit. *See also* Business cycle; Growth cycle; Limit cycle
  closed, 85, 284, 316, 319, 327, 366
  and cross-dual dynamics, 41
  periodic, 171–172, 303–304, 315, 363

Oscillatory motions, 171
Output-capital ratio, 213, 301–302, 305, 310, 330, 365
Output-inflation feedback, 162–163, 170
Overshooting, 161, 388
  of interest rate, 236
  mechanisms, 283
  phenomenon, 143
Overtime work, 223

Perfect competition, 218
Perfect foresight. *See* Hyperperfect foresight; Myopic perfect foresight; Rational expectations
Persistent cyclical movements, 55
Phillips curve, 92, 212, 235, 322
  and current inflation, 309
  expectations augmented, 107, 281, 303, 308
  nominal/money wage, 81, 87, 91, 190, 193, 208, 275, 299
  nonlinear, 90
  real wage, 107, 174, 198, 200, 204, 207, 280, 289
  in Tobin model, 163–164
  vertical, 109
Phillips loops, 331, 381
Pigou effect, 134, 139, 140
Poincaré-Bendixson theorem
  and cross-dual dynamics, 40–42
  and Goodwin model, 86, 89
  and Kaldor model, 74
  and Rose model, 93, 95
Point-in-time jumps, 199
Policy rules, 253
Pontryagin's maximum principle, 110, 117
Population growth, 90, 104, 110, 119
Portfolio equilibrium, 307
Prediction errors, 160–161
Price deflator of capital, 376
Price flexibility
  and destabilizing effect, 171
  and instability in the medium run, 147
Price predictor, 262
Price setting of firms, 308
Price and wage adjustments, 165, 169
Production function
  Cobb-Douglas, 109–110, 214, 285
  neoclassical, 105, 133, 193, 249–250
Profit rate, 301, 306, 320, 365
  expected, 353, 360
Profit share, 301–302
Profit squeeze(s), 274, 282–283, 286, 301, 329
Proportional savings function, 63
Psychological experiments and expectations, 151

Quadratic loss function, 156
Quantity theory of money, 206

R & D models of endogenous growth, 116
Random shocks, 159–160
Random walk, 113
Rate of capital depreciation, 166, 305
Rate of interest
  and expected rate of profit, 354
  and IS-LM dynamics, 141–142
  and Keynesian adjustment process, 138
  level of, 358
  and market clearing, 135
  and money supply jump, 201, 204, 236
  nominal, 162, 166–167, 191, 193, 233, 284, 299, 303, 306, 350–351
  per unit of calendar time, 234
  real, 163, 203–205, 233, 237, 284, 286, 302, 305–306, 320, 328, 349
  in steady state, 168
Rate of profit
  and investment, 166, 275, 302, 306
  net, 277
Rate of return, 275, 282, 306, 329, 345–346
  differentials, 271, 282
Rational expectations
  and AD-AS growth models, 189–196
  and adaptive expectations, 150–153
  asymptotically, 273, 290
  and irreducible uncertainty, 347
  and learning, 341
  methology, 227–228
  and Stein's model, 290
Real balances per capital, 67
Real business cycles (RBC), 112–115
Real rate of return
  on bonds, 275
  on capital, 306, 329, 345–346
Real wage
  approximation, 199, 207–208
  effect, 169–171
  movement, 216
Reference oscillations, 380–381, 383, 386, 390

Regression forecasts, 156–162
Relative risk aversion, coefficient of, 110, 117–118
Relaxation oscillations
in Cagan model, 78, 80
in generalized Cagan model, 257, 259–260
in Kaldor model, 76
Repressed inflation, 218
Retention ratio, 124, 357, 363–364
Returns to scale, 37, 46–47
Risk cost, 124–125
Risk of overprediction, 324
Risk premium, 306, 346, 366
Romer, P., 118, 120–121
Romer model, 120
Root mean-square prediction error, 160
Rose, H., 90–92, 95, 281
Rose model, 90–95, 281
Routh-Hurwitz conditions
and Goodwin model, 83
and Keynes-Goodwin model, 313–314
and Keynesian adjustment process, 139
and Keynesian growth model, 244
and price flexibility, 169, 178, 181
and wage flexibility, 145

Saddlepath (in)stability phenomenon, 254
Saddlepoint
and cross-dual dynamics, 40, 42
and dual dynamics, 45
in Harrod model, 65
in intertemporal Solow model, 111
in modified Tobin model, 174, 180
in Romer model, 120
Sales expectations, 64
Sargent, T., 80, 136, 165, 167, 189, 193–194, 196, 254–259, 261, 274, 279, 302
Sargent model, 162, 166–167, 192, 212, 227, 233, 277, 305
Saving
and capital accumulation, 273
government, 276
and investment, 269, 274, 302
in Keynes-Wicksell model, 275
plans 272–273
predetermined, 277
private, 276
rate of, 273
sensitivity to real wages, 279
Savings and monetary growth, 279–281
Say's law, 82
Self-reference, 344–345, 360
Separation of investment and saving decisions, 302
Separation theorem, 122–123
Shadow price of capital stock, 120
Share prices, 349
Share of profits, 301
and inflationary pressure, 220
Share of wages, 220
Short run, 131
neutrality, 195, 202–203, 208, 280
Sluggish adjustment of the labor force, 242
Sluggish price adjustment, 246
Sluggish wages and stability, 170
Solow, R., 105
Solowian adjustment paths, 208
Solowian supply side dynamics, 200
Solow model, 105–109
intertemporal version, 109–112
Solow residual, 113–115
Stability
and Keynes-Goodwin model, 333
and Keynes-Wicksell model, 279
local asymptotic, 37–38, 47, 83
and price/wage adjustment speeds, 170
universal asymptotic, 51
and wage/price flexibility, 216
Stability corridor, 98. *See also* Corridor stability
and cross-dual dynamics, 41, 43
and Harrodian growth, 68
Stable limit cycle, 98, 216, 223, 245, 257, 304
Stable node, 72
Stable private sector, 281
Stable spiral, 72
Stagflationary process, 222
State of confidence, 342, 349, 355, 358–362, 365, 368–369
State dependent reaction functions, 86
Statically endogenous variables, 194, 197, 250
Steady state inflation, 70, 312, 320
Stein, J., 272, 289–292
Stochastic growth, 112–115
Stochastic noise, 160
Stochastic optimization problem, 113
Stock equilibrium, 350
Stock of knowledge, 115–116, 118
Subcritical bifurcation, 98, 216

and cross-dual dynamics, 41–42
and Keynes-Goodwin model, 316
Supercritical bifurcation, 216, 245
and cross-dual dynamics, 41–42
and Keynes-Goodwin model, 316
Supply side Keynesianism, 271–297

Target markup rate, 309
Tâtonnement
adjustment process, 36, 57
dynamics, 59
Taxes, net of interest, 193, 276–277
Technical change
growth rate of, 110
Harrod-neutral, 109
Technology shocks, 112–115
Temporary equilibrium
in AD-AS growth model, 237
and financial markets, 351
functions, 355, 358
in Keynes-Goodwin model, 303
under myopic perfect foresight, 173
in Sargent/Tobin model, 166
Three-phase structure of business cycle, 222
Time horizon of expectations, 323
Time preference, 110, 118
Tobin, J., 147–148, 163–164, 167, 175
Tobin model, 162–166, 170, 172, 175, 180
Tobin's *q*, 134, 349
Transversality condition(s), 110–111, 119
Trend
in capital structure, 378–389
deviations, 305, 330
productivity, 310

Ultra short run, 135, 138
Uncertainty, 342–344, 347
Underutilization, 96
Unemployment, 104, 114, 131, 147, 169, 286, 301, 331
Unit wage costs, 210, 242
Unstable node, 71–72, 93
Unstable spiral, 72
Utility function
with constant elasticity preference, 110, 118
loglinear, 113
Utilization, 124, 305, 308–310, 342, 358, 361
Uzawa, H., 122

Variable speed of adjustment, 161
Variables
dynamically endogenous, 194, 197, 250
statically endogenous, 194, 197, 250
Viability
of Cagan model, 78
and Classical growth dynamics, 81–90
and IS-LM growth dynamics, 217
of multiplier-accelerator growth, 69
of price-quantity dynamics, 40, 43, 45
of Rose model, 93
and sluggish adjustment of prices, 246

Wage bill, and output prices, 162
Wage flexibility and stability, 94, 131–146
Wage share, 97, 286, 301–302, 310–312, 331
dynamic, 96
Wallace, N., 80, 254–259, 261
Walras' law, 35
Walrasian adjustment(s), 34–43, 133–137
Warranted rate of growth, 64
Wealth allocation function, 79
Wicksellian price adjustment equation, 276
Wicksell-Keynes-Phillips (WKP) model, 163